International Litigation and Arbitration

Practice and Planning

Carolina Academic Press
Law Casebook Series
Advisory Board

❦

Gary J. Simson, Chairman
Cornell Law School

Raj K. Bhala
The George Washington University Law School

John C. Coffee, Jr.
Columbia University School of Law

Randall Coyne
University of Oklahoma Law Center

John S. Dzienkowski
University of Texas School of Law

Robert M. Jarvis
Shepard Broad Law Center
Nova Southeastern University

Vincent R. Johnson
St. Mary's University School of Law

Thomas G. Krattenmaker
Director of Research
Federal Communications Commission

Michael A. Olivas
University of Houston Law Center

Michael P. Scharf
New England School of Law

Peter M. Shane
Dean, University of Pittsburgh School of Law

Emily L. Sherwin
University of San Diego School of Law

John F. Sutton, Jr.
University of Texas School of Law

David B. Wexler
University of Arizona College of Law

International Litigation and Arbitration

Practice and Planning

Third Edition

Russell J. Weintraub
Professor of Law
Holder of the Ben H. & Kitty King Powell Chair
University of Texas School of Law

Carolina Academic Press
Durham, North Carolina

Copyright © 2001
Russell J. Weintraub
All rights reserved

ISBN 0-89089-972-X
LCCN 00-110351

Carolina Academic Press
700 Kent Street
Durham, North Carolina 27701
Telephone: (919) 489-7486
Fax: (919)493-5668
email: cap@cap-press.com
www.cap-press.com

Printed in the United States of America

To my best friend and dearest love, my wife, Zelda

Summary of Contents

Contents
Preface
Acknowledgments

1. SUING FOREIGN DEFENDANTS IN UNITED STATES COURTS — 1

Section 1. Problems of In Personam and In Rem Jurisdiction — 1
Section 2. Agreements to Litigate or Arbitrate Abroad — 47
Section 3. Enjoining Suit Abroad — 89
Section 4. Service of Process — 96
Section 5. Taking of Evidence — 119
Section 6. Currency Conversion — 163

2. SUITS BY FOREIGN PLAINTIFFS — 173

Section 1. Forum Shopping and Forum Non Conveniens — 173
Section 2. Erie, Reverse Erie, and Litigation Strategy — 207

3. RECOGNITION OF JUDGMENTS — 227

Section 1. Bases for Non-Recognition — 227
Section 2. Judgments Enforcing Public Law — 248
Section 3. The Uniform Act — 251

4. THE ACT OF STATE DOCTRINE — 261

Section 1. Application and Exceptions — 261
Section 2. Intangible Property — 274

5. FOREIGN SOVEREIGN IMMUNITY — 281

Section 1. The Foreign Sovereign Immunities Act — 281
Section 2. Commercial or Governmental — 300
Section 3. Enforcing a Judgment — 319

6. EXTRATERRITORIAL APPLICATION OF UNITED STATES LAW — 335

Section 1. Antitrust Law — 335
Section 2. Securities Law — 388
Section 3. Other Problems — 397

7. CIVIL SUITS FOR ATROCITIES THAT VIOLATE INTERNATIONAL LAW — 403

Section 1. The Alien Tort Claims Act — 403
Section 2. The Torture Victim Protection Act — 413

8. DAMAGES RESULTING FROM INTERNATIONAL FLIGHTS: THE WARSAW CONVENTION — 427

Section 1. Current and Proposed Recovery Rules — 427
Section 2. Defining Convention Terms and Determining Preemption — 444

9. INTERNATIONAL CHILD ABDUCTION — 463

Section 1. Duty to Return the Child — 463
Section 2. Exceptions to the Duty to Return — 481

10. LETTERS OF CREDIT — 487

Section 1. Compliance with Terms of the Letter — 489
Section 2. Enjoining Payment — 495
Section 3. Political Risks — 504

11. ARBITRATION — 513

Section 1. Conventions and Model Law — 514
Section 2. Judicial Assistance and Interference — 541
Section 3. Awards of the Iran-United States Claims Tribunal — 551

Contents

Preface	xix
Acknowledgments	xxi

1. SUING FOREIGN DEFENDANTS IN UNITED STATES COURTS — 1

Section 1. Problems of In Personam and In Rem Jurisdiction — 1

Helicopteros Nacionales de Colombia v. Hall, 466 U.S. 408 (1984) — 1
Notes. U.S. amicus brief in Helicopteros; foreign defendants' vulnerability to suit despite Helicopteros; obsolete precedent relied on in Helicopteros; Calvo clauses — 6
Asahi Metal Industry Co. v. Superior Court, 480 U.S. 102 (1987) — 7
Notes. Implications of Asahi for injured users; split of authority concerning "stream of commerce"; Japanese jurisdiction cases; use of national contacts in Federal Rule 4(k)(2). — 14
Choice of Law — 17
European Economic Community Convention on Jurisdiction and the Enforcement of Judgments in Civil and Commercial Matters, (Brussels Convention) — 19
Notes. Ratification of Brussels Convention; Lugano Convention; relevance of the provisions of the EEC Convention to assessing the reasoning in Asahi; jurisdiction under the Brussels Convention; exorbitant bases for jurisdiction under Convention; transient presence as basis for jurisdiction; differences between jurisdiction under Convention and in U.S. — 28
Miller v. Honda Motor Co., 779 F.2d 769 (1st Cir. 1985) — 30
Notes. Piercing the corporate veil — 33
Shaffer v. Heitner, 433 U.S. 186 (1977) — 34
Notes. Uses of in rem jurisdiction that survive Shaffer; English "Mareva" injunction compared; local procedure may not permit pre-judgment seizure; due process requirements affected by interest at risk; likelihood that Shaffer will be overruled or limited. — 44
Louring v. Kuwait, Boulder Shipping Co., 455 F. Supp. 630 (D. Conn. 1977) — 45
Notes. Meaning of "no other forum"; possibility that fewer forum contacts needed for in rem than for in personam jurisdiction — 47

Section 2. Agreements to Litigate or Arbitrate Abroad — 47

The Bremen v. Zapata Off-Shore Co., 407 U.S. 1 (1972) — 47

Notes. Exculpatory clauses invalid under German law; enforcement of forum-selection clauses in cruise tickets; drafting of a choice-of-forum clause; limitation of vessel owner's liability; the forum-selection clause in Carbon Black	54
Vimar Seguros y Reaseguros, S.A. v. M/V. Sky Reefer, 515 U.S. 528 (1995)	57
Notes. Enforcement of forum-selection clauses; denial of interlocutory appeal for refusal to enforce	60
Scherk v. Alberto-Culver Co., 417 U.S. 506 (1974)	61
Notes. Overruling of Wilco v. Swan; enforcement of arbitral awards under Foreign Sovereign Immunities Act and Act of State Doctrine; enforcement of forum-selection clauses against U.S. investors in Lloyd's	68
United Nations Convention on the Recognition and Enforcement of Foreign Arbitral Awards ("New York" Convention)	69
Notes. New York Convention widely ratified; Inter-American Convention on International Commercial Arbitration ("Panama" Convention); construction of Convention and Federal Arbitration Act; drafting of arbitration clause; local awards not considered as "domestic"	71
Mitsubishi Motors Corp. v. Soler Chrysler-Plymouth, Inc., 473 U.S. 614 (1985)	77
Notes. Enforcement of arbitration awards and agreements; comments on Mitsubishi	85
Rhone Mediterranee Compagnia Francese v. Lauro, 712 F.2d 50 (3rd Cir. 1983)	86
Notes. Standard for enforcement of agreement to arbitrate; "time" and "bareboat" charters	89
Section 3. Enjoining Suit Abroad	**89**
Gannon v. Payne, 706 S.W.2d 304 (Tex. 1986)	89
Notes. "Parallel proceedings" and the Conflict of Jurisdiction Model Act; antisuit injunctions and stays of proceedings; parallel proceedings under Brussels Convention; comparative law on parallel proceedings	92
Section 4. Service of Process	**96**
Hague Convention on the Service Abroad of Judicial and Extrajudicial Documents in Civil or Commercial Matters	96
Notes. Sources of multilateral conventions affecting international litigation; Service Convention provision for reopening judgment; treatment of controversial issues in multilateral conventions; Inter-American Convention on Letters Rogatory	101
Service abroad under Federal Rule of Civil Procedure 4	102
Note. Interpretation of Rule 4	102
Volkswagenwerk Aktiengesellschaft v. Schlunk, 486 U.S. 694 (1988)	103
Notes. Special Commission report on Schlunk; refusal of service when request forwarded by U.S. attorney; "send" in Article 10(a) and Japanese position on mail service; American form of notification au parquet; due process notice requirements; whether Service Convention is mandatory	109
Federal Trade Commission v. Compagnie de Saint-Gobain-Pont-A-Mousson, 636 F.2d 1300 (D.C. Cir. 1980)	110

Notes. Legislation conflicting with international law; jus cogens;
  amendment of FTC service provisions   118

Section 5. Taking of Evidence   119

  Hague Convention on the Taking of Evidence Abroad in Civil or
    Commercial Matters   119
  Société Nationale Industrielle Aérospatiale v. United States District
    Court, 482 U.S. 522 (1987)   126
  Notes. Special Commission report on Aérospatiale; abandoned proposal to
    amend FRCP 26(a); critique of conclusion that "may" indicates that
    Convention is optional; reservations under Article 23; discovery in aid
    of foreign proceedings under 28 U.S.C. § 1782; "GmbH"; lower court
    decisions after Aérospatiale; discovery in England; "Anton Piller"
    order; civil law discovery   136
  Restatement (Third) of the Foreign Relations Law of the
    United States § 442   139
  Notes. Court supervision of discovery of evidence located abroad; effect
    of blocking statutes on discovery orders and sanctions   140
  Societe Internationale Pour Participations Industrielles et Commerciales,
    S.A. v. Rogers, 357 U.S. 197 (1958)   140
  Notes. How burden of proof may be affected by blocking statute; settlement
    of principal case; lifting of Swiss banking secrecy laws; effect of blocking
    statutes on decision to order production and on sanctions for
    disobedience   146
  In re Uranium Antitrust Litigation, 480 F.Supp. 1138 (N.D. Ill. 1979) 146
  Note. "Balancing test" for ordering discovery and for extraterritorial
    application of law   152
  United States v. First Nat'l Bank of Chicago, 699 F.2d 341 (7th Cir. 1983) 152
  Notes. Use of "Second" and "Third" in referring to Restatements of Foreign
    Relations; deliberate use of foreign blocking statute; discovery on the
    jurisdictional issue; ordering discovery in violation of foreign law 155
  In re Asbestos Insurance Coverage Cases, [1985] 1 W.L.R. 331
    (House of Lords)   157
  Note. England permits discovery in U.S. in aid of English proceedings 162

Section 6. Currency Conversion   163

  Note. Analysis of currency-conversion problem   163
  In re Good Hope Chemical Corp., 747 F.2d 806 (1st Cir. 1984)   165
  Notes. Supreme Court precedent on currency conversion; "F.A.S" and
    Guide to Incoterms; effect on U.S. judgment of payment of English
    judgment   170

2. SUITS BY FOREIGN PLAINTIFFS   173

  Section 1. Forum Shopping and Forum Non Conveniens   173
  Piper Aircraft Co. v. Reyno, 454 U.S. 235 (1981)   173
  Notes. Why an American forum is attractive to foreigners; disparity between
    awards within EEC; tactical use of transfers between federal courts; review

of ruling on forum non conveniens motion; state forum
non conveniens standards; defamation as exception to attractiveness
of United States forum; obligation of courts in a magnet forum; Friendship,
Commerce, and Navigation treaties; examples of courts applying public
and private convenience factors 182
Harrison v. Wyeth Laboratories, 510 F. Supp. 1 (E.D. Pa. 1980) 188
Note. Conditions on granting forum non conveniens motion 191
In re Union Carbide Corp. Gas Plant Disaster at Bhopal, India,
809 F.2d 195 (2d Cir.) 192
Notes. Uniform Foreign Money-Judgments Act; review of denial of forum
non conveniens motion; collateral attack on Bophal settlement; forum's
granting relief after forum non conveniens dismissal; India as inadequate
forum; waiver of limitations that ran before suit in forum 198
Lubbe v. Cape PLC, [2000] 1 W.L.R. 1545 (H.L.) 200
Notes. Implications of eliminating public factors from forum
non conveniens analysis; "substantial justice" as a factor;
Japan eliminates public factors 206

Section 2. Erie, Reverse Erie, and Litigation Strategy 207

Sibaja v. Dow Chemical Co., 757 F.2d 1215 (11th Cir. 1985) 207
Notes. Options available to foreign plaintiffs when their suits are dismissed
in federal court; the Erie Doctrine and forum non conveniens; states that
do not permit forum non conveniens dismissals or apply the doctrine
restrictively as magnet forums; tactics to prevent removal to federal court. 210
Chick Kam Choo v. Exxon Corp., 486 U.S. 140 (1988) 214
Notes. Result in Chick Kam Choo in Texas court; "reverse-Erie" doctrine not
applicable to forum non conveniens; Anti-Injunction Act not applicable
when no ongoing state proceeding; "strangers" exception to Act 218
Smith Kline & French Laboratories Ltd v. Bloch,
[1983] 2 All E.R. 72 (Ct. App.) 219
Notes. Lord Denning's views on forum shopping; development of forum
non conveniens in England; forum non conveniens under the Brussels
Convention; foreign anti-suit injunction as alternative to forum
non conveniens dismissal 224

3. RECOGNITION OF JUDGMENTS 227

Section 1. Bases for Non-Recognition 227

Hilton v. Guyot, 159 U.S. 113 (1895) 227
Notes. Reciprocity as basis for judgment recognition; "intrinsic,"
"extrinsic" fraud; change in French law 231
Somportex Ltd. v. Philadelphia Chewing Gum Corp.,
453 F.2d 435 (3rd Cir. 1971) 232
Notes. Collateral attack under the Brussels Convention; jura novit curia;
recognition of inconsistent judgments; exorbitant bases for jurisdiction;
failed bilateral judgments treaty between United States and United Kingdom;
res judicata effect of failed collateral attack; registration of U.S. judgments

in Canada; enforcement of foreign decree freezing assets in the United States; extra-territorial service under United Kingdom law; law applicable to judgment recognition in federal courts 236

Jet Holdings Inc. v. Patel, [1988] 3 W.L.R. 295 (Ct. App.) 239

Notes. English bases for recognizing personal jurisdiction in foreign courts; English requirement of "substantial justice"; English view of "presence" as a basis for jurisdiction; recognition of judgments for punitive damages; English view of collateral attack for fraud; application of Brussels Convention in parallel proceeding to enforce judgment from outside EU; recognition of foreign judgments; Hague Conference judgment-recognition project 244

Section 2. Judgments Enforcing Public Law 248

United States of America v. Inkley, [1988] 3 W.L.R. 304 (Ct. App.) 248
Notes. Recognition of judgments for taxes and family support 251

Section 3. The Uniform Act 251

Uniform Foreign Money-Judgments Recognition Act 251
Notes. Fraud as basis for collateral attack; "public policy" as basis for nonrecognition 253
Royal Bank of Canada v. Trentham Corp., 665 F.2d 515 (5th Cir. 1981) 254
Note. Variety of reciprocity requirements in some versions of Money-Judgments Act 256
Detamore v. Sullivan, 731 S.W.2d 122 (Tex. Civ. App.-Houston 1987) 257
Note. Notice and opportunity to be heard under Money-Judgments Act 258

4. THE ACT OF STATE DOCTRINE 261

Section 1. Application and Exceptions 261

Banco Nacional de Cuba v. Sabbatino, 376 U.S. 398 (1964) 261
Notes. The "Hickenlooper" amendment; result on remand; application of letter-of-credit proviso; "a claim of title or other right to property"; requirement of act by sovereign authority; "commercial" exception; Litvinov Assignment; application of doctrine; Libertad Act; arbitration involving sovereigns 271

Section 2. Intangible Property 274

Allied Bank International v. Banco Credito Agricola de Cartago, 757 F.2d 516, (2d Cir. 1985) 274
Notes. "Situs" of a debt; scope of Act of State doctrine; "sovereign risk" and bank deposits in foreign branches 277

5. FOREIGN SOVEREIGN IMMUNITY 281

Section 1. The Foreign Sovereign Immunities Act 281

Foreign Sovereign Immunities Act	281
Notes. Other Code provisions affecting suits with foreign sovereigns; when an "agency or instrumentality" is "a citizen of the United States"; time for determining sovereign status; choice of law under the FSIA; distinctions in FSIA between treatment of "foreign state" and "agency or instrumentality"; relationship between commercial and tort exceptions; pooling and tiering to determine sovereign ownership; application of the FSIA to individuals; "organ of a foreign state"; burden of proof; Bankruptcy Act provisions	289
Verlinden B.V. v. Central Bank of Nigeria, 461 U.S. 480 (1983)	295
Notes. Grounds for jurisdiction in Verlinden; background of Act	300

Section 2. Commercial or Governmental — 300

Republic of Argentina v. Weltover, 504 U.S. 607 (1992)	300
Notes. Due process limits on personal jurisdiction under Act; sovereign immunity in the United Kingdom; "direct effect"	303
Saudi Arabia v. Nelson, 507 U.S. 349 (1993)	305
Notes. "Direct effect"; commercial activity in U.S.	311
International Association of Machinists v. OPEC, 649 F.2d 1354 (9th Cir. 1981)	312
Note. Act is sole basis for jurisdiction over foreign sovereign	316
MOL, Inc. v. Peoples Republic of Bangladesh, 736 F.2d 1326 (9th Cir. 1984)	316
Notes. Choice between decision on act of state and sovereign immunity grounds; commercial-governmental distinction	318

Section 3. Enforcing a Judgment — 319

Letelier v. Republic of Chile, 748 F.2d 790 (2d Cir. 1984)	319
Notes. International Commission award re Letelier; why LAN was not joined; discretionary function exception; implied waiver of immunity by violation of jus cogens standard; state-sponsored terrorism amendment of FSIA	324
Joseph v. Office of the Consulate General of Nigeria, 830 F.2d 1018 (9th Cir. 1987)	326
Notes. Drafting of lease to foreign consulate; use of state law to determine "scope of employment"; distinctions between consular and diplomatic immunity; discretionary function exemption; hiring as commercial activity; waiver of diplomatic immunity; implied waiver of sovereign immunity; International Organizations Immunities Act	332

6. EXTRATERRITORIAL APPLICATION OF UNITED STATES LAW — 335

Section 1. Antitrust Law — 335

Restatement (Third) The Foreign Relations Law of the United States §§ 401, 402, 403, 415, 416	335

Notes. "Jurisdiction to enforce"; "effects" basis for jurisdiction to prescribe; "passive personality" principle; universal jurisdiction; § 403's multi-factor reasonableness standard; intended but no actual effect	337
Timberlane Lumber Co. v. Bank of America, 549 F.2d 597 (9th Cir. 1976)	339
Notes. Decision after remand in Timberlane; range of opinion on proper territorial reach of U.S. antitrust law	345
Laker Airways Ltd. v. Sabena, Belgian World Airlines, 731 F.2d 909 (D.C. Cir. 1984)	347
Note. Territoriality and nationality as bases for jurisdiction to prescribe	353
Agreement Between the United States and the United Kingdom Concerning Air Services ["Bermuda II"]	353
Note. Relevance of Treaty to antitrust suit	354
British Airways Board v. Laker Airways Ltd, [1985] 1 A.C.58 (1984) (House of Lords)	355
Notes. English and Australian "Clawback" Acts; enjoining suit by Laker's liquidator; settlement of Laker litigation	361
Hartford Fire Insurance Co. v. California, 509 U.S. 764 (1993)	362
Notes. Ambiguity of Justice Souter's opinion; Justice Scalia's treatment of § 403; relevance of McCarron-Ferguson exemption; Ninth Circuit retains tripartite analysis	369
British Nylon Spinners v. Imperial Chemical Industries, [1953] 1 Ch. 19	371
Notes. Subsequent proceedings in British Nylon Spinners; Judge Ryan's findings concerning what British Nylon Spinners knew at time of purchase	373
McGlinchy v. Shell Chemical Co., 845 F.2d 802 (9th Cir. 1988)	374
Notes. Effect of 15 U.S.C. § 6a on Timberlane; purpose of § 6a.	377
Antitrust Enforcement Guidelines for International Operations-1995	377
Notes. Sovereign compulsion as defense; recommendation of Organization for Economic Cooperation and Development (OECD) on the extraterritorial application of antitrust law	379
Lucchino v. Foreign Countries of Brazil, et al, 476 A.2d 1369 (Pa. Cmwlth. Ct. 1984)	379
Note. Pennsylvania "buy America" statute; United States-Germany Treaty of Friendship; state legislation that interferes with foreign affairs	381
Japan-United States: Agreement on Semiconductor Trade (1986)	382
European Community Declaration Concerning Japanese-United States Agreement on Semiconductor Trade	384
Notes. Subsequent Japan-U.S. semiconductor agreements; antitrust agreements between U.S. and EU, Australia, France, Germany, Canada; International Antitrust Enforcement Assistance Act; recognition of "effects" doctrine abroad; The Court of Justice of the European Communities applies EU antitrust law to foreign producers (The "Wood Pulp Case"); U.S. companies obtain antitrust remedies against other U.S. companies from EU Commission; EU Merger Control Rules; comparative antitrust law	385
Section 2. Securities Law	388
Zoelsch v. Arthur Andersen & Co., 824 F.2d 27 (D.C. Cir. 1987)	388

Notes. Application of U.S. securities law to protect U.S. and foreign investors; agreements between the U.S. and Switzerland and the U.S. and Japan on cooperation in enforcement of securities laws; modification of requirement of U.S. registration for foreign securities offered to U.S. investors — 394

Section 3. Other Problems — 397

Restatement (Third) The Foreign Relations Law of the United States § 414 — 397
Notes. Distinction between branches and subsidiaries; The U.S.S.R.-Western Europe Pipeline incident; acts of U.S. regulatory agencies affecting operations abroad; Iran & Libyan Sanctions Act; Cuban Liberty & Democratic Solidarity Act; extraterritorial application of other U.S. public laws — 398

7. CIVIL SUITS FOR ATROCITIES THAT VIOLATE INTERNATIONAL LAW — 403

Section 1. The Alien Tort Claims Act — 403

Filartiga v. Pena-Irala, 630 F.2d 876 (2d Cir. 1980) — 403
Notes. State responsibility for acts of individuals; construction and application of the ATCA; choice of law under the ATCA; federal question jurisdiction although state or foreign law applies; codification in the United Kingdom of the European Convention on Human Rights — 408

Section 2. The Torture Victim Protection Act — 413

Torture Victim Protection Act — 413
Note. Time limitations under the TVPA — 414
Kadic v. Karadzic, 70 F.3d 232 (2d Cir. 1995) — 415
Notes. Jurisdiction over Karadzic; judgments against Karadzic; international criminal tribunals; immunity of individuals under the FSIA; international law as federal law; head-of-state immunity — 424

8. DAMAGES RESULTING FROM INTERNATIONAL FLIGHTS: THE WARSAW CONVENTION — 427

Section 1. Current and Proposed Recovery Rules — 427

The Warsaw Convention — 427
Civil Aeronautics Board Order Concerning Hague Protocol and Montreal Agreement — 433
Note. Protocols amending Warsaw Convention; IATA agreement removing liability limits for personal injury and death; proposed Montreal Convention — 435
Montreal Convention — 436
Note. Recovery under the Montreal Convention; plaintiff strategy; important issues under IATA Agreement and Montreal Convention — 443

Section 2. Defining Convention Terms and Determining Preemption — 444

Air France v. Saks, 470 U.S. 392 (1985)	444
Note. Meaning of "accident"	449
Eastern Airlines, Inc. v. Floyd, 499 U.S. 530 (1991)	450
Zicherman v. Korean Air Lines Co., Ltd., 516 U.S. 217 (1996)	454
Notes. Choice of law under Warsaw Convention; amendment of Death on the High Seas Act to permit recovery of nonpecuniary damages	457
El Al Israel Airlines, Ltd. v. Tseng, 525 U.S. 155 (1999)	457
Notes. Defining Convention terms	459

9. INTERNATIONAL CHILD ABDUCTION — 463

Section 1. Duty to Return the Child — 463

Hague Convention on the Civil Aspects of International Child Abduction — 463
Notes. United States ratification; implementing legislation and regulations; return under Uniform Child Custody Jurisdiction Act and Uniform Child Custody Jurisdiction and Enforcement Act; Inter-American Convention on International Repatriation of Children; European Convention on Recognition and Enforcement of Decisions Concerning Custody of Children and on Restoration of Custody of Children; applicable law when both Hague and European Conventions are in force — 469
Friedrich v. Friedrich, 983 F.2d 1396 (6th Cir. 1993) — 472
Notes. The duty to return; "habitual residence"; problems of enforcement in some signatory countries; decision on remand in Friedrich — 477

Section 2. Exceptions to the Duty to Return — 481

Tahan v. Duquette; 613 A.2d 486 (N.J. App. 1992) — 481
Notes. "Intolerable situation"; child's objections; acquiescence in removal; rights of fugitive from justice — 483

10. LETTERS OF CREDIT — 487

Introduction: Operation of letters of credit; U.S. banks' inability to guaranty; Uniform Customs and Practice for Documentary Credits; UCC Article 5; Convention on Independent Guarantees and Standby Letters of Credit; International Standby Practices — 487

Section 1. Compliance with Terms of the Letter — 489

Banco Espanol de Credito v. State Street Bank and Trust Co., 385 F.2d 230 (1st Cir. 1967) — 489
Notes. Strict compliance; high percentage of document discrepancy and rejection; "advising bank", "confirming bank", "nominated bank", "drawee bank"; inspection certificates; jurisdiction in wrongful dishonor suit — 493

Section 2. Enjoining Payment — 495

Trans Meridian Trading Inc. v. Empresa Nacional de Comercializacion
de Insumos, 829 F.2d 949 (9th Cir. 1987)   495
Notes. Enjoining payment on a letter of credit   500
Foxboro Co. v. Arabian American Oil Co., 805 F.2d 34 (1st Cir. 1986)   502

Section 3. Political Risks   504

Note. Problems arising from letters of credit issued before the revolution in favor of Iranian beneficiaries   504
Harris Corp. v. National Iranian Radio and Television, 691 F.2d 1344 (11th Cir. 1982)   504
Declaration of Algeria Concerning Settlement of Claims by the United States and Iran   510

11. ARBITRATION   513

Introduction: reasons to prefer arbitration to litigation   513

Section 1. Conventions and Model Law   514

Inter-American Convention on International Commercial Arbitration   514
Notes. Ratification of Inter-American Convention; comparison of Inter-American and New York Conventions; North American Free Trade Agreement   515
Convention on the Settlement of Investment Disputes Between States and Nationals of Other States   516
Notes. Ratification; immunity of a State from execution   527
UNCITRAL Model Law on International Commercial Arbitration   528
Notes. Use of Model Law; "ex aequo et bono", "amiable compositeur", "lex mercatoria"; enforcing agreements that arbitrators apply lex mercatoria   539

Section 2. Judicial Assistance and Interference   541

Introduction. Court review of arbitration awards; developments in England   541
Pioneer Shipping Ltd. v. B.T.P. Tioxide Ltd. ("The Nema") [1981] 2 All E.R. 1030 (House of Lords)   542
Notes. English standards for appeal from award; interim judicial assistance; stay of confirmation of award; exclusion from Brussels Convention   547

Section 3. Awards of the Iran-United States Claims Tribunal   551

Ministry of Defense of Islamic Republic of Iran v. Gould Inc. 887 F.2d 1357 (9th Cir. 1989)   551
Notes. Tendency to enforce international arbitral awards; relevance of awards of Iran-U.S. Claims Tribunal   556

Preface

The volume of international civil litigation and arbitration continues to increase. Lawyers outside the huge firms that conduct the lion's share of international practice are likely if not now, soon, to be faced with the problem of asserting claims by or against foreign parties. Moreover, a lawyer must know what issues arise in international practice in order to draft agreements that put the client in the best tactical position should there be a dispute.

These materials survey the problems arising in international litigation and arbitration. The focus is on proceedings in the United States, but much comparative material is provided.

Two subjects that might logically have been included receive only incidental treatment-choice of law and admiralty. Coverage of those topics is left to courses in conflict of laws and admiralty. There is a note on "Choice of Law" in the first section of Chapter 1, which is intended to provide background for those who have not studied the subject.

This book focuses on current problems and developments, but is not designed as a practice manual. The purpose is to explore the issues raised by international practice. The issues are likely to be with us one hundred years from now, although the methods of dealing with them will have changed dozens of times.

With regard to form, the omission of text is indicated by * * *. Citations and footnotes are omitted without indication. When a footnote is retained, it bears its original number.

Acknowledgments

Before the publication of the First Edition, I had been teaching from temporary editions of these materials for almost ten years. Many colleagues taught from these materials or read them and made helpful comments. Users of both the first and second editions have commented on the book. I am grateful to these colleagues for assisting me in shaping the contents. I am indebted also to my students, here and abroad, who joined with me in discussion and argument. A special thanks to my secretary, Consuelo Akin, for her hard work and the mastering of new skills for accessing data bases.

Chapter 1

Suing Foreign Defendants in United States Courts

Section 1: Problems of In Personam and In Rem Jurisdiction

Helicopteros Nacionales de Colombia, S.A. v. Hall
466 U.S. 408 (1984)

Justice BLACKMUN delivered the opinion of the Court.

We granted certiorari in this case to decide whether the Supreme Court of Texas correctly ruled that the contacts of a foreign corporation with the State of Texas were sufficient to allow a Texas state court to assert jurisdiction over the corporation in a cause of action not arising out of or related to the corporation's activities within the State.

I

Petitioner Helicopteros Nacionales de Colombia, S.A., (Helicol) is a Colombian corporation with its principal place of business in the city of Bogota in that country. It is engaged in the business of providing helicopter transportation for oil and construction companies in South America. On January 26, 1976, a helicopter owned by Helicol crashed in Peru. Four United States citizens were among those who lost their lives in the accident. Respondents are the survivors and representatives of the four decedents.

At the time of the crash, respondents' decedents were employed by Consorcio, a Peruvian consortium, and were working on a pipeline in Peru. Consorcio is the alter-ego of a joint venture named Williams-Sedco-Horn (WSH). The venture had its headquarters in Houston, Texas. Consorcio had been formed to enable the venturers to enter into a contract with Petro Peru, the Peruvian state-owned oil company. Consorcio was to construct a pipeline for Petro Peru running from the interior of Peru westward to the Pacific Ocean. Peruvian law forbade construction of the pipeline by any non-Peruvian entity.

Consorcio/WSH needed helicopters to move personnel, materials, and equipment into and out of the construction area. In 1974, upon request of Consorcio/WSH, the chief executive officer of Helicol, Francisco Restrepo, flew to the United States and conferred in Houston with representatives of the three joint venturers. At that meeting, there was a discussion of prices, availability, working conditions, fuel, supplies, and housing. Restrepo represented that Helicol could have the first helicopter on the job in 15 days. The Consorcio/WSH representatives decided to accept the contract proposed by Restrepo. Helicol began performing before the agreement was formally signed in Peru on November 11, 1974. The contract was written in Spanish on official government stationery and provided that the residence of all the parties would be Lima, Peru. It further stated that controversies arising out of the contract would be submitted to the jurisdiction of Peruvian courts. In addition, it provided that Consorcio/WSH would make payments to Helicol's account with the Bank of America in New York City.

Aside from the negotiation session in Houston between Restrepo and the representatives of Consorcio/WSH, Helicol had other contacts with Texas. During the years 1970-1977, it purchased helicopters (approximately 80% of its fleet), spare parts, and accessories for more than $4,000,000 from Bell Helicopter Company in Fort Worth. In that period, Helicol sent prospective pilots to Fort Worth for training and to ferry the aircraft to South America. It also sent management and maintenance personnel to visit Bell Helicopter in Fort Worth during the same period in order to receive "plant familiarization" and for technical consultation. Helicol received into its New York City and Panama City, Fla., bank accounts over $5,000,000 in payments from Consorcio/WSH drawn upon First City National Bank of Houston.

Beyond the foregoing, there have been no other business contacts between Helicol and the State of Texas. Helicol never has been authorized to do business in Texas and never has had an agent for the service of process within the State. It never has performed helicopter operations in Texas or sold any product that reached Texas, never solicited business in Texas, never signed any contract in Texas, never had any employee based there, and never recruited an employee in Texas. In addition, Helicol never has owned real or personal property in Texas and never has maintained an office or establishment there. Helicol has maintained no records in Texas and has no shareholders in that State. None of the respondents or their decedents were domiciled in Texas, but all of the decedents were hired in Houston by Consorcio/WSH to work on the Petro Peru pipeline project.

The Texas Court of Civil Appeals, Houston, First District, reversed the judgment of the District Court, holding that in personam jurisdiction over Helicol was lacking. 616 S.W.2d 247 (Tex.1981). The Supreme Court of Texas, with three Justices dissenting, initially affirmed the judgment of the Court of Civil Appeals. Seven months later, however, on motion for rehearing, the court withdrew its prior opinions and, again with three Justices dissenting, reversed the judgment of the intermediate court. 638 S.W.2d 870 (Tex.1982). In ruling that the Texas courts had in personam jurisdiction, the Texas Supreme Court first held that the State's long arm statute reaches as far as the Due Process Clause of the Fourteenth Amendment permits. Id., at 872. Thus, the only question remaining for the court to decide was whether it was consistent with the Due Process Clause for Texas courts to assert in personam jurisdiction over Helicol. Ibid.

* * *

Even when the cause of action does not arise out of or relate to the foreign corporation's activities in the forum State, due process is not offended by a State's subjecting the corporation to its in personam jurisdiction when there are sufficient contacts between the State and the foreign corporation. *Perkins v. Benguet Consolidated Mining Co.*, 342 U.S. 437, (1952); see *Keeton v. Hustler Magazine, Inc.*, 465 U.S. 770, 779-780 (1984). In *Perkins*, the Court addressed a situation in which state courts had asserted general jurisdiction over a defendant foreign corporation. During the Japanese occupation of the Philippine Islands, the president and general manager of a Philippine mining corporation maintained an office in Ohio from which he conducted activities on behalf of the company. He kept company files and held directors' meetings in the office, carried on correspondence relating to the business, distributed salary checks drawn on two active Ohio bank accounts, engaged an Ohio bank to act as transfer agent, and supervised policies dealing with the rehabilitation of the corporation's properties in the Philippines. In short, the foreign corporation, through its president, "ha[d] been carrying on in Ohio a continuous and systematic, but limited, part of its general business," and the exercise of general jurisdiction over the Philippine corporation by an Ohio court was "reasonable and just." 342 U.S., at 438, 445.

All parties to the present case concede that respondents' claims against Helicol did not "arise out of," and are not related to, Helicol's activities within Texas.[10] We thus must explore the nature of Helicol's contacts with the State of Texas to determine whether they constitute the kind of continuous and systematic general business contacts the Court found to exist in *Perkins*. We hold that they do not.

It is undisputed that Helicol does not have a place of business in Texas and never has been licensed to do business in the State. Basically, Helicol's contacts with Texas consisted of sending its chief executive officer to Houston for a contract negotiation session; accepting into its New York bank account checks drawn on a Houston bank; purchasing helicopters, equipment, and training services from Bell Helicopter for substantial sums; and sending personnel to Bell's facilities in Fort Worth for training.

The one trip to Houston by Helicol's chief executive officer for the purpose of negotiating the transportation-services contract with Consorcio/WSH cannot be described or regarded as a contact of a "continuous and systematic" nature, as Perkins described it, see also *International Shoe Co. v. Washington*, 326 U.S. [310], at 320 [1945], and thus cannot support an assertion of in personam jurisdiction over Helicol by a Texas court. Similarly, Helicol's acceptance from Consorcio/WSH of checks drawn on a Texas bank is of negligible significance for purposes of determining whether Helicol had sufficient contacts in Texas. There is no indication that Helicol ever requested that the checks be

---

10.* * * The dissent suggests that we have erred in drawing no distinction between controversies that "relate to" a defendant's contacts with a forum and those that "arise out of" such contacts. This criticism is somewhat puzzling, for the dissent goes on to urge that, for purposes of determining the constitutional validity of an assertion of specific jurisdiction, there really should be no distinction between the two.

We do not address the validity or consequences of such a distinction because the issue has not been presented in this case. Respondents have made no argument that their cause of action either arose out of or is related to Helicol's contacts with the State of Texas. Absent any briefing on the issue, we decline to reach the questions (1) whether the terms "arising out of" and "related to" describe different connections between a cause of action and a defendant's contacts with a forum, and (2) what sort of tie between a cause of action and a defendant's contacts with a forum is necessary to a determination that either connection exists. Nor do we reach the question whether, if the two types of relationship differ, a forum's exercise of personal jurisdiction in a situation where the cause of action "relates to," but does not "arise out of," the defendant's contacts with the forum should be analyzed as an assertion of specific jurisdiction.

drawn on a Texas bank or that there was any negotiation between Helicol and Consorcio/WSH with respect to the location or identity of the bank on which checks would be drawn. Common sense and everyday experience suggest that, absent unusual circumstances, the bank on which a check is drawn is generally of little consequence to the payee and is a matter left to the discretion of the drawer. Such unilateral activity of another party or a third person is not an appropriate consideration when determining whether a defendant has sufficient contacts with a forum State to justify an assertion of jurisdiction.

The Texas Supreme Court focused on the purchases and the related training trips in finding contacts sufficient to support an assertion of jurisdiction. We do not agree with that assessment, for the Court's opinion in *Rosenberg Bros. & Co. v. Curtis Brown Co.*, 260 U.S. 516 (1923) (Brandeis, J., for a unanimous tribunal), makes clear that purchases and related trips, standing alone, are not a sufficient basis for a State's assertion of jurisdiction.

The defendant in *Rosenberg* was a small retailer in Tulsa, Okla., who dealt in men's clothing and furnishings. It never had applied for a license to do business in New York, nor had it at any time authorized suit to be brought against it there. It never had an established place of business in New York and never regularly carried on business in that State. Its only connection with New York was that it purchased from New York wholesalers a large portion of the merchandise sold in its Tulsa store. The purchases sometimes were made by correspondence and sometimes through visits to New York by an officer of the defendant. The Court concluded: "Visits on such business, even if occurring at regular intervals, would not warrant the inference that the corporation was present within the jurisdiction of [New York]." Id., at 518.

This Court in *International Shoe* acknowledged and did not repudiate its holding in *Rosenberg*. See 326 U.S., at 318. In accordance with *Rosenberg*, we hold that mere purchases, even if occurring at regular intervals, are not enough to warrant a State's assertion of in personam jurisdiction over a nonresident corporation in a cause of action not related to those purchase transactions.[12] Nor can we conclude that the fact that Helicol sent personnel into Texas for training in connection with the purchase of helicopters and equipment in that State in any way enhanced the nature of Helicol's contacts with Texas. The training was a part of the package of goods and services purchased by Helicol from Bell Helicopter. The brief presence of Helicol employees in Texas for the purpose of attending the training sessions is no more a significant contact than were the trips to New York made by the buyer for the retail store in *Rosenberg*. See also *Kulko v. California Superior Court*, 436 U.S. [84], at 93 [1978] (basing California jurisdiction on 3 day and 1 day stopovers in that State "would make a mockery of" due process limitations on assertion of personal jurisdiction).

---

12. This Court in *International Shoe* cited *Rosenberg* for the proposition that "the commission of some single or occasional acts of the corporate agent in a state sufficient to impose an obligation or liability on the corporation has not been thought to confer upon the state authority to enforce it." 326 U.S., at 318. Arguably, therefore, *Rosenberg* also stands for the proposition that mere purchases are not a sufficient basis for either general or specific jurisdiction. Because the case before us is one in which there has been an assertion of general jurisdiction over a foreign defendant, we need not decide the continuing validity of *Rosenberg* with respect to an assertion of specific jurisdiction, i.e., where the cause of action arises out of or relates to the purchases by the defendant in the forum State.

III

We hold that Helicol's contacts with the State of Texas were insufficient to satisfy the requirements of the Due Process Clause of the Fourteenth Amendment.[13] Accordingly, we reverse the judgment of the Supreme Court of Texas.

It is so ordered.

Justice BRENNAN, dissenting.

* * *

As a foreign corporation that has actively and purposefully engaged in numerous and frequent commercial transactions in the State of Texas, Helicol clearly falls within the category of nonresident defendants that may be subject to that forum's general jurisdiction. Helicol not only purchased helicopters and other equipment in the State for many years, but also sent pilots and management personnel into Texas to be trained in the use of this equipment and to consult with the seller on technical matters. Moreover, negotiations for the contract under which Helicol provided transportation services to the joint venture that employed the respondents' decedents also took place in the State of Texas. Taken together, these contacts demonstrate that Helicol obtained numerous benefits from its transaction of business in Texas. In turn, it is eminently fair and reasonable to expect Helicol to face the obligations that attach to its participation in such commercial transactions. Accordingly, on the basis of continuous commercial contacts with the forum, I would conclude that the Due Process Clause allows the State of Texas to assert general jurisdiction over petitioner Helicol.

The Court also fails to distinguish the legal principles that controlled our prior decisions in Perkins and Rosenberg. In particular, the contacts between petitioner Helicol and the State of Texas, unlike the contacts between the defendant and the forum in each of those cases, are significantly related to the cause of action alleged in the original suit filed by the respondents. Accordingly, in my view, it is both fair and reasonable for the Texas courts to assert specific jurisdiction over Helicol in this case.

By asserting that the present case does not implicate the specific jurisdiction of the Texas courts, the Court necessarily removes its decision from the reality of the actual facts presented for our consideration. Moreover, the Court refuses to consider any distinction between contacts that are "related to" the underlying cause of action and contacts that "give rise" to the underlying cause of action. In my view, however, there is a substantial difference between these two standards for asserting specific jurisdiction. Thus, although I agree that the respondents' cause of action did not formally "arise out of" specific activities initiated by Helicol in the State of Texas, I believe that the wrongful death claim filed by the respondents is significantly related to the undisputed contacts between Helicol and the forum. On that basis, I would conclude that the Due Process Clause allows the Texas courts to assert specific jurisdiction over this particular action.

---

13. As an alternative to traditional minimum-contacts analysis, respondents suggest that the Court hold that the State of Texas had personal jurisdiction over Helicol under a doctrine of "jurisdiction by necessity." See *Shaffer v. Heitner*, 433 U.S. 186, 211, n. 37 (1977) [infra page 34]. We conclude, however, that respondents failed to carry their burden of showing that all three defendants could not be sued together in a single forum. It is not clear from the record, for example, whether suit could have been brought against all three defendants in either Colombia or Peru. We decline to consider adoption of a doctrine of jurisdiction by necessity—a potentially far-reaching modification of existing law—in the absence of a more complete record.

* * *

Limiting the specific jurisdiction of a forum to cases in which the cause of action formally arose out of the defendant's contacts with the State would subject constitutional standards under the Due Process Clause to the vagaries of the substantive law or pleading requirements of each State. For example, the complaint filed against Helicol in this case alleged negligence based on pilot error. Even though the pilot was trained in Texas, the Court assumes that the Texas courts may not assert jurisdiction over the suit because the cause of action "did not 'arise out of,' and [is] not related to," that training. If, however, the applicable substantive law required that negligent training of the pilot was a necessary element of a cause of action for pilot error, or if the respondents had simply added an allegation of negligence in the training provided for the Helicol pilot, then presumably the Court would concede that the specific jurisdiction of the Texas courts was applicable.

* * *

Notes

1. The United States submitted an amicus brief in *Helicopteros* stating that "the United States is concerned that the ability of American firms to compete in world trade markets could be adversely affected because foreign corporations might be dissuaded from purchasing American products if the mere purchases of products in the United States—together with training in the United States as part of the purchase agreement—is sufficient to subject foreign businesses to the jurisdiction of American courts for causes of action totally unrelated to their purchases." Brief for the United States as Amicus Curiae, pp. 1-2.

2. *Helicopteros* appears to sharply limit the use of general jurisdiction over corporations, perhaps limiting it to corporations incorporated in, having their principal place of business in, or having a certificate to do business in, the forum. [But see Siemer v. Learjet Acquisition Corp., 966 F.2d 179 (5th Cir. 1992), cert. denied, 506 U.S..1080 (1993) (certificate to do business and appointment of agent for service of process is not sufficient for general jurisdiction).] Nevertheless, some American courts continue to base general jurisdiction on activities in the forum that have been characterized as "tenuous." See Peter Hay, Flexibility Versus Predictability and Uniformity in Choice of Law, 226 Recueil des cours 314 n. 20 (1991 Hague Academy of International Law). See United Rope Distributors, Inc. v. Kimberly Line, 785 F. Supp. 446 (S.D.N.Y. 1992) (in suit for loss of cargo, jurisdiction over the vessel's owner is upheld based on the owner's use of a forum bank to receive substantially all its income and pay substantially all its expenses); Schlobohm v. Schapiro, 784 S.W.2d 355, at 357 (Tex. 1990) (finding general jurisdiction over a Pennsylvania resident and citing *Helicopteros* for the proposition that general jurisdiction is available "where the defendant's activities in the forum are continuing and systematic"); Temperature Systems, Inc. v. Bill Pepper, Inc., 854 S.W.2d 669 (Tex. App.—Dallas, 1993, writ dism'd by agreement), (general jurisdiction upheld over a Wisconsin corporation based on purchases from Texas sellers and exchanges of equipment with other Texas Carrier dealers, *Helicopteros* not cited).

If the trial court rejects the defendant's motion to dismiss for lack of jurisdiction, this is not a final order and defendant cannot appeal in federal and most state courts. The Texas Legislature has enacted legislation permitting an interlocutory appeal from a denial of defendant's special appearance. Tex. Civ. Prac. & Rem. C. §51.014(7). State courts are split as to whether mandamus or some other extraordinary remedy is available to the defendant, or whether the defendant must wait to appeal after trial and final judgment. See State ex rel Connor v. McGough, 546 N.E.2d 407 (Ohio 1989) (writ of prohibition granted). In federal court, if the trial judge states in the order denying the motion to dismiss for lack of personal jurisdiction "that such order involves a controlling question of law as to which there is substantial ground for difference of opinion and that an immediate appeal from the order may materially advance the ultimate termination of the litigation... [t]he Court of Appeals... may thereupon, in its discretion, permit an appeal to be taken from such order." 28 U.S.C. § 1292(b). Certifications for an interlocutory appeal are rarely made and even more rarely granted. For the two years, 1994 and 1995, in the Second Circuit there were only "35 motions for leave to appeal under §1292(b), of which only eight were granted." Koehler v. Bank of Bermuda, Ltd., 101 F.3d 863, 866 (2d Cir. 1996) (refusing to entertain interlocutory appeal of the denial of bank's motion to dismiss for lack of personal jurisdiction).

3. Justice Blackmun relied upon Rosenberg Bros. & Co. Inc. v. Curtis Brown Co., decided 22 years before International Shoe Co. v. Washington ended reliance on the fiction of "presence," on which *Rosenberg* is based, and opened the way to jurisdiction based on causes of action arising out of or connected to the defendant's "minimum contacts" with the forum. Immediately after the passage from *International Shoe* that Justice Blackmun quotes in note 12 of his opinion, *International Shoe* indicates that *Rosenberg* is being cited as an example of the confusion caused by the "presence" fiction, by citing other cases in which acts in the forum subjected the defendant to jurisdiction, and finally repudiates statements, such as that found in *Rosenberg*, that it is irrelevant if the suit arises out of forum contacts. (*International Shoe* 326 U.S. at 329). *Rosenberg* was relied upon in the United States' amicus brief cited in note 1. (amicus brief at pp. 5-6).

Justice Brennan's dissent states that in *Rosenberg* the "contacts between the defendant and the forum [were not] significantly related to the cause of action...." In that case, suit was to recover the price of goods ordered by the defendant's president on one of his visits to plaintiff's plant in Rochester, New York. The goods were shipped F.O.B. Rochester. Some of the goods were returned, but none were paid for. Brief for Plaintiff in Error, pp. 3-4.

4. The opinion states that "Peruvian law forbade construction of the pipeline by any non-Peruvian entity." Contracts with Central and South American countries often contain "Calvo clauses," named after Carlos Calvo, a nineteenth century Argentine diplomat. These clauses state that the contracting parties submit to the same treatment as citizens of the country in which the contract is performed and waive any rights as aliens to the protection of any foreign country. The United States takes the position that such clauses cannot preclude its right to assert a claim based on state responsibility for injury to an American citizen. Donald R. Shea, The Calvo Clause 16, 200 (1955); Restatement (Third) of the Foreign Relations Laws of the United States § 713, cmt. g (1987).

Asahi Metal Industry Co., v. Superior Court
480 U.S. 102 (1987)

Justice O'CONNOR announced the judgment of the Court and delivered the unanimous opinion of the Court with respect to Part I, the opinion of the Court with respect to Part II-B, in which the Chief Justice, Justice BRENNAN, Justice WHITE, Justice MARSHALL, Justice BLACKMUN, Justice POWELL, and Justice STEVENS join, and an opinion with respect to Parts II-A and III, in which the Chief Justice, Justice POWELL, and Justice SCALIA join.

This case presents the question whether the mere awareness on the part of a foreign defendant that the components it manufactured, sold, and delivered outside the United States would reach the forum State in the stream of commerce constitutes "minimum contacts" between the defendant and the forum State such that the exercise of jurisdiction "does not offend 'traditional notions of fair play and substantial justice.'" *International Shoe Co. v. Washington*, 326 U.S. 310, 316 (1945), quoting *Milliken v. Meyer*, 311 U.S. 457, 463 (1940).

I

On September 23, 1978, on Interstate Highway 80 in Solano County, California, Gary Zurcher lost control of his Honda motorcycle and collided with a tractor. Zurcher was severely injured, and his passenger and wife, Ruth Ann Moreno, was killed. In September 1979, Zurcher filed a product liability action in the Superior Court of the State of California in and for the County of Solano. Zurcher alleged that the 1978 accident was caused by a sudden loss of air and an explosion in the rear tire of the motorcycle, and alleged that the motorcycle tire, tube, and sealant were defective. Zurcher's complaint named, *inter alia*, Cheng Shin Rubber Industrial Co., Ltd. (Cheng Shin), the Taiwanese manufacturer of the tube. Cheng Shin in turn filed a cross-complaint seeking indemnification from its codefendants and from petitioner, Asahi Metal Industry Co., Ltd. (Asahi), the manufacturer of the tube's valve assembly. Zurcher's claims against Cheng Shin and the other defendants were eventually settled and dismissed, leaving only Cheng Shin's indemnity action against Asahi.

California's long-arm statute authorizes the exercise of jurisdiction "on any basis not inconsistent with the Constitution of this state or of the United States." Cal.Civ.Proc.Code Ann. § 410.10 (West 1973). Asahi moved to quash Cheng Shin's service of summons, arguing the State could not exert jurisdiction over it consistent with the Due Process Clause of the Fourteenth Amendment.

In relation to the motion, the following information was submitted by Asahi and Cheng Shin. Asahi is a Japanese corporation. It manufactures tire valve assemblies in Japan and sells the assemblies to Cheng Shin, and to several other tire manufacturers, for use as components in finished tire tubes. Asahi's sales to Cheng Shin took place in Taiwan. The shipments from Asahi to Cheng Shin were sent from Japan to Taiwan. Cheng Shin bought and incorporated into its tire tubes 150,000 Asahi valve assemblies in 1978; 500,000 in 1979; 500,000 in 1980; 100,000 in 1981; and 100,000 in 1982. Sales to Cheng Shin accounted for 1.24 percent of Asahi's income in 1981 and 0.44 percent in 1982. Cheng Shin alleged that approximately 20 percent of its sales in the United States are in California. Cheng Shin purchases valve assemblies from other suppliers as well, and sells finished tubes throughout the world.

In 1983 an attorney for Cheng Shin conducted an informal examination of the valve stems of the tire tubes sold in one cycle store in Solano County. The attorney declared that of the approximately 115 tire tubes in the store, 97 were purportedly manufactured in Japan or Taiwan, and of those 97, 21 valve stems were marked with the circled letter "A", apparently Asahi's trademark. Of the 21 Asahi valve stems, 12 were incorporated into Cheng Shin tire tubes. The store contained 41 other Cheng Shin tubes that incorporated the valve assemblies of other manufacturers. An affidavit of a manager of Cheng Shin whose duties included the purchasing of component parts stated: "In discussions with Asahi regarding the purchase of valve stem assemblies the fact that my

Company sells tubes throughout the world and specifically the United States has been discussed. I am informed and believe that Asahi was fully aware that valve stem assemblies sold to my Company and to others would end up throughout the United States and in California." An affidavit of the president of Asahi, on the other hand, declared that Asahi "has never contemplated that its limited sales of tire valves to Cheng Shin in Taiwan would subject it to lawsuits in California." The record does not include any contract between Cheng Shin and Asahi.

Primarily on the basis of the above information, the Superior Court denied the motion to quash summons, stating: "Asahi obviously does business on an international scale. It is not unreasonable that they defend claims of defect in their product on an international scale."

The Court of Appeal of the State of California issued a peremptory writ of mandate commanding the Superior Court to quash service of summons. The court concluded that "it would be unreasonable to require Asahi to respond in California solely on the basis of ultimately realized foreseeability that the product into which its component was embodied would be sold all over the world including California."

The Supreme Court of the State of California reversed and discharged the writ issued by the Court of Appeal. The court observed: "Asahi has no offices, property or agents in California. It solicits no business in California and has made no direct sales [in California]." Moreover, "Asahi did not design or control the system of distribution that carried its valve assemblies into California." Nevertheless, the court found the exercise of jurisdiction over Asahi to be consistent with the Due Process Clause. It concluded that Asahi knew that some of the valve assemblies sold to Cheng Shin would be incorporated into tire tubes sold in California, and that Asahi benefited indirectly from the sale in California of products incorporating its components. The court considered Asahi's intentional act of placing its components into the stream of commerce—that is, by delivering the components to Cheng Shin in Taiwan—coupled with Asahi's awareness that some of the components would eventually find their way into California, sufficient to form the basis for state court jurisdiction under the Due Process Clause.

We granted certiorari, and now reverse.

II

A

* * *

Applying the principle that minimum contacts must be based on an act of the defendant, the Court in *World-Wide Volkswagen Corp. v. Woodson*, 444 U.S. 286 (1980), rejected the assertion that a consumer's unilateral act of bringing the defendant's product into the forum State was a sufficient constitutional basis for personal jurisdiction over the defendant.

* * *

Since *World-Wide Volkswagen,* lower courts have been confronted with cases in which the defendant acted by placing a product in the stream of commerce, and the stream eventually swept defendant's product into the forum State, but the defendant did nothing else to purposefully avail itself of the market in the forum State. Some courts have understood the Due Process Clause, as interpreted in *World-Wide Volkswagen*, to allow an exercise of personal jurisdiction to be based on no more than the defendant's act of placing the product in the stream of commerce. Other courts have understood the Due Process Clause and the above-quoted language in *World-Wide Volkswagen* to require the action of the defendant to be more purposefully directed at the forum State than the mere act of placing a product in the stream of commerce.

The reasoning of the Supreme Court of California in the present case illustrates the former interpretation of *World-Wide Volkswagen*. The Supreme Court of California held that, because the stream of commerce eventually brought some valves Asahi sold Cheng Shin into California, Asahi's awareness that its valves would be sold in California was sufficient to permit California to exercise jurisdiction over Asahi consistent with the requirements of the Due Process Clause. The Supreme Court of California's position was consistent with those courts that have held that mere foreseeability or awareness was a constitutionally sufficient basis for personal jurisdiction if the defendant's product made its way into the forum State while still in the stream of commerce. See *Bean Dredging Corp. v. Dredge Technology Corp.*, 744 F.2d 1081 (CA5 1984); *Hedrick v. Daiko Shoji Co.*, 715 F.2d 1355 (CA9 1983).

Other courts, however, have understood the Due Process Clause to require something more than that the defendant was aware of its product's entry into the forum State through the stream of commerce in order for the State to exert jurisdiction over the defendant. In the present case, for example, the State Court of Appeal did not read the Due Process Clause, as interpreted by *World-Wide Volkswagen*, to allow "mere foreseeability that the product will enter the forum state [to] be enough by itself to establish jurisdiction over the distributor and retailer." In *Humble v. Toyota Motor Co.*, 727 F.2d 709 (CA8 1984), an injured car passenger brought suit against Arakawa Auto Body Company, a Japanese corporation that manufactured car seats for Toyota. Arakawa did no business in the United States; it had no office, affiliate, subsidiary, or agent in the United States; it manufactured its component parts outside the United States and delivered them to Toyota Motor Company in Japan. The Court of Appeals, adopting the reasoning of the District Court in that case, noted that although it "does not doubt that Arakawa could have foreseen that its product would find its way into the United States," it would be "manifestly unjust" to require Arakawa to defend itself in the United States. Id., at 710-711, quoting 578 F.Supp. 530, 533 (ND Iowa 1982). See also *Hutson v. Fehr Bros., Inc.*, 584 F.2d 833 (CA8 1978); see generally *Max Daetwyler Corp. v. R. Meyer*, 762 F.2d 290, 299 (CA3 1985) (collecting "stream of commerce" cases in which the "manufacturers involved had made deliberate decisions to market their products in the forum state").

We now find this latter position to be consonant with the requirements of due process. The "substantial connection," *Burger King [Corp. v. Rudzewicz]*, 471 U.S. [462], at 475 [1985] *McGee [v. International Life Ins. Co.]*, 355 U.S. [220], at 223 [1957] between the defendant and the forum State necessary for a finding of minimum contacts must come about by an action of the defendant purposefully directed toward the forum State. *Burger King*, supra, 471 U.S., at 476; *Keeton v. Hustler Magazine, Inc.*, 465 U.S. 770, 774 (1984). The placement of a product into the stream of commerce, without more, is not an act of the defendant purposefully directed toward the forum State. Additional conduct of the defendant may indicate an intent or purpose to serve the market in the forum State, for example, designing the product for the market in the forum State, advertising in the forum State, establishing channels for providing regular advice to customers in the forum State, or marketing the product through a distributor who has agreed to serve as the sales agent in the forum State. But a defendant's awareness that the stream of commerce may or will sweep the product into the forum State does not convert the mere act of placing the product into the stream into an act purposefully directed toward the forum State.

Assuming, arguendo, that respondents have established Asahi's awareness that some of the valves sold to Cheng Shin would be incorporated into tire tubes sold in California, respondents have not demonstrated any action by Asahi to purposefully avail itself of the California market. Asahi does not do business in California. It has no office, agents, employees, or property in California. It does not advertise or otherwise solicit business in California. It did not create, control, or employ the distribution system that brought its valves to California. There is no evidence that Asahi designed its product in anticipation of sales in California. On the basis of these facts, the exertion of personal jurisdiction over Asahi by the Superior Court of California* exceeds the limits of due process.

B

The strictures of the Due Process Clause forbid a state court to exercise personal jurisdiction over Asahi under circumstances that would offend "'traditional notions of fair play and substantial justice.'" *International Shoe Co. v. Washington*, 326 U.S., at 316; quoting *Milliken v. Meyer*, 311 U.S., at 463.

We have previously explained that the determination of the reasonableness of the exercise of jurisdiction in each case will depend on an evaluation of several factors. A court must consider the burden on the defendant, the interests of the forum State, and the plaintiff's interest in obtaining relief. It must also weigh in its determination "the interstate judicial system's interest in obtaining the most efficient resolution of controversies; and the shared interest of the several States in furthering fundamental substantive social policies." *World-Wide Volkswagen*, 444 U.S., at 292 (citations omitted).

A consideration of these factors in the present case clearly reveals the unreasonableness of the assertion of jurisdiction over Asahi, even apart from the question of the placement of goods in the stream of commerce.

Certainly the burden on the defendant in this case is severe. Asahi has been commanded by the Supreme Court of California not only to traverse the distance between Asahi's headquarters in Japan and the Superior Court of California in and for the County of Solano, but also to submit its dispute with Cheng Shin to a foreign nation's judicial system. The unique burdens placed upon one who must defend oneself in a foreign legal system should have significant weight in assessing the reasonableness of stretching the long arm of personal jurisdiction over national borders.

When minimum contacts have been established, often the interests of the plaintiff and the forum in the exercise of jurisdiction will justify even the serious burdens placed on the alien defendant. In the present case, however, the interests of the plaintiff and the forum in California's assertion of jurisdiction over Asahi are slight. All that remains is a claim for indemnification asserted by Cheng Shin, a Taiwanese corporation, against

---

*. We have no occasion here to determine whether Congress could, consistent with the Due Process Clause of the Fifth Amendment, authorize federal court personal jurisdiction over alien defendants based on the aggregate of national contacts, rather than on the contacts between the defendant and the State in which the federal court sits.

Asahi. The transaction on which the indemnification claim is based took place in Taiwan; Asahi's components were shipped from Japan to Taiwan. Cheng Shin has not demonstrated that it is more convenient for it to litigate its indemnification claim against Asahi in California rather than in Taiwan or Japan.

Because the plaintiff is not a California resident, California's legitimate interests in the dispute have considerably diminished. The Supreme Court of California argued that the State had an interest in "protecting its consumers by ensuring that foreign manufacturers comply with the state's safety standards." The State Supreme Court's definition of California's interest, however, was overly broad. The dispute between Cheng Shin and Asahi is primarily about indemnification rather than safety standards. Moreover, it is not at all clear at this point that California law should govern the question whether a Japanese corporation should indemnify a Taiwanese corporation on the basis of a sale made in Taiwan and a shipment of goods from Japan to Taiwan. *Phillips Petroleum Co. v. Shutts*, 472 U.S. 797, 821-822, 105 S.Ct. 2965, 2979-2980, 86 L.Ed.2d 628 (1985); *Allstate Insurance Co. v. Hague*, 449 U.S. 302, 312-313, 101 S.Ct. 633, 639-640, 66 L.Ed.2d 521 (1981). The possibility of being haled into a California court as a result of an accident involving Asahi's components undoubtedly creates an additional deterrent to the manufacture of unsafe components; however, similar pressures will be placed on Asahi by the purchasers of its components as long as those who use Asahi components in their final products, and sell those products in California, are subject to the application of California tort law.

World-Wide Volkswagen also admonished courts to take into consideration the interests of the "several States," in addition to the forum State, in the efficient judicial resolution of the dispute and the advancement of substantive policies. In the present case, this advice calls for a court to consider the procedural and substantive policies of other nations whose interests are affected by the assertion of jurisdiction by the California court. The procedural and substantive interests of other nations in a state court's assertion of jurisdiction over an alien defendant will differ from case to case. In every case, however, those interests, as well as the Federal interest in Government's foreign relations policies, will be best served by a careful inquiry into the reasonableness of the assertion of jurisdiction in the particular case, and an unwillingness to find the serious burdens on an alien defendant outweighed by minimal interests on the part of the plaintiff or the forum State. "Great care and reserve should be exercised when extending our notions of personal jurisdiction into the international field." *United States v. First National City Bank*, 379 U.S. 378, 404, 85 S.Ct. 528, 542, 13 L.Ed.2d 365 (1965) (Harlan, J., dissenting). See Born, Reflections on Judicial Jurisdiction in International Cases, to be published in 17 Ga.J. Int'l & Comp. L. 1 (1987).

Considering the international context, the heavy burden on the alien defendant, and the slight interests of the plaintiff and the forum State, the exercise of personal jurisdiction by a California court over Asahi in this instance would be unreasonable and unfair.

III

Because the facts of this case do not establish minimum contacts such that the exercise of personal jurisdiction is consistent with fair play and substantial justice, the judgment of the Supreme Court of California is reversed, and the case is remanded for further proceedings not inconsistent with this opinion.

It is so ordered.

Justice BRENNAN, with whom Justice WHITE, Justice MARSHALL, and Justice BLACKMUN join, concurring in part and concurring in the judgment.

I do not agree with the interpretation in Part II-A of the stream-of-commerce theory, nor with the conclusion that Asahi did not "purposely avail itself of the California market." I do agree, however, with the Court's conclusion in Part II-B that the exercise of personal jurisdiction over Asahi in this case would not comport with "fair play and substantial justice," *International Shoe Co. v. Washington*, 326 U.S. 310, 320 (1945). This is one of those rare cases in which "minimum requirements inherent in the concept of 'fair play and substantial justice'...defeat the reasonableness of jurisdiction even [though] the defendant has purposefully engaged in forum activities." *Burger King Corp. v. Rudzewicz*, 471 U.S. 462, 477-478 (1985). I therefore join Parts I and II-B of the Court's opinion, and write separately to explain my disagreement with Part II-A.

Part II-A states that "a defendant's awareness that the stream of commerce may or will sweep the product into the forum State does not convert the mere act of placing the product into the stream into an act purposefully directed toward the forum State." Under this view, a plaintiff would be required to show "[a]dditional conduct" directed toward the forum before finding the exercise of jurisdiction over the defendant to be consistent with the Due Process Clause. I see no need for such a showing, however. The stream of commerce refers not to unpredictable currents or eddies, but to the regular and anticipated flow of products from manufacture to distribution to retail sale. As long as a participant in this process is aware that the final product is being marketed in the forum State, the possibility of a lawsuit there cannot come as a surprise. Nor will the litigation present a burden for which there is no corresponding benefit. A defendant who has placed goods in the stream of commerce benefits economically from the retail sale of the final product in the forum State, and indirectly benefits from the State's laws that regulate and facilitate commercial activity. These benefits accrue regardless of whether that participant directly conducts business in the forum State, or engages in additional conduct directed toward that State. Accordingly, most courts and commentators have found that jurisdiction premised on the placement of a product into the stream of commerce is consistent with the Due Process Clause, and have not required a showing of additional conduct.

The endorsement in Part II-A of what appears to be the minority view among Federal Courts of Appeals represents a marked retreat from the analysis in *World-Wide Volkswagen v. Woodson*, 444 U.S. 286 (1980).

* * *

Justice STEVENS, with whom Justice WHITE and Justice BLACKMUN join, concurring in part and concurring in the judgment.

The judgment of the Supreme Court of California should be reversed for the reasons stated in Part II-B of the Court's opinion. While I join Parts I and II-B, I do not join Part II-A for two reasons. First, it is not necessary to the Court's decision. An examination of minimum contacts is not always necessary to determine whether a state court's assertion of personal jurisdiction is constitutional. See *Burger King Corp. v. Rudzewicz*, 471 U.S. 462, 476-478 (1985). Part II-B establishes, after considering the factors set forth in *World-Wide Volkswagen Corp. v. Woodson*, 444 U.S. 286, 292, (1980), that California's exercise of jurisdiction over Asahi in this case would be "unreasonable and unfair." This finding alone requires reversal; this case fits within the rule that "minimum requirements inherent in the concept of 'fair play and substantial justice' may defeat the reasonableness of jurisdiction even if the defendant has purposefully engaged in forum activities." *Burger King*, 471 U.S., at 477- 478 (quoting *International Shoe Co. v. Washington*, 326 U.S. 310, 320 (1945)). Accordingly, I see no reason in this case for the plurality to articulate "purposeful direction" or any other test as the nexus between an act of a defendant and the forum State that is necessary to establish minimum contacts.

Second, even assuming that the test ought to be formulated here, Part II-A misapplies it to the facts of this case. * * * Whether or not [Asahi's] conduct rises to the level of purposeful availment requires a constitutional determination that is affected by the volume, the value, and the hazardous character of the components. In most circumstances I would be inclined to conclude that a regular course of dealing that results in deliveries of over 100,000 units annually over a period of several years would constitute "purposeful availment" even though the item delivered to the forum State was a standard product marketed throughout the world.

* * *

Notes

1. Hedrick v. Daiko Shoji Co., 715 F.2d 1355 (9th Cir. 1983), modified, 733 F.2d 1335 (9th Cir. 1984), is cited with disapproval in Justice O'Connor's opinion in *Asahi*. An Oregon longshoreman was injured in an Oregon port while working on a ship owned by a Japanese company. A defective splice in a wire rope parted, causing a boom to strike the longshoreman. He sued the shipowner and another Japanese company that had manufactured the splice. The splice maker won dismissal at trial on the ground of lack of jurisdiction. The Ninth Circuit reversed, distinguishing this case from *World-Wide Volkswagen* on the ground that the "probability that the part sold to an ocean carrier will be used in a foreign port is not fortuitous. It is certain." The court also indicated that the liability of the shipowner would depend on whether the jury found the shipowner negligent in using a poorly designed splice or in not detecting the defect. How may *Asahi*'s disapproval of *Hedrick* affect recovery by injured users?

2. Hutson v. Fehr Bros., 584 F.2d 833, (8th Cir. 1978), cert. denied, 439 U.S. 983 (1978), is cited with approval in Justice O'Connor's opinion in *Asahi*. Lumberyard employees were injured in the forum when a chain broke. The chain traveled from an unknown Yugoslavian manufacturer, to an Italian corporation, to a British corporation, to the British corporation's American subsidiary, to the local retailer. The Eighth Circuit held that jurisdiction could not be obtained over the Italian corporation, which had given exclusive North American resale rights to its British customer. How may *Asahi*'s approval of *Hutson* affect recovery by injured users?

3. Notes 1 and 2 refer to part IIA of Justice O'Connor's opinion, which got four votes. There has been a split of authority in subsequent cases as to whether lower courts must follow this part of the opinion and its restrictive view of "stream of commerce." See Boit v. Gar-Tec Products, Inc., 967 F.2d 671 (1st Cir. 1992), which follows IIA to deny jurisdiction over the American importer of a paint stripper that caused property damage, when the importer distributed the stripper though a mail order catalogue company. *Boit* states that "those circuits that have squarely addressed the stream-of-commerce issue since *Asahi* have adopted Justice O'Connor's plurality view," citing cases from the 1st, 8th, and 11th circuits. The statement in *Boit* that all circuits "since *Asahi* have adopted Justice O'Connor's plurality view" restricting jurisdiction based on a "stream of commerce" theory, is not true of the Fifth Circuit. See Ham v. La Cienga Music Co., 4 F.3d 413 (5th Cir. 1993) (stating that the Fifth Circuit will continue to fol-

low its pre-*Asahi* cases absent rejection by a Supreme Court majority). Moreover, *Boit's* inclusion of the Eighth Circuit is thrown into doubt by two Eighth Circuit decisions. Barone v. Rich Bros. Interstate Display Fireworks Co., 25 F.3d 610, 614 (8th Cir. 1994), held that a seller may not insulate itself from jurisdiction by utilizing a multi-level distribution system and noted that five justices in *Asahi* did not share Justice O'Connor's view. Vandelune v. 4B Elevator Components Unlimited, 148 F.3d 943, 947-48 (8th Cir.), cert. denied, 525 U.S. 1018 (1998), upheld jurisdiction in Iowa over the British manufacturer of a grain elevator component and stated that "whether introducing products into the 'stream of commerce' satisfies the due process requirement of minimum contacts in a product liability case.... remains an open question." Pennzoil Products Co. v. Colelli & Associates, Inc., 149 F.3d 197 (3rd Cir. 1998) notes the split of authority among circuits as to whether they should follow part IIA of Asahi and concludes that "[m]ost courts of appeals...have avoided choosing one position over the other." The court also finds it unnecessary to choose between Justice O'Connor's and Justice Brennan's views on the stream of commerce in order to uphold jurisdiction over Colelli. Kernan v.Kurz-Hastings, Inc., 175 F.3d 236 (2d Cir. 1999), also finds its unnecessary to decide whether it should follow IIA. The court upholds jurisdiction of a federal district court in New York over a Japanese manufacturer of a machine that injured a worker in New York. The manufacturer's corporate predecessor had given a Pennsylvania distributor the exclusive right to sell the manufacturer's products in North America. The worker sued the Pennsylvania distributor who impleaded the manufacturer for contribution and indemnity. The court stated: "even assuming *arguendo* that we were to adopt the *Asahi* plurality's more restrictive view [of stream of commerce], we would still conclude that the 'exclusive sales rights' agreement constitutes the type of purposeful action sufficient to support a finding of minimum contacts." Id. at 244.

State courts are also split on whether they will follow IIA. CSR Ltd. V. Link, 925 S.W.2d 591 (Tex. 1996), denied jurisdiction to injured users in reliance on Justice O'Connor's statement that "placement of a product into the stream, without more, is not an act of the defendant purposefully directed toward the forum state." The defendant, an Australian company, had sold raw asbestos to a manufacturer F.O.B Australia and the manufacturer shipped the asbestos to its Texas factory. The plaintiffs were workers at the factory suffering from asbestos caused illnesses. The court stated that "foreseeability [that the manufacturer would use the asbestos in Texas] alone cannot create minimum contacts between [the Australian seller] and Texas." Another case denying jurisdiction over the same Australian asbestos producer and relying on IIA is Anderson v. Metropolitan Life Ins. Co., 694 A.2d 701 (R.I. 1997). In Anderson, Johns-Manville used the raw asbestos outside of Rhode Island to manufacture products. Johns-Manville then shipped the products to Rhode Island where the asbestos injured the plaintiffs. On the other hand, the following state decisions note IIA did not receive the vote of a majority of the Justices and refuse to apply IIA's requirement that, in addition to foreseeing that its product is likely to reach the forum in the ordinary course of distribution, there be some "action of the defendant purposefully directed toward the forum State." Showa Denko K.K. v. Pangle, 414 S.E.2d 658 (Ga. App. 1991), Ga. cert. denied (1992); Cox v. Hozelock, Ltd., 411 S.E.2d 640 (N.C. App. 1992), review denied, 414 S.E.2d 752 (N.C. 1992); Hill v. Showa Denko K.K., 425 S.E.2d 609 (W. Va. 1992).

4. In Goto v. Malaysian Airline System Berhad, 35 Minshu 1224 (1981), the Japanese Supreme Court upheld jurisdiction over the Malaysian Airline in a suit for breach of an air transportation contract resulting in the death of plaintiffs' husband and father. The crash occurred in Malaysia on a domestic Malaysian flight. The court indicated that in international cases, jurisdiction is based on rules of reason for maintaining impartiality,

fairness, and speediness. These requirements are met if the Japanese court has jurisdiction over the foreign party in accordance with the Japanese Code of Civil Procedure's venue provisions including the defendant's residence, the place where the defendant has a place of business (the provision applicable in *Goto*—the defendant had an office in Tokyo although this office had no connection to the relevant transportation contract), where the defendant's property is located, and "a place of tort" (art. 15, CCP).

In Family Co. Ltd. v. Miyahara, [1998] H.J. (1626) 74, translation in Japanese Annual Int'l L. 117 (1998), the Supreme Court of Japan limited *Goto*. The court held that Japanese courts did not have jurisdiction of a Japanese company's suit to recover funds from an individual residing in Frankfurt. The company had given the Frankfurt resident the funds to purchase goods for the company. The court affirmed the principal of jurisdiction set out in *Goto* and stated: "However, if we find some exceptional circumstances, where a trial in a Japanese court would result in contradicting the ideas of promoting fairness between the parties and equitable and prompt administration of justice, the international adjudicatory jurisdiction of the Japanese court should be denied." The court found such exceptional circumstances in this case. The contract between the parties was made in Germany, defendant had his home in principal place of business in Germany for more than 20 years, and much of the evidence relevant to the defense is in Germany.

In Mukoda v. The Boeing Co. (Far Eastern Air Transport Case), 604 Hanrei Taimuzu (The Law Times Report) 138 (1986), summary and partial English translation in 31 Japanese Annual Int'l Law 216 (1988), the Tokyo District Court dismissed a wrongful death suit against United States defendants even though, under the Japanese Civil Code, venue was proper. The action was dismissed for reasons resembling the common law doctrine of forum non conveniens. The decedents were passengers on a Far Eastern Air Transport (FEAT) airplane that crashed on Taiwan. The defendants were Boeing, the plane's manufacturer, and United Air Lines, which had sold the craft to FEAT, a Taiwanese company. The plaintiffs had first sued in the United States. That suit was dismissed on forum non conveniens grounds on condition that the defendants submit to the jurisdiction of a Taiwanese court, make their employees available to testify there, waive any statute of limitations defense, and consent to satisfying any Taiwanese judgment. The Tokyo District Court held that it would entertain suits if venue were proper, unless "special circumstances [existed indicating that] sustaining the Japanese court's jurisdiction would result in contradicting the ideas of promoting impartiality between the parties and fair and prompt administration of justice." The court found that there were such special circumstances. Suit in Japan was unfair because evidence and witnesses located in Taiwan were important. A Japanese court could not obtain this evidence or these witnesses by judicial assistance because there were no diplomatic relations with Taiwan. It was not unjust to make the plaintiffs proceed in Taiwan because their interests were protected by the conditions imposed on the defendants when the United States court dismissed the case.

For a discussion by a distinguished Japanese professor of the jurisdiction of Japanese courts in international litigation, see Masato Dogauchi, Concurrent Litigations in Japan and the United States, 37 Japanese Annual Int'l L. 72 (1994).

5. In footnote * page 11, Justice O'Connor leaves open the question whether Congress could "authorize federal court personal jurisdiction over alien defendants based on the aggregate of national contacts...." Federal Rule of Civil Procedure 4(k)(2), which took effect on December 1, 1993, permits accumulating national contacts to obtain jurisdiction over defendants to pursue federal claims. In order to do this, the defendant must "not [be] subject to the jurisdiction of the courts of general jurisdiction of any

state." Will this quoted requirement reverse the usual tactical position of the parties? United States v. Swiss American Bank, Ltd., 191 F.3d 30 (1st Cir. 1999), rules that a plaintiff seeking to use 4(k)(2) must make a prima facie showing that it has satisfied the requirements of 4(k)(2). If the plaintiff makes out this prima facie case, the burden shifts to the defendant to produce evidence which shows either than one or more specific states exist in which it would be subject to suit or that its contacts with the United States are constitutionally insufficient.

World Tanker Carriers Corp. v. M/V Ya Mawlaya, 99 F.3d 717 (5th Cir. 1996), held that Rule 4(k)(2) applied to a suit under general maritime law. The court said that the issue controlling application of the Rule was whether federal substantive law applied even when no federal statute applied and the court did not have "federal question" jurisdiction under 28 U.S.C. § 1331.

United States Securities and Exchange Commission v. Carrillo, 115 F.3d 1540 (11th Cir. 1997), upheld personal jurisdiction over a Costa Rican corporation and two of its Costa Rican officers in an action by the SEC for fraudulent offer and sale of securities to U.S. residents. The court held "that the applicable forum for minimum contacts purposes is the United States in cases where, as here, the court's personal jurisdiction is invoked based on a federal statute authorizing nationwide or worldwide service of process."

Choice of Law

Justice O'Connor states that "it is not at all clear at this point that California law should govern the question whether a Japanese corporation should indemnify a Taiwanese corporation on the basis of a sale made in Taiwan and a shipment of goods from Japan to Taiwan" and cites two cases concerning constitutional limits on choice of law. This is the first of many references in the materials to choice of law. Choice of law is not a primary focus of these materials because there is a separate course, conflict of laws, devoted to that subject. A little background for those who have not had a course in conflict of laws may be helpful.

With the exception of a few countries that will apply their own law whenever they accept jurisdiction of a case, each legal system has a set of rules that determine what law to apply to controversies that have contacts with more than one jurisdiction. These are "choice-of-law rules." Until the 1960s, these rules, not only in the United States, but also abroad, were territorial rules. They selected a key event in a transaction, put a pin in the map where that event occurred, and, subject to certain exceptions such as "public policy," applied the law of that place. For example, in 1960 the choice-of-law rule in United States jurisdictions for torts was to apply the law of the place of injury. In contracts, the law was less monolithic and several rules contended, sometimes within the same state. Common contract choice-of-law rules were place of making, place of performance, the law intended by the parties, and, particularly on the issue of invalidity for usury, a rule that broke the territorial mold—the law that would validate the agreement. A common term for territorial analysis of choice-of-law problems was the "vested rights" approach. This term referred to the theory that in the course of a transaction, rights vested at a particular moment, and it is these rights that are enforced by a court either at the situs of the vesting or elsewhere.

Beginning in the 1960s, influenced by academic commentators, most United States courts have replaced the territorial choice-of-law rules with what might be called "consequences-based" rules. Under this approach, courts select law in a manner that best accommodates the purposes underlying the rules of states most likely to bear the long-range consequences of the choice. If only one state is likely to bear these consequences, its law applies.

An illustration may be helpful. Husband and Wife live in a state in which spouses may sue one another for negligence. On a pleasure drive with Wife as driver and Husband as passenger, their car hits a tree in a neighboring state where there is marital immunity for negligent injury. [The problem is chosen for illustrative simplicity, not practicality. Only a handful of states retain marital immunity. See Heino v. Harper, 759 P.2d 253, 255 n. 1 (Or. 1988) (5 states).] Up until 1960, with the exception of a few states that had recharacterized this problem as one of "family law" rather than "tort," United States courts would have applied the law of the place of injury in this case. This means that if Husband sued Wife in a court at their marital domicile, Husband would lose because the immunity rule of the neighboring state would have been applied. As of January 1, 2000, however, courts in at least 39 states plus the District of Columbia and Puerto Rico would apply the law of the marital domicile and allow recovery. See Russell J. Weintraub, Commentary on the Conflict of Laws § 6.18 n.171 (4th ed. 2000) (citing cases from thirty-nine states, the District of Columbia, and Puerto Rico). The reason is that under a consequences-based approach, if its law is not applied, the place of injury is not likely to suffer the consequences that its marital immunity rule is designed to prevent (marital discord and collusion between Husband and Wife against Wife's liability insurer). Any discord will be at the marital domicile. If the anti-collusion policy is designed to keep down insurance rates, recovery will primarily affect rates in the rating district where the car is principally garaged. On the other hand, the marital domicile is likely to experience the consequences if its policy preferring compensation of Husband is not given effect. In an extreme case, the family may need public support if compensation is not available from the liability insurer. In any event, the marital domicile will experience the subtle and not-so-subtle effects of martial immunity for negligently inflicted harm.

Some terms used for this consequences-based approach to choice of law are "interest analysis" and "most significant relationship test." This approach not only has been adopted by most United States jurisdictions, but also has influenced recent choice-of-law developments in many foreign countries, including Australia, the United Kingdom, and the codes of Western and Eastern Europe. See Michael C. Pryles, "Reflections on the False Conflict in the Choice of Law Process," 11 Sydney L. Rev. 284 (1987); U.K.: Private International Law (Miscellaneous Provisions) Act 1995, pt. III §§ 11, 12 (presumption that the applicable law is that of the place of injury is rebutted if it is "substantially more appropriate" to apply the law of another country); C.G.J. Morse, "Choice of Law in Tort: A Comparative Survey," 32 Am. J. Comp. L. 51 (1984).

Justice O'Connor's suggestion that California law should not determine whether there is contribution between Cheng Shin and Asahi, assuming both are liable for the harm caused, makes sense under a consequences-based approach to choice of law. Does she, however, overlook another choice-of-law problem—what law determines the underlying liability on which contribution is based? The only way to guarantee that California products liability law is applied to determine Asahi's liability to the injured users, is to litigate the case in California.

Convention On Jurisdiction and Enforcement of Judgments in Civil and Commercial Matters, (European Economic Community) ["Brussels Convention"]

[Consolidated and updated version of the Brussels Convention of 1968 and the Protocol of 1971, following the 1989 accession of Spain and Portugal. Official J. E.C., C 189, V. 33, July 28, 1990. pp. 1-34, reprinted 29 I.L.M. 1413 (1990)]

Title I: Scope

Article 1

This Convention shall apply in civil and commercial matters whatever the nature of the court or tribunal. It shall not extend, in particular, to revenue, customs or administrative matters.

The Convention shall not apply to:

(1) the status or legal capacity of natural persons, rights in property arising out of a matrimonial relationship, wills and succession;

(2) bankruptcy, proceedings relating to the winding up of insolvent companies or other legal persons, judicial arrangements, compositions and analogous proceedings;

(3) social security;

(4) arbitration.

Title II: Jurisdiction

Section 1: General Provisions

Article 2

Subject to the provisions of this Convention, persons domiciled in a Contracting State shall, whatever their nationality, be sued in the courts of that State.

Persons who are not nationals of the State in which they are domiciled shall be governed by the rules of jurisdiction applicable to nationals of that State.

Article 3

Persons domiciled in a Contracting State may be sued in the courts of another Contracting State only by virtue of the rules set out in Sections 2 to 6 of this Title.

In particular the following provisions shall not be applicable as against them:

in Belgium: Article 15 of the civil code (Code civil—Burgerlijk Wetboek) and Article 638 of the judicial code (Code judiciaire—Gerechtelijk Wetboek),

in Denmark: Article 246(2), (3) of the law on civil procedure (Lov om rettens pleje),

in the Federal Republic of Germany: Article 23 of the code of civil procedure (Zivilprozeßordnung),

in Greece: Article 40 of the code of civil procedure

in France: Articles 14 and 15 of the civil code (Code civil), in Ireland: the rules which enable jurisdiction to be founded on the document instituting the proceedings having been served on the defendant during his temporary presence in Ireland,

in Italy: Articles 2 and 4, Nos. 1 and 2 of the code of civil procedure (Codice di procedura civile),

in Luxembourg: Articles 14 and 15 of the civil code (Code civil),

in the Netherlands: Articles 126(3) and 127 of the code of civil procedure (Wetboek van Burgerlijke Rechtsvordering),

in Portugal: Article 65(1)(c), Article 65(2) and Article 65A(c) of the code of civil procedure (Código de Processo Civil) and Article 11 of the code of labour procedure (Código de Processo de Trabalho),

in the United Kingdom: the rules which enable jurisdiction to be founded on:

(a) the document instituting the proceedings having been served on the defendant during his temporary presence in the United Kingdom; or

(b) presence within the United Kingdom of property belonging to the defendant; or

(c) the seizure by the plaintiff of property situated in the United Kingdom.

Article 4

If the defendant is not domiciled in a Contracting State, the jurisdiction of the courts of each Contracting State shall, subject to the provisions of Article 16, be determined by the law of that State.

As against such a defendant, any person domiciled in a Contracting State may, whatever his nationality, avail himself in that State of the rules of jurisdiction there in force, and in particular those specified in the second paragraph of Article 3, in the same way as the nationals of that State.

Section 2: Special Jurisdiction

Article 5

A person domiciled in a Contracting State may, in another Contracting State, be sued:

(1) in matters relating to a contract, in the courts for the place of performance of the obligation in question; in matters relating to individual contracts of employment, this place is that where the employee habitually carries out his work, or if the employee does not habitually carry out his work in any one country, the employer may also be sued in the courts for the place where the business which engaged the employee was or is now situated;

(2) in matters relating to maintenance, in the courts for the place where the maintenance creditor is domiciled or habitually resident or, if the matter is ancillary to proceedings concerning the status of a person, in the court which, according to its own law, has jurisdiction to entertain those proceedings, unless that jurisdiction is based solely on the nationality of one of the parties;

(3) in matters relating to tort, delict or quasi-delict, in the courts for the place where the harmful event occurred;

(4) as regards a civil claim for damages or restitution which is based on an act giving rise to criminal proceedings, in the court seised of those proceedings, to the extent that that court has jurisdiction under its own law to entertain civil proceedings;

(5) as regards a dispute arising out of the operations of a branch, agency or other establishment, in the courts for the place in which the branch, agency or other establishment is situated;

(6) as settlor, trustee or beneficiary of a trust created by the operation of a statute, or by a written instrument, or created orally and evidenced in writing, in the courts of the Contracting State in which the trust is domiciled;

(7) as regards a dispute concerning the payment of remuneration claimed in respect of the salvage of a cargo or freight, in the court under the authority of which the cargo or freight in question:

(a) has been arrested to secure such payment, or

(b) could have been so arrested, but bail or other security has been given;

provided that this provision shall apply only if it is claimed that the defendant has an interest in the cargo or freight or had such an interest at the time of salvage.

Article 6

A person domiciled in a Contracting State may also be sued:

(1) where he is one of a number of defendants, in the courts for the place where any one of them is domiciled;

(2) as a third party in an action on a warranty or guarantee or in any other third party proceedings, in the court seised of the original proceedings, unless these were instituted solely with the object of removing him from the jurisdiction of the court which would be competent in his case;

(3) on a counter-claim arising from the same contract or facts on which the original claim was based, in the court in which the original claim is pending.

(4) in matters relating to a contract, if the action may be combined with an action against the same defendant in matters relating to rights *in rem* in immovable property, in the court of the Contracting State in which the property is situated.

Section 3: Jurisdiction in Matters Relating to Insurance

[These provisions provide that an insurer may be sued either in the State where it is domiciled or where the policy-holder is domiciled, and in the case of liability insurance, where the harmful event occurred. The insurer is permitted to sue an insured or beneficiary only where they are domiciled. With a few exceptions, the provisions of the Section may not be departed from by an agreement entered into before the dispute has arisen.]

Section 4: Jurisdiction over Consumer Contracts

Article 13

In proceedings concerning a contract concluded by a person for a purpose which can be regarded as being outside his trade or profession, hereinafter called "the consumer," jurisdiction shall be determined by this Section, without prejudice to the provisions of Articles 4 and 5(5), if it is:

(1) a contract for the sale of goods on instalment credit terms, or

(2) a contract for a loan repayable by instalments, or for any other form of credit, made to finance the sale of goods, or

(3) any other contract for the supply of goods or a contract for the supply of services, and

(a) in the State of the consumer's domicile the conclusion of the contract was preceded by a specific invitation addressed to him or by advertising, and

(b) the consumer took in that State the steps necessary for the conclusion of the contract.

Where a consumer enters into a contract with a party who is not domiciled in a Contracting State but has a branch, agency or other establishment in one of the Contracting States, that party shall, in disputes arising out of the operations of the branch, agency or establishment, be deemed to be domiciled in that State.

This Section shall not apply to contracts of transport.

Article 14

A consumer may bring proceedings against the other party to a contract either in the courts of the Contracting State in which that party is domiciled or in the courts of the Contracting State in which he is himself domiciled.

Proceedings may be brought against a consumer by the other party to the contract only in the courts of the Contracting State in which the consumer is domiciled.

These provisions shall not affect the right to bring a counterclaim in the court in which, in accordance with this Section, the original claim is pending.

Article 15

The provisions of this Section may be departed from only by an agreement:

(1) which is entered into after the dispute has arisen, or

(2) which allows the consumer to bring proceedings in courts other than those indicated in this Section, or

(3) which is entered into by the consumer and the other party to the contract, both of whom are at the time of conclusion of the contract domiciled or habitually resident in the sameContracting State, and which confers jurisdiction on the courts of that State, provided that such an agreement is not contrary to the law of that State.

Section 5: Exclusive Jurisdiction

Article 16

The following courts shall have exclusive jurisdiction, regardless of domicile:

(1) (a) in proceedings which have as their object rights *in rem* in immovable property or tenancies of immovable property, the courts of the Contracting State in which the property is situated;

(b) however, in proceedings which have as their object tenancies of immovable property concluded for temporary private use for a maximum period of six consecutive months, the courts of the Contracting State in which the defendant is domiciled shall also have jurisdiction, provided that the landlord and the tenant are natural persons and are domiciled in the same Contracting State;

(2) in proceedings which have as their object the validity of the constitution, the nullity or the dissolution of companies or other legal persons or associations of natural or legal persons, or the decisions of their organs, the courts of the Contracting State in which the company, legal person or association has its seat;

(3) in proceedings which have as their object the validity of entries in public registers, the courts of the Contracting State in which the register is kept;

(4) in proceedings concerned with the registration or validity of patents, trade marks, designs, or other similar rights required to be deposited or registered, the courts of the Contracting State in which the deposit or registration has been applied for, has taken place or is under the terms of an international convention deemed to have taken place;

(5) in proceedings concerned with the enforcement of judgments, the courts of the Contracting State in which the judgment has been or is to be enforced.

Section 6: Prorogation of Jurisdiction

Article 17

If the parties, one or more of whom is domiciled in a Contracting State, have agreed that a court or the courts of a Contracting State are to have jurisdiction to settle any disputes which have arisen or which may arise in connection with a particular legal relationship, that court or those courts shall have exclusive jurisdiction. Such an agreement conferring jurisdiction shall be either:

(a) in writing or evidenced in writing; or

(b) in a form which accords with practices which the parties have established between themselves; or

(c) in international trade or commerce, in a form which accords with a usage of which the parties are or ought to have been aware and which in such trade or commerce is widely known to, and regularly observed by, parties to contracts of the type involved in the particular trade or commerce concerned.

Where such an agreement is concluded by parties, none of whom is domiciled in a Contracting State, the courts of other Contracting States shall have no jurisdiction over their disputes unless the court or courts chosen have declined jurisdiction.

The court or courts of a Contracting State on which a trust instrument has conferred jurisdiction shall have exclusive jurisdiction in any proceedings brought against a settlor, trustee or beneficiary, if relations between these persons or their rights or obligations under the trust are involved.

Agreements or provisions of a trust instrument conferring jurisdiction shall have no legal force if they are contrary to the provisions of Articles 12 or 15, or if the courts whose jurisdiction they purport to exclude have exclusive jurisdiction by virtue of Article 16.

If an agreement conferring jurisdiction was concluded for the benefit of only one of the parties, that party shall retain the right to bring proceedings in any other court which has jurisdiction by virtue of this Convention.

In matters relating to individual contracts of employment an agreement conferring jurisdiction shall have legal force only if entered into after the dispute has arisen or if the employee invokes it to seise courts other than those for the defendant's domicile or those specified in Article 5(1).

Article 18

Apart from jurisdiction derived from other provisions of this Convention, a court of a Contracting State before whom a defendant enters an appearance shall have jurisdiction. This rule shall not apply where appearance was entered solely to contest the jurisdiction, or where another court has exclusive jurisdiction by virtue of Article 16.

Section 7: Examination as to Jurisdiction and Admissibility

Article 19

Where a court of a Contracting State is seised of a claim which is principally concerned with a matter over which the courts of another Contracting State have exclusive jurisdiction by virtue of Article 16, it shall declare of its own motion that it has no jurisdiction.

Article 20

Where a defendant domiciled in one Contracting State is sued in a court of another Contracting State and does not enter an appearance, the court shall declare of its own motion that it has no jurisdiction unless its jurisdiction is derived from the provisions of this Convention.

The court shall stay the proceedings so long as it is not shown that the defendant has been able to receive the document instituting the proceedings or an equivalent document in sufficient time to enable him to arrange for his defence, or that all necessary steps have been taken to this end.

The provisions of the foregoing paragraph shall be replaced by those of Article 15 of the Hague Convention of 15 November 1965 on the service abroad of judicial and extrajudicial documents in civil or commercial matters, if the document instituting the proceedings or notice thereof had to be transmitted abroad in accordance with that Convention.

Section 8: Lis Pendens—Related Actions

Article 21

Where proceedings involving the same cause of action and between the same parties are brought in the courts of different Contracting States, any court other than the court first seised shall of its own motion stay its proceedings until such time as the jurisdiction of the court first seised is established.

Where the jurisdiction of the court first seised is established, any court other than the court first seised shall decline jurisdiction in favour of that court.

Article 22

Where related actions are brought in the courts of different Contracting States, any court other than the court first seised may, while the actions are pending at first instance, stay its proceedings.

A court other than the court first seised may also, on the application of one of the parties, decline jurisdiction if the law of that court permits the consolidation of related actions and the court first seised has jurisdiction over both actions.

For the purposes of this article, actions are deemed to be related where they are so closely connected that it is expedient to hear and determine them together to avoid the risk of irreconcilable judgments resulting from separate proceedings.

Article 23

Where actions come within the exclusive jurisdiction of several courts, any court other than the court first seised shall decline jurisdiction in favour of that court.

Section 9: Provisional, Including Protective, Measures

Article 24

Application may be made to the courts of a Contracting State for such provisional, including protective, measures as may be available under the law of that State, even if, under this Convention, the courts of another Contracting State have jurisdiction as to the substance of the matter.

Title III: Recognition and Enforcement

Article 25

For the purposes of this Convention, "judgment" means any judgment given by a court or tribunal of a Contracting State, whatever the judgment may be called, including a decree, order, decision or writ of execution, as well as the determination of costs or expenses by an officer of the court.

Section 1: Recognition

Article 26

A judgment given in a Contracting State shall be recognized in the other Contracting States without any special procedure being required.

Any interested party who raises the recognition of a judgment as the principal issue in a dispute may, in accordance with the procedures provided for in Sections 2 and 3 of this Title, apply for a decision that the judgment be recognized.

If the outcome of proceedings in a court of a Contracting State depends on the determination of an incidental question of recognition that court shall have jurisdiction over that question.

Article 27

A judgment shall not be recognized:

(1) if such recognition is contrary to public policy in the State in which recognition is sought;

(2) where it was given in default of appearance, if the defendant was not duly served with the document which instituted the proceedings or with an equivalent document in sufficient time to enable him to arrange for his defence;

(3) if the judgment is irreconcilable with a judgment given in a dispute between the same parties in the State in which recognition is sought;

(4) if the court of the State of origin, in order to arrive at its judgment, has decided a preliminary question concerning the status or legal capacity of natural persons, rights in property arising out of a matrimonial relationship, wills or succession in a way that conflicts with a rule of the private international law of the State in which the recognition is sought, unless the same result would have been reached by the application of the rules of private international law of that State;

(5) if the judgment is irreconcilable with an earlier judgment given in a non-contracting State involving the same cause of action and between the same parties, provided that this latter judgment fulfills the conditions necessary for its recognition in the State addressed.

Article 28

Moreover, a judgment shall not be recognized if it conflicts with the provisions of Sections 3, 4 or 5 of Title II, or in a case provided for in Article 59.

In its examination of the grounds of jurisdiction referred to in the foregoing paragraph, the court or authority applied to shall be bound by the findings of fact on which the court of the State in which the judgment was given based its jurisdiction.

Subject to the provisions of the first paragraph, the jurisdiction of the court of the State of origin may not be reviewed; the test of public policy referred to in point 1 of Article 27, may not be applied to the rules relating to jurisdiction.

Article 29

Under no circumstances may a foreign judgment be reviewed as to its substance.

Article 30

A court of a Contracting State in which recognition is sought of a judgment given in another Contracting State may stay the proceedings if an ordinary appeal against the judgment has been lodged.

A court of a Contracting State in which recognition is sought of a judgment given in Ireland or the United Kingdom may stay the proceedings if enforcement is suspended in the State of origin, by reason of an appeal.

Section 2: Enforcement

Article 31

A judgment given in a Contracting State and enforceable in that State shall be enforced in another Contracting State when, on the application of any interested party, it has been declared enforceable there.

However, in the United Kingdom, such a judgment shall be enforced in England and Wales, in Scotland, or in Northern Ireland when, on the application of any interested party, it has been registered for enforcement in that part of the United Kingdom.

* * *

Article 34

The court applied to shall give its decision without delay; the party against whom enforcement is sought shall not at this stage of the proceedings be entitled to make any submissions on the application.

The application may be refused only for one of the reasons specified in Articles 27 and 28.

* * *

Article 36

If enforcement is authorized, the party against whom enforcement is sought may appeal against the decision within one month of service thereof.

If that party is domiciled in a Contracting State other than that in which the decision authorizing enforcement was given, the time for appealing shall be two months and shall run from the date of service, either on him in person or at his residence. No extension of time may be granted on account of distance.

* * *

Title V: General Provisions

Article 52

In order to determine whether a party is domiciled in the Contracting State whose courts are seised of a matter, the Court shall apply its internal law.

If a party is not domiciled in the State whose courts are seised of the matter, then, in order to determine whether the party is domiciled in another Contracting State, the court shall apply the law of that State.

Article 53

For the purposes of this Convention, the seat of a company or other legal person or association of natural or legal persons shall be treated as its domicile. However, in order to determine that seat, the court shall apply its rules of private international law.

In order to determine whether a trust is domiciled in the Contracting State whose courts are seised of the matter, the court shall apply its rules of private international law.

* * *

Title VII: Relationship to Other Conventions

* * *

Article 59

This Convention shall not prevent a Contracting State from assuming, in a convention on the recognition and enforcement of judgments, an obligation towards a third State not to recognize judgments given in other Contracting States against defendants domiciled or habitually resident in the third State where, in cases provided for in Article 4, the judgment could only be founded on a ground of jurisdiction specified in the second paragraph of Article 3.

However, a Contracting State may not assume an obligation towards a third State not to recognize a judgment given in another Contracting State by a court basing its jurisdiction on the presence within that State of property belonging to the defendant, or the seizure by the plaintiff of property situated there:

(1) if the action is brought to assert or declare proprietary or possessory rights in that property, seeks to obtain authority to dispose of it, or arises from another issue relating to such property, or

(2) if the property constitutes the security for a debt which is the subject-matter of the action.

* * *

Notes

1. As of January 1, 2000, 15 countries were members of the European Union: Austria, Belgium, Denmark, Finland, France, Germany, Greece, Ireland, Italy, Luxembourg, Netherlands, Portugal, Spain, Sweden, and United Kingdom. Austria, Finland, and Sweden joined on January 1, 1995. The Lugano Convention, done Sept. 16, 1988, 1988 O.J. (L.319) 9, reprinted 28 I.L.M. 620, extends the provisions of the Convention to three members of the European Free Trade Association (EFTA): Iceland, Norway, and Switzerland. EFTA countries have duty-free access to the EEC market for their manufactured exports.

Luxembourg and Switzerland do not recognize jurisdiction over their domiciliaries based on Article 5(1). In their courts, Austria, Germany, Spain, and Switzerland do not permit jurisdiction under Articles 6(2) and 10 (permitting the insurer to be joined in proceedings that the injured party has brought against the insured), but they will recognize judgments of other Contracting States based on these provisions.

The Commission of the European Communities has published a proposal for an Act by the Council of the European Union establishing a Convention on Jurisdiction and the Recognition and Enforcement of Judgments based on the existing Convention (the "Brussels Convention") but containing numerous amendments. For example, current Article 2 relating to general jurisdiction is amended by referring to Article 57 (formerly Article 53) for the definition of the domicile of legal persons. Article 57 eliminates former Article 53's reference to the forum's rules of private international law and provides that "a company or other legal person or association of natural or legal persons is domiciled at the place where it has its statutory seat, central administration, or principal place of business." The Treaty of Amsterdam, in force in the EU since May 1, 1999, gives the EU Council power to thus replace the Brussels Convention. The U.K., Ireland, and Denmark have not adhered to this portion of the Treaty. The proposal for the Council Regulation is found on the following Web site, last visited August 22, 2000: <http://europa.eu.int/eur-lex/en/com/dat/1999/en_599PC0348.html>.

2. Are the provisions of the EEC Convention on Jurisdiction and the Enforcement of Judgments, particularly Articles 5 and 6, relevant to assessing the reasoning in *Asahi*? A 1971 Protocol to the Brussels Convention gave the Court of Justice of the European Communities jurisdiction to rule on interpretations of the Convention. Only governments and EU institutions can bring cases directly in the Court and national courts can refer points of European law. In 1989 the EU added a Court of First Instance to hear cases brought by firms and individuals.

In Zelger v. Salinitri, [1980] E.C.R. 89, the Court of Justice declared: "The provisions of Article 5 * * * introduce a criterion for jurisdiction, the selection of which is at the option of the plaintiff and which is justified by the existence of a direct link between the dispute and the court called upon to take cognizance of it." (Id. at 96).

Handelskwekerij G. J. Bier v. Mines de Potasse d'Alsace, [1976] E.C.R. 1735, held that a Netherlands horticultural company could bring suit under Article 5(3) in the Netherlands for damage to its seedbeds caused by defendant's alleged discharging of pollutants into the Rhine River in France. The Court declared that "the defendant may be sued, at the option of the plaintiff, either in the courts for the place where the damage occurred or in the courts for the place of the event which gives rise to and is at the origin of that damage." (Id. at 1749).

Dumez Batiment SA v. Hessische Landesbank, [1990] E.C.R. I-49 (Case 220/88), further defined Article 5(3)'s reference to "the place where the harmful event occurred." French parent companies claimed that German banks had wrongfully refused to provide construction financing to the French companies' German subsidiaries. The French companies sued the German banks in France contenting that where they suffered financial loss and therefore "where the damages occurred.". The Court held that the French courts did not have jurisdiction under 5(3) stating that *Bier*'s reference to "where the damage occurred" "can be understood only as indicating the place where the event giving rise to the damage, and entailing tortious, delictual or quasi-delictual liability, directly produced its harmful effects upon the person who is the immediate victim of that event."

In Shevill v. Presse Alliance S.A., [1995] E.C.R. I-415 (Case C-68/93), the Court of Justice of the European Communities interpreted article 5(3) in the context of multistate libel. The Court stated that "the victim of a libel by a newspaper article distributed in several contracting states may bring an action for damages against the publisher either before the courts * * * of the place where the publisher...is established, which has jurisdiction to award damages for all the harm caused by the defamation, or before the courts of each contracting state in which the publication was distributed, and where the victim claims to have suffered injury to his reputation, which have jurisdiction to rule solely in respect of the harm caused in the state of the court seised."

Compare with *Shevill*, Keeton v. Hustler Magazine, 465 U.S. 770 (1984), in which plaintiff was permitted to sue the magazine for libel in New Hampshire. The plaintiff did not reside in New Hampshire, where only a small percentage of the magazines were sold. New Hampshire was the only state in which the statute of limitations had not run. Keeton v. Hustler Magazine, 549 A.2d 1187 (N.H. 1988), then held that a New Hampshire court would apply the New Hampshire statute of limitations to permit recovery for harm suffered in any state where the magazine was published.

In July 1998, while on a trip to Europe with other United States judges to improve judicial cooperation, Justice O'Connor stated that the Supreme Court of the United States would "be more inclined to look at decisions of the [Court of Justice of the European Communities] on substantive issues * * * and perhaps use them and cite them in future decisions." Nat'l L.J. 7/20/98 A14, col. 1.

3. Of the bases for jurisdiction that Art. 3 provides may not be used against persons domiciled in contracting states, the most notorious are the French provisions permitting any French national (extended by Art. 4 ¶ 2 to anyone domiciled in France) to acquire personal jurisdiction over any defendant, and the German provisions under which the presence of property confers personal jurisdiction over the owner. Why do the EEC and Lugano Conventions render these exorbitant bases for jurisdiction more threatening to companies and persons not domiciled in the contracting states? What advantages do Arts 3, 4, and 59 give contracting states in negotiating bilateral judgment-recognition treaties with non-contracting states?

The German Federal Supreme Court has narrowed the scope of personal jurisdiction based on the presence of defendant's assets, requiring that in addition to the location of assets, there must be a sufficient connection between the litigation and Germany. Judgment of July 2, 1991, BGH, 1991 Neue Juristische Wochenschrift [NJW] 3092. The Munich Court of Appeals has affirmed a district court's rejection of jurisdiction in a suit by a Saudi-Arabian plaintiff against a United States airline, which had assets in Germany. The court noted that the suit, based on a contract between the parties, had no connection with Germany and that Germany was not the only jurisdiction in which the plaintiff could obtain a judgment that would be enforced in Germany. Judgment of October 7, 1992, OLG München, 1993 Recht der internationalen Wirtschaft [RIW] 66.

There are other EEC and EFTA countries that provide for personal jurisdiction over the owner of assets within the country. See, Austria, Jurisdiktionsnorm art. 99 (but there can be no disproportion between the value of the local assets and the amount in controversy); Denmark, Act on Civil Procedure art. 246(2); Greece, Code of Civil Procedure art. 40; Switzerland, Bundesgesetz Ober Das Internationale Privatrecht (IPEG) of Dec. 18, 1987, SR 291 art. 4.

4. Burnham v. Superior Court, 495 U.S. 604 (1990) held that service on a defendant while transiently present in the forum is constitutionally sufficient to confer personal jurisdiction. Justice Scalia announced the judgment of a unanimous court, although only Chief Justice Rehnquist and Justice Kennedy concurred in his reasoning. Justice Scalia said that presence as a basis for jurisdiction did not violate due process because, if long and continued use was not a sufficient basis for determining what was constitutional, the only substitute would be "each Justice's subjective assessment of what is fair and just." Do the provisions of Art. 3 of the EEC Convention on Jurisdiction and Judgments provide an objective basis for arguing that transient presence is not a proper basis for personal jurisdiction?

5. Note 2, supra, suggests that *Asahi* would be decided differently under the Brussels Convention. Suits to enforce support obligations are another area in which the Convention confers jurisdiction that the United States Supreme Court has held violates due process. Article 5(2) permits jurisdiction "where the maintenance creditor is domiciled or habitually resident." The Court of Justice of the European Communities has held that article 5(2) permits an Irish resident to sue a Belgium resident in Ireland for child support even though paternity is denied by the defendant and the question of paternity is a preliminary issue in the proceedings. Farrell v. Long, [1997] E.C.R. I-1683 (EC case C-295/95). Kulko v. Superior Court, 436 U.S. 84 (1978) held that a father's acquiescence in his child's desire to move to California to live with the mother did not give California courts jurisdiction over the father in a suit to increase child-support payments.

Miller v. Honda Motor Co.
779 F.2d 769 (1st Cir. 1985)

Before BOWNES, TORRUELLA and TIMBERS, Circuit Judges.

TORRUELLA, Circuit Judge.

The issue presented by this case is whether we will expand the reach of our recent decision in *Howse v. Zimmer Manufacturing Co., Inc.*, 757 F.2d 448 (1st Cir.1985), a case involving the service of process requirements of Mass. Gen. Laws Ann. ch. 223 §38, for the purpose of permitting the acquisition of in personam jurisdiction over a foreign corporation which lacks any direct contacts with this jurisdiction. Because we believe that *Howse* delineates the outer limits of what is permitted by the due process clause, we reject the invitation proffered by appellants and affirm the district court's decision to the effect that in personam jurisdiction is lacking over defendant/appellee Honda Motor

Co., Ltd. (Honda). Since jurisdictional controversies are so fact-dependent, we commence with a summary of the relevant particulars.

Plaintiffs/appellants Marion and Donald Miller (Miller) are residents of Massachusetts. In February, 1980, the Millers, while vacationing in Bermuda, rented a Honda PC 50 moped from Smatt's Cycle Livery, Ltd. (Smatt), a Bermudian enterprise. Mrs. Miller had an accident while using the vehicle, sustaining serious injuries which resulted in a quadriplegic condition. She will, in all probability, be confined to a bed or wheelchair the rest of her life, totally dependent on others for all aspects of her care, even for breathing, for which she requires the use of a respirator.

The vehicle in question was manufactured for Honda, a Japanese company, by another company located in Taiwan, Koyo Kogyo Co., Ltd. (Koyo). Honda had the moped shipped to Bermuda via Asia and South America. There it was sold to Honda Livery, Ltd. (Honda Bermuda), a Bermuda corporation. Honda Bermuda then sold it to Smatt's who, as indicated, was the owner of the moped when the accident occurred.

The Millers brought a products liability suit against Honda in the United States District Court for the District of Massachusetts. The suit was dismissed, the court ruling that the facts were insufficient to justify an assertion of personal jurisdiction over Honda.

The record is uncontroverted that Honda-manufactured vehicles, and other products are sold in Massachusetts by authorized dealers who purchase them from a California corporation, American Honda Motor Co., Inc. (American Honda). American Honda is a wholly-owned subsidiary of Honda. Honda, however, conducts no direct business activities in Massachusetts and has no offices, bank accounts nor employees located therein. Nor has it entered into any franchise or distributorship agreements in Massachusetts or with any business entity located in that state. There is not even any allegation that Honda's employees have ever visited Massachusetts.

The record is uncontradicted that Honda's direct involvement with goods destined for the North American market ends dockside in Japan with the sale of these goods to Honda American, which is the company that sells to the Massachusetts dealers. American Honda is also the company that has contacts with Massachusetts normally associated with the granting of in personam jurisdiction over a foreign corporation. It is not, however, a party defendant in this suit. We surmise that the reason for this is that American Honda has no Bermuda connection, and more importantly, because American Honda cannot be charged with the manufacturing defects, having had no apparent intervention with that end of the business. The Millers rely on *Howse v. Zimmer Manufacturing Co., Inc., supra,* in their attempt to acquire Massachusetts jurisdiction over Honda. Unfortunately, as indicated, that case is not applicable.

Howse, although extremely liberal in allowing the assumption of jurisdiction, is clearly distinguishable from the present situation. Howse, a Massachusetts resident, suffered a broken hip while in Spain. He underwent surgery in a United States naval hospital in that country during which a "nail and plate" implant, allegedly manufactured by Zimmer, was inserted into his hip. Upon his return to the United States, Howse sued Zimmer in Massachusetts, alleging that the fracture improperly healed due to defects in the implant. Zimmer, a Delaware corporation with its principal place of business in Indiana, had none of the contacts which are traditionally thought to establish personal jurisdiction under § 38. As in the present case, Zimmer was neither registered in, nor did it have a traditional type of agent in the Massachusetts. It manufactured no products there nor did it have an office, bank accounts, nor employees located there. It had not entered into franchises or distributorship agreements in Massachusetts. Its products were sold in Massachusetts exclusively by a representative, Docherty Associates, Inc., which did business under the name Zimmer Docherty Associates. The district court found that there was no personal jurisdiction over Zimmer. We reversed.

Two important distinguishing features appear in *Howse* that are absent in the present situation, however. First, Zimmer engaged in a systematic pattern of activities in Massachusetts closely approximating the regular conduct of domestic enterprises:

> [T]o us most significantly, Zimmer is "always" sending representatives to Massachusetts to confer with surgeons concerning the development of new products and specific need products. We think this pattern of extensive instate activities removes Zimmer from the category of defendant encountered in *Caso*.... While the case is close, the fact that Zimmer representatives are constantly in and out of Massachusetts in order to deal directly with customers, coupled with the sizeable sales volume and other factors removes this from the "mere solicitation" and "solicitation plus" category....

Howse, supra at 452-453, (emphasis supplied) (footnote omitted).

Second, we noted, that payments for the products sold in Massachusetts was always made directly to Zimmer in Indiana, even when the Massachusetts dealer, Zimmer Docherty Associates, filled the order from his in-state inventory.

Both of these factors are missing from the present situation. This is not to say, of course, that the mere absence of these conditions, if other traditionally relevant indicia are present, would by themselves defeat jurisdiction. As previously indicated, these controversies are highly fact-specific and all evidence must be carefully weighed and evaluated before concluding whether or not there is jurisdiction. What is clear from the record is that permitting the acquisition of in *personam* jurisdiction over Honda in this case would offend all notions of fair play and due process. *See World-Wide Volkswagen Corp. v. Woodson*, 444 U.S. 286 (1980); *International Shoe Co. v. Washington*, 326 U.S. 310 (1945). In the present case Zimmer's equivalent is American Honda, not Honda. Honda is one step further removed than Zimmer, a gap which, at least under the circumstances before us, can not be bridged.

Appellants make one additional claim as an alternate ground for finding jurisdiction. They urge that we apply the doctrine of corporate disregard and find that American Honda is in fact an agent of its Japanese parent. The Supreme Judicial Court of Massachusetts has stated that the fiction of corporate separateness should be disregarded only:

> a) when there is active and direct participation by the representatives of one corporation, apparently exercising some form of pervasive control in the activities of another, and there is *some fraudulent or injurious consequence of the intercorporate relationship*, or (b) when there is a confused intermingling of activity of two or more corporations engaged in a common enterprise with substantial disregard of the separate nature of the corporate entities, or serious ambiguity about the manner and capacity in which various corporations and their respective representatives are acting.

My Bread Baking Co. v. Cumberland Farms Inc., 353 Mass. 614, 619, 233 N.E.2d 748, 752 (1968). (Emphasis ours). *See also Westcott Constructions Corp. v. Cumberland Const. Co., Inc.*, 3 Mass.App. 294, 297-98, 328 N.E.2d 522, 525 (1975); *Willis v. American Permac, Inc.*, 541 F.Supp. 118, 122 (D.Mass.1982).

The district court found that the affairs of Honda and American Honda were not so intertwined as to demonstrate that the two corporations are, in reality, a single entity subject to the application of the doctrine in question. The evidence in the record supports this conclusion.

Although there is common membership on the board of directors by two officers, the day to day operational decisions of each company are made by separate groups of corporate officers. Of the twenty-four officers and directors at Honda, only one is from American Honda, its president, and his involvement is limited to attending board meetings in Japan. Of fourteen directors and officers of American Honda, the chairman of the board is also the executive vice-president of Honda, but he has no involvement in running the operations of American Honda and receives reports when he visits American Honda in California for meetings. At those meetings, only the affairs of American Honda are discussed. Honda reimburses American Honda for warranty repairs. It also charged American Honda interest for delayed payments. American Honda controls its own advertising and marketing schemes, and the types of goods it feels are appropriate for the American market. Last, but not least, American Honda maintains a completely separate system for personnel management, financial planning, and real estate planning.

Appellants' argument primarily rests on equity. Mrs. Miller's severe physical limitations preclude her traveling to Bermuda to litigate this action there; it would present no significant burden for Honda to litigate in Massachusetts. Such an argument, although emotive, cannot deter us from being fair to all parties. It would be contrary to long established legal doctrine to apply the corporate disregard doctrine to the relationship between Honda and American Honda. Even where there is a common control of a group of separate corporations engaged in a single enterprise, failure to meet the criteria established in *My Bread Baking Co.*, supra, will defeat any attempt to pierce the corporate veil. *See NCR Credit Corporation v. Underground Camera, Inc.*, 581 F.Supp. 609, 612 (D.Mass.1984). After all, there is nothing fraudulent or against public policy in limiting one's liability by the appropriate use of corporate insulation. While sympathetic to the appellants' tragedy, we cannot find any legal basis for assumption of in personam jurisdiction over Honda. For these reasons the decision of the district court is

Affirmed.

Notes

1. The court rejects the request that it pierce the corporate veil between Honda Japan and Honda United States applying standards that it takes from Massachusetts cases, citing *My Bread*, *Wescott*, and *Willis*. The issue in *My Bread* was whether the parent was liable for the subsidiary's conversion; in *Wescott*, whether parent and subsidiary could bid on the same public contract; in *Willis*, whether the parent was liable for the subsidiary's breach of contract. Only in *Willis* was the issue of personal jurisdiction even incidentally involved, because if the parent were liable, there would be specific jurisdiction over the parent. Should the same standard for piercing the corporate veil be used to ascribe the actions of the subsidiary to the parent for purposes of liability and for the purposes of personal jurisdiction?

2. Even though the request to pierce the corporate veil for purposes of jurisdiction failed in *Miller*, this is a device often used by plaintiffs' attorneys asserting jurisdiction over foreign defendants. This tactic is far more likely to succeed in American courts than in European courts. See Professor Hay's Hague lecture, cited in note 2 following *Helicopteros*, at p. 314.

One reason that plaintiffs' attorneys assert jurisdiction over foreign defendants based on the activities of a U.S. subsidiary is that discovery on this jurisdictional issue may prove embarrassing to the defendant on matters unrelated to the case and thus create pressure for settlement. Jazini v. Nissan Motor Co., 148 F.3d 181 (2d Cir. 1998), discusses discovery in order to pierce the corporate veil. Plaintiffs, New York residents, were injured when a Nissan automobile crashed while one of them was driving it in Iran. They sued Nissan Japan in federal district court in New York alleging that Nissan Japan was subject to jurisdiction there because of the activities of its wholly owned subsidiary, Nissan U.S. Plaintiffs alleged that Nissan U.S. "is able to act as would its parent, were [Nissan Japan] directly present in the State of New York." This allegation, if proven, would meet the New York standard for piercing the corporate veil. Nevertheless, before discovery the district court dismissed the complaint for lack of jurisdiction. The Second Circuit affirmed stating that plaintiffs had not pleaded sufficient facts to entitle them to discovery on the jurisdictional issue: "This conclusory statement is but a restatement, with slight changes, of the legal standard for determining agency enunciated in [New York cases]. It states no facts supporting that conclusion and does not constitute a prima facie showing of agency....If the [plaintiffs'] allegations were sufficient to establish a prima facie case of jurisdiction over Nissan Japan, and thus subject the latter to discovery—which the [plaintiffs] stated at the district court hearing would be '[r]ather extensive'—it would not be difficult for a plaintiff suing a multinational foreign corporation in the federal courts in New York, to make similar conclusory non-fact-specific jurisdictional allegations and thus obtain extensive discovery on that issue." Before discovery how can the plaintiff plead specific facts concerning relations between parent and subsidiary? Federal Rule of Civil Procedure 11(b) provides: "By presenting to the court (whether by signing, filing, submitting, or later advocating) a pleading, written motion, or other paper, an attorney or unrepresented party is certifying that to the best of the person's knowledge, information, and belief, formed after an inquiry reasonable under the circumstances...(3) the allegations and other factual contentions have evidentiary support or, if specifically so identified, are likely to have evidentiary support after a reasonable opportunity for further investigation or discovery." Rule 11(c) provides monetary sanctions for violation including penalties and payment of opponent's "reasonable attorneys' fees and other expenses."

In Sar Schotte GmbH v. Parmus Rothchild Sarl, (Case 218/86), [1987] E.C.R. 4905, the Court of Justice of the European Communities held that "Article 5(5) [of the Brussels Convention] must be interpreted as applying to a case in which a legal entity established in a Contracting State maintains no dependent branch, agency or other establishment in another Contracting State but nevertheless pursues its activities there through an independent company with the same name and identical management which negotiates and conducts business in its name and which it uses as an extension of itself."

Shaffer v. Heitner
433 U.S. 186 (1977)

Mr. Justice MARSHALL delivered the opinion of the Court.

The controversy in this case concerns the constitutionality of a Delaware statute that allows a court of that State to take jurisdiction of a lawsuit by sequestering any property of the defendant that happens to be located in Delaware. Appellants contend that the sequestration statute as applied in this case violates the Due Process Clause of the Fourteenth Amendment both because it permits the state courts to exercise jurisdiction despite the absence of sufficient contacts among the defendants, the litigation, and the State of Delaware and because it authorizes the deprivation of defendants' property without providing adequate procedural safeguards. We find it necessary to consider only the first of these contentions.

I

Appellee Heitner, a nonresident of Delaware, is the owner of one share of stock in the Greyhound Corp., a business incorporated under the laws of Delaware with its principal place of business in Phoenix, Ariz. On May 22, 1974, he filed a shareholder's derivative suit in the Court of Chancery for New Castle County, Del., in which he named as defendants Greyhound, its wholly owned subsidiary Greyhound Lines, Inc.,[1] and 28 present or former officers or directors of one or both of the corporations. In essence, Heitner alleged that the individual defendants had violated their duties to Greyhound by causing it and its subsidiary to engage in actions that resulted in the corporations being held liable for substantial damages in a private antitrust suit and a large fine in a criminal contempt action. The activities which led to these penalties took place in Oregon.

Simultaneously with his complaint, Heitner filed a motion for an order of sequestration of the Delaware property of the individual defendants pursuant to Del.Code Ann., Tit. 10, § 366 (1975). This motion was accompanied by a supporting affidavit of counsel which stated that the individual defendants were nonresidents of Delaware. The affidavit identified the property to be sequestered as

> "common stock, 3% Second Cumulative Preferred Stock and stock unit credits of the Defendant Greyhound Corporation, a Delaware corporation, as well as all options and all warrants to purchase said stock issued to said individual Defendants and all contractual [sic] obligations, all rights, debts or credits due or accrued to or for the benefit of any of the said Defendants under any type of written agreement, contract or other legal instrument of any kind whatever between any of the individual Defendants and said corporation."

The requested sequestration order was signed the day the motion was filed. Pursuant to that order, the sequestrator "seized" approximately 82,000 shares of Greyhound common stock belonging to 19 of the defendants, and options belonging to another 2 defendants. These seizures were accomplished by placing "stop transfer" orders or their equivalents on the books of the Greyhound Corp. So far as the record shows, none of the certificates representing the seized property was physically present in Delaware. The stock was considered to be in Delaware, and so subject to seizure, by virtue of Del.Code Ann., Tit. 8, § 169 (1975), which makes Delaware the situs of ownership of all stock in Delaware corporations.

All 28 defendants were notified of the initiation of the suit by certified mail directed to their last known addresses and by publication in a New Castle County newspaper. The 21 defendants whose property was seized (hereafter referred to as appellants) responded by entering a special appearance for the purpose of moving to quash service of process and to vacate the sequestration order. They contended that the ex parte sequestration procedure did not accord them due process of law and that the property seized was not capable of attachment in Delaware. In addition, appellants asserted that under

---

1. Greyhound Lines, Inc., is incorporated in California and has its principal place of business in Phoenix, Ariz.

the rule of *International Shoe Co. v. Washington*, 326 U.S. 310 (1945), they did not have sufficient contacts with Delaware to sustain the jurisdiction of that State's courts.

* * *

II

The Delaware courts rejected appellants' jurisdictional challenge by noting that this suit was brought as a quasi in rem proceeding. Since quasi in rem jurisdiction is traditionally based on attachment or seizure of property present in the jurisdiction, not on contacts between the defendant and the State, the courts considered appellants' claimed lack of contacts with Delaware to be unimportant.

* * *

If a court's jurisdiction is based on its authority over the defendant's person, the action and judgment are denominated "in personam" and can impose a personal obligation on the defendant in favor of the plaintiff. If jurisdiction is based on the court's power over property within its territory, the action is called "in rem" or "quasi in rem." The effect of a judgment in such a case is limited to the property that supports jurisdiction and does not impose a personal liability on the property owner, since he is not before the court.[17]

* * *

[I]n the well-known case of *Harris v. Balk*, 198 U.S. 215 (1905), Epstein, a resident of Maryland, had a claim against Balk, a resident of North Carolina. Harris, another North Carolina resident, owed money to Balk. When Harris happened to visit Maryland, Epstein garnished his debt to Balk. Harris did not contest the debt to Balk and paid it to Epstein's North Carolina attorney. When Balk later sued Harris in North Carolina, this Court held that the Full Faith and Credit Clause, U.S. Const., Art. IV, § 1, required that Harris' payment to Epstein be treated as a discharge of his debt to Balk. This Court reasoned that the debt Harris owed Balk was an intangible form of property belonging to Balk, and that the location of that property traveled with the debtor. By obtaining personal jurisdiction over Harris, Epstein had "arrested" his debt to Balk, 198 U.S., at 223, and brought it into the Maryland court.

* * *

We think that the time is ripe to consider whether the standard of fairness and substantial justice set forth in *International Shoe* should be held to govern actions *in rem* as well as *in personam*.

III

The case for applying to jurisdiction in rem the same test of "fair play and substantial justice" as governs assertions of jurisdiction in personam is simple and straightforward.

---

17. "A judgment *in rem* affects the interests of all persons in designated property. A judgment *quasi in rem* affects the interests of particular persons in designated property. The latter is of two types. In one the plaintiff is seeking to secure a pre-existing claim in the subject property and to extinguish or establish the nonexistence of similar interests of particular persons. In the other the plaintiff seeks to apply what he concedes to be the property of the defendant to the satisfaction of a claim against him. Restatement, Judgments, 5-9." *Hanson v. Denckla*, 357 U.S. 235, 246 n. 12, (1958).

As did the Court in *Hanson*, we will for convenience generally use the term "*in rem*" in place of "in rem and quasi *in rem*."

It is premised on recognition that "[t]he phrase, 'judicial jurisdiction over a thing', is a customary elliptical way of referring to jurisdiction over the interests of persons in a thing." Restatement (Second) of Conflict of Laws § 56, Introductory Note (1971) (hereafter Restatement). This recognition leads to the conclusion that in order to justify an exercise of jurisdiction in rem, the basis for jurisdiction must be sufficient to justify exercising "jurisdiction over the interests of persons in a thing."[23] The standard for determining whether an exercise of jurisdiction over the interests of persons is consistent with the Due Process Clause is the minimum-contacts standard elucidated in *International Shoe*.

This argument, of course, does not ignore the fact that the presence of property in a State may bear on the existence of jurisdiction by providing contacts among the forum State, the defendant, and the litigation. For example, when claims to the property itself are the source of the underlying controversy between the plaintiff and the defendant,[24] it would be unusual for the State where the property is located not to have jurisdiction. In such cases, the defendant's claim to property located in the State would normally[25] indicate that he expected to benefit from the State's protection of his interest. The State's strong interests in assuring the marketability of property within its borders and in providing a procedure for peaceful resolution of disputes about the possession of that property would also support jurisdiction, as would the likelihood that important records and witnesses will be found in the State. The presence of property may also favor jurisdiction in cases such as suits for injury suffered on the land of an absentee owner, where the defendant's ownership of the property is conceded but the cause of action is otherwise related to rights and duties growing out of that ownership.

It appears, therefore, that jurisdiction over many types of actions which now are or might be brought in rem would not be affected by a holding that any assertion of state-court jurisdiction must satisfy the *International Shoe* standard.[30] For the type of *quasi in rem* action typified by *Harris v. Balk* and the present case, however, accepting the proposed analysis would result in significant change. These are cases where the property which now serves as the basis for state-court jurisdiction is completely unrelated to the plaintiff's cause of action. Thus, although the presence of the defendant's property in a State might suggest the existence of other ties among the defendant, the State, and the litigation, the presence of the property alone would not support the State's jurisdiction. If those other ties did not exist, cases over which the State is now thought to have jurisdiction could not be brought in that forum.

Since acceptance of the *International Shoe* test would most affect this class of cases, we examine the arguments against adopting that standard as they relate to this category

---

23. It is true that the potential liability of a defendant in an in rem action is limited by the value of the property, but that limitation does not affect the argument. The fairness of subjecting a defendant to state-court jurisdiction does not depend on the size of the claim being litigated. Cf. *Fuentes v. Shevin*, 407 U.S. [67], at 88-90 [1972]

24. This category includes true *in rem* actions and the first type of *quasi in rem* proceedings. See n. 17, supra.

25. In some circumstances the presence of property in the forum State will not support the inference suggested in text. Cf., e. g., Restatement § 60, Comments c, d; Note, The Power of a State to Affect Title in a Chattel Atypically Removed to It, 47 Colum.L.Rev. 767 (1947).

30. Cf. Smit, The Enduring Utility of In Rem Rules: A Lasting Legacy of Pennoyer v. Neff, 43 Brooklyn L. Rev. 600 (1977). We do not suggest that jurisdictional doctrines other than those discussed in text, such as the particularized rules governing adjudications of status, are inconsistent with the standard of fairness.

of litigation. Before doing so, however, we note that this type of case also presents the clearest illustration of the argument in favor of assessing assertions of jurisdiction by a single standard. For in cases such as *Harris* and this one, the only role played by the property is to provide the basis for bringing the defendant into court. Indeed, the express purpose of the Delaware sequestration procedure is to compel the defendant to enter a personal appearance. In such cases, if a direct assertion of personal jurisdiction over the defendant would violate the Constitution, it would seem that an indirect assertion of that jurisdiction should be equally impermissible.

The primary rationale for treating the presence of property as a sufficient basis for jurisdiction to adjudicate claims over which the State would not have jurisdiction if *International Shoe* applied is that a wrongdoer

> "should not be able to avoid payment of his obligations by the expedient of removing his assets to a place where he is not subject to an in personam suit." Restatement § 66, Comment a.

This justification, however, does not explain why jurisdiction should be recognized without regard to whether the property is present in the State because of an effort to avoid the owner's obligations. Nor does it support jurisdiction to adjudicate the underlying claim. At most, it suggests that a State in which property is located should have jurisdiction to attach that property, by use of proper procedures, as security for a judgment being sought in a forum where the litigation can be maintained consistently with *International Shoe*. Moreover, we know of nothing to justify the assumption that a debtor can avoid paying his obligations by removing his property to a State in which his creditor cannot obtain personal jurisdiction over him. The Full Faith and Credit Clause, after all, makes the valid *in personam* judgment of one State enforceable in all other States.

It might also be suggested that allowing in rem jurisdiction avoids the uncertainty inherent in the International Shoe standard and assures a plaintiff of a forum.[37] We believe, however, that the fairness standard of International Shoe can be easily applied in the vast majority of cases. Moreover, when the existence of jurisdiction in a particular forum under *International Shoe* is unclear, the cost of simplifying the litigation by avoiding the jurisdictional question may be the sacrifice of "fair play and substantial justice." That cost is too high.

* * *

We therefore conclude that all assertions of state-court jurisdiction must be evaluated according to the standards set forth in *International Shoe* and its progeny.

IV

The Delaware courts based their assertion of jurisdiction in this case solely on the statutory presence of appellants' property in Delaware. Yet that property is not the subject matter of this litigation, nor is the underlying cause of action related to the property. Appellants' holdings in Greyhound do not, therefore, provide contacts with Delaware sufficient to support the jurisdiction of that State's courts over appellants. If it exists, that jurisdiction must have some other foundation.

---

37. This case does not raise, and we therefore do not consider, the question whether the presence of a defendant's property in a State is a sufficient basis for jurisdiction when no other forum is available to the plaintiff.

Appellee Heitner did not allege and does not now claim that appellants have ever set foot in Delaware. Nor does he identify any act related to his cause of action as having taken place in Delaware. Nevertheless, he contends that appellants' positions as directors and officers of a corporation chartered in Delaware provide sufficient "contacts, ties, or relations", *International Shoe Co. v. Washington*, 326 U.S., at 319, with that State to give its courts jurisdiction over appellants in this stockholder's derivative action. This argument is based primarily on what Heitner asserts to be the strong interest of Delaware in supervising the management of a Delaware corporation. That interest is said to derive from the role of Delaware law in establishing the corporation and defining the obligations owed to it by its officers and directors. In order to protect this interest, appellee concludes, Delaware's courts must have jurisdiction over corporate fiduciaries such as appellants.

This argument is undercut by the failure of the Delaware Legislature to assert the state interest appellee finds so compelling. Delaware law bases jurisdiction, not on appellants' status as corporate fiduciaries, but rather on the presence of their property in the State. Although the sequestration procedure used here may be most frequently used in derivative suits against officers and directors, the authorizing statute evinces no specific concern with such actions. Sequestration can be used in any suit against a nonresident, and reaches corporate fiduciaries only if they happen to own interests in a Delaware corporation, or other property in the State. But as Heitner's failure to secure jurisdiction over seven of the defendants named in his complaint demonstrates, there is no necessary relationship between holding a position as a corporate fiduciary and owning stock or other interests in the corporation. If Delaware perceived its interest in securing jurisdiction over corporate fiduciaries to be as great as Heitner suggests, we would expect it to have enacted a statute more clearly designed to protect that interest.

Moreover, even if Heitner's assessment of the importance of Delaware's interest is accepted, his argument fails to demonstrate that Delaware is a fair forum for this litigation. The interest appellee has identified may support the application of Delaware law to resolve any controversy over appellants' actions in their capacities as officers and directors. But we have rejected the argument that if a State's law can properly be applied to a dispute, its courts necessarily have jurisdiction over the parties to that dispute.

> "[The State] does not acquire...jurisdiction by being the 'center of gravity' of the controversy, or the most convenient location for litigation. The issue is personal jurisdiction, not choice of law. It is resolved in this case by considering the acts of the [appellants]." *Hanson v. Denckla*, 357 U.S. 235, 254 (1958).

Appellee suggests that by accepting positions as officers or directors of a Delaware corporation, appellants performed the acts required by *Hanson v. Denckla*. He notes that Delaware law provides substantial benefits to corporate officers and directors, and that these benefits were at least in part the incentive for appellants to assume their positions. It is, he says, "only fair and just" to require appellants, in return for these benefits, to respond in the State of Delaware when they are accused of misusing their power.

But like Heitner's first argument, this line of reasoning establishes only that it is appropriate for Delaware law to govern the obligations of appellants to Greyhound and its stockholders. It does not demonstrate that appellants have "purposefully avail[ed themselves] of the privilege of conducting activities within the forum State," *Hanson v. Denckla, supra*, at 253; in a way that would justify bringing them before a Delaware tribunal. Appellants have simply had nothing to do with the State of Delaware. Moreover, appellants had no reason to expect to be haled before a Delaware court. Delaware, unlike some States, has not enacted a statute that treats acceptance of a directorship as consent to jurisdiction in the State. And "[i]t strains reason...to suggest that anyone buying securities in a corporation formed in Delaware 'impliedly consents' to subject himself to Delaware's...jurisdiction on any cause of action." Folk & Moyer, [Sequestration in Delaware: A Constitutional Analysis, 73 Colum. L. Rev. 749 (1973)] at 785. Appellants, who were not required to acquire interests in Greyhound in order to hold their positions, did not by acquiring those interests surrender their right to be brought to judgment only in States with which they had had "minimum contacts."

The Due Process Clause

> "does not contemplate that a state may make binding a judgment...against an individual or corporate defendant with which the state has no contacts, ties, or relations." *International Shoe Co. v. Washington*, 326 U.S., at 319.

Delaware's assertion of jurisdiction over appellants in this case is inconsistent with that constitutional limitation on state power. The judgment of the Delaware Supreme Court must, therefore, be reversed.

It is so ordered.

Mr. Justice REHNQUIST took no part in the consideration or decision of this case.

Mr. Justice POWELL, concurring.

I agree that the principles of *International Shoe Co. v. Washington*, 326 U.S. 310 (1945), should be extended to govern assertions of in rem as well as in personam jurisdiction in a state court. I also agree that neither the statutory presence of appellants' stock in Delaware nor their positions as directors and officers of a Delaware corporation can provide sufficient contacts to support the Delaware courts' assertion of jurisdiction in this case.

I would explicitly reserve judgment, however, on whether the ownership of some forms of property whose situs is indisputably and permanently located within a State may, without more, provide the contacts necessary to subject a defendant to jurisdiction within the State to the extent of the value of the property. In the case of real property, in particular, preservation of the common-law concept of quasi in rem jurisdiction arguably would avoid the uncertainty of the general International Shoe standard without significant cost to "'traditional notions of fair play and substantial justice.'" Id., at 316, quoting *Milliken v. Meyer*, 311 U.S. 457, 463 (1940).

Subject to the foregoing reservation, I join the opinion of the Court.

Mr. Justice STEVENS, concurring in the judgment.

The Due Process Clause affords protection against "judgments without notice." *International Shoe Co. v. Washington*, 326 U.S. 310, 324 (opinion of Black, J.). Throughout our history the acceptable exercise of *in rem* and *quasi in rem* jurisdiction has included a procedure giving reasonable assurance that actual notice of the particular claim will be conveyed to the defendant. Thus, publication, notice by registered mail, or extraterritorial personal service has been an essential ingredient of any procedure that serves as a substitute for personal service within the jurisdiction.

The requirement of fair notice also, I believe, includes fair warning that a particular activity may subject a person to the jurisdiction of a foreign sovereign. If I visit another State, or acquire real estate or open a bank account in it, I knowingly assume some risk that the State will exercise its power over my property or my person while there. My contact with the State, though minimal, gives rise to predictable risks.

Perhaps the same consequences should flow from the purchase of stock of a corporation organized under the laws of a foreign nation, because to some limited extent one's property and affairs then become subject to the laws of the nation of domicile of the corporation. As a matter of international law, that suggestion might be acceptable because a foreign investment is sufficiently unusual to make it appropriate to require the investor to study the ramifications of his decision. But a purchase of securities in the domestic market is an entirely different matter.

One who purchases shares of stock on the open market can hardly be expected to know that he has thereby become subject to suit in a forum remote from his residence and unrelated to the transaction. As a practical matter, the Delaware sequestration statute creates an unacceptable risk of judgment without notice. Unlike the 49 other States, Delaware treats the place of incorporation as the situs of the stock, even though both the owner and the custodian of the shares are elsewhere. Moreover, Delaware denies the defendant the opportunity to defend the merits of the suit unless he subjects himself to the unlimited jurisdiction of the court. Thus, it coerces a defendant either to submit to personal jurisdiction in a forum which could not otherwise obtain such jurisdiction or to lose the securities which have been attached. If its procedure were upheld, Delaware would, in effect, impose a duty of inquiry on every purchaser of securities in the national market. For unless the purchaser ascertains both the State of incorporation of the company whose shares he is buying, and also the idiosyncrasies of its law, he may be assuming an unknown risk of litigation. I therefore agree with the Court that on the record before us no adequate basis for jurisdiction exists and that the Delaware statute is unconstitutional on its face.

How the Court's opinion may be applied in other contexts is not entirely clear to me. I agree with Mr. Justice Powell that it should not be read to invalidate *quasi in rem* jurisdiction where real estate is involved. I would also not read it as invalidating other long-accepted methods of acquiring jurisdiction over persons with adequate notice of both the particular controversy and the fact that their local activities might subject them to suit. My uncertainty as to the reach of the opinion, and my fear that it purports to decide a great deal more than is necessary to dispose of this case, persuade me merely to concur in the judgment.

Mr. Justice BRENNAN, concurring in part and dissenting in part.

I join Parts I-III of the Court's opinion. I fully agree that the minimum-contacts analysis developed in *International Shoe Co. v. Washington*, 326 U.S. 310 (1945), represents a far more sensible construct for the exercise of state-court jurisdiction than the patchwork of legal and factual fictions that has been generated from the decision in *Pennoyer v. Neff*, 95 U.S. 714 (1878). It is precisely because the inquiry into minimum contacts is now of such overriding importance, however, that I must respectfully dissent from Part IV of the Court's opinion.

I

* * *

In my view, a purer example of an advisory opinion is not to be found. True, appellants do not deny having received actual notice of the action in question. However, notice is but one ingredient of a proper assertion of state-court jurisdiction. The other is a statute authorizing the exercise of the State's judicial power along constitutionally permissible grounds which henceforth means minimum contacts. As of today, § 366 is not such a law. Recognizing that today's decision fundamentally alters the relevant jurisdictional ground rules, I certainly would not want to rule out the possibility that Delaware's courts might decide that the legislature's overriding purpose of securing the personal appearance in state courts of defendants would best be served by reinterpreting its statute to permit state jurisdiction on the basis of constitutionally permissible contacts rather than stock ownership. Were the state courts to take this step, it would then become necessary to address the question of whether minimum contacts exist here. But in the present posture of this case, the Court's decision of this important issue is purely an abstract ruling.

* * *

II

Nonetheless, because the Court rules on the minimum-contacts question, I feel impelled to express my view. While evidence derived through discovery might satisfy me that minimum contacts are lacking in a given case, I am convinced that as a general rule a state forum has jurisdiction to adjudicate a shareholder derivative action centering on the conduct and policies of the directors and officers of a corporation chartered by that State. Unlike the Court, I therefore would not foreclose Delaware from asserting jurisdiction over appellants were it persuaded to do so on the basis of minimum contacts.

* * *

I, of course, am not suggesting that Delaware's varied interests would justify its acceptance of jurisdiction over any transaction touching upon the affairs of its domestic corporations. But a derivative action which raises allegations of abuses of the basic management of an institution whose existence is created by the State and whose powers and duties are defined by state law fundamentally implicates the public policies of that forum.

To be sure, the Court is not blind to these considerations. It notes that the State's interests "may support the application of Delaware law to resolve any controversy over appellants' actions in their capacities as officers and directors." But this, the Court argues, pertains to choice of law, not jurisdiction. I recognize that the jurisdictional and choice-of-law inquiries are not identical. *Hanson v. Denckla*, 357 U.S. 235, 254 (1958). But I would not compartmentalize thinking in this area quite so rigidly as it seems to me the Court does today, for both inquiries "are often closely related and to a substantial degree depend upon similar considerations." Id., at 258 (Black, J., dissenting). In either case an important linchpin is the extent of contacts between the controversy, the parties, and the forum State. While constitutional limitations on the choice of law are by no means settled, see, e. g., *Home Ins. Co. v. Dick*, 281 U.S. 397 (1930), important considerations certainly include the expectancies of the parties and the fairness of governing the defendants' acts and behavior by rules of conduct created by a given jurisdiction. See, e. g., Restatement (Second) of Conflict of Laws §6 (1971) (hereafter Restatement). These same factors bear upon the propriety of a State's exercising jurisdiction over a legal dispute. At the minimum, the decision that it is fair to bind a defendant by a State's laws and rules should prove to be highly relevant to the fairness of permitting that same State to accept jurisdiction for adjudicating the controversy.

Furthermore, I believe that practical considerations argue in favor of seeking to bridge the distance between the choice-of-law and jurisdictional inquiries. Even when a court would apply the law of a different forum, as a general rule it will feel less knowledgeable and comfortable in interpretation, and less interested in fostering the policies of that foreign jurisdiction, than would the courts established by the State that provides the applicable law. Obviously, such choice-of-law problems cannot entirely be avoided in a diverse legal system such as our own. Nonetheless, when a suitor seeks to lodge a suit in a State with a substantial interest in seeing its own law applied to the transaction in question, we could wisely act to minimize conflicts, confusion, and uncertainty by adopting a liberal view of jurisdiction, unless considerations of fairness or efficiency strongly point in the opposite direction.

This case is not one where, in my judgment, this preference for jurisdiction is adequately answered. Certainly nothing said by the Court persuades me that it would be unfair to subject appellants to suit in Delaware. The fact that the record does not reveal whether they "set foot" or committed "act[s] related to [the] cause of action" in Delaware, is not decisive, for jurisdiction can be based strictly on out-of-state acts having foreseeable effects in the forum State. I have little difficulty in applying this principle to nonresident fiduciaries whose alleged breaches of trust are said to have substantial damaging effect on the financial posture of a resident corporation. Further, I cannot understand how the existence of minimum contacts in a constitutional sense is at all affected by Delaware's failure statutorily to express an interest in controlling corporate fiduciaries. To me this simply demonstrates that Delaware did not elect to assert jurisdiction to the extent the Constitution would allow. Nor would I view as controlling or even especially meaningful Delaware's failure to exact from appellants their consent to be sued. Once we have rejected the jurisdictional framework created in *Pennoyer v. Neff*, I see no reason to rest jurisdiction on a fictional outgrowth of that system such as the existence of a consent statute, expressed or implied.

I, therefore, would approach the minimum-contacts analysis differently than does the Court. Crucial to me is the fact that appellants[7] voluntarily associated themselves with the State of Delaware, "invoking the benefits and protections of its laws", *Hanson v. Denckla*, 357 U.S., at 253; *International Shoe Co. v. Washington*, 326 U.S., at 319, by entering into a long-term and fragile relationship with one of its domestic corporations. They thereby elected to assume powers and to undertake responsibilities wholly derived from that State's rules and regulations, and to become eligible for those benefits that Delaware law makes available to its corporations' officials. E. g., Del. Code Ann., Tit. 8, § 143 (1975) (interest-free loans); § 145 (1975 ed. and Supp.1976) (indemnification). While it is possible that countervailing issues of judicial efficiency and the like might clearly favor a different forum, they do not appear on the meager record before us;[8] and, of course, we are concerned solely with "minimum" contacts, not the "best" contacts. I thus do not believe that it is unfair to insist that appellants make themselves available to suit in a competent forum that Delaware might create for vindication of its important public policies directly pertaining to appellants' fiduciary associations with the State.

---

7. Whether the directors of the out-of-state subsidiary should be amenable to suit in Delaware may raise additional questions. It may well require further investigation into such factors as the degree of independence in the operations of the two corporations, the interrelationship of the managers of parent and subsidiary in the actual conduct under challenge, and the reasonable expectations of the subsidiary directors that the parent State would take an interest in their behavior. While the present record is not illuminating on these matters, it appears that all appellants acted largely in concert with respect to the alleged fiduciary misconduct, suggesting that overall jurisdiction might fairly rest in Delaware.

8. And, of course, if a preferable forum exists elsewhere, a State that is constitutionally entitled to accept jurisdiction nonetheless remains free to arrange for the transfer of the litigation under the doctrine of forum non conveniens. See, *e.g.*, *Broderick v. Rosner*, 294 U.S. 629, 643 (1935); *Gulf Oil Corp. v. Gilbert*, 330 U.S. 501, 504 (1947).

Notes

1. Note the 4 uses of in rem or quasi in rem jurisdiction that survive *Shaffer*. One of these uses, pre-trial seizure of property in a state without jurisdiction over the defendant pending suit in a state with personal jurisdiction, is new, the need for which was created by *Shaffer*. This is similar to, but distinguishable from the English "Mareva" injunction. [Named for Mareva Compania Naviera S.A. of Panama v. International Bulk Carriers, S.A. [1980] 1 All E. R. 213 (C.A. 1975), in which a shipowner sued a charterer for breach of contract and in an ex parte proceeding, enjoined the defendant from removing funds from a London bank.] The Mareva injunction, unlike the pre-trial seizure referred to in *Shaffer*, assumes personal jurisdiction over the person enjoined. The Mareva injunction has been used not only to freeze assets in England pending litigation in England, but also to freeze assets in England pending litigation in another country (X v. Y., [1989] 3 All E. R. 689 (Q.B.)) and even to freeze assets outside of England pending litigation outside of England (Derby & Co. v. Weldon, [1989] 2 W.L.R. 412 (C.A.)) Mercedes-Benz AG v. Leiduck, [1995] 3 All E.R. 929 (P.C., appeal from Hong Kong), emphasized that a Mareva injunction operates in personam and could not be issued to freeze assets in a forum that did not have jurisdiction over the owner. The plaintiff had sought the injunction in Hong Kong to assure that assets there would be available to satisfy a judgment rendered in Monaco.

Although *Shaffer* states that it is constitutional to seize property in one jurisdiction while suing the defendant in another jurisdiction, the rules of procedure at the property's situs may not permit this remedy. Brittingham v. Ayala, 995 S.W.2d 199 (Tex. App.-San Antonio, 1999, rev. denied) held that a Texas court has no power to enjoin defendant from transferring assets in Texas pending the outcome of a suit against defendant in Mexico. Grupo Mexicano de Desarrollo, S.A. v. Alliance Bond Fund, Inc., 527 U.S. 308 (1999), holds that federal courts have no power to grant pre-judgment relief preventing the defendant from transferring assets in which the plaintiff does not claim a lien or equitable interest. The court noted that in England there are over 1,000 applications for Mareva injunctions every month. Thus in federal court, with rare exception, the plaintiff may not even seize property in a federal district while suing the defendant in the same district.

Credit Agricole Indosuez v. Rossiyskiy Kredit Bank, 729 N.E.2d 683 (N.Y. 2000): Foreign banks sued Rossiyskiy, a Russian bank, to recover payment of principal and interest on debentures issued by Rossiyskiy. Rossiyskiy had defaulted in payment. Under the terms of the debentures, Rossiyskiy had agreed to submit to the jurisdiction of New York courts. Rossiyskiy had transferred its principal assets to another Russian bank. The plaintiffs moved for an order of attachment and a temporary injunction against defendant's further transfer of assets. The trial and intermediate appellate courts granted the motion. Held: Reversed. Unsecured contract creditors, whose ultimate objective is attaining an enforceable money judgment, are not entitled to a preliminary injunction to restrain the debtor's asset transfers. The court noted the availability of world-wide Mareva injunctions in England and stated: "the widespread use of this remedy would drastically unbalance existing creditors' and debtors' rights under the present Federal and State statutory and decisional schemes, and substantially interfere with the sovereignty and debtor/creditor/bankruptcy laws of, and the rights of interested domiciliaries in, foreign countries." Id. at 689.

2. In note 23 of his opinion, Justice Marshall states that the fact that "the potential liability of a defendant in an *in rem* action is limited by the value of the property" does not affect the due process argument, and cites "Cf. Fuentes v. Shevin." Does *Fuentes*

support or contradict this statement? That case held unconstitutional statutes that permitted pre-trial seizure of assets without notice or hearing. The opinion stated that due process required "a prior hearing of some kind" (407 U.S. at 84) but then stated that "[l]eeway remains to develop a form of hearing that will minimize unnecessary cost and delay while preserving the fairness and effectiveness of the hearing in preventing seizures of goods where the party seeking the writ has little probability of succeeding on the merits of the dispute." (Id. at 97 n. 33). Would such a prima facie showing of merit in the complaint meet due process standards if the issue were not temporary seizure but final judgment depriving the defendant of all interest in the property?

In *Shaffer*, Justice Marshall rejects the argument that Delaware could assert in personam jurisdiction over the defendants. He points out that Delaware did not have a long-arm statute applicable to malfeasance of directors and therefore the defendants "had no reason to expect to be haled before a Delaware court." It this unfair surprise argument tenable if a long-arm statute can be applied retroactively? McGee v. International Life Insurance Co., 355 U.S. 220 (1957) approved the retroactive application of a statute conferring jurisdiction over a Texas company that had insured the life of a California resident and had failed to pay the death benefit. Justice Black stated that "[t]he statute was remedial, in the purest sense of that term, and neither enlarged nor impaired [the insurer's] substantive rights or obligations under the contract.... [Defendant] had no vested right not to be sued in California."

3. Justice Scalia's reasoning in Burnham v. Superior Court, 495 U.S. 604 (1990), discussed in note 4 following the EEC Jurisdiction and Judgments Convention, (long and continued use equals constitutional) is inconsistent with an expansive reading of Shaffer v. Heitner. Perhaps there are sufficient votes on the current Supreme Court to limit *Shaffer* to intangible property that has no reasonable nexus with the forum (the situation in *Shaffer*) or whose location the defendant cannot knowingly and voluntarily control (Harris v. Balk, discussed in *Shaffer*). In addition to Rehnquist and Kennedy, who joined in Scalia's *Burnham* reasoning, Stevens renews in *Burnham* his opposition to giving *Shaffer* an "unnecessarily broad reach." Is Souter, Thomas, or Ginsburg, the fifth vote? Nevertheless, it will take a courageous or foolhardy attorney to make the attempt because of the threat of monetary sanctions under 42 U.S.C. § 1983 if the attempt fails. Section 1983 provides that "[e]very person who, under color of any statute...of any State...subjects...any citizen to the deprivation of any rights...secured by the Constitution...shall be liable to the party injured." See Pinsky v. Duncan, 79 F.3d 306 (2d Cir. 1996), dealing with recovery under § 1983 for prejudgment attachment of realty.

Louring v. Kuwait Boulder Shipping Co.
455 F. Supp. 630 (D. Conn. 1977)

NEWMAN, District Judge.

Defendant moves to dissolve a garnishment and dismiss this action, which was removed from state court, on the ground that the garnishment was improper and the Court lacks jurisdiction. Following oral argument on those motions, plaintiff moved for judgment on the ground that defendant had submitted itself to the Court's jurisdiction, but had failed to answer the underlying complaint.

Plaintiff alleges that he is a citizen of the state of Connecticut, and that he has an interest in the defendant, a corporation organized and existing under the laws of Kuwait. Plaintiff commenced this action in the Connecticut state courts because of a dispute with the defendant over the alleged non-payment of a sum of money. In order to obtain jurisdiction over the defendant, whose principal place of business is Safat, Kuwait, plaintiff prepared an application for a pre-judgment remedy with the intention of garnishing a debt owed to defendant by Boulder Shipping Company, a Connecticut corporation, which then maintained an office in Greenwich. This procedure is authorized by Conn.Gen.Stat. §52-278e.

* * *

Until very recently it was well established that the presence of property in a state gave the courts of that state, and the appropriate federal court, following a valid removal, jurisdiction to adjudicate rights to the property without regard to the relationship of the underlying dispute and the property owner to the forum. However, the Supreme Court has ruled in *Shaffer v. Heitner*, 433 U.S. 186 (1977), that the valid assertion of in rem and quasi in rem jurisdiction is, to an extent not entirely defined, subject to the minimum contacts requirement of the due process clause. By letters to the Court the plaintiff and the defendant have urged differing interpretations of Shaffer to the facts of this case.

The Supreme Court's opinion in *Shaffer* explicitly left open the question whether the presence of a defendant's property in a state is a sufficient basis for jurisdiction "when no other forum is available to the plaintiff." 433 U.S. at 211 n. 37. Presumably, the Court had in mind a case such as this, where the defendant is outside the territorial jurisdiction of any of the fifty states, in the sheikdom of Kuwait. While *Shaffer* leaves the issue open, its rationale does not support application of a minimum contacts test to a case such as this. The Court was persuaded to apply the standards of *International Shoe* to quasi in rem jurisdiction in part because an In personam judgment could be obtained "in a forum where the litigation can be maintained consistently with *International Shoe*," 433 U.S. at 210, and because the state in which the property is located would then be obliged to honor such a judgment under the full faith and credit clause. Ibid. These arguments plainly contemplate a defendant over whom In personam jurisdiction can be obtained in one of the fifty states. Defendant has made no claim here that it is subject to jurisdiction in some state other than Connecticut.

Moreover, under the reasoning suggested by Mr. Justice Stevens, the activity of the defendant has given it "fair warning" that it may be subjected to suit somewhere in the United States. By transacting business with the garnishee, defendant plainly took the risk that debts owed the defendant by the garnishee might provide the basis for the assertion of jurisdiction. Even if the defendant could be more substantially "found" in another state, there is no unfairness in calling upon a foreign corporation to defend in Connecticut to the extent of a debt accruing in Connecticut. A Kuwait corporation cannot claim disadvantage in defending in Connecticut rather than some other state.

Finally, even if there are not the minimum contacts needed to satisfy *International Shoe* (though there may well be), there are surely sufficient contacts to make the assertion of *quasi in rem* jurisdiction over a foreign corporation fair even under *Shaffer*. From deposition testimony it appears that the garnishee was acting as agent for the defendant in Connecticut and the chief executive officer of the defendant has been present in the Connecticut offices of the garnishee on a number of occasions.

* * *

Notes

1. Is the court's position that "no other forum" means no other forum in the United States, consistent with note 13 in Helicopteros [page 1 supra] (decided 7 years after Louring)? Is it consistent with the next principal case, Bremen (decided 5 years before Louring), which decried "the parochial concept that all disputes must be resolved under our laws and in our courts"?

2. The suggestion in the last paragraph of Louring that fewer forum contacts may suffice for quasi in rem jurisdiction than for in personam jurisdiction, seems inconsistent with note 23 of Justice Marshall's opinion in *Shaffer*. [Page 34 supra.] Is note 23 cogent? See note 2 in the notes following *Shaffer*. [Page 44 supra.]

Section 2: Agreements to Litigate or Arbitrate Abroad

The Bremen v. Zapata Off-Shore Company
407 U.S. 1 (1972)

Mr. Chief Justice BURGER delivered the opinion of the Court.

We granted certiorari to review a judgment of the United States Court of Appeals for the Fifth Circuit declining to enforce a forum-selection clause governing disputes arising under an international towage contract between petitioners and respondent. The circuits have differed in their approach to such clauses. For the reasons stated hereafter, we vacate the judgment of the Court of Appeals.

In November 1967, respondent Zapata, a Houston-based American corporation, contracted with petitioner Unterweser, a German corporation, to tow Zapata's ocean-going, self-elevating drilling rig Chaparral from Louisiana to a point off Ravenna, Italy, in the Adriatic Sea, where Zapata had agreed to drill certain wells.

Zapata had solicited bids for the towage, and several companies including Unterweser had responded. Unterweser was the low bidder and Zapata requested it to submit a contract, which it did. The contract submitted by Unterweser contained the following provision, which is at issue in this case:

"Any dispute arising must be treated before the London Court of Justice."

In addition the contract contained two clauses purporting to exculpate Unterweser from liability for damages to the towed barge.[2]

After reviewing the contract and making several changes, but without any alteration in the forum-selection or exculpatory clauses, a Zapata vice president executed the con-

---

2. The General Towage Conditions of the contract included the following:
"1...[Unterweser and its] masters and crews are not responsible for defaults and/or errors in the navigation of the tow.
"2...
"b) Damages suffered by the towed object are in any case for account of its Owners."
In addition, the contract provided that any insurance of the Chaparral was to be "for account of" Zapata. Unterweser's initial telegraphic bid had also offered to "arrange insurance covering

tract and forwarded it to Unterweser in Germany, where Unterweser accepted the changes, and the contract became effective.

On January 5, 1968, Unterweser's deep sea tug Bremen departed Venice, Louisiana, with the Chaparral in tow bound for Italy. On January 9, while the flotilla was in international waters in the middle of the Gulf of Mexico, a severe storm arose. The sharp roll of the Chaparral in Gulf waters caused its elevator legs, which had been raised for the voyage, to break off and fall into the sea, seriously damaging the Chaparral. In this emergency situation Zapata instructed the Bremen to tow its damaged rig to Tampa, Florida, the nearest port of refuge.

On January 12, Zapata, ignoring its contract promise to litigate "any dispute arising" in the English courts, commenced a suit in admiralty in the United States District Court at Tampa, seeking $3,500,000 damages against Unterweser in personam and the Bremen in rem, alleging negligent towage and breach of contract. Unterweser responded by invoking the forum clause of the towage contract, and moved to dismiss for lack of jurisdiction or on forum non conveniens grounds, or in the alternative to stay the action pending submission of the dispute to the "London Court of Justice". Shortly thereafter, in February, before the District Court had ruled on its motion to stay or dismiss the United States action, Unterweser commenced an action against Zapata seeking damages for breach of the towage contract in the High Court of Justice in London, as the contract provided. Zapata appeared in that court to contest jurisdiction, but its challenge was rejected, the English courts holding that the contractual forum provision conferred jurisdiction.[4]

In the meantime, Unterweser was faced with a dilemma in the pending action in the United States court at Tampa. The six-month period for filing action to limit its liability to Zapata and other potential claimants was about to expire, but the United States District Court in Tampa had not yet ruled on Unterweser's motion to dismiss or stay Zapata's action. On July 2, 1968, confronted with difficult alternatives, Unterweser filed an action to limit its liability in the District Court in Tampa. That court entered the customary injunction against proceedings outside the limitation court, and Zapata refiled its initial claim in the limitation action.

---

towage risk for rig if desired." As Zapata had chosen to be self-insured on all its rigs, the loss in this case was not compensated by insurance.

4. Zapata appeared specially and moved to set aside service of process outside the country. Justice Karminski of the High Court of Justice denied the motion on the ground the contractual choice-of-forum provision conferred jurisdiction and would be enforced, absent a factual showing it would not be "fair and right" to do so. He did not believe Zapata had made such a showing, and held that it should be required to "stick to [its] bargain." The Court of Appeal dismissed an appeal on the ground that Justice Karminski had properly applied the English rule. Lord Justice Willmer stated that rule as follows:

"The law on the subject, I think, is not open to doubt...It is always open to parties to stipulate...that a particular Court shall have jurisdiction over any dispute arising out of their contract. Here, the parties chose to stipulate that disputes were to be referred to the 'London Court,' which I take as meaning the High Court in this country. Prima facie it is the policy of the Court to hold parties to the bargain into which they have entered...But that is not an inflexible rule, as was shown, for instance, by the case of The Fehmarn, (1957) 1 Lloyd's Rep. 511; (C.A.) (1957) 2 Lloyd's Rep. 551..."

"I approach the matter, therefore, in this way, that the Court has a discretion, but it is a discretion which, in the ordinary way and in the absence of strong reason to the contrary, will be exercised in favour of holding parties to their bargain. The question is whether sufficient circumstances have been shown to exist in this case to make it desirable, on the grounds of balance of convenience, that proceedings should not take place in this country..." [1968] 2 Lloyd's Rep. 158, 162-163.

It was only at this juncture, on July 29, after the six-month period for filing the limitation action had run, that the District Court denied Unterweser's January motion to dismiss or stay Zapata's initial action. In denying the motion, that court relied on the prior decision of the Court of Appeals in *Carbon Black Export, Inc. v. The Monrosa*, 254 F.2d 297 (CA5 1958), cert. dismissed, 359 U.S. 180 (1959). In that case the Court of Appeals had held a forum-selection clause unenforceable, reiterating the traditional view of many American courts that "agreements in advance of controversy whose object is to oust the jurisdiction of the courts are contrary to public policy and will not be enforced." 254 F.2d, at 300-301. Apparently concluding that it was bound by the *Carbon Black* case, the District Court gave the forum-selection clause little, if any, weight. Instead, the court treated the motion to dismiss under normal forum non conveniens doctrine applicable in the absence of such a clause, citing *Gulf Oil Corp. v. Gilbert*, 330 U.S. 501 (1947). Under that doctrine "unless the balance is strongly in favor of the defendant, the plaintiff's choice of forum should rarely be disturbed." Id., at 508. The District Court concluded: "the balance of conveniences here is not strongly in favor of [Unterweser] and [Zapata's] choice of forum should not be disturbed."

Thereafter, on January 21, 1969, the District Court denied another motion by Unterweser to stay the limitation action pending determination of the controversy in the High Court of Justice in London and granted Zapata's motion to restrain Unterweser from litigating further in the London court. The District Judge ruled that, having taken jurisdiction in the limitation proceeding, he had jurisdiction to determine all matters relating to the controversy. He ruled that Unterweser should be required to "do equity" by refraining from also litigating the controversy in the London court, not only for the reasons he had previously stated for denying Unterweser's first motion to stay Zapata's action, but also because Unterweser had invoked the United States court's jurisdiction to obtain the benefit of the Limitation Act.

On appeal, a divided panel of the Court of Appeals affirmed, and on rehearing en banc the panel opinion was adopted, with six of the 14 en banc judges dissenting. As had the District Court, the majority rested on the *Carbon Black* decision, concluding that "at the very least" that case stood for the proposition that a forum-selection clause "will not be enforced unless the selected state would provide a more convenient forum than the state in which suit is brought." From that premise the Court of Appeals proceeded to conclude that, apart from the forum-selection clause, the District Court did not abuse its discretion in refusing to decline jurisdiction on the basis of forum non conveniens. It noted that (1) the flotilla never "escaped the Fifth Circuit's mare nostrum, and the casualty occurred in close proximity to the district court"; (2) a considerable number of potential witnesses, including Zapata crewmen, resided in the Gulf Coast area; (3) preparation for the voyage and inspection and repair work had been performed in the Gulf area; (4) the testimony of the Bremen crew was available by way of deposition; (5) England had no interest in or contact with the controversy other than the forum-selection clause. The Court of Appeals majority further noted that Zapata was a United States citizen and "[t]he discretion of the district court to remand the case to a foreign forum was consequently limited"—especially since it appeared likely that the English courts would enforce the exculpatory clauses.[8] In the Court of Appeals' view, enforcement of such clauses would be contrary to public policy in American courts under *Bisso v. Inland Waterways Corp.*, 349 U.S. 85 (1955), and *Dixilyn Drilling*

---

8. The record contains an undisputed affidavit of a British solicitor stating an opinion that the exculpatory clauses of the contract would be held "prima facie valid and enforceable" against Zapata

Corp. v. Crescent Towing & Salvage Co., 372 U.S. 697 (1963). Therefore, "[t]he district court was entitled to consider that remanding Zapata to a foreign forum, with no practical contact with the controversy, could raise a bar to recovery by a United States citizen which its own convenient courts would not countenance."

We hold, with the six dissenting members of the Court of Appeals, that far too little weight and effect were given to the forum clause in resolving this controversy. For at least two decades we have witnessed an expansion of overseas commercial activities by business enterprises based in the United States. The barrier of distance that once tended to confine a business concern to a modest territory no longer does so. Here we see an American company with special expertise contracting with a foreign company to tow a complex machine thousands of miles across seas and oceans. The expansion of American business and industry will hardly be encouraged if, notwithstanding solemn contracts, we insist on a parochial concept that all disputes must be resolved under our laws and in our courts. Absent a contract forum, the considerations relied on by the Court of Appeals would be persuasive reasons for holding an American forum convenient in the traditional sense, but in an era of expanding world trade and commerce, the absolute aspects of the doctrine of the *Carbon Black* case have little place and would be a heavy hand indeed on the future development of international commercial dealings by Americans. We cannot have trade and commerce in world markets and international waters exclusively on our terms, governed by our laws, and resolved in our courts.

Forum-selection clauses have historically not been favored by American courts. Many courts, federal and state, have declined to enforce such clauses on the ground that they were "contrary to public policy," or that their effect was to "oust the jurisdiction" of the court. Although this view apparently still has considerable acceptance, other courts are tending to adopt a more hospitable attitude toward forum-selection clauses. This view, advanced in the well-reasoned dissenting opinion in the instant case, is that such clauses are prima facie valid and should be enforced unless enforcement is shown by the resisting party to be "unreasonable" under the circumstances.[11] We believe this is the correct doctrine to be followed by federal district courts sitting in admiralty. It is merely the other side of the proposition recognized by this Court in *National Equipment Rental, Ltd. v. Szukhent*, 375 U.S. 311 (1964), holding that in federal courts a party may validly consent to be sued in a jurisdiction where he cannot be found for service of process through contractual designation of an 'agent' for receipt of process in that jurisdiction. In so holding, the Court stated:

---

in any action maintained in England in which Zapata alleged that defaults or errors in Unterweser's tow caused the casualty and damage to the Chaparral.

In addition, it is not disputed that while the limitation fund in the District Court in Tampa amounts to $1,390,000, the limitation fund in England would be only slightly in excess of $80,000 under English law.

11. E.g., Central Contracting Co. v. Maryland Casualty Co., 367 F.2d 341 (CA3 1966); Anastasiadis v. S.S. Little John, 346 F.2d 281 (CA5 1965) (by implication); Wm. H. Muller & Co. v. Swedish American Line Ltd., 224 F.2d 806 (CA2), cert. denied, 350 U.S. 903 (1955); Cerro de Pasco Copper Corp. v. Knut Knutsen, O.A.S., 187 F.2d 990 (CA2 1951); Central Contracting Co. v. C. E. Youngdahl & Co., 418 Pa. 122, 209 A.2d 810 (1965). The *Muller* case was overruled in Indussa Corp. v. S.S. Ranborg, 377 F.2d 200 (CA2 1967), insofar as it held that the forum clause was not inconsistent with the 'lessening of liability' provision of the Carriage of Goods by Sea Act, 46 U.S.C. § 1303(8), which was applicable to the transactions in *Muller, Indussa*, and *Carbon Black*. That Act is not applicable in this case.

"[I]t is settled...that parties to a contract may agree in advance to submit to the jurisdiction of a given court to permit notice to be served by the opposing party, or even to waive notice altogether." Id., at 315-316.

This approach is substantially that followed in other common-law countries including England. It is the view advanced by noted scholars and that adopted by the Restatement of the Conflict of Laws. It accords with ancient concepts of freedom of contract and reflects an appreciation of the expanding horizons of American contractors who seek business in all parts of the world. Not surprisingly, foreign businessmen prefer, as do we, to have disputes resolved in their own courts, but if that choice is not available, then in a neutral forum with expertise in the subject matter. Plainly, the courts of England meet the standards of neutrality and long experience in admiralty litigation. The choice of that forum was made in an arm's-length negotiation by experienced and sophisticated businessmen, and absent some compelling and countervailing reason it should be honored by the parties and enforced by the courts.

The argument that such clauses are improper because they tend to "oust" a court of jurisdiction is hardly more than a vestigial legal fiction. It appears to rest at core on historical judicial resistance to any attempt to reduce the power and business of a particular court and has little place in an era when all courts are overloaded and when businesses once essentially local now operate in world markets. It reflects something of a provincial attitude regarding the fairness of other tribunals. No one seriously contends in this case that the forum-selection clause "ousted" the District Court of jurisdiction over Zapata's action. The threshold question is whether that court should have exercised its jurisdiction to do more than give effect to the legitimate expectations of the parties, manifested in their freely negotiated agreement, by specifically enforcing the forum clause.

There are compelling reasons why a freely negotiated private international agreement, unaffected by fraud, undue influence, or overweening bargaining power, such as that involved here, should be given full effect. In this case, for example, we are concerned with a far from routine transaction between companies of two different nations contemplating the tow of a extremely costly piece of equipment from Louisiana across the Gulf of Mexico and the Atlantic Ocean, through the Mediterranean Sea to its final destination in the Adriatic Sea. In the course of its voyage, it was to traverse the waters of many jurisdictions. The Chaparral could have been damaged at any point along the route, and there were countless possible ports of refuge. That the accident occurred in the Gulf of Mexico and the barge was towed to Tampa in an emergency were mere fortuities. It cannot be doubted for a moment that the parties sought to provide for a neutral forum for the resolution of any disputes arising during the tow. Manifestly much uncertainty and possibly great inconvenience to both parties could arise if a suit could be maintained in any jurisdiction in which an accident might occur or if jurisdiction were left to any place where the Bremen or Unterweser might happen to be found.[15] The elimination of all such uncertainties by agreeing in advance on a forum acceptable to both parties is an indispensable element in international trade, commerce, and con-

---

15. At the very least, the clause was an effort to eliminate all uncertainty as to the nature, location, and outlook of the forum in which these companies of differing nationalities might find themselves. Moreover, while the contract here did not specifically provide that the substantive law of England should be applied, it is the general rule in English courts that the parties are assumed, absent contrary indication, to have designated the forum with the view that it should apply its own

tracting. There is strong evidence that the forum clause was a vital part of the agreement, and it would be unrealistic to think that the parties did not conduct their negotiations, including fixing the monetary terms, with the consequences of the forum clause figuring prominently in their calculations. Under these circumstances, as Justice Karminski reasoned in sustaining jurisdiction over Zapata in the High Court of Justice, "[t]he force of an agreement for litigation in this country, freely entered into between two competent parties, seems to me to be very powerful."

Thus, in the light of present-day commercial realities and expanding international trade we conclude that the forum clause should control absent a strong showing that it should be set aside. Although their opinions are not altogether explicit, it seems reasonably clear that the District Court and the Court of Appeals placed the burden on Unterweser to show that London would be a more convenient forum than Tampa, although the contract expressly resolved that issue. The correct approach would have been to enforce the forum clause specifically unless Zapata could clearly show that enforcement would be unreasonable and unjust, or that the clause was invalid for such reasons as fraud or overreaching. Accordingly, the case must be remanded for reconsideration.

We note, however, that there is nothing in the record presently before us that would support a refusal to enforce the forum clause. The Court of Appeals suggested that enforcement would be contrary to the public policy of the forum under *Bisso v. Inland Waterways Corp.*, 349 U.S. 85 (1955), because of the prospect that the English courts would enforce the clauses of the towage contract purporting to exculpate Unterweser from liability for damages to the Chaparral. A contractual choice-of-forum clause should be held unenforceable if enforcement would contravene a strong public policy of the forum in which suit is brought, whether declared by statute or by judicial decision. See, e.g., *Boyd v. Grand Trunk W.R. Co.*, 338 U.S. 263 (1949). It is clear, however, that whatever the proper scope of the policy expressed in *Bisso*, it does not reach this case. *Bisso* rested on considerations with respect to the towage business strictly in American waters, and those considerations are not controlling in an international commercial agreement.

* * *

In the course of its ruling on Unterweser's second motion to stay the proceedings in Tampa, the District Court did make a conclusory finding that the balance of convenience was "strongly" in favor of litigation in Tampa. However, as previously noted, in making that finding the court erroneously placed the burden of proof on Unterweser to show that the balance of convenience was strongly in its favor. Moreover, the finding falls far short of a conclusion that Zapata would be effectively deprived of its day in court should it be forced to litigate in London. Indeed, it cannot even be assumed that it would be placed to the expense of transporting its witnesses to London. It is not unusual for important issues in international admiralty cases to be dealt with by deposition. Both the District Court and the Court of Appeals majority appeared satisfied that Unterweser could receive a fair hearing in Tampa by using deposition testimony of its witnesses from distant places, and there is no reason to conclude that Zapata could not use deposition testimony to equal advantage if forced to litigate in London as it bound itself to do. Nevertheless, to allow Zapata opportunity to carry its heavy burden of showing not only that the balance of convenience is strongly in favor of trial in Tampa

---

law. See, e.g., Tzortzis v. Monark Line A/B, (1968) 1 W.L.R. 406 (CA); see generally 1 T. Carver, Carriage by Sea 496-497 (that is, that it will be far more inconvenient for Zapata to litigate in London than it will be for Unterweser to litigate in Tampa), but also that a London trial will be so manifestly and gravely inconvenient to Zapata that it will be effectively deprived of a meaningful day in court, we remand for further proceedings.

Zapata's remaining contentions do not require extended treatment. It is clear that Unterweser's action in filing its limitation complaint in the District Court in Tampa was, so far as Zapata was concerned, solely a defensive measure made necessary as a response to Zapata's breach of the forum clause of the contract. When the six-month statutory period for filing an action to limit its liability had almost run without the District Court's having ruled on Unterweser's initial motion to dismiss or stay Zapata's action pursuant to the forum clause, Unterweser had no other prudent alternative but to protect itself by filing for limitation of its liability. Its action in so doing was a direct consequence of Zapata's failure to abide by the forum clause of the towage contract. There is no basis on which to conclude that this purely necessary defensive action by Unterweser should preclude it from relying on the forum clause it bargained for.

For the first time in this litigation, Zapata has suggested to this Court that the forum clause should not be construed to provide for an exclusive forum or to include in rem actions. However, the language of the clause is clearly mandatory and all-encompassing; the language of the clause in the *Carbon Black* case was far different.

* * *

Vacated and remanded.

Mr. Justice WHITE, concurring.

I concur in the opinion and judgment of the Court except insofar as the opinion comments on the issues which are remanded to the District Court. In my view these issues are best left for consideration by the District Court in the first instance.

Mr. Justice DOUGLAS, dissenting.

* * *

All in all, the District Court judge exercised his discretion wisely in enjoining petitioners from pursuing the litigation in England.*

I would affirm the judgment below.

---

*. It is said that because these parties specifically agreed to litigate their disputes before the London Court of Justice, the District Court, absent "unreasonable" circumstances, should have honored that choice by declining to exercise its jurisdiction. The forum-selection clause, however, is part and parcel of the exculpatory provision in the towing agreement which, as mentioned in the text, is not enforceable in American courts. For only by avoiding litigation in the United States could petitioners hope to evade the *Bisso* doctrine. Judges in this country have traditionally been hostile to attempts to circumvent the public policy against exculpatory agreements. For example, clauses specifying that the law of a foreign place (which favors such releases) should control have regularly been ignored. Thus, in The Kensington, 183 U.S. 263, the Court held void an exemption from liability despite the fact that the contract provided that it should be construed under Belgian law which was more tolerant. And see E. Gerli & Co. v. Cunard S.S. Co., 48 F.2d 115, 117 (CA2); Oceanic Steam Nav. Co. v. Corcoran, 9 F.2d 724, 731 (CA2); In re Lea Fabrics, Inc., 226 F.Supp. 232, 237 (D.C.N.J.); F. A Straus & Co. v. Canadian P.R. Co., 254 N.Y. 407, 173 N.E. 564; Siegelman v. Cunard White Star, 221 F.2d 189, 199 (CA2) (Frank, J., dissenting). 6A A. Corbin on Contracts § 1446 (1962).

The instant stratagem of specifying a foreign forum is essentially the same as invoking a foreign law of construction except that the present circumvention also requires the American party to travel across an ocean to seek relief. Unless we are prepared to overrule *Bisso* we should not countenance

Notes

1. Atlantic Harvesters of Namibia (PTY) Ltd. v. Unterweser Reederei GMBH of Bremen, [1986] 4 South African L.R. 865, involving the same German towing company as The Bremen v. Zapata, refused to enforce exculpatory clauses, similar to those in the contract with Zapata. The court found that the clauses were invalid under German law, and that German law applied.

2. With regard to the court's suggestion in *Bremen*, that a forum-selection clause should not be given effect if the result of "overweening bargaining power," Carnival Cruise Lines v. Shute, 499 U.S. 585 (1991) held enforceable a clause inserted in the "terms and conditions" of a cruise ticket limiting suit to the courts of Florida, where the defendant had its principal place of business. The clause was the 8th of 9 conditions on the first page of the ticket form (there were 25 conditions in all) and was printed in the same small type as the other conditions. The suit had been brought by a husband and wife in a federal court in Washington state, where the claimants lived and had purchased their tickets. The claim was based on injuries to the wife resulting from a slip on deck while the ship was in international waters off of Mexico. The couple had boarded the ship in Los Angeles.

Carnival Cruise Lines also had implications for decisions under the Carriage of Goods by Sea Act, such as the next principal case, *The Sky Reefer*, because the majority construed language in the Vessel Owner's Liability Act, 46 U.S.C. App. § 183c ("[i]t shall be unlawful to insert in any contract any provision purporting to lessen, weaken, or avoid the right of any claimant to a trial by court of competent jurisdiction") as not invalidating forum-selection clauses. This aspect of *Carnival* was briefly abrogated by Congress, which amended § 183c to insert "any" before "court." Pub. L. No. 102-587 § 3006, 106 Stat. 5039, 5068. A subsequent amendment restored the original wording. Pub. L. No. 103-206. *Compagno v. Commodore Cruise Line, Ltd.*, 1994 WL 462997 (U.S. Dist. Ct. E.D. La. 1994) held that the restoration of the pre-*Carnival* wording of the Vessel Owner's Liability Act was intended to cancel the prior amendment's abrogation of *Carnival* and discussed the legislative history of the amendments.

Effron v. Sun Line Cruises, Inc., 67 F.3d 7 (2d Cir. 1995) enforced a cruise ticket clause requiring suit in Athens, Greece. The plaintiff had purchased her ticket through a New York travel agent and was injured on a cruise in South American waters.

How would *Carnival* be decided under the EEC Jurisdiction and Judgments Convention (Brussels Convention)? See Articles 13-15, supra pages 21-22. Article 13 provides coverage under Section 4 if the contract is for the supply of goods or services and the conclusion of the contract was preceded by advertising there and the consumer there concluded the contract. In *Carnival*, the Shutes obtained the cruise tickets through their local travel agent. *Carnival* had promoted its cruises in that state. Articles 14 and 15 provide that the consumer's ability to sue at his domicile cannot be abrogated by an agree-

---

devices designed solely for the purpose of evading its prohibition.

It is argued, however, that one of the rationales of the *Bisso* doctrine, "to protect those in need of goods or services from being overreached by others who have power to drive hard bargains" (349 U.S., at 91), does not apply here because these parties may have been of equal bargaining stature. Yet we have often adopted prophylactic rules rather than attempt to sort the core cases from the marginal ones. In any event, the other objective of the *Bisso* doctrine, to "discourage negligence by making wrongdoers pay damages" (Ibid.) applies here and in every case regardless of the relative bargaining strengths of the parties.

ment unless the agreement is made after dispute has arisen. Article 13 excludes "contracts of transport" from Section 4. Is the cruise ticket a "contract of transport" or one for something else, such as entertainment? The European Union Convention on the Law Applicable to Contracts (Rome Convention), 19 June 1980 (80/934/EEC), provides in article 5(2) that "a choice of law made by the parties shall not have the result of depriving the consumer of the protection afforded to him by the mandatory rules of the law of the country in which he has his habitual residence." The protection does not apply to "a contract of carriage" (art. 5(4)(a), but does apply "to a contract, which, for an inclusive price, provides for a combination of travel and accommodation." (Art. 5(5)).

3. *Bremen* suggests that drafters of agreements concerning transnational or interstate transactions should give serious consideration to including a choice-of-forum clause. Two other clauses that should be considered are a choice-of-law clause and a clause consenting to jurisdiction in the chosen forum. If the choice of forum is exclusive, a consent to jurisdiction there seems implied, but in matters of such importance, this should not be left to implication.

The choice-of-forum clause should be clear that the parties are promising to sue in the selected forum and nowhere else. In case of ambiguity, an American court will not interpret a consent to jurisdiction ("prorogation" clause) as a promise not to sue elsewhere ("derogation" clause). See, e.g., Citro Florida, Inc. v. Citrovale, S.A., 760 F.2d 1231 (11th Cir. 1985); Keaty v. Freeport Indonesia, Inc., 503 F.2d 955 (5th Cir. 1974) (ambiguity construed against drafter). Note that this American distinction between prorogation and derogation is not reflected in the EEC Convention on Jurisdiction and Judgments, supra section 1. See article 17, first sentence, page 23 supra.

Poorly drafted forum-selection clauses are likely to result in litigation to determine their meaning. For example, if the forum chosen is a federal court, is transfer to another federal court under 28 U.S.C. § 1404(a) permitted? See Plum Tree, Inc. v. Stockment, 488 F.2d 754 (3d Cir. 1973) (transfer permitted). If suit is brought in a state court in the chosen forum, can the defendant remove to federal court? See Spatz v. Nascone, 364 F. Supp. 967 (W.D. Pa 1973) (removal not permitted). An arbitration clause is a one kind of forum-selection clause. Mitsubishi Motors Corp. v. Soler Chrysler-Plymouth, Inc., a principal case infra this section, involved an arbitration clause which did not cover all the parties or issues and the meaning of which was contested at every stage of the litigation. In Carbon Black Export v. The S. S. Monrosa, discussed in both *Bremen* and the next principal case, the forum-selection clause (quoted in the notes following the next case) was held not to cover in rem actions.

It is possible to learn from the cases construing forum-selection clauses and to draft a clause removing the ambiguities that these cases address? Consider the following clause:

> Any action arising from or in any way related to this transaction shall be brought only in the state courts in the first judicial district of the state of New York and both parties agree that they shall not seek forum non conveniens dismissal of any action so brought and shall not seek removal to federal court or, if removal is effected despite this agreement, they shall not move for transfer from the federal district in New York to which the case has been removed. This forum-selection agreement applies no matter what the form of action, whether in rem, in personam, or any other, and no matter what the theory of the action, whether tort, contract, or any other, or whether based on any statute, rule, or regulation, now existing or hereafter enacted. If either party is sued

without that party's consent or collusion in another forum, that party may implead the other party to this agreement for contribution or indemnity.

Hough v. P&O Containers Ltd., [1998] 3 W.L.R. 851, [1998] 2 All E.R. 978 (Q.B., Admiralty 1998), resolves a conflict between two articles of the Brussels Convention. Article 6(2) gives a court jurisdiction over third parties impleaded for indemnity or contribution. Article 17 gives effect to a forum selection clause. Hough holds that a third party may not be impleaded for indemnity if this is contrary to a forum-selection clause in an agreement between the third party and the defendant seeking to implead the third party. As indicated in the sample clause above, a well-drafted forum selection clause will address the issue of whether it prevents impleader if one of the parties is sued by a third party in a forum other than that agreed upon.

Evolution Online Systems, Inc. v. Koninklijke PTT Nederland N.V., 145 F.3d 505 (2d Cir. 1998), indicates the effect of a forum clause on forum non conveniens analysis. The agreement to litigate in the Netherlands removed the strong presumption in favor of allowing a New York firm to sue in its home forum.

4. The *Bremen* opinion refers to the "limitation fund" in federal court and to the owner's filing of a "limitation action." 46 U.S.C. chapter 8 covers "Limitation of Vessel Owner's Liability." Under 46 U.S.C. § 183(a), subject to certain exceptions, the liability of the vessel owner for loss of cargo "without the privity or knowledge of such owner... shall not...exceed the amount or value of the interest of such owner in such vessel, and her freight then pending." 46 U.S.C § 185 gives the owner 6 months after notice of claim to petition for limitation of liability under chapter 8.

Other maritime countries also permit shipowners to limit damages, but most of those countries base their limits not on the value of the ship, but on its tonnage. Under the United States limitation procedure, the value of the vessel is calculated after the accident. See Petition of Chadade Steamship Co. (*The Yarmouth Castle*), 266 F. Supp. 517, 519 (S.D. Fla. 1967) (following sinking of cruise ship, shipowner attempts to limit bond to $33,000, "the suggested value of the strippings of the Yarmouth Castle together with passage money" to cover claims other than injury and death); G. Gilmore & C. Black, Jr., The Law of Admiralty 940 (2d ed. 1975). The value of the ship before the accident is likely to exceed the amount available under foreign law. Therefore United States limitations law is likely to favor the shipowner if the ship is sunk and favor the cargo claimants if the ship emerges from the accident without serious damage. The difference may be substantial, as in In re Complaint of K.S. Line Corp. (*The Swibon*), 596 F. Supp. 1268 (D. Alaska 1984), in which one Korean ship survived a collision that sank another Korean vessel. The United States limitations were almost $9,000,000 greater than the Korean limitations.

If there are claims for injury or death and the value of the ship after the accident is not sufficient to pay these claims, the limit of recovery for these claims is increased to "$420 per ton of such vessel's tonnage." 46 U.S.C. § 183(b).

5. In *The Bremen*, the court says that "the language of the clause in the *Carbon Black* case was far different." The clause there read "no legal proceedings may be brought against the captain or shipowners or their agents except in Genoa."

In footnote 11, the court states that the Carriage of Goods by Sea Act was not applicable. It was not applicable because the drilling rig was not a "good" and the towage contract was not a bill of lading. Union Ins. Soc'y. of Canton, Ltd. v. S.S. Elikon, 642 F.2d

721, 724 (4th Cir. 1981). The next principal case holds that forum selection clauses will be enforced against cargo interests even when the Act applies.

6. *The Pioneer Container*, [1994] 2 All E.R. 250 (P.C., appeal from Hong Kong), enforced against cargo owners a clause in the bills of lading selecting Taiwan as the exclusive forum even though time limitations had expired in Taiwan. The Privy Council held that the plaintiffs were unreasonable in allowing time to run out in Taiwan without issuing a protective writ there.

Vimar Seguros y Reaseguros, S.A. v. M/V Sky Reefer
515 U.S. 528 (1995)

Justice KENNEDY delivered the opinion of the Court.

[A New York partnership purchased Moroccan oranges and lemons. The carrier issued a bill of lading to the shipper, which the shipper gave to the purchaser. The bill of lading provided that the contract of shipment "shall be governed by Japanese law" and that "any dispute arising from this Bill of Lading shall be referred to arbitration in Tokyo." When the fruit arrived, the purchaser discovered that it had been damaged during the voyage and brought suit against the owner of the vessel in personam and against the vessel in rem.

The district court granted the defendants' motion to stay judicial proceedings and to compel arbitration. The First Circuit affirmed on the ground that even if the arbitration clause was void under section 3(8) of the Carriage of Goods by Sea Act (COGSA), it was enforceable under the Federal Arbitration Act (FAA). COGSA section 3(8) invalidated any clause in a contract of carriage that resulted in "lessening" the liability of the carrier or the ship for loss or damage to goods. The Supreme Court granted certiorari.]

II

The parties devote much of their argument to the question whether COGSA or the FAA has priority. "[W]hen two statutes are capable of co-existence," however, "it is the duty of the courts, absent a clearly expressed congressional intention to the contrary, to regard each as effective." Morton v. Mancari, 417 U.S. 535, 551 (1974). There is no conflict unless COGSA by its own terms nullifies a foreign arbitration clause, and we choose to address that issue rather than assume nullification arguendo, as the Court of Appeals did. We consider the two arguments made by petitioner. The first is that a foreign arbitration clause lessens COGSA liability by increasing the transaction costs of obtaining relief. The second is that there is a risk foreign arbitrators will not apply COGSA.

A

The leading case for invalidation of a foreign forum selection clause is the opinion of the Court of Appeals for the Second Circuit in Indussa Corp. v. S.S. Ranborg, 377 F.2d 200 (1967) (en banc). The court there found that COGSA invalidated a clause designating a foreign judicial forum because it "puts 'a high hurdle' in the way of enforcing liability, and thus is an effective means for carriers to secure settlements lower than if cargo [owners] could sue in a convenient forum," id., at 203 (citation omitted). The court observed "there could be no assurance that [the foreign court] would apply [COGSA] in the same way as would an American tribunal subject to the uniform control of the Supreme Court," id., at 203-204. Following *Indussa*, the Courts of Appeals without exception have invalidated foreign forum selection clauses under § 3(8). * * *

The determinative provision in COGSA, examined with care, does not support the arguments advanced first in *Indussa* and now by the petitioner. Section 3(8) of COGSA provides as follows:

> "Any clause, covenant, or agreement in a contract of carriage relieving the carrier or the ship from liability for loss or damage to or in connection with the goods, arising from negligence, fault, or failure in the duties or obligations provided in this section, or lessening such liability otherwise than as provided in this chapter, shall be null and void and of no effect." 46 U.S.C.App. § 1303(8).

The liability that may not be lessened is "liability for loss or damage arising from negligence, fault, or failure in the duties or obligations provided in this section." The statute thus addresses the lessening of the specific liability imposed by the Act, without addressing the separate question of the means and costs of enforcing that liability. The difference is that between explicit statutory guarantees and the procedure for enforcing them, between applicable liability principles and the forum in which they are to be vindicated. * * *

Petitioner's contrary reading of § 3(8) is undermined by the Court's construction of a similar statutory provision in Carnival Cruise Lines, Inc. v. Shute, 499 U.S. 585(1991). [See page 54 supra, note 2]. * * *

If the question whether a provision lessens liability were answered by reference to the costs and inconvenience to the cargo owner, there would be no principled basis for distinguishing national from foreign arbitration clauses. Even if it were reasonable to read § 3(8) to make a distinction based on travel time, airfare, and hotels bills, these factors are not susceptible of a simple and enforceable distinction between domestic and foreign forums. Requiring a Seattle cargo owner to arbitrate in New York likely imposes more costs and burdens than a foreign arbitration clause requiring it to arbitrate in Vancouver. It would be unwieldy and unsupported by the terms or policy of the statute to require courts to proceed case by case to tally the costs and burdens to particular plaintiffs in light of their means, the size of their claims, and the relative burden on the carrier.

Our reading of "lessening such liability" to exclude increases in the transaction costs of litigation also finds support in the goals of the Brussels Convention for the Unification of Certain Rules Relating to Bills of Lading, 51 Stat. 233 (1924) (Hague Rules), on which COGSA is modeled. Sixty-six countries, including the United States and Japan, are now parties to the Convention, see Department of State, Office of the Legal Adviser, Treaties in Force: A List of Treaties and Other International Agreements of the United States in Force on January 1, 1994, p. 367 (June 1994), and it appears that none has interpreted its enactment of § 3(8) of the Hague Rules to prohibit foreign forum selection clauses, see Sturley, International Uniform Laws in National Courts: The Influence of Domestic Law in Conflicts of Interpretation, 27 Va.J.Int'l L. 729, 776-796 (1987). The English courts long ago rejected the reasoning later adopted by the *Indussa* court. See Maharani Woolen Mills Co. v. Anchor Line, [1927] 29 Lloyd's List L. Rep. 169 (C.A.) (Scrutton, L.J.) ("[T]he liability of the carrier appears to me to remain exactly the same under the clause. The only difference is a question of procedure—where shall the law be enforced?—and I do not read any clause as to procedure as lessening liability"). And other countries that do not recognize foreign forum selection clauses rely on specific provisions to that effect in their domestic versions of the Hague Rules, see, e.g., Sea-Carriage of Goods Act 1924, §9(2) (Australia); Carriage of Goods by Sea Act, No. 1 of 1986, §3 (South Africa). In light of the fact that COGSA is the culmination of a multilateral effort "to establish uniform ocean bills of lading to govern the rights and liabilities of carriers and shippers inter se in international trade," Robert C. Herd & Co. v. Krawill Machinery Corp., 359 U.S. 297, 301, 79 S.Ct. 766, 769, 3 L.Ed.2d 820 (1959), we decline to interpret our version of the Hague Rules in a manner contrary to every other nation to have addressed this issue. See Sturley, supra, at 736 (conflicts in the interpretation of the Hague Rules not only destroy aesthetic symmetry in the international legal order but impose real costs on the commercial system in the Rules govern).

It would also be out of keeping with the objects of the Convention for the courts of this country to interpret COGSA to disparage the authority or competence of international forums for dispute resolution. Petitioner's skepticism over the ability of foreign arbitrators to apply COGSA or the Hague Rules, and its reliance on this aspect of Indussa, supra, must give way to contemporary principles of international comity and commercial practice. * * *

B

Petitioner's second argument against enforcement of the Japanese arbitration clause is that there is no guarantee foreign arbitrators will apply COGSA. This objection raises a concern of substance. The central guarantee of §3(8) is that the terms of a bill of landing may not relieve the carrier of the obligations or diminish the legal duties specified by the Act. The relevant question, therefore, is whether the substantive law to be applied will reduce the carrier's obligations to the cargo owner below what COGSA guarantees.

Petitioner argues that the arbitrators will follow the Japanese Hague Rules, which, petitioner contends, lessen respondents' liability in at least one significant respect. The Japanese version of the Hague Rules, it is said, provides the carrier with a defense based on the acts or omissions of the stevedores hired by the shipper. * * *

Whatever the merits of petitioner's comparative reading of COGSA and its Japanese counterpart, its claim is premature. At this interlocutory stage it is not established what law the arbitrators will apply to petitioner's claims or that petitioner will receive diminished protection as a result. The arbitrators may conclude that COGSA applies of its own force or that Japanese law does not apply so that, under another clause of the bill of lading, COGSA controls. Respondents seek only to enforce the arbitration agreement. The district court has retained jurisdiction over the case and "will have the opportunity at the award-enforcement stage to ensure that the legitimate interest in the enforcement of the laws has been addressed." Mitsubishi Motors, 473 U.S., at 638; cf. 1 Restatement (Third) of Foreign Relations Law of the United States §482(2)(d) (1986) ("A court in the United States need not recognize a judgment of the court of a foreign state if the judgment itself, is repugnant to the public policy of the United States"). Were there no subsequent opportunity for review and were we persuaded that "the choice-of-forum and choice-of-law clauses operated in tandem as a prospective waiver of a party's right to pursue statutory remedies , we would have little hesitation in condemning the agreement as against public policy." Mitsubishi Motors, supra, at 637, n. 19. Cf. Knott v. Botany Mills, 179 U.S. 69 (1900) (nullifying choice-of-law provision under the Harter Act, the statutory precursor to COGSA, where British law would give effect to provision in bill of lading that purported to exempt carrier from liability for damage to goods caused by carrier's negligence in loading and stowage of cargo); The

Hollandia, [1983] A.C. 565, 574-575 (H.L.1982) (noting choice of forum clause "does not ex facie offend against article III, paragraph 8," but holding clause unenforceable where "the foreign court chosen as the exclusive forum would apply a domestic substantive law which would result in limiting the carrier's liability to the sum lower than that to which he would be entitled if [English COGSA] applied"). Under the circumstances of this case, however, the First Circuit was correct to reserve judgment on the choice-of-law question, 29 F.3d, at 729, n. 3, as it must be decided in the first instance by the arbitrator, cf. Mitsubishi Motors, supra, 473 U.S., at 637, n. 19. As the District Court has retained jurisdiction, mere speculation that the foreign arbitrators might apply Japanese law which, depending on the proper construction of COGSA, might reduce respondents' legal obligations, does not in and of itself lessen liability under COGSA § 3(8).

Because we hold that foreign arbitration clauses in bills of lading are not invalid under COGSA in all circumstances, both the FAA and COGSA may be given full effect. The judgment of the Court of Appeals is affirmed, and the case is remanded for further proceedings consistent with this opinion.

Justice BREYER took no part in the consideration or decision of this case.

[Justice O'Connor concurred in the judgment on the ground that arbitration was involved and stated that she would not overrule Indussa Corp. v. S.S. Ranborg, 377 F.2d 200 (2d Cir. 1967). Justice Stevens dissented. Justice Breyer took no part.]

Notes

1. Banque Francaise du Commerce Exterieur v. Rio Grande Trading, Inc., 17 Bankr. R. 134 (S.D. Tex. 1981). Rio Grande and Banque entered into an agreement that, in exchange for Banque's standby letters of credit in favor of Rio Grande's suppliers, Rio Grande would assign Banque its accounts receivable. The agreement recited that it was governed by French law and that all disputes "arising in connection with the present agreement shall be submitted to the exclusive jurisdiction of the Tribunal of Commerce of Paris." Rio Grande filed a voluntary petition in bankruptcy. Banque petitioned the bankruptcy court to lift an order staying all other proceedings in order to permit Banque to prosecute an action in the Tribunal of Commerce of Paris to determine its rights. The petition was denied on the ground that the choice-of-forum clause contravened the strong United States public policy for determination of all claims in the bankruptcy court.

In re Maxwell Communication Corp., 93 F.3d 1036 (2d Cir. 1996) holds that "the doctrine of international comity supports deferring to the courts and laws of England," where parallel bankruptcy proceedings were pending, and affirms dismissal of claims under the United States Bankruptcy Code for avoidance of pre-petition transfers. The court declared that "England has the strongest connection to the present litigation."

In re Simon, 153 F.3d 991 (9th Cir. 1998), cert. denied, 525 U.S. 1141 (1999), refused to vacate a California Bankruptcy Court's order enjoining a collection action against the bankrupt's property in Hong Kong. The court distinguished *Maxwell* on the ground that in *Simon* there was no competing bankruptcy proceeding abroad.

On May 30, 1997, the United Nations Commission on International Trade Law (UNCITRAL) adopted the final text of a Model Law on Cross-Border Insolvency, 36 I.L.M. 1386 (1997). Article 21(2) provides that upon recognition of a foreign insolvency proceeding a court "may, at the request of the foreign representative, entrust the distribution of all or part of the debtor's assets located in this State to the foreign representative or another person designated by the court, provided that the court is satisfied that the interests of creditors in this State are adequately protected." Id. at 1395.

2. Evans Marshall & Co., Ltd. v. Bertola S.A., [1973] 1 All Eng. R. 992 (C.A.), reversed on another issue, [1976] 2 Lloyd's R. 17 (H.L.). An agreement with Bertola made Evans Marshall, an English company, the exclusive distributor in the U.K. of Bertola's wine. The agreement provided that any claim between the parties would be "submitted to the Barcelona Court of Justice." Bertola terminated the agreement and appointed another English company as its distributor. Evans Marshall sued in England, joining Bertola and the other English company, to enjoin breach of the agreement. Bertola objected to suit on the basis of the forum-choosing clause. This objection was overruled on the ground that both defendants could not be sued in Spain and the Spanish courts would not grant the injunctions sought.

3. Lauro Lines S.R.L. v. Chasser, 490 U.S. 495 (1989) held that refusal of the trial judge to enforce a forum-selection clause and dismiss the case was interlocutory and not appealable; that if the trial judge erred, defendant's right to be sued by passengers only in Naples was "adequately vindicable" by appeal after final judgment.

4. Mitsui & Co. (USA) v. Mira M/V, 111 F.3d 33 (5th Cir. 1997) enforced a clause in a bill of lading that required all disputes to be adjudicated in London, England, and refused to restrict the holding of Sky Reefer to foreign arbitration clauses. Fireman's Fund Ins. Co. v. Cho Yang Shipping Co., 131 F.3d 1336 (9th Cir. 1997), cert. denied, 525 U.S. 921 (1998), enforced a clause in the bill of lading requiring litigation in Korea even though the plaintiff's in rem action against the vessel upon which damage occurred would not be available in Korea. The court found that Korean law imposed obligations on the carrier equal to those of COGSA.

Scherk v. Alberto-Culver Co.
417 U.S. 506 (1974

Mr. Justice STEWART delivered the opinion of the Court.

Alberto-Culver Co., the respondent, is an American company incorporated in Delaware with its principal office in Illinois. It manufactures and distributes toiletries and hair products in this country and abroad. During the 1960's Alberto-Culver decided to expand its overseas operations, and as part of this program it approached the petitioner Fritz Scherk, a German citizen residing at the time of trial in Switzerland. Scherk was the owner of three interrelated business entities, organized under the laws of Germany and Liechtenstein, that were engaged in the manufacture of toiletries and the licensing of trademarks for such toiletries. An initial contact with Scherk was made by a representative of Alberto-Culver in Germany in June 1967, and negotiations followed at further meetings in both Europe and the United States during 1967 and 1968. In February 1969 a contract was signed in Vienna, Austria, which provided for the transfer of the ownership of Scherk's enterprises to Alberto-Culver, along with all rights held by these enterprises to trademarks in cosmetic goods. The contract contained a number of express warranties whereby Scherk guaranteed the sole and unencumbered ownership of these trademarks. In addition, the contract contained an arbitration clause providing that "any controversy or claim [that] shall arise out of this agreement or the breach thereof" would be referred to arbitration before the International Chamber of Commerce in Paris, France, and that "[t]he laws of the State of Illinois, U.S.A. shall apply to and govern this agreement, its interpretation and performance."

The closing of the transaction took place in Geneva, Switzerland, in June 1969. Nearly one year later Alberto-Culver allegedly discovered that the trademark rights purchased under the contract were subject to substantial encumbrances that threatened to give others superior rights to the trademarks and to restrict or preclude Alberto-Culver's use of them. Alberto-Culver thereupon tendered back to Scherk the property that had been transferred to it and offered to rescind the contract. Upon Scherk's refusal, Alberto-Culver commenced this action for damages and other relief in a Federal District Court in Illinois, contending that Scherk's fraudulent representations concerning the status of the trademark rights constituted violations of § 10(b) of the Securities Exchange Act of 1934, 48 Stat. 891, 15 U.S.C. § 78j(b), and Rule 10b-5 promulgated thereunder, 17 CFR § 240.10b-5.

In response, Scherk filed a motion to dismiss the action for want of personal and subject-matter jurisdiction as well as on the basis of forum non conveniens, or, alternatively, to stay the action pending arbitration in Paris pursuant to the agreement of the parties. Alberto-Culver, in turn, opposed this motion and sought a preliminary injunction restraining the prosecution of arbitration proceedings.[2] On December 2, 1971, the District Court denied Scherk's motion to dismiss, and, on January 14, 1972, it granted a preliminary order enjoining Scherk from proceeding with arbitration. In taking these actions the court relied entirely on this Court's decision in *Wilko v. Swan*, 346 U.S. 427, which held that an agreement to arbitrate could not preclude a buyer of a security from seeking a judicial remedy under the Securities Act of 1933, in view of the language of § 14 of that Act, barring "[a]ny condition, stipulation, or provision binding any person acquiring any security to waive compliance with any provision of this subchapter..." 48 Stat. 84, 15 U.S.C. § 77n. The Court of Appeals for the Seventh Circuit, with one judge dissenting, affirmed, upon what it considered the controlling authority of the *Wilko* decision. 484 F.2d 611. Because of the importance of the question presented we granted Scherk's petition for a writ of certiorari.

I

The United States Arbitration Act, now 9 U.S.C. § 1 et seq., reversing centuries of judicial hostility to arbitration agreements, was designed to allow parties to avoid "the costliness and delays of litigation," and to place arbitration agreements "upon the same footing as other contracts..." H.R.Rep.No.96, 68th Cong., 1st Sess., 1, 2 (1924); see also S.Rep.No.536, 68th Cong., 1st Sess. (1924). Accordingly the Act provides that an arbitration agreement such as is here involved "shall be valid, irrevocable, and enforceable, save upon such grounds as exist at law or in equity for the revocation of any contract." 9 U.S.C. § 2.[5] The Act also provides in § 3 for a stay of proceedings in a case where a court is satisfied that the issue before it is arbitrable under the agreement, and § 4 of the Act

---

2. Scherk had taken steps to initiate arbitration in Paris in early 1971. He did not, however, file a formal request for arbitration with the International Chamber of Commerce until November 9, 1971, almost five months after the filing of Alberto-Culver's complaint in the Illinois federal court.

5. Section 2 of the Arbitration Act renders "valid, irrevocable, and enforceable" written arbitration provisions "in any maritime transaction or a contract evidencing a transaction involving commerce...," as those terms are defined in § 1. In Bernhardt v. Polygraphic Co., 350 U.S. 198, this Court held that the stay provisions of § 3 apply only to the two kinds of contracts specified in §§ 1 and 2. Since the transaction in this case constituted "commerce...with foreign nations," 9 U.S.C. § 1, the Act clearly covers this agreement.

directs a federal court to order parties to proceed to arbitration if there has been a "failure, neglect, or refusal" of any party to honor an agreement to arbitrate.

In *Wilko v. Swan, supra,* this Court acknowledged that the Act reflects a legislative recognition of the "desirability of arbitration as an alternative to the complications of litigation," 346 U.S., at 431, but nonetheless declined to apply the Act's provisions. That case involved an agreement between Anthony Wilko and Hayden, Stone & Co., a large brokerage firm, under which Wilko agreed to purchase on margin a number of shares of a corporation's common stock. Wilko alleged that his purchase of the stock was induced by false representations on the part of the defendant concerning the value of the shares, and he brought suit for damages under § 12(2) of the Securities Act of 1933, 15 U.S.C. § 77l. The defendant responded that Wilko had agreed to submit all controversies arising out of the purchase to arbitration, and that this agreement, contained in a written margin contract between the parties, should be given full effect under the Arbitration Act.

The Court found that "[t]wo policies, not easily reconcilable, are involved in this case." 346 U.S., at 438. On the one hand, the Arbitration Act stressed "the need for avoiding the delay and expense of litigation," id., at 431, and directed that such agreements be "valid, irrevocable, and enforceable" in federal courts. On the other hand, the Securities Act of 1933 was "[d]esigned to protect investors" and to require "issuers, underwriters, and dealers to make full and fair disclosure of the character of securities sold in interstate and foreign commerce and to prevent fraud in their sale," by creating "a special right to recover for misrepresentation..." 346 U.S., at 431 (footnote omitted). In particular, the Court noted that § 14 of the Securities Act, 15 U.S.C. § 77n, provides:

> "Any condition, stipulation, or provision binding any person acquiring any security to waive compliance with any provision of this subchapter or of the rules and regulations of the Commission shall be void."

The Court ruled that an agreement to arbitrate "is a 'stipulation,' and [that] the right to select the judicial forum is the kind of 'provision' that cannot be waived under § 14 of the Securities Act." 346 U.S., at 434-435. Thus, Wilko's advance agreement to arbitrate any disputes subsequently arising out of his contract to purchase the securities was unenforceable under the terms of § 14 of the Securities Act of 1933.

Alberto-Culver, relying on this precedent, contends that the District Court and Court of Appeals were correct in holding that its agreement to arbitrate disputes arising under the contract with Scherk is similarly unenforceable in view of its contentions that Scherk's conduct constituted violations of the Securities Exchange Act of 1934 and rules promulgated thereunder. For the reasons that follow, we reject this contention and hold that the provisions of the Arbitration Act cannot be ignored in this case.

* * *

[T]he respondent's reliance on *Wilko* in this case ignores the significant and, we find, crucial differences between the agreement involved in *Wilko* and the one signed by the parties here. Alberto-Culver's contract to purchase the business entities belonging to Scherk was a truly international agreement. Alberto-Culver is an American corporation with its principal place of business and the vast bulk of its activity in this country, while Scherk is a citizen of Germany whose companies were organized under the laws of Germany and Liechtenstein. The negotiations leading to the signing of the contract in Austria and to the closing in Switzerland took place in the United States, England, and Germany, and involved consultations with legal and trademark experts from each of those countries and from Liechtenstein. Finally, and most significantly, the subject matter of the contract concerned the sale of business enterprises organized under the laws of and primarily situated in European countries, whose activities were largely, if not entirely, directed to European markets.

Such a contract involves considerations and policies significantly different from those found controlling in *Wilko*. In *Wilko*, quite apart from the arbitration provision, there was no question but that the laws of the United States generally, and the federal securities laws in particular, would govern disputes arising out of the stock-purchase agreement. The parties, the negotiations, and the subject matter of the contract were all situated in this country, and no credible claim could have been entertained that any international conflict-of-laws problems would arise. In this case, by contrast, in the absence of the arbitration provision considerable uncertainty existed at the time of the agreement, and still exists, concerning the law applicable to the resolution of disputes arising out of the contract.[9]

Such uncertainty will almost inevitably exist with respect to any contract touching two or more countries, each with its own substantive laws and conflict-of-laws rules. A contractual provision specifying in advance the forum in which disputes shall be litigated and the law to be applied is, therefore, an almost indispensable precondition to achievement of the orderliness and predictability essential to any international business transaction. Furthermore, such a provision obviates the danger that a dispute under the agreement might be submitted to a forum hostile to the interests of one of the parties or unfamiliar with the problem area involved.

A parochial refusal by the courts of one country to enforce an international arbitration agreement would not only frustrate these purposes, but would invite unseemly and mutually destructive jockeying by the parties to secure tactical litigation advantages. In the present case, for example, it is not inconceivable that if Scherk had anticipated that Alberto-Culver would be able in this country to enjoin resort to arbitration he might have sought an order in France or some other country enjoining Alberto-Culver from proceeding with its litigation in the United States. Whatever recognition the courts of this country might ultimately have granted to the order of the foreign court, the dicey atmosphere of such a legal no-man's-land would surely damage the fabric of international commerce and trade, and imperil the willingness and ability of businessmen to enter into international commercial agreements.[11]

---

9. Together with his motion for a stay pending arbitration, Scherk moved that the complaint be dismissed because the federal securities laws do not apply to this international transaction, cf. *Leasco Data Processing Equipment Corp. v. Maxwell*, 468 F.2d 1326 (CA2 1972). Since only the order granting the injunction was appealed, this contention was not considered by the Court of Appeals and is not before this Court.

11. The dissenting opinion argues that our conclusion that *Wilko* is inapplicable to the situation presented in this case will vitiate the force of that decision because parties to transactions with many more direct contacts with this country than in the present case will nonetheless be able to invoke the "talisman" of having an "international contract." Concededly, situations may arise where the contacts with foreign countries are so insignificant or attenuated that the holding in *Wilko* would meaningfully apply. Judicial response to such situations can and should await future litigation in concrete cases. This case, however, provides no basis for a judgment that only United States laws and United States courts should determine this controversy in the face of a solemn agreement between the parties that such controversies be resolved elsewhere. The only contact between the United States and the transaction involved here is the fact that Alberto-Culver is an American corporation and the occurrence of some—but by no means the greater part—of the pre-contract negotiations in this country. To determine that "American standards of fairness," must nonetheless govern the controversy demeans the standards of justice elsewhere in the world, and unnecessarily exalts the primacy of United States law over the laws of other countries.

The exception to the clear provisions of the Arbitration Act carved out by *Wilko* is simply inapposite to a case such as the one before us. In Wilko the Court reasoned that "[w]hen the security buyer, prior to any violation of the Securities Act, waives his right to sue in courts, he gives up more than would a participant in other business transactions. The security buyer has a wider choice of courts and venue. He thus surrenders one of the advantages the Act gives him..." 346 U.S., at 435. In the context of an international contract, however, these advantages become chimerical since, as indicated above, an opposing party may by speedy resort to a foreign court block or hinder access to the American court of the purchaser's choice.[12]

[The Court characterizes an agreement to arbitrate as "a specialized kind of forum-selection clause" dealt with in *The Bremen v. Zapata Off-Shore Co.*, 407 U.S. 1 (1972).][14]

For all these reasons we hold that the agreement of the parties in this case to arbitrate any dispute arising out of their international commercial transaction is to be respected and enforced by the federal courts in accord with the explicit provisions of the Arbitration Act.[15]

---

12. The dissenting opinion raises the specter that our holding today will leave American investors at the mercy of multinational corporations with "vast operations around the world..." Our decision, of course, has no bearing on the scope of the substantive provisions of the federal securities laws for the simple reason that the question is not presented in this case.

14. In *The Bremen* we noted that forum-selection clauses "should be given full effect" when "a freely negotiated private international agreement [is] unaffected by fraud..." 407 U.S., at 13. This qualification does not mean that any time a dispute arising out of a transaction is based upon an allegation of fraud, as in this case, the clause is unenforceable. Rather, it means that an arbitration or forum-selection clause in a contract is not enforceable if the inclusion of that clause in the contract was the product of fraud or coercion. Cf. *Prima Paint Corp. v. Flood & Conklin Mfg. Co.*, 388 U.S. 395. Although we do not decide the question, presumably the type of fraud alleged here could be raised, under Art. V of the Convention on the Recognition and Enforcement of Foreign Arbitral Awards, see n. 15, infra, in challenging the enforcement of whatever arbitral award is produced through arbitration. Article V (2)(b) of the Convention provides that a country may refuse recognition and enforcement of an award if "recognition or enforcement of the award would be contrary to the public policy of that country."

15. Our conclusion today is confirmed by international developments and domestic legislation in the area of commercial arbitration subsequent to the *Wilko* decision. On June 10, 1958, a special conference of the United Nations Economic and Social Council adopted the Convention on the Recognition and Enforcement of Foreign Arbitral Awards. In 1970 the United States acceded to the treaty, (1970) 3 U.S.T. 2517, T.I.A.S. No. 6997, and Congress passed Chapter 2 of the United States Arbitration Act, 9 U.S.C. § 201 et seq., in order to implement the Convention. Section 1 of the new chapter, 9 U.S.C. § 201, provides unequivocally that the Convention "shall be enforced in United States courts in accordance with this chapter." The goal of the Convention, and the principal purpose underlying American adoption and implementation of it, was to encourage the recognition and enforcement of commercial arbitration agreements in international contracts and to unify the standards by which agreements to arbitrate are observed and arbitral awards are enforced in the signatory countries. See Convention on the Recognition and Enforcement of Foreign Arbitral Awards, S. Exec. Doc. E, 90th Cong., 2d Sess. (1968): Quigley, Accession by the United States to the United Nations Convention on the Recognition and Enforcement of Foreign Arbitral Awards, 70 Yale L.J. 1049 (1961). Article II(1) of the Convention provides: "Each Contracting State shall recognize an agreement in writing under which the parties undertake to submit to arbitration all or any differences which have arisen or which may arise between them in respect of a defined legal relationship, whether contractual or not, concerning a subject matter capable of settlement by arbitration." In their discussion of this Article, the delegates to the Convention voiced frequent concern that courts of signatory countries in which an agreement to arbitrate is sought to be enforced should not be permitted to decline enforcement of such agreements on the basis of parochial views of their desirability or in a manner that would diminish the mutually binding nature of the agreements. See G. Haight, Convention on the Recognition and Enforcement of Foreign Arbitral Awards: Summary

Accordingly, the judgment of the Court of Appeals is reversed and the case is remanded to that court with directions to remand to the District Court for further proceedings consistent with this opinion. It is so ordered.

Mr. Justice DOUGLAS, with whom Mr. Justice BRENNAN, Mr. Justice WHITE, and Mr. Justice MARSHALL concur, dissenting.

* * *

There has been much support for arbitration of disputes; and it may be the superior way of settling some disagreements. If A and B were quarreling over a trade-mark and there was an arbitration clause in the contract, the policy of Congress in implementing the United Nations Convention on the Recognition and Enforcement of Foreign Arbitral Awards, as it did in 9 U.S.C. § 201 et seq., would prevail. But the Act does not substitute an arbiter for the settlement of disputes under the 1933 and 1934 Acts. Art. II(3) of the Convention says: "The court of a Contracting State, when seized of an action in a matter in respect of which the parties have made an agreement within the meaning of this article, shall, at the request of one of the parties, refer the parties to arbitration, unless it finds that the said agreement is null and void, inoperative or incapable of being performed."[5] (1970) 3 U.S.T. 2517, 2519, T.I.A.S. No. 6997.

But § 29(a) of the 1934 Act makes agreements to arbitrate liabilities under § 10 of the Act "void" and "inoperative." Congress has specified a precise way whereby big and small investors will be protected and the rules under which the Alberto-Culvers of this Nation shall operate. They or their lawyers cannot waive those statutory conditions, for our corporate giants are not principalities of power but guardians of a host of wards unable to care for themselves. It is these wards that the 1934 Act tries to protect. Not a word in the Convention governing awards adopts the standards which Congress has passed to protect the investors under the 1934 Act. It is peculiarly appropriate that we adhere to *Wilko*—more so even than when *Wilko* was decided. Huge foreign investments are being made in our companies. It is important that American standards of fairness in security dealings govern the destinies of American investors until Congress changes these standards.

* * *

It has been recognized that the 1934 Act, including the protections of Rule 10b-5, applies when foreign defendants have defrauded American investors, particularly when, as alleged here, they have profited by virtue of proscribed conduct within our boundaries. This is true even when the defendant is organized under the laws of a foreign country, is conducting much of its activity outside the United States, and is therefore governed largely by foreign law. The language of § 29 of the 1934 Act does not immu-

---

Analysis of Record of United Nations Conference, May/June 1958, pp. 24-28 (1958). Without reaching the issue of whether the Convention, apart from the considerations expressed in this opinion, would require of its own force that the agreement to arbitrate be enforced in the present case, we think that this country's adoption and ratification of the Convention and the passage of Chapter 2 of the United States Arbitration Act provide strongly persuasive evidence of congressional policy consistent with the decision we reach today.

5. The Convention also permits that arbitral awards not be recognized and enforced when a court in the country where enforcement is sought finds that "[t]he recognition or enforcement of the award would be contrary to the public policy of that country." Art. V(2)(b); (1970) 3 U.S.T. 2517, 2520, T.I.A.S. No. 6997. It also provides that recognition of an award may be refused when the arbitration agreement "is not valid under the law to which the parties have subjected it," in this case the laws of Illinois. Art. V(1)(a). See n. 10, *infra*.

nize such international transactions, and the United Nations Convention provides that a forum court in which a suit is brought need not enforce an agreement to arbitrate which is "void" and "inoperative" as contrary to its public policy.[10] When a foreign corporation undertakes fraudulent action which subjects it to the jurisdiction of our federal securities laws, nothing justifies the conclusion that only a diluted version of those laws protects American investors.

* * *

The loss of the proper judicial forum carries with it the loss of substantial rights.[11]

* * *

The virtue of certainty in international agreements may be important, but Congress has dictated that when there are sufficient contacts for our securities laws to apply, the policies expressed in those laws take precedence. Section 29 of the 1934 Act, which renders arbitration clauses void and inoperative, recognizes no exception for fraudulent dealings which incidentally have some international factors. The Convention makes provision for such national public policy in Art. II(3). Federal jurisdiction under the 1934 Act will attach only to some international transactions, but when it does, the protections afforded investors such as Alberto-Culver can only be full-fledged.

---

10. A summary of the conference proceedings which led to the adoption of the United Nations Convention was prepared by G. W. Haight, who served as a member of the International Chamber of Commerce delegation to the conference. Haight, Convention on the Recognition and Enforcement of Foreign Arbitral Awards: Summary Analysis of Record of United Nations Conference, May/June 1958 (1958). When Art. II(3) was being discussed, the Israeli delegate pointed out that while a court could, under the draft Convention as it then stood, refuse enforcement of an award which was incompatible with public policy, "the court had to refer parties to arbitration whether or not such reference was lawful or incompatible with public policy." Id., at 27. The German delegate observed that this difficulty arose from the omission in Art. II(3) "of any words which would relate the arbitral agreement to an arbitral award capable of enforcement under the convention." *Ibid*.

Haight continues: "When the German proposal was put to a vote, it failed to obtain a two-thirds majority (13 to 9) and the Article was thus adopted without any words linking agreements to the awards enforceable under the Convention. Nor was this omission corrected in the Report of the Drafting Committee (L. 61), *although the obligation to refer parties to arbitration was (and still is) qualified by the clause "unless it finds that the agreement is null and void, inoperative or incapable of being performed."*

"As the applicable law is not indicated, courts may under this wording be allowed some latitude: *they may find an agreement incapable of performance if it offends the law or the public policy of the forum*. Apart from this limited opening, the Conference appeared unwilling to qualify the broad undertaking not only to recognize but also to give effect to arbitral agreements." Id., at 28 (emphasis added).

Whatever "concern" the delegates had that signatories to the Convention "not be permitted to decline enforcement of such agreements on the basis of parochial views of their desirability," it would seem that they contemplated that a court may decline to enforce an agreement which offends its law or public policy. The Court also attempts to treat this case as only a minor variation of *The Bremen v. Zapata Off-Shore Co.*, 407 U.S. 1. In that case, however, the Court, per Mr. Chief Justice Burger explicitly stated:

"A contractual choice-of-forum clause should be held unenforceable if enforcement would contravene a strong public policy of the forum."

11. The agreement in this case provided that the "laws of the State of Illinois" are applicable. Even if the arbitration court should read this clause to require application of Rule 10b-5's standards, Alberto-Culver's victory would be Pyrrhic. The arbitral court may improperly interpret the substantive protections of the Rule, and if it does its error will not be reviewable as would the error of a federal court. And the ability of Alberto-Culver to prosecute its claim would be eviscerated by lack of discovery. These are the policy considerations which underlay *Wilko* and which apply to the instant case as well.

Notes

1. Wilco v. Swan, 346 U.S. 427 (1953), discussed in *Scherk*, was overruled by Rodriguez De Quijas v. Shearson/American Exp., Inc., 490 U.S. 477 (1989), which held (5-4) that a predispute agreement to arbitrate claims under the Securities Act of 1933 is enforceable and does not require resolution of the claims only in a judicial forum.

2. In 1988, the Foreign Sovereign Immunities Act [see infra chapter 5] was amended by adding § 1605(a)(6). The amendment allows the enforcement of arbitral awards and the confirmation of arbitral awards against a sovereign if the arbitration takes place in the United States, is under a treaty signed by the United States, or the underlying claim could have been brought in the United States under existing provisions of the FSIA. Section 1610 of the FSIA was also amended by adding subsection (a)(6) allowing attachment of property in the United States of a foreign state used for commercial activity if attachment is in aid of execution of a judgment based on an arbitral award and is not contrary to the arbitration agreement.

At the same time, the Federal Arbitration Act was amended by adding 9 U.S.C. § 15, which provides that enforcement of arbitration agreements, confirmation of an arbitral award, and execution on judgments based on such confirmations "shall not be refused on the basis of the Act of State doctrine." [See infra chapter 4].

3. Riley v. Kingsley Underwriting Agencies, Ltd., 969 F.2d 953 (10th Cir.), cert. denied, 506 U.S. 1021 (1992). An American who became a member of the British LLoyd's insurance syndicate and lost large amounts of money, sued Lloyd's and other English defendants for violations of federal and state securities laws. The suit was dismissed on the basis of clauses in the membership agreement selecting English courts and arbitration as the exclusive forum and providing for the application of English law. Similar results were reached in Richards v. Lloyd's of London, 135 F.3d 1289 (9th Cir. En Banc), cert. denied, 525 U.S. 943 (1998) and Roby v. Corporation of Lloyd's, 996 F2d 1353 (2d Cir. 1993), cert. denied, 510 U.S. 945 (1993), suits by American investors who participated in a Lloyd's insurance syndicate to their great regret. *Roby* states in dictum that "if the [plaintiffs] were able to show that available remedies in England are insufficient to deter British issuers from exploiting American investors through fraud, misrepresentation or inadequate disclosure, we would not hesitate to condemn the choice of law, forum selection and arbitration clauses as against public policy." The court concludes, however, that the plaintiffs failed to make such a showing. Stamm v. Barclays Bank of New York, 153 F.3d 30 (2d Cir. 1998), reaffirms the holding in *Roby* even though the Securities and Exchange Commission has changed its position and now urges the court to find that the clauses choosing English law and forum are unenforceable waivers of the protection of U.S. securities laws. Haynsworth v. The Corporation, 121 F.3d 956 (5th Cir. 1997), cert. denied, 523 U.S. 1072 (1998) and Lipcon v. Underwriters at Lloyd's, 148 F.3d 1285 (11th Cir. 1998), cert. denied, 525 U.S. 1093 (1999), enforced the choice clauses against Names who had previously signed agreements that did not contain the clauses. The courts rejected the argument that Lloyd's had not adequately called attention to the changes and that this failure constituted fraud that directly affected the forum clause itself.

On March 5, 2000, opening arguments began in the London High Court of Justice in the suit by Names, including Americans, against Lloyd's seeking damages of $237 million.

Do the rulings in the Lloyd's cases conflict with the statement by the Supreme Court of the United States in note 19 of Mitsubishi Motors Corp. v. Soler Chrysler Plymouth,

Inc., infra page 82, "that in the event the choice-of-forum and choice-of-law clauses operated in tandem as a prospective waiver of a party's right to pursue statutory remedies for antitrust violations, we would have little hesitation in condemning the agreement as against public policy." The Court repeated this statement in Vimar Seguros y Reaseguros, S.A. v. M/V Sky Reefer, supra p. 59. See Darrell Hall, No Way Out: An Argument Against Permitting Parties to Opt Out of U.S. Securities Laws in International Transactions, 97 Colum. L. Rev. 57, 86-87 (1997) (stating that courts should not have enforced the forum-selection clause in the suits by Names against Lloyd's unless Lloyd's could demonstrate that the English courts would consider the Names' claims under U.S. securities law).

Baker v. LeBoeuf, Lamb, Leiby & Macrae, 105 F.3d 1102 (6th Cir. 1997) held that the Lloyd's forum-selection clause did not prevent suit in the United States against a law firm. The Lloyd's agreement required the plaintiffs to grant the firm a power of attorney concerning U.S. tax matters. The plaintiffs contend that the firm improperly executed on their behalf an agreement with the U.S. Commissioner of Internal Revenue.

Canadian courts in Victoria and Ontario and a court in New Zealand have enforced forum-selection clauses against Lloyds' Names. See Peter Nygh, Transnational Fraud, in Transnational Tort Litigation: Jurisdictional Principles 82, 87-88 (Campbell McLachlan & Peter Nygh eds., 1996).

United Nations Convention on the Recognition and Enforcement of Foreign Arbitral Awards
Opened for signature June 10, 1958, 21 UST 2517, 330 UNTS 3

(The United States ratified this Convention in 1970 with the following reservation: "The United States of America will apply the Convention, on the basis of reciprocity, to the recognition and enforcement of only those awards made in the territory of another Contracting State only to differences arising out of legal relationships, whether contractual or not, which are considered as commercial under the national law of the United States.")

Article I

1. This Convention shall apply to the recognition and enforcement of arbitral awards made in the territory of a State other than the State where the recognition and enforcement of such awards are sought, and arising out of differences between persons, whether physical or legal. It shall also apply to arbitral awards not considered as domestic awards in the State where their recognition and enforcement are sought.

2. The term "arbitral awards" shall include not only awards made by arbitrators appointed for each case but also those made by permanent arbitral bodies to which the parties have submitted.

3. When signing, ratifying or acceding to this Convention, or notifying extension under Article X hereof, any State may on the basis of reciprocity declare that it will apply the Convention to the recognition and enforcement of awards made only in the territory of another Contracting State. It may also declare that it will apply the Convention only to differences arising out of legal relationships, whether contractual or not, which are considered as commercial under the national law of the State making such declaration.

Article II

1. Each Contracting State shall recognize an agreement in writing under which the parties undertake to submit to arbitration all or any differences which have arisen or which may arise between them in respect of a defined legal relationship, whether contractual or not, concerning a subject matter capable of settlement by arbitration.

2. The term "agreement in writing" shall include an arbitral clause in a contract or an arbitration agreement, signed by the parties or contained in an exchange of letters or telegrams.

3. The court of a Contracting State, when seized of an action in a matter in respect of which the parties have made an agreement within the meaning of this article, shall, at the request of one of the parties, refer the parties to arbitration, unless it finds that the said agreement is null and void, inoperative or incapable of being performed.

Article III

Each Contracting State shall recognize arbitral awards as binding and enforce them in accordance with the rules of procedure of the territory where the award is relied upon, under the conditions laid down in the following articles. There shall not be imposed substantially more onerous conditions or higher fees or charges on the recognition or enforcement of arbitral awards to which this Convention applies than are imposed on the recognition or enforcement of domestic arbitral awards.

Article IV

1. To obtain the recognition and enforcement mentioned in the preceding article, the party applying for recognition and enforcement shall, at the time of the application, supply:

(a) The duly authenticated original award or a duly certified copy thereof;

(b) The original agreement referred to in Article II or a duly certified copy thereof.

2. If the said award or agreement is not made in an official language of the country in which the award is relied upon, the party applying for recognition and enforcement of the award shall produce a translation of these documents into such language. The translation shall be certified by an official or sworn translator or by a diplomatic or consular agent.

Article V

1. Recognition and enforcement of the award may be refused, at the request of the party against whom it is invoked, only if that party furnishes to the competent authority where the recognition and enforcement is sought, proof that:

(a) The parties to the agreement referred to in Article II were, under the law applicable to them, under some incapacity, or the said agreement is not valid under the law to which the parties have subjected it or, failing any indication thereon, under the law of the country where the award was made; or

(b) The party against whom the award is invoked was not given proper notice of the appointment of the arbitrator or of the arbitration proceedings or was otherwise unable to present his case; or

(c) The award deals with a difference not contemplated by or not falling within the terms of the submission to arbitration, or it contains decisions on matters beyond the scope of the submission to arbitration, provided that, if the decisions on matters submitted to arbitration can be separated from those not so submitted, that part of the award which contains decisions on matters submitted to arbitration may be recognized and enforced; or

(d) The composition of the arbitral authority or the arbitral procedure was not in accordance with the agreement of the parties, or, failing such agreement, was not in accordance with the law of the country where the arbitration took place; or

(e) The award has not yet become binding on the parties, or has been set aside or suspended by a competent authority of the country in which, or under the law of which, that award was made.

2. Recognition and enforcement of an arbitral award may also be refused if the competent authority in the country where recognition and enforcement is sought finds that:

(a) The subject matter of the difference is not capable of settlement by arbitration under the law of that country; or

(b) The recognition or enforcement of the award would be contrary to the public policy of that country.

Article VI

If an application for the setting aside or suspension of the award has been made to a competent authority referred to in Article V(1)(e), the authority before which the award is sought to be relied upon may, if it considers it proper, adjourn the decision on the enforcement of the award and may also, on the application of the party claiming enforcement of the award, order the other party to give suitable security.

Article VII

1. The provisions of the present Convention shall not affect the validity of multilateral or bilateral agreements concerning the recognition and enforcement of arbitral awards entered into by the Contracting States nor deprive any interested party of any right he may have to avail himself of an arbitral award in the manner and to the extent allowed by the law or the treaties of the country where such award is sought to be relied upon.

2. The Geneva Protocol on Arbitration Clauses of 1923 and the Geneva Convention on the Execution of Foreign Arbitral Awards of 1927 [27 LNTS 157; 92 LNTS 301] shall cease to have effect between Contracting States on their becoming bound and to the extent that they become bound, by this Convention.

* * *

Article XIV

A Contracting State shall not be entitled to avail itself of the present Convention against other Contracting States except to the extent that it is itself bound to apply the Convention.

* * *

Notes

1. As of January 1, 2000, 109 countries had ratified the United Nations Convention on the Recognition and Enforcement of Foreign Arbitral Awards. (The Convention and a list of parties is found in a note following 9 U.S.C.A. §201.) It is sometimes called the "New York" Convention. Note that the title of the New York Convention is misleading

since the convention covers enforcement of arbitral agreements as well as arbitral awards. See article II(3).

The United States has also ratified the Inter-American Convention on International Commercial Arbitration, sometimes called the "Panama" Convention, which is set out in chapter 11. As of January 1, 2000, 11 other countries had also ratified both the New York and Panama conventions. (Argentina, Chile, Colombia, Costa Rica, Ecuador, Guatemala, Mexico, Panama, Peru, Uruguay, and Venezuela.) 9 U.S.C. § 305 provides that "[w]hen the requirements for application of both the [Panama] and [New York conventions] are met, determination as to which Convention applies shall, unless otherwise expressly agreed, be made as follows: (a) If a majority of the parties to the arbitration agreement are citizens of a State or States that have ratified or acceded to the [Panama] Convention and are member States of the Organization of American States, the [Panama] Convention shall apply. (2) In all other cases the [New York Convention] shall apply."

The United States reservation, limiting the New York Convention to "commercial" relationships, excludes matrimonial and custody disputes and disputes excluded under the United States Arbitration Act, 9 U.S.C. § 1 ("contracts of employment of seamen, railroad employees, or any other class of workers engaged in foreign or interstate commerce"). Most circuits that have considered the problem have construed the words "contracts of any other class of workers engaged in foreign or interstate commerce" narrowly to apply only to "workers actually engaged in the movement of goods in interstate commerce in the same way that seamen and railroad workers are." Asplundh Tree Expert Co. v. Bates, 71 F.3d 592, 600 (6th Cir. 1995). Accord, Maryland Casualty Co. v. Realty Advisory Board on Labor Relations, 107 F.3d 979 (2d Cir. 1997); Cole v. Burns Int'l Security Services, 105 F.3d 1465 (D.C. Cir. 1997). Craft v. Campbell Soup Co., 177 F.3d 1083 (9th Cir. 1999), however, refuses to follow cases that it cites from the 3rd, 4th, and 10th circuits that have given a narrow construction to the 9 U.S.C. § 1 exclusion and holds that the Federal Arbitration Act does not apply to any labor or employment contract. The United States Supreme Court has granted certiorari in another Ninth Circuit case that follows *Craft*. Circuit City Stores, Inc. v. Adams, 194 F.3d 1070 (9th Cir. 1999), cert. granted, 120 S.Ct. 2004 (2000).

2. Scrutiny of the UN Arbitration Convention suggests topics that should be covered in the arbitration clause:

(a) Scope: what issues shall be submitted to arbitration? See article V(1)(c). This is perhaps the most important point. See *Mitsubishi Motors*, the next principal case, and compare the "dragnet" forum-selection clause set out in note 3 following *Bremen*.

First Options of Chicago, Inc. v. Kaplan, 514 U.S. 938 (1995), concerning a dispute between United States parties, holds that one of the issues that the parties may submit to arbitration is whether a dispute is arbitrable. If the parties did not agree to submit the arbitrability question itself to arbitration, and the arbitrators decide that the parties have agreed to arbitrate a dispute, a court to whom the decision is appealed should independently decide the arbitrability issue. If, however, there is "clear and unmistakable" (Id. at 1924) evidence that the parties have agreed to arbitrate arbitrability, "the court will set aside [the arbitrators' decision that an issue is arbitrable] only in very unusual circumstances. See, e.g. 9 U.S.C. § 10." Id. at 1923. 9 U.S.C. § 10 permits a United States district court to vacate an arbitration award procured by "corruption, fraud, or undue means," or for arbitrator "misbehavior by which rights of any party have been prejudiced," or "where the arbitrators exceeded their powers." See William W. Park, The Arbitrability Dicta in First Options v. Kaplan: What Sort of Kompetenz-Kompetenz Has Crossed the Atlantic?, 12 J. London Court of Int'l Arbitration 137 (1996); Shirin Philipp, Is the Supreme Court Bucking the Trend? First Options v. Kaplan in Light of European Reform Initiatives in Arbitration Law, 14 B.U. Int'l L.J. 119, 131 (1996) (stating that "Article 16 [of the Model Law on International Commercial Arbitration, infra page 528] does not address [the competence of an arbitral tribunal to finally determine its own jurisdiction] where parties have explicitly agreed to arbitrate the question of arbitrability").

(b) Where? This is the one of the keys to applicability of the convention under article I(1).

(c) How are arbitrators to be appointed? See article I(2). Two methods are often used: each party chooses one arbitrator and these two arbitrators choose a third to preside; the arbitrator or arbitrators are chosen from a panel designated by the arbitral institution referred to in the agreement.

(d) In what language will the arbitration be conducted? See article IV(2).

(e) What law will govern the arbitration? See article V(1)(a).

If the law of the chosen state limits the power of arbitrators or the scope of arbitration, dispute settlement is likely to take a prolonged detour to litigate the interaction of the parties' agreement to arbitrate, their choice-of-law clause, and the arbitration law of the chosen state. See Mastrobuono v. Shearson Lehman Hutton, Inc., 514 U.S. 52 (1995) (choice of New York law does not include New York rule that arbitrators cannot assess punitive damages); Volt Information Sciences v. Board of Trustees of Stanford University, 489 U.S. 468 (1989) (choice of California law included California rule that a court may stay arbitration in a case involving parties to an arbitration agreement and other litigants who have not agreed to arbitrate). A choice-of-law clause in an arbitration agreement should exclude the law of the chosen state that governs the powers of arbitrators, the scope of arbitration, or the power of courts to stay arbitration).

In 1994 The International Institute for the Unification of Private Law (UNIDROIT), with headquarters in Rome, published the UNIDROIT Principles of International Commercial Contracts.<http://www.UNIDROIT/org/english/principles/contents.htm>. The Principles codify the lex mercatoria (law merchant), consisting of the customs and practices of participants in international commercial transactions. There is disagreement as to whether the parties have the power to choose law that is not that of some state, such as the UNIDROIT Principles. The parties are given this power by the Rules of the International Chamber of Commerce and by the Mexico Treaty on the Law Applicable to Contracts, but not by The European Convention on the Law Applicable to Contractual Obligations (the "Rome Convention). The parties should be able to choose the UNIDROIT Principles because this is simply a way of incorporating by reference matters that the parties are free to spell out at length. Article 1.4 of the Principles states: "Nothing in these Principles shall restrict the application of mandatory rules...."

(f) What procedure will the arbitrators follow? See article V(1)(d). This is often covered by reference to the rules of a specified arbitral institution such as the International Chamber of Commerce, the American Arbitration Association, The London Court of Arbitration, The Japan Commercial Arbitration Association, The Arbitration Association of the Stockholm Chamber of Commerce, the Inter-American Commercial Arbitration Commission, or the Society of Maritime Arbitrators.

Scrutiny of the Model Law on International Commercial Arbitration in Chapter 11, page 528, suggests various details of procedure that might be included in the arbitration agreement.

(g) Expert witnesses: may the arbitral tribunal appoint them? Are there limits on the number called by each party? See article 26.

(h) Waiver: If suit is brought and the other party does not request reference to arbitration until after submitting the first statement on the substance of the dispute, does the party waive the right to demand arbitration? If not, when does waiver occur? See article 8(1); Alan Scott Rau, The UNCITRAL Model Law in State and Federal Courts: The Case of "Waiver," 6 Amer. Rev. Int'l Arbitration 223 (1995).

Recent cases have litigated the waiver issue when the arbitration agreement does not cover waiver. S&R Co. of Kingston v. Latona Trucking, Inc., 159 F.3d 80 (2d Cir. 1998), cert. dism'd, 120 S. Ct. 629 (1999), held that in the light of extensive pre-trial discovery and motions, the trial court properly decided the issue of waiver rather than referring it to an arbitrator, and that the trial court properly found a waiver of the right to arbitration despite the fact that the arbitration agreement incorporated by reference a rule of the American Arbitration Association that stated "[n]o judicial proceeding by a party relating to the subject matter of the arbitration shall be deemed a waiver of the party's right to arbitrate." In re Bruce Terminix Co., 988 S.W.2d 702 (Tex. 1998), found no waiver even after filing an answer to the complaint and serving discovery requests.

(i) Judicial assistance: Do the parties consent to pre-award attachment and other interim measures? See article 9.

(j) Other details of procedure: Do the parties consent to consolidation of related arbitrations? What shall be the nature and scope of discovery? Shall there be a transcript of proceedings? See article 19(1).

Other topics that the parties should considered for coverage in the arbitration agreement are the court that will enter a judgment on the award (permitted by 9 U.S.C. §9), the standard for fixing the arbitrators' fees, allocation and allowability of the costs of arbitration (see J. Gillis Wetter & Charl Priem, Costs and Their Allocation in International Commercial Arbitrations, 2 Amer. Rev. Int'l Arbitration 249 (1992); John Yukio Gotanda, Awarding Costs and Attorneys' Fees in International Commercial Arbitrations, 21 Mich. J. Int'l L. 1 (1999)), whether the parties agree not to contest the award (See Michael H. Strub, Jr., Resisting Enforcement of Foreign Arbitral Awards Under Article V(1)(e) and Article VI of the New York Convention: A Proposal for Effective Guidelines, 68 Texas L. Rev. 1031 (1990)), and whether the award will have collateral estoppel effect in favor of third persons. The parties can eliminate a difficult issue by agreeing on what interest will be paid on any award, both before the award is made and after the award but before payment. See John Y. Golanda, Awarding Interest in International Arbitration, 90 Am. J. Int'l L. 40 (1996). The parties may wish to agree that evidence produced and the proceedings and award shall be confidential. See Charles S. Baldwin, IV, Protecting Confidential and Proprietary Commercial Information in International Arbitration, 31 Texas Int'l L.J. 451, 492-93 (1996) (providing a form for a confidentiality agreement). If both the New York and Panama conventions are applicable, the parties must choose the New York convention if they wish it to apply (see 9 U.S.C. §305, supra note 1).

As with other parts of their agreement, the parties should determine whether all aspects of the arbitration clause will be valid under the applicable law. For example, English Arbitration Act 1950 § 18(3) invalidates a pre-dispute, but not post-dispute, agreement under which each party bears its own costs.

See Stephen R. Bond, How to Draft an Arbitration Clause, 6 No.2 J. Int'l Arbitration 65 (1989); Marc Blessing, Drafting Arbitration Clauses, 5 Am. Rev. Int'l Arbitration 54 (1994).

3. The second sentence of Article I(1) of the Arbitration Convention refers to "arbitral awards not considered as domestic awards in the State where their recognition and enforcement are sought" even though, as the first sentence requires, not "made in the territory of a State other than the State where the recognition and enforcement [is] sought." France and Germany were the countries primarily responsible for the "not considered as domestic" language. They do not regard an award rendered in their country as "domestic" if made under the arbitration procedure of a foreign country. See Paolo Contini, International Commercial Arbitration: The United Nations Convention on the Recognition and Enforcement of Foreign Arbitral Awards, 8 Am. J. Comp. L. 283, 292-93 (1959); Albert Jan van den Berg, The New York Arbitration Convention of 1958: Towards a Uniform Judicial Interpretation, 23 (Kluwer, Netherlands, 1981). The United States and other countries opposed this provision.

Nevertheless, Bergesen v. Joseph Mueller Corp., 710 F.2d 928 (2d Cir. 1983) held the Convention applicable to an arbitration held in New York between Norwegian and Swiss parties under the procedures of the American Arbitration Association. This extended the Convention beyond even the circumstance in which France and Germany, the sponsors of the "not domestic" language, would have applied it. The court based its result partly on the fact that when enacting 9 U.S.C. § 202, Congress did not also exclude arbitral awards involving foreign parties rendered within the United States. (Id. at 933). 9 U.S.C. § 202 provides: "An arbitration agreement or arbitral award arising out of a legal relationship..which is considered as commercial...falls under the Convention. An agreement or award rising out of such a relationship which is entirely between citizens of the United States shall be deemed not to fall under the Convention unless that relationship involves property located abroad, envisages performance or enforcement abroad, or has some other reasonable relation with one or more foreign states." The Court also noted that § 206 permits a district court having jurisdiction under the chapter intended to implement the Convention to direct that arbitration be held in the United States. 710 F.2d at 933. The court dismissed the United States reservation as providing "little reason for us to construe the accession in narrow terms." Smith/Enron Cogeneration Limited Partnership, Inc. v. Smith Cogneration, Int'l, Inc., 198 F.3d 88 (2d Cir. 1999), cert. filed, May 19, 2000, extended *Bergesen* and applied Article II of the Convention to order arbitration in the United States of a dispute between United States and foreign parties concerning construction an operation of a power plant abroad even though none of the foreign jurisdictions involved were signatories of the Convention. The court held that the reciprocity requirement in the United States reservation to the Convention is satisfied when the award is granted in a Contracting State.

Is *Bergesen*'s construction of "not considered as domestic" correct? A possible interpretation of the United States reservation to the Convention, quoted on page 69, is that it imposes only the requirements of reciprocity and commercial subject matter but does not require that the award be made abroad. For this reading of the reservation, see Lander Co. v. MMP Investments, Inc., 107 F.3d 476, 482 (7th Cir.) (Posner, J.), cert. denied, 522 U.S. 811 (1997).

The second sentence of §202, quoted above in the second paragraph of this note, can be read as limiting what would otherwise be the too-broad inclusion by the first sentence of all commercial relationships. If read in this manner, §202 has no application to foreign awards and would not violate article 1, which applies the Convention to all "arbitral awards made in the territory of a State other than the State where recognition and enforcement of such awards are sought." Industrial Risk Insurers v. M.A.N. Gutehoffnunshutte GmbH, 141 F.3d 1434 (11th Cir. 1998), cert. denied, 525 U.S. 1068 (1999), read §202 "to define all arbitral awards not 'entirely between citizens of the United States' as 'non-domestic' for purposes of Article I of the Convention." The court held that the Convention applied to "an arbitral award granted to a foreign corporation by an arbitral panel sitting in the United States and applying American federal or state law." See also Alan Scott Rau, The New York Convention in American Courts, 7 Am. Rev. Int'l Arb. 213, 231 (1996) (stating that §202 "must be understood as the American definition of 'non-domestic' awards").

Why does it make a difference whether the New York Convention applies to an arbitration agreement otherwise covered by the Federal Arbitration Act? In *Bergesen,* supra, the issue was the statute of limitations. 9 U.S.C. §207, which implements the Convention, provides a three-year limitation for getting an award confirmed. In *Lander,* supra, the issue was the ability to contest an arbitration award. 9 U.S.C. §12, which does not apply if the Convention applies, allows only three months for a judicial challenge to an arbitration award. If a party fails to make a timely motion to vacate an arbitration award, that party loses the right to oppose enforcement of the award. The New York Convention has no provision for seeking to vacate an award and a party can raise the bases in Article V for denying enforcement. In *Industrial Risk Insurers,* supra, the issue was grounds for denying enforcement to an award. Under the Federal Arbitration Act, a court can deny enforcement of a domestic award on the ground that the award is "arbitrary and capricious." There is no such basis in Article V of the Convention for denying enforcement. But see Alghanim & Sons, v. Toys "R" US, Inc., 126 F.3d 15, 18-23 (2d Cir. 1997), cert. denied, 522 U.S. 1111 (1998), stating that although a United States court may refuse enforcement of an award rendered in another signatory country only under one of the grounds set out in Article V, a U.S. court can vacate an award rendered in the U.S. for "manifest disregard of the law" even though the award is covered by the Convention. Nevertheless, the court affirmed confirmation of the award on the ground that the party seeking to vacate the award had not demonstrated "manifest disregard."

There is likely to be federal subject matter jurisdiction whether or not the Convention applies on the ground of diversity of citizenship, but if not, there is jurisdiction if the Convention applies but not if the award is domestic. 9 U.S.C. §9 provides that parties can specify in their arbitration agreement a court to confirm the award and that if "no court is specified in the agreement...then such application may be made to the United States court in and for the district within such award was made." This section has not been interpreted as providing an independent basis for federal jurisdiction if there is no other basis for federal jurisdiction, such as diversity, admiralty, or federal question other than the Federal Arbitration Act. See Charles Alan Wright et al, 13B Federal Practice and Procedure §3569 at 170-71 (1984).

4. Europcar Italia, S.p.A v. Maiellano Tours, Inc., 156 F.3d 310 (2d Cir. 1998), lists six factors that affect a court's discretion under Article VI of the New York Convention to adjourn enforcement proceedings pending appeal of an arbitration award in the originating country. The factors include "the status of the foreign proceedings and the estimated time for those proceedings to be resolved" and "whether the award...will receive greater scrutiny in the foreign proceedings under a less deferential standard of review."

5. Article VII of the Convention states that the Convention does not "deprive any interested party of any right he may have to avail himself of an arbitral award in the manner and to the extent allowed by the law or the treaties of the country where such award is sought to be relied upon." Baker Marine (Nigeria), Ltd. v. Chevron (Nigeria) Ltd, 191 F.3d 194 (1999) held that this language does not compel a U.S. court to confirm an award made in Nigeria that had been set aside by a Nigerian court on a ground not available under U.S. law. Nor had the party seeking to enforce the award demonstrated by a U.S. court should exercise the discretion it may have under Article V(1)(e) to recognize the award. In re Arbitration of Certain Controversies between Chromalloy Aeroservices and the Arab Republic of Egypt, 939 F. Supp. 907 (D.D.C. 1996), enforced an Egyptian arbitration award after an Egyptian court had nullified it. The court held that because the ground invoked by the Egyptian court to nullify the award would not exist under U.S. law, Article VII gave the recipient of the award a right to have the award recognized and enforced. *Baker* distinguished but not repudiate *Chromalloy*. The distinction was that in *Chromalloy* the party opposing the award had agreed that the award could not "be made subject to any appeal or other recourse." Therefore recognizing the Egyptian judgment in that case "would be contrary to the United States policy favoring arbitration." *Baker*, 191 F.3d at 197 n.3. The has been much adverse criticism of *Chromalloy*. See, e.g., Richard W. Hulbert, Further Observations on Chromalloy: A Contract Misconstrued, a Law Misapplied, and an Opportunity Foregone, 13 ICSID Rev.—Foreign Investment L.J. 124 (1998); William W. Park, Duty and Discretion in International Arbitration, 93 Am. J. Int'l L. 805, 807-08 (1999).

Mitsubishi Motors Corporation v. Soler Chrysler-Plymouth, Inc.
473 U.S. 614 (1985)

Justice BLACKMUN delivered the opinion of the Court.

The principal question presented by these cases is the arbitrability, pursuant to the Federal Arbitration Act, 9 U.S.C. §1 et seq., and the Convention on the Recognition and Enforcement of Foreign Arbitral Awards (Convention), [1970] 21 U.S.T. 2517, T.I.A.S. No. 6997, of claims arising under the Sherman Act, 15 U.S.C. §1 et seq., and encompassed within a valid arbitration clause in an agreement embodying an international commercial transaction.

I

Petitioner-cross-respondent Mitsubishi Motors Corporation (Mitsubishi) is a Japanese corporation which manufactures automobiles and has its principal place of business in Tokyo, Japan. Mitsubishi is the product of a joint venture between, on the one hand, Chrysler International, S.A. (CISA), a Swiss corporation registered in Geneva and wholly owned by Chrysler Corporation, and, on the other, Mitsubishi Heavy Industries, Inc., a Japanese corporation. The aim of the joint venture was the distribution through Chrysler dealers outside the continental United States of vehicles manufactured by Mitsubishi and bearing Chrysler and Mitsubishi trademarks. Respondent-cross-petitioner Soler Chrysler-Plymouth, Inc. (Soler), is a Puerto Rico corporation with its principal place of business in Pueblo Viejo, Guaynabo, Puerto Rico.

On October 31, 1979, Soler entered into a Distributor Agreement with CISA which provided for the sale by Soler of Mitsubishi-manufactured vehicles within a designated area, including metropolitan San Juan. On the same date, CISA, Soler, and Mitsubishi entered into a Sales Procedure Agreement (Sales Agreement) which, referring to the Distributor Agreement, provided for the direct sale of Mitsubishi products to Soler and governed the terms and conditions of such sales. Paragraph VI of the Sales Agreement, labeled "Arbitration of Certain Matters," provides:

"All disputes, controversies or differences which may arise between [Mitsubishi] and [Soler] out of or in relation to Articles I-B through V of this Agreement or for the breach thereof, shall be finally settled by arbitration in Japan in accordance with the rules and regulations of the Japan Commercial Arbitration Association."

* * *

Soler ran into serious difficulties in meeting the expected sales volume, and by the spring of 1981 it felt itself compelled to request that Mitsubishi delay or cancel shipment of several orders. About the same time, Soler attempted to arrange for the transshipment of a quantity of its vehicles for sale in the continental United States and Latin America. Mitsubishi and CISA, however, refused permission for any such diversion, citing a variety of reasons, and no vehicles were transshipped. Attempts to work out these difficulties failed. Mitsubishi eventually withheld shipment of 966 vehicles, apparently representing orders placed for May, June, and July 1981 production, responsibility for which Soler disclaimed in February 1982.

The following month, Mitsubishi brought an action against Soler in the United States District Court for the District of Puerto Rico under the Federal Arbitration Act and the Convention. Mitsubishi sought an order, pursuant to 9 U.S.C. §§ 4 and 201, to compel arbitration in accord with paragraph VI of the Sales Agreement. Shortly after filing the complaint, Mitsubishi filed a request for arbitration before the Japan Commercial Arbitration Association.

Soler denied the allegations and counterclaimed against both Mitsubishi and CISA. It alleged numerous breaches by Mitsubishi of the Sales Agreement, raised a pair of defamation claims, and asserted causes of action under the Sherman Act, 15 U.S.C. § 1 et seq.; the federal Automobile Dealers' Day in Court Act, 70 Stat. 1125, 15 U.S.C. § 1221 et seq.; the Puerto Rico competition statute, P.R.Laws Ann., Tit. 10, § 257 et seq. (1976); and the Puerto Rico Dealers' Contracts Act, P.R.Laws Ann., Tit. 10, § 278 et seq. (1978 and Supp.1983). In the counterclaim premised on the Sherman Act, Soler alleged that Mitsubishi and CISA had conspired to divide markets in restraint of trade. To effectuate the plan, according to Soler, Mitsubishi had refused to permit Soler to resell to buyers in North, Central, or South America vehicles it had obligated itself to purchase from Mitsubishi; had refused to ship ordered vehicles or the parts, such as heaters and defoggers, that would be necessary to permit Soler to make its vehicles suitable for resale outside Puerto Rico; and had coercively attempted to replace Soler and its other Puerto Rico distributors with a wholly owned subsidiary which would serve as the exclusive Mitsubishi distributor in Puerto Rico.

After a hearing, the District Court ordered Mitsubishi and Soler to arbitrate each of the issues raised in the complaint and in all the counterclaims save two and a portion of a third. [7] With regard to the federal antitrust issues, it recognized that the Courts of Ap-

---

7. The District Court found that the arbitration clause did not cover the fourth and sixth counterclaims, which sought damages for defamation, or the allegations in the seventh counterclaim concerning discriminatory treatment and the establishment of minimum-sales volumes. Accordingly, it retained jurisdiction over those portions of the litigation. In addition, because no arbitration agreement between Soler and CISA existed, the court retained jurisdiction, insofar as they

peals, following *American Safety Equipment Corp. v. J.P. Maguire & Co.*, 391 F.2d 821 (CA2 1968), uniformly had held that the rights conferred by the antitrust laws were "of a character inappropriate for enforcement by arbitration," quoting *Wilko v. Swan*, 201 F.2d 439, 444 (CA2 1953), rev'd, 346 U.S. 427 (1953). The District Court held, however, that the international character of the Mitsubishi-Soler undertaking required enforcement of the agreement to arbitrate even as to the antitrust claims. It relied on *Scherk v. Alberto-Culver Co.*, 417 U.S. 506, 515-520 (1974), in which this Court ordered arbitration, pursuant to a provision embodied in an international agreement, of a claim arising under the Securities Exchange Act of 1934 notwithstanding its assumption, arguendo, that *Wilko*, which held nonarbitrable claims arising under the Securities Act of 1933, also would bar arbitration of a 1934 Act claim arising in a domestic context.

The United States Court of Appeals for the First Circuit affirmed in part and reversed in part. 723 F.2d 155 (1983). It first rejected Soler's argument that Puerto Rico law precluded enforcement of an agreement obligating a local dealer to arbitrate controversies outside Puerto Rico. It also rejected Soler's suggestion that it could not have intended to arbitrate statutory claims not mentioned in the arbitration agreement. Assessing arbitrability "on an allegation-by-allegation basis," *id.*, at 159, the court then read the arbitration clause to encompass virtually all the claims arising under the various statutes, including all those arising under the Sherman Act.

Finally, after endorsing the doctrine of *American Safety*, precluding arbitration of antitrust claims, the Court of Appeals concluded that neither this Court's decision in *Scherk* nor the Convention required abandonment of that doctrine in the face of an international transaction. 723 F.2d, at 164-168. Accordingly, it reversed the judgment of the District Court insofar as it had ordered submission of "Soler's antitrust claims" to arbitration. Affirming the remainder of the judgment, the court directed the District Court to consider in the first instance how the parallel judicial and arbitral proceedings should go forward.

We granted certiorari primarily to consider whether an American court should enforce an agreement to resolve antitrust claims by arbitration when that agreement arises from an international transaction.

II

At the outset, we address the contention raised in Soler's cross-petition that the arbitration clause at issue may not be read to encompass the statutory counterclaims stated in its answer to the complaint. * * * Soler reasons that, because it falls within the class for whose benefit the federal and local antitrust laws and dealers' Acts were passed, but the arbitration clause at issue does not mention these statutes or statutes in general, the clause cannot be read to contemplate arbitration of these statutory claims.

We do not agree, for we find no warrant in the Arbitration Act for implying in every contract within its ken a presumption against arbitration of statutory claims. The Act's centerpiece provision makes a written agreement to arbitrate "in any maritime transaction or a contract evidencing a transaction involving commerce...valid, irrevocable, and enforceable, save upon such grounds as exist at law or in equity for the revocation

---

sought relief from CISA, over the first, second, third, and ninth counterclaims, which raised claims under the Puerto Rico Dealers' Contracts Act, the federal Automobile Dealers' Day in Court Act, the Sherman Act, and the Puerto Rico competition statute, respectively. These aspects of the District Court's ruling were not appealed and are not before this Court.

of any contract." 9 U.S.C. §2. The "liberal federal policy favoring arbitration agreements," Moses H. Cone Memorial Hospital v. Mercury Construction Corp., 460 U.S. 1, 24 (1983), manifested by this provision and the Act as a whole, is at bottom a policy guaranteeing the enforcement of private contractual arrangements....* * * "The Arbitration Act establishes that, as a matter of federal law, any doubts concerning the scope of arbitrable issues should be resolved in favor of arbitration, whether the problem at hand is the construction of the contract language itself or an allegation of waiver, delay, or a like defense to arbitrability." Id. at 24-25.

* * *

In sum, the Court of Appeals correctly conducted a two-step inquiry, first determining whether the parties' agreement to arbitrate reached the statutory issues, and then, upon finding it did, considering whether legal constraints external to the parties' agreement foreclosed the arbitration of those claims. We endorse its rejection of Soler's proposed rule of arbitration-clause construction.

III

We now turn to consider whether Soler's antitrust claims are nonarbitrable even though it has agreed to arbitrate them. In holding that they are not, the Court of Appeals followed the decision of the Second Circuit in *American Safety Equipment Corp. v. J.P. Maguire & Co.*, 391 F.2d 821 (1968). Notwithstanding the absence of any explicit support for such an exception in either the Sherman Act or the Federal Arbitration Act, the Second Circuit there reasoned that "the pervasive public interest in enforcement of the antitrust laws, and the nature of the claims that arise in such cases, combine to make...antitrust claims...inappropriate for arbitration." *Id.*, at 827-828. We find it unnecessary to assess the legitimacy of the *American Safety* doctrine as applied to agreements to arbitrate arising from domestic transactions. As in *Scherk v. Alberto-Culver Co.*, 417 U.S. 506 (1974), we conclude that concerns of international comity, respect for the capacities of foreign and transnational tribunals, and sensitivity to the need of the international commercial system for predictability in the resolution of disputes require that we enforce the parties' agreement, even assuming that a contrary result would be forthcoming in a domestic context.

* * *

The Bremen and *Scherk* establish a strong presumption in favor of enforcement of freely negotiated contractual choice-of-forum provisions. Here, as in *Scherk*, that presumption is reinforced by the emphatic federal policy in favor of arbitral dispute resolution. And at least since this Nation's accession in 1970 to the Convention, see [1970] 21 U.S.T. 2517, T.I.A.S. 6997, and the implementation of the Convention in the same year by amendment of the Federal Arbitration Act,[16] that federal policy applies with special force in the field of international commerce. Thus, we must weigh the concerns of *American Safety* against a strong belief in the efficacy of arbitral procedures for the resolution of international commercial disputes and an equal commitment to the enforcement of freely negotiated choice-of-forum clauses.

At the outset, we confess to some skepticism of certain aspects of the *American Safety* doctrine. As distilled by the First Circuit, 723 F.2d, at 162, the doctrine comprises four ingredients. First, private parties play a pivotal role in aiding governmental enforcement of the antitrust laws by means of the private action for treble damages. Second, "the

---

16. Act of July 31, 1970, Pub.L. 91-368, 84 Stat. 692, codified at 9 U.S.C. §§201-208.

strong possibility that contracts which generate antitrust disputes may be contracts of adhesion militates against automatic forum determination by contract." Third, antitrust issues, prone to complication, require sophisticated legal and economic analysis, and thus are "ill-adapted to strengths of the arbitral process, i.e., expedition, minimal requirements of written rationale, simplicity, resort to basic concepts of common sense and simple equity." Finally, just as "issues of war and peace are too important to be vested in the generals,...decisions as to antitrust regulation of business are too important to be lodged in arbitrators chosen from the business community—particularly those from a foreign community that has had no experience with or exposure to our law and values." See *American Safety*, 391 F.2d, at 826-827.

Initially, we find the second concern unjustified. The mere appearance of an antitrust dispute does not alone warrant invalidation of the selected forum on the undemonstrated assumption that the arbitration clause is tainted. A party resisting arbitration of course may attack directly the validity of the agreement to arbitrate. See *Prima Paint Corp. v. Flood & Conklin Mfg. Co.*, 388 U.S. 395 (1967). Moreover, the party may attempt to make a showing that would warrant setting aside the forum-selection clause—that the agreement was "[a]ffected by fraud, undue influence, or overweening bargaining power"; that "enforcement would be unreasonable and unjust"; or that proceedings "in the contractual forum will be so gravely difficult and inconvenient that [the resisting party] will for all practical purposes be deprived of his day in court." *The Bremen*, 407 U.S., at 12, 15, 18. But absent such a showing—and none was attempted here—there is no basis for assuming the forum inadequate or its selection unfair.

Next, potential complexity should not suffice to ward off arbitration. We might well have some doubt that even the courts following *American Safety* subscribe fully to the view that antitrust matters are inherently insusceptible to resolution by arbitration, as these same courts have agreed that an undertaking to arbitrate antitrust claims entered into after the dispute arises is acceptable. And the vertical restraints which most frequently give birth to antitrust claims covered by an arbitration agreement will not often occasion the monstrous proceedings that have given antitrust litigation an image of intractability. In any event, adaptability and access to expertise are hallmarks of arbitration. The anticipated subject matter of the dispute may be taken into account when the arbitrators are appointed, and arbitral rules typically provide for the participation of experts either employed by the parties or appointed by the tribunal. Moreover, it is often a judgment that streamlined proceedings and expeditious results will best serve their needs that causes parties to agree to arbitrate their disputes; it is typically a desire to keep the effort and expense required to resolve a dispute within manageable bounds that prompts them mutually to forgo access to judicial remedies. In sum, the factor of potential complexity alone does not persuade us that an arbitral tribunal could not properly handle an antitrust matter.

For similar reasons, we also reject the proposition that an arbitration panel will pose too great a danger of innate hostility to the constraints on business conduct that antitrust law imposes. International arbitrators frequently are drawn from the legal as well as the business community; where the dispute has an important legal component, the parties and the arbitral body with whose assistance they have agreed to settle their dispute can be expected to select arbitrators accordingly.[18] We decline to indulge the pre-

---

18. We are advised by Mitsubishi and amicus International Chamber of Commerce, without contradiction by Soler, that the arbitration panel selected to hear the parties' claims here is composed of three Japanese lawyers, one a former law school dean, another a former judge, and the third a practicing attorney with American legal training who has written on Japanese antitrust law.

sumption that the parties and arbitral body conducting a proceeding will be unable or unwilling to retain competent, conscientious, and impartial arbitrators.

We are left, then, with the core of the *American Safety* doctrine—the fundamental importance to American democratic capitalism of the regime of the antitrust laws. Without doubt, the private cause of action plays a central role in enforcing this regime. As the Court of Appeals pointed out:

"A claim under the antitrust laws is not merely a private matter. The Sherman Act is designed to promote the national interest in a competitive economy; thus, the plaintiff asserting his rights under the Act has been likened to a private attorney-general who protects the public's interest." 723 F.2d, at 168, quoting *American Safety*, 391 F.2d, at 826.

The treble-damages provision wielded by the private litigant is a chief tool in the antitrust enforcement scheme, posing a crucial deterrent to potential violators.

The importance of the private damages remedy, however, does not compel the conclusion that it may not be sought outside an American court.

* * *

There is no reason to assume at the outset of the dispute that international arbitration will not provide an adequate mechanism. To be sure, the international arbitral tribunal owes no prior allegiance to the legal norms of particular states; hence, it has no direct obligation to vindicate their statutory dictates. The tribunal, however, is bound to effectuate the intentions of the parties. Where the parties have agreed that the arbitral body is to decide a defined set of claims which includes, as in these cases, those arising from the application of American antitrust law, the tribunal therefore should be bound to decide that dispute in accord with the national law giving rise to the claim. Cf. *Wilko v. Swan*, 346 U.S., at 433- 434.[19] And so long as the prospective litigant effectively may

---

The Court of Appeals was concerned that international arbitrators would lack "experience with or exposure to our law and values." 723 F.2d, at 162. The obstacles confronted by the arbitration panel in this case, however, should be no greater than those confronted by any judicial or arbitral tribunal required to determine foreign law. See, *e.g.*, Fed. Rule Civ.Proc. 44.1. Moreover, while our attachment to the antitrust laws may be stronger than most, many other countries, including Japan, have similar bodies of competition law. See, *e.g.*, 1 Law of Transnational Business Transactions, ch. 9 (Banks, Antitrust Aspects of International Business Operations), § 9.03[7] (V. Nanda ed. 1984); H. Iyori & A. Uesugi, The Antimonopoly Laws of Japan (1983).

19. In addition to the clause providing for arbitration before the Japan Commercial Arbitration Association, the Sales Agreement includes a choice-of-law clause which reads: "This Agreement is made in, and will be governed by and construed in all respects according to the laws of the Swiss Confederation as if entirely performed therein." The United States raises the possibility that the arbitral panel will read this provision not simply to govern interpretation of the contract terms, but wholly to displace American law even where it otherwise would apply. Brief for United States as Amicus Curiae 20. The International Chamber of Commerce opines that it is "[c]onceivabl[e], although we believe it unlikely, [that] the arbitrators could consider Soler's affirmative claim of anticompetitive conduct by CISA and Mitsubishi to fall within the purview of this choice-of-law provision, with the result that it would be decided under Swiss law rather than the U.S. Sherman Act." Brief for International Chamber of Commerce as Amicus Curiae 25. At oral argument, however, counsel for Mitsubishi conceded that American law applied to the antitrust claims and represented that the claims had been submitted to the arbitration panel in Japan on that basis. The record confirms that before the decision of the Court of Appeals the arbitral panel had taken these claims under submission.

We therefore have no occasion to speculate on this matter at this stage in the proceedings, when Mitsubishi seeks to enforce the agreement to arbitrate, not to enforce an award. Nor need we consider now the effect of an arbitral tribunal's failure to take cognizance of the statutory cause of action on the claimant's capacity to reinitiate suit in federal court. We merely note that in the event the

vindicate its statutory cause of action in the arbitral forum, the statute will continue to serve both its remedial and deterrent function.

Having permitted the arbitration to go forward, the national courts of the United States will have the opportunity at the award-enforcement stage to ensure that the legitimate interest in the enforcement of the antitrust laws has been addressed. The Convention reserves to each signatory country the right to refuse enforcement of an award where the "recognition or enforcement of the award would be contrary to the public policy of that country." Art. V(2)(b), 21 U.S.T., at 2520. While the efficacy of the arbitral process requires that substantive review at the award-enforcement stage remain minimal, it would not require intrusive inquiry to ascertain that the tribunal took cognizance of the antitrust claims and actually decided them.

As international trade has expanded in recent decades, so too has the use of international arbitration to resolve disputes arising in the course of that trade. The controversies that international arbitral institutions are called upon to resolve have increased in diversity as well as in complexity. Yet the potential of these tribunals for efficient disposition of legal disagreements arising from commercial relations has not yet been tested. If they are to take a central place in the international legal order, national courts will need to "shake off the old judicial hostility to arbitration," *Kulukundis Shipping Co. v. Amtorg Trading Corp.*, 126 F.2d 978, 985 (CA2 1942), and also their customary and understandable unwillingness to cede jurisdiction of a claim arising under domestic law to a foreign or transnational tribunal. To this extent, at least, it will be necessary for national courts to subordinate domestic notions of arbitrability to the international policy favoring commercial arbitration. See *Scherk, supra.*

Accordingly, we "require this representative of the American business community to honor its bargain," *Alberto-Culver Co. v. Scherk*, 484 F.2d 611, 620 (CA7 1973) (Stevens, J., dissenting), by holding this agreement to arbitrate "enforce[able]...in accord with the explicit provisions of the Arbitration Act." *Scherk*, 417 U.S., at 520. The judgment of the Court of Appeals is affirmed in part and reversed in part, and the cases are remanded for further proceedings consistent with this opinion.

Justice POWELL took no part in the decision of these cases.

Justice STEVENS, with whom Justice BRENNAN joins, and with whom Justice MARSHALL joins except as to Part II, dissenting.

* * *

In my opinion, (1) a fair construction of the language in the arbitration clause in the parties' contract does not encompass a claim that auto manufacturers entered into a conspiracy in violation of the antitrust laws; (2) an arbitration clause should not normally be construed to cover a statutory remedy that it does not expressly identify; (3) Congress did not intend §2 of the Federal Arbitration Act to apply to antitrust claims; and (4) Congress did not intend the Convention on the Recognition and Enforcement of Foreign Arbitral Awards to apply to disputes that are not covered by the Federal Arbitration Act.

International Comity

It is clear then that the international obligations of the United States permit us to honor Congress' commitment to the exclusive resolution of antitrust disputes in the

---

choice-of-forum and choice-of-law clauses operated in tandem as a prospective waiver of a party's right to pursue statutory remedies for antitrust violations, we would have little hesitation in condemning the agreement as against public policy.

federal courts. The Court today refuses to do so, offering only vague concerns for comity among nations. The courts of other nations, on the other hand, have applied the exception provided in the Convention, and refused to enforce agreements to arbitrate specific subject matters of concern to them.[35]

It may be that the subject-matter exception to the Convention ought to be reserved—as a matter of domestic law—for matters of the greatest public interest which involve concerns that are shared by other nations. The Sherman Act's commitment to free competitive markets is among our most important civil policies. This commitment, shared by other nations which are signatory to the Convention,[36] is hardly the sort of parochial concern that we should decline to enforce in the interest of international comity. Indeed, the branch of Government entrusted with the conduct of political relations with foreign governments has informed us that the "United States' determination that federal antitrust claims are nonarbitrable under the Convention...is not likely to result in either surprise or recrimination on the part of other signatories to the Convention." Brief for United States as *Amicus Curiae* 30.

* * *

The Court's repeated incantation of the high ideals of "international arbitration" creates the impression that this case involves the fate of an institution designed to implement a formula for world peace. But just as it is improper to subordinate the public interest in enforcement of antitrust policy to the private interest in resolving commercial disputes, so is it equally unwise to allow a vision of world unity to distort the importance of the selection of the proper forum for resolving this dispute. Like any other mechanism for resolving controversies, international arbitration will only succeed if it is realistically limited to tasks it is capable of performing well—the prompt and inexpensive resolution of essentially contractual disputes between commercial partners. As for matters involving the political passions and the fundamental interests of nations, even the multilateral convention adopted under the auspices of the United Nations recognizes that private international arbitration is incapable of achieving satisfactory results.

In my opinion, the elected representatives of the American people would not have us dispatch an American citizen to a foreign land in search of an uncertain remedy for the violation of a public right that is protected by the Sherman Act. This is especially so when there has been no genuine bargaining over the terms of the submission, and the arbitration remedy provided has not even the most elementary guarantees of fair process. Consideration of a fully developed record by a jury, instructed in the law by a federal judge, and subject to appellate review, is a surer guide to the competitive character of a commercial practice than the practically unreviewable judgment of a private arbitrator.

---

35. For example, the Cour de Cassation in Belgium has held that disputes arising under a Belgian statute limiting the unilateral termination of exclusive distributorships are not arbitrable under the Convention in that country, *Audi-NSU Auto Union A.G. v. S.A. Adelin Petit & Cie.* (1979), in 5 Yearbook Commercial Arbitration 257, 259 (1980), and the Corte di Cassazione in Italy has held that labor disputes are not arbitrable under the Convention in that country, *Compagnia Generale Construzioni v Piersanti*, [1980] Foro Italiano I 190, in 6 Yearbook Commercial Arbitration 229, 230 (1981).

36. For example, the Federal Republic of Germany has a vigorous antitrust program, and prohibits the enforcement of predispute agreements to arbitrate such claims under some circumstances. See Act Against Restraints of Competition §91(1), in 1 Organisation for Economic Co-operation and Development, Guide to Legislation on Restrictive Business Practices, Part D, p. 49 (1980). See also 2 G. Delaume, Transnational Contracts § 13.06, p. 31, and n. 3 (1982).

Unlike the Congress that enacted the Sherman Act in 1890, the Court today does not seem to appreciate the value of economic freedom. I respectfully dissent.

Notes

1. Under the influence of *Mitsubishi*, lower courts have favored enforcement of international arbitration agreements even when public law claims are made. See Genesco, Inc. v. T. Kakiuchi & Co., Ltd., 815 F.2d 840 (2d Cir. 1987), ordering arbitration of a claim under the Racketeer Influenced & Corrupt Organizations Acts (RICO), 18 U.S.C. § 1962, against a Japanese supplier. In the same spirit, courts have construed arbitration clauses broadly to cover disputes not clearly within their scope. Republic of Nicaragua v. Standard Fruit Co., 937 F.2d 469 (9th Cir. 1991), cert. denied, 112 S. Ct. 1294 (1992), held that the issue of whether an agreement in principle was a binding contract was subject to arbitration, stating that "where the parties admit to signing a document that contains an arbitration provisions...all questions regarding breach of the agreement must be referred to arbitration." (937 F.2d at 477). J.J. Ryan & Sons, Inc. v. Rhone Poulenc Textile, S.A., 863 F.2d 315, 321-22 (4th Cir. 1988) states:

> The International Chamber of Commerce's recommended clause which provides for arbitration of "[a]ll disputes arising in connection with the present contract" must be construed to encompass a broad scope of arbitrable issues. The recommended clause does not limit arbitration to the literal interpretation or performance of the contract. It embraces every dispute between the parties having a significant relationship to the contract regardless of the label attached to the dispute.

Does this mean that it is not desirable to draft a "dragnet" arbitration clause similar to the choice-of-forum clause in note 3 following *Bremen*? Tracer Research Corp. v. National Environmental Services Co., 42 F.3d 1292 (9th Cir. 1994), cert. dism'd, 515 U.S. 1187 (1995), held that an arbitration clause covering "any controversy or claim arising out of this Agreement" but not containing the words "relating to," did not cover a tort claim against a former licensee for misappropriation of trade secrets. In Seifert v. U.S. Home Corp., 750 So.2d 633 (Fla. 1999), a contract for purchase of a house contained an arbitration agreement covering "any controversy or claim arising under or related to this agreement or to the property." The court held that the agreement was ambiguous and did not cover a tort claim for wrongful death based on alleged faulty construction of the house.

Kotam Electronics, Inc. v. JBL Consumer Products, Inc., 93 F.3d 724 (11th Cir. 1996) (en banc), cert. denied 519 U.S. 1110 (1997), held that in the light of *Mitsubishi* and the statement in Shearson/American Express, Inc. v. McMahon, 482 U.S. 220, 239 (1987), that "much of [Mitsubishi's] reasoning is equally applicable" to domestic claims, domestic antitrust disputes are arbitrable. The court cites decisions in accord from the Second, Fifth, Seventh, and Ninth Circuits that the *American Safety* doctrine should no longer be followed.

2. Comments on the wisdom of *Mitsubishi*'s enforcement of the agreement to arbitrate have been mixed. See, e.g, Sharon L. Cloud, Mitsubishi and the Arbitrability of Antitrust Claims: Did the Supreme Court Throw the Baby Out with the Bathwater?, 18 Law & Pol'y Int'l Bus. 341, 369 (1986) (stating that "[t]he majority's international and commercial zeal gave rise to an understandable but ill-considered position"); Robert B. von Mehren, From Vynior's Case to Mitsubishi: The Future of Arbitration and Public

Law, 12 Brook. J. Int'l L. 583, 622 (1986) (stating that "[t]he *Mitsubishi* decision is not perfect; it is, however,... good").

For discussion of *Mitsubishi* as well as cases decided under the Hague Service and Evidence Conventions (infra sections 4 and 5), see Russell J. Weintraub, The Need for Awareness of International Standards When Construing Multilateral Conventions: The Arbitration, Evidence, and Service Conventions, 28 Tex. Int'l L.J. 441 (1993).

3. Soleimany v. Soleimany, 3 W.L.R. 811 (Ct. App. 1998) refused on the ground of public policy to enforce an arbitration award for breach of a contract to export and sell Iranian carpets. The transaction violated Iranian revenue laws and export controls.

Rhone Mediterranee Compagnia Francese v. Lauro
712 F.2d 50 (3rd Cir. 1983)

GIBBONS, Circuit Judge.

Rhone Mediterranee Compagnia Francese di Assicurazioni E Riassicurazioni (Rhone), a casualty insurer, appeals from an order of the District Court of the Virgin Islands staying Rhone's action pending arbitration. The action results from a fire loss which occurred when the vessel Angelina Lauro burned at the dock of the East Indian Co. Ltd. in Charlotte Amalie, St. Thomas. At the time of the fire the vessel was under time charter to Costa Armatori S.P.A. (Costa), an Italian Corporation. Rhone insured Costa and reimbursed it for property and fuel losses totaling over one million dollars. Rhone, as subrogee of Costa, sued the owner of the vessel, Achille Lauro (Lauro), and its master, Antonio Scotto di Carlo, alleging breach of the Lauro-Costa time charter, unseaworthiness, and negligence of the crew. The district court granted defendants' motion for a stay of the action pending arbitration, and Rhone appeals. The defendants have moved to dismiss the appeal for lack of an appealable order. We hold that we have appellate jurisdiction, and we affirm.

* * *

As subrogee, Rhone stands in place of its insured, the time charterer Costa. In the time charter contract there is a clause:

23. Arbitration

> Any dispute arising under the Charter to be referred to arbitration in London (or such other place as may be agreed according to box 24) one arbitrator to be nominated by the Owners and the other by the Charterers, and in case the Arbitrators shall not agree then to the decision of an Umpire to be appointed by them, the award of the Arbitrators or the Umpire to be final and binding upon both parties.

Box 24

> Place of arbitration (only to be filled in if place other than London agreed (cl. 23)) NAPOLI

* * *

What Rhone does contend is that under the terms of the Convention the arbitration clause in issue is unenforceable. Rhone's argument proceeds from a somewhat ambiguous provision in Article II section 3 of the Convention:

The court of a Contracting State, when seized of an action in a matter in respect of which the parties have made an agreement within the meaning of this article, shall, at the request of one of the parties, refer the parties to arbitration, unless it finds that the said agreement is null and void, inoperative or incapable of being performed.

Ambiguity occurs from the fact that no reference appears in section 3 to what law determines whether "said agreement...is null and void, inoperative or incapable of being performed."

Rhone contends that when the arbitration clause refers to a place of arbitration, here Naples, Italy, the law of that place is determinative. It then relies on the affidavit of an expert on Italian law which states that in Italy an arbitration clause calling for an even number of arbitrators is null and void, even if, as in this case, there is a provision for their designation of a tie breaker.

The ambiguity in Article II section 3 of the Convention with respect to governing law contrasts with Article V, dealing with enforcement of awards. Section 1(a) of Article V permits refusal of recognition and enforcement of an award if the "agreement is not valid under the law to which the parties have subjected it or, failing any indication thereon, under the law of the country where the award was made." Section 1(e) of Article V permits refusal of recognition and enforcement if "[t]he award has not yet become binding on the parties, or has been set aside or suspended by a competent authority of the country in which, or under the law of which, that award was made." Section 1(d) of Article V permits refusal of enforcement if "[t]he composition of the arbitral authority or the arbitral procedure was not in accordance with the agreement of the parties, or, failing such agreement, was not in accordance with the law of the country where the arbitration took place." Thus Article V unambiguously refers the forum in which enforcement of an award is sought to the law chosen by the parties, or the law of the place of the award.

Rhone and the defendants suggest different conclusions that should be drawn from the differences between Article II and Article V. Rhone suggests that the choice of law rule of Article V should be read into Article II. The defendants urge that in the absence of a specific reference Article II should be read so as to permit the forum, when asked to refer a dispute to arbitration, to apply its own law respecting validity of the arbitration clause.

There is some treaty history suggesting that a proposal to incorporate in Article II choice of law language similar to that in Article V was rejected because delegates to the United Nations organization which drafted it were concerned that a forum might then have an obligation to enforce arbitration clauses regardless of its "local" law. G. Haight, *Convention on the Recognition and Enforcement of Foreign Arbitral Awards: Summary Analysis of Record of U.N. Conference*, May/June 1958 at 27-28. It thus appears that the ambiguity in Article II section 3 is deliberate. How it should be resolved has been a matter of concern to commentators, who suggest, variously, that the forum state should look to its own law and policy, to the rules of conflicts of laws, or to the law of the place of execution of the agreement.

None of the limited secondary literature sheds so clear a light as to suggest a certain answer. However, we conclude that the meaning of Article II section 3 which is most consistent with the overall purposes of the Convention is that an agreement to arbitrate is "null and void" only (1) when it is subject to an internationally recognized defense such as duress, mistake, fraud, or waiver, *see Ledee v. Ceramiche Ragno*, 684 F.2d 184

(1st Cir.1982); *I.T.A.D. Associates, Inc. v. Podar Brothers*, 636 F.2d 75 (4th Cir.1981), or (2) when it contravenes fundamental policies of the forum state. The "null and void" language must be read narrowly, for the signatory nations have jointly declared a general policy of enforceability of agreements to arbitrate.

* * *

In other words, signatory nations have effectively declared a joint policy that presumes the enforceability of agreements to arbitrate. Neither the parochial interests of the forum state, nor those of states having more significant relationships with the dispute, should be permitted to supersede that presumption. The policy of the Convention is best served by an approach which leads to upholding agreements to arbitrate. The rule of one state as to the required number of arbitrators does not implicate the fundamental concerns of either the international system or forum, and hence the agreement is not void.

Rhone urges that this rule may result in a Neopolitan arbitration award which, because of Italy's odd number of arbitrators rule, the Italian courts would not enforce. The defendants insist that even in Italy this procedural rule on arbitration is waivable and a resulting award will be enforced. Even if that is not the law of Italy, however, Rhone's objection does not compel the conclusion that we should read Article II section 3 as it suggests. The parties did agree to a non-judicial dispute resolution mechanism, and the basic purpose of the Convention is to discourage signatory states from disregarding such agreements. Rhone is not faced with an Italian public policy disfavoring arbitration, but only with an Italian procedural rule of arbitration which may have been overlooked by the drafters of the time charter agreement. Certainly the parties are free to structure the arbitration so as to comply with the Italian procedural rule by having the designated arbitrators select a third member before rather than after impasse. Even if that is not accomplished an award may still result, which can be enforced outside Italy.

Rhone urges that Article V section 1(d) prohibits such enforcement outside Italy, because it refers a non-Italian forum to the law of Italy. We disagree. Section 1 says only that "enforcement of an award may be refused" on the basis of the law of the country where it was made. Where, as here, the law of such a country generally favors enforcement of arbitration awards, and the defect is at best one of a procedural nature, Article V, section 1 certainly permits another forum to disregard the defect and enforce. That is especially the case when defendants come before the court and, relying on Article II, seek a stay of the action in favor of arbitration. They will hardly be in a position to rely on Italy's odd number of arbitrators rule if Rhone seeks to enforce an award in the District Court of the Virgin Islands.[3]

The forum law implicitly referenced by Article II section 3 is the law of the United States, not the local law of the Virgin Islands or of a state. That law favors enforcement of arbitration clauses. *Scherk v. Alberto-Culver Co.*, 417 U.S. 506 (1974); *Becker Autoradio U.S.A. Inc. v. Becker Autoradiowerk GmbH*, 585 F.2d 39 (3d Cir.1978). Indeed, "[a]n action or proceeding falling under the Convention shall be deemed to arise under the laws and treaties of the United States." 9 U.S.C. §203. Such an action would be removable from a state court. 9 U.S.C. §205. The removal section has no application, of course, to

---

3. Had Rhone so requested it would have been proper for the district court to condition its stay order on the defendants' agreement to reform the arbitration clause so as to satisfy Italy's procedural requirement. Since no such request was made we do not consider whether, had it been made, we would remand for such a modification.

the District Court of the Virgin Islands, which exercises the jurisdiction of the United States District Courts in all cases arising under the treaties and laws of the United States. 48 U.S.C. § 1612 (1976 & Supp. V 1981). Since no federal law imposes an odd number of arbitrators rule—the only defect relied upon by Rhone—the district court did not err in staying the suit for breach of the time charter agreement pending arbitration. Moreover since the duty to provide a seaworthy vessel and to operate it non-negligently arises out of the charter relationship, it was proper to stay the entire case.

The order staying the action in the District Court of the Virgin Islands was in compliance with the Convention and with the law of the United States. It will be in all respects affirmed.

Notes

1. The court holds that article II (3) of the New York Convention is to be applied in the light of the law of the United States forum in determining when an agreement to arbitrate is "null and void, inoperative or incapable of being performed." The court also decides that under United States law, these words require "an internationally recognized defense such as duress, mistake, fraud or waiver." Is not the proper formula that stated in *Bremen*, which *Mitsubishi* assumes is applicable to agreements to arbitrate under the New York Convention? The *Bremen* standard for enforcing a forum-selection clause might be summarized as follows: a forum selection clause is enforceable unless the party wishing to sue in violation of the clause demonstrates that trial in the agreed forum "will be so manifestly and gravely inconvenient that [the party] will be effectively deprived of a meaningful day in court," with 2 exceptions: (1) the clause is affected "by fraud, undue influence, or overweening bargaining power," or (2) "enforcement would contravene a strong public policy of the forum." For discussion of lower court opinions elaborating on the *Bremen* standards for enforcement of forum-selection clauses, see Linda S. Mullenix, Another Choice of Forum, Another Choice of Law: Consensual Adjudicatory Procedure in Federal Court, 57 Fordham L. Rev. 291, 356-60 (1988).

2. The opinion refers to the lease of the vessel as a "time charter." Under a "time charter," the ship is leased with crew. Under a "bareboat charter," the ship is leased without crew.

Section 3: Enjoining Suit Abroad

Gannon v. Payne
706 S.W.2d 304 (Tex. 1986)

KILGARLIN, Justice.

At issue is whether a party to a pending Texas lawsuit may be enjoined from taking any action in a lawsuit he subsequently filed in a foreign jurisdiction in which some of the same parties and same issues are involved. The trial court granted Robert B. Payne a temporary injunction prohibiting Fred G. Gannon from pursuing a suit in the Court of Queen's Bench, Alberta, Canada. The court of appeals originally held that the trial court had abused its discretion and ordered the temporary injunction be dissolved. However, on rehearing, the court withdrew its earlier opinion and, with one justice dissenting, upheld the temporary injunction.

* * *

We reverse the judgment of the court of appeals and order the injunction dissolved.

The genesis of the current litigation is a joint venture of Gannon and Payne for oil and gas production in Alberta Province. Under their agreement, the two were to share equally in the costs and profits of the venture. Through negotiations with a Canadian corporation, Paddon-Hughes Development Company, Gannon acquired a 50% interest in an oil and gas lease in Canada. For some nineteen distribution payments, between June 1970 and December 1971, Gannon and Payne shared equally in the profits from the oil and gas lease. However, beginning with the twentieth payment, Gannon unilaterally reduced Payne's share of the profits by 5%.

Upon discovering that Gannon had reduced the percentage, Payne sued Gannon in Canada. In the Canadian judgment, dated January 18, 1980, Gannon was ordered to account and pay to Payne any amounts previously deducted from Payne's share of the profits. Following two unsuccessful appeals, the judgment became final against Gannon. On August 30, 1982, Payne again sued Gannon, this time in the Dallas County court that subsequently granted the injunction in question. Approximately two years after Payne filed his Texas suit, Gannon sued for a declaratory judgment in the Canadian court to obtain a ruling on whether some of the matters raised by Payne in the Texas action had already been decided in the prior Canadian suit. Payne then filed his application for a temporary injunction seeking to prohibit Gannon from prosecuting or taking any action in the Canadian suit.

The question to be decided by the reviewing court in an appeal of a temporary injunction is whether the trial court abused its discretion in issuing the injunction. Whether a Texas trial court may properly enjoin persons subject to its jurisdiction from proceeding with litigation pending in a foreign country is a question of first impression for this court.

Texas state courts do have the power to restrain persons from proceeding with suits filed in other courts of this state. The general rule is that when a suit is filed in a court of competent jurisdiction, that court is entitled to proceed to judgment and may protect its jurisdiction by enjoining the parties to a suit subsequently filed in another court of this state.

Obviously, anti-suit injunctions prohibiting litigants from proceeding in out-of-state courts necessarily involve two sovereigns with concurrent jurisdiction to decide the controversy. For this reason, the courts of this state have consistently recognized that the power to enjoin proceedings pending in a foreign jurisdiction should be exercised sparingly and only by reason of very special circumstances.

When the sovereigns involved are not sister states but a state and a foreign nation, the policy of allowing parallel court proceedings to continue simultaneously requires more scrupulous adherence. Thus, the question presented to this court is not whether the Texas trial court possessed the inherent power to issue such an injunction, but whether the trial court's action was proper and within its discretion. In answering this, we note that cases discussing the propriety of an injunction prohibiting prosecution of an action in a foreign country likewise almost unanimously recognize the caveat of limited use. Ordinarily parallel actions should be allowed to proceed simultaneously. "[O]nly in the most compelling circumstance does a court have discretion to issue an anti-suit injunction." *Laker Airways Limited v. Sabena, Belgian World Airlines*, 731 F.2d 909, 926, 927 (D.C.Cir.1984).

As the issue is not jurisdiction, the propriety of the injunction depends upon what weight we will ascribe to the principle of comity. In *Hilton v. Guyot*, 159 U.S. 113, 163-64 (1895), the United States Supreme Court wrote:

> "Comity," in the legal sense, is neither a matter of absolute obligation, on the one hand, nor of mere courtesy and good will, upon the other. But it is the recognition which one nation allows within its territory to the legislative, executive or judicial acts of another nation, having due regard both to international duty and convenience, and to the rights of its own citizens or of other persons who are under the protection of its laws.

In Texas, comity has been described as "a principle of mutual convenience whereby one state or jurisdiction will give effect to the laws and judicial decisions of another." *New Process Steel Corp. v. Steel Corporation of Texas*, 638 S.W.2d at 524 [Tex. App.—Houston [1st Dist.] 1982, no writ].

No state or nation can demand that its laws have effect beyond the limits of its sovereignty. *Hilton v. Guyot*, 159 U.S. at 163; *Laker Airways v. Sabena, Belgian World Airlines*, 731 F.2d at 937. Only comity can compel courts to act in a manner designed to advance the rule of law among and between nations. An anti-suit injunction necessarily restricts a foreign court's ability to exercise its jurisdiction. The foreign court cannot be compelled to recognize such an injunction, and if it responds by issuing a similar injunction, no party may be able to obtain a remedy. *Laker Airways v. Sabena, Belgian World Airlines*, 731 F.2d at 927.

There are no precise guidelines for determining the appropriateness of an anti-suit injunction or for deciding whether comity should be invoked. The circumstances of each situation must be carefully examined to determine whether the injunction is required to prevent an irreparable miscarriage of justice. Id. Some courts have issued anti-suit injunctions to protect their own jurisdiction or to prevent evasion of important public policies of the forum nation. Other courts have enjoined the prosecution of foreign actions to prevent a multiplicity of suits or to protect a party from vexatious or harassing litigation.

In our case, the trial court did not find and Payne does not allege that Gannon attempted to subvert an important public policy of this state by filing his suit in Canada. In its order granting Payne's requested temporary injunction, the trial court specifically found: (1) the primary purpose of the Canadian action was to interfere with the processes and jurisdiction of the Texas court; (2) Payne had incurred costs of $24,000 in prosecuting the Texas action which would be wasted if the temporary injunction were not granted; (3) a multiplicity of suits would result without the temporary injunction; (4) Gannon's action altered the status quo; and (5) the two suits presented a risk of inconsistent judgments.

In his pleading filed in the Canadian court, Gannon requested "A Judgment, Order or Declaration permanently enjoining Payne from suing the Plaintiffs." However, in an amended motion to stay proceedings in the Texas court, Gannon stipulated that he would eliminate his request for injunctive relief in the Canadian suit. The Texas trial court could have delayed issuing its injunction and allowed Gannon an opportunity to comply with this stipulation. In any case, the trial court could have more narrowly drawn its injunction to permit proceedings that were not inconsistent with its continued jurisdiction. Moreover, there is no evidence the Canadian court has attempted to carve out exclusive jurisdiction in this case. We must rely on the court system of a sister common law jurisdiction to recognize the same rule of comity we now apply.

The trial court's concerns about a multiplicity of suits and a risk of inconsistent judgments do not support this anti-suit injunction. As noted, some courts have upheld the issuance of an anti-suit injunction on these grounds. However, if the principle of comity is to have any application, a single parallel proceeding filed in a party's home country cannot justify issuing an anti-suit injunction. Likewise, the possibility of inconsistent judgments does not justify an injunction. Once a final judgment is reached in one of the actions, the second forum is usually obliged to respect the prior adjudication under the rules regarding the enforcement of foreign judgments. Thus, even if both proceedings continue, there should be only one judgment recognized in both forums.

There is no indication that the Canadian suit is vexatious or harassing. The trial court found that Payne had incurred costs of $24,000 in prosecuting the Texas action, and if the injunction were not granted, those expenses would be wasted and additional expenses incurred. However, Payne's expenses in prosecuting the Texas action are not wasted when the Canadian and Texas actions are allowed to proceed simultaneously. Moreover, that further expenses will be incurred by Payne is not a sufficient reason to grant an anti-suit injunction. If additional expense were a sufficient reason for granting an injunction, an injunction would be proper in every case.

Only in exceptional situations should a trial court issue an injunction prohibiting a foreign citizen from prosecuting an action in his home country. Those circumstances do not exist here. This is especially so because prior litigation between Gannon and Payne occurred in Canada, and the issues of the prior Canadian suit and the Texas action are similar. Respect for the principle of comity compels us to conclude that the trial court abused its discretion in granting the temporary injunction. Accordingly, we reverse the judgment of the court of appeals and order the temporary injunction dissolved.

Notes

1. The "parallel proceedings" rule directs that if two or more nations have jurisdiction in cases involving the same dispute, each suit should proceed until judgment is reached in one of the suits. Once judgment is reached in one of the suits, all other nations, including those with concurrent jurisdiction, are supposed to recognize and enforce the judgment under principles of res judicata and the rules of enforcement of judgments. The International Law and Practice Section of the ABA, however, has drafted and proposed for adoption by any jurisdiction that will have it, The Conflict of Jurisdiction Model Act. Under this Act, the forum is directed to refuse to recognize a foreign judgment made by one of two or more courts litigating the same dispute unless, within 6 months of notice of duplicate proceedings, an application for determination of "an adjudicating forum" is made to the first known court of competent jurisdiction. Only the judgments of the forum adjudicated as proper in this determination proceeding will be recognized, if the determination is in accordance with criteria set out in the Model Act. These factors are designed to select the most convenient place for trial. If no such determination proceeding has been held, courts of the forum adopting the statute shall make their own determination using the same factors and recognize only the judgment of the foreign state determined to be "the proper adjudicating forum." Would you recommend adoption of this Model Act? Connecticut has enacted the Model Act. Conn. G.S.Ann. § 50a200-03. What effect with this have on the ability to get Connecticut judgments recognized in countries that require reciprocity before they will recognize foreign judgments? How can the parties to an international transaction avoid parallel proceedings should a future dispute arise?

2. *Gau Shan Co., Ltd v. Bankers Trust Co.*, 956 F.2d 1349 (6th Cir. 1992), held that the trial court abused its discretion when it enjoined parallel litigation in Hong Kong:

> The circuits are split concerning the proper standards to be applied, in the context of considerations of international comity, in determining whether a foreign antisuit injunction should be issued. The Ninth and Fifth Circuits hold that a duplication of the parties and issues, alone, is generally sufficient to justify the issuance of such an injunction. These courts rely primarily upon considerations of vexatiousness or oppressiveness in a race to judgment in the foreign forum as sufficient grounds for an injunction. But the Second and D.C. Circuits have held that the standard for granting a foreign antisuit injunction is whether the injunction is necessary to prevent evasion of the forum court's jurisdiction or to prevent evasion of the forum court's important public policies. [The court adopts the view of the Second and D.C. Circuits.]

956 F.2d at 1352-53. *China Trade and Development Corp. v. M/V Choong Yong*, 837 F.2d 33 (2d Cir. 1987), reversed the trial court's enjoining of parallel action in Korea, but gave two examples of instances in which the foreign action would threaten the forum's jurisdiction and therefore injunction of that action would be proper: (1) the forum proceedings are in rem or quasi in rem; (2) one party attempts in foreign litigation to enjoin the other party from proceeding with the action in the forum. (Id. at 36-37). *Allendale Mutual Ins. Co. v. Bull Data Systems, Inc.*, 10 F.3d 425 (7th Cir. 1993) affirmed enjoining a French insured from continuing a suit in France to recover under a fire insurance policy. The insurer had sued in an Illinois federal court for a declaration that the fire was caused by arson committed by the insured and therefore not covered by the policy. In discussing the difference between circuits in enjoining duplicative litigation abroad, the court states: "When we say we lean toward the laxer standard [that enjoins suit abroad if there is a duplication of parties and issues] we do not mean that international comity should have no weight in the balance; we do not interpret the "lax" cases as assigning it no weight.... Just as we don't think the 'lax' cases would refuse to consider tangible evidence of a threat to comity, so we don't think the 'strict' cases [that require a showing of irreparable harm before enjoining suit abroad] would refuse to weigh against such a threat [to comity] substantial U.S. interests." Id. at. 431-32.

Haaruis v. Kunnan Enterprises, Ltd., 177 F.3d 1007 (D.C. Cir. 1998), affirmed a U.S. bankruptcy court's enjoining continuation of a law suit filed in federal district court against a Taiwanese corporation that was in reorganization in Taiwan. The court noted that 11 U.S.C. § 304 allows a representative of a foreign bankruptcy or reorganization to petition a U.S. bankruptcy court to "enjoin the commencement or continuation of any action against a debtor with respect to property involved in [the foreign proceeding]." The court held that § 304 did not require the debtor to have property in the U.S.

Neuchatel Swiss General Ins. Co. v. Lufthansa Airlines, 925 F.2d 1193 (9th Cir. 1991) held that it was error for the district court to stay an action against an airline for lost cargo pending the outcome of parallel proceedings in Geneva, Switzerland. The court held that absent "exceptional circumstances" United States federal courts have no discretion to defer to parallel proceedings either in this country or abroad. *Turner Entertainment Co. v. Degeto Film GmbH*, 25 F.3d 1512 (11th Cir. 1994), held that once the foreign court reaches a judgment, proceedings in the forum should be stayed pending completion of the foreign action. In *Turner*, the German court had not yet ruled on appeal or on the fee that the German licensee had to pay to the American licensor.

Compare cases dealing with parallel litigation in the United States rather than abroad. Northwest Airlines, Inc. v. American Airlines, Inc., 989 F.2d 1002 (8th Cir. 1993) holds that the Minnesota Federal District Court did not abuse its discretion in enjoining American Airlines from proceeding with a lawsuit that it filed against Northwest in the Federal District Court for the Northern District of Texas after Northwest had sued in Minnesota. "The discretionary power of the federal court in which the first-filed action is pending to enjoin the parties from proceeding with a later-filed action in another federal court is firmly established." 989 F.2d. at 1004. See also Cajun Elec. Power Co-op v. Triton Coal Co., 590 So.2d 813 at 818 (La. App. 4 Cir. 1991), enjoining subsequently filed parallel litigation in a Wyoming state court: "The two suits are clearly duplicative and permitting both suits to continue only thwarts the legitimate effort to avoid a multiplicity of lawsuits for the benefit of both of the litigants and the courts."

For surveys of how United States courts react to parallel litigation, both domestic and foreign, see Margarita Treviño de Coale, Stay, Dismiss, Enjoin, or Abstain?: A Survey of Foreign Parallel Litigation in the Federal Courts of the United States, 17 B.U. Int'l L.J. 79 (1999); James P. George, Parallel Litigation, 51 Baylor L. Rev. 769 (1999).

3. Note article 21 of the EEC Jurisdiction and Judgments Convention barring parallel proceedings in contracting states. See Overseas Union Ins. Ltd. v. New Hampshire Ins. Co., [1992] 2 W.L.R. 586 (Ct. Of Justice of the European Communities, 1991) (article 21 applies to any proceeding in a court of a contracting state even though one of the parties is not domiciled in a contracting state); Owens Bank Ltd. v. Bracco, [1994] 2 W.L.R. 759 (Ct. of Justice of the European Communities, 1994) (article 21 does not apply to proceedings in contracting states concerning the recognition and enforcement of judgments given in non-contracting states); Neste Chemicals SA v. DK Line SA, [1994] 3 All E.R. 180 (Ct. App.) (an English court is "seised" of the proceeding within the meaning of article 21 when the writ is served and not when the court ordered service of process out of the jurisdiction); Continental Bank NA v. Aeokos Cia Naviera SA, [1994] 2 All E.R. 540 (article 21 does not require a court to stay proceedings if the parties have agreed that the forum shall have exclusive jurisdiction under article 17).

In Sarrio S.A. v. Kuwait Investment Authority, [1999] 1 AC 32, [1997] 3 W.L.R. 1143 (H.L.), the plaintiff, a Spanish company, sued defendants in Spain to recover damages for refusal to purchase shares in plaintiff's business and then sued defendants in England to recover damages for negligent misrepresentations in the course of negotiations for the sale. The House of Lords held that an English court should decline jurisdiction under article 22 of the Brussels Convention because the English suit is "related" to the Spanish action and stated: "[T]here should be a broad commonsense approach to the question whether the actions in question are related, bearing in mind the objective of the article, applying the simple wide test set out in [paragraph three of] article 22 and refraining from an over-sophisticated analysis of the matter." 3 W.L.R. at 1149.

4. Foreign courts have adopted a variety of positions with regard to enjoining parties before them from suing abroad. For the United Kingdom position see Smith Kline & French Labs. Ltd. v. Bloch, [1983] 2 All E.R. 72 (Ct. App.), infra page 219; SNI Aérospatiale v. Lee Kui Jak, [1987] 2 All E.R. 510 (P.C.), infra page 225 note 4; British Airways Board v. Laker Airways Ltd., [1985] 1 A.C. 58 (H.L. 1984), infra page 355; Midland Bank v. Laker Airways, [1986] 1 All E.R. 526 (Ct. App.), infra page 362 note 2. Airbus Industrie G.I.E. v. Patel, [1999] 1 A.C. 119 (H.L. 1998) is a recent House of Lords opinion in which the court reversed an injunction barring suit in Texas. The suit was for the wrongful death of British citizens who had resided in London but were of Indian origin.

The deaths resulted from an airplane crash in India. The parties seeking to enjoin the Texas lawsuit were the designers and manufacturers of the aircraft. An Indian court had previously enjoined the Texas suit but was unable to enforce the injunction because the defendants were outside the jurisdiction of that court. The court held that enjoining the Texas suit would be inconsistent with international comity because "the English forum [does not] have a sufficient interest in, or connection with, the matter in question to justify the indirect interference with the foreign court which an anti-suit injunction entails." The action of the Texas court was not so outrageous as to deprive it of the respect normally required by comity even though at the relevant time Texas did not permit forum non conveniens dismissals and India was the natural forum.

The leading Canadian case on anti-suit injunctions is Amchem Products Inc. v. British Columbia (Workers' Compensation Board), 102 D.L.R.4th 96 (Can. S. Ct. 1993). Amchem reversed the granting of an injunction by a British Columbia trial judge who order British Columbia claimants to desist from pursuing their claims for asbestosis injuries in a Texas state court. With one exception, the defendants in the Texas action were United States companies. Amchem held that a court should enjoin suit in foreign countries only if the court is the natural forum for the trial of the action and the injunction does not deprive the plaintiff of any advantages in the foreign forum that the plaintiff has any reasonable expectation of being able to enjoy. Amchem stated that "[a] party can have no reasonable expectations of advantages available in a jurisdiction with which the party and the subject-matter of the litigation [have] little or no connection."

An important Australian case on anti-suit injunctions is CSR Ltd. v. Cigna Ins. Australia Ltd., [1997] 146 A.L.R. 402 (High Ct. of Austl.). A New South Wales (NSW) trial judge had enjoined further proceedings in a United States lawsuit and denied a motion to stay the Australian proceedings. The High Court of Australia set aside these orders and stayed proceedings in Australia pending the outcome of the U.S. proceedings. Cigna Insurance had disclaimed coverage of claims against its insured, CSR, a company dealing in asbestos products. CSR sued Cigna in a federal district court in New Jersey to recover on the insurance policies for the claims of injuries caused by asbestos products in the U.S. The CSR plaintiffs were the U.S. parent and the Australian subsidiary. The Cigna defendants were the Australian parent and the U.S. subsidiary. CSR U.S. also sued Cigna U.S. for treble damages under the Sherman Act. The Cigna companies then sued the CSR companies in NSW for a declaration of no coverage with regard to both U.S. and Australian claims. The High Court found that the U.S. proceedings were not vexatious or oppressive and declared that "the power to grant injunctions in restraint of foreign proceedings should be exercised with caution" because it "interferes with the processes of the foreign court and may well be perceived as a breach of comity by that court." The court also held that an Australian court should grant a forum non conveniens stay or dismissal only "if the Australian court is a clearly inappropriate forum." The court found that NSW was a clearly inappropriate forum because the U.S. proceedings were pending when Cigna sued in NSW and the Sherman Act claim for treble damages could not pursued in Australia.

Masato Dogauchi, Concurrent Litigations in Japan and the United States, 37 Japanese Ann. Int'l L. 72, 92 (1994), states that no Japanese court has ruled on whether it should enjoin foreign proceedings and concludes that a Japanese court would deny a request for such an injunction.

Section 4: Service of Process

Hague Convention on the Service Abroad of Judicial and Extrajudicial Documents in Civil or Commercial Matters

Opened for signature Nov. 15, 1965 20 U.S.T. 361, 658 UNTS 163
[ratified by the United States in 1969]

The States signatory to the present Convention,

Desiring to create appropriate means to ensure that judicial and extrajudicial documents to be served abroad shall be brought to the notice of the addressee in sufficient time,

Desiring to improve the organization of mutual judicial assistance for that purpose by simplifying and expediting the procedure,

Have resolved to conclude a Convention to this effect and have agreed upon the following provisions:

Article 1

The present Convention shall apply in all cases, in civil or commercial matters, where there is occasion to transmit a judicial or extrajudicial document for service abroad.

This Convention shall not apply where the address of the person to be served with the document is not known.

Chapter I: Judicial Documents

Article 2

Each contracting State shall designate a Central Authority which will undertake to receive requests for service coming from other contracting States and to proceed in conformity with the provisions of Articles 3 to 6.

Each State shall organise the Central Authority in conformity with its own law.

Article 3

The authority or judicial officer competent under the law of the State in which the documents originate shall forward to the Central Authority of the State addressed a request conforming to the model annexed to the present Convention, without any requirement of legalisation or other equivalent formality.

The document to be served or a copy thereof shall be annexed to the request. The request and the document shall both be furnished in duplicate.

Article 4

If the Central Authority considers that the request does not comply with the provisions of the present Convention it shall promptly inform the applicant and specify its objections to the request.

Article 5

The Central Authority of the State addressed shall itself serve the document or shall arrange to have it served by an appropriate agency, either—

(a) by a method prescribed by its internal law for the service of documents in domestic actions upon persons who are within its territory, or

(b) by a particular method requested by the applicant, unless such a method is incompatible with the law of the State addressed.

Subject to sub-paragraph (b) of the first paragraph of this article, the document may always be served by delivery to an addressee who accepts it voluntarily.

If the document is to be served under the first paragraph above, the Central Authority may require the document to be written in, or translated into, the official language or one of the official languages of the State addressed.

That part of the request, in the form attached to the present Convention, which contains a summary of the document to be served, shall be served with the document.

Article 6

The Central Authority of the State addressed or any authority which it may have designated for that purpose, shall complete a certificate in the form of the model annexed to the present Convention.

The certificate shall state that the document has been served and shall include the method, the place and the date of service and the person to whom the document was delivered. If the document has not been served, the certificate shall set out the reasons which have prevented service.

The applicant may require that a certificate not completed by a Central Authority or by a judicial authority shall be countersigned by one of these authorities.

The certificate shall be forwarded directly to the applicant.

Article 7

The standard terms in the model annexed to the present Convention shall in all cases be written either in French or in English. They may also be written in the official language, or in one of the official languages, of the State in which the documents originate.

The corresponding blanks shall be completed either in the language of the State addressed or in French or in English.

Article 8

Each contracting State shall be free to effect service of judicial documents upon persons abroad, without application of any compulsion, directly through its diplomatic or consular agents.

Any State may declare that it is opposed to such service within its territory, unless the document is to be served upon a national of the State in which the documents originate.

Article 9

Each contracting State shall be free, in addition, to use consular channels to forward documents, for the purpose of service, to those authorities of another contracting State which are designated by the latter for this purpose.

Each contracting State may, if exceptional circumstances so require, use diplomatic channels for the same purpose.

Article 10

Provided the State of destination does not object, the present Convention shall not interfere with—

(a) the freedom to send judicial documents, by postal channels, directly to persons abroad,

(b) the freedom of judicial officers, officials or other competent persons of the State of origin to effect service of judicial documents directly through the judicial officers, officials or other competent persons of the State of destination,

(c) the freedom of any person interested in a judicial proceeding to effect service of judicial documents directly through the judicial officers, officials or other competent persons of the State of destination.

Article 11

The present Convention shall not prevent two or more contracting States from agreeing to permit, for the purpose of service of judicial documents, channels of transmission other than those provided for in the preceding articles and, in particular, direct communication between their respective authorities.

Article 12

The service of judicial documents coming from a contracting State shall not give rise to any payment or reimbursement of taxes or costs for the services rendered by the State addressed.

The applicant shall pay or reimburse the costs occasioned by—

(a) the employment of a judicial officer or of a person competent under the law of the State of destination,

(b) the use of a particular method of service.

Article 13

Where a request for service complies with the terms of the present Convention, the State addressed may refuse to comply therewith only if it deems that compliance would infringe its sovereignty or security.

It may not refuse to comply solely on the ground that, under its internal law, it claims exclusive jurisdiction over the subject-matter of the action or that its internal law would not permit the action upon which the application is based.

The Central Authority shall, in case of refusal, promptly inform the applicant and state the reasons for the refusal.

Article 14

Difficulties which may arise in connection with the transmission of judicial documents for service shall be settled through diplomatic channels.

Article 15

Where a writ of summons or an equivalent document had to be transmitted abroad for the purpose of service, under the provisions of the present Convention, and the defendant has not appeared, judgment shall not be given until it is established that—

(a) the document was served by a method prescribed by the internal law of the State addressed for the service of documents in domestic actions upon persons who are within its territory, or

(b) the document was actually delivered to the defendant or to his residence by another method provided for by this Convention, and that in either of these cases the service or the delivery was effected in sufficient time to enable the defendant to defend.

Each contracting State shall be free to declare that the judge, notwithstanding the provisions of the first paragraph of this article, may give judgment even if no certificate of service or delivery has been received, if all the following conditions are fulfilled—

(a) the document was transmitted by one of the methods provided for in this Convention,

(b) a period of time of not less than six months, considered adequate by the judge in the particular case, has elapsed since the date of the transmission of the document,

(c) no certificate of any kind has been received, even though every reasonable effort has been made to obtain it through the competent authorities of the State addressed.

Notwithstanding the provisions of the preceding paragraphs the judge may order, in case of urgency, any provisional or protective measures.

Article 16

When a writ of summons or an equivalent document had to be transmitted abroad for the purpose of service, under the provisions of the present Convention, and a judgment has been entered against a defendant who has not appeared, the judge shall have the power to relieve the defendant from the effects of the expiration of the time for appeal from the judgment if the following conditions are fulfilled—

(a) the defendant, without any fault on his part, did not have knowledge of the document in sufficient time to defend, or knowledge of the judgment in sufficient time to appeal, and

(b) the defendant has disclosed a prima facie defence to the action on the merits.

An application for relief may be filed only within a reasonable time after the defendant has knowledge of the judgment.

Each contracting State may declare that the application will not be entertained if it is filed after the expiration of a time to be stated in the declaration, but which shall in no case be less than one year following the date of the judgment.

This article shall not apply to judgments concerning status or capacity of persons.

Chapter II: Extrajudicial Documents

Article 17

Extrajudicial documents emanating from authorities and judicial officers of a contracting State may be transmitted for the purpose of service in another contracting State by the methods and under the provisions of the present Convention.

Chapter III: General Clauses

Article 18

Each contracting State may designate other authorities in addition to the Central Authority and shall determine the extent of their competence.

The applicant shall, however, in all cases, have the right to address a request directly to the Central Authority.

Federal States shall be free to designate more than one Central Authority.

Article 19

To the extent that the internal law of a contracting State permits methods of transmission, other than those provided for in the preceding articles, of documents coming from abroad, for service within its territory, the present Convention shall not affect such provisions.

* * *

Article 29

Any State may, at the time of signature, ratification or accession, declare that the present Convention shall extend to all the territories for the international relations of which it is responsible, or to one or more of them. Such a declaration shall take effect on the date of entry into force of the Convention for the State concerned.

At any time thereafter, such extensions shall be notified to the Ministry of Foreign Affairs of the Netherlands.

The Convention shall enter into force for the territories mentioned in such an extension on the 60th day after the notification referred to in the preceding paragraph.

* * *

Designations and Declarations Made on the Part of the United States in Connection with the Deposit of the United States Ratification

"1. In accordance with Article 2, the United States Department of State is designated as the Central Authority to receive requests for service from other Contracting States and to proceed in conformity with Articles 3 to 6.

"2. In accordance with Article 6, in addition to the United States Department of State, the United States Department of Justice and the United States Marshal or Deputy Marshal for the judicial district in which service is made are designated for the purpose of completing the certificate in the form annexed to the Convention.

"3. In accordance with the second paragraph of Article 15, it is declared that the judge may, notwithstanding the provisions of the first paragraph of Article 15, give judgment even if no certificate of service or delivery has been received, if all the conditions specified in subdivisions (a), (b) and (c) of the second paragraph of Article 15 are fulfilled.

"4. In accordance with the third paragraph of Article 16, it is declared that an application under Article 16 will not be entertained if it is filed (a) after the expiration of the period within which the same may be filed under the procedural regulations of the court in which the judgment has been entered, or (b) after the expiration of one year following the date of the judgment, whichever is later.

"5. In accordance with Article 29, it is declared that the Convention shall extend to all the States of the United States, the District of Columbia, Guam, Puerto Rico, and the Virgin Islands."

Notes

1. The Service Convention is a product of the Hague Conference on Private International Law, which was established in 1893 and joined by the United States in 1964. The Hague Conference is one of three major sources of multilateral conventions affecting international litigation. The other two, products of which have already appeared in these materials, are the United Nations (Arbitration Convention) and the European Economic Community (Convention on Jurisdiction and Judgments). The Organization of American States is becoming more active and successful in promulgating conventions, such as the Panama Arbitration Convention, and may vie with the EEC as a source of regional conventions.

2. Article 16(1)(b) requires that the defendant disclose "a prima facie defence" before reopening a judgment entered without notice or opportunity to be heard. This accords with due process because article 15 paragraph 2 requires that a reasonable effort has been made to give notice. See Mullane v. Central Hanover Bank & Trust Co., 339 U.S. 306, 317 (1950) (holding that published notice suffices for persons "whose interests or whereabouts could not with due diligence be ascertained"). This requirement distinguishes the Convention procedure from the procedure declared unconstitutional in Peralta v. Heights Medical Center, Inc., 485 U.S. 80 (1988), under which the defendant had to allege and prove a meritorious defense to make a collateral attack on a default judgment even if no reasonable effort had been made to give notice.

3. The Service Convention is typical of successful multilateral conventions in the two ways in which it treats controversial issues. One way is to set out basic provisions that all signatories must approve (articles 1-7) and then permit additional methods of service to which signatories may object (articles 8 and 10). The second way is leave important terms undefined. For example, "civil" is not defined. The United Kingdom and the United States regard "civil" as referring to any proceeding that is not criminal. Germany and France do not regard "civil" as referring to any application of public law, such as the subpoena served by the Federal Trade Commission in FTC v. Compagnie de Saint-Gobain, a principal case infra this section.

4. On August 27, 1988, the United States ratified the Inter-American Convention on Letters Rogatory. Senate Treaty Doc. 98-27; 14 I.L.M. 339 (1975) (Convention); 18 I.L.M. 1238 (1979)(Protocol). Article 4 of the Convention permits a party to send a document to the other country's central authority, but article 1 of the protocol requires that this be through the sending country's central authority.

Kreimerman v. Casa Veerkamp, S.A. de C.V., 22 F.3d 634 (5th Cir.), cert. denied, 513 U.S. 1016 (1994), held that the Inter-American Convention on Letters Rogatory was designed to facilitate service of letters rogatory and was not the exclusive means of effecting service on the defendants. The court noted that article 2 of the Convention stated that it "shall apply to letters rogatory" rather than to all means of serving process. Id. at 639. Plaintiffs had served Mexican defendants by mail through the Texas Secretary of State under the Texas long-arm statute. The trial court quashed this service, and, after plaintiffs were unsuccessful in a lengthy attempt to serve defendants under the Convention, dismissed the action. The Fifth Circuit reversed and remanded "with instruction to consider whether the only other method of service of process attempted by the plaintiffs—service under the Texas long-Arm Statute—comports with the principles of comity, Fed. R. Civ. P. 4 (especially 4(f)), and any other applicable legal principles of domestic or international law." Id. at 647. Accord, Laino v. Cuprum S.A. de C.V., 235 A.D.2d 25, 663 N.Y.S.2d 275 (1997).

Federal Rule of Civil Procedure 4

(f) Service Upon Individuals in a Foreign Country. Unless otherwise provided by federal law, service upon an individual from whom a waiver has not been obtained and filed, other than an infant or an incompetent person, may be effected in a place not within any judicial district of the United States:

(1) by any internationally agreed means reasonably calculated to give notice, such as those means authorized by the Hague Convention on the Service Abroad of Judicial and Extrajudicial Documents; or

(2) if there is no internationally agreed means of service or the applicable international agreement allows other means of service, provided that service is reasonably calculated to give notice:

> (A) in the manner prescribed by the law of the foreign country for service in that country in an action in any of its courts of general jurisdiction; or

> (B) as directed by the foreign authority in response to a letter rogatory or letter of request; or

> (C) unless prohibited by the law of the foreign country, by

>> (i) delivery to the individual personally of a copy of the summons and the complaint; or

>> (ii) any form of mail requiring a signed receipt, to be addressed and dispatched by the clerk of the court to the party to be served; or

(3) by other means not prohibited by international agreement as may be directed by the court.

Note

Rule 4(f), above, took effect on December 3, 1993. Rule 4(d), which imposes costs of service of summons on a defendant who, when requested to do so, does not waive service, applies only to "a defendant located within the United States." For comment on the new rule, see Stephen B. Burbank, The Reluctant Partner: Making Procedural Law for International Civil Litigation, 57 Law & Contemp. Probs. 103, 121, 145 (Summer 1994) (stating that the rulemakers did not include persons expert in international litigation and that "[t]he way to deal with difficulties in effecting service under the Hague Convention is through diplomatic channels" and not by unilateral methods).

Silvious v. Pharaon, 54 F.3d 697 (11th Cir. 1995), holds that Rule 4(f) does not prevent service in the United States on an agent of the defendant under Rule 4(e), even though the defendant is abroad. Rule 4(e) covers "service upon individuals within a judicial district of the United States."

Volkswagenwerk Aktiengesellschaft v. Schlunk
486 U.S. 694 (1988)

Justice O'CONNOR delivered the opinion of the Court.

This case involves an attempt to serve process on a foreign corporation by serving its domestic subsidiary which, under state law, is the foreign corporation's involuntary agent for service of process. We must decide whether such service is compatible with the Convention on Service Abroad of Judicial and Extrajudicial Documents in Civil and Commercial Matters, Nov. 15, 1965 (Hague Service Convention), [1969] 20 U.S.T. 361, T.I.A.S. No. 6638.

I

The parents of respondent Herwig Schlunk were killed in an automobile accident in 1983. Schlunk filed a wrongful death action on their behalf in the Circuit Court of Cook County, Illinois. Schlunk alleged that Volkswagen of America, Inc. (VWoA), had designed and sold the automobile that his parents were driving, and that defects in the automobile caused or contributed to their deaths. Schlunk also alleged that the driver of the other automobile involved in the collision was negligent; Schlunk has since obtained a default judgment against that person, who is no longer a party to this lawsuit. Schlunk successfully served his complaint on VWoA, and VWoA filed an answer denying that it had designed or assembled the automobile in question. Schlunk then amended the complaint to add as a defendant Volkswagen Aktiengesellschaft (VWAG), which is the petitioner here. VWAG, a corporation established under the laws of the Federal Republic of Germany, has its place of business in that country. VWoA is a wholly owned subsidiary of VWAG. Schlunk attempted to serve his amended complaint on VWAG by serving VWoA as VWAG's agent.

VWAG filed a special and limited appearance for the purpose of quashing service. VWAG asserted that it could be served only in accordance with the Hague Service Convention, and that Schlunk had not complied with the Convention's requirements. The Circuit Court denied VWAG's motion. It first observed that VWoA is registered to do business in Illinois and has a registered agent for receipt of process in Illinois. The court then reasoned that VWoA and VWAG are so closely related that VWoA is VWAG's agent for service of process as a matter of law, notwithstanding VWAG's failure or refusal to appoint VWoA formally as an agent. The court relied on the facts that VWoA is a wholly owned subsidiary of VWAG, that a majority of the members of the board of directors of VWoA are members of the board of VWAG, and that VWoA is by contract the exclusive importer and distributor of VWAG products sold in the United States. The court concluded that, because service was accomplished within the United States, the Hague Service Convention did not apply.

The Circuit Court certified two questions to the Appellate Court of Illinois. For reasons similar to those given by the Circuit Court, the Appellate Court determined that VWoA is VWAG's agent for service of process under Illinois law, and that the service of process in this case did not violate the Hague Service Convention. After the Supreme Court of Illinois denied VWAG leave to appeal, VWAG petitioned this Court for a writ of certiorari to review the Appellate Court's interpretation of the Hague Service Convention. We granted certiorari to address this issue, which has given rise to disagreement among the lower courts.

II

The Hague Service Convention is a multilateral treaty that was formulated in 1964 by the Tenth Session of the Hague Conference of Private International Law. The Convention revised parts of the Hague Conventions on Civil Procedure of 1905 and 1954. The revision was intended to provide a simpler way to serve process abroad, to assure that defendants sued in foreign jurisdictions would receive actual and timely notice of suit, and to facilitate proof of service abroad. Representatives of all 23 countries that were members of the Conference approved the Convention without reservation. Thirty-two countries, including the United States and the Federal Republic of Germany, have ratified or acceded to the Convention.

The primary innovation of the Convention is that it requires each state to establish a central authority to receive requests for service of documents from other countries. 20 U.S.T. 362, T.I.A.S. 6638, Art. 2. Once a central authority receives a request in the proper form, it must serve the documents by a method prescribed by the internal law of the receiving state or by a method designated by the requester and compatible with that law. Art. 5. The central authority must then provide a certificate of service that conforms to a specified model. Art. 6. A state also may consent to methods of service within its boundaries other than a request to its central authority. Arts. 8-11, 19. The remaining provisions of the Convention that are relevant here limit the circumstances in which a default judgment may be entered against a defendant who had to be served abroad and did not appear, and provide some means for relief from such a judgment. Arts. 15, 16.

Article 1 defines the scope of the Convention, which is the subject of controversy in this case. It says: "The present Convention shall apply in all cases, in civil or commercial matters, where there is occasion to transmit a judicial or extrajudicial document for service abroad." 20 U.S.T., at 362. The equally authentic French version says, "La présente Convention est applicable, en matière civile ou commerciale, dans tous les cas où un acte judiciaire ou extrajudiciaire doit être transmis à l'étranger pour y être signifié ou notifié." Ibid. This language is mandatory, as we acknowledged last Term in *Société Nationale Industrielle Aérospatiale v. United States District Court*, 482 U.S. 522, 534, n. 15 (1987). By virtue of the Supremacy Clause, U.S. Const., Art. VI, the Convention preempts inconsistent methods of service prescribed by state law in all cases to which it applies. Schlunk does not purport to have served his complaint on VWAG in accordance with the Convention. Therefore, if service of process in this case falls within Article 1 of the Convention, the trial court should have granted VWAG's motion to quash.

When interpreting a treaty, we "begin 'with the text of the treaty and the context in which the written words are used.'" in *Société Nationale*, supra, at 534 (quoting *Air France v. Saks*, 470 U.S. 392, 397 (1985)). Other general rules of construction may be brought to bear on difficult or ambiguous passages. " 'Treaties are construed more liberally than private agreements, and to ascertain their meaning we may look beyond the written words to the history of the treaty, the negotiations, and the practical construction adopted by the parties.' " *Air France v. Saks*, supra, at 396 (quoting *Choctaw Nation of Indians v. United States*, 318 U.S. 423, 431-432 (1943)).

The Convention does not specify the circumstances in which there is "occasion to transmit" a complaint "for service abroad." But at least the term "service of process" has a well-established technical meaning. Service of process refers to a formal delivery of documents that is legally sufficient to charge the defendant with notice of a pending action. The legal sufficiency of a formal delivery of documents must be measured against some standard. The Convention does not prescribe a standard, so we almost necessarily must refer to the internal law of the forum state. If the internal law of the forum state defines the applicable method of serving process as requiring the transmittal of documents abroad, then the Hague Service Convention applies.

The negotiating history supports our view that Article 1 refers to service of process in the technical sense. The committee that prepared the preliminary draft deliberately used a form of the term "notification" (formal notice), instead of the more neutral term "remise" (delivery), when it drafted Article 1. Then, in the course of the debates, the negotiators made the language even more exact. The preliminary draft of Article 1 said that the present Convention shall apply in all cases in which there are grounds to transmit or to give formal notice of a judicial or extrajudicial document in a civil or commercial matter to a person staying abroad. To be more precise, the delegates decided to add a form of the juridical term "signification" (service), which has a narrower meaning than "notification" in some countries, such as France, and the identical meaning in others, such as the United States. The delegates also criticized the language of the preliminary draft because it suggested that the Convention could apply to transmissions abroad that do not culminate in service. The final text of Article 1, supra, eliminates this possibility and applies only to documents transmitted for service abroad. The final report confirms that the Convention does not use more general terms, such as delivery or transmission, to define its scope because it applies only when there is both transmission of a document from the requesting state to the receiving state, and service upon the person for whom it is intended.

The negotiating history of the Convention also indicates that whether there is service abroad must be determined by reference to the law of the forum state.

* * *

VWAG protests that it is inconsistent with the purpose of the Convention to interpret it as applying only when the internal law of the forum requires service abroad. One of the two stated objectives of the Convention is "to create appropriate means to ensure that judicial and extrajudicial documents to be served abroad shall be brought to the notice of the addressee in sufficient time." 20 U.S.T., at 362. The Convention cannot assure adequate notice, VWAG argues, if the forum's internal law determines whether it applies. VWAG warns that countries could circumvent the Convention by defining methods of service of process that do not require transmission of documents abroad. Indeed, VWAG contends that one such method of service already exists and that it troubled the Conference: *notification au parquet*.

Notification au parquet permits service of process on a foreign defendant by the deposit of documents with a designated local official. Although the official generally is supposed to transmit the documents abroad to the defendant, the statute of limitations begins to run from the time that the official receives the documents, and there allegedly is no sanction for failure to transmit them. At the time of the 10th Conference, France, the Netherlands, Greece, Belgium, and Italy utilized some type of *notification au parquet*.

There is no question but that the Conference wanted to eliminate *notification au parquet*. It included in the Convention two provisions that address the problem. Article 15 says that a judgment may not be entered unless a foreign defendant received adequate and timely notice of the lawsuit. Article 16 provides means whereby a defendant who did not receive such notice may seek relief from a judgment that has become final. Like Article 1, however, Articles 15 and 16 apply only when documents must be transmitted abroad for the purpose of service. VWAG argues that, if this determination is made according to the internal law of the forum state, the Convention will fail to eliminate variants of *notification au parquet* that do not expressly require transmittal of documents to foreign defendants. Yet such methods of service of process are the least likely to provide a defendant with actual notice.

The parties make conflicting representations about whether foreign laws authorizing *notification au parquet* command the transmittal of documents for service abroad within the meaning of the Convention. The final report is itself somewhat equivocal. It says that, although the strict language of Article 1 might raise a question as to whether the Convention regulates *notification au parquet*, the understanding of the drafting Commission, based on the debates, is that the Convention would apply. Although this statement might affect our decision as to whether the Convention applies to *notification au parquet*, an issue we do not resolve today, there is no comparable evidence in the negotiating history that the Convention was meant to apply to substituted service on a subsidiary like VWoA, which clearly does not require service abroad under the forum's internal law. Hence neither the language of the Convention nor the negotiating history contradicts our interpretation of the Convention, according to which the internal law of the forum is presumed to determine whether there is occasion for service abroad.

Nor are we persuaded that the general purposes of the Convention require a different conclusion. One important objective of the Convention is to provide means to facilitate service of process abroad. Thus the first stated purpose of the Convention is "to create" appropriate means for service abroad, and the second stated purpose is "to improve the organization of mutual judicial assistance for that purpose by simplifying and expediting the procedure." 20 U.S.T., at 362. By requiring each state to establish a central authority to assist in the service of process, the Convention implements this enabling function. Nothing in our decision today interferes with this requirement.

VWAG correctly maintains that the Convention also aims to ensure that there will be adequate notice in cases in which there is occasion to serve process abroad. Thus compliance with the Convention is mandatory in all cases to which it applies and Articles 15 and 16 provide an indirect sanction against those who ignore it. Our interpretation of the Convention does not necessarily advance this particular objective, inasmuch as it makes recourse to the Convention's means of service dependent on the forum's internal law. But we do not think that this country, or any other country, will draft its internal laws deliberately so as to circumvent the Convention in cases in which it would be appropriate to transmit judicial documents for service abroad. For example, there has been no question in this country of excepting foreign nationals from the protection of our Due Process Clause. Under that Clause, foreign nationals are assured of either personal service, which typically will require service abroad and trigger the Convention, or substituted service that provides "notice reasonably calculated, under all the circumstances, to apprise interested parties of the pendency of the action and afford them an opportunity to present their objections." *Mullane v. Central Hanover Bank & Trust Co.*, 339 U.S. 306 (1950).

Furthermore, nothing that we say today prevents compliance with the Convention even when the internal law of the forum does not so require. The Convention provides simple and certain means by which to serve process on a foreign national. Those who eschew its procedures risk discovering that the forum's internal law required transmittal of documents for service abroad, and that the Convention therefore provided the exclusive means of valid service. In addition, parties that comply with the Convention ultimately may find it easier to enforce their judgments abroad. For these reasons, we anticipate that parties may resort to the Convention voluntarily, even in cases that fall outside the scope of its mandatory application.

III

In this case, the Illinois long-arm statute authorized Schlunk to serve VWAG by substituted service on VWoA, without sending documents to Germany. VWAG has not petitioned for review of the Illinois Appellate Court's holding that service was proper as a matter of Illinois law. VWAG contends, however, that service on VWAG was not complete until VWoA transmitted the complaint to VWAG in Germany. According to VWAG, this transmission constituted service abroad under the Hague Service Convention.

VWAG explains that, as a practical matter, VWoA was certain to transmit the complaint to Germany to notify VWAG of the litigation. Indeed, as a legal matter, the Due Process Clause requires every method of service to provide "notice reasonably calculated, under all the circumstances, to apprise interested parties of the pendency of the action and afford them an opportunity to present their objections." *Mullane v. Central Hanover Bank & Trust Co.*, supra, at 314. VWAG argues that, because of this notice requirement, every case involving service on a foreign national will present an "occasion to transmit a judicial...document for service abroad" within the meaning of Article 1. VWAG emphasizes that in this case, the Appellate Court upheld service only after determining that "the relationship between VWAG and VWoA is so close that it is certain that VWAG 'was fully apprised of the pendency of the action' by delivery of the summons to VWoA." 145 Ill.App.3d, at 606, 105 Ill.Dec., at 47, 503 N.E.2d, at 1053 (quoting *Maunder v. DeHavilland Aircraft of Canada, Ltd.*, 102 Ill.2d 342, 353, 80 Ill.Dec. 765, 771, 466 N.E.2d 217, 223, cert. denied, 469 U.S. 1036 (1984).

We reject this argument. Where service on a domestic agent is valid and complete under both state law and the Due Process Clause, our inquiry ends and the Convention has no further implications. Whatever internal, private communications take place between the agent and a foreign principal are beyond the concerns of this case. The only transmittal to which the Convention applies is a transmittal abroad that is required as a necessary part of service. And, contrary to VWAG's assertion, the Due Process Clause does not require an official transmittal of documents abroad every time there is service on a foreign national. Applying this analysis, we conclude that this case does not present an occasion to transmit a judicial document for service abroad within the meaning of Article 1. Therefore the Hague Service Convention does not apply, and service was proper. The judgment of the Appellate Court is

Affirmed.

Justice BRENNAN, with whom Justice MARSHALL and Justice BLACKMUN join, concurring in the judgment.

* * *

I do not join the Court's opinion because I find it implausible that the Convention's framers intended to leave each contracting nation, and each of the 50 States within our Nation, free to decide for itself under what circumstances, if any, the Convention would control. Rather, in my view, the words "service abroad," read in light of the negotiating history, embody a substantive standard that limits a forum's latitude to deem service complete domestically.

* * *

The negotiating history and the uniform interpretation announced by our own negotiators confirm that the Convention limits a forum's ability to deem service "domestic," thereby avoiding the Convention's terms. Admittedly, the Convention does not precisely define the contours. But that imprecision does not absolve us of our responsibility to apply the Convention mandatorily, any more than imprecision permits us to discard the words "due process of law," U.S. Const., Amend. 14, § 1. And however difficult it might be in some circumstances to discern the Convention's precise limits, it is remarkably easy to conclude that the Convention does not prohibit the type of service at issue here. Service on a wholly owned, closely controlled subsidiary is reasonably calculated to reach the parent "in due time" as the Convention requires. That is, in fact, what our own Due Process Clause requires, see *Mullane v. Central Hanover Bank & Trust Co.*, 339 U.S. 306, 314-315 (1950), and since long before the Convention's implementation our law has permitted such service. This is significant because our own negotiators made clear to the Senate their understanding that the Convention would require no major changes in federal or state service-of-process rules. Thus, it is unsurprising that nothing in the negotiating history suggests that the contracting nations were dissatisfied with the practice at issue here, which they were surely aware, much less that they intended to abolish it like they intended to abolish *notification au parquet*. And since notice served on a wholly owned domestic subsidiary is infinitely more likely to reach the foreign parent's attention than was notice served *au parquet* (or by any other procedure that the negotiators singled out for criticism) there is no reason to interpret the Convention to bar it.

My difference with the Court does not affect the outcome of this case, and, given that any process emanating from our courts must comply with due process, it may have little practical consequence in future cases that come before us. But cf. S.Exec.Rep. No. 6, at 15 (statement by Philip W. Amram suggesting that Convention may require "a minor change in the practice of some of our States in long-arm and automobile accident cases" where "service on the appropriate official need be accompanied only by a minimum effort to notify the defendant"). Our Constitution does not, however, bind other nations haling our citizens into their courts. Our citizens rely instead primarily on the forum nation's compliance with the Convention, which the Senate believed would "provide increased protection (due process) for American Citizens who are involved in litigation abroad." Id., at 3. And while other nations are not bound by the Court's pronouncement that the Convention lacks obligatory force, after today's decision their courts will surely sympathize little with any United States national pleading that a judgment violates the Convention because (notwithstanding any local characterization) service was "abroad."

It is perhaps heartening to "think that [no] countr[y] will draft its internal laws deliberately so as to circumvent the Convention in cases in which it would be appropriate to transmit judicial documents for service abroad," ante, at 2112, although from the defendant's perspective "circumvention" (which, according to the Court, entails no more than exercising a prerogative not to be bound) is equally painful whether deliberate or not. The fact remains, however, that had we been content to rely on foreign notions of fair play and substantial justice, we would have found it unnecessary, in the first place, to participate in a Convention "to ensure that judicial...documents to be served abroad [would] be brought to the notice of the addressee in sufficient time," 20 U.S.T., at 362.

Notes

1. In April, 1989 a Special Commission, consisting of representatives of the signatories of the Hague Service Convention, was convened by the Secretary General of the Hague Conference on Private International Law and a report published by the Permanent Bureau of the Conference. 28 I.L.M. 1556 (1989). The report covered comments of the delegates on problems that had arisen under the Service Convention. The *Schlunk* case was discussed. The delegates voiced concern over "the danger of permitting domestic service upon a person who had not been expressly designated as an agent to receive service of process [because] [s]uch service might not fulfill the purposes of the Convention which were to assure timely notice of the legal action..." The delegates thought that the practical effect of *Schlunk* on future U.S. cases "would probably be rather limited" and adopted "a wait-and-see attitude."

Another problem noted in the report was that under Article 3, the United Kingdom and Israel have refused service requests when forwarded by U.S. attorneys. Other states, including Germany, accept such requests if there is reference to the U.S. law or rule of court granting this authority to an attorney.

2. The word "send" in Article 10(a) has created a split of authority in United States courts. Some courts have held that "send" is the same as the word "service" used in the other provisions. Other courts have held that the use of "send" means that service by mail, even in a country that does not object to use of 10(a), is limited to sending subsequent documents after service of process has been obtained by means of the central authority. See Bankston v. Toyota Motor Corp., 889 F.2d 172 (8th Cir. 1989), which takes this latter view, that service under 10(a) is improper, and collects authority both ways.

The Legal Adviser to the United States Department of State, Alan J. Kreczko, in a letter to the Administrative Office of United States Courts and the National Center for State Courts, stated that *Bankston* was in error. 30 I.L.M. 260 (1991). The report of the Special Commission, discussed in note 1, supports the Legal Adviser's view, stating that "theoretical doubts about [whether article 10(a) included service] were unjustified."

At the meeting of the Special Commission referred to in note 1, above, the Japanese delegation made the following statement: "Japan has made it clear that no objection to use of postal channels for sending judicial documents to persons in Japan does not necessarily imply that the sending by such method is considered valid service in Japan; it merely indicates that Japan does not consider it as infringement of its sovereign power."

The Legal Adviser's letter referred to this statement and interpreted it to mean that although Japan did not consider service by mail inconsistent with the Convention, "a judgment by a court in the United States based on service on the defendant in Japan by mail...may well not be capable of recognition and enforcement in Japan by the courts of that country."

3. Two courts have held service completed when made on a local official for communication abroad, thus creating an American form of *notification au parquet*. Melia v. Les Grands Chais de France, 135 F.R.D. 28 (D. R.I. 1991) (service on Secretary of State); Kawasaki Heavy Indus., Ltd. v. Superior Court of Guam, 1990 WL 320758 (service on Director of Revenue and Taxation). Other courts, however, have distinguished the service provisions of the state in which they sit from the Illinois statute at issue in *Schlunk*, and have held service incomplete until delivered abroad. Fleming v. Yamaha Motor Corp., U.S.A., 774 F. Supp. 992 (W.D. Va. 1991); McClenon v. Nissan Motor Corp.

U.S.A., 726 F. Supp. 822 (N.D. Fla. 1989); Weinstein v. Volkswagen of America, Inc., 1989 WL 35950 (E.D.N.Y. 1989).

4. Justice Brennan differs from the majority in that he would add to Justice O'Connor's statement that "service on a domestic agent is valid and complete under both state law and the Due Process Clause," the statement that this service "is reasonably calculated to reach the parent 'in due time' as the Convention requires." This addition would not be necessary if, as Justice Brennan next states, "[t]hat is, in fact, what our Due Process Clause requires." The case he cites, Mullane v. Central Hanover Bank & Trust Co., 339 U.S. 306 (1950), held that published notice, which was not likely to result in actual notice, was sufficient as to beneficiaries of a common trust "whose interests or whereabouts could not with due diligence be ascertained." Id. at 317. The court held that service on known beneficiaries could not be made by "means less likely than the mails to apprise them of its pendency." Id. at 318. The court noted that personal service on known beneficiaries would be even more likely to give actual notice but said this was not necessary because there were a large number of beneficiaries and "notice reasonably certain to reach most of those interested in objecting is likely to safeguard the interests of all." Id. at 319. The same might be said of published notice to unknown beneficiaries, but the statement was not made in this context. The case, therefore, stands for the proposition that due process may permit giving notice in a manner not "reasonably calculated to reach the [defendant] in due time" if no method more likely to result in actual notice is reasonably available.

5. France and the Netherlands have enacted legislation requiring service under the Convention to supplement notification au parquet. Cornelis D. van Boeschoten, Hague Conference Conventions and the United States: A European View, 57 Law & Contemp. Probs. 47, 55-56 (Summer 1994).

6. Professor Smit does not agree with the Court in *Schlunk* that the Service Convention is "mandatory" when a document is served abroad. Hans Smit, Recent Developments in International Litigation, 35 S. Tex. L. Rev. 215, 222 n.35 (1994) (stating that Article I "does not provide that the Convention shall apply exclusively. It says merely that it is applicable, not that it must be followed").

Federal Trade Commission v. Compagnie de Saint-Gobain- Pont-A-Mousson

636 F.2d 1300 (D.C. Cir. 1980)

WILKEY, Circuit Judge:

This case addresses a narrow issue of broad international consequence: did Congress expressly or impliedly authorize the Federal Trade Commission (FTC or Commission) to serve its investigatory subpoenas directly upon citizens of other countries by means of registered mail? Although on the surface this question appears to rest solely upon statutory interpretation, our answer to it is primarily guided by our recognition of established and fundamental principles of international law.

Federal courts have long acknowledged that the investigatory and regulatory reach of domestic agencies may, and often must, extend across national boundaries. This court has previously recognized that those agencies may under certain circumstances compel production of documents located abroad. We cannot, however, simply assume from these precedents that Congress intended to authorize regulatory agencies in general and the FTC in particular to employ any and all methods to serve compulsory process when conducting their investigations. When an American regulatory agency directly serves its compulsory process upon a citizen of a foreign country, the act of service itself constitutes an exercise of American sovereign power within the area of the foreign country's territorial sovereignty. Though some techniques of service may prove less obnoxious than others to foreign sensibilities, our recognition of those sensibilities must affect our willingness to infer congressional authorization for a particular mode of service from an otherwise silent statute. In the face of the foreign country's direct protest to the mode of service employed here, and in the absence of clear congressional intent at the time this subpoena was served to authorize that manner of exercise of American sovereign power, we decline to infer the necessary statutory authority for the FTC's chosen mode of subpoena service.

I. Background

Since 1977 the FTC has been engaged in a nonpublic antitrust investigation of the U.S. fiberglass insulation industry to determine whether a number of fiberglass manufacturers and distributors have engaged in acts or practices in violation of section 5 of the FTC Act. One of the principal targets of the FTC investigation has been Compagnie de Saint-Gobain-Pont-à-Mousson (SGPM), a French holding company headquartered in Paris, but with a general delegate based in New York City. In September 1977 the Commission issued four identical subpoenas duces tecum directing SGPM to produce specified classes of documents relevant to the investigation. One copy of the subpoena was served by registered mailing to SGPM's corporate headquarters in Paris. * * * When SGPM refused to comply with the subpoenas, the Commission petitioned the district court for an enforcement order * * * Finding the subpoena relevant to the Commission's inquiry and the mode of service to be proper, the district court issued the requested order enforcing the subpoena on 29 September 1978.

On appeal from the district court's denial of SGPM's motion to stay the enforcement order, this court remanded the record to the district court. * * * At the time we cautioned the district court to pay special attention to whether its construction of the relevant statutes conformed to accepted principles of international law, "since Congress is customarily presumed, unless a plain intention appears to the contrary, to avoid conflict with such principles as well as with the Constitution."

* * *

For reasons articulated below, we vacate * * * the enforcement order.

* * *

II: Analysis

The sole issue to be resolved on this appeal is the propriety of the technique employed by the FTC to serve its subpoena abroad namely, registered mailing to a foreign citizen on foreign soil. We will begin by examining whether, at the time service was attempted, the language of the FTC Act expressly authorized service by registered mail of FTC subpoenas abroad and whether the legislative history of the FTC Act and similarly worded statutes revealed any congressional intent to authorize such a mode of service. Next, after clarification of two distinctions blurred by the opinion below, we reject the district court's conclusions that accepted principles of international law condone the mode of subpoena service employed here. We then suggest that basic canons of statutory construction do not permit authority for such a mode of subpoena service to be inferred from the FTC's general jurisdictional mandates to investigate and regulate foreign and interstate commerce. We conclude that, at the time the subpoena was served, Congress intended to authorize the FTC to employ only those customary and legitimate methods of service of compulsory process commonly employed by American courts and administrative agencies when serving its subpoenas abroad. Because service of compulsory process by registered mail had not customarily proved a legitimate means of summoning a third-party witness to appear, with or without documents, in an agency investigation, we find that the method of service employed by the FTC in this case was unauthorized and hence invalid.

* * *

We find the district court's opinion unconvincing because of its failure to draw two distinctions of critical importance in international law: the first, based on the type of document being served; the second, based on the type of jurisdiction being invoked. By failing to draw these crucial distinctions, the district court failed to give adequate weight to fundamental principles of international law which disfavor methods of extraterritorial subpoena service circumventing official channels of judicial assistance, oppose judicial enforcement of investigatory subpoenas abroad, and prohibit the particular manner of subpoena service employed here.

B: The Legitimacy of the FTC's Method of Service Under International Law

1: The Nature of the Document Served

As one of several targets of an FTC investigation which remains in a preliminary phase, SGPM has neither the status of an accused in a criminal action nor the status of a defendant in a civil action. Although as a result of the agency investigation, SGPM may eventually be named a defendant in a civil action, presently it is merely a third-party witness on notice of its potential status as a party defendant. The FTC's subpoena duces tecum and accompanying letter ought not, therefore, be viewed merely as a summons giving notice of a complaint initiating a lawsuit against SGPM. Rather, the FTC's issuance of a subpoena and the district court's enforcement thereof, represent a classic exercise of compulsory process, intended to secure the personal appearance of and production of documents by an otherwise unwilling witness through threat of judicial sanctions for noncompliance.

The distinction between service of notice and service of compulsory process is a crucial one under principles of both domestic and international law. When an agency serves a party with notice of the pendency of an action, it thereby supplies the recipient with information upon which he may base a decision to act or not. When an agency serves compulsory process upon a third-party witness, regardless of the technique of service employed, it effectively compels that witness to do something and threatens him with sanctions should he choose not to comply.

* * *

When the individual being served is not an American on U.S. soil but a foreign subject on foreign soil, the distinction between the service of notice and the service of compulsory process takes on added significance. When process in the form of summons and complaint is served overseas, the informational nature of that process renders the act of service relatively benign. When compulsory process is served, however, the act of service itself constitutes an exercise of one nation's sovereignty within the territory of another sovereign. Such an exercise constitutes a violation of international law. Given its informational nature, service of process from the United States into a foreign country by registered mail may thus be viewed as the least intrusive means of service i. e., the device which minimizes the imposition upon the local authorities caused by official U.S. government action within the boundaries of the local state. Given the compulsory nature of a subpoena, however, subpoena service by direct mail upon a foreign citizen on foreign soil, without warning to the officials of the local state and without initial request for or prior resort to established channels of international judicial assistance,[69] is perhaps maximally intrusive. Not only does it represent a deliberate bypassing of the official authorities of the local state, it allows the full range of judicial sanctions for non-compliance with an agency subpoena to be triggered merely by a foreign citizen's unwillingness to comply with directives contained in an ordinary registered letter.

* * *

2: The Nature of the Jurisdiction Invoked by the FTC's Service

The exercise of jurisdiction by any governmental body in the United States is subject to limitations reflecting principles of international and constitutional law, as well as the strictures of the particular statute governing that body's conduct. When more than one nation is involved, jurisdictional issues are often elusive. Some jurisdiction which American governmental bodies might exercise consistently with the U.S. Constitution and laws could violate international law, while some exercises of jurisdiction to which international law does not object may violate the Constitution or laws of the United States. The jurisdictional questions posed by this case are peculiarly complex because the jurisdiction of three institutions is at issue: the jurisdiction of the nations involved, under international law, to require production of documents by a French citizen on French soil; the jurisdiction of the federal courts to enforce the agency's subpoena; and the jurisdiction of the agency to effect service of its subpoena by registered mail.

---

69. We should note here that direct service of American subpoenas abroad does not always violate international law. A nation may give general consent to service of compulsory process upon its nationals by another nation's government agencies by signing an international convention. See, e. g., Multilateral Convention on the Service Abroad of Judicial and Extrajudicial Documents in Civil and Commercial Matters, done 15 November 1965, (1969) 20 U.S.T. 361, T.I.A.S. No. 6638, 658 U.N.T.S. (hereinafter Hague Convention). The Hague Convention specifically recognizes, however, a signatory's right to refuse to honor any particular foreign request for service of judicial documents "if it deems that compliance would infringe its sovereignty or security." Id. at art. XIII. See also note 136 infra. Alternatively, a nation may consent to a particular request for service, and specify an appropriate procedural mechanism whereby the serving nation's compulsory process may be served on its own citizens, thus minimizing the infringement upon its own sovereignty caused by the service itself. One example of specific consent occurred in November 1961, when the Swiss Embassy delivered an aide-memoire to the Department of State protesting the service by mail of judicial documents on Swiss residents by a U.S. government agency. Observing that "the service of judicial documents on persons residing in Switzerland is, under Swiss law, a governmental function to be exercised exclusively by the appropriate Swiss authorities," and that "service of such documents by mail constitutes an infringement of Switzerland's sovereign powers, which is incompatible with international law," the aide-memoire requested that "documents destined for Switzerland should be transmitted by the U.S. Embassy in Berne to the Federal Division of Police." The Department of State officially apologized to the Swiss Embassy for its inadvertent violation of applicable Swiss law and directed the responsible American agency to "avoid any future transmittals of such documents in a manner inconsistent with Swiss law." Dept. of State, MS file 711.33 1/11 -1661, 28 Nov. 1961, reprinted in Contemporary Practice of the United States Relating to International Law, 56 Am.J. Int'l L. 793, 794 (1962).

* * *

If a state should enforce a rule which it does not have jurisdiction to enforce, it violates international law, thus giving rise to a claim by the state adversely affected which may then be adjudicated in an appropriate international forum. This would be true even if the state had jurisdiction to prescribe the rule in the first place.

* * *

Two separate conferences of the International Law Association have also studied this problem and reached the same conclusion that the district court's proposed enforcement of the administrative subpoena, by compelling the conduct in France of French nationals, would violate international law. The Fifty-First Conference, held in Tokyo, initially concluded that:

> It is difficult to find any authority under international law for the issuance of orders compelling the production of documents from abroad. The documents are admittedly located in the territory of another State. To assume jurisdiction over documents located abroad *in advance of a finding of effect upon commerce* raises the greatest doubts among non-Americans as to the validity of such orders.[94]

* * *

By this analysis, the district court's enforcement of the FTC's subpoenas so served would clearly extend American enforcement jurisdiction beyond the limits of its prescriptive jurisdiction. As such, the district court's enforcement order violated a fundamental principle of international law.

* * *

The district court, however, apparently viewed the central issue in the case as whether or not the power of the FTC to serve process abroad could validly be inferred from its broad investigatory and regulatory jurisdiction. The court read *Blackmer v. United States*[107] as "unequivocally conclud[ing] that the lawful exercise of jurisdiction confers the authority to effect service."[108] It then postulated that since the *Blackmer* Court had upheld Congress' power expressly to authorize issuance of subpoenas abroad, it must have also approved Congress' power to secure service of those subpoenas. By delegating its subpoena power to the FTC, the district court concluded, Congress by implication must have delegated to the agency authority to effect subpoena service in any permissible manner.

Such an analysis fundamentally misreads the Supreme Court's jurisdictional findings in *Blackmer*, as a review of the history of that case will demonstrate. Upon discovery of the Teapot Dome scandal in 1923, a number of the prominent Americans involved, among them Harry Blackmer, fled to France. To compel their testimony in the subsequent criminal proceedings, Congress passed the Walsh Act authorizing the federal district courts to compel the attendance of American witnesses abroad in connection with domestic criminal proceedings. The statute expressly authorized service of judicial subpoenas outside the United States and specified the means of service to be employed. Pursuant to the Act, the Supreme Court of the District of Columbia issued a subpoena

---

94. Report of the Fifty-First Conference, International Law Association 403, 407 (Tokyo 1964) (emphasis added).

107. 284 U.S. 421, 52 S.Ct. 252, 76 L.Ed. 375 (1932).

108. FTC v. Compagnie De Saint-Gobain-Pont-A-Mousson, 493 F.Supp. 286, 293 (D.D.C.1980).

which was served upon Blackmer in the statutorily authorized fashion, requiring Blackmer to appear as a witness at a criminal trial. When Blackmer failed to respond, he was found in contempt of court. The U. S. Supreme Court affirmed the contempt conviction and upheld the statute against a due process attack solely on the grounds that Blackmer "was, and continued to be, a citizen of the United States."

The *Blackmer* Court found the statute consistent with both the Constitution and international law for two reasons. With respect to the exercise of the United States' prescriptive authority over Blackmer, the Court found "there is no question of international law, but solely of the purport of the municipal law which establishes the duties of the citizen in relation to his own government," namely, the duty "which the citizen owes to his government... to support the administration of justice by attending its courts and giving his testimony whenever he is properly summoned." With respect to the exercise of the United States' adjudicative authority over Blackmer, the Court held that the trial court's authority to give Blackmer constitutionally required notice was a necessary adjunct of its judicial power over him, which in turn was independently based upon the contact provided by his American citizenship.

* * *

In direct contradistinction to *Blackmer*, in this case the personal jurisdiction of both the district court and the agency over the respondent is not at issue: the court has secured personal jurisdiction over the respondent by proper service of process and, misguidedly or not, the respondent has conceded that the documents being sought are subject to the personal jurisdiction of the agency. The relevant issues under international law, therefore, are whether the FTC has properly served its subpoena and whether the court exceeded its enforcement jurisdiction by enforcing that subpoena.

* * *

In view of the international interests at stake, we suggest that, at the time of service, the best reading of congressional intent with regard to permissible modes of subpoena service was one authorizing the FTC to use all customary and legitimate methods of service of compulsory process commonly employed by American courts and administrative tribunals. Such a reading would have imposed the requirement of personal service found in Federal Rule of Civil Procedure 45(c), governing permissible methods of subpoena service by a federal court, upon FTC subpoenas as well. It would have further required that wherever possible, an agency attempting subpoena service on foreign citizens residing on foreign soil should make initial resort through established diplomatic channels or procedures authorized by international convention.[136]

* * *

Should the FTC be able to obtain personal service upon the president, an officer, or a director of SGPM within the territorial boundaries of the United States, it could validly obtain a judicial enforcement order for that subpoena. Furthermore, we take judicial

---

136. The Hague Convention, note 69 supra, establishes standard procedures for service of judicial and extrajudicial documents in the territory of one contracting nation in aid of private commercial or civil litigation taking place in another contracting nation. * * * France is a signatory of the Convention.
* * *
Even if the Hague Convention does not apply to service by a United States government agency, see First Affidavit of Professor Covey T. Oliver, attached to SGPM Brief on Remand, at 5-6; Second Affidavit of Professor Pierre Mayer, attached to SGPM Brief on Remand, at 9, service by some other channel mutually acceptable to both governments is not precluded.

notice of a recent congressional amendment to the FTC Act, enacted after the subpoena challenged here issued, which apparently gives the FTC express authority to serve its civil investigative demands upon "any person who is not found within the territorial jurisdiction of any court of the United States, in such manner as the Federal Rules of Civil Procedure prescribe for service in a foreign nation." Because we are concerned here solely with interpreting the congressional intent underlying the FTC Act as it existed at the time of the challenged service, we need not express any opinion at this time as to whether the FTC could now lawfully serve its compulsory process abroad by registered mail as a civil investigative demand governed by the terms of the amended provision. We note only that, even if expressly authorized by statute, such a mode of service might still be subject to a due process attack if the witness so served both refused to concede the personal jurisdiction of the agency and lacked the requisite minimum contacts with the United States. Furthermore, under the principles of international law discussed above, such a manner of statutory service might still violate international law.

Even if the agency could accomplish proper service by the means we have described, the issue of whether it could actually obtain the documents in question is far from settled. Proper service of the FTC's subpoena would merely create an obligation upon SGPM under American law to furnish the documents. The zeal with which American litigators have recently engaged in antitrust discovery abroad and the willingness of American courts to order production of foreign documents have not only triggered international controversy[143] and academic debate; they have prompted passage of a fresh wave of foreign non-disclosure laws as well.[145] Indeed, since the instant litigation began, the French government has enacted a statute which would not only subject SGPM to criminal and monetary penalties for producing the documents sought here,[146] but

---

143. See, e. g., the reaction of the British House of Lords to American government support of Westinghouse's efforts to take the testimony of British witnesses to an alleged uranium price-fixing conspiracy. *Rio Tinto Zinc Corp. v. Westinghouse Elec. Corp.*, (1978) 2 W.L.R. 81 (House of Lords).

145. At the close of 1979, six foreign states and two Canadian provinces had enacted "blocking statutes," designed to protect their citizens against official inquiries by authorities of other states. Foreign nondisclosure statutes have been of two types the first, providing that a government official may, in his discretion, prohibit the production of a class of documents, see, e. g., Foreign Proceedings (Prohibition of Certain Evidence Act), 1976, Austl. Acts No. 121, §5, and the second, prohibiting production of any documents requested by a foreign tribunal unless those documents are of a type normally sent out of the province in the regular course of business, see, e. g., Business Concerns Records Act, 1964, Que.Rev.Stat. c. 278 (1964). The British legislature has recently enacted legislation of the first type, see Protection of Trading Interests Act, 1980, c. 11 §2, 20 Mar. 1980, while the French government has promulgated in the last few months legislation of the second type, see notes 146-47 infra.

146. French Law No. 80-538, titled "Law concerning the communication of documents or information of an economic, commercial, industrial, financial or technical nature to aliens, whether natural or artificial persons," provides in Article 1:

Without prejudice to international treaties or agreements, a natural person of French nationality or customarily residing on French territory, *or director, representative, agent or official of an artificial person with headquarters or an establishment on French territory*, shall *not communicate* in writing, orally, or in any other form, regardless of place, *to the public authorities of another country documents or information of an economic, commercial, industrial, financial or technical nature where such communication is liable to threaten France's sovereignty*, security or basic economic interests or the public order, as defined by the administering authority when necessary.

Journal Officiel de la Republique Francaise (17 July 1980) (translation provided by SGPM; uncontroverted by FTC) (emphasis added).

Article 3 of that law further specifies:

Without prejudice to more serious penalties provided by law, any violations of articles 1

would also potentially subject the FTC to criminal penalties under French law merely for "ask[ing] for...information of an economic, commercial, industrial, financial or technical nature that may constitute proof with a view to legal or administrative proceedings in another country."[147] Though we express no view here as to whether SGPM's noncompliance with a properly served subpoena would be excused in light of the French statute[148] the potentially dire consequences of properly obtained service for both the agency and the respondent influence our decision strictly to construe the congressional intent underlying the statutory provisions relevant here. Without granting undue deference to the mandate of foreign nondisclosure laws, we note simply that where two constructions of a statute are possible, the one less likely to conflict directly with regulations of other nations should be chosen.

III: CONCLUSION

Finding the Commission's investigatory subpoena to be improperly served under the Federal Trade Commission Act, as we have construed it in conformity with general principles of international law, we order that the district court's enforcement orders * * * be vacated and that the case be dismissed by the district court. The order of dismissal should also prescribe that all documents and copies submitted by SGPM to the FTC responsive to the improperly served subpoena be returned to SGPM within sixty days after entry of judgment, and that all notes, extracts, or other records derived from such documents be destroyed.

So Ordered.

McGOWAN, Circuit Judge, concurring separately.

I concur in the result. In doing so, however, I do not find it necessary to explore the jurisdictional distinctions and the intricacies of international law which bulk so large in the majority opinion.

This case was greatly simplified by the fact that no issue was presented with respect to the power of the Federal Trade Commission to compel the production by appellant

---

and 1a of this law shall be punishable by two to six months' imprisonment and a fine of from 10,000 to 120,000 francs ($2,500 to $30,000) or either one of these two penalties alone.
Id.
147. Article 1a of the French statute provides:
Without prejudice to international treaties or agreements and to current laws and regulations, a person *shall not ask for*, seek or communicate in writing, orally, or in any other form, *documents or information of an economic, commercial, industrial, financial or technical nature that may constitute proof with a view to legal or administrative proceedings in another country* or in the framework of such proceedings.
Id. (emphasis added).
Thus, not only would the FTC's act of delivering its subpoena threaten French sovereignty, its request for the documents would itself constitute a prima facie violation of French law subject to enforcement by criminal penalties.
148. The district court would first have to determine whether the French statute was applicable to this subpoena (which issued prior to the passage of the French law) and to those subpoenaed documents which, though under the control of SGPM, may be within the territorial jurisdiction of the United States. Furthermore, the district court would have to consider whether SGPM had made good-faith efforts to secure the permission of the French government to produce the documents despite the French statute, and then weigh the respective interests of the United States and France.
In view of the interpretation of French law which would be necessary, see notes 146-47 supra, a district court might see fit to defer to the judgment of a foreign court regarding the applicability of the law.

corporation of documents located in the country of its nationality, France. The claim, rather, was only that the Commission had not been clothed by Congress with the authority to serve its investigative subpoena by registered mail directed to appellant at its general corporate headquarters in Paris. Effective service of that subpoena, so it was argued by appellant, could only be made by personal service of it upon an officer or director of appellant within the United States.

The service of an investigative subpoena on a foreign national in a foreign country seems to me to be a sufficiently significant act as to require that Congress should speak to it clearly. I am not, therefore, prepared, as was the District Court, to infer the requisite authority from the breadth of Congress's power to reach foreign documents in the exercise of its power to regulate interstate and foreign commerce, or from a general delegation by Congress to the Commission of rulemaking authority.

* * *

Notes

1. Judge Wilkey states "Congress is customarily presumed, unless a plain intention appears to the contrary, to avoid conflict with [principles of international law] as well as with the Constitution." Murray v. The Schooner Charming Betsy, 6 U.S. (2 Cranch) 64, 118 (1804) contained an early statement of this canon of construction: "an act of Congress ought never to be construed to violate the law of nations if any other possible construction remains." The canon implies that legislation would prevail if constitutional, even if in violation of international law. Cf. Committee of United States Citizens Living in Nicaragua v. Reagan, 859 F.2d 929, 935-36 (D.C. Cir. 1988) (dismissing suit to enjoin funding of "Contras" in Nicaragua):

> Here the alleged violation [of international law] is the law that Congress enacted and that the President signed, appropriating funds for the Contras. When our government's two political branches, acting together, contravene an international legal norm, does this court have any authority to remedy the violation? The answer is "no" if the type of international obligation that Congress and the President violate is either a treaty or a rule of customary international law. If, on the other hand, Congress and the President violate a peremptory norm (or *jus cogens*), the domestic legal consequences are unclear. We need not resolve this uncertainty, however, for we find that the principles appellants characterize as peremptory norms of international law are not recognized as such by the community of nations. Thus... none of the claims that appellants derive from violations of international law can succeed in this court.

46 U.S.C. App. § 1903 declares it unlawful for any person on board a vessel subject to the jurisdiction of the U.S. to possess a controlled substance with the intent to manufacture or distribute the substance. A vessel "subject to the jurisdiction of the U.S." includes a vessel registered in a country or located in the territorial waters of a country that has consented to the enforcement of U.S. law by the U.S. Subsection (d) provides: "Any person charged with a violation of this section shall not have standing to raise the claim of failure to comply with international law as a basis for a defense."

The Japanese Constitution, Art. 98, paragraph 2, requires faithful observance of treaties concluded by Japan and of established international law. Article 55 of the French Constitution provides that "treaties or agreements duly ratified or approved shall, upon publication, prevail over Acts of Parliament, subject, in regard to each agreement or treaty, to its application by the other party."

See Vienna Convention on the Law of Treaties, opened for signature May 23, 1969, art. 53, U.N. Doc. A/Conf. 39/27, 8 I.L.M. 679 (1969): "A treaty is void if, at the time of its conclusion, it conflicts with a peremptory norm of general international law... [which] is a norm accepted and recognized by the international community of States as a whole as a norm from which no derogation is permitted..."; Restatement (Third) Foreign Relations Law of the United States (1986) §102 Reporters' Notes 6 [Copyright 1987 by the American Law Institute. Reprinted with the permission of The American Law Institute.]:

> There is general agreement that the principles of the United Nations Charter prohibiting the use of force are *jus cogens*. It has been suggested that norms that create "international crimes" and obligate all states to proceed against violations are also peremptory. Such norms might include rules prohibiting genocide, slave trade and slavery, apartheid and other gross violations of human rights, and perhaps attacks on diplomats.

2. As the court notes, 15 U.S.C. §57b-1 was amended in 1980 to permit the Federal Trade Commission to serve a subpoena duces tecum "upon any person who is not found within the territorial jurisdiction of any court of the United States, in such manner as the Federal Rules of Civil Procedure prescribe for service in a foreign nation." Id. (c)(7)(B). Until its amendment in 1993 [see supra page 102], Federal Rule of Civil Procedure 4(i)(1)(D) permitted service in a foreign country "by any form of mail, requiring a signed receipt."

Section 5: Taking of Evidence

Hague Convention on the Taking of Evidence Abroad in Civil or Commercial Matters

Opened for signature March 18, 1970, 23 U.S.T. 2555, 847 UNTS 231
[ratified by the United States in 1972]

The States signatory to the present Convention.

Desiring to facilitate the transmission and execution of Letters of Request and to further the accommodation of the different methods which they use for this purpose,

Desiring to improve mutual judicial co-operation in civil or commercial matters,

Have resolved to conclude a Convention to this effect and have agreed upon the following provisions—

Chapter I: Letters of Request

Article 1

In civil or commercial matters a judicial authority of a Contracting State may, in accordance with the provisions of the law of that State, request the competent authority of another Contracting State, by means of a Letter of Request, to obtain evidence, or to perform some other judicial act.

A Letter shall not be used to obtain evidence which is not intended for use in judicial proceedings, commenced or contemplated.

The expression "other judicial act" does not cover the service of judicial documents or the issuance of any process by which judgments or orders are executed or enforced, or orders for provisional or protective measures.

Article 2

A Contracting State shall designate a Central Authority which will undertake to receive Letters of Request coming from a judicial authority of another Contracting State and to transmit them to the authority competent to execute them. Each State shall organize the Central Authority in accordance with its own law.

Letters shall be sent to the Central Authority of the State of execution without being transmitted through any other authority of that State.

Article 3

A Letter of Request shall specify—

(a) the authority requesting its execution and the authority requested to execute it, if known to the requesting authority;

(b) the names and addresses of the parties to the proceedings and their representatives, if any;

(c) the nature of the proceedings for which the evidence is required, giving all necessary information in regard thereto;

(d) the evidence to be obtained or other judicial act to be performed. Where appropriate, the Letter shall specify, inter alia—

(e) the names and addresses of the persons to be examined;

(f) the questions to be put to the persons to be examined or a statement of the subject-matter about which they are to be examined;

(g) the documents or other property, real or personal, to be inspected;

(h) any requirement that the evidence is to be given on oath or affirmation, and any special form to be used;

(i) any special method or procedure to be followed under Article 9

A Letter may also mention any information necessary for the application of Article 11.

No legalization or other like formality may be required.

Article 4

A Letter of Request shall be in the language of the authority requested to execute it or be accompanied by a translation into that language.

Nevertheless, a Contracting State shall accept a Letter in either English or French, or a translation into one of these languages, unless it has made the reservation authorized by Article 33.

A contracting State which has more than one official language and cannot, for reasons of internal law, accept Letters in one of these languages for the whole of its territory, shall, by declaration, specify the language in which the Letter or translation thereof shall be expressed for execution in the specified parts of its territory. In case of failure to comply with this declaration, without justifiable excuse, the costs of translation into the required language shall be borne by the State of origin.

A Contracting State may, by declaration, specify the language or languages other than those referred to in the preceding paragraphs, in which a Letter may be sent to its Central Authority.

Any translation accompanying a Letter shall be certified as correct, either by a diplomatic officer or consular agent or by a sworn translator or by any other person so authorized in either State.

Article 5

If the Central Authority considers that the request does not comply with the provisions of the present Convention, it shall promptly inform the authority of the State of origin which transmitted the Letter of Request, specifying the objections to the Letter.

Article 6

If the authority to whom a Letter of Request has been transmitted is not competent to execute it, the Letter shall be sent forthwith to the authority in the same State which is competent to execute it in accordance with the provisions of its own law.

Article 7

The requesting authority shall, if it so desires, be informed of the time when, and the place where, the proceedings will take place, in order that the parties concerned, and their representatives, if any, may be present. This information shall be sent directly to the parties or their representatives when the authority of the State of origin so requests.

Article 8

A Contracting State may declare that members of the judicial personnel of the requesting authority of another Contracting State may be present at the execution of a Letter of Request. Prior authorization by the competent authority designated by the declaring State may be required.

Article 9

The judicial authority which executes a Letter of Request shall apply its own law as to the methods and procedures to be followed.

However, it will follow a request of the requesting authority that a special method or procedure be followed, unless this is incompatible with the internal law of the State of execution or is impossible of performance by reason of its internal practice and procedure or by reason of practical difficulties.

A Letter of Request shall be executed expeditiously.

Article 10

In executing a Letter of Request the requested authority shall apply the appropriate measures of compulsion in the instances and to the same extent as are provided by its internal law for the execution of orders issued by the authorities of its own country or of requests made by parties in internal proceedings.

Article 11

In the execution of a Letter of Request the person concerned may refuse to give evidence insofar as he has a privilege or duty to refuse to give the evidence—

(a) under the law of the State of execution; or

(b) under the law of the State of origin, and the privilege or duty has been specified in the Letter, or, at the instance of the requested authority, has been otherwise confirmed to that authority by the requesting authority.

A Contracting State may declare that, in addition, it will respect privileges and duties existing under the law of States other than the State of origin and the State of execution, to the extent specified in that declaration.

Article 12

The execution of a Letter of Request may be refused only to the extent that—

(a) in the State of execution the execution of the Letter does not fall within the functions of the judiciary; or

(b) the State addressed considers that its sovereignty or security would be prejudiced thereby.

Execution may not be refused solely on the ground that under its internal law the State of execution claims exclusive jurisdiction over the subject-matter of the action or that its internal law would not admit a right of action on it.

Article 13

The documents establishing the execution of the Letter of Request shall be sent by the requested authority to the requesting authority by the same channel which was used by the latter.

In every instance where the Letter is not executed in whole or in part, the requesting authority shall be informed immediately through the same channel and advised of the reasons.

Article 14

The execution of the Letter of Request shall not give rise to any reimbursement of taxes or costs of any nature.

Nevertheless, the State of execution has the right to require the State of origin to reimburse the fees paid to experts and interpreters and the costs occasioned by the use of a special procedure requested by the State of origin under Article 9, paragraph 2.

The requested authority whose law obliges the parties themselves to secure evidence, and which is not able itself to execute the Letter, may, after having obtained the consent of the requesting authority, appoint a suitable person to do so. When seeking this consent the requested authority shall indicate the approximate costs which would result from this procedure. If the requesting authority gives its consent it shall reimburse any costs incurred; without such consent the requesting authority shall not be liable for the costs.

Chapter II: Taking of Evidence by Diplomatic Officers, Consular Agents and Commissioners

Article 15

In a civil or commercial matter, a diplomatic officer or consular agent of a Contracting State may, in the territory of another Contracting State and within the area where he exercises his functions, take the evidence without compulsion of nationals of a State which he represents in aid of proceedings commenced in the courts of a State which he represents.

A Contracting State may declare that evidence may be taken by a diplomatic officer or consular agent only if permission to that effect is given upon application made by him or on his behalf to the appropriate authority designated by the declaring State.

Article 16

A diplomatic officer or consular agent of a Contracting State may, in the territory of another Contracting State and within the area where he exercises his functions, also take the evidence, without compulsion, of nationals of the State in which he exercises his functions or of a third State, in aid of proceedings commenced in the courts of a State which he represents, if—

(a) a competent authority designated by the State in which he exercises his functions has given its permission either generally or in the particular case, and

(b) he complies with the conditions which the competent authority has specified in the permission.

A Contracting State may declare that evidence may be taken under this article without its prior permission.

Article 17

In a civil or commercial matter, a person duly appointed as a commissioner for the purpose may, without compulsion, take evidence in the territory of a Contracting State in aid of proceedings commenced in the courts of another Contracting State if—

(a) a competent authority designated by the State where the evidence is to be taken has given its permission either generally or in the particular case; and

(b) he complies with the conditions which the competent authority has specified in the permission.

A Contracting State may declare that evidence may be taken under this article without its prior permission.

Article 18

A Contracting State may declare that a diplomatic officer, consular agent or commissioner authorized to take evidence under Articles 15, 16 or 17, may apply to the competent authority designated by the declaring State for appropriate assistance to obtain the evidence by compulsion. The declaration may contain such conditions as the declaring State may see fit to impose.

If the authority grants the application it shall apply any measures of compulsion which are appropriate and are prescribed by its law for use in internal proceedings.

Article 19

The competent authority, in giving the permission referred to in Articles 15, 16 or 17, or in granting the application referred to in Article 18, may lay down such conditions as it deems fit, inter alia, as to the time and place of the taking of the evidence. Similarly it may require that it be given reasonable advance notice of the time, date and place of the taking of the evidence; in such a case a representative of the authority shall be entitled to be present at the taking of the evidence.

Article 20

In the taking of evidence under any article of this chapter persons concerned may be legally represented.

Article 21

Where a diplomatic officer, consular agent or commissioner is authorized under Articles 15, 16 or 17 to take evidence—

(a) he may take all kinds of evidence which are not incompatible with the law of the State where the evidence is taken or contrary to any permission granted pursuant to the above Articles, and shall have power within such limits to administer an oath or take an affirmation;

(b) a request to a person to appear or to give evidence shall, unless the recipient is a national of the State where the action is pending, be drawn up in the language of the place where the evidence is taken or be accompanied by a translation into such language;

(c) the request shall inform the person that he may be legally represented and, in any State that has not filed a declaration under Article 18, shall also inform him that he is not compelled to appear or to give evidence;

(d) the evidence may be taken in the manner provided by the law applicable to the court in which the action is pending provided that such manner is not forbidden by the law of the State where the evidence is taken;

(e) a person requested to give evidence may invoke the privileges and duties to refuse to give the evidence contained in Article 11.

Article 22

The fact that an attempt to take evidence under the procedure laid down in this chapter has failed, owing to the refusal of a person to give evidence, shall not prevent an application being subsequently made to take the evidence in accordance with Chapter I.

Chapter III: General Clauses

Article 23

A Contracting State may at the time of signature, ratification or accession, declare that it will not execute Letters of Request issued for the purpose of obtaining pre-trial discovery of documents as known in Common Law countries.

Article 24

A Contracting State may designate other authorities in addition to the Central Authority and shall determine the extent of their competence. However, Letters of Request may in all cases be sent to the Central Authority.

Federal States shall be free to designate more than one Central Authority.

Article 25

A Contracting State which has more than one legal system may designate the authorities of one of such systems, which shall have exclusive competence to execute Letters of Request pursuant to this Convention.

Article 26

A Contracting State, if required to do so because of constitutional limitations, may request the reimbursement by the State of origin of fees and costs, in connection with the execution of Letters of Request, for the service of process necessary to compel the appearance of a person to give evidence, the costs of attendance of such persons, and the cost of any transcript of the evidence.

Where a State has made a request pursuant to the above paragraph, any other Contracting State may request from that State the reimbursement of similar fees and costs.

Article 27

The provisions of the present Convention shall not prevent a Contracting State from—

(a) declaring that Letters of Request may be transmitted to its judicial authorities through channels other than those provided for in Article 2;

(b) permitting, by internal law or practice, any act provided for in this Convention to be performed upon less restrictive conditions;

(c) permitting, by internal law or practice, methods of taking evidence other than those provided for in this Convention.

* * *

Article 33

A State may, at the time of signature, ratification or accession exclude, in whole or in part, the application of the provisions of paragraph 2 of Article 4 and of Chapter II. No other reservation shall be permitted.

Each Contracting State may at any time withdraw a reservation it has made; the reservation shall cease to have effect on the 60th day after notification of the withdrawal.

When a State has made a reservation, any other State affected thereby may apply the same rule against the reserving State.

Article 34

A State may at any time withdraw or modify a declaration.

Article 35

A Contracting State shall, at the time of the deposit of its instrument of ratification or accession, or at a later date, inform the Ministry of Foreign Affairs of the Netherlands of the designation of authorities, pursuant to Articles 2, 8, 24 and 25.

A Contracting State shall likewise inform the Ministry, where appropriate, of the following—

(a) the designation of the authorities to whom notice must be given, whose permission may be required, and whose assistance may be invoked in the taking of evidence by diplomatic officers and consular agents, pursuant to Articles 15, 16 and 18 respectively;

(b) the designation of the authorities whose permission may be required in the taking of evidence by commissioners pursuant to Article 17 and of those who may grant the assistance provided for in Article 18;

(c) declarations pursuant to Articles 4, 8, 11, 15, 16, 17, 18, 23 and 27;

(d) any withdrawal or modification of the above designations and declarations;

(e) the withdrawal of any reservation.

Article 36

Any difficulties which may arise between Contracting States in connection with the operation of this Convention shall be settled through diplomatic channels.

* * *

Société Nationale Industrielle Aérospatiale v. United States District Court
482 U.S. 522 (1987)

Justice STEVENS delivered the opinion of the Court.

The United States, the Republic of France, and 15 other Nations have acceded to the Hague Convention on the Taking of Evidence Abroad in Civil or Commercial Matters, opened for signature, Mar. 18, 1970, 23 U.S.T. 2555, T.I.A.S. No. 7444. This Convention—sometimes referred to as the "Hague Convention" or the "Evidence Convention"—prescribes certain procedures by which a judicial authority in one contracting state may request evidence located in another contracting state. The question presented in this case concerns the extent to which a federal district court must employ the procedures set forth in the Convention when litigants seek answers to interrogatories, the production of documents, and admissions from a French adversary over whom the court has personal jurisdiction.

I

The two petitioners are corporations owned by the Republic of France. They are engaged in the business of designing, manufacturing, and marketing aircraft. One of their planes, the "Rallye," was allegedly advertised in American aviation publications as "the World's safest and most economical STOL plane."[3] On August 19, 1980, a Rallye crashed in Iowa, injuring the pilot and a passenger. Dennis Jones, John George, and Rosa George brought separate suits based upon this accident in the United States District Court for the Southern District of Iowa, alleging that petitioners had manufactured and sold a defective plane and that they were guilty of negligence and breach of warranty.

---

3. The term "STOL," an acronym for "short takeoff and landing," "refers to a fixed-wing aircraft that either takes off or lands with only a short horizontal run of the aircraft." Douglas v. United States, 206 Ct.Cl. 96, 99, 510 F.2d 364, 365, cert. denied, 423 U.S. 825 (1975).

Petitioners answered the complaints, apparently without questioning the jurisdiction of the District Court. With the parties' consent, the cases were consolidated and referred to a Magistrate.

Initial discovery was conducted by both sides pursuant to the Federal Rules of Civil Procedure without objection. When plaintiffs served a second request for the production of documents pursuant to Rule 34, a set of interrogatories pursuant to Rule 33, and requests for admission pursuant to Rule 36, however, petitioners filed a motion for a protective order. The motion alleged that because petitioners are "French corporations, and the discovery sought can only be found in a foreign state, namely France," the Hague Convention dictated the exclusive procedures that must be followed for pretrial discovery. In addition, the motion stated that under French penal law, the petitioners could not respond to discovery requests that did not comply with the Convention.

The Magistrate denied the motion insofar as it related to answering interrogatories, producing documents, and making admissions. After reviewing the relevant cases, the Magistrate explained:

> "To permit the Hague Evidence Convention to override the Federal Rules of Civil Procedure would frustrate the courts' interests, which particularly arise in products liability cases, in protecting United States citizens from harmful products and in compensating them for injuries arising from use of such products."

The Magistrate made two responses to petitioners' argument that they could not comply with the discovery requests without violating French penal law. Noting that the law was originally "inspired to impede enforcement of United States antitrust laws," and that it did not appear to have been strictly enforced in France, he first questioned whether it would be construed to apply to the pretrial discovery requests at issue. Second, he balanced the interests in the "protection of United States citizens from harmful foreign products and compensation for injuries caused by such products" against France's interest in protecting its citizens "from intrusive foreign discovery procedures." The Magistrate concluded that the former interests were stronger, particularly because compliance with the requested discovery will "not have to take place in France" and will not be greatly intrusive or abusive.

Petitioners sought a writ of mandamus from the Court of Appeals for the Eighth Circuit under Federal Rule of Appellate Procedure 21(a). Although immediate appellate review of an interlocutory discovery order is not ordinarily available, the Court of Appeals considered that the novelty and the importance of the question presented, and the likelihood of its recurrence, made consideration of the merits of the petition appropriate. 782 F.2d 120 (1986). It then held that "when the district court has jurisdiction over a foreign litigant the Hague Convention does not apply to the production of evidence in that litigant's possession, even though the documents and information sought may physically be located within the territory of a foreign signatory to the Convention." Id., at 124. The Court of Appeals disagreed with petitioners' argument that this construction would render the entire Hague Convention "meaningless," noting that it would still serve the purpose of providing an improved procedure for obtaining evidence from nonparties. Id., at 125. The court also rejected petitioners' contention that considerations of international comity required plaintiffs to resort to Hague Convention procedures as an initial matter ("first use"), and correspondingly to invoke the federal discovery rules only if the treaty procedures turned out to be futile. The Court of Appeals believed that the potential overruling of foreign tribunals' denial of discovery would do more to defeat than to promote international comity. Id., at 125-126. Finally, the Court of Appeals concluded that objections based on the French penal statute should be considered in two stages: first, whether the discovery order was proper even though compliance may require petitioners to violate French law; and second, what sanctions, if any, should be imposed if petitioners are unable to comply. The Court of Appeals held that the Magistrate properly answered the first question and that it was premature to address the second.[10] The court therefore denied the petition for mandamus. We granted certiorari.

II

In the District Court and the Court of Appeals, petitioners contended that the Hague Evidence Convention "provides the exclusive and mandatory procedures for obtaining documents and information located within the territory of a foreign signatory." 782 F.2d, at 124.[11] We are satisfied that the Court of Appeals correctly rejected this extreme position. We believe it is foreclosed by the plain language of the Convention. Before discussing the text of the Convention, however, we briefly review its history.

The Hague Conference on Private International Law, an association of sovereign states, has been conducting periodic sessions since 1893. S.Exec. Doc. A, 92d Cong., 2d Sess. p. V (1972) (S.Exec. Doc. A). The United States participated in those sessions as an observer in 1956 and 1960, and as a member beginning in 1964 pursuant to congressional authorization. In that year Congress amended the Judicial Code to grant foreign litigants, without any requirement of reciprocity, special assistance in obtaining evidence in the United States. In 1965 the Hague Conference adopted a Convention on the Service Abroad of Judicial and Extrajudicial Documents in Civil or Commercial Matters (Service Convention), 20 U.S.T. 361, T.I.A.S. No. 6638, to which the Senate gave its advice and consent in 1967. The favorable response to the Service Convention, coupled with the longstanding interest of American lawyers in improving procedures for obtaining evidence abroad, motivated the United States to take the initiative in proposing that an evidence convention be adopted.

* * *

The Convention was fairly summarized in the Secretary of State's letter of submittal to the President:

"The willingness of the Conference to proceed promptly with work on the evidence convention is perhaps attributable in large measure to the difficulties encountered by courts and lawyers in obtaining evidence abroad from countries with markedly different legal systems. Some countries have insisted on the exclusive use of the complicated, dilatory and expensive system of letters rogatory or letters of request. Other countries have refused adequate judicial assistance because of the absence of a treaty or conven-

---

10. "The record before this court does not indicate whether the Petitioners have notified the appropriate French Minister of the requested discovery in accordance with Article 2 of the French Blocking Statute, or whether the Petitioners have attempted to secure a waiver of prosecution from the French government. Because the Petitioners are corporations owned by the Republic of France, they stand in a most advantageous position to receive such a waiver. However, these issues will only be relevant should the Petitioners fail to comply with the magistrate's discovery order, and we need not presently address them." 782 F.2d, at 127.

11. The Republic of France likewise takes the following position in this case:
"THE HAGUE CONVENTION IS THE EXCLUSIVE MEANS OF DISCOVERY IN TRANSNATIONAL LITIGATION AMONG THE CONVENTION'S SIGNATORIES UNLESS THE SOVEREIGN ON WHOSE TERRITORY DISCOVERY IS TO OCCUR CHOOSES OTHERWISE." Brief for Republic of France as Amicus Curiae 4.

tion regulating the matter. The substantial increase in litigation with foreign aspects arising, in part, from the unparalleled expansion of international trade and travel in recent decades had intensified the need for an effective international agreement to set up a model system to bridge differences between the common law and civil law approaches to the taking of evidence abroad.

"Civil law countries tend to concentrate on commissions rogatories, while common law countries take testimony on notice, by stipulation and through commissions to consuls or commissioners. Letters of request for judicial assistance from courts abroad in securing needed evidence have been the exception, rather than the rule. The civil law technique results normally in a resume of the evidence, prepared by the executing judge and signed by the witness, while the common law technique results normally in a verbatim transcript of the witness's testimony certified by the reporter.

"Failure by either the requesting state or the state of execution fully to take into account the differences of approach to the taking of evidence abroad under the two systems and the absence of agreed standards applicable to letters of request have frequently caused difficulties for courts and litigants. To minimize such difficulties in the future, the enclosed convention, which consists of a preamble and forty-two articles, is designed to:

"1. Make the employment of letters of request a principal means of obtaining evidence abroad;

"2. Improve the means of securing evidence abroad by increasing the powers of consuls and by introducing in the civil law world, on a limited basis, the concept of the commissioner;

"3. Provide means for securing evidence in the form needed by the court where the action is pending; and

"4. Preserve all more favorable and less restrictive practices arising from internal law, internal rules of procedure and bilateral or multilateral conventions.

"What the convention does is to provide a set of minimum standards with which contracting states agree to comply. Further, through articles 27, 28 and 32, it provides a flexible framework within which any future liberalizing changes in policy and tradition in any country with respect to international judicial cooperation may be translated into effective change in international procedures. At the same time it recognizes and preserves procedures of every country which now or hereafter may provide international cooperation in the taking of evidence on more liberal and less restrictive bases, whether this is effected by supplementary agreements or by municipal law and practice."

III

In arguing their entitlement to a protective order, petitioners correctly assert that both the discovery rules set forth in the Federal Rules of Civil Procedure and the Hague Convention are the law of the United States. This observation, however, does not dispose of the question before us; we must analyze the interaction between these two bodies of federal law. Initially, we note that at least four different interpretations of the relationship between the federal discovery rules and the Hague Convention are possible. Two of these interpretations assume that the Hague Convention by its terms dictates the extent to which it supplants normal discovery rules. First, the Hague Convention might be read as requiring its use to the exclusion of any other discovery procedures whenever evidence located abroad is sought for use in an American court. Second, the Hague

Convention might be interpreted to require first, but not exclusive, use of its procedures. Two other interpretations assume that international comity, rather than the obligations created by the treaty, should guide judicial resort to the Hague Convention. Third, then, the Convention might be viewed as establishing a supplemental set of discovery procedures, strictly optional under treaty law, to which concerns of comity nevertheless require first resort by American courts in all cases. Fourth, the treaty may be viewed as an undertaking among sovereigns to facilitate discovery to which an American court should resort when it deems that course of action appropriate, after considering the situations of the parties before it as well as the interests of the concerned foreign state.

* * *

We reject the first two of the possible interpretations as inconsistent with the language and negotiating history of the Hague Convention. The preamble of the Convention specifies its purpose "to facilitate the transmission and execution of Letters of Request" and to "improve mutual judicial co-operation in civil or commercial matters." The preamble does not speak in mandatory terms which would purport to describe the procedures for all permissible transnational discovery and exclude all other existing practices.[15] The text of the Evidence Convention itself does not modify the law of any contracting state, require any contracting state to use the Convention procedures, either in requesting evidence or in responding to such requests, or compel any contracting state to change its own evidence-gathering procedures.

The Convention contains three chapters. Chapter I, entitled "Letters of Requests," and chapter II, entitled "Taking of Evidence by Diplomatic Officers, Consular Agents and Commissioners," both use permissive rather than mandatory language. Thus, Article 1 provides that a judicial authority in one contracting state "may" forward a letter of request to the competent authority in another contracting state for the purpose of obtaining evidence. Similarly, Articles 15, 16, and 17 provide that diplomatic officers, consular agents, and commissioners "may...without compulsion," take evidence under certain conditions. The absence of any command that a contracting state must use Convention procedures when they are not needed is conspicuous.

Two of the Articles in chapter III, entitled "General Clauses," buttress our conclusion that the Convention was intended as a permissive supplement, not a pre-emptive replacement, for other means of obtaining evidence located abroad. Article 23 expressly authorizes a contracting state to declare that it will not execute any letter of request in aid of pretrial discovery of documents in a common-law country. Surely, if the Convention had been intended to replace completely the broad discovery powers that the common-law courts in the United States previously exercised over foreign litigants subject to their jurisdiction, it would have been most anomalous for the common-law contract-

---

15. The Hague Conference on Private International Law's omission of mandatory language in the preamble is particularly significant in light of the same body's use of mandatory language in the preamble to the Hague Service Convention, 20 U.S.T. 361, T.I.A.S. No. 6638. Article 1 of the Service Convention provides: "The present Convention shall apply in all cases, in civil or commercial matters, where there is occasion to transmit a judicial or extrajudicial document for service abroad." Id., at 362, T.I.A.S. No. 6638. * * * [T]he Service Convention was drafted before the Evidence Convention, and its language provided a model exclusivity provision that the drafters of the Evidence Convention could easily have followed had they been so inclined. Given this background, the drafters' election to use permissive language instead is strong evidence of their intent.

ing parties to agree to Article 23, which enables a contracting party to revoke its consent to the treaty's procedures for pretrial discovery.[22]

In the absence of explicit textual support, we are unable to accept the hypothesis that the common-law contracting states abjured recourse to all pre-existing discovery procedures at the same time that they accepted the possibility that a contracting party could unilaterally abrogate even the Convention's procedures. Moreover, Article 27 plainly states that the Convention does not prevent a contracting state from using more liberal methods of rendering evidence than those authorized by the Convention. Thus, the text of the Evidence Convention, as well as the history of its proposal and ratification by the United States, unambiguously supports the conclusion that it was intended to establish optional procedures that would facilitate the taking of evidence abroad. See Amram, The Proposed Convention on the Taking of Evidence Abroad, 55 A.B.A.J. 651, 655 (1969); President's Letter of Transmittal, Sen. Exec. Doc. A, p. III.

An interpretation of the Hague Convention as the exclusive means for obtaining evidence located abroad would effectively subject every American court hearing a case involving a national of a contracting state to the internal laws of that state. Interrogatories and document requests are staples of international commercial litigation, no less than of other suits, yet a rule of exclusivity would subordinate the court's supervision of even the most routine of these pretrial proceedings to the actions or, equally, to the inactions of foreign judicial authorities.

* * *

We conclude accordingly that the Hague Convention did not deprive the District Court of the jurisdiction it otherwise possessed to order a foreign national party before it to produce evidence physically located within a signatory nation.[25]

IV

While the Hague Convention does not divest the District Court of jurisdiction to order discovery under the Federal Rules of Civil Procedure, the optional character of

---

22. Thirteen of the seventeen signatory states have made declarations under Article 23 of the Convention that restrict pretrial discovery of documents. See 7 Martindale-Hubbell Law Directory (pt. VII) 15-19 (1986).

25. The opposite conclusion of exclusivity would create three unacceptable asymmetries. First, within any lawsuit between a national of the United States and a national of another contracting party, the foreign party could obtain discovery under the Federal Rules of Civil Procedure, while the domestic party would be required to resort first to the procedures of the Hague Convention. This imbalance would run counter to the fundamental maxim of discovery that "[m]utual knowledge of all the relevant facts gathered by both parties is essential to proper litigation." *Hickman v. Taylor*, 329 U.S. 495, 507 (1947). Second, a rule of exclusivity would enable a company which is a citizen of another contracting state to compete with a domestic company on uneven terms, since the foreign company would be subject to less extensive discovery procedures in the event that both companies were sued in an American court. Petitioners made a voluntary decision to market their products in the United States. They are entitled to compete on equal terms with other companies operating in this market. But since the District Court unquestionably has personal jurisdiction over petitioners, they are subject to the same legal constraints, including the burdens associated with American judicial procedures, as their American competitors. A general rule according foreign nationals a preferred position in pretrial proceedings in our courts would conflict with the principle of equal opportunity that governs the market they elected to enter. Third, since a rule of first use of the Hague Convention would apply to cases in which a foreign party is a national of a contracting state, but not to cases in which a foreign party is a national of any other foreign state, the rule would confer an unwarranted advantage on some domestic litigants over others similarly situated.

the Convention procedures sheds light on one aspect of the Court of Appeals' opinion that we consider erroneous. That court concluded that the Convention simply "does not apply" to discovery sought from a foreign litigant that is subject to the jurisdiction of an American court. 782 F.2d, at 124.

* * *

Nevertheless, the text of the Convention draws no distinction between evidence obtained from third parties and that obtained from the litigants themselves; nor does it purport to draw any sharp line between evidence that is "abroad" and evidence that is within the control of a party subject to the jurisdiction of the requesting court. Thus, it appears clear to us that the optional Convention procedures are available whenever they will facilitate the gathering of evidence by the means authorized in the Convention. Although these procedures are not mandatory, the Hague Convention does "apply" to the production of evidence in a litigant's possession in the sense that it is one method of seeking evidence that a court may elect to employ. See Briefs of Amici Curiae for the United States and the SEC 9-10, the Federal Republic of Germany 5-6, the Republic of France 8-12, and the Government of the United Kingdom and Northern Ireland 8.

V

Petitioners contend that even if the Hague Convention's procedures are not mandatory, this Court should adopt a rule requiring that American litigants first resort to those procedures before initiating any discovery pursuant to the normal methods of the Federal Rules of Civil Procedure. The Court of Appeals rejected this argument because it was convinced that an American court's order ultimately requiring discovery that a foreign court had refused under Convention procedures would constitute "the greatest insult" to the sovereignty of that tribunal. 782 F.2d, at 125-126. We disagree with the Court of Appeals' view. It is well known that the scope of American discovery is often significantly broader than is permitted in other jurisdictions, and we are satisfied that foreign tribunals will recognize that the final decision on the evidence to be used in litigation conducted in American courts must be made by those courts. We therefore do not believe that an American court should refuse to make use of Convention procedures because of a concern that it may ultimately find it necessary to order the production of evidence that a foreign tribunal permitted a party to withhold.

Nevertheless, we cannot accept petitioners' invitation to announce a new rule of law that would require first resort to Convention procedures whenever discovery is sought from a foreign litigant. Assuming, without deciding, that we have the lawmaking power to do so, we are convinced that such a general rule would be unwise. In many situations the Letter of Request procedure authorized by the Convention would be unduly time consuming and expensive, as well as less certain to produce needed evidence than direct use of the Federal Rules.[26] A rule of first resort in all cases would therefore be inconsistent with the overriding interest in the "just, speedy, and inexpensive determination" of litigation in our courts. See Fed.Rule Civ.Proc. 1.

* * *

---

26. We observe, however, that in other instances a litigant's first use of the Hague Convention procedures can be expected to yield more evidence abroad more promptly than use of the normal procedures governing pre-trial civil discovery. In those instances, the calculations of the litigant will naturally lead to a first-use strategy.

We therefore decline to hold as a blanket matter that comity requires resort to Hague Evidence Convention procedures without prior scrutiny in each case of the particular facts, sovereign interests, and likelihood that resort to those procedures will prove effective.[29]

Some discovery procedures are much more "intrusive" than others. In this case, for example, an interrogatory asking petitioners to identify the pilots who flew flight tests in the Rallye before it was certified for flight by the Federal Aviation Administration, or a request to admit that petitioners authorized certain advertising in a particular magazine, is certainly less intrusive than a request to produce all of the "design specifications, line drawings and engineering plans and all engineering change orders and plans and all drawings concerning the leading edge slats for the Rallye type aircraft manufactured by the Defendants." Even if a court might be persuaded that a particular document request was too burdensome or too "intrusive" to be granted in full, with or without an appropriate protective order, it might well refuse to insist upon the use of Convention procedures before requiring responses to simple interrogatories or requests for admissions. The exact line between reasonableness and unreasonableness in each case must be drawn by the trial court, based on its knowledge of the case and of the claims and interests of the parties and the governments whose statutes and policies they invoke.

American courts, in supervising pretrial proceedings, should exercise special vigilance to protect foreign litigants from the danger that unnecessary, or unduly burdensome, discovery may place them in a disadvantageous position. Judicial supervision of discovery should always seek to minimize its costs and inconvenience and to prevent improper uses of discovery requests. When it is necessary to seek evidence abroad, how-

---

29. The French "blocking statute," does not alter our conclusion. It is well settled that such statutes do not deprive an American court of the power to order a party subject to its jurisdiction to produce evidence even though the act of production may violate that statute. See *Societe Internationale Pour Participations Industrielles et Commerciales, S.A. v. Rogers*, 357 U.S. 197, 204-206 (1958). Nor can the enactment of such a statute by a foreign nation require American courts to engraft a rule of first resort onto the Hague Convention, or otherwise to provide the nationals of such a country with a preferred status in our courts. It is clear that American courts are not required to adhere blindly to the directives of such a statute. Indeed, the language of the statute, if taken literally, would appear to represent an extraordinary exercise of legislative jurisdiction by the Republic of France over a United States district judge, forbidding him or her to order any discovery from a party of French nationality, even simple requests for admissions or interrogatories that the party could respond to on the basis of personal knowledge. It would be particularly incongruous to recognize such a preference for corporations that are wholly owned by the enacting nation. Extraterritorial assertions of jurisdiction are not one-sided. While the District Court's discovery orders arguably have some impact in France, the French blocking statute asserts similar authority over acts to take place in this country. The lesson of comity is that neither the discovery order nor the blocking statute can have the same omnipresent effect that it would have in a world of only one sovereign. The blocking statute thus is relevant to the court's particularized comity analysis only to the extent that its terms and its enforcement identify the nature of the sovereign interests in nondisclosure of specific kinds of material. The American Law Institute has summarized this interplay of blocking statutes and discovery orders: "[W]hen a state has jurisdiction to prescribe and its courts have jurisdiction to adjudicate, adjudication should (subject to generally applicable rules of evidence) take place on the basis of the best information available... [Blocking] statutes that frustrate this goal need not be given the same deference by courts of the United States as substantive rules of law at variance with the law of the United States." See Restatement, § 437, Reporter's Note 5, pp. 41, 42. "On the other hand, the degree of friction created by discovery requests... and the differing perceptions of the acceptability of American-style discovery under national and international law, suggest some efforts to moderate the application abroad of U.S. procedural techniques, consistent with the overall principle of reasonableness in the exercise of jurisdiction." Id., at 42.

ever, the district court must supervise pretrial proceedings particularly closely to prevent discovery abuses. For example, the additional cost of transportation of documents or witnesses to or from foreign locations may increase the danger that discovery may be sought for the improper purpose of motivating settlement, rather than finding relevant and probative evidence. Objections to "abusive" discovery that foreign litigants advance should therefore receive the most careful consideration. In addition, we have long recognized the demands of comity in suits involving foreign states, either as parties or as sovereigns with a coordinate interest in the litigation. See *Hilton v. Guyot*, 159 U.S. 113 (1895). American courts should therefore take care to demonstrate due respect for any special problem confronted by the foreign litigant on account of its nationality or the location of its operations, and for any sovereign interest expressed by a foreign state. We do not articulate specific rules to guide this delicate task of adjudication.[30]

VI

In the case before us, the Magistrate and the Court of Appeals correctly refused to grant the broad protective order that petitioners requested. The Court of Appeals erred, however, in stating that the Evidence Convention does not apply to the pending discovery demands. This holding may be read as indicating that the Convention procedures are not even an option that is open to the District Court. It must be recalled, however, that the Convention's specification of duties in executing states creates corresponding rights in requesting states; holding that the Convention does not apply in this situation would deprive domestic litigants of access to evidence through treaty procedures to which the contracting states have assented. Moreover, such a rule would deny the foreign litigant a full and fair opportunity to demonstrate appropriate reasons for employing Convention procedures in the first instance, for some aspects of the discovery process.

Accordingly, the judgment of the Court of Appeals is vacated, and the case is remanded for further proceedings consistent with this opinion.

Justice BLACKMUN, with whom Justice BRENNAN, Justice MARSHALL, and Justice O'CONNOR join, concurring in part and dissenting in part.

Some might well regard the Court's decision in this case as an affront to the nations that have joined the United States in ratifying the Hague Convention on the Taking of Evidence Abroad in Civil or Commercial Matters.

* * *

I do agree with the Court's repudiation of the positions at both extremes of the spectrum with regard to the use of the Convention. Its rejection of the view that the Convention is not "applicable" at all to this case is surely correct: the Convention clearly ap-

---

30. Under the Hague Convention, a letter of request must specify "the evidence to be obtained or other judicial act to be performed," Art. 3, and must be in the language of the executing authority or be accompanied by a translation into that language. Art. 4, 23 U.S.T., at 2558-2559, T.I.A.S. 7444. Although the discovery request must be specific, the party seeking discovery may find it difficult or impossible to determine in advance what evidence is within the control of the party urging resort to the Convention and which parts of that evidence may qualify for international judicial assistance under the Convention. This information, however, is presumably within the control of the producing party from which discovery is sought. The district court may therefore require, in appropriate situations, that this party bear the burden of providing translations and detailed descriptions of relevant documents that are needed to assure prompt and complete production pursuant to the terms of the Convention.

plies to litigants as well as to third parties, and to requests for evidence located abroad, no matter where that evidence is actually "produced." The Court also correctly rejects the far opposite position that the Convention provides the exclusive means for discovery involving signatory countries. I dissent, however, because I cannot endorse the Court's case-by-case inquiry for determining whether to use Convention procedures and its failure to provide lower courts with any meaningful guidance for carrying out that inquiry. In my view, the Convention provides effective discovery procedures that largely eliminate the conflicts between United States and foreign law on evidence gathering. I therefore would apply a general presumption that, in most cases, courts should resort first to the Convention procedures. An individualized analysis of the circumstances of a particular case is appropriate only when it appears that it would be futile to employ the Convention or when its procedures prove to be unhelpful.

* * *

There are, however, some situations in which there is legitimate concern that certain documents cannot be made available under Convention procedures. Thirteen nations have made official declarations pursuant to Article 23 of the Convention, which permits a contracting state to limit its obligation to produce documents in response to a letter of request. These reservations may pose problems that would require a comity analysis in an individual case, but they are not so all-encompassing as the majority implies—they certainly do not mean that a "contracting party could unilaterally abrogate... the Convention's procedures." First, the reservations can apply only to letters of request for documents. Thus, an Article 23 reservation affects neither the most commonly used informal Convention procedures for taking of evidence by a consul or a commissioner nor formal requests for depositions or interrogatories. Second, although Article 23 refers broadly to "pre-trial discovery," the intended meaning of the term appears to have been much narrower than the normal United States usage.[21] The contracting parties for the most part have modified the declarations made pursuant to Article 23 to limit their reach.[22] See 7 Martindale-Hubbell Law Directory (pt. VII) 14-19 (1986). Indeed, the

---

21. The use of the term "pre-trial" seems likely to have been the product of a lack of communication. According to the United States delegates' report, at a meeting of the Special Commission on the Operation of the Evidence Convention held in 1978, delegates from civil-law countries revealed a "gross misunderstanding" of the meaning of "pre-trial discovery," thinking that it is something used before the institution of a suit to search for evidence that would lead to litigation. Report of the United States Delegation, 17 Int'l Legal Materials 1417, 1421 (1978). This misunderstanding is evidenced by the explanation of a French commentator that the "pre-trial discovery" exception was a reinforcement of the rule in Article 1 of the Convention that a letter of request "shall not be used to obtain evidence which is not intended for use in judicial proceedings, commenced or contemplated" and by his comment that the Article 23 exception referred to the collection of evidence in advance of litigation. Gouguenheim, Convention sur l'obtention des preuves à l'étranger en matière civile et commerciale, 96 Journal du Droit International 315, 319 (1969).

22. France has recently modified its declaration as follows: "The declaration made by the Republic of France pursuant to Article 23 relating to letters of request whose purpose is 'pre-trial discovery of documents' does not apply so long as the requested documents are limitatively enumerated in the letter of request and have a direct and clear nexus with the subject matter of the litigation." * * * Letter from J.B. Raimond, Minister of Foreign Affairs, France, to van den H.H. Broek, Minister of Foreign Affairs, The Netherlands (Dec. 24, 1986). The Danish declaration is more typical: "The declaration made by the Kingdom of Denmark in accordance with article 23 concerning 'Letters of Request issued for the purpose of obtaining pre-trial discovery of documents' shall apply to any Letter of Request which requires a person: a) to state what documents relevant to the proceedings to which the Letter of Request relates are, or have been, in his possession, other than particular documents specified in the Letter of Request; or b) to produce any documents other than particular doc-

emerging view of this exception to discovery is that it applies only to "requests that lack sufficient specificity or that have not been reviewed for relevancy by the requesting court." Oxman, The Choice Between Direct Discovery and Other Means of Obtaining Evidence Abroad: The Impact of the Hague Evidence Convention, 37 U. Miami L.Rev., at 777. Thus, in practice, a reservation is not the significant obstacle to discovery under the Convention that the broad wording of Article 23 would suggest.

* * *

Use of the Convention would help develop methods for transnational litigation by placing officials in a position to communicate directly about conflicts that arise during discovery, thus enabling them to promote a reduction in those conflicts. In a broader framework, courts that use the Convention will avoid foreign perceptions of unfairness that result when United States courts show insensitivity to the interests safeguarded by foreign legal regimes. Because of the position of the United States, economically, politically, and militarily, many countries may be reluctant to oppose discovery orders of United States courts. Foreign acquiescence to orders that ignore the Convention, however, is likely to carry a price tag of accumulating resentment, with the predictable long-term political cost that cooperation will be withheld in other matters. Use of the Convention is a simple step to take toward avoiding that unnecessary and undesirable consequence.

* * *

Notes

1. At the meeting of the same Special Commission referred to in Note 1 following *Schlunk*, there was extended discussion of *Aérospatiale*. Many delegates expressed the view that the decision was wrong and its concentration on U.S. sources was parochial. The Report simply noted these criticisms and "encouraged any States which have made...the reservation under Article 23 to limit the scope of such reservation." The Report also noted that "although some [lower federal court] decisions since *Aérospatiale* did not lead to the application of the Convention, courts in the US are undergoing a process of education..." The Commission's conclusion was "that in all Contracting States, whatever their views as to its exclusive application, priority should be given to the procedures offered by the Convention when evidence located abroad is being sought."

2. The Federal Rules Advisory Committee proposed an amendment to Federal Rule of Civil Procedure 26(a) adopting Justice's Blackmun's views in *Aérospatiale* and requiring use of the Evidence Convention unless "discovery conducted by such methods is inadequate." Reprinted in 127 F.R.D. 237, 318 (1989). The proposal triggered strong opposition and was abandoned. It now appears that there will be no revision of Rule 26 regarding the *Aérospatiale* problem. The only reference to the Evidence Convention is in proposed Rule 28(b), which deals with persons before whom depositions may be taken

---

uments which are specified in the Letter of Request, and which are likely to be in his possession." Declaration of July 23, 1980, 7 Martindale-Hubbell Law Directory (pt. VII) 15 (1986). The Federal Republic of Germany, Italy, Luxembourg, and Portugal continue to have unqualified Article 23 declarations, id., at 16-18, but the German Government has drafted new regulations that would "permit pretrial production of specified and relevant documents in response to letters of request." Brief for Anschuetz & Co. GmbH and Messerschmitt-Boelkow-Blohm GmbH as Amici Curiae 21.

in foreign countries: "Depositions may be taken in a foreign country (1) pursuant to any applicable treaty or convention..."

3. Justice Stevens focuses on the Convention's use of "may" rather than "shall" to buttress his conclusion that use of the Convention is optional. "May" appears in each of the four articles describing the four different methods of obtaining evidence from abroad under the Convention: article 1, letters of request; article 15, diplomatic officers taking evidence of the officers' own nationals; article 16, diplomatic officers taking evidence of nationals of other countries; article 17, commissioners taking evidence. Given these four permissible methods of obtaining evidence, would it make literal sense to state that any one of them "shall" be used?

4. Given the widespread distaste for American-style pre-trial discovery, article 23's impact is modest. First, article 23 refers only to "pre-trial discovery of documents," not to interrogatories or depositions. Second, of the 33 jurisdictions that, as of August 10, 2000, have ratified the Evidence Convention, twelve have made unmodified declarations under article 23. (Argentina, Australia, Bulgaria, Germany, Italy, Luxembourg, Monaco, Poland, Portugal, South Africa, Spain, and Macau (a special administrative region of China)). Seven have made no article 23 declaration. (Barbados, Czech Republic, Latvia, Slovakia, Israel, United States, and Venezuela). Fourteen have modified their article 23 declarations to permit enforcement of requests for specifically identified, relevant documents. (China, Cyprus, Denmark, Estonia, Finland, France, Hong Kong (a special administrative region of China), Mexico, Netherlands, Norway, Singapore, Sweden, Switzerland, and United Kingdom). Ten of these fourteen add a condition that the person requested cannot be asked to identify relevant documents. (Cyprus, Denmark, Finland, Hong Kong, Netherlands, Norway, Singapore, Sweden, Switzerland, and United Kingdom).

5. Justice Stevens' opinion refers to the fact that in 1964 "Congress amended the Judicial Code to grant foreign litigants, without any requirement of reciprocity, special assistance in obtaining evidence in the United States." One of sections amended is 28 U.S.C. § 1782(a):

> The district court of the district in which a person resides or is found may order him to give his testimony or statement or to produce a document or other thing for use in a proceeding in a foreign or international tribunal. The order may be made pursuant to a letter rogatory issued, or request made, by a foreign or international tribunal or upon the application of any interested person....

In re Application of Malev Hungarian Airlines, 964 F.2d 97 (2d Cir. 1992), cert. denied, 506 U.S. 861 (1992), permitted a foreign party, defending a suit brought in Hungary, to depose employees of the American plaintiff and obtain documents, and held that it was not necessary that the 1782 applicant first request such discovery in the Hungarian court. In re Application of Asta Medica, S.A., 981 F.2d 1 (1st Cir. 1992), however, held that "a litigant requesting assistance under Section 1782 has to show that the information sought in the United States would be discoverable under foreign law" (981 F.2d at 7), otherwise "a United States party involved in litigation in a foreign country with limited pre-trial discovery will be placed at a substantial disadvantage vis-à-vis the foreign party" (id. at 5) and "foreign countries may be offended by the use of United States procedure to circumvent their own procedures and laws." (Id. at 6). In the light of *Asta Medica*, which agreed with similar rulings in the 3rd and 11th circuits, if the evidence is not discoverable under foreign law, is the foreign applicant's alternative to file a suit in the United States parallel to the foreign proceedings? For the contrary view, that under § 1782 it is not necessary to make a threshold showing that the discovery sought would be available under the laws of the foreign jurisdiction, see In re Application of Bayer, 146 F.3d 188 (2d Cir. 1998).

In re Letter Rogatory from the First Court of First Instance in Civil Matters, Caracas, Venezuela, 42 F.3d 308, 310-11 (5th Cir. 1995), although approving of a determination whether the evidence would be discoverable in the foreign forum when the request comes from a foreign litigant, holds that "no such discoverability determination is required" when the request comes from a foreign court because the purpose of requiring discoverability abroad is "fear of offending the forum nation by furthering a scheme to obviate that nation's discovery rules." Suppose, however, the foreign court would not permit the requested discovery but would admit the evidence discovered in the United States? See South Carolina Ins. Co. v. Assurantie Maatschappij de Zeven Provincien NV, [1986] 3 W.L.R. 398 (H.L.) noted infra page 162. Europa S.A. v. R. Esmerian, Inc., 51 F.3d 1095, 1100 (2d Cir. 1995), holds that "a district court's inquiry into the discoverability of requested materials should consider only authoritative proof that a foreign tribunal would reject evidence obtained with the aid of section 1782." See Jeffery A. Wortman, In search of Discovery: The Split Between the Circuits Surrounding a Threshold Discoverability Requirement to Provide Assistance under 28 U.S.C. § 1782, 30 Tex. Int'l L.J. 583 (1995).

In re Request for Int'l Judicial Assistance for the Federative Republic of Brazil, 963 F.2d 702 (2d Cir. 1991), held that 28 U.S.C. § 1782 may be invoked in advance of foreign adjudicative proceedings only when such proceedings are imminent, but notes that the D.C. Circuit has a "more relaxed standard" that the foreign proceedings "be within reasonable contemplation."

National Broadcasting Co. v. Bear Stearns & Co., 165 F.3d 184 (2d Cir. 1999), held that a private arbitral panel in Mexico is not "a foreign or international tribunal" and therefore § 1782 does not apply to facilitate discovery in that proceeding. Accord, Application of the Republic of Kazakhstan v. Biedermann International, 168 F.3d 880 (5th Cir. 2000). For the contrary view see Hans Smit, American Assistance to Litigation in Foreign and International Tribunals: Section 1782 of Title 28 of the U.S.C. Revisited, 25 Syracuse J. Intl L & Com. 1, 6-8 (1998).

6. The reference in footnote 29 of Justice Steven's opinion to the Restatement is to a tentative draft of Restatement (Third) of Foreign Relations Law of the United States. The provision referred to is § 442 in the final version and is set out before the next principal case. The wording of the Reporter's Note referred to is slightly changed.

7. The letters "GmbH" after the names of German amici curiae in footnote 22 of Justice Blackmun's opinion, appear frequently in these materials. They stand for the words "Gessellschaft mit beschränkter Haftung," meaning "company with limited liability," similar to "Inc." after the name of an American company.

8. Lower court cases following *Aérospatiale* have generally echoed the majority's hostility to the Convention. Hudson v. Hermann Pfauter GmbH & Co., 117 F.R.D. 33 (N.D.N.Y. 1987) started out in the opposite direction by expressing a preference for Justice Blackmun's analysis (id. at 37) and placing the burden of proof "on the party opposing the use of Convention procedures." (Id. at 38). A long line of subsequent cases, however, places the burden of proof on the proponent of Convention procedures. See, e.g., Doster v. Carl Schenk A.G., 141 F.R.D. 50, 51 (M.D. N.C. 1991). Some courts have simply rejected Convention procedures to avoid discovery delay. See, e.g., Benton Graphics v. Uddeholm Corp., 118 F.R.D. 386, 391 (D. N.J. 1987).

9. The United Kingdom's article 23 reservation (see note 4 supra) and the many references that will appear in English cases in these materials to pre-trial discovery in

United States courts as a "fishing expedition," are ironic in the light of Order 24, rule 1, Rules of the Supreme Court, for England and Wales: "After the close of pleadings in an action begun by writ there shall...be discovery by the parties to the action of the documents which are or have been in their possession, custody or power relating to matters in question in the action." 1 Supreme Court Practice 432 (1992).

Under new English procedural rules, prospective litigants are expected to cooperate in discovery before filing an action. Courts have discretion to order pre-action discovery "where such disclosure is desirable to dispose fairly of the anticipated proceedings, avoid the need for litigation or save costs." Edward Hood, It's Changing Over There, March/April 2000 Business Law 10, 12.

Under an "Anton Piller order" (referring to Anton Piller K.G. v. Manufacturing Processes Ltd., [1976] 1 All E.R. 779 (Ct. App. 1975)), a party may obtain, after ex parte application, a decree permitting the applicant to enter the other party's premises and inspect, remove, or make copies of documents. There is a requirement that the applicant for an Anton Piller order show a prima facie case and the likelihood that the other party would destroy evidence if given notice before the order issued. See Alexander J. Black, "Pretrial Discovery in Scotland, England and Canada," 39 Netherlands Int'l L. Rev. 267, 280 (1992).

It is the civil law practice to develop a case ("dossier de plaidoirie" or "pleading file" in France) through a series of hearings, eliminating the common-law contrast between pre-trial discovery and evidence presented during trial.

Restatement (Third) of Foreign Relations Law of the United States (1986)

[Copyright 1987 by The American Law Institute. Reprinted with the permission of the American Law Institute.]

§ 442. Requests for Disclosure: Law of the United States

(1)(a) A court or agency in the United States, when authorized by statute or rule of court, may order a person subject to its jurisdiction to produce documents, objects, or other information relevant to an action or investigation, even if the information or the person in possession of the information is outside the United States.

(b) Failure to comply with an order to produce information may subject the person to whom the order is directed to sanctions, including finding of contempt, dismissal of a claim or defense, or default judgment, or may lead to a determination that the facts to which the order was addressed are as asserted by the opposing party.

(c) In deciding whether to issue an order directing production of information located abroad, and in framing such an order, a court or agency in the United States should take into account the importance to the investigation or litigation of the documents or other information requested; the degree of specificity of the request; whether the information originated in the United States; the availability of alternative means of securing the information; and the extent to which noncompliance with the request would undermine important interests of the United States, or compliance with the request would undermine important interests of the state where the information is located.

(2) If disclosure of information located outside the United States is prohibited by a law, regulation, or order of a court or other authority of the state in which the information or prospective witness is located, or of the state of which a prospective witness is a national,

> (a) a court or agency in the United States may require the person to whom the order is directed to make a good faith effort to secure permission from the foreign authorities to make the information available;
>
> (b) a court or agency should not ordinarily impose sanctions of contempt, dismissal, or default on a party that has failed to comply with the order for production, except in cases of deliberate concealment or removal of information or of failure to make a good faith effort in accordance with paragraph (a);
>
> (c) a court or agency may, in appropriate cases, make findings of fact adverse to a party that has failed to comply with the order for production, even if that party has made a good faith effort to secure permission from the foreign authorities to make the information available and that effort has been unsuccessful.

Notes

1. The reference in subsection 1(a) to a "court or agency" suggests that in the event of discovery of evidence located abroad, a court should supervise the process and take a more active role than is normally the case under Federal Rules of Civil Procedure. Rule 26(b)(1) provides that the "[p]arties may obtain discovery" in conformity with the Rules without leave of the court. Rule 34, as quoted in the next principal case, was amended in 1970 to dispense with the need for a court order. The use of the term "relevant" in 1(a) suggests that discovery of evidence abroad should meet a higher standard than permitted by FRCP 26(b)(1), which provides that "[t]he information sought need not be admissible at the trial if the information sought appears reasonably calculated to lead to the discovery of admissible evidence." Perhaps, in view of the House of Lords opinion in In re Asbestos Insurance Coverage Cases, principal case infra this section, 1(a) should say "relevant and admissible."

2. Subsection (2) is addressed to the next topic, the effect of blocking statutes on discovery orders and sanctions. Subsection 2(c) permits "findings of fact adverse to a party that has failed to comply" with a discovery order, even if that party has made a good faith effort to obtain a waiver of a foreign blocking statute. Comment f states that "[s]uch a finding does not reflect a shift in the burden of proof, and is appropriate only when there is reason to believe that the information, if disclosed, would support a finding adverse to the noncomplying party…." Does this accurately reflect the standards set out in the next principal case?

Societe Internationale Pour Participations Industrielles Et Commerciales, S.A. v. Rogers
357 U.S. 197 (1958)

Mr. Justice HARLAN delivered the opinion of the Court.

The question before us is whether, in the circumstances of this case, the District Court erred in dismissing, with prejudice, a complaint in a civil action as to a plaintiff that had failed to comply fully with a pretrial production order.

This issue comes to us in the context of an intricate litigation. Section 5(b) of the Trading with the Enemy Act, 50 U.S.C. Appendix, § 5(b), sets forth the conditions under which the United States during a period of war or national emergency may seize " * * * any property or interest of any foreign country or national * * *." Acting under this section, the Alien Property Custodian during World War II assumed control of assets which were found by the Custodian to be "owned by or held for the benefit of" I.G. Farbenindustrie, a German firm and a then enemy national. These assets, valued at more than $100,000,000, consisted of cash in American banks and approximately 90% of the capital stock of General Aniline & Film Corporation, a Delaware corporation. In 1948 petitioner, a Swiss holding company also known as I. G. Chemie or Interhandel, brought suit under §9(a) of the Trading with the Enemy Act, 50 U.S.C.Appendix, §9(a), against the Attorney General, as successor to the Alien Property Custodian, and the Treasurer of the United States, to recover these assets. This section authorizes recovery of seized assets by "[a]ny person not an enemy or ally of enemy" to the extent of such person's interest in the assets. Petitioner claimed that it had owned the General Aniline stock and cash at the time of vesting and hence, as the national of a neutral power, was entitled under §9(a) to recovery.

The Government both challenged petitioner's claim of ownership and asserted that in any event petitioner was an "enemy" within the meaning of the Act since it was intimately connected with I. G. Farben and hence was affected with "enemy taint" despite its "neutral" incorporation. More particularly, the Government alleged that from the time of its incorporation in 1928, petitioner had conspired with I. G. Farben, H. Sturzenegger & Cie, a Swiss banking firm, and others "[t]o conceal, camouflage, and cloak the ownership, control and domination by I. G. Farben of properties and interests located in countries, including the United States, other than Germany, in order to avoid seizure and confiscation in the event of war between such countries and Germany."

At an early stage of the litigation the Government moved under Rule 34 of the Federal Rules of Civil Procedure, 28 U.S.C.A., for an order requiring petitioner to make available for inspection and copying a large number of the banking records of Sturzenegger & Cie. Rule 34, in conjunction with Rule 26(b), provides that upon a motion "showing good cause therefor," a court may order a party to produce for inspection nonprivileged documents relevant to the subject matter of pending litigation "* * * which are in his possession, custody, or control * * *." In support of its motion the Government alleged that the records sought were relevant to showing the true ownership of the General Aniline stock and that they were within petitioner's control because petitioner and Sturzenegger were substantially identical. Petitioner did not dispute the general relevancy of the Sturzenegger documents but denied that it controlled them. The District Court granted the Government's motion, holding, among other things, that petitioner's "control" over the records had been prima facie established.

Thereafter followed a number of motions by petitioner to be relieved of production on the ground that disclosure of the required bank records would violate Swiss penal laws and consequently might lead to imposition of criminal sanctions, including fine and imprisonment, on those responsible for disclosure. The Government in turn moved under Rule 37(b)(2) of the Federal Rules of Civil Procedure to dismiss the complaint because of petitioner's noncompliance with the production order. During this period the Swiss Federal Attorney, deeming that disclosure of these records in accordance with the production order would constitute a violation of Article 273 of the Swiss Penal Code, prohibiting economic espionage, and Article 47 of the Swiss Bank Law, relating to secrecy of banking records, "confiscated" the Sturzenegger records. This "confiscation" left possession of the records in Sturzenegger and amounted to an interdiction on

Sturzenegger's transmission of the records to third persons. The upshot of all this was that the District Court, before finally ruling on petitioner's motion for relief from the production order and on the Government's motion to dismiss the complaint, referred the matter to a Special Master for findings as to the nature of the Swiss laws claimed by petitioner to block production and as to petitioner's good faith in seeking to achieve compliance with the court's order.

The Report of the Master bears importantly on our disposition of this case. It concluded that the Swiss Government had acted in accordance with its own established doctrines in exercising preventive police power by constructive seizure of the Sturzenegger records, and found that there was "* * * no proof, or any evidence at all of collusion between plaintiff and the Swiss Government in the seizure of the papers herein." Noting that the burden was on petitioner to show good faith in its efforts to comply with the production order, and taking as the test of good faith whether petitioner had attempted all which a reasonable man would have undertaken in the circumstances to comply with the order, the Master found that "* * * the plaintiff has sustained the burden of proof placed upon it and has shown good faith in its efforts [to comply with the production order] in accordance with the foregoing test."

These findings of the Master were confirmed by the District Court. Nevertheless the court, in February 1953, granted the Government's motion to dismiss the complaint * * *. [To allow petitioner more time to obtain waivers from the Swiss Government, the effective date of the dismissal order was twice suspended, once by the District Court and once by the Court of Appeals. Although further documents were released during this period, petitioner did not fully comply with the District Court's order. The District Court directed final dismissal of the action, the Court of Appeals affirmed, and certiorari was granted.]

I

We consider first petitioner's contention that the District Court erred in issuing the production order because the requirement of Rule 34, that a party ordered to produce documents must be in "control" of them, was not here satisfied. Without intimating any view upon the merits of the litigation, we accept as amply supported by the evidence the findings of the two courts below that, apart from the effect of Swiss law, the Sturenegger documents are within petitioner's control. The question then becomes: Do the interdictions of Swiss law bar a conclusion that petitioner had "control" of these documents within the meaning of Rule 34?

We approach this question in light of the findings below that the Swiss penal laws did in fact limit petitioner's ability to satisfy the production order because of the criminal sanctions to which those producing the records would have been exposed. Still we do not view this situation as fully analogous to one where documents required by a production order have ceased to exist or have been taken into the actual possession of a third person not controlled by the party ordered to produce, and without that party's complicity. The "confiscation" of these records by the Swiss authorities adds nothing to the dimensions of the problem under consideration, for possession of the records stayed where it was and the possibility of criminal prosecution for disclosure was of course present before the confiscation order was issued.

In its broader scope, the problem before us requires consideration of the policies underlying the Trading with the Enemy Act. If petitioner can prove its record title to General Aniline stock, it certainly is open to the Government to show that petitioner itself is the captive of interests whose direct ownership would bar recovery. This possibility of enemy taint of nationals of neutral powers, particularly of holding companies with intricate financial structures, which asserted rights to American assets was of deep concern to the Congress when it broadened the Trading with the Enemy Act in 1941 " * * * to reach enemy interests which masqueraded under those innocent fronts." *Clark v. Uebersee Finanz-Korp.*, 332 U.S. 480, 485.

In view of these considerations, to hold broadly that petitioner's failure to produce the Sturzenegger records because of fear of punishment under the laws of its sovereign precludes a court from finding that petitioner had "control" over them, and thereby from ordering their production, would undermine congressional policies made explicit in the 1941 amendments, and invite efforts to place ownership of American assets in persons or firms whose sovereign assures secrecy of records. The District Court here concluded that the Sturzenegger records might have a vital influence upon this litigation insofar as they shed light upon petitioner's confused background. Petitioner is in a most advantageous position to plead with its own sovereign for relaxation of penal laws or for adoption of plans which will at the least achieve a significant measure of compliance with the production order, and indeed to that end it has already made significant progress. United States courts should be free to require claimants of seized assets who face legal obstacles under the laws of their own countries to make all such efforts to the maximum of their ability where the requested records promise to bear out or dispel any doubt the Government may introduce as to true ownership of the assets.

We do not say that this ruling would apply to every situation where a party is restricted by law from producing documents over which it is otherwise shown to have control. Rule 34 is sufficiently flexible to be adapted to the exigencies of particular litigation. The propriety of the use to which it is put depends upon the circumstances of a given case, and we hold only that accommodation of the Rule in this instance to the policies underlying the Trading with the Enemy Act justified the action of the District Court in issuing this production order.

II

We consider next the source of the authority of a District Court of dismiss a complaint for failure of a plaintiff to comply with a production order. The District Court found power to dismiss under Rule 37(b)(2)(iii) of the Federal Rules of Civil Procedure as well as in the general equity powers of a federal court.

* * *

Rule 37 describes the consequences of a refusal to make discovery. Subsection (b), which is entitled "Failure to Comply With Order," provides in pertinent part:

"(2) * * * If any party * * * refuses to obey * * * an order made under Rule 34 to produce any document or other thing for inspection * * *, the court may make such orders in regard to the refusal as are just, and among others the following:

"(iii) An order striking out pleadings or parts thereof * * *, or dismissing the action or proceeding or any part thereof * * *."

* * *

For purposes of subdivision (b)(2) of Rule 37, we think that a party "refuses to obey" simply by failing to comply with an order. So construed the Rule allows a court all the flexibility it might need in framing an order appropriate to a particular situation. Whatever its reasons, petitioner did not comply with the production order. Such reasons, and the willfulness or good faith of petitioner, can hardly affect the fact of noncompliance and are relevant only to the path which the District Court might follow in dealing with petitioner's failure to comply.

III

We turn to the remaining question, whether the District Court properly exercised its powers under Rule 37(b) by dismissing this complaint despite the findings that petitioner had not been in collusion with the Swiss authorities to block inspection of the Sturzenegger records, and had in good faith made diligent efforts to execute the production order.

* * *

The provisions of Rule 37 which are here involved must be read in light of the provisions of the Fifth Amendment that no person shall be deprived of property without due process of law, and more particularly against the opinions of this Court in *Hovey v. Elliott*, 167 U.S. 409, and *Hammond Packing Co. v. State of Arkansas*, 212 U.S. 322. These decisions establish that there are constitutional limitations upon the power of courts, even in aid of their own valid processes, to dismiss an action without affording a party the opportunity for a hearing on the merits of his cause. The authors of Rule 37 were well aware of these constitutional considerations. See Notes of Advisory Committee on Rules, Rule 37, 28 U.S.C. (1952 ed.) p. 4325, 28 U.S.C.A.

In *Hovey v. Elliott*, supra, it was held that due process was denied a defendant whose answer was struck, thereby leading to a decree *pro confesso* without a hearing on the merits, because of his refusal to obey a court order pertinent to the suit. This holding was substantially modified by *Hammond Packing Co. v. State of Arkansas*, supra, where the Court ruled that a state court, consistently with the Due Process Clause of the Fourteenth Amendment, could strike the answer of and render a default judgment against a defendant who refused to produce documents in accordance with a pretrial order. The *Hovey* case was distinguished on grounds that the defendant there was denied his right to defend "as a mere punishment"; due process was found preserved in *Hammond* on the reasoning that the State simply utilized a permissible presumption that the refusal to produce material evidence "* * * was but an admission of the want of merit in the asserted defense." 212 U.S. at pages 350-351. But the Court took care to emphasize that the defendant had not been penalized "* * * for a failure to do that which it may not have been in its power to do." All the State had required "was a bona fide effort to comply with an order * * *, and therefore any reasonable showing of an inability to comply would have satisfied the requirements * * *" of the order. 212 U.S. at page 347.

These two decisions leave open the question whether Fifth Amendment due process is violated by the striking of a complaint because of a plaintiff's inability, despite good-faith efforts, to comply with a pretrial production order. The presumption utilized by the Court in the Hammond case might well falter under such circumstances. Certainly substantial constitutional questions are provoked by such action. Their gravity is accented in the present case where petitioner, though cast in the role of plaintiff, cannot be deemed to be in the customary role of a party invoking the aid of a court to vindicate rights asserted against another. Rather petitioner's position is more analogous to that of a defendant, for it belatedly challenges the Government's action by now protesting against a seizure and seeking the recovery of assets which were summarily possessed by the Alien Property Custodian without the opportunity for protest by any party claiming that seizure was unjustified under the Trading with the Enemy Act. Past decisions of this Court emphasize that this summary power to seize property which is believed to be enemy-owned is rescued from constitutional invalidity under the Due Process and Just Compensation Clauses of the Fifth Amendment only by those provisions of the Act which afford a non-enemy claimant a later judicial hearing as to the propriety of the seizure.

The findings below, and what has been shown as to petitioner's extensive efforts at compliance, compel the conclusion on this record that petitioner's failure to satisfy fully the requirements of this production order was due to inability fostered neither by its own conduct nor by circumstances within its control. It is hardly debatable that fear of criminal prosecution constitutes a weighty excuse for nonproduction, and this excuse is not weakened because the laws preventing compliance are those of a foreign sovereign. Of course this situation should be distinguished from one where a party claims that compliance with a court's order will reveal facts which may provide the basis for criminal prosecution of that party under the penal laws of a foreign sovereign thereby shown to have been violated. Cf. *United States v. Murdock*, 284 U.S. 141, 149. Here the findings below establish that the very fact of compliance by disclosure of banking records will itself constitute the initial violation of Swiss laws.

* * *

In view of the findings in this case, the position in which petitioner stands in this litigation, and the serious constitutional questions we have noted, we think that Rule 37 should not be construed to authorize dismissal of this complaint because of petitioner's noncompliance with a pretrial production order when it has been established that failure to comply has been due to inability, and not to willfulness, bad faith, or any fault of petitioner.

This is not to say that petitioner will profit through its inability to tender the records called for. In seeking recovery of the General Aniline stock and other assets, petitioner recognizes that it carries the ultimate burden of proof of showing itself not to be an "enemy" within the meaning of the Trading with the Enemy Act. The Government already has disputed its right to recovery by relying on information obtained through seized records of I. G. Farben, documents obtained through petitioner, and depositions taken of persons affiliated with petitioner. It may be that in a trial on the merits, petitioner's inability to produce specific information will prove a serious handicap in dispelling doubt the Government might be able to inject into the case. It may be that in the absence of complete disclosure by petitioner, the District Court would be justified in drawing inferences unfavorable to petitioner as to particular events. So much indeed petitioner concedes. But these problems go to the adequacy of petitioner's proof and should not on this record preclude petitioner from being able to contest on the merits.

On remand, the District Court possesses wide discretion to proceed in whatever manner it deems most effective. It may desire to afford the Government additional opportunity to challenge petitioner's good faith. It may wish to explore plans looking towards fuller compliance. Or it may decide to commence at once trial on the merits. We decide only that on this record dismissal of the complaint with prejudice was not justified. The judgment of the Court of Appeals is reversed and the case is remanded to the District Court for further proceedings in conformity with this opinion.

Judgment of Court of Appeals reversed and case remanded to the District Court with directions.

Mr. Justice CLARK took no part in the consideration or decision of this case.

Notes

1. "Burden of proof" can be separated into its two components of litigation risk, the risk of non-production of evidence and the risk of non-persuasion of the fact finder by the evidence that is produced. There are three possibilities as to how burden of proof can be affected because a party, despite good faith efforts, is unable to secure a waiver of a foreign blocking statute. One, the entire burden may be shifted to that party, both the risk of non-production and the risk of non-persuasion. Two, the risk of non-persuasion only may be shifted, the risk of non-production remaining on the party who otherwise would have it. Three, no part of the burden of proof is shifted and the party who cannot secure the waiver and produce evidence simply suffers the natural consequence of being unable to rebut evidence introduced by the other party.

Which if these three possibilities is reflected in the preceding principal case? Which is reflected in Restatement of Foreign Relations § 442?

The principal case was settled in 1964 by a sale of General Aniline stock, with 30 per cent of the proceeds going to Interhandel and the rest to the United States. See Societe Internationale v. Kennedy, 231 F. Supp. 132 (D.D.C. 1964); Andreas F. Lowenfeld, International Litigation and the Quest for Reasonableness 149 (1996).

2. A Swiss federal decree of December 16, 1996 lifted the banking secrecy laws for the purpose of investigating assets that were transferred to Swiss companies or persons during the Nazi regime.

3. The preceding principal case focuses on what sanctions are permitted for failure to obey an order to produce evidence when that failure is caused by a foreign blocking statute. The next two cases examine how such a statute may affect the decision to issue the order in the first place.

In re Uranium Antitrust Litigation
480 F.Supp. 1138 (N.D. Ill. 1979)

Memorandum Decision

MARSHALL, District Judge.

On February 27, 1979, we entered Joint Pretrial Order No. 5 in an effort to narrow and ripen the issues surrounding the parties' discovery demands for documents located in foreign countries. We ordered that, by March 28, 1979, all parties should either comply with outstanding discovery demands for "foreign documents" or file restated objections to the production of such documents, including specific and particularized objections to demands for any such documents whose production was said to be forbidden by foreign law. The term "foreign documents" was defined to include all documents whose disclosure was in any way affected by foreign law.

* * *

Ten * * * defendants have raised foreign law objections and have withheld foreign documents. Those defendants are Rio Algom Corporation (Rio U.S.), Engelhard Minerals and Chemicals Corporation (Engelhard), Denison Mines, Ltd. (Denison Canada), Denison Mines, Inc. (Denison U.S.), Gulf Oil Corporation (Gulf), Gulf Minerals Canada Limited (GMCL), Getty Oil Company (Getty), Utah International, Inc. (Utah), Noranda Mines, Ltd. (Noranda), and Federal Resources Corporation (Federal). In the three TVA actions, in which eight of the thirteen named defendants have appeared, seven of the active defendants have invoked foreign nondisclosure laws as a bar to production. Only one of those defendants, Uranerz Canada Ltd. (Uranerz), is not a defendant in the Westinghouse action.

Westinghouse has moved for production orders pursuant to Rule 37(a), F.R.Civ.P., against the ten non-producing defendants listed above, and TVA has similarly moved against the seven non-producing defendants in its case. The following table connects each defendant with the country whose foreign law is invoked as a bar to production. Defendants who are named in both the Westinghouse and TVA motions are identified by an asterisk (*)

Canada	Australia	Switzerland	South Africa
Denison Canada*	Engelhard*	Gulf*	Engelhard*
Denison U.S.	Getty	GMCL*	
Federal	Noranda*		
Rio U.S.*	Utah		
Uranerz			
Noranda*			
Gulf*			
GMCL*			

Five sets of foreign laws are involved. Three of those are regulations or statutes of Canada, Australia and South Africa which were enacted or modified during the period from 1976 to 1978 for the express purpose of frustrating the jurisdiction of the United States courts over the activities of the alleged international uranium cartel. Those laws generally prohibit the production of any document relating to uranium marketing activities from 1972 through 1975 and also prohibit communications that would result in the disclosure of the contents of such documents. The fourth statute is the Ontario Business Records Protection Act, which was enacted in Canada in 1947. That Act forbids the production of any business records requested by a foreign tribunal if a provincial court issues an order to that effect. Because no such order has been sought or issued to date, this Act has little or no applicability here. The final statutes are Articles 162 and 273 of the Swiss Penal Code, which prohibit the disclosure of a "business or manufacturing secret." Because a violation can be avoided if a person with a secrecy interest in some matter consents to its disclosure, and because Gulf and GMCL expect to secure all necessary consents within a short span of time, the Swiss statutes also have limited applicability here. All of these statutes impose criminal penalties for their violation, including fines and imprisonment.

* * *

The parties have offered differing views on the proper standards to be applied in deciding whether to issue a production order for documents located in a country which prohibits their removal or disclosure. Plaintiffs argue that Rule 37 requires a bifurcated two-step procedure for compelling production and imposing sanctions. They contend that the question of whether a discovery order should issue is solely a matter of American law; foreign nondisclosure laws are only relevant in deciding whether sanctions should be imposed for non-compliance. Defendants argue that we should instead use a balancing test to consider all circumstances, including foreign law, before entering an order compelling discovery. We take a middle course between these opposing positions, finding that a number of factors must be considered before issuing a production order, but that the inquiry is not as comprehensive as defendants suggest.

At the outset, we should identify the type of jurisdiction exercised by a court in issuing an order to produce foreign documents. In the field of foreign relations law, two types of jurisdiction have been defined. Prescriptive jurisdiction refers to the capacity of a state under international law to make a rule of law. It is exemplified by the enactment of the Federal Rules of Civil Procedure, e.g., Rule 37. Enforcement jurisdiction, on the other hand, refers to the capacity of a state under international law to enforce a rule of law. When a court enters an order compelling production of documents under Rule 37, it exercises its enforcement jurisdiction. Restatement, Second, Foreign Relations Law of the United States, § 6 (1965); Onkelinx, Conflict of International Jurisdiction: Ordering the Production of Documents in Violation of the Law of the Situs, 64 Nw.L.Rev. 487, 495 (1969). The jurisdiction of American courts is unquestioned when they order their own nationals to produce documents located within this country. But jurisdiction is less certain when American courts order a defendant to produce documents located abroad, especially when the country in which the documents are situated prohibits their disclosure.

As a general rule, a court has the power to order a person subject to its jurisdiction to perform an act in another state. Restatement, Second, Conflict of Laws, § 53 (1971). There are two preconditions for the exercise of this power. First, the court must have personal jurisdiction over the person. Second, the person must have control over the documents. *United States v. First National City Bank*, 396 F.2d 897, 900-01 (2d Cir. 1968); *In Re Grand Jury Subpoenas Duces Tecum Addressed to Canadian International Paper Co.*, 72 F.Supp. 1013 (S.D.N.Y.1947). The location of the documents is irrelevant. 72 F.Supp. at 1020.

On the issue of control, there are certain corollary principles which apply to multinational corporations. The test for determining whether an American court can order an American parent corporation to produce the documents of its foreign subsidiary was stated in *In Re Investigation of World Arrangements*, 13 F.R.D. 280, 285 (D.D.C.1952): "[I]f a corporation has power, either directly or indirectly, through another corporation or series of corporations, to elect a majority of the directors of another corporation, such corporation may be deemed a parent corporation and in control of the corporation whose directors it has the power to elect to office." Thus, for example, if the parent owns more than 50% Of the foreign subsidiary's stock, it possesses the necessary control. W. Fugate, Foreign Commerce and the Antitrust Laws, 116 (2d ed. 1973).

The test is less clear in situations where an order is directed to the American subsidiary of a foreign corporation to produce documents from its head office located abroad. One court has held that a subpoena duces tecum was enforceable if it was served on the subsidiary's offices in the United States, even though the corporation's board of directors had passed a resolution prohibiting the removal of the requested records from Canada and even though all the board members were residents of Canada. *In Re Grand Jury Subpoenas Duces Tecum*, supra, 72 F.Supp. at 1020. The court's reasoning as to how the American officers had control over the withheld documents seems to rest on the theory that it was sufficient that the documents were in the possession of the corporation and that a subpoena had been served on some of its officers. See Onkelinx, supra, 64 Nw.L.Rev. at 505-06. More helpful guidance can be drawn from *Societe Internationale v. McGranery*, 111 F.Supp. 435, 440-42 (D.D.C.1953), in which the court held that plaintiff, a Swiss corporation, had control over the papers of its Swiss-based bank,

H. Sturzenegger & Cie.[3] The court attached significance to the fact that Sturzenegger was a director and officer of plaintiff and was "perhaps" a dominant personality in plaintiff's affairs. After an extensive examination of the corporate affiliations of the two partners, the court concluded that "[t]hrough the interlocked web of corporate organization, management and finance there runs the thread of a fundamental identity of individuals in the pattern of control." 111 F.Supp. at 442. Thus, the issue of control is more a question of fact than of law, and it rests on a determination of whether the defendant has practical and actual managerial control over, or shares such control with, its affiliate, regardless of the formalities of corporate organization.

Once personal jurisdiction over the person and control over the documents by the person are present, a United States court has power to order production of the documents. The existence of a conflicting foreign law which prohibits the disclosure of the requested documents does not prevent the exercise of this power. This proposition has been accepted by both the American Law Institute (Restatement, Second, Foreign Relations Law of the United States, §39), and by the Supreme Court, *Societe Internationale v. Rogers*, 357 U.S. 197 (1958). However, American courts should not ignore the fact that such a law exists. When two states, both having jurisdiction, prescribe inconsistent conduct, American courts have developed certain rules of self-restraint governing the appropriate exercise of their power. *United States v. First National City Bank*, supra, 396 F.2d at 901. Because *Societe Internationale* dominates the field and sets forth the pertinent considerations to be weighed when such conflicts arise, we analyze it at length.

* * *

To summarize the preceding discussion, we have concluded that we possess the power to enter an order against defendants under Rule 37(a) compelling them to produce documents located abroad if the particular defendant is within the personal jurisdiction of this court and has control over the requested documents. *Societe* teaches that the decision whether to exercise that power is a discretionary one which is informed by three main factors: 1) the importance of the policies underlying the United States statute which forms the basis for the plaintiffs' claims; 2) the importance of the requested documents in illuminating key elements of the claims; and 3) the degree of flexibility in the foreign nation's application of its nondisclosure laws. Relying on the Court's additional suggestion that each case must depend upon its particular facts, several defendants urge that we consider several other factors that we have not yet discussed. However, in the circumstances of this case, we find that these other factors are of limited or no utility.

Several defendants cite the Restatement, Second, Foreign Relations Law of the United States, §40(a) or rely on broad notions of "international comity" for the proposition that we should balance the vital national interests of the United States and the foreign countries to determine which interests predominate. Aside from the fact that the judiciary has little expertise, or perhaps even authority, to evaluate the economic and social policies of a foreign country, such a balancing test is inherently unworkable in this case. The competing interests here display an irreconcilable conflict on precisely

---

3. The court's holding on the control issue was accepted both by the Court of Appeals, Societe Internationale v. Brownell, 96 U.S.App.D.C. 232, 236, 225 F.2d 532, 536 (D.C.Cir. 1955), and by the Supreme Court, Societe Internationale v. Rogers, 357 U.S. 197, 204, 78 S.Ct. 1087, 2 L.Ed.2d 1255 (1958).

the same plane of national policy. Westinghouse seeks to enforce this nation's antitrust laws against an alleged international marketing arrangement among uranium producers, and to that end has sought documents located in foreign countries where those producers conduct their business. In specific response to this and other related litigation in the American courts, three foreign governments have enacted nondisclosure legislation which is aimed at nullifying the impact of American antitrust legislation by prohibiting access to those same documents. It is simply impossible to judicially "balance" these totally contradictory and mutually negating actions.

All defendants rely on a line of Second Circuit cases which were decided after *Societe* and which suggest that a district court should not order production if the order would cause a party to violate a foreign law. *First National City Bank v. Internal Revenue Service*, 271 F.2d 616 (2d Cir. 1959); *Ings v. Ferguson*, 282 F.2d 149 (2d Cir. 1960); *Application of Chase Manhattan Bank*, 297 F.2d 611 (2d Cir. 1962). Plaintiffs rely in turn on a Tenth Circuit decision which takes a contrary view. *Arthur Andersen & Co. v. Finesilver*, 546 F.2d 338 (10th Cir. 1976). We believe that the Tenth Circuit decision is more closely in harmony with the principles established in *Societe*.

Gulf and Uranerz urge that the production orders sought by plaintiffs are barred by the act of state doctrine because they would interfere with the conduct of our foreign relations by the Executive Branch. However, the act of state doctrine is not applicable here. That doctrine bars an American court from questioning the validity of the act of a foreign sovereign when that act is done within the sovereign's territory. *Underhill v. Hernandez*, 168 U.S. 250 (1897); *Banco Nacional de Cuba v. Sabbatino*, 376 U.S. 398 (1964). Plaintiffs have not challenged the validity of any of the foreign nondisclosure laws which are relied on by defendants. The issue is not whether those laws are valid, but rather, conceding their validity, whether they excuse defendants from complying with a production order.

Many defendants ask us to consider communications from foreign governments to the U. S. State Department which have protested the issuance of production orders by American courts in similar circumstances. We believe those communications are relevant to the decision whether to issue a production order only insofar as they indicate the degree of accommodation or adjustment which the foreign government may be willing to make in its nondisclosure laws. We reserve any further consideration of these communications to the hearing on sanctions, if that becomes necessary.

Finally we have on this question as we have on another question been benefited with statements amici curiae from the Governments of Canada, Australia, South Africa and Switzerland. By far the most extensive of these is the Canadian statement which urges that we defer to the critical importance which Canada attaches to its national policies and regulations. But as we have earlier observed a balancing test is inherently unworkable in this case, and were it not we would be hard pressed not to accede to the strong national policy of this country to enforce vigorously its antitrust laws.

* * *

We now examine whether all defendants are within the personal jurisdiction of this court and have control over the requested documents, so that we possess the requisite power to issue an order under Rule 37(a) compelling production of their foreign documents. Only Noranda has raised an objection based on lack of in personam jurisdiction. Five defendants Engelhard, Noranda, Denison U.S., Rio U.S. and Uranerz deny that they control the requested documents.

* * *

We have now determined that, with certain exceptions regarding Denison U.S. and Uranerz, we have the power to issue a production order under Rule 37(a) against the eleven resisting defendants that are the subjects of plaintiffs' motions. The remaining question is whether we should exercise our discretionary power to issue those orders, after weighing the three factors described earlier in this memorandum. We conclude that we should.

The first consideration is the strength of the Congressional policies underlying the statute which forms the basis for plaintiffs' action. Plaintiffs' complaint challenges activities by the defendants which, if true, would constitute massive violations of this nation's antitrust laws. "These laws have long been considered cornerstones of this nation's economic policies, have been vigorously enforced and the subject of frequent interpretation by our Supreme Court." *United States v. First National City Bank*, 396 F.2d 897, 903 (2d Cir. 1968). "They are as important to the preservation of economic freedom and our free-enterprise system as the Bill of Rights is to the protection of our fundamental personal freedoms." *United States v. Topco Associates, Inc.*, 405 U.S. 596, 610 (1972). More specifically, Congressional concern with the very practices at issue here, and with the antitrust implications of those practices, is evidenced by extensive subcommittee investigations into the alleged international uranium cartel. See Hearings Before the Subcommittee on Oversight and Investigation of the House Committee on Interstate and Foreign Commerce, 95th Cong., 1st Sess. (1977). Governmental concern with this issue achieved choate form when the Justice Department convened a grand jury which eventually charged Gulf with criminal antitrust violations arising out of the same transactions identified by Westinghouse. The existence of this public enforcement action does not supplant plaintiffs' private civil action. Indeed, Congress specifically intended to encourage civil antitrust actions by allowing private litigants to gain certain estoppel advantages from government antitrust actions. From these indicators, it is clear that the policies supporting an inquiry into corporate activities and structure are at least as weighty, and probably stronger, with the antitrust statutes here than they were with the Trading with the Enemy Act in *Societe Internationale*.

The second consideration is whether the requested documents are crucial to the determination of a key issue in the litigation. Plaintiffs' showing on this factor is simply overwhelming.

* * *

The third consideration involves an appraisal of the chances for flexibility in a country's application of its nondisclosure laws. The degree of leniency in the application of the nondisclosure laws varies from country to country. South Africa has taken the most flexible position. It has allowed Westinghouse to inspect Utah's uranium-related documents in that country, and is currently considering a request from Engelhard to allow a similar inspection of its documents. Australia has rejected all past requests for a waiver of its regulations, but interprets its laws as authorizing the Attorney General to grant such waivers. The Attorney General is presently considering requests for waivers from Engelhard, Getty and Utah. Canada has taken a completely inflexible position. It has consistently rejected all requests for waivers, stating that its government officials have no authority to grant them. It has opposed Westinghouse's unsuccessful efforts to secure letters rogatory from a Canadian court for production of uranium-related documents. It has rejected all requests to modify or amend the regulations and has refused to give any assurances of non-prosecution for any violations. Canada has also sent numerous diplomatic notes to the U.S. State Department in which it has expressed a firm position that any disclosure of documents covered by its regulations would be inimical to its national interests. Canada's position has not been relaxed by its amicus submission.

On balance, we have concluded the issuance of Rule 37(a) orders is required. The entry of such orders may lead to a further narrowing of the defendants' foreign law objections. That process has already been evidenced by the increased disclosures which have occurred since Westinghouse filed the present motions. Even if some defendants subsequently conclude, as they now suggest, that they have already done everything within their powers to comply with such an order, we do not think an order at this time would be a futile gesture. The order will serve to declare Westinghouse's right to the discovery it seeks, thereby framing the competing interests of the United States and the foreign governments on a plane where the potential moderation of the exercise of their conflicting enforcement jurisdictions can be meaningfully considered. We do not seek to force any defendant to violate foreign law. But we do seek to make each defendant feel the full measure of each sovereign's conflicting commands, so that, in the words of Chief Judge Kaufman of the Second Circuit, it now "must confront...the need to 'surrender to one sovereign or the other the privileges received therefrom' or, alternatively a willingness to accept the consequences." *United States v. First National City Bank*, 396 F.2d 897, 905 (2d Cir. 1968).

Accordingly, plaintiffs' motions to compel Utah, Gulf, GMCL, Noranda, Denison Canada, Engelhard, Getty, Federal, and Rio U.S. to produce foreign documents are granted in their entirety and are granted in part and denied in part as to Uranerz and are denied as to Denison U.S. Defendants' alternative objections to production of foreign documents on grounds such as attorney-client privilege and overbroad definitions are reserved for ruling at such time as defendants announce their ability to comply with this order. Production hereunder to be made on or before January 2, 1980.

* * *

Note

The principal case rejects a "balancing test" for ordering discovery in the face of a foreign blocking statute. The next case, decided four years later by the Court of Appeals in the same circuit, adopts a balancing test. A similar disagreement about the feasibility of a balancing approach, is reflected in cases in chapter 6 dealing with the extraterritorial application of United States law.

United States v. First National Bank of Chicago
699 F.2d 341 (7th Cir. 1983)

Before SPRECHER and BAUER, Circuit Judges, and FAIRCHILD, Senior Circuit Judge.

FAIRCHILD, Senior Circuit Judge.

The district court granted enforcement of an Internal Revenue Service summons directed to First National Bank of Chicago, seeking disclosure of certain records in First Chicago's branch bank in Athens, Greece. We decide that First Chicago has adequately demonstrated that compliance will subject its employees to the risk of substantial criminal penalties under Greek law, and that a balancing of relevant competing interests weighs against compelling disclosure at this time. We therefore reverse the judgment of the district court, but remand for consideration of an order requiring First Chicago to make a good faith effort to secure permission to make the information available.

I: The Facts

On September 24, 1979, Internal Revenue Service Officer Earl Tripplett issued a summons to the First National Bank of Chicago ("First Chicago") requiring production of bank statements of Christ and Helen Panos for the month of June 1978 and the balance of funds in their account at the Athens, Greece, branch of First Chicago on June 19, 1978. (The Panoses now reside in Greece.)

First Chicago refused to furnish the requested information, stating:

> [O]ur Greek counsel has informed us that under the Greek Bank Secrecy Act, any and all of our employees—whether in Greece or elsewhere—who reveal exact account information about depositors of our Branch in Athens to any third party may be subject under the Act to criminal penalties, including, inter alia, not less than a six-month prison sentence. He further informs us that in two very recent Greek court decisions, it has been made clear that this Act does indeed apply to branches of foreign banks doing business in Greece.

However, in what it termed an effort to cooperate as much as possible without jeopardizing the welfare of its employees, First Chicago did advise the IRS that only one account for the Panoses existed, and that during the month of June 1978 the balance was "in the range of 40,000 Greek drachmas" (approximately $1,100 American money).

Thereafter, the IRS filed a petition in the district court to enforce the summons. Upon First Chicago's failure to respond timely to an order to show cause, the court, on May 7, 1980, ordered compliance.

First Chicago then filed a motion to vacate the enforcement order, arguing that disclosure would expose its employees to penal sanctions under Greek law.

* * *

II: The Merits

'First Chicago does not argue that the Government failed to make out a prima facie case for enforcement. And indeed there is no suggestion that the summons did not relate to a proper purpose, albeit levy and collection rather than determination of tax liability, that the material sought was irrelevant or already within the Commissioner's possession, or that necessary administrative steps remained to be taken. Rather, First Chicago urges that cause has been established for denying enforcement, notwithstanding the Government's prima facie showing. As we view the case, the arguments raised on appeal fall into two categories. First, whether First Chicago has sufficiently proved that Greek law forbids, under penalty of imprisonment, disclosure of the information in question. Second, whether (if it has so demonstrated) it should nonetheless be compelled to comply with the IRS summons.

* * *

We hold that First Chicago has adequately proved that [Greek law] forbids, under penalty of imprisonment, disclosure of the information the IRS seeks to compel.

The fact that foreign law may subject a person to criminal sanctions in the foreign country if he produces certain information does not automatically bar a domestic court from compelling production. Rather what is required is a sensitive balancing of the competing interests at stake. A number of circuits have utilized a test derived from the Restatement (Second) Foreign Relations Law of the United States (1965). See *United States v. Vetco Inc.*, 644 F.2d 1324, 1331 (9th Cir.1981), and cases cited therein. Section 40 of the Restatement provides:

> §40. Limitations on Exercise of Enforcement Jurisdiction. Where two states have jurisdiction to prescribe and enforce rules of law and the rules they may prescribe require inconsistent conduct upon the part of a person, each state is required by international law to consider, in good faith, moderating the exercise of its enforcement jurisdiction, in light of such factors as (a) vital national interests of each of the states, (b) the extent and the nature of the hardship that inconsistent enforcement actions would impose upon the person, (c) the extent to which the required conduct is to take place in the territory of the other state, (d) the nationality of the person, and (e) the extent to which enforcement by action of either state can reasonably be expected to achieve compliance with the rule prescribed by that state.

Applying the test just set forth, we conclude that it was an abuse of discretion to enter an unqualified order compelling production, particularly where there is no indication of the rationale of the decision.

It seems clear that the critical act of initially conveying the information would take place in Greece (factor (c)), and highly probable that persons of Greek nationality would make the initial disclosure (factor (d)). Factor (b), extent and nature of hardship, bears great weight. Those acting in Greece would be exposed to criminal liability, not merely a fine, but imprisonment. Comment c to § 40 of the Restatement observes:

> In determining whether to refrain from exercising jurisdiction, a state must give special weight to the nature of the penalty that may be imposed by the other state. A state will be less likely to refrain from exercising its jurisdiction when the consequence of obedience to its order will be a civil liability abroad. Similarly, a state will be less likely to exercise jurisdiction, where there is a possibility that obedience to its command may put an alien in jeopardy under the criminal laws of his own country, than it will if one of its own nationals may be subjected to foreign liability under similar circumstances.

We think it significant in weighing the hardship factor that the Bank employees who would be exposed to penalty and First Chicago, which would be ordering its Greek employees to act unlawfully, are involved only as neutral sources of information and not as taxpayers or adverse parties in litigation.

Although the interest of the United States in collecting taxes is of importance to the financial integrity of the nation, the interest of Greece, served by its bank secrecy law is also important, and so conceded by Government counsel (factor (a)). In connection with this factor it seems significant that the amount of tax liability of the Panoses has already been determined, the information is sought as a step toward levy and collection, the amount of the asset is comparatively small, and there are legal restrictions on the conversion and export of Greek funds.

We note further that Restatement (Second) of the Foreign Relations Law of the United States is being revised, and the substance of § 40, with some modification, is being reflected in § 403 of Tentative Draft No. 2 and §§ 419 and 420 of Tentative Draft No. 3, Foreign Relations Law of the United States (Revised).

Section 419(1) provides that "A person may not ordinarily be required by authority of the United States...to do an act outside the United States prohibited by the law of the state where the act is to be done." Section 420 deals specifically with court ordered production of information located outside the United States. Section 420(2) provides that "If disclosure of information located outside the United States is prohibited by a law or regulation of the state in which the information or prospective witness is located...the person to whom the order is directed may be required by the court to make a good faith effort to secure permission from the foreign authorities to make the information available."

In the case before us, we note that Article 3 of the Greek Act provides what seems to be a closely limited exception. The question whether this exception would be liberally construed in a case like the present does not appear to have been explored, and it seems to us that a reasonable, good faith effort to explore it might fairly be imposed on First Chicago. The furnishing of information by the Greek branch to the home office may possibly not be considered an offense, and a reasonable, good faith effort to determine that question of law might fairly be imposed on First Chicago. If the information came into the possession of First Chicago employees in the United States without violation of law in Greece, the result of the balancing test might well be different.

First Chicago tells us that the United States and Greece have a treaty, Convention Between The United States of America And The Kingdom Of Greece For The Avoidance Of Double Taxation And The Prevention Of Fiscal Evasion With Respect To Taxes On Income, entered into on February 10, 1950 and ratified in 1953, and that the IRS maintains a regional representative in Europe to coordinate efforts to collect delinquent taxes through diplomatic means. We are not aware of the Government's position as to the relevancy of either of these facts to the problem with which we are confronted.

On remand, the district court is directed to conduct further inquiry consistent with this opinion and to consider whether to issue an order requiring First Chicago to make a good faith effort to receive permission from the Greek authorities to produce the information specified in the summons.

We are aware that the Eleventh Circuit has reached a different result in a case involving a bank which was apparently a neutral source of information, as here. *In re Grand Jury Proceedings*, 691 F.2d 1384 (11th Cir.1982). In that case, however, the court of appeals had the benefit of findings by the district court, including a finding that the bank had not made a good faith effort to comply with the subpoena. The information was sought by a grand jury conducting a tax and narcotics investigation, so that the interest of the United States in the grand jury process of investigation and enforcement of its criminal laws was involved as well as its interest in determination and collection of taxes. There was evidence, though contested, that all banking transactions for the foreign branch could be handled by the United States branch. The foreign law (Bahamian) was different from the Greek law involved here in that disclosure with the consent of the customer would not be a criminal offense, and the power of a Bahamian court to permit disclosure did not appear to be as strictly limited. We consider the decision distinguishable.

The order appealed from is REVERSED, and the cause REMANDED for further proceedings.

Notes

1. The subject matter of §40 of The Restatement (Second) of Foreign Relations Law, quoted in the preceding case, is now covered in §403 of the Restatement (Third), set

out in chapter 6. The court also quotes from § 420 of a tentative draft of the Restatement (Third), which, in final form, is § 442, set out supra in this section.

The Restatement (Second) of Foreign Relations Law, despite its title, was the first restatement on this subject. "Second" refers not to the chronology of this restatement, but to the fact that it was published at a time when many of the second versions of earlier restatements, such as Torts, were being published. The working title for the Restatement (Third) was "Revised."

2. A court is likely to impose severe sanctions for failure to comply with discovery orders if the court finds that, although discovery is barred by the law of the country where records are stored, the party refusing to make discovery deliberately stored the records there to take advantage of the law preventing disclosure. See General Atomic Co. v. Exxon Nuclear Co., Inc., 90 F.R.D. 290 (S.D. Cal. 1981); United Nuclear Corp. v. General Atomic Co., 629 P.2d 231 (N.M. 1980), appeal dism'd & cert. denied, 451 U.S. 901 (1981).

In re Westinghouse Corp., 563 F.2d 992 (10th Cir. 1977) decided it was error to hold a non-party in contempt for failure to produce records held abroad when foreign law would impose criminal sanctions for disclosure and when the non-party had shown its good faith by seeking waivers from foreign officials.

All the cases in this note involved the alleged uranium antitrust conspiracy (see In re Uranium Antitrust Litigation, principal case supra) and Canadian law forbidding disclosure.

3. A defendant who contests personal jurisdiction is sometimes ordered to submit to discovery on matters affecting the jurisdictional issue, such as defendant's contacts with the forum. See Leasco Data Processing Equipment Corp. v. Maxwell, 468 F.2d 1326 (2d Cir. 1971). Suppose the defendant claims that discovery on the jurisdictional issue is forbidden by foreign law? Then the concern manifested in cases like Societe Internationale v. Rogers, principal case supra, for avoiding harsh sanctions on a party prevented by foreign law from making discovery combines with the concern manifested in cases like Leasco, to avoid undue burdens on the defendant before a decision that there is jurisdiction over the defendant. This issues are more likely to be combined in the future if United States Supreme Court decisions, like Asahi Metal Ind. v. Superior Ct., principal case supra, place significant restrictions on exercise of personal jurisdiction over foreign defendants.

Insurance Corp. of Ireland, Ltd. v. Compagnie des Bauxites de Guinee, 456 U.S. 694 (1982). Suit was brought in a Pennsylvania United States District Court against foreign insurance companies. Defendants moved to dismiss on the ground there was no personal jurisdiction over them, but refused to obey the court's discovery orders on this issue. As a sanction for disobedience, the court shifted the burden of proof on the jurisdictional issue from plaintiff to defendants. The Supreme Court held this consistent with due process and not an abuse of discretion. What act of the defendants made it fair and reasonable to compel discovery on the jurisdictional issue when it had not yet been decided that the defendants had the requisite contacts with the forum for personal jurisdiction?

Canada Trust Co. v. Stolzenberg, [1997] 1 W.L.R. 1582 (Ct. App. 1997), holds that the English High Court of Justice has the power to order discovery on the issue of personal jurisdiction.

4. Volkswagen, A.G. v. Valdez, 909 S.W.2d 900 (Tex. 1995), applied § 442 and held that the trial court had abused its discretion in ordering the German automobile manu-

facturer to produce its current corporate telephone book, which contained names, job titles, direct corporate telephone numbers, and the private home numbers of managers. Production of the telephone book would violate German privacy laws. Germany submitted an amicus brief stating that its interests would be undermined by production. The court noted that there were "numerous alternative means" of discovering the names of persons who had information concerning alleged defects in the automobile. Moreover, the book was of little importance because it was sought merely to double check information obtained in previous discovery requests.

In re Grand Jury Proceedings, 40 F.3d 959 (9th Cir. 1994), cert. denied, 515 U.S. 1132 (1995), applies §403 [set out infra page 336], not §442, to affirm a district court's order holding in contempt an Austrian citizen residing in the United States. The Austrian was the subject of a grand jury investigation into possible violations of U.S. tax laws. The court ordered him to sign a disclosure directive to Austrian banks authorizing them to release information concerning his accounts. He refused. The court held that even if compelling him to sign the consent directive violated Austrian law "international comity does not preclude enforcement [because] the United State's interest in [disclosure] outweighs Austria's interest in preventing [disclosure]." Id. at 965-66.

5. In Brannigan v. Davison, [1996] 3 W.L.R. 859 (P.C. 1996) (appeal taken from N.Z.), the Privy Council adopted the following test to determine whether a witness should be compelled to answer questions in New Zealand when the answers would expose him to criminal penalties in The Cook Islands: "weighing all the consequences of the refusal to give evidence: the adverse consequences to the inquiry if the questions are not answered, and the adverse consequences to the witness if he is compelled to answer." Id. at 868.

In Re Asbestos Insurance Coverage Cases
[1985] 1 W.L.R. 331, (House of Lords)

LORD FRASER OF TULLYBELTON. My Lords, these appeals raise two questions under §2 of the Evidence (Procedure in Other Jurisdictions) Act 1975. The questions relate to letters rogatory issued out of the Superior Court of California for the City of San Francisco requesting the assistance of the High Court in England, and to orders made by the High Court in response to that request. One question relates to orders for witnesses to attend before an examiner in England for oral examination. The other relates to an order for production of documents.

The respondents are four American corporations, or groups of corporations, who manufacture asbestos. They are engaged in litigation in the United States of America against insurers with whom they had a large number of insurance policies to cover asbestos-related claims. Five actions have been raised in the Superior Court of California in San Francisco and they are collectively referred to as "the co-ordination proceedings". The insurers named in the titles to the five actions are merely a few of the many insurers involved and in each action certain underwriters at Lloyd's of London are also parties. In four of the actions, one or other of the respondents is the plaintiff and the defendants are insurers or, in one case, American insurance brokers. In the fifth action one of the insurers is the plaintiff and one of the respondents is the defendant. But nothing turns on the forms of the particular actions. The appellants are Sedgwick Group Plc and two of its subsidiary companies (collectively referred to as "Sedgwick"), who together represent, as a result of amalgamations or otherwise, the final brokers through whom all the relevant policies with Lloyd's underwriters in London were arranged, and three individuals who are or were at the material time directors of those brokers.

Each of the respondents is faced with claims from persons who say that they are suffering from asbestos-related injuries, and who seek compensation for these injuries and in some cases for damage to property. In the co-ordination proceedings the respondents seek declarations and damages and in some cases injunctive relief and rectification against the insurers, including Lloyd's underwriters. There are many thousands of claims and their total amount is very large. The respondents allege that the insurers have failed or declined to defend actions brought by the claimants for compensation, or to indemnify the respondents against the claims.

The issues in the co-ordination proceedings include the following: (1) whether certain of the policies which are alleged to exist, dating back as far as 1920, exist at all (2) the extent of the cover actually placed by the respondents with Sedgwick and in particular whether the insurance cover extends only to claims based on asbestos-related disease which manifested itself during the policy period or is provided only under policies which relate to the period of inhalation or ingestion (3) the construction of certain of the policies issued by Lloyd's underwriters to the respondents through the agency of Sedgwick, including the level of loss at which liability of "excess" underwriters arises and (4) whether the respondents failed to disclose to the underwriters the extent of their knowledge of the risk of asbestos-related injury.

The orders now under appeal were made by McNeill J. on 25 July 1984. He ordered the three individual appellants to attend before examiners to give oral testimony. As regards the production of documents, he made an order against Sedgwick giving effect to all the requests in the letters rogatory, except those in two paragraphs and certain others which were not pursued by the pursuant respondents. The Court of Appeal (Eveleigh, O'Connor and Slade L.JJ.) unanimously dismissed the appeals by the three individual appellants against the orders relating to oral testimony, and allowed in part Sedgwick's appeal against the order relating to production of documents. Slade L.J. gave a dissenting judgment in respect of the documents and would have allowed Sedgwick's appeal in relation to all the documents in issue. The appellants have now appealed by leave of this House.

On 11 February 1985 the House allowed the appeal in respect of documents and dismissed the appeal in respect of oral evidence. The reasons for the decision were not stated on that day, owing to the urgency of announcing the decision so that it could be carried into effect before the trial began in California early in March. We intimated that the reasons would be given later, and that we now do.

The 1975 Act was passed in order, inter alia, to give effect to the principles of the Convention on the Taking of Evidence abroad in Civil or Commercial Matters which was ratified by the United Kingdom in 1976. The 1975 Act was fully considered by this House in *Rio Tinto Zinc Corp. v Westinghouse Electric Corp.* [1978] 1 All ER 434 at 444, [1978] AC 547 at 612, where Lord Wilberforce said:

> ...I am of opinion that following the spirit of the 1975 Act which is to enable judicial assistance to be given to foreign courts, the letters rogatory ought to be given effect to so far as possible...

> I respectfully agree and I approach the present appeal with that admonition in mind.

Section 1 of the 1975 Act (reading it short) provides:

> Where an application is made to the High Court... for an order for evidence to be obtained in [England], and the court is satisfied—(a) that the application is made in pursuance of a request issued by or on behalf of a court or tribunal ("the requesting court") exercising jurisdiction... in a country or territory outside the United Kingdom and (b) that the evidence to which the application relates is to be obtained for the purposes of civil proceedings which either have been instituted before the requesting court or whose institution before that court is contemplated, the High Court... shall have the powers conferred on it by the following provisions of this Act.

Section 2(1) provides that the High Court shall have power by order to make such provision for obtaining evidence in England as may appear to the court to be appropriate for the purpose of giving effect to the request in pursuance of which an application has been made under § 1. Subsection (2) of § 2, so far as relevant, provides that an order under the section "may... make provision—(a) for the examination of witnesses, either orally or in writing (b) for the production of documents..." Subsection (3) is not material in the present appeal. Subsection (4) is the subsection which is directly in point here and I must quote it in full as follows:

> An order under this section shall not require a person—(a) to state what documents relevant to the proceedings to which the application for the order relates are or have been in his possession, custody or power or (b) to produce any documents other than particular documents specified in the order as being documents appearing to the court making the order to be, or to be likely to be, in his possession, custody or power.

Two preliminary observations fall to be made on subsection (4). It was evidently passed in order to give effect to the United Kingdom government's reservation, made in accordance with art 23 of the convention when it ratified the convention, declaring that "the United Kingdom will not execute letters of request issued for the purpose of obtaining pre-trial discovery of documents". While that is the explanation for the presence of subsection (4) in the 1975 Act, I do not consider that it assists directly in the construction of the subsection so far as this appeal is concerned. The wide-ranging nature of pre-trial discovery in the United States of America was explained by Lord Wilberforce in *Westinghouse*, but there is no question of the letters of request which are before the House in this appeal having been issued for the purpose of obtaining pre-trial discovery. The time for such discovery is long past, the trial is due to begin in California about one month after the date on which we heard the appeal.

* * *

Production of documents

It will be convenient to consider first Sedgwick's appeal against the order for production of documents. This appeal is limited to the order so far as it gives effect to paragraphs (b) and (g) and the first part of paragraph (j) of the letters of request. (McNeill J. had already refused the request for documents under the second part of paragraph (j).) These paragraphs are in the following terms:

> (b) The written instructions from the plaintiffs or their agents to Sedgwick to obtain the insurance policies set forth in exhibit 1 hereto...
>
> (g) The written instructions to Sedgwick from the plaintiffs or their agents to obtain the insurance policies referred to in (f) above...

(j) The exemplars of Price, Forbes & Co. Ltd.'s excess comprehensive personal injury and property damage "umbrella" liability policies in use in the London insurance market during the period 1950 through 1966...

Paragraphs (b) and (g) raise exactly the same point and can be considered together. Exhibit 1 referred to in paragraph (b) is a list of policies identified by their numbers and by the numbers of brokers' slips. Paragraph (g) refers back to paragraph (f) which in turn refers to exhibit 4 where the dates during which predecessors of certain of the respondents are said to have effected policies are stated. The question is whether paragraphs (b) and (g) of the letters specify "particular documents" and thus comply with §2(4)(b) of the 1975 Act. McNeill J. held that they did so. The majority of the Court of Appeal upheld that view, but Slade L.J. dissented, holding that they did not particularise the documents.

The meaning of the expression "particular documents specified in the order" in subsection (4)(b) was considered by several of the noble and learned Lords who took part in the *Westinghouse* decision. They were all emphatic that the expression should be given a strict construction. Having regard to the purpose of subsection (4), which, as I have already mentioned, is to preclude pre-trial discovery, it is to be construed so as not to permit mere "fishing" expeditions. Lord Wilberforce said ([1978] 1 All ER 434 at 442, [1978] AC 547 at 609):

> These provisions, and especially the words "particular documents specified in the order" (replacing "documents to be mentioned in the order" in the [Foreign Tribunals Evidence Act 1856]) together with the expressed duty of the English court to decide that the documents are or are likely to be in the possession, custody or power of the person called on to produce, show in my opinion that a strict attitude is to be taken by English courts in giving effect to foreign requests for the production of documents by non-party witnesses. They are, in the words of Lord Goddard C.J., not to countenance "fishing" expeditions: *Radio Corp. of America v Rauland Corp.* [1956] 1 All ER 549 at 554, [1956] 1 QB 618 at 649.

Lord Diplock expressed perhaps an even more restrictive view of the effect of subsection (4)(b) where he said ([1978] 1 All ER 434 at 463, [1978] AC 547 at 635):

> The requirements of subsection (4)(b), however, are not in my view satisfied by the specification of classes of documents. What is called for is the specification of "particular documents" which I would construe as meaning individual documents separately described.

I do not think that by the words "separately described" Lord Diplock intended to rule out a compendious description of several documents provided that the exact document in each case is clearly indicated. If I may borrow (and slightly amplify) the apt illustration given by Slade L.J. in the present case, an order for production of the respondents' "monthly bank statements for the year 1984 relating to his current account" with a named bank would satisfy the requirements of the paragraph, provided that the evidence showed that regular monthly statements had been sent to the respondent during the year and were likely to be still in his possession. But a general request for "all the respondent's bank statements in 1984" would in my view refer to a class of documents and would not be admissible.

The second test of particular documents is that they must be actual documents, about which there is evidence which has satisfied the judge that they exist, or at least that they did exist, and that they are likely to be in the respondents' possession. Actual documents are to be contrasted with conjectural documents, which may or may not exist. In *Westinghouse* [1978] 1 All ER 434 at 470, [1978] AC 547 at 644 I said:

> The reference to "any" documents in the sweeping-up words in the schedule to the letters rogatory suggests to me that the draftsmen did not know whether such documents were in existence or not. Accordingly the words seem to be an attempt to circumvent § 2(4)(a) of the 1975 Act, an attempt which should not be allowed to succeed.

In my opinion the terms of paragraphs (b) and (g) of the letters rogatory in the present case fail both these tests. They fail the second test because there was no evidence that there was usually a single document or set of documents by which written instructions for policies from the plaintiffs or their agents were transmitted to Sedgwick. The only document to which our attention was called as being a specimen of such instruction related to the renewal of a policy and it is certainly not a definite instruction. It is addressed to one of the firms now represented by Sedgwick and it includes the following paragraph:

> We would ask you specifically to remove from the renewal [a particular provision] as this is not in keeping with the umbrella form as now written. We look forward to hearing from you on this subject by cable as soon as possible, after the receipt of this memorandum.

That appears to be a request or inquiry which might well have led to correspondence and discussion about the terms of the final policy. Moreover, for all that appears from the evidence, it is possible that instructions for some policies may have been given verbally and that there were no written instructions for those policies. In an affidavit sworn by the attorney for one of the respondents, he states his belief that—

> it is necessarily the case that Sedgwick must have received instructions [NB not "written instructions"] to proceed as it did and *on this basis* have reason to believe that Sedgwick possesses the documents... referred to in [paragraph (b) of the letters rogatory]. (My emphasis.)

In the light of the evidence as a whole paragraphs (b) and (g) are in effect calls for production of "written instructions if any", that is to say for conjectural documents which may or may not exist. In *Westinghouse* Lord Wilberforce was willing to extend "particular documents specified" to include replies to letters "where replies must have been sent" (see [1978] 1 All ER 434 at 443, [1978] AC 547 at 611). I would go that far with him, but I would not extend the expression to documents which may or may not exist.

For much the same reasons I am of opinion that these paragraphs of the letters rogatory also fail the first test in respect that they do not refer to particular documents at all. In effect they refer to "all or any documents falling within the class consisting of written instructions". The class is ill-defined and in my view there is room for some doubt whether the specimen document that I have mentioned relating to renewal of a policy falls within the class or not. I would therefore hold that paragraphs (b) and (g) should not be made the subjects of the order for production of documents.

With regard to paragraph (j) the words "exemplars" is not one that is in common use and its meaning is not altogether clear to me. For the present purpose the evidence shows that "exemplars" is used to describe the standard forms of what were called "umbrella" policies which were developed by Sedgwick in conjunction with others, and which varied from time to time. The first part of paragraph (j) gives no indication of the dates on which the exemplars were amended or different exemplars of umbrella policies that were in use at any time during the period from 1950 to the end of 1966. That is in my opinion clearly a description of a class of documents and not of particular documents. Moreover, the class is not clearly defined by the opening words of paragraph (j), which refer to "exemplars of Price, Forbes & Co. Ltd.'s...'umbrella'...policies". There is nothing to show how their policies are to be distinguished from policies of other firms; the distinction might be important having regard to evidence that they "and...other Sedgwick companies" were responsible, "in conjunction with one or more North American brokers, for developing, drafting and marketing these umbrella policies". This paragraph therefore fails the first test.

Oral testimony

The appeals from the three individual appellants against orders to give oral evidence were presented on the basis that the California judge who issued the letters rogatory had been misled into overestimating the evidence that these appellants could give. For example, it is said that Mr. Crane, whose experience of insurance is limited to dealing with claims, has been asked to give evidence about placement of risks, underwriting, drafting and interpretation of policies and other matters of which he has no direct knowledge. I am not impressed by this argument. Each of these three appellants admits that he is in a position to give some evidence that is relevant to the co-ordination proceedings. It may be that they will be asked for evidence about matters which are outwith their experience, and which they are not qualified to deal with. If so, they can say so. It would be quite inappropriate, even if it were possible, for this House or any English court to determine in advance the matters relevant to the issues before the Californian courts on which each of these witnesses is in a position to give evidence. As Lord Keith said in *Westinghouse* [1978] 1 All ER 434 at 478, [1978] AC 547 at 654:

> In the face of a statement of letters rogatory that a certain person is a necessary witness for the applicant, I am of opinion that the court of request should not be astute to examine the issues in the action and the circumstances of the case with excessive particularity for the purpose of determining in advance whether the evidence of that person will be relevant and admissible. That is essentially a matter for the requesting court.

[Counsel for the appellants] appreciated the difficulty in the way of this House if it tried to determine the matters on which oral evidence would be relevant and admissible in the Californian proceedings, and, in order to meet the difficulty, he suggested that the letters rogatory should be sent back to the Californian court to be reconsidered by the judge there with a view to their being amended and restricted. I am not in favour of that course. It would cause delay, which is an important matter as the trial in California is due to begin early in March 1985. Quite apart from the delay, the Californian judge might not be persuaded to restrict the scope of the letters rogatory to the extent that would satisfy the appellants, or at all, and there would be no satisfactory way of resolving any difference between his view and the views of the English court. I would refuse the appeals against the orders relating to oral evidence.

* * *

Note

South Carolina Ins. Co. v. Assurantie Maatschappij de Zeven Provincien NV, [1986] 3 W.L.R. 398 (H.L.). A United States insurance company sued defendant insurers on their reinsurance contracts. Plaintiff was asked to produce documents held by plaintiff's business associates and underwriting agents in the United States, but the request was refused. The defendants, in order to investigate possible defenses of misrepresentation and non-disclosure, filed a petition for discovery in a United States district court pursuant to 28 U.S.C. § 1782 (discovery for use in a foreign court). The United States action was against persons not parties in the English case. The House of Lords held that the defendants should not have been enjoined from continuing the United States proceedings, even though English procedure would not compel pre-trial discovery from nonparties. There was no showing that the United States action interfered with the English litigation. This case somewhat weakens one of the bases for the decision in *Asta Medica*, in note 5 following *Aérospatiale*, supra page 137.

Section 6. Currency Conversion

Note

A: Why Conversion is Necessary

Suppose that a buyer repudiates a contract to buy machinery. The contract calls for payment in German marks. In the few years between the time that the payment was originally due and the date judgment is rendered, the dollar has depreciated compared with the mark. When payment was due, the number of marks called for in the contract could have been purchased with $4 million, but on the date of judgment, $6 million is required. Thus, if a judgment against the buyer is in dollars, it matters a good deal whether the "breach day" or "judgment day" is picked as the date to covert dollars to marks.

B: Position of the Parties on Time for Conversion

As a matter of tactics, in the example just given, the foreign creditor will want conversion at the later date, and the debtor, or in bankruptcy, the other creditors, will want conversion at the earlier date. (The example is based on In re Good Hope Chemical Corp., infra). This will be the tactical position of creditor and debtor whenever the dollar depreciates with regard to the foreign currency between breach and judgment. When the dollar has appreciated with regard to the foreign currency, the tactical position of the parties is reversed: the foreign creditor wants a breach day conversion, and the United States debtor wants judgment day conversion.

C: Losses from Currency Fluctuations as Consequential Damages

Damage to the creditor, caused by changes in the relative value of currencies, could be treated as any other consequential damage for breach of contract. In choosing between the day payment was due ("breach day") and the day judgment is rendered ("judgment day"), a court would choose breach day if, compared with the foreign currency in which the debt is owed, the dollar has appreciated, and would choose judgment day if the dollar has depreciated. This is the position taken by the Restatement (Third) Foreign Relations Law of the United States § 823, comment c (1987). For a case following the Restatement (Third), see El Universal v. Phoenician Imports, Inc., 802

S.W.2d 799 (Tex. App.—Corpus Christi, 1990, writ denied), which awards judgment to a Mexican newspaper against a Texas advertiser that did not pay its bill, converting the peso obligation to dollars at the date of the breach. The peso had depreciated relative to the dollar during the period between the day payment was due and the date of judgment. Accord with regard to tort damages, Aker Verdal A/S v. Neil F. Lampson, Inc., 828 P.2d 610 (Wash. App. 1992). Art. 6.1.9(1) of the UNIDROIT Principles of International Commercial Contracts, published by the International Institute for the Unification of Private Law, gives the obligee a choice between requiring payment at the exchange rate "prevailing either when payment is due or at the time of actual payment."

This creditor-favoring rule should be subject to the usual requirement that the creditor exert reasonable efforts to mitigate damages. It may be that if not now, some day, reasonable efforts to mitigate will include hedging in currency markets when substantial sums are payable from foreign debtors or in foreign funds. Cf. Brane v. Roth, 590 N.E.2d 587 (Ind. App. 1st Dist. 1992) (shareholders in grain co-operative recover against the directors for losses caused by failure to use grain futures to hedge against falling prices).

Is the creditor-favoring rule, treating losses from currency fluctuations as foreseeable consequential damages, justified? Within the same country, under the rule of "nominalism," a debtor who repays a fixed obligation after a period of inflation, is allowed to benefit from the fact that it borrowed dear currency and is repaying in cheap currency. Why should the international debtor be treated differently? The intra-country example assumes that the debtor pays on time. If not, pre-judgment interest rates may reflect the high interest rates that accompanied the inflation. See also Ronald A. Brand, "Exchange Loss Damages and the Uniform Foreign-Money Claims Act: The Emperor Hasn't All His Clothes," 23 Law & Policy in Int'l Bus. 1, 43 (1991) (stating that "the complexities of multiple-currency transactions make [application of the principle of nominalism] inappropriate").

D: U.S. Judgments in Foreign Currency

Millangos v. George Frank (Textiles), Ltd., [1975] 3 All E.R. 801 (H.L.) affirmed a judgment in Swiss francs. It is debatable whether a United States court can render a judgment in foreign currency. The Restatement (Third) Foreign Relations Law § 823(1), the Uniform Foreign-Money Claims Act, §§ 4(a), 7(a) 13 Unif. L. Ann. 72 (2000 Supp.) (adopted in 20 states, the District of Columbia, and the Virgin Islands), and a New York statute, N.Y. Jud. Law § 27(b) (McKinney Supp. 1992) assume that U.S. judgments can be in foreign currency. [But 31 U.S.C. § 371, before its recodification, read: "The money of account of the United States shall be expressed in dollars...and all proceedings in the courts shall be kept and had in conformity with this regulation." This is recodified in 31 U.S.C. § 5101 omitting the reference to "all accounts" and "all proceedings in courts." The Reviser's Note states that these words were "omitted as surplus" and the "Explanation" note preceding new title 31 states that the recodification "made no substantive change."] In re Oil Spill by the Amoco Cadiz off the Coast of France on March 16, 1978, 954 F.2d 1279 (7th Cir. 1992), ordered entry of a judgment in francs. Rendering U.S. judgments in foreign currency would not, however, solve the conversion date problem. As a practical matter, unless a complex double conversion were used, a U.S. judgment in foreign currency would result in a judgment day conversion and, if one adopts the Foreign Relations Restatement's position that losses resulting from shifts in the relative value of currencies should be treated as foreseeable consequential damages, would be unfair to the foreign creditor if the dollar has appreciated since breach day. The Restatement recognizes this and states that the judgment should be in foreign currency only when judgment day conversion would be proper. Restatement (Third) Foreign Relations Law § 823 comment b. There is no such flexibility in the Uniform and New York statutes. For adverse criticism on this ground of the Uniform Foreign-Money Claims Act, see the article by Ronald A. Brand, supra this note, and Suzanne Raggio Westerheim, "The Uniform Foreign-Money Claims Act: No Solution to an Old Problem," 69 Tex. L. Rev. 1203 (1991).

Professor Mann states that Restatement § 823 "introduces into a purely procedural rule an element of substantive justice which the applicable proper law should care for." F.A. Mann, The Legal Aspect of Money 351 (5th ed. 1992). He notes that a "rule permitting the recovery of damages for the loss caused by the depreciation of foreign money" has been adopted in many countries. Id. at 353. Should § 823 be applied if there is no precedent on the issue in the foreign country because such damages have not been claimed?

This note has considered how the currency-conversion problem might be approached if analyzed de novo. Now for what the courts have wrought.

In re Good Hope Chemical Corp.
747 F.2d 806 (1st Cir. 1984), cert. denied, 471 U.S. 1102 (1985)

LEVIN H. CAMPBELL, Chief Judge.

In 1974, Good Hope Chemical Corporation ("Good Hope"), a Texas corporation and the Chapter XI debtor, contracted with Koerver & Lersch ("K & L"), a West German manufacturer of specially fabricated equipment, to construct two sets of heat exchangers for use in an ammonia plant Good Hope was to build in Ingleside, Texas. The contract was formed by a series of telexes between Good Hope's purchasing agent, M.W. Kellogg Co. ("Kellogg"), and K & L in West Germany. The first telex, from Kellogg to K & L, advised K & L to "enter good hope chemical purchase orders" and quoted a purchase price in dollars. K & L's reply telex, however, stated:

> we confirm to have booked your order for the supply of heat exchangers strictly in accordance with your telex... with the following exception: all prices in the purchase order to be in German marks as follows: [list of figures omitted] two plants have been ordered at a total price of 13.046.540,-German marks. If the purchase order is made out in dollars, it will not be accepted...
>
> ...the dollar prices in your purchase order have been worked out at a rate of one German mark equal to 0.394 dollars and have been used for comparison reason only.

According to K & L, it was unwilling to enter into the contract unless it provided for payment of a fixed number of marks because K & L expected to, and did, incur all costs of the contract in German marks, and because K & L's offices were in Germany, it had no investments outside of Germany, and it was unwilling to shoulder the risk of foreign exchange fluctuations. Subsequent communications and purchase order modifications reflected the understanding that K & L would receive a fixed number of German marks for the heat exchangers.

The parties arranged for Good Hope to pay K & L in three installments: 30 percent 90 days after placement of the order, 30 percent 180 days after placement of the order, and the balance on shipment of the exchangers to Good Hope, F.A.S., a German or

Dutch port. Good Hope was to notify its bank of the amount of marks owed K & L. Good Hope's American bank would then arrange a date for exchange with K & L's German bank. On that date, Good Hope's bank would wire marks to the German bank, which would credit K & L's account with that number of marks. Good Hope's bank would debit Good Hope's account by the number of dollars needed to buy the marks. Thus, Good Hope would not know the actual dollar cost to it of the heat exchangers until it had paid for them.

Good Hope never made any payments under the contract. On October 31, 1975, after K & L had substantially completed the exchangers but before it shipped them, Good Hope filed a voluntary petition for reorganization under Chapter XI of the Bankruptcy Act. K & L filed its proofs of claims in December 1975.

* * *

On June 12, 1980, in accordance with a stipulation agreed to by Good Hope, K & L, and the creditors' committee, the bankruptcy court allowed K & L's claim in the total amount of the United States dollar equivalent of DM 11,055,121 for damages for the rejected executory contract. This figure represents the final contract price minus the net proceeds K & L realized from the resale to Pemex.

After a hearing on January 20, 1983, the bankruptcy judge rejected Good Hope's creditors' committee's argument that the appropriate date for determining the exchange rate is the date of the contract breach, which it asserted to be October 31, 1975. Instead, the court adopted K & L's suggestion that the exchange rate on the date of judgment—June 12, 1980—should govern the computation of the judgment amount.

The consequence of choosing the exchange rate prevailing on the judgment date, as opposed to the breach date as declared by the committee, is a substantially larger dollar judgment.

Date	Exchange Rate	Claim in Dollars
October 31, 1975 (filing of petition, asserted breach date)	0.3913	$4,325,869
June 12, 1980 (allowance of claim)	0.5679	$6,278,203

* * *

The United States District Court for the District of Massachusetts affirmed the exchange rate selected by the bankruptcy court. The creditors' committee now appeals to this court.

I

The creditors' committee first argues that the contract's reference to marks served only to adjust the amount of dollars payable; dollars, they contend, were to be the medium of payment under the contract. The facts, however, indicate that the reverse is true.

* * *

II

A harder question is what date determines the exchange rate for converting damages, computed in marks, into a dollar judgment. See *Frontera Transportation Co. v. Abaunza*, 271 F. 199 (5th Cir.1921); Note, Conversion Date of Foreign Money Obligation, 65 Colum. L. Rev. 490 (1965) ("It is a settled principle of Anglo-American law that judgments for money damages must be rendered in the currency of the forum.") (footnote omitted).

The parties, as well as the bankruptcy court and the district court, agree that the question of what date's exchange rate controls turns on the interpretation of two Supreme Court cases, *Hicks v. Guinness*, 269 U.S. 71 (1925), and *Deutsche Bank Filiale Nurnberg v. Humphrey*, 272 U.S. 517 (1926).

In *Hicks*, a German firm owed a debt to an American company. Although the debt was to be paid in America, the obligation was stated in German marks. The Court, employing what became known as the breach day rule, held that the American company had a claim for dollars as of the date the contract was breached and thus the conversion rate prevailing on that date should apply:

> The debt was due to an American creditor and was to be paid in the United States. When the contract was broken by a failure to pay, the American firm had a claim here, not for the debt, but, at its option, for damages in dollars. It no longer could be compelled to accept marks. It had a right to say to the debtors "You are too late to perform what you promised, and we want the dollars to which we have a right by the law here in force…The event has come to pass upon which your liability becomes absolute as fixed by law."…The loss for which the plaintiff is entitled to be indemnified is "the loss of what the contractor would have had if the contract had been performed,"…it happens at the moment when the contract is broken, just as it does when a tort is committed, and the plaintiff's claim is for the amount of that loss valued in money at that time.

Hicks, 269 U.S. at 80.

By contrast, the Court one year later in *Deutsche Bank* used what has been labelled the judgment day rule. In *Deutsche Bank*, a German bank refused to return marks on deposit when the American depositor demanded them. The money was held by the Alien Property Custodian after World War I and the depositor sued in the United States under the Trading with the Enemy Act to recover his money. The Court held that the amount owed should be converted at the rate in effect on the date of judgment, stating:

> In this case, unlike *Hicks v. Guinness*, 269 U.S. 71, at the date of the demand the German Bank owed no duty to the plaintiff under our law. It was not subject to our jurisdiction and the only liability that it incurred by its failure to pay was that which the German law might impose…A suit in this country is based upon an obligation existing under the foreign law at the time when the suit is brought, and the obligation is not enlarged by the fact that the creditor happens to be able to catch his debtor here…We may assume that when the Bank failed to pay on demand its liability was fixed at a certain number of marks both by the terms of the contract and by the German law—but we also assume that it was fixed in marks only, not at the extrinsic value that those marks then had in commodities or in the currency of another country. On the contrary, we repeat, it was and continued to be a liability in marks alone and was open to satisfaction by the payment of that number of marks, at any time, with

whatever interest might have accrued, however much the mark might have fallen in value as compared with other things... An obligation in terms of the currency of a country takes the risk of currency fluctuations and whether the creditor or debtor profits by the change the law takes no account of it... Obviously, in fact a dollar or a mark may have different values at different times but to the law that establishes it it is always the same. If the debt had been due here and the value of dollars had dropped before suit was brought the plaintiff could recover no more dollars on that account. A foreign debtor should be no worse off.

Deutsche Bank, 272 U.S. at 518-19 (citations omitted).

As the district court correctly noted, courts and commentators have drawn from *Hicks* and *Deutsche Bank* disparate formulas for determining when to apply the judgment or breach day rules. Two principal approaches have emerged. The first is a rather mechanical approach that focuses on the place of payment. It requires that the judgment day rule apply when the contractual obligation is payable in a foreign country in that country's currency, and the breach day rule apply when the payment is to be made in the United States. The district court questioned this formula. It indicated that it would have rejected it were it not for this court's decision in *Gutor International AG v. Raymond Packer Co.*, 493 F.2d 938, 943 (1st Cir.1974). But the court read *Gutor* as requiring it to follow the above rule. While we understand the court's quandary, we do not believe that *Gutor* mandates such an approach. In *Gutor* we merely acquiesced in a formulation advanced by one side without effective opposition from the other. The issue was never litigated.

Now that the issue is squarely before us, we agree with the district court that a second approach, while more complex, conforms better with the Court's language in *Hicks* and *Deutsche Bank* and the weight of authority. This approach looks to the jurisdiction in which the plaintiff's cause of action arose to determine which rule is applicable. The judgment day rule applies only when the obligation arises entirely under foreign law. If, however, at the time of breach the plaintiff has a cause of action arising in this country under American law, the breach day rule applies.

* * *

The second approach follows logically from the language of both *Hicks* and *Deutsche Bank*. Thus the Court said in *Hicks*,

> When the contract was broken by a failure to pay, the American firm had a claim *here*, not for the debt, but, at its option, for damages in dollars.

269 U.S. at 80 (emphasis added).

This language contrasts with that in *Deutsche Bank*, where the Court said,

> In this case, unlike *Hicks*..., at the date of the demand the German Bank owed no duty to the plaintiff *under our law*. It was not subject to our jurisdiction and the only liability it incurred by its failure to pay was that which German law might impose Here we are lending our Courts to enforce an obligation (as we should put it, to pay damages,) arising from German law alone and ought to enforce no greater obligation than exists by that law at the moment when the suit is brought.

272 U.S. at 518-20 (emphasis added)

* * *

The weight of authority endorses our reading of *Hicks* and *Deutsche Bank*.

***

In this case, the bankruptcy court and the parties were in agreement that Good Hope's cause of action arose under American law. The "choice of law" approach mandates, therefore, that the rate of exchange in effect on the breach date prevail.

III

Our decision to apply the breach date does not, however, end the matter. Given Good Hope's bankruptcy, it is not obvious what date constitutes the date of breach. The district court believed that section 63(c), 11 U.S.C. § 103(c) (1976), required that the actual date of breach—assumed to be the date upon which the contract was rejected, May 9, 1980,[7]—relates back to the date the petition was filed on October 31, 1975. K & L argues that the relation back rule's rationale in bankruptcy has no applicability in this context. It also asserts that any "fictional" breach of the contract on October 31, 1975, did not give rise to an obligation enforceable against Good Hope on that date, and thus October 31, 1975 cannot be the determinative date under *Hicks*. See *Hicks*, 269 U.S. at 80 (upon breach "[t]he event has come to pass upon which your liability becomes absolute as fixed by law"). See also *Zimmerman [v. Sutherland]*, 274 U.S. [253] at 256 [1927], (upon breach, "there arose a present liability in dollars"). Assumedly, they are contending that the date upon which Good Hope's liability became definite was (and thus the breach date should be) the date the contract was actually and finally rejected, May 9, 1980.

We find merit in K & L's contention. The *Hicks* Court believed that the fixation of liability is important because the plaintiff's loss, its expectancy from the contract, "happens when the contract is broken...and the plaintiff's claim is for the amount of loss valued in money at that time." Here the breach was complete, and the compensable loss incurred, only when the contract was rejected on May 9, 1980, not before. In this case, the relation back rule would disrupt the *Hicks* Court's attempt to give the plaintiff his expectancy as of the date his loss became definite.[8] The relation back rule is necessary in bankruptcy because without it a Chapter XI debtor would be required to reject an executory contract immediately upon filing or have its obligation for damages upon rejection during the bankruptcy case treated as an administrative expense entitled to priority under section 64(a)(1), 11 U.S.C. § 104(a)(1) (1976). This rationale for the operation of

---

7. The Act provides that a Plan of Arrangement may include "provisions for the rejection of any executory contract." Bankruptcy Act § 357(2), 11 U.S.C. § 757(2) (1976). Chemical's Plan provided that all executory contracts would be rejected as of confirmation on May 9, 1980.

8. The object of the breach day rule is to restore the plaintiff to the position he would have enjoyed had the contract not been breached. See *Hicks*, 269 U.S. at 80 ("The loss for which the plaintiff is entitled to be indemnified is 'the loss of what the contractor would have had if the contract had been performed' "); Note, Conversion Date of Foreign Money Obligations, 65 Colum.L.Rev. 490, 493 (1965). The breach day rule, however, may fail to fully compensate plaintiffs like K & L who would have retained the foreign currency, which appreciated in value relative to the dollar, had the agreement been performed. To put K & L as nearly as possible in the position it would have enjoyed had the contract not been breached, we would have to use the judgment day rate of exchange, a result not reconcilable with our reading of Supreme Court precedent. We recognize that more flexibility in determining the "breach date" for the purpose of awarding full compensation in cases like this, i.e., permitting a court to use the judgment day rate of exchange in order to give the plaintiff its full measure of expectancy damages, might be desirable. But we also believe that because this is a rule governing commercial transactions, the parties' interest in a clearly defined rule, which affords them some degree of certainty, should be weighted heavily. Thus, we believe that the "breach date" selected should indeed be the date at which the contract is broken and the loss incurred, rather than some other date that gives plaintiffs like K & L the fullest possible recovery.

section 63(c) has no applicability to the conversion rate issue. We recognize that the creditors' committee petitioned in 1975 to have the K & L contracts rejected, and they argue that they should not be made to suffer because of subsequent currency fluctuations. But we think that K & L is entitled to the conversion rate in effect when the contract was actually broken.

We hold therefore that the actual breach date—the date upon which the contract was rejected, May 9, 1980—is controlling. The rate of conversion prevailing on that date should be applied to the damages estimation to yield the dollar judgment amount.

The judgment of the district court is vacated and the matter is remanded for revaluation of K & L's claim in accordance with the exchange rate in effect on May 9, 1980.

So ordered.

Notes

1. The two United States Supreme Court decisions discussed in *Good Hope Chemical* (*Hicks* and *Deutsche Bank*) involved cases in which, between breach and judgment, German currency had depreciated drastically in relation to United States currency. At the time of *Hicks* and *Deutsche Bank*, in suits between German creditors and German debtors, the German courts were engaged in a practice of equitable revaluation of debts to protect creditors against this depreciation. There is no indication that the United States Supreme Court was aware of this. See Nussbaum, Money in the Law 206-211 (rev. ed. 1950). Should the German practice have made a difference in the results in *Hicks* or *Deutsche Bank*, or both?

2. In note 8 of the opinion, *Good Hope Chemical* refers to a more flexible approach. What might this be?

3. In *Good Hope Chemical*, the contracts called for the exchangers to be shipped "F.A.S., a German or Dutch port." The Uniform Commercial Code §2-319(2) defines "F.A.S." as "free alongside" and states that it "is a delivery term under which the seller must (a) at his own expense and risk deliver the goods alongside the vessel in the manner usual in that port or on a dock designated and provided by the buyer; and (b) obtain and tender a receipt for the goods in exchange for which the carrier is under a duty to issue a bill of lading." UCC §2-319 (4) makes it clear the "unless otherwise agreed" a F.A.S. sale is a cash-against-documents sale and "the buyer must make payment against tender of the required documents."

Perhaps more importantly for international sales, "F.A.S" is defined in Guide to Incoterms 2000 published by the International Chamber of Commerce. The Guide to Incoterms definition is consistent with the UCC provision (except that the Guide defines F.A.S. as "free alongside ship," not, as in the UCC "free alongside"). The Guide to Incoterms is a model of clarity, not only defining the various shipping terms used in international commercial transactions in a manner that can be understood by business persons who are not lawyers, but also accompanying each definition with colored diagrams demonstrating at exactly what point in the shipment the seller's risk of loss and costs end and the buyer's commences.

4. 11 U.S.C. §103(c), now §356(g)(1), referred to by the court in *Good Hope Chemical*, provided that rejection of a contract by the trustee in bankruptcy "constitutes a breach immediately before the date of the filing of the petition."

5. Competex, S.A. v. Labow, 783 F.2d 333 (2d Cir. 1986). The plaintiff obtained a judgment in England in pounds. The plaintiff then sued the judgment debtor in New York federal court and obtained a judgment in dollars enforcing the English judgment. Between and after the two judgments, the pound depreciated with respect to the dollar. The judgment debtor paid the English judgment in pounds and moved for a declaration that the American judgment was satisfied. The motion was denied. Held: affirmed. The American judgment in dollars can be satisfied only by paying the amount of that judgment and the payment in pounds should be credited against that judgment at the conversion date prevailing at the date of payment, leaving a balance of $236,000. This is the result the court predicted that a New York court would reach and, under Erie R.R. v. Tompkins, 304 U.S. 64 (1938), state law controlled.

Chapter 2

Suits by Foreign Plaintiffs

Section 1: Forum Shopping and Forum Non Conveniens

Piper Aircraft Co. v. Reyno
454 U.S. 235 (1981)

Justice MARSHALL delivered the opinion of the Court.

These cases arise out of an air crash that took place in Scotland. Respondent, acting as representative of the estates of several Scottish citizens killed in the accident, brought wrongful-death actions against petitioners that were ultimately transferred to the United States District Court for the Middle District of Pennsylvania. Petitioners moved to dismiss on the ground of forum non conveniens. After noting that an alternative forum existed in Scotland, the District Court granted their motions. 479 F.Supp. 727 (1979). The United States Court of Appeals for the Third Circuit reversed. 630 F.2d 149 (1980). The Court of Appeals based its decision, at least in part, on the ground that dismissal is automatically barred where the law of the alternative forum is less favorable to the plaintiff than the law of the forum chosen by the plaintiff. Because we conclude that the possibility of an unfavorable change in law should not, by itself, bar dismissal, and because we conclude that the District Court did not otherwise abuse its discretion, we reverse.

I

A

In July 1976, a small commercial aircraft crashed in the Scottish highlands during the course of a charter flight from Blackpool to Perth. The pilot and five passengers were killed instantly. The decedents were all Scottish subjects and residents, as are their heirs and next of kin. There were no eyewitnesses to the accident. At the time of the crash the plane was subject to Scottish air traffic control.

The aircraft, a twin-engine Piper Aztec, was manufactured in Pennsylvania by petitioner Piper Aircraft Co. (Piper). The propellers were manufactured in Ohio by petitioner Hartzell Propeller, Inc. (Hartzell). At the time of the crash the aircraft was registered in Great Britain and was owned and maintained by Air Navigation and Trading Co., Ltd. (Air Navigation). It was operated by McDonald Aviation, Ltd. (McDonald), a Scottish air taxi service. Both Air Navigation and McDonald were organized in the United Kingdom. The wreckage of the plane is now in a hangar in Farnsborough, England.

The British Department of Trade investigated the accident shortly after it occurred. A preliminary report found that the plane crashed after developing a spin, and suggested that mechanical failure in the plane or the propeller was responsible. At Hartzell's request, this report was reviewed by a three-member Review Board, which held a 9-day adversary hearing attended by all interested parties. The Review Board found no evidence of defective equipment and indicated that pilot error may have contributed to the accident. The pilot, who had obtained his commercial pilot's license only three months earlier, was flying over high ground at an altitude considerably lower than the minimum height required by his company's operations manual.

In July 1977, a California probate court appointed respondent Gaynell Reyno administratrix of the estates of the five passengers. Reyno is not related to and does not know any of the decedents or their survivors; she was a legal secretary to the attorney who filed this lawsuit. Several days after her appointment, Reyno commenced separate wrongful-death actions against Piper and Hartzell in the Superior Court of California, claiming negligence and strict liability. Air Navigation, McDonald, and the estate of the pilot are not parties to this litigation. The survivors of the five passengers whose estates are represented by Reyno filed a separate action in the United Kingdom against Air Navigation, McDonald, and the pilot's estate. Reyno candidly admits that the action against Piper and Hartzell was filed in the United States because its laws regarding liability, capacity to sue, and damages are more favorable to her position than are those of Scotland. Scottish law does not recognize strict liability in tort. Moreover, it permits wrongful-death actions only when brought by a decedent's relatives. The relatives may sue only for "loss of support and society."

On petitioners' motion, the suit was removed to the United States District Court for the Central District of California. Piper then moved for transfer to the United States District Court for the Middle District of Pennsylvania, pursuant to 28 U.S.C. § 1404(a).[4] Hartzell moved to dismiss for lack of personal jurisdiction, or in the alternative, to transfer. In December 1977, the District Court quashed service on Hartzell and transferred the case to the Middle District of Pennsylvania. Respondent then properly served process on Hartzell.

B

In May 1978, after the suit had been transferred, both Hartzell and Piper moved to dismiss the action on the ground of forum non conveniens. The District Court granted these motions in October 1979. It relied on the balancing test set forth by this Court in *Gulf Oil Corp. v. Gilbert*, 330 U.S. 501 (1947), and its companion case, *Koster v. Lumbermens Mut. Cas. Co.*, 330 U.S. 518 (1947). In those decisions, the Court stated that a plaintiff's choice of forum should rarely be disturbed. However, when an alternative forum has jurisdiction to hear the case, and when trial in the chosen forum would "establish...oppressiveness and vexation to a defendant...out of all proportion to plaintiff's convenience," or when the "chosen forum [is] inappropriate because of considerations affecting the court's own administrative and legal problems," the court may, in the exercise of its sound discretion, dismiss the case. *Koster*, supra, at 524. To guide trial

---

4. Section 1404(a) provides: "For the convenience of parties and witnesses, in the interest of justice, a district court may transfer any civil action to any other district or division where it might have been brought."

court discretion, the Court provided a list of "private interest factors" affecting the convenience of the litigants, and a list of "public interest factors" affecting the convenience of the forum. *Gilbert,* supra, 330 U.S. at 508- 509.[6]

After describing our decisions in *Gilbert* and *Koster,* the District Court analyzed the facts of these cases. It began by observing that an alternative forum existed in Scotland; Piper and Hartzell had agreed to submit to the jurisdiction of the Scottish courts and to waive any statute of limitations defense that might be available. It then stated that plaintiff's choice of forum was entitled to little weight. The court recognized that a plaintiff's choice ordinarily deserves substantial deference. It noted, however, that Reyno "is a representative of foreign citizens and residents seeking a forum in the United States because of the more liberal rules concerning products liability law," and that "the courts have been less solicitous when the plaintiff is not an American citizen or resident, and particularly when the foreign citizens seek to benefit from the more liberal tort rules provided for the protection of citizens and residents of the United States." 479 F.Supp., at 731.

The District Court next examined several factors relating to the private interests of the litigants, and determined that these factors strongly pointed towards Scotland as the appropriate forum. Although evidence concerning the design, manufacture, and testing of the plane and propeller is located in the United States, the connections with Scotland are otherwise "overwhelming." Id., at 732. The real parties in interest are citizens of Scotland, as were all the decedents. Witnesses who could testify regarding the maintenance of the aircraft, the training of the pilot, and the investigation of the accident—all essential to the defense—are in Great Britain. Moreover, all witnesses to damages are located in Scotland. Trial would be aided by familiarity with Scottish topography, and by easy access to the wreckage.

The District Court reasoned that because crucial witnesses and evidence were beyond the reach of compulsory process, and because the defendants would not be able to implead potential Scottish third-party defendants, it would be "unfair to make Piper and Hartzell proceed to trial in this forum." Id., at 733. The survivors had brought separate actions in Scotland against the pilot, McDonald, and Air Navigation. "[I]t would be fairer to all parties and less costly if the entire case was presented to one jury with available testimony from all relevant witnesses." Ibid. Although the court recognized that if trial were held in the United States, Piper and Hartzell could file indemnity or contribution actions against the Scottish defendants, it believed that there was a significant risk of inconsistent verdicts.[7]

The District Court concluded that the relevant public interests also pointed strongly towards dismissal. The court determined that Pennsylvania law would apply to Piper

---

6. The factors pertaining to the private interests of the litigants included the "relative ease of access to sources of proof; availability of compulsory process for attendance of unwilling, and the cost of obtaining attendance of willing, witnesses; possibility of view of premises, if view would be appropriate to the action; and all other practical problems that make trial of a case easy, expeditious and inexpensive." *Gilbert,* 330 U.S., at 508. The public factors bearing on the question included the administrative difficulties flowing from court congestion; the "local interest in having localized controversies decided at home"; the interest in having the trial of a diversity case in a forum that is at home with the law that must govern the action; the avoidance of unnecessary problems in conflict of laws, or in the application of foreign law; and the unfairness of burdening citizens in an unrelated forum with jury duty. Id., at 509.

7. The District Court explained that inconsistent verdicts might result if petitioners were held liable on the basis of strict liability here, and then required to prove negligence in an indemnity action in Scotland. Moreover, even if the same standard of liability applied, there was a danger that different juries would find different facts and produce inconsistent results.

and Scottish law to Hartzell if the case were tried in the Middle District of Pennsylvania. As a result, "trial in this forum would be hopelessly complex and confusing for a jury." Id., at 734. In addition, the court noted that it was unfamiliar with Scottish law and thus would have to rely upon experts from that country. The court also found that the trial would be enormously costly and time-consuming; that it would be unfair to burden citizens with jury duty when the Middle District of Pennsylvania has little connection with the controversy; and that Scotland has a substantial interest in the outcome of the litigation.

In opposing the motions to dismiss, respondent contended that dismissal would be unfair because Scottish law was less favorable. The District Court explicitly rejected this claim. It reasoned that the possibility that dismissal might lead to an unfavorable change in the law did not deserve significant weight; any deficiency in the foreign law was a "matter to be dealt with in the foreign forum." Id., at 738.

C

On appeal, the United States Court of Appeals for the Third Circuit reversed and remanded for trial. The decision to reverse appears to be based on two alternative grounds. First, the Court held that the District Court abused its discretion in conducting the Gilbert analysis. Second, the Court held that dismissal is never appropriate where the law of the alternative forum is less favorable to the plaintiff.

* * *

We granted certiorari in these cases to consider the questions they raise concerning the proper application of the doctrine of forum non conveniens.

II

The Court of Appeals erred in holding that plaintiffs may defeat a motion to dismiss on the ground of forum non conveniens merely by showing that the substantive law that would be applied in the alternative forum is less favorable to the plaintiffs than that of the present forum. The possibility of a change in substantive law should ordinarily not be given conclusive or even substantial weight in the forum non conveniens inquiry.

We expressly rejected the position adopted by the Court of Appeals in our decision in *Canada Malting Co. v. Paterson Steamships, Ltd.*, 285 U.S. 413, (1932). That case arose out of a collision between two vessels in American waters. The Canadian owners of cargo lost in the accident sued the Canadian owners of one of the vessels in Federal District Court. The cargo owners chose an American court in large part because the relevant American liability rules were more favorable than the Canadian rules. The District Court dismissed on grounds of forum non conveniens. The plaintiffs argued that dismissal was inappropriate because Canadian laws were less favorable to them. This Court nonetheless affirmed:

> "We have no occasion to enquire by what law the rights of the parties are governed, as we are of the opinion that, under any view of that question, it lay within the discretion of the District Court to decline to assume jurisdiction over the controversy...'[T]he court will not take cognizance of the case if justice would be as well done by remitting the parties to their home forum.'" Id., at 419-420, quoting *Charter Shipping Co. v. Bowring, Jones & Tidy*, 281 U.S. 515, 517 (1930).

The Court further stated that "[t]here was no basis for the contention that the District Court abused its discretion." 285 U.S., at 423.

It is true that *Canada Malting* was decided before *Gilbert*, and that the doctrine of forum non conveniens was not fully crystallized until our decision in that case.[13] However, *Gilbert* in no way affects the validity of *Canada Malting*. Indeed, by holding that the central focus of the forum non conveniens inquiry is convenience, *Gilbert* implicitly recognized that dismissal may not be barred solely because of the possibility of an unfavorable change in law. Under *Gilbert*, dismissal will ordinarily be appropriate where trial in the plaintiff's chosen forum imposes a heavy burden on the defendant or the court, and where the plaintiff is unable to offer any specific reasons of convenience supporting his choice. If substantial weight were given to the possibility of an unfavorable change in law, however, dismissal might be barred even where trial in the chosen forum was plainly inconvenient.

The Court of Appeals' decision is inconsistent with this Court's earlier forum non conveniens decisions in another respect. Those decisions have repeatedly emphasized the need to retain flexibility. In *Gilbert*, the Court refused to identify specific circumstances "which will justify or require either grant or denial of remedy." 330 U.S., at 508. Similarly, in *Koster*, the Court rejected the contention that where a trial would involve inquiry into the internal affairs of a foreign corporation, dismissal was always appropriate. "That is one, but only one, factor which may show convenience." 330 U.S., at 527. And in *Williams v. Green Bay & Western R. Co.*, 326 U.S. 549, 557 (1946), we stated that we would not lay down a rigid rule to govern discretion, and that "[e]ach case turns on its facts." If central emphasis were placed on any one factor, the forum non conveniens doctrine would lose much of the very flexibility that makes it so valuable.

In fact, if conclusive or substantial weight were given to the possibility of a change in law, the forum non conveniens doctrine would become virtually useless. Jurisdiction and venue requirements are often easily satisfied. As a result, many plaintiffs are able to choose from among several forums. Ordinarily, these plaintiffs will select that forum whose choice-of-law rules are most advantageous. Thus, if the possibility of an unfavorable change in substantive law is given substantial weight in the forum non conveniens inquiry, dismissal would rarely be proper.

* * *

The Court of Appeals' approach is not only inconsistent with the purpose of the forum non conveniens doctrine, but also poses substantial practical problems. If the

---

13. The doctrine of forum non conveniens has a long history. It originated in Scotland, see Braucher, The Inconvenient Federal Forum, 60 Harv.L.Rev. 908, 909-911 (1947), and became part of the common law of many States, see id., at 911-912; Blair, The Doctrine of Forum Non Conveniens in Anglo-American Law, 29 Colum L. Rev. 1 (1929). The doctrine was also frequently applied in federal admiralty actions. See, e. g., Canada Malting Co. v. Paterson Steamships, Ltd.; see also Bickel, The Doctrine of Forum Non Conveniens As Applied in the Federal Courts in Matters of Admiralty, 35 Cornell L.Q. 12 (1949). In Williams v. Green Bay & Western R. Co., 326 U.S. 549 (1946), the Court first indicated that motions to dismiss on grounds of forum non conveniens could be made in federal diversity actions. The doctrine became firmly established when Gilbert and Koster were decided one year later.

In previous forum non conveniens decisions, the Court has left unresolved the question whether under Erie R. Co. v. Tompkins, 304 U.S. 64 (1938), state or federal law of forum non conveniens applies in a diversity case. Gilbert, 330 U.S., at 509; Koster, 330 U.S., at 529; Williams v. Green Bay & Western R. Co., supra, 326 U.S., at 551, 558-559. The Court did not decide this issue because the same result would have been reached in each case under federal or state law. The lower courts in these cases reached the same conclusion: Pennsylvania and California law on forum non conveniens dismissals are virtually identical to federal law. See 630 F.2d, at 158. Thus, here also, we need not resolve the Erie question.

possibility of a change in law were given substantial weight, deciding motions to dismiss on the ground of forum non conveniens would become quite difficult. Choice-of-law analysis would become extremely important, and the courts would frequently be required to interpret the law of foreign jurisdictions. First, the trial court would have to determine what law would apply if the case were tried in the chosen forum, and what law would apply if the case were tried in the alternative forum. It would then have to compare the rights, remedies, and procedures available under the law that would be applied in each forum. Dismissal would be appropriate only if the court concluded that the law applied by the alternative forum is as favorable to the plaintiff as that of the chosen forum. The doctrine of forum non conveniens, however, is designed in part to help courts avoid conducting complex exercises in comparative law. As we stated in *Gilbert*, the public interest factors point towards dismissal where the court would be required to "untangle problems in conflict of laws, and in law foreign to itself." 330 U.S., at 509.

Upholding the decision of the Court of Appeals would result in other practical problems. At least where the foreign plaintiff named an American manufacturer as defendant,[17] a court could not dismiss the case on grounds of forum non conveniens where dismissal might lead to an unfavorable change in law. The American courts, which are already extremely attractive to foreign plaintiffs,[18] would become even more attractive. The flow of litigation into the United States would increase and further congest already crowded courts.

The Court of Appeals based its decision, at least in part, on an analogy between dismissals on grounds of forum non conveniens and transfers between federal courts pursuant to §1404(a). In *Van Dusen v. Barrack*, 376 U.S. 612 (1964), this Court ruled that a §1404(a) transfer should not result in a change in the applicable law. Relying on dictum in an earlier Third Circuit opinion interpreting *Van Dusen*, the court below held that that principle is also applicable to a dismissal on forum non conveniens grounds. However, §1404(a) transfers are different than dismissals on the ground of forum non conveniens.

---

17. In fact, the defendant might not even have to be American. A foreign plaintiff seeking damages for an accident that occurred abroad might be able to obtain service of process on a foreign defendant who does business in the United States. Under the Court of Appeals' holding, dismissal would be barred if the law in the alternative forum were less favorable to the plaintiff—even though none of the parties are American, and even though there is absolutely no nexus between the subject matter of the litigation and the United States.

18. First, all but 6 of the 50 American States—Delaware, Massachusetts, Michigan, North Carolina, Virginia, and Wyoming—offer strict liability. 1 CCH Prod. Liability Rep. §4016 (1981). Rules roughly equivalent to American strict liability are effective in France, Belgium, and Luxembourg. West Germany and Japan have a strict liability statute for pharmaceuticals. However, strict liability remains primarily an American innovation. Second, the tort plaintiff may choose, at least potentially, from among 50 jurisdictions if he decides to file suit in the United States. Each of these jurisdictions applies its own set of malleable choice-of-law rules. Third, jury trials are almost always available in the United States, while they are never provided in civil law jurisdictions. G. Gloss, Comparative Law 12 (1979); J. Merryman, The Civil Law Tradition 121 (1969). Even in the United Kingdom, most civil actions are not tried before a jury. 1 G. Keeton, The United Kingdom: The Development of its Laws and Constitutions 309 (1955). Fourth, unlike most foreign jurisdictions, American courts allow contingent attorney's fees, and do not tax losing parties with their opponents' attorney's fees. R. Schlesinger, Comparative Law: Cases, Text, Materials 275-277 (3d ed. 1970); Orban, Product Liability: A Comparative Legal Restatement—Foreign National Law and the EEC Directive, 8 Ga.J.Int'l & Comp.L. 342, 393 (1978). Fifth, discovery is more extensive in American than in foreign courts. R. Schlesinger, supra, at 307, 310, and n. 33.

Congress enacted § 1404(a) to permit change of venue between federal courts. Although the statute was drafted in accordance with the doctrine of forum non conveniens, see Revisor's Note, H.R.Rep. No. 308, 80th Cong., 1st Sess., A132 (1947); H.R.Rep. No. 2646, 79th Cong., 2d Sess., A127 (1946), it was intended to be a revision rather than a codification of the common law. *Norwood v. Kirkpatrick*, 349 U.S. 29 (1955). District courts were given more discretion to transfer under § 1404(a) than they had to dismiss on grounds of forum non conveniens. Id., at 31-32.

The reasoning employed in *Van Dusen v. Barrack* is simply inapplicable to dismissals on grounds of forum non conveniens. That case did not discuss the common-law doctrine. Rather, it focused on "the construction and application" of § 1404(a). 376 U.S., at 613. Emphasizing the remedial purpose of the statute, *Barrack* concluded that Congress could not have intended a transfer to be accompanied by a change in law. Id., at 622. The statute was designed as a "federal housekeeping measure," allowing easy change of venue within a unified federal system. Id., at 613. The Court feared that if a change in venue were accompanied by a change in law, forum-shopping parties would take unfair advantage of the relaxed standards for transfer. The rule was necessary to ensure the just and efficient operation of the statute.

We do not hold that the possibility of an unfavorable change in law should never be a relevant consideration in a forum non conveniens inquiry. Of course, if the remedy provided by the alternative forum is so clearly inadequate or unsatisfactory that it is no remedy at all, the unfavorable change in law may be given substantial weight; the district court may conclude that dismissal would not be in the interests of justice. In these cases, however, the remedies that would be provided by the Scottish courts do not fall within this category. Although the relatives of the decedents may not be able to rely on a strict liability theory, and although their potential damages award may be smaller, there is no danger that they will be deprived of any remedy or treated unfairly.

III

The Court of Appeals also erred in rejecting the District Court's *Gilbert* analysis. The Court of Appeals stated that more weight should have been given to the plaintiff's choice of forum, and criticized the District Court's analysis of the private and public interests. However, the District Court's decision regarding the deference due plaintiff's choice of forum was appropriate. Furthermore, we do not believe that the District Court abused its discretion in weighing the private and public interests.

A

The District Court acknowledged that there is ordinarily a strong presumption in favor of the plaintiff's choice of forum, which may be overcome only when the private and public interest factors clearly point towards trial in the alternative forum. It held, however, that the presumption applies with less force when the plaintiff or real parties in interest are foreign.

The District Court's distinction between resident or citizen plaintiffs and foreign plaintiffs is fully justified. In *Koster*, the Court indicated that a plaintiff's choice of forum is entitled to greater deference when the plaintiff has chosen the home forum. 330 U.S., at 524. When the home forum has been chosen, it is reasonable to assume that this choice is convenient. When the plaintiff is foreign, however, this assumption is much less reasonable. Because the central purpose of any forum non conveniens inquiry is to ensure that the trial is convenient, a foreign plaintiff's choice deserves less deference.

B

The forum non conveniens determination is committed to the sound discretion of the trial court. It may be reversed only when there has been a clear abuse of discretion; where the court has considered all relevant public and private interest factors, and where its balancing of these factors is reasonable, its decision deserves substantial deference. *Gilbert,* 330 U.S., at 511-512; *Koster,* 330 U.S., at 531. Here, the Court of Appeals expressly acknowledged that the standard of review was one of abuse of discretion. In examining the District Court's analysis of the public and private interests, however, the Court of Appeals seems to have lost sight of this rule, and substituted its own judgment for that of the District Court.

(1)

In analyzing the private interest factors, the District Court stated that the connections with Scotland are "overwhelming." 479 F.Supp., at 732. This characterization may be somewhat exaggerated. Particularly with respect to the question of relative ease of access to sources of proof, the private interests point in both directions. As respondent emphasizes, records concerning the design, manufacture, and testing of the propeller and plane are located in the United States. She would have greater access to sources of proof relevant to her strict liability and negligence theories if trial were held here.[25] However, the District Court did not act unreasonably in concluding that fewer evidentiary problems would be posed if the trial were held in Scotland. A large proportion of the relevant evidence is located in Great Britain.

The Court of Appeals found that the problems of proof could not be given any weight because Piper and Hartzell failed to describe with specificity the evidence they would not be able to obtain if trial were held in the United States. It suggested that defendants seeking forum non conveniens dismissal must submit affidavits identifying the witnesses they would call and the testimony these witnesses would provide if the trial were held in the alternative forum. Such detail is not necessary. Piper and Hartzell have moved for dismissal precisely because many crucial witnesses are located beyond the reach of compulsory process, and thus are difficult to identify or interview. Requiring extensive investigation would defeat the purpose of their motion. Of course, defendants must provide enough information to enable the District Court to balance the parties' interests. Our examination of the record convinces us that sufficient information was provided here. Both Piper and Hartzell submitted affidavits describing the evidentiary problems they would face if the trial were held in the United States.

The District Court correctly concluded that the problems posed by the inability to implead potential third-party defendants clearly supported holding the trial in Scotland. Joinder of the pilot's estate, Air Navigation, and McDonald is crucial to the presentation of petitioners' defense. If Piper and Hartzell can show that the accident was

---

25. In the future, where similar problems are presented, district courts might dismiss subject to the condition that defendant corporations agree to provide the records relevant to the plaintiff's claims.

caused not by a design defect, but rather by the negligence of the pilot, the plane's owners, or the charter company, they will be relieved of all liability. It is true, of course, that if Hartzell and Piper were found liable after a trial in the United States, they could institute an action for indemnity or contribution against these parties in Scotland. It would be far more convenient, however, to resolve all claims in one trial. The Court of Appeals rejected this argument. Forcing petitioners to rely on actions for indemnity or contributions would be "burdensome" but not "unfair." 630 F.2d, at 162. Finding that trial in the plaintiff's chosen forum would be burdensome, however, is sufficient to support dismissal on grounds of forum non conveniens.

(2)

The District Court's review of the factors relating to the public interest was also reasonable. On the basis of its choice-of-law analysis, it concluded that if the case were tried in the Middle District of Pennsylvania, Pennsylvania law would apply to Piper and Scottish law to Hartzell. It stated that a trial involving two sets of laws would be confusing to the jury. It also noted its own lack of familiarity with Scottish law. Consideration of these problems was clearly appropriate under *Gilbert*; in that case we explicitly held that the need to apply foreign law pointed towards dismissal.[29] The Court of Appeals found that the District Court's choice-of-law analysis was incorrect, and that American law would apply to both Hartzell and Piper. Thus, lack of familiarity with foreign law would not be a problem. Even if the Court of Appeals' conclusion is correct, however, all other public interest factors favored trial in Scotland.

Scotland has a very strong interest in this litigation. The accident occurred in its airspace. All of the decedents were Scottish. Apart from Piper and Hartzell, all potential plaintiffs and defendants are either Scottish or English. As we stated in *Gilbert*, there is "a local interest in having localized controversies decided at home." 330 U.S., at 509. Respondent argues that American citizens have an interest in ensuring that American manufacturers are deterred from producing defective products, and that additional deterrence might be obtained if Piper and Hartzell were tried in the United States, where they could be sued on the basis of both negligence and strict liability. However, the incremental deterrence that would be gained if this trial were held in an American court is likely to be insignificant. The American interest in this accident is simply not sufficient to justify the enormous commitment of judicial time and resources that would inevitably be required if the case were to be tried here.

IV

The Court of Appeals erred in holding that the possibility of an unfavorable change in law bars dismissal on the ground of forum non conveniens. It also erred in rejecting the District Court's *Gilbert* analysis. The District Court properly decided that the pre-

---

29. Many forum non conveniens decisions have held that the need to apply foreign law favors dismissal. See, e. g., *Calavo Growers of California v. Belgium*, 632 F.2d 963, 967 (CA2 1980), *cert. denied*, 449 U.S. 1084 (1981); *Schertenleib v. Traum*, 589 F.2d, at 1165. Of course, this factor alone is not sufficient to warrant dismissal when a balancing of all relevant factors shows that the plaintiff's chosen forum is appropriate. See, e. g., *Founding Church of Scientology v. Verlag*, 175 U.S.App.D.C., at 409, 536 F.2d, at 436; *Burt v. Isthmus Development Co.*, 218 F.2d 353, 357 (CA5), cert. denied, 349 U.S. 922 (1955).

sumption in favor of the respondent's forum choice applied with less than maximum force because the real parties in interest are foreign. It did not act unreasonably in deciding that the private interests pointed towards trial in Scotland. Nor did it act unreasonably in deciding that the public interests favored trial in Scotland. Thus, the judgment of the Court of Appeals is

Reversed.

Justice POWELL took no part in the decision of these cases.

Justice O'CONNOR took no part in the consideration or decision of these cases.

Justice WHITE, concurring in part and dissenting in part.

I join Parts I and II of the Court's opinion. However, like Justice BRENNAN and Justice STEVENS, I would not proceed to deal with the issues addressed in Part III. To that extent, I am in dissent.

Justice STEVENS, with whom Justice BRENNAN joins, dissenting.

In No. 80-848, only one question is presented for review to this Court:

> "Whether, in an action in federal district court brought by foreign plaintiffs against American defendants, the plaintiffs may defeat a motion to dismiss on the ground of forum non conveniens merely by showing that the substantive law that would be applied if the case were litigated in the district court is more favorable to them than the law that would be applied by the courts of their own nation." Pet. for Cert. in No. 80-848, p. i.

In No. 80-883, the Court limited its grant of certiorari, see 450 U.S. 909, 101 S.Ct. 1346, 67 L.Ed.2d 33, to the same question:

> "Must a motion to dismiss on grounds of forum non conveniens be denied whenever the law of the alternate forum is less favorable to recovery than that which would be applied by the district court?" Pet. for Cert. in No. 80-883, p. i.

I agree that this question should be answered in the negative. Having decided that question, I would simply remand the case to the Court of Appeals for further consideration of the question whether the District Court correctly decided that Pennsylvania was not a convenient forum in which to litigate a claim against a Pennsylvania company that a plane was defectively designed and manufactured in Pennsylvania.

Notes

1. In footnote 18, Justice Marshall lists the factors that make an American forum so attractive to foreigners injured abroad. Some of these same factors are repeated in more colorful language by Lord Denning in Smith Kline & French Labs v. Bloch, later in this chapter, page 219. In *Piper*, the plaintiff "candidly admits" that suit was brought in the United States "because its laws regarding liability, capacity to sue, and damages are more favorable to her position than are those of Scotland." Lord Denning suggests that the primary motive may have been the "heavy damages" that an American jury might award. Although choice of law considerations may be significant (in *Piper*, the Third Circuit decided that United States Law would apply whereas a Scottish court would probably apply Scottish law), it is the American jury, in Denning's words, "prone to award fabulous damages," coupled with the ease of access to court provided by the contingent fee, that is the major attraction of American courts.

The fact that damage awards in the United States are higher than in the country where the foreign plaintiff was injured, affects more than the number of suits filed and litigated to judgment here. It influences settlements of claims. Under what has become known as "the mid-Atlantic formula," claims of European plaintiffs injured in Europe are being settled at figures above the likely recovery in the foreign forum. The amount of the settlement turns on the probability that jurisdiction over the defendant could have been obtained in the United States and that a motion for forum non conveniens dismissal would not be successful. See Eugene J. Silva, "Practical Views on Stemming the Tide of Foreign Plaintiffs and Concluding Mid-Atlantic Settlements," 28 Texas Int'l L.J. 479 (1993).

Even if an American court decides that foreign law applies, including foreign heads of damages, it is, surprisingly to the uninitiated, the prevailing choice-of-law doctrine that determination of the amount to be awarded under these heads (e.g. pain and suffering), is "procedural" to be determined under the procedure of the American forum. Foreign levels of recovery are irrelevant to this determination. See Restatement (Second) Conflict of Laws (1969) § 171, comment f: "The forum will follow its own local practices in determining whether the damages awarded by a jury are excessive"; 1 Albert Venn Dicey & J.H.C. Morris, The Conflict of Laws 170 (Lawrence Collins et al. eds. 13th ed. 2000): "A distinction must be drawn between remoteness and heads of damages, which are questions of substance governed by the *lex causae*, and the measure or quantification of damages, which is a question of procedure governed by the *lex fori*." Courts usually treat statutory limits on damages as substantive. But see Stevens v. Head, 176 C.L.R. 433 (Austl. 1993) (holding that the New South Wales statutory limit on non-economic damages is "procedural" and that Queensland law should be applied by a Queensland court). Occasionally a court has treated a judicially imposed limit on damages as sufficiently specific as to be substantive. See Cunningham v. Quaker Oats Co., 107 F.R.D. 66 (W.D. N.Y. 1985) (will apply as the equivalent of a statutory cap on recovery, the declaration of the Canadian Supreme Court that $100,000 is the "upper limit" of recovery for one element of damages, but will not apply the general level of Canadian recoveries to another element of damages). There are a few cases in which a court has treated quantification of damages as substantive. See Bhatnagar v. Surrendra Overseas Ltd., 52 F.3d 1220, 1235 (3d Cir. 1995) (vacating award of non-pecuniary damages with instruction to "reassess those damages in accordance with Indian law"); Archuleta v. Valencia, 871 P.2d 198 (Wyo. 1994) (applying Colorado law to determine whether the jury's verdict was inadequate).

The prevailing rule that quantification of damages is procedural is undesirable because it affects the choice of forum. Gasperini v. Center for Humanities, Inc., 518 U.S. 415 (1996), may facilitate a change. The United States Supreme Court unanimously agreed that "[t]he Second Circuit correctly recognized that when New York substantive law governs a claim for relief, New York law and decisions guide the allowable damages." Id. at 2224. In *Gasperini*, the relevant state law was that of the state in which the federal court was sitting. If, under the choice-of-law rules of that state, the law of another state governed substantive issues, but the courts of the forum state took the traditional view that quantification of damages under sister-state heads was procedural and governed by forum standards, a federal court would be forced to follow. Cf. Klaxon Co. v. Stentor Elec. Mfg. Co., 313 U.S. 487, 496 (1941) (holding that whether prejudgment interest is treated as substantive or procedural for choice-of-law purposes is governed by the law of the state in which the federal court is sitting and that a federal court sitting in Delaware cannot apply New York law on this issue unless a Delaware state court would do so). A federal court could reject a state's procedural characterization of a conflicts issue if this characterization was unconstitutional, but traditional procedural characterizations, though arguably wrong under modern choice-of-law analysis, are unlikely to be declared unconstitutional. See Sun Oil Co. v. Wortman, 486 U.S. 717 (1988) (holding that Kansas may characterize time limitations as procedural and permit recovery that would be time-barred in the states whose law applies to substantive issues). Nevertheless, *Gasperini* strongly supports the contention that, when reviewing jury awards, state courts should apply the standards of another jurisdiction if that jurisdiction's law governs the substantive issues in the case. If a state court does so, *Gasperini* unanimously holds that a federal district judge must also compare the verdict with awards in that other jurisdiction.

American jury awards may be influenced, not by an officious zeal to do good with someone else's money, but by a realization, as Lord Denning notes in *Smith Kline,* that a large contingent fee (and expenses) will be deducted from what the plaintiff receives, and by the fact that because the United States does not have "a strong welfare state system," injured plaintiffs are likely to have to rely solely on torts recovery for compensation, support, and medical treatment. See Basil S. Markesinis, Litigation-Mania in England, Germany and the U.S.A.: Are We So Very Different?, 49 Cambridge L. J. 233, 243 (1990).

Even within the European Economic Community, average awards differ greatly from country to country, and forum shopping for the highest recovery is common. The shopping is within the jurisdictional provisions of the EEC Jurisdiction and Judgments Convention, set out in chapter 1. (Article 2 (general jurisdiction), articles 5-6 (long-arm jurisdiction), articles 13-15 (consumer contracts)). Davies Arnold Cooper, a London firm of solicitors, has constructed a chart showing that for loss of sight in one eye to a medical student who is a single woman, aged 20, average product liability awards range from over $150,000 in Ireland, through $25,000 in France, to less than $10,000 in Greece. See "The Legal Profession," The Economist, July 18 1992, survey section at 8.

2. In footnote 17, Justice Marshall states that under the Third Circuit's rule, forum non conveniens "dismissal would be barred if the law in the alternative forum were less favorable to the plaintiff even though none of the parties are American, and even though there is absolutely no nexus between the subject matter of the litigation and the United States." This statement fails to take account of the difference between the internal law of the American forum and its choice-of-law rules. There is no likelihood that an American court would apply American tort law under the facts supposed, even if the case were litigated here.

3. Justice Marshall refers to the doctrine of Van Dusen v. Barrack that when a diversity case is transferred under 28 U.S.C. §1404(a) from a federal district court in one state to a federal district court in another state, the transferee court applies whatever law would be applied by the state courts in the state where the transferor court is located. This is a significant exception to the rule that in diversity a federal court applies to non-federal issues the law of the state in which its sits. (One exception to the *Barrack* rule is when the case is transferred under 28 U.S.C. §1631 for lack of jurisdiction. The law of the transferee state applies.)

Two cases provide dramatic contrasts in the tactical use of the *Barrack* rule:

Ferens v. John Deere Co., 494 U.S. 516 (1990). Ferens was injured in Pennsylvania by a harvester manufactured by Deere. After the Pennsylvania two-year tort statute of limitations had run, Ferens filed suit in a Pennsylvania federal court based on contract and warranty claims, for which the limitations had not run. He brought suit in a Mississippi federal court on the tort claims. Mississippi had a six-year statute of limitations, which a Mississippi state court would apply it to the Pennsylvania tort because, under the Mississippi conflicts rule, the limitations would be "procedural." Ferens then moved in the Mississippi federal court for a 1404(a) transfer of his tort action to the Pennsylvania district court where the contract and warranty claims were pending. This motion was granted and the Supreme Court held that under *Barrack*, Ferens took with him the six-year Mississippi statute of limitations. (The *Ferens* ploy is no longer available in Mississippi because the legislature has passed a "borrowing statute" that on the facts of *Ferens* would apply the Pennsylvania limitations. Miss. Code Ann. § 15-1-65 (Supp.))

In re Air Crash Disaster at Boston, 399 F. Supp. 1106 (D. Mass. 1975). New Hampshire residents boarded an airplane in New Hampshire and were killed when the plane crashed in Massachusetts. Massachusetts had a $200,000 limit on wrongful death recovery. Some of the suits for the wrongful death of the New Hampshire residents were filed in New Hampshire federal court and some in Massachusetts federal court. The New Hampshire suits were then consolidated with the Massachusetts suits under 28 U.S.C. § 1407 for coordinated pretrial proceedings. The Massachusetts choice-of-law rule chose Massachusetts law as governing the claims of the New Hampshire claimants, but a New Hampshire court would apply New Hampshire law. Even though the transfer to Massachusetts was under 1407, rather than 1404(a), the court assumed the *Barrack* rule governed. Consequently, the suits filed in Massachusetts were subject to the Massachusetts limit on damages, but not the suits filed in New Hampshire.

4. Despite *Piper Aircraft*, some federal circuit courts, while reciting the "abuse of discretion" standard, have re-examined the trial court's analysis and reversed forum non conveniens dismissals of suits brought against American defendants by foreign plaintiffs injured abroad. See Lony v. E.I. DuPont De Nemours & Co., 935 F.2d 604, 613 (3rd Cir. 1991) (defendant "has not carried its 'heavy burden' to prove that [the German plaintiff's] choice of a forum with proper jurisdiction must be rejected in favor of a German court"); William L. Reynolds, "The Proper Forum for a Suit: Transnational Forum Non Conveniens and Counter-Suit Injunctions in the Federal Courts," 70 Texas L. Rev. 1663, 1686 (1992).

5. State courts differ in their readiness to follow *Piper Aircraft* and dismiss suits brought against American defendants by foreigners injured abroad. See Stangvik v. Shiley Inc., 819 P.2d 14 (Cal. 1991) (affirming a forum non conveniens stay of suits brought by families of Swedish and Norwegian patients who died after heart valve implants failed); Picketts v. International Playtex, Inc., 576 A.2d 518, 525 (Conn. 1990) (reversing forum non conveniens dismissal of action for wrongful death of Canadian who used product in Canada, stating that "[w]hile the weight to be given the choice of a domestic forum by foreign plaintiffs is diminished, their entitlement to a preference does not disappear entirely").

Ison v. E.I. Dupont de Nemours & Co., 729 A.2d 832 (Del. 1999) reversed the trial court's forum non conveniens dismissal of a product liability suit brought by foreign nationals whose children suffered birth defects in New Zealand and Great Britain. The court stated that although the presumption in favor of a plaintiff's choice of forum "is not as strong in the case of a foreign national plaintiff," the defendant did not show the "overwhelming hardship" that would justify dismissal.

Myers v. The Boeing Co., 794 P.2d 1272 (Wash. 1990), affirmed a forum non conveniens dismissal of a suit by Japanese nationals against a Washington manufacturer for wrongful deaths resulting from a plane crash in Japan. The court approved the trial court's finding "that the balance of private and public interest factors weighs heavily in favor of trial of damages in Japan" but "took this opportunity to expressly decline to adopt Reyno.... because it simply is not necessary. Proper application of the Gulf Oil [private and public interest] factors alone will lead to fair and equitable results." (Id. at 1280-81).

6. The United States is not a magnet forum for all suits. A claim for defamation would be subject to the strict constitutional limits imposed by the Supreme Court. See New York Times v. Sullivan, 376 U.S. 254 (1964) (a public official cannot recover damages for a defamatory falsehood relating to his official conduct unless he proves that the statement was made with actual malice); Gertz v. Robert Welch, Inc., 418 U.S. 323 (1974) (when assessing damages for libel of a private individual, states may not impose liability without fault and may not permit recovery of presumed or punitive damages unless liability is based on knowledge of falsity or reckless disregard for the truth). Cf. Bachchan v. India Abroad Publications, Inc., 585 N.Y.S.2d 661 (N.Y. Sup. Ct. 1992) (refuse recognition of English libel judgment on the ground that recognition would be repugnant to the forum's public policy in the light of limits on such recoveries required by the First Amendment of the United States Constitution); Matusevitch v. Telnikoff, 877 F. Supp. 1 (D.D.C. 1995) (same).

Do courts in a magnet forum have an obligation to examine their rules and procedures and modify those that are luring claimants from forums that are more appropriate for adjudicating the matters in dispute? England has been a magnet forum for defamation actions. These suits are among the few in which England has retained a jury trial in civil matters [Supreme Court Act 1981, Part III, §69(1) (providing for jury trial on issues of fraud, libel, slander, malicious prosecution, and false imprisonment)] and jury awards have typically been generous. Two opinions by European Community tribunals and two by the English Court of Appeal, however, have made England a less attractive forum for defamation suits.

In Shevill v. Presse Alliance S.A., [1995] 2 W.L.R. 499 (Ct. J. E.C., Case C-68/93) the Court of Justice of the European Communities interpreted article 5(3) of the European Union Convention on Jurisdiction and Enforcement of Judgments (p. 20, supra) to permit a victim of libel to sue in any country where the libel was published and caused harm, but if the forum is not the defendant's domicile, the plaintiff may recover only for harm caused in that country. Thus England will no longer be an attractive forum for foreigners libeled in England but incurring most of their damages elsewhere. In Tolstoy Milosslavsky v. United Kingdom, [1995] 20 E.H.R.R. 442, the European Court of Human Rights held that an English libel award of 1.5 million pounds was not "necessary in a democratic society" to protect the "reputation or rights of others" and therefore it interfered with the defendant's exercise of his right to freedom of expression as guaranteed by Article 10(1) of the European Convention for the Protection of Human Rights and Fundamental Freedoms [Opened for signature Nov. 4, 1950, 213 U.N.T.S. 221, entered into force Sept. 3, 1953]. In Rantzen v. Mirror Group Newspapers Ltd., [1993] 3 W.L.R. 953, the English Court of Appeal exercised powers recently granted to it by legislation and court rules to substitute a sum of £110,000 for a jury libel award of 250,000 pounds. Finally, John v. MGN Ltd., [1996], All E.R. 35 (Ct. App.), reduced a libel award by seventy-five percent and stated that in future cases libel juries should be informed of the maximum conventional awards for pain and suffering and loss of amenity set by English judges in personal injury cases, and should be instructed to take these personal injury awards into account in arriving at a verdict in libel cases. The Court also indicated than after it has reviewed a sufficient number of libel awards, courts and counsel in libel cases can refer to the awards approved or substituted by the Court of Appeal.

On the other hand, one feature of United States law that has made it a magnet forum, the contingent fee, is now available in England and Wales. Courts and Legal Services Act 1990, c. 41, pt. II, § 58 (permitting a "conditional fee" except in specified proceedings); Conditional Fee Agreements Order 1995 (SI 1995 No. 1674) (specifying proceedings in which conditional fee agreements are permitted, including those "in which there is a claim for damages in respect of personal injuries or death").

7. The United States has treaties of "Friendship, Commerce, and Navigation" (FCN) with approximately 25 foreign countries. (FCN is a generic name for these treaties, although the title of a specific treaty may differ. For example, the treaty with Luxembourg is entitled "Treaty of Friendship, Establishment, and Navigation," 14 U.S.T. 251, TIAS 5306.) These treaties typically contain clauses that guarantee the citizens of each country "national treatment with respect to having access to courts of justice both in pursuit of and in defense of rights." For the conclusion that these treaties prevent a United States court from forum non conveniens dismissal of a suit brought by a citizen of a FCN-treaty country unless it would dismiss on similar grounds a suit brought by a nonresident U.S. citizen, see Alan Jay Stevenson, Forum Non Conveniens and Equal Access Under FCN Treaties: A Foreign Plaintiff's Rights, 13 Hastings Int'l & Comp. L. Rev. 267, 277-78 (1990).

8. Forum non conveniens dismissals and stays have been granted even though, because of the availability of a contingent fee, legal aid, or a jury trial, the forum is more favorable to the plaintiff than the alternative foreign jurisdiction. See Magnin v. Teledyne Continental Motors, 91 F.3d 1424 (11th Cir. 1996) (affirming forum non conveniens dismissal of wrongful death suit for French decedent although France provides neither a contingent fee nor a jury trial); Murray v. British Broadcasting Corp., 81 F.3d 287 (2d Cir. 1996) (affirming dismissal of English plaintiff's suit although England does not permit a contingent fee for the copyright infringement and unfair competition action); Connelly v. R.T.Z. Corp. PLC, [1996] 2 W.L.R. 251 (C.A.) (dismissing appeal of stay although the plaintiff can obtain legal aid for his suit in England but not in Namibia, referring to the language of the Legal Aid and Advice Act 1949 § 1(7)(b) that "the rights conferred by this... Act... shall not affect the rights or liabilities of other parties").

Taylor v. LSI Logic Corp., 689 A.2d 1196 (Del. 1997), reversed a forum non conveniens dismissal by a trial judge who found that Canada would be a more appropriate forum. The suit was by a Canadian shareholder of a Canadian subsidiary who brought suit against the U.S. parent company to enjoin the parent's acquisition of the public minority interest in the Canadian subsidiary. A factor that the court stated weighed in favor of plaintiff's choice of the Delaware forum was that rules of discovery are more restrictive in Canada.

9. As Justice Marshall states in footnote 29 of his opinion in the principal case, "the need to apply foreign law favors dismissal [but] this factor alone is not sufficient to warrant dismissal when a balancing of all relevant factors shows that the plaintiff's chosen forum is appropriate." See Boosey & Hawkes Music Publishers, Ltd. v. Walt Disney Co., 145 F.3d 481 (2d Cir. 1998) (reversing a forum non conveniens dismissal despite the need to apply foreign copyright law because a U.S. forum could dispose of all claims against the licensee whereas dismissal would require the plaintiff to sue in eighteen countries); Peregrine Myanmar Ltd. v. Segal, 89 F.3d 41 (2d Cir. 1996) (affirming denial of forum non conveniens dismissal motion although Hong Kong law applies); Salabaschew v. TRW, Inc., 654 N.E.2d 387 (Ohio App. 1995), appeal not allowed, 650 N.E.2d 481 (Ohio 1995) (holding that, although French law applied, the trial court's dismissal was an abuse of discretion).

10. For cases that reached different results with regard to forum non conveniens dismissal of a suit by a U.S. citizen suing to recovery for wrongful death suffered abroad,

see Iragorri v. International Elevator, Inc., 203 F.3d 8 (1st Cir. 2000) (affirming dismissal); Guidi v. Inter-Continental Hotels Corp., 224 F.3d 142 (2d Cir. 2000) (reversing dismissal). See also Scottish Air International Inc. v. British Caledonian Group, 81 F.3d 1224 (2d Cir. 1996) (affirming dismissal of a suit to compel British airline to place plaintiff on its board of directors, finding that both private and public factors rebutted the strong presumption in favor of a United States citizen's choice of a United States forum).

Gemini Capital Group, Inc. v. Yap Fishing corp., 150 F.3d 1088 (9th Cir. 1998) affirmed a forum non conveniens dismissal of a California corporation's suit in Hawaii, stating that the trial court properly gave plaintiff's choice of forum "less deference" than would have been given to a Hawaiian plaintiff suing in its home state. Contra, *Guidi* supra at 147 (U.S. plaintiff has "home forum" in any federal district).

Harrison v. Wyeth Laboratories Division of American Home Products Corp.
510 F. Supp. 1 (E.D. Pa. 1980), aff'd w.o. opinion, 676 F.2d 685 (3d Cir. 1982)

MEMORANDUM OPINION AND ORDER

WEINER, District Judge.

Plaintiffs in these actions are all citizens and residents of the United Kingdom. They each allege that they purchased oral contraceptives within the United Kingdom, used them in accordance with the directions and instructions, and as a direct and proximate result of such usage suffered injury, damages, and/or death. Presently before this Court is the defendant's motion to dismiss on grounds of forum non conveniens. For the reasons to follow, the motion is granted, subject to the defendant's agreement to the conditions specified in this memorandum and order.

I

Plaintiffs allege that defendant has its principle place of business in Pennsylvania, and is engaged in the development, testing, manufacture, production, sale, marketing, promotion and advertising of the oral contraceptives Ovram-30, Ovram, and Ovranette.

Plaintiffs allege that defendant caused the marketing, sale and distribution of the drugs in the United Kingdom and either actually produced and manufactured the drugs marketed in the United Kingdom themselves, or did so through others by agency, license, or otherwise. Plaintiffs allege that defendant was negligent in its conduct of these activities, and in its failure to give reasonable or adequate warning concerning the serious risk of which it had knowledge associated with the use of these drugs.

Defendant has submitted the affidavit of David Gibbens, the Secretary of John Wyeth & Brothers Limited (JWB), incorporated under the laws of the United Kingdom, a wholly owned subsidiary of American Home Products Corporation (AHPC). According to the affidavit, JWB is a sub-licensee of AHPC and pays royalties to AHPC for use of synthetic progestrogens, for which AHPC holds the exclusive license, in the contraceptives it manufactures, including Ovram-30, Ovram, and Ovranette. The affidavit states that all three of the drugs are manufactured, packaged and labelled in the United Kingdom by, or on behalf of, JWB for distribution in the United Kingdom and Ireland. The affidavit further states that JWB received product licenses under the laws of the

United Kingdom authorizing distribution and marketing of the drugs. Defendant argues that the litigation could and should more conveniently and appropriately be brought in the United Kingdom, as that country is the domicile of the plaintiffs, and the situs of the licensing, manufacture, packaging, prescription, purchase, and ingestion of the drugs. Defendant contends that the activities complained of did not occur in Pennsylvania, and Pennsylvania has no legitimate interest in regulating the conduct of its citizens beyond its borders. Defendant reasons that the marketing decisions were made in light of British regulation and law, and should be judged by the standards of the community affected by the allegedly tortious activity. Thus they argue that the more appropriate forum is a court in the United Kingdom.

Plaintiffs argue that while it may well be true that the particular drugs which caused the injury in these cases were actually manufactured and sold in the United Kingdom, such facts are not dispositive of its claim. Plaintiffs contend that the alleged tortious conduct consisted of marketing the drugs and placing them in the stream of commerce with knowledge that the warning accompanying the drugs was inadequate, thus creating an unreasonable risk of harm, irrespective of where the drugs were sold. Plaintiffs claim that the fundamental manufacturing and marketing decision, conceiving the formula for the drugs, the knowledge of the risks involved, the alleged withholding of adequate warning, and the distribution of the drugs, all were made by defendant in Pennsylvania. Plaintiffs argue that the alleged tortious acts occurred in Pennsylvania, and that Pennsylvania has an interest in and direct concern with the safety of products which emanate from its borders and with conduct which occurs within Pennsylvania which may cause harm to others, regardless of where that harm may have occurred. Plaintiffs thus contend that under Pennsylvania choice of law rules, the law of Pennsylvania would apply in this case.

* * *

II

A

The local interest in having this localized issue decided at home is strong. A Court versed in the law that must govern the case and familiar with the people and the community in which the law is to govern, is better able to establish the appropriate legal standards and apply them to the facts of the case.

After careful consideration we have decided that these cases would be more conveniently and appropriately heard in the courts of the United Kingdom. Even assuming arguendo that all production and marketing decisions were made by defendant in Pennsylvania and not by JWB in the United Kingdom, Pennsylvania's interest in the regulation of the conduct of drug manufacturers and the safety of drugs produced and distributed within its borders does not extend so far as to include such regulation of conduct on drugs produced or distributed in foreign countries. Questions as to the safety of drugs marketed in a foreign country are properly the concern of that country; the courts of the United States are ill-equipped to set a standard of product safety for drugs sold in other countries. The issues raised here concern the knowledge, if any, of an allegedly unreasonable risk, and the sufficiency of the warning of that risk to users of the product. Both the British and the American governments have established requirements as to the standards of safety for drugs and the adequacy of any warnings to be given in connection with its use. Each government must weigh the merits of permitting the drug's use and the necessity of requiring a warning. Each makes its own determination as to the standards of degree of safety and duty of care. This balancing of the overall benefits to be derived from a product's use with the risk of harm associated with that use is peculiarly suited to a forum of the country in which the product is to be used. Each country has its own legitimate concerns and its own unique needs which must be factored into its process of weighing the drug's merits, and which will tip the balance for it one way or the other. The United States should not impose its own view of the safety, warning, and duty of care required of drugs sold in the United States upon a foreign country when those same drugs are sold in that country. Here, that foreign country is the United Kingdom, a society in some aspects similar to our own in a standard of living, beliefs, and values. At issue here is, among other things, the delivery of medical care and drugs, oral contraceptives, a category of drugs long considered controversial in the United States for reasons of health and morals. It is therefore tempting for us to believe that our standards of product safety and care, if more stringent than their own, ought to apply to the British in order to afford the British people a higher degree of protection from possibly harmful products.

The impropriety of such an approach would be even more clearly seen if the foreign country involved was, for example, India, a country with a vastly different standard of living, wealth, resources, level of health care and services, values, morals and beliefs than our own. Most significantly, our two societies must deal with entirely different and highly complex problems of population growth and control. Faced with different needs, problems and resources in our example India may, in balancing the pros and cons of a drug's use, give different weight to various factors than would our society, and more easily conclude that any risks associated with the use of a particular oral contraceptive are far outweighed by its overall benefits to India and its people. Should we impose our standards upon them in spite of such differences? We think not.

Furthermore, fairness to the defendant mandates that defendant's conduct be judged by the standards of the community affected by its actions.

In addition, defendant claims to have complied by the dictates of the British government's requirements as to drug safety and warnings standards. While it may be true in most states in this country that compliance with the minimum government requirements does not necessarily constitute compliance with the duty of care which a manufacturer owes users of its products, it is manifestly unfair to the defendant, as well as an inappropriate usurpation of a foreign court's proper authority to decide a matter of local interest, for a court in this country to set a higher standard of care than is required by the government of the country in which the product is sold and used.

Finally, under Pennsylvania choice of law rules, it is clear that the applicable law here is that of the United Kingdom. A federal court sitting in a diversity case must apply the choice of law rules of the forum state. *Klaxon Co. v. Stentor Electric Manufacturing Co.*, 313 U.S. 487 (1941). Pennsylvania has adopted the "most significant relationship" test for determining which law to apply. *Griffith v. United Air Lines, Inc.*, 416 Pa. 1, 203 A.2d 796 (1964). This flexible approach permits analysis of the policies and interests underlying the particular issue before the court, and gives the place having the most interest in the problem paramount control over the legal issues arising out of a particular factual context and thereby allows the forum to apply the policy of the jurisdiction most intimately concerned with the outcome of the particular litigation. 416 Pa. at 21-22, 203 A.2d at 805-806. We have already shown that the United Kingdom, and not Pennsylvania, has the greater interest in the control of drugs distributed and consumed in the United Kingdom.

Hence, it is the jurisdiction most intimately concerned with the outcome of this litigation and its law would be applied even if these cases were to be heard in this forum.

B

We turn now to consideration of the availability of an alternative forum, and to practical questions of process, expense, production of witnesses and evidence, and enforceability of judgment.

Defendant argues that the alternative forum prerequisite is met by the availability of an action in the United Kingdom against AHPC's subsidiary, JWB, and that even if defendant is not subject to United Kingdom jurisdiction, the availability of JWB makes it unnecessary for plaintiffs to include defendant in any action against JWB. We do not agree. We are not sure if a suit against the subsidiary, JWB, is sufficient to constitute an adequate alternative forum for this suit, brought by plaintiffs against this defendant. As we have explained, this action is more appropriately heard and decided by a British court. But in dismissing this action as a matter of convenience, we should not insulate this defendant from judicial determination of its alleged liability and from the consequences of its actions by placing it beyond the reach of the plaintiffs and of the courts of this or any other jurisdiction. An action against JWB may or may not fully protect plaintiffs as regards their claims against defendant for the alleged tortious conduct of defendant.

* * *

Accordingly, defendant must agree to submit to the jurisdiction of the courts of the United Kingdom in any civil action timely instituted there against JWB on the claims alleged herein. In addition, important evidence, both documents and witnesses, may be located in Pennsylvania and under the control of defendant. This evidence must be available to plaintiffs and to the courts in any action brought on these claims in the United Kingdom if the courts of the United Kingdom are to constitute an alternative forum in which plaintiffs can receive a fair adjudication. Accordingly, defendant must agree to make available, at its own expense, any documents, witnesses, or other evidence under its control that are needed for fair adjudication of any actions brought in the United Kingdom by plaintiffs on their claims. Finally, so that any judgment rendered against defendant in the United Kingdom on plaintiffs' claims will have effect, defendant must agree to pay any judgment so rendered.

* * *

Note

If the defendant prevails on the forum non conveniens motion, the next point of contention is the conditions on which the motion will be granted. *Harrison* and the next case, *Union Carbide*, provide an interesting contrast with regard to these conditions. What conditions were imposed in *Harrison* that defendant avoided in *UnionCarbide*? What condition was imposed in *Union Carbide* that was not imposed in *Harrison*?

In re Union Carbide Corporation Gas Plant Disaster at Bhopal, India

809 F.2d 195 (2d Cir.), cert. denied, 484 U.S. 871 (1987)

Before MANSFIELD, PRATT and ALTIMARI, Circuit Judges.

MANSFIELD, Circuit Judge:

This appeal raises the question of whether thousands of claims by citizens of India and the Government of India arising out of the most devastating industrial disaster in history—the deaths of over 2,000 persons and injuries of over 200,000 caused by lethal gas known as methyl isocyanate which was released from a chemical plant operated by Union Carbide India Limited (UCIL) in Bhopal, India—should be tried in the United States or in India. The Southern District of New York, John F. Keenan, Judge, granted the motion of Union Carbide Corporation (UCC), a defendant in some 145 actions commenced in federal courts in the United States, to dismiss these actions on grounds of forum non conveniens so that the claims may be tried in India, subject to certain conditions. The individual plaintiffs appeal from the order and the court's denial of their motion for a fairness hearing on a proposed settlement. UCC and the Union of India (UOI), a plaintiff, cross-appeal. We eliminate two of the conditions imposed by the district court and in all other respects affirm that court's orders.

The accident occurred on the night of December 2-3, 1984, when winds blew the deadly gas from the plant operated by UCIL into densely occupied parts of the city of Bhopal. UCIL is incorporated under the laws of India. Fifty and nine-tenths percent of its stock is owned by UCC, 22% is owned or controlled by the government of India, and the balance is held by approximately 23,500 Indian citizens. The stock is publicly traded on the Bombay Stock Exchange. The company is engaged in the manufacture of a variety of products, including chemicals, plastics, fertilizers and insecticides, at 14 plants in India and employs over 9,000 Indian citizens. It is managed and operated entirely by Indians in India.

Four days after the Bhopal accident, on December 7, 1984, the first of some 145 purported class actions in federal district courts in the United States was commenced on behalf of victims of the disaster. On January 2, 1985, the Judicial Panel on Multidistrict Litigation assigned the actions to the Southern District of New York where they became the subject of a consolidated complaint filed on June 28, 1985.

In the meantime, on March 29, 1985, India enacted the Bhopal Gas Leak Disaster (Processing of Claims) Act, granting to its government, the UOI, the exclusive right to represent the victims in India or elsewhere. Thereupon the UOI, purporting to act in the capacity of parens patriae, and with retainers executed by many of the victims, on April 8, 1985, filed a complaint in the Southern District of New York on behalf of all victims of the Bhopal disaster, similar to the purported class action complaints already filed by individuals in the United States. The UOI's decision to bring suit in the United States was attributed to the fact that, although numerous lawsuits (by now, some 6,500) had been instituted by victims in India against UCIL, the Indian courts did not have jurisdiction over UCC, the parent company, which is a defendant in the United States actions. The actions in India asserted claims not only against UCIL but also against the UOI, the State of Madhya Pradesh, and the Municipality of Bhopal, and were consolidated in the District Court of Bhopal.

By order dated April 25, 1985, Judge Keenan appointed a three-person Executive Committee to represent all plaintiffs in the pre-trial proceedings. It consisted of two lawyers representing the individual plaintiffs and one representing the UOI. On July 31, 1985, UCC moved to dismiss the complaints on grounds of forum non conveniens, the plaintiffs' lack of standing to bring the actions in the United States, and their purported attorneys' lack of authority to represent them. After several months of discovery related to forum non conveniens, the individual plaintiffs and the UOI opposed UCC's motion. After hearing argument on January 3, 1986, the district court, on May 12, 1986, 634 F.Supp. 842, in a thoroughly reasoned 63-page opinion granted the motion, dismissing the lawsuits before it on condition that UCC:

(1) consent to the jurisdiction of the courts of India and continue to waive defenses based on the statute of limitations,

(2) agree to satisfy any judgment rendered by an Indian court against it and upheld on appeal, provided the judgment and affirmance "comport with the minimal requirements of due process," and

(3) be subject to discovery under the Federal Rules of Civil Procedure of the United States.

On June 12, 1986, UCC accepted these conditions subject to its right to appeal them; and on June 24, 1986, the district court entered its order of dismissal. In September 1986 the UOI, acting pursuant to its authority under the Bhopal Act, brought suit on behalf of all claimants against UCC and UCIL in the District Court of Bhopal, where many individual suits by victims of the disaster were then pending.

In its opinion dismissing the actions the district court analyzed the forum non conveniens issues, applying the standards and weighing the factors suggested by the Supreme Court in *Gulf Oil Corp. v. Gilbert*, 330 U.S. 501 (1947), and *Piper Aircraft Co. v. Reyno*, 454 U.S. 235 (1981). * * * Judge Keenan reviewed thoroughly the affidavits of experts on India's law and legal system, which described in detail its procedural and substantive aspects, and concluded that, despite some of the Indian system's disadvantages, it afforded an adequate alternative forum for the enforcement of plaintiffs' claims.

* * *

In two areas bearing upon the adequacy of the Indian forum the district court decided to impose somewhat unusual conditions on the transfer of the American cases to India. One condition dealt with pre-trial discovery. Indian courts, following the British pattern, permit parties to have pre-trial discovery of each other through written interrogatories, liberal inspection of documents and requests for admissions. Non-party witnesses can be interviewed and summoned to appear at trial or to produce documents. See India Code Civ.Proc., Order 16, Rule 6. Witnesses unable to appear at trial are sometimes permitted to give evidence by means of affidavits. See id. Order 19. Discovery in India, however, as in Britain, is limited to evidence that may be admitted at trial. Litigants are not permitted to engage in wide-ranging discovery of the type authorized by Fed.R.Civ.P. 26(b), which allows inquiry into any unprivileged matter that could reasonably lead to the discovery of admissible evidence.

Judge Keenan, concluding that the Indian system might limit the victims' access to sources of proof, directed that dismissal of the actions on grounds of forum non conveniens must be conditioned on UCC's consent to discovery of it in accordance with the Federal Rules of Civil Procedure after the cases were transferred to India. He added, "While the Court feels that it would be fair to bind the plaintiffs to American discovery rules, too, it has no authority to do so."

Another condition imposed by the district court upon dismissal on grounds of forum non conveniens dealt with the enforceability in the United States of any judgment rendered by an Indian court in the cases. Judge Keenan, expressing the view that an Indian judgment might possibly not be enforceable in the United States, provided in his order that UCC must "agree to satisfy any judgment rendered by an Indian court, and if applicable, upheld by an appellate court in that country, where such judgment and affirmance comport with the minimal requirements of due process."

As the district court found, the record shows that the private interests of the respective parties weigh heavily in favor of dismissal on grounds of forum non conveniens. The many witnesses and sources of proof are almost entirely located in India, where the accident occurred, and could not be compelled to appear for trial in the United States.

* * *

The vast majority of material witnesses and documentary proof bearing on causation of and liability for the accident is located in India, not the United States, and would be more accessible to an Indian court than to a United States court. The records are almost entirely in Hindi or other Indian languages, understandable to an Indian court without translation. The witnesses for the most part do not speak English but Indian languages understood by an Indian court but not by an American court. These witnesses could be required to appear in an Indian court but not in a court of the United States. Although witnesses in the United States could not be subpoenaed to appear in India, they are comparatively few in number and most are employed by UCC which, as a party, would produce them in India, with lower overall transportation costs than if the parties were to attempt to bring hundreds of Indian witnesses to the United States. Lastly, Judge Keenan properly concluded that an Indian court would be in a better position to direct and supervise a viewing of the Bhopal plant, which was sealed after the accident. Such a viewing could be of help to a court in determining liability issues.

After a thorough review, the district court concluded that the public interest concerns, like the private ones, also weigh heavily in favor of India as the situs for trial and disposition of the cases. The accident and all relevant events occurred in India. The victims, over 200,000 in number, are citizens of India and located there. The witnesses are almost entirely Indian citizens. The Union of India has a greater interest than does the United States in facilitating the trial and adjudication of the victims' claims. Despite the contentions of plaintiffs and amici that it would be in the public interest to avoid a "double standard" by requiring an American parent corporation (UCC) to submit to the jurisdiction of American courts, India has a stronger countervailing interest in adjudicating the claims in its courts according to its standards rather than having American values and standards of care imposed upon it.

India's interest is increased by the fact that it has for years treated UCIL as an Indian national, subjecting it to intensive regulations and governmental supervision of the construction, development and operation of the Bhopal plant, its emissions, water and air pollution, and safety precautions. Numerous Indian government officials have regularly conducted on-site inspections of the plant and approved its machinery and equipment, including its facilities for storage of the lethal methyl isocyanate gas that escaped and caused the disaster giving rise to the claims. Thus India has considered the plant to be an Indian one and the disaster to be an Indian problem. It therefore has a deep interest in ensuring compliance with its safety standards. Moreover, plaintiffs have conceded that in view of India's strong interest and its greater contacts with the plant, its operations, its employees, and the victims of the accident, the law of India, as the place where the tort occurred, will undoubtedly govern. In contrast, the American interests are relatively minor. Indeed, a long trial of the 145 cases here would unduly burden an already overburdened court, involving both jury hardship and heavy expense. It would face the court with numerous practical difficulties, including the almost impossible task of attempting to understand extensive relevant Indian regulations published in a foreign language and the slow process of receiving testimony of scores of witnesses through interpreters.

Having made the foregoing findings, Judge Keenan dismissed the actions against UCC on grounds of forum non conveniens upon the conditions indicated above, after obtaining UCC's consent to those conditions subject to its right to appeal the order. After the plaintiffs filed their notice of appeal, UCC and the Union of India filed cross appeals.

Upon these appeals, the plaintiffs continue to oppose the dismissal. The Union of India, however, has changed its position and now supports the district court's order. UCC, as it did in the district court, opposes as unfair the condition that it submit to discovery pursuant to the Federal Rules of Civil Procedure without reciprocally obligating the plaintiffs and Union of India to be subject to discovery on the same basis so that both sides might be treated equally, giving each the same access to the facts in the others' possession.

Upon argument of the appeal, UCC also took the position that the district court's order requiring it to satisfy any Indian court judgment was unfair unless some method were provided, such as continued availability of the district court as a forum, to ensure that any denial of due process by the Indian courts could be remedied promptly by the federal court here rather than delay resolution of the issue until termination of the Indian court proceedings and appeal, which might take several years. UCC's argument in this respect was based on the sudden issuance by the Indian court in Bhopal of a temporary order freezing all of UCC's assets, which could have caused it irreparable injury if it had been continued indefinitely,[3] and by the conflict of interest posed by the UOI's position in the Indian courts where, since the UOI would appear both as a plaintiff and a defendant, it might as a plaintiff voluntarily dismiss its claims against itself as a defendant or, as a co-defendant with UCC, be tempted to shed all blame upon UCC even though the UOI had in fact been responsible for supervision, regulation and safety of UCIL's Bhopal plant.

DISCUSSION

* * *

Having reviewed Judge Keenan's detailed decision, in which he thoroughly considered the comparative adequacy of the forums and the public and private interests involved, we are satisfied that there was no abuse of discretion in his granting dismissal of the action. On the contrary, it might reasonably be concluded that it would have been an abuse of discretion to deny a forum non conveniens dismissal. Practically all relevant factors demonstrate that transfer of the cases to India for trial and adjudication is both fair and just to the parties.

* * *

In requiring that UCC consent to enforceability of an Indian judgment against it, the district court proceeded at least in part on the erroneous assumption that, absent such a

---

[3]. The Indian court's temporary restraining order has since been dissolved upon UCC's agreement to maintain sufficient assets to satisfy a judgment rendered against it in India.

requirement, the plaintiffs, if they should succeed in obtaining an Indian judgment against UCC, might not be able to enforce it against UCC in the United States. The law, however, is to the contrary. Under New York law, which governs actions brought in New York to enforce foreign judgments, see *Island Territory of Curacao v. Solitron Devices, Inc.*, 489 F.2d 1313, 1318 (2d Cir.1973), cert. denied, 416 U.S. 986 (1974), a foreign-country judgment that is final, conclusive and enforceable where rendered must be recognized and will be enforced as "conclusive between the parties to the extent that it grants or denies recovery of a sum of money" except that it is not deemed to be conclusive if:

1. the judgment was rendered under a system which does not provide impartial tribunals or procedures compatible with the requirements of due process of law;

2. the foreign court did not have personal jurisdiction over the defendant.

Art. 53, Recognition of Foreign Country Money Judgments, 7B N.Y.Civ.Prac.L. & R. §§ 5301-09 (McKinney 1978). Although § 5304 further provides that under certain specified conditions a foreign country judgment need not be recognized,[4] none of these conditions would apply to the present cases except for the possibility of failure to provide UCC with sufficient notice of proceedings or the existence of fraud in obtaining the judgment, which do not presently exist but conceivably could occur in the future.[5]

UCC contends that Indian courts, while providing an adequate alternative forum, do not observe due process standards that would be required as a matter of course in this country. As evidence of this apprehension it points to the haste with which the Indian court in Bhopal issued a temporary order freezing its assets throughout the world and the possibility of serious prejudice to it if the UOI is permitted to have the double and conflicting status of both plaintiff and co-defendant in the Indian court proceedings. It argues that we should protect it against such denial of due process by authorizing Judge Keenan to retain the authority, after forum non conveniens dismissal of the cases here, to monitor the Indian court proceedings and be available on call to rectify in some undefined way any abuses of UCC's right to due process as they might occur in India.

UCC's proposed remedy is not only impractical but evidences an abysmal ignorance of basic jurisdictional principles, so much so that it borders on the frivolous. The dis-

---

4. Section 5304 provides in pertinent part: (b) Other grounds for non-recognition. A foreign country judgment need not be recognized if:
   1. the foreign court did not have jurisdiction over the subject matter;
   2. the defendant in the proceedings in the foreign court did not receive notice of the proceedings in sufficient time to enable him to defend;
   3. the judgment was obtained by fraud;
   4. the cause of action on which the judgment is based is repugnant to the public policy of this state;
   5. the judgment conflicts with another final and conclusive judgment;
   6. the proceeding in the foreign court was contrary to an agreement between the parties under which the dispute in question was to be settled otherwise than by proceedings in that court; or
   7. in the case of jurisdiction based only on personal service, the foreign court was a seriously inconvenient forum for the trial of the action.

5. New York's article 53 is based upon the Uniform Foreign Money-Judgments Recognition Act, see 13 U.L.A. 263 (1962). * * * An Indian money judgment could be enforced against UCC in New York by means of either an action on the judgment or a motion for summary judgment in lieu of complaint. In either case, once converted into a New York judgment, the judgment would be enforceable as a New York judgment, and thus entitled to the full faith and credit of New York's sister states.

trict court's jurisdiction is limited to proceedings before it in this country. Once it dismisses those proceedings on grounds of forum non conveniens it ceases to have any further jurisdiction over the matter unless and until a proceeding may some day be brought to enforce here a final and conclusive Indian money judgment. Nor could we, even if we attempted to retain some sort of supervisory jurisdiction, impose our due process requirements upon Indian courts, which are governed by their laws, not ours. The concept of shared jurisdictions is both illusory and unrealistic. The parties cannot simultaneously submit to both jurisdictions the resolution of the pre-trial and trial issues when there is only one consolidated case pending in one court. Any denial by the Indian courts of due process can be raised by UCC as a defense to the plaintiffs' later attempt to enforce a resulting judgment against UCC in this country.

We are concerned, however, that as it is written the district court's requirement that UCC consent to the enforcement of a final Indian judgment, which was imposed on the erroneous assumption that such a judgment might not otherwise be enforceable in the United States, may create misunderstandings and problems of construction. Although the order's provision that the judgment "comport with the *minimal* requirements of due process" (emphasis supplied) probably is intended to refer to "due process" as used in the New York Foreign Country Money Judgments Law and others like it, there is the risk that it may also be interpreted as providing for a lesser standard than we would otherwise require. Since the court's condition with respect to enforceability of any final Indian judgment is predicated on an erroneous legal assumption and its "due process" language is ambiguous, and since the district court's purpose is fully served by New York's statute providing for recognition of foreign-country money judgments, it was error to impose this condition upon the parties.

We also believe that the district court erred in requiring UCC to consent (which UCC did under protest and subject to its right of appeal) to broad discovery of it by the plaintiffs under the Federal Rules of Civil Procedure when UCC is confined to the more limited discovery authorized under Indian law. We recognize that under some circumstances, such as when a moving defendant unconditionally consents thereto or no undiscovered evidence of consequence is believed to be under the control of a plaintiff or co-defendant, it may be appropriate to condition a forum non conveniens dismissal on the moving defendant's submission to discovery under the Federal Rules without requiring reciprocal discovery by it of the plaintiff. See, e.g., *Piper Aircraft v. Reyno*, supra, 454 U.S. at 257 n. 25 (suggesting that district courts can condition dismissal upon a defendant's agreeing to provide all relevant records); *Ali v. Offshore Co.*, 753 F.2d 1327, 1334 n. 16 (5th Cir.1985) (same); *Boskoff v. Transportes Aereos Portugueses*, 17 Av. Cas. (CCH) 18,613, at 18,616 (N.D.Ill.1983) (accepting defendant's voluntary commitment to provide discovery in foreign forum according to Federal Rules). Basic justice dictates that both sides be treated equally, with each having equal access to the evidence in the possession or under the control of the other. Application of this fundamental principle in the present case is especially appropriate since the UOI, as the sovereign government of India, is expected to be a party to the Indian litigation, possibly on both sides.

For these reasons we direct that the condition with respect to the discovery of UCC under the Federal Rules of Civil Procedure be deleted without prejudice to the right of the parties to have reciprocal discovery of each other on equal terms under the Federal Rules, subject to such approval as may be required of the Indian court in which the case will be pending. If, for instance, Indian authorities will permit mutual discovery pursuant to the Federal Rules, the district court's order, as modified in accordance with this opinion, should not be construed to bar such procedure. In the absence of such a court-sanctioned agreement, however, the parties will be limited by the applicable discovery rules of the Indian court in which the claims will be pending.

As so modified the district court's order is affirmed.

Notes

1. The Uniform Foreign Money-Judgments Act, referred to by the court in footnote 5, is set out in chapter 3, page 251. How does the New York version differ from the Uniform Act?

2. The Second Circuit concludes not only that Judge Keenan did not abuse his discretion in granting a forum non conveniens dismissal, but also that "it might reasonably be concluded that it would have been an abuse of discretion to deny a forum non conveniens dismissal." There are many practical difficulties, however, in obtaining meaningful review of a denial of a motion for forum non conveniens dismissal. Van Cauwenberghe v. Biard, 486 U.S. 517 (1988), held that the denial of a forum non conveniens motion is not subject to immediate appeal under 28 U.S.C. § 1291, which limits the appellate jurisdiction of federal courts of appeals to "final decisions of the district courts." In re Air Crash Disaster Near New Orleans, 821 F.2d 1147 (5th Cir. 1987), cert. granted and judgment vacated for further consideration, 490 U.S. 1032 (1989), remanded for reconsideration of damages, otherwise reinstated, 883 F.2d 17 (5th Cir. 1982), held that the trial court had not abused its discretion in denying the motion for dismissal and discussed the difficulties in obtaining review of such a denial:

"As with all decisions that are reviewed for abuses of discretion, it is difficult to formulate a list of examples which will be always abuses of discretion. We can say with certainty that a district court abuses its discretion when it summarily denies or grants a motion to dismiss without either written or oral explanation. We can also state that a district court abuses its discretion when it fails to address and balance the relevant principles and factors of the doctrine of forum non conveniens. See Gates Learjet Corp. v. Jensen, 743 F.2d 1325, 1334 (9th Cir. 1984) (court's failure to consider private factors and two public factors in deciding forum non conveniens motion was abuse of discretion), cert. denied, 471 U.S. 1066 (1985); La Seguridad v. Transytur Line, 707 F.2d 1304, 1308 (11th Cir. 1983) (district court's dismissal of plaintiff's action without balancing private and public factors or specifying facts supporting dismissal was abuse of discretion); Founding Church of Scientology v. Verlag, 536 F.2d 429, 436 (D.C.Cir. 1976) (district court's weighing of only disadvantages of one forum was abuse of discretion). Beyond these two examples, we cannot list which decisions will be adjudged abuses of discretion and which will not. Simply stated, our duty as an appellate court in reviewing forum non conveniens decisions is to review the lower court's decisionmaking process and conclusion and determine if it is reasonable, our duty is not to perform a de novo analysis and make the initial determination for the district court.

"In deciding whether a district court's denial of a motion to dismiss for forum non conveniens was an abuse of discretion, we may also need to consider an additional factor—the effect, if any, of a subsequent trial of the case. The denial of a motion to dismiss for forum non conveniens is not a final order under 28 U.S.C. § 1291 and, therefore, is not immediately appealable. An unsuccessful defendant may seek certification for an interlocutory appeal pursuant to 28 U.S.C. § 1292(b), or if this is denied, the defendant can petition this court for a writ of mandamus. The decision to certify an interlocutory appeal pursuant to section 1292(b) is within the discretion of the trial court and unappealable. Our intervention in this decision by way of a writ of mandamus is very rare. Hence initial appellate review of a denial of a motion to dismiss for forum non conveniens may sometimes follow a trial on the merits. In the present cases the district court refused to certify an interlocutory appeal of the forum non conveniens issue and we refused to issue a writ of mandamus. Pan American, therefore, had to go to trial in the forum selected by the plaintiffs without review of the district court's ruling, as may many defendants whose motions to dismiss for forum non conveniens fail.

"The fact that a trial on the merits has occurred in the plaintiff's selected forum does have some effect on our decision of whether the district court abused its discretion in maintaining the action before it. Unless the defendant can show that he was greatly prejudiced by the fact that the trial occurred in the particular forum selected by the plaintiff, we believe the trial's occurrence and completion bolsters the district court's original decision to deny the motion to dismiss. A defendant might establish prejudice by showing key evidence or witnesses were unavailable during trial or that it did not receive a fair trial because of the forum's animosity or prejudice toward it. By pointing out such prejudice, the defendant raises an inference that the trial court's decision to deny the motion was erroneous. In any event the fact that trial on the merits has occurred, following a denial of a motion to dismiss for forum non conveniens, may be a factor to be considered on appeal in deciding whether the trial court abused its discretion. It may often times, however, not come into play if the private and public factors otherwise support the lower court's decision."

Id. at 1166-68. *Van Cauwenberghe*, supra this note, also states that if the trial judge exercises his discretion to certify denial of a forum non conveniens motion for interlocutory appeal, the "court of appeals may then, in its discretion, determine whether the order warrants prompt review." 486 U.S. at 530.

For a rare example of reversal after trial and judgment for abuse of discretion in denying forum non conveniens dismissal, see Gonzalez v. Naviera Neptuno A.A., 832 F.2d 876, 881 (5th Cir. 1987) (defendant had shown "sufficient prejudice" resulting from "difficulties associated with obtaining foreign witnesses or their deposition testimony"). *Gonzalez* also suggests that a trial judge who denies a motion for forum non conveniens dismissal "should be hospitable to applications for interlocutory appeal under 28 U.S.C. 1292(b)." Id. at 881.

3. In an action filed in a Texas state court, removed to federal court, and then transferred to New York, the Second Circuit held that Indian plaintiffs had no standing to make a collateral attack on the fairness of the Indian government's settlement of the claims in the principal case. The court held that, "although the act of state doctrine [see Chapter 4] is not precisely applicable here" for reasons similar to those underlying that doctrine, it would not be appropriate to "pass judgment on [the Indian government's] determination" that its citizens interests were best served by the Indian government's exclusive representation of their claims. Moreover, the issue of whether the Indian government's act must be respected "is a question of federal common law binding on state and federal courts alike." Bi v. Union Carbide Chem. & Plastics Co. Inc., 984 F.2d 582, 586 (2d Cir. 1993), cert. denied, 510 U.S. 862 (1993).

4. The court in the principal case states that UCC's proposal that the trial judge "retain the authority, after forum non conveniens dismissal..., to monitor the Indian court proceedings...evidences an abysmal ignorance of basic jurisdictional principles." But see Borden Inc. v. Meiji Milk Products Co., 919 F.2d 822 (2d Cir. 1990), cert. denied, 500 U.S. 953 (1991) (modifying trial court's forum non conveniens dismissal of

plaintiff's breach of contract action so that plaintiff may re-apply for a preliminary injunction if a Japanese court does not decide plaintiff's application within 60 days after it is submitted).

5. Bhatnagar v. Surrendra Overseas Ltd., 52 F.3d 1220 (3d Cir. 1995) affirmed the district court's refusal to grant a forum non conveniens dismissal of a suit brought by an Indian national against an Indian shipping company for personal injuries suffered on the high seas. The court stated that "delay [in Indian courts] of the magnitude described by the [plaintiffs'] experts' affidavits *can* render an alternative forum inadequate as matter of law," but added "it is likely that future defendants will develop a record (if such can be made) adequate to support dismissal in similar circumstances."

6. One of the conditions imposed in the principal case was that defendant "waive defenses bases on the statute of limitations." This apparently refers to Indian time limitations that may have expired either before or after plaintiffs sued in the United States. Courts typically impose such a blanket waiver. Waiver of limitations abroad that ran after the suit in the U.S. is perhaps justified by plaintiff's reliance on being able to sue here. Waiver of limitations that ran abroad before the plaintiff sued here, however, may reward forum shopping for a longer statute of limitations. There is some authority that the defendant need waive only limitations that ran in the alternative forum after the plaintiff sued in the forum that dismisses. See Gschwind v. Cessna Aircraft Co., 161 F.3d 602, 607 (10th Cir. 1998) (affirming dismissal that required defendants to waive only "limitations defenses that would not have been available to them in France on the day [plaintiff] filed her initial complaint in" the U.S. and citing cases in accord); Kinney System Inc. v. Continental Ins. Co., 674 So.2d 86, 94 (Fla. 1996) (adopting federal standard of forum non conveniens and attaching an Appendix with rules to govern dismissals under the new standard including the following: "In moving for forum non conveniens dismissal, defendants shall be deemed to automatically stipulate that the action will be treated in the new forum as though it had been filed in that forum on the date it was filed in Florida").

If limitations ran in the "alternative forum" before the plaintiff sued in the U.S. is there an alternative forum as required for a forum non conveniens dismissal? Perhaps the answer to this objection to limited waiver is that the plaintiff can choose between (1) dismissal and attempting to find some reason why limitations have not run abroad, or (2) a judgment on the merits for the defendant under the foreign limitations. Although U.S. courts have traditionally treated time limitations as "procedural" and rewarded forum shoppers with the forum's longer period (See, e.g. Ferens v. Johns Deere Co., 494 U.S. 516 (1990), supra Note 3 page 184), there is a trend to treating limitations as substantive and applying foreign shorter limitations if choice-of-law analysis points to foreign law for this purpose. See, e.g., Restatement (Second) Conflict of Laws § 142(2) (1988 Revision); Uniform Conflict of Laws—Limitations Act, 12 U.L.A. 155 (1996) (as of January 1, 2000, in force in five states).

Lubbe v. Cape PLC
[2000] 1 W.L.R. 1545 (House of Lords)

[Lubbe and four other claimants sued Cape PLC, an English corporation, for personal injuries and deaths resulting from exposure to asbestos fibers while working for Cape's South African subsidiary in the manufacture of asbestos products or while living in a contaminated area near the subsidiary's factory. Claimants contended that Cape knew that asbestos fibers were dangerous but failed to ensure that the subsidiary observed proper safety precautions. In 1989 Cape sold all its interests in the subsidiary and other South African companies. Since then it has had no assets in South Africa.

One of the claimants, suing as personal representative of her deceased husband, is a British citizen resident in England. All other claimants are South African citizens resident in South Africa. Most are black and poor. The trial judge stayed the action on the basis of forum non conveniens. The Court of Appeal reversed and removed the stay. Then over 3,000 additional claimants filed suit in another action and over 800 additional claimants gave instructions to English solicitors to sue. All claims were consolidated into a group action. The trial court again stayed the action on the basis of forum non conveniens. This time the Court of Appeal affirmed. The House of Lords allowed the claimants' appeal (reversed) and removed the stay.]

LORD BINGHAM OF CORNHILL

* * *

The Applicable Principles

* * * In Spiliada [Maritime Corp. v. Cansulex Ltd., [1987] A.C. 460] it was stated (at page 476): "The basic principle is that a stay will only be granted on the ground of forum non conveniens where the court is satisfied that there is some other available forum, having competent jurisdiction, which is the appropriate forum for the trial of the action, i.e. in which the case may be tried more suitably for the interests of all the parties and the ends of justice."

In applying this principle the court's first task is to consider whether the defendant who seeks a stay is able to discharge the burden resting upon him not just to show that England is not the natural or appropriate forum for the trial but to establish that there is another available forum which is clearly or distinctly more appropriate than the English forum. In this way, proper regard is had to the fact that jurisdiction has been founded in England as of right. At this first stage of the inquiry the court will consider what factors there are which point in the direction of another forum. If the court concludes at that stage that there is no other available forum which is clearly more appropriate for the trial of the action, that is likely to be the end of the matter. But if the court concludes at that stage that there is some other available forum which prima facie is more appropriate for the trial of the action it will ordinarily grant a stay unless the plaintiff can show that there are circumstances by reason of which justice requires that a stay should nevertheless not be granted. In this second stage the court will concentrate its attention not only on factors connecting the proceedings with the foreign or the English forum but on whether the plaintiff will obtain justice in the foreign jurisdiction. The plaintiff will not ordinarily discharge the burden lying upon him by showing that he will enjoy procedural advantages, or a higher scale of damages or more generous rules of limitation if he sues in England; generally speaking, the plaintiff must take a foreign forum as he finds it, even if it is in some respects less advantageous to him than the English forum. It is only if the plaintiff can establish that substantial justice will not be done in the appropriate forum that a stay will be refused.

This is not an easy condition for a plaintiff to satisfy, and it is not necessarily enough * * *

The Present Cases

The issues in the present cases fall into two segments. The first segment concerns the responsibility of the defendant as a parent company for ensuring the observance of proper standards of health and safety by its overseas subsidiaries. Resolution of this issue will be likely to involve an inquiry into what part the defendant played in controlling the operations of the group, what its directors and employees knew or ought to have known, what action was taken and not taken, whether the defendant owed a duty of care to employees of group companies overseas and whether, if so, that duty was broken. Much of the evidence material to this inquiry would, in the ordinary way, be documentary and much of it would be found in the offices of the parent company, including minutes of meetings, reports by directors and employees on visits overseas and correspondence.

The second segment of the cases involves the personal injury issues relevant to each individual: diagnosis, prognosis, causation (including the contribution made to a plaintiff's condition by any sources of contamination for which the defendant was not responsible) and special damage. Investigation of these issues would necessarily involve the evidence and medical examination of each plaintiff and an inquiry into the conditions in which that plaintiff worked or lived and the period for which he did so. Where the claim is made on behalf of a deceased person the inquiry would essentially the same, although probably more difficult.* * *

The brunt of the plaintiffs' argument on these appeals to the House has been directed not against the decisions [below] on the first stage of the *Spiliada* test but against their conclusion that the plaintiffs had not shown that substantial justice would not be done in the more appropriate South African forum.

Funding

The plaintiffs submitted that legal aid in South Africa had been withdrawn for personal injury claims, that there was no reasonable likelihood of any lawyer or group of lawyers being able or willing to fund proceedings of this weight and complexity under the contingency fee arrangements permitted in South Africa since April 1999 and that there was no other available source of funding open to the plaintiffs. These were, they argued, proceedings which could not be effectively prosecuted without legal representation and adequate funding. To stay proceedings in England, where legal representation and adequate funding are available, in favour of the South African forum where they are not would accordingly deny the plaintiffs any realistic prospect of pursuing their claims to trial.

The defendant roundly challenged these assertions. Reliance was placed on the facts that the plaintiffs had not applied for legal aid in South Africa before its withdrawal and had made no determined effort to obtain funding in South Africa. Even if legal aid was no longer available in South Africa, contingency fee agreements were now permissible and it was unrealistic to suppose that South African counsel and attorneys would be any less ready to act than English counsel and solicitors if the claims were judged to have a reasonable prospect of success. If contingency fee arrangements could not be made in South Africa because South African counsel and attorneys did not judge the claims to have a reasonable prospect of success, that did not involve a denial of justice to the plaintiffs. In any event there were other potential sources of assistance available to the plaintiffs in South Africa.

The material placed before the House (and the lower courts) relevant to these issues is very extensive and cannot conveniently be summarised. The following conclusions are in my opinion to be drawn from it:

1) The proceedings as now constituted can only be handled efficiently, cost- effectively and expeditiously on a group basis. It is impossible at this stage to predict with accuracy

what procedural directions might on that basis be given in future (although the directions could only relate to the conduct of proceedings in England). Obvious possibilities include the trial of a preliminary issue on the parent company responsibility question and the trial of selected lead cases to test the outcome in different factual situations. It would be very highly desirable, if possible, to avoid determination of these claims on a plaintiff by plaintiff basis.

2) The plaintiffs' claims raise a serious legal issue concerning the duty of the defendant as a parent company, and it would be necessary to decide whether that duty was governed by English or South African law. If a duty were held to exist, there would be a serious factual issue whether the defendant was in breach of it. If the plaintiffs were successful on these questions, the personal injury issues would have, even in the context of a group action, to be investigated, prepared and quantified. This would be a heavy and difficult task. It could only be done by, or under the supervision of, professional lawyers. It would call for high quality expert advice and evidence, certainly on medical and industrial issues, very possibly on other issues also. * * *

3) A possibility must exist that the proceedings may culminate in settlement. The plaintiffs confidently predict such an outcome if they succeed on the parent company responsibility issue. But the defendant has given no indication that the claims will not be fully contested. In the *Spiliada* case Staughton J. thought it right to decide the stay application on the assumption that there would be a trial, and it would seem to me wrong in principle to reject a submission that justice will not be done in a foreign forum on the basis of a speculative assumption that, if a stay is granted, proceedings in the foreign forum will culminate in a just settlement without the need for a trial.

4)* * *Despite suggestions to the contrary there is no evidence that legal aid might be made available in South Africa to fund this potentially protracted and expensive litigation. Written submissions on behalf of the Republic of South Africa contain no hint that public funds might, exceptionally, be made available to fund it.

5) The South African Contingency Fees Act (No. 66 of 1997) sanctioned a new regime similar (although not identical) to that governing conditional fees in this country. It enables counsel and attorneys to undertake work for plaintiffs on the basis that if the claim is successful they will receive a fee in excess of that ordinarily chargeable, and that they receive nothing if the claim fails. This regime does not apply to the fees of expert witnesses, who may not be engaged on the basis that they are paid only if the plaintiff by whom they are called is successful.

6) If these proceedings were stayed in favour of the more appropriate forum in South Africa the probability is that the plaintiffs would have no means of obtaining the professional representation and the expert evidence which would be essential if these claims were to be justly decided. This would amount to a denial of justice. In the special and unusual circumstances of these proceedings, lack of the means, in South Africa, to prosecute these claims to a conclusion provides a compelling ground, at the second stage of the Spiliada test, for refusing to stay the proceedings here.

7) [T]he absence, as yet, of developed procedures for handling group actions in South Africa reinforces the submissions made by the plaintiffs on the funding issue. It is one thing to embark on and fund a heavy group action where the procedures governing the conduct of the proceedings are known to and understood by experienced judges and practitioners. It may be quite another where the exercise is novel and untried. There must then be an increased likelihood of interlocutory decisions which are contentious, with the likelihood of appeals and delay. It cannot be assumed that all judges will re-

spond to this new procedural challenge in the same innovative spirit. The exercise of jurisdiction by the South African High Court through separate territorial divisions, while not a potent obstacle in itself, could contribute to delay, uncertainty and cost. The procedural novelty of these proceedings, if pursued in South Africa, must in my view act as a further disincentive to any person or body considering whether or not to finance the proceedings.

Third Parties

[Below] it was contended by the defendant and accepted as a factor pointing towards the appropriateness of the South African forum that the defendant, if sued there, could make and enforce claims against third parties who could be shown to have contributed to the plaintiffs' condition, whereas it might be difficult to join such parties and enforce judgments if the actions were pursued here. The plaintiffs have sought to meet this point by questioning whether, in truth, the defendant has disclosed any potential claim against an identified third party with assets or insurance sufficient to meet any significant claim; by relying on Court of Appeal authority for the proposition that a defendant is only liable for such proportion of a plaintiff's damage as he is shown to have caused; and by formally undertaking, in asbestos (but not mesothelioma) cases, to limit their claim to compensation for loss and damage for asbestos-related disease to such sum as would reflect the proportion of a plaintiff's total asbestos exposure as was shown to be the defendant's responsibility. The courts below were in my judgment right to treat the third party consideration as one strengthening the appropriateness of the South African forum, but I am persuaded by the plaintiffs' response that the refusal of a stay will not expose the defendant to a significant risk of prejudice so long as any new claimants are admitted to the group only upon their binding themselves by the undertaking of the present plaintiffs.* * *

Public Interest

Both the plaintiffs and the defendant placed reliance on public interest considerations as strengthening their contentions that these proceedings should be tried in the forum for which they respectively contended. I agree with my noble and learned friend Lord Hope of Craighead, for the reasons which he gives, that public interest considerations not related to the private interests of the parties and the ends of justice have no bearing on the decision which the court has to make. Where a catastrophe has occurred in a particular place, the facts that numerous victims live in that place, that the relevant evidence is to be found there and that site inspections are most conveniently and inexpensively carried out there will provide factors connecting any ensuing litigation with the court exercising jurisdiction in that place. These are matters of which the *Spiliada* test takes full account.

Conclusion

I would dismiss the defendant's appeal against the decision of the first Court of Appeal. I would allow the plaintiffs' appeal against the decision of the second Court of Appeal and remove the stay which that court upheld. The defendant must bear the costs of both appeals, and also the costs of the proceedings before Buckley J. and the second Court of Appeal.

LORD HOPE OF CRAIGHEAD

My Lords,

I have had the advantage of reading in draft the speech of my noble and learned friend Lord Bingham of Cornhill. I agree with it, and for the reasons which he has given I too would allow the claimants' appeals * * *. I should however like to add some observations on two matters that were raised in the course of the argument about the doctrine of forum non conveniens.

Available forum

It is clear that the decision of the first Court of Appeal to refuse a stay was much influenced by the view which they formed about the defendant's submission that the South African courts were available to the plaintiffs because it had offered during the hearing before the judge to submit to the jurisdiction of those courts. It was not suggested to the judge that there were any reasons for doubting that this offer had removed the difficulty that the defendant was not otherwise subject to the jurisdiction of the South African courts as it was neither present nor had any assets in South Africa. But in the Court of Appeal it was contended that the offer was objectionable, for two reasons. The first was that the courts in South Africa were not available at the time when the plaintiffs brought their proceedings in England, as the defendant did not indicate its willingness to be sued in South Africa until after the proceedings had been brought. The second was that the effect of treating the South African courts as available in these circumstances was to give the defendant a choice of jurisdiction, enabling it to elect for the court that was more favourable to it and thus indulge in forum shipping.* * *

The approach that is to be taken to this question has been examined in a number of Scottish cases to which it may be helpful to refer, as the underlying principles which Lord Goff of Chieveley described in the *Spiliada* case were derived from the Scottish authorities. * * * In the light of these authorities I would have regarded the undertakings which were offered by the defendant in this case as sufficient to satisfy the requirement that the alternative forum in South Africa was available because it had undertaken to submit to the jurisdiction of the courts of that country. Nothing turns on the time when the undertakings were given. It is sufficient that they were before the judge when he was considering the question of forum non conveniens. As for the suggestion that the defendant was choosing its jurisdiction and thus indulging in a kind of forum shopping, this overlooks the fact that the issue as to forum non conveniens is for the court itself to resolve. It is not a matter that is left to the choice of the defender. Furthermore the court resolves the issue by looking to the intrests of all parties and the ends of justice. * * *

Public Interest

In my opinion the principles on which the doctrine of forum non conveniens rest leave no room for considerations of public interest or public policy which cannot be related to the private interests of any the parties or the ends of justice in the case which is before the court. * * *

The proper approach therefore is to start from the proposition that a claimant who is able to establish jurisdiction against the defendant as of right in this country is entitled to call upon the courts of this country to exercise that jurisdiction. So, if the plea of forum non conveniens cannot be sustained on the ground that the case may be tried more suitably in the other forum, in the words of Lord Kinnear in Sim v. Robinow (1892) 19 R. 665, 668, "for the interests of all the parties and for the ends of justice", the jurisdiction must be exercised—however desirable it may be on grounds of public interest or public policy that the litigation should be conducted elsewhere and not in the

English courts. On the other hand, if the interests of all parties and the ends of justice require that the action in this country should be stayed, a stay ought to be granted however desirable it may be on grounds of public interest or public policy that the action should be tried here. I would therefore decline to follow those judges in the United States who would decide issues as to where a case ought to be tried on broad grounds of public policy: see Union Carbide Corporation Gas Plant Disaster at Bhopal (1986) 634 F. Supp. 842 and Piper Aircraft Company v. Reyno (1981) 454 U.S. 235. I respectfully agree with Deane J.'s observation in Oceanic Sun Line Special Shipping Company Inc. v. Fay [1988] 165 C.L.R. 197, 255 that the court is not equipped to conduct the kind of inquiry and assessment of the international as well as the domestic implications that would be needed if it were to follow that approach.

However tempting it may be to give effect to concerns about the expense and inconvenience to the administration of justice of litigating actions such as these in this country on the one hand or in South Africa on the other, the argument must be resolved upon an examination of their effect upon the interests of the parties who are before the court and securing the ends of justice in their case. I would hold that considerations of policy which cannot be dealt with in this way should be left out of account in the application to the case of the *Spiliada* principles.

[Lords HOBHOUSE OF WOODBOROUGH, STEYN, and HOFFMANN, join in both opinions.]

Notes

1. Lord Hope states that "the principles on which the doctrine of forum non conveniens rest leave no room for considerations of public interest or public policy *which cannot be related to the private interests of any the parties or the ends of justice in the case which is before the court.*" (Emphasis added.) Can any or all of the public policy factors enumerated in footnote 6 of Piper Aircraft v. Reyno, supra page 175, "be related to the private interests of any the parties or the ends of justice"? As indicated in Note 6, supra page 186, England has abolished jury trial in most civil cases.

2. In what sort of jurisdiction are public interest factors likely to be less important in forum non conveniens decisions—a jurisdiction with overloaded dockets or one with light dockets?

3. David W. Robertson, Forum Non Conveniens in America and England: "A Rather Fantastic Fiction," 103 L.Q. Rev. 398 (1987), reports the results of a postal survey of lawyers whose attempts to sue in the United States on behalf of foreign clients were aborted by forum non conveniens dismissals. Professor Robertson received responses relating to fifty-five personal injury actions and thirty commercial cases. He assumed that the nine personal injury and three commercial cases in which the lawyers reported that they "did not know" if the client took further action were cases in which the claim had been abandoned. He then reports:

> If that assumption is made, then in the foregoing sample of cases 49 per cent. (27/55) of the personal injury plaintiffs and 27 per cent. (8/30) of the commercial plaintiffs gave up the claim or sold it for next to nothing (10 per cent. of its potential value or less). Only 7 per cent. (4/55) of the personal injury plaintiffs and 17 per cent. (5/30) of the commercial plaintiffs achieved anything like full satisfaction (51 per cent. or more). (Id. at 420.)

Are these results surprising given the fact that the plaintiffs had brought suit in the United States seeking higher recoveries and lower costs than were available in their home courts? What is "full satisfaction" of these claims; what an American jury would award or what would be a normal recovery in the plaintiffs' home courts? In the context of the principal case, do these results indicate "substantial justice" was not done in the alternative forums and that the courts should have refused the forum non conveniens motions?

4. A Japanese court may dismiss a case even though it has jurisdiction over the parties if there are "special circumstances" that would render retention of jurisdiction a violation of principles of justice. In accord with the principal case, "the factors considered in the Japanese 'special circumstances' method are all private ones in accordance with the distinction between public and private in the doctrine of *forum non conveniens* in the United States." Masato Dogauchi, Concurrent Litigations in Japan and the United States, 37 Japanese Ann. Int'l L. 72, 86 (1994).

Section 2: Erie, Reverse Erie, and Litigation Strategy

Sibaja v. Dow Chemical Co.
757 F.2d 1215 (11th Cir.), cert. denied, 474 U.S. 948 (1985)

Before TJOFLAT and VANCE, Circuit Judges, and ATKINS, District Judge.

PER CURIAM:

The district court dismissed this diversity case under the doctrine of forum non conveniens. The plaintiffs appeal, claiming that the *Erie*[1] doctrine required the court to apply the state forum non conveniens rule which would have precluded the dismissal. We affirm.

I

The plaintiffs are fifty-eight Costa Rican agricultural workers. They claim to have been sterilized as a result of their exposure in Costa Rica to pesticides manufactured by either Dow Chemical Company or Shell Oil Company. In May 1983, they sued these companies in Florida state court, seeking damages under product liability theories of negligence, strict liability in tort and implied warranty. The Florida court had personal jurisdiction over the defendants because they were qualified to transact business in the State of Florida. Fla.Stat. § 48.091 (1983).[2]

The defendants removed the case to the U.S. District Court for the Southern District of Florida, pursuant to 28 U.S.C. § 1332(a)(2) (1982), and, thereafter, moved to dismiss

---

1. See Erie Railroad Co. v. Tompkins, 304 U.S. 64 (1938).
2. Dow Chemical Company and Shell Oil Company are major international corporations. They are subject to jurisdiction over their persons in the courts of every state and several foreign countries, including Costa Rica. The plaintiffs chose to sue them in Florida.

the action on the ground of forum non conveniens. They argued that the plaintiffs should prosecute their claims in the courts of Costa Rica: the plaintiffs are Costa Rican citizens; they were injured in Costa Rica; and substantially all of the evidence and witnesses are in Costa Rica. Furthermore, Florida's choice of law rule would require the district court to apply the substantive law of Costa Rica.

The plaintiffs, in response, argued that the *Erie* doctrine requires a federal district court, sitting in a diversity case, to apply the state forum non conveniens rule rather than the federal rule. Florida precludes the dismissal of an action under the doctrine, where one of the parties is a resident, therefore, the plaintiffs continued, the district court transgressed the *Erie* rule in dismissing the action.

The district court, after weighing the traditional forum non conveniens factors, concluded that the convenience of the parties, the witnesses and the court, and the interests of justice, dictated that the case be dismissed, and it granted the defendants' motion. In appealing, the plaintiffs do not dispute the district court's interpretation of the doctrine, as it has been applied in the federal courts, and they do not dispute the court's weighing of the relevant factors. They also do not dispute that this case presents a paradigm for the invocation of the doctrine. Their argument is, purely, that *Erie* requires the application of the state rule because this is a diversity case.

II

The doctrine of forum non conveniens authorizes a trial court to decline to exercise its jurisdiction, even though the court has venue, where it appears that the convenience of the parties and the court, and the interests of justice indicate that the action should be tried in another forum. The doctrine derives from the court's inherent power, under article III of the Constitution, to control the administration of the litigation before it and to prevent its process from becoming an instrument of abuse, injustice and oppression. As the Supreme Court observed nearly 100 years ago, "the equitable powers of courts of law over their own process, to prevent abuses, oppression, and injustice, are inherent and equally extensive and efficient." *Gumbel v. Pitkin*, 124 U.S. 131, 144 (1888).

The doctrine of forum non conveniens is but one manifestation of that inherent power. The doctrine addresses "whether the actions brought are vexatious or oppressive or whether the interests of justice require that the trial be had in a more appropriate forum." *Koster v. Lumbermens Mutual Casualty Co.*, 330 U.S. 518, 530 (1947). Under the federal standard, "dismissal will ordinarily be appropriate where trial in the plaintiff's chosen forum imposes a heavy burden on the defendant or the court, and where the plaintiff is unable to offer any specific reasons of convenience supporting his choice." *Piper Aircraft Co. v. Reyno*, 454 U.S. 235, 249 (1981).

The court's inherent power to protect the integrity of its process through forum non conveniens is similar to the court's inherent power to punish contempt. Of the latter, the Supreme Court has written:

> It is essential to the administration of justice. The courts of the United States, when called into existence and vested with jurisdiction over any subject, at once become possessed of the power. So far as the inferior federal courts are concerned, however, it is not beyond the authority of Congress; but the attributes which inhere in that power and are inseparable from it can neither be abrogated nor rendered practically inoperative. That it may be regulated within limits not precisely defined may not be doubted.

Michaelson v. United States, 266 U.S. 42, 65-66 (1924). We think this statement applies with equal force to the authority of a federal district court to dismiss an action for want of an appropriate forum.

The Court's interest in controlling its crowded docket also provides a basis for the Court's inherent power to dismiss on grounds of forum non conveniens: "the 'chosen forum [is] inappropriate because of considerations affecting the court's own administrative and legal problems.'" *Piper Aircraft Co. v. Reyno*, 454 U.S. at 241 (quoting *Koster v. Lumbermens Mutual Casualty Co.*, 330 U.S. at 524. "Administrative difficulties follow for courts when litigation is piled up in congested centers instead of being handled at its origin. Jury duty is a burden that ought not to be imposed upon the people of a community which has no relation to the litigation." *Gulf Oil Corp. v. Gilbert*, 330 U.S. 501, 508-09 (1947). The forum non conveniens doctrine is "designed in part to help courts avoid conducting complex exercises in comparative law," *Piper Aircraft Co.*, 454 U.S. at 251, an exercise the court below would have to undertake if it litigated this case on the merits.

The plaintiffs acknowledge, as they must, the court's inherent power to dismiss a case for the purposes expressed in the doctrine. They insist, however, that *Erie* precludes a court from invoking this power if its invocation would control the "outcome" of the parties' controversy.

The *Erie* rule holds that neither Congress nor the courts have the constitutional authority to promulgate the substantive rule of law that controls the controversy in a diversity case:

> There is no federal general common law. Congress has no power to declare substantive rules of common law applicable in a state whether they be local in their nature or "general," be they commercial law or a part of the law of torts. And no clause in the Constitution purports to confer such a power upon the federal courts.

Erie Railroad v. Tompkins, 304 U.S. 64, 78 (1938). It is obvious that the district court here, in deciding the merits of the defendants' motions to dismiss, did not explicitly promulgate a state common law rule. The question thus becomes whether the court did so by implication. We think not.

We recognize that the application of the federal, rather than the state, forum non conveniens rule alters the outcome of this case. Under Florida law, the plaintiffs would litigate their claims to a conclusion on the merits; under federal law, they are precluded from reaching the merits. They are, in effect, consigned to the Costa Rican courts for trial. This does not mean, however, that, in dismissing their case, the federal court fashioned a state substantive rule in violation of *Erie*.

The forum non conveniens doctrine is a rule of venue, not a rule of decision. The doctrine provides "simply that a court may resist imposition upon its jurisdiction even when jurisdiction is authorized by the letter of [the law]." *Gulf Oil Corp. v. Gilbert*, 330 U.S. at 507. In contrast, "rules of decision" are the "substantive" law of the state, the "legal rules [which] determine the outcome of a litigation." *Guaranty Trust Co. v. York*, 326 U.S. 99, 109 (1945). It is true that a judge-made rule may qualify as a rule of decision if it substantially affects the "character or result of a litigation." *Hanna v. Plumer*, 380 U.S. 460, 467 (1965). But the trial court's decision, under the circumstances presented here, whether to exercise its jurisdiction and decide the case was not a decision going to the character and result of the controversy. Rather, it was a decision that oc-

curred before, and completely apart from, any application of state substantive law. A trial court only reaches the state rule of decision, relating to the character and result of the litigation, once it has decided to try the case and determine whether the plaintiff has a valid claim for relief. We hold, accordingly, that the district court's application of the doctrine of forum non conveniens in this case did not operate as a state substantive rule of law and thus transgress *Erie's* constitutional prohibition. The judgment of the district court is therefore
AFFIRMED.

Notes

1. The court states that the plaintiffs are "consigned to the Costa Rican courts for trial." The plaintiffs, however, brought suit in a Texas state court. Defendants could not remove to federal court because Shell Oil Company, one of the defendants, had its principal place of business in Texas. [28 U.S.C. § 1332(c)(1) provides that a corporation is deemed a citizen of a state where it is either incorporated or has its principal place of business; 28 U.S.C. § 1441(b) provides that a case cannot be removed from state court under federal diversity jurisdiction if any defendant is a citizen of the state in which suit is brought. Torres v. Southern Peru Copper Corp., 113 F.3d 540 (5th Cir. 1997), held that a corporation incorporated in Delaware with its principal place of business in Peru, is a citizen for diversity purposes only of the state in which it is incorporated, and that there was diversity of citizenship jurisdiction of a suit by Peruvian citizens against the company.] The trial court granted a forum non conveniens dismissal, but the dismissal was reversed on the ground that a Texas statute precluded application of that doctrine. Dow Chem. Co. v. Alfaro, 786 S.W.2d 674 (Tex. 1990), cert. denied, 498 U.S. 1024 (1991). The statute, Tex. Civ. Prac. & Rem. Code § 71.031(a) provided: "An action for damages for the death or personal injury of a citizen of this state, of the United States, or of a foreign country, may be enforced in the courts of this state, although the wrongful act, neglect, or default causing the death or injury takes place in a foreign state or country * * *" The claims of the Costa Rican farm workers were then settled. The Texas code was amended effective September 1, 1993 to permit forum non conveniens dismissals. Tex. Civ. Prac. & Rem. Code Ann. § 71.051(a).

The plaintiffs also sued again in Florida state court, this time joining a new defendant that was a Florida company, Dole Fresh Fruit Company. The case was removed to federal district court, the removal upheld on the ground that joinder of Dole was fraudulent, and forum non conveniens dismissal again ordered. (Calbaceta v. Standard Fruit Co., 667 F. Supp. 833 (S.D. Fla. 1987)), but the circuit court reversed and remanded for determination of the fraudulent joinder claim under Costa Rican law. Cabalceta v. Standard Fruit Co., 883 F.2d 1553 (11th Cir. 1989).

2. The 1st, 5th and 9th circuits agree with *Sibaja* that a federal court in a diversity case applies federal and not state forum non conveniens doctrine. Royal Bed & Spring Co., Inc., v. Famossul Industria e Comercio de Moveis, Ltda., 906 F.2d 45 (1st Cir. 1990); In re Air Crash Disaster Near New Orleans, 821 F.2d 1147 (5th Cir. 1987), cert. granted and judgment vacated for reconsideration on another issue, 490 U.S. 1032 (1989), remanded for reconsideration of damages) otherwise reinstated, 883 F.2d 17 (5th Cir. 1982); Ravelo Monegro v.Rosa, 211 F.3d 509, 512 (9th Cir. 2000).(but noting "that the result in this case would likely be the same if we applied California's law of forum non conveniens"). Cf. Chambers v. Nasco, Inc., 501 U.S. 32, 44 (1991) (in holding that a federal court has inherent power to assess as sanctions for bad-faith conduct, attorney's fees and related expenses, the court gives as another example of "a federal

court's inherent power," that "[i]t may dismiss an action on grounds of *forum non conveniens*"). See also Rivendell Forest Prod., Ltd. v. Canadian Pacific, Ltd., 2 F.3d 990, 992 (10th Cir. 1993) (stating that federal law controls, but not discussing why it makes a difference and reversing the dismissal for abuse of discretion); Miller v. Davis, 507 F.2d 308 (6th Cir. 1974) (refusing to follow a Kentucky rule denying jurisdiction over foreign trusts because the rule is based on "notions of *in personam* jurisdiction and choice of law that no longer predominate" [at 314] and adding "insofar as [the Kentucky rule] rests on considerations of venue, including the doctrine of *forum non conveniens*, this is considered a 'procedural' matter within the policy of *Erie*" [at 316]); 15 Charles A. Wright et al., Federal Practice and Procedure §3828 at 293-94 (2d ed. 1986) (stating that federal court need not follow state forum non conveniens doctrine).

It is doubtful that Learned Hand's statement in Weiss v. Routh, 149 F.2d 193 (2d Cir. 1945), that "we should follow the New York decisions" (at 195) extends beyond the special rule denying jurisdiction over the "internal affairs" of a foreign corporation, or whether, if it does, the decision is viable. Judge Hand looks to New York law on the issue of what constitutes "internal affairs within the meaning of the rule." 149 F.2d at 195-96. Gilbert v. Gulf Oil Corp., 153 F.2d 883 (2d Cir. 1946), rev'd on other grounds, 330 U.S. 501 (1947), explains Weiss v. Routh as dealing with the internal affairs rule and states that "New York law should not control" with regard to the application of forum non conveniens. Id. at 885. Schertenleib v. Traum, 589 F.2d 1156 (2d Cir. 1978) assumes that the *Erie* question is open in the Second Circuit and indicates that it need not decide the issue because the New York and federal rules would reach the same result on forum non conveniens in this case. Id. at 1162 n.13.

Miskow v. Boeing Co., 664 F.2d 205 (9th Cir. 1981), cert. denied, 455 U.S. 1020 (1982), noted that it need not decide the *Erie* issue because a California state court had already dismissed this case, as did the federal court, but adds cryptically: "If we were in doubt, the plaintiff-appellants would have a difficult burden to convince this court that it should not follow the state court's determination." Id. at 1162 n.13. This statement is made in the context of a state-court dismissal.

Do you agree that a federal court sitting in diversity should be able to grant a motion for forum non conveniens dismissal when the state in which it is sitting would not? In *Sibaja*, the court decided that Florida courts would apply Costa Rican law. Suppose, however, Florida courts would apply Florida law and Costa Rican courts would apply Costa Rican law, which was less favorable to plaintiffs? See Klaxon Co. v. Stentor Electric Mfg. Co., 313 U.S. 487 (1941) (in diversity cases, a federal court must apply the choice-of-law rules of the state in which it is sitting). See Allan R. Stein, Erie and Court Access, 100 Yale L.J. 1935, 1968-2006 (1991) (suggesting that whether a federal court need follow state forum non conveniens policy turns on whether state policies worthy of deference are undercut by dismissal and whether there exist countervailing federal policies that justify frustration of state policy).

Permitting a federal court with diversity jurisdiction to apply a federal forum non conveniens doctrine, is of tactical significance in those states that have no such doctrine, or apply the doctrine more restrictively. *Delaware* requires a showing of "overwhelming hardship" to the defendant before a court may grant a forum non conveniens dismissal. See Ison v. E.I. Dupont de Nemours & Co., 729 A.2d 832 (Del. 1999). *Georgia* rejects the forum non conveniens doctrine, basing its refusal on Ga. Code Ann. §1-2-6(a)(6), which provides that "[t]he rights of citizens include, without limitation the following:...the right to appeal to the courts." The Georgia courts have interpreted this to include both resident and non-resident Georgia citizens and therefore, because of the privileges and immunities clause of the United States Constitution, to include United States citizens who are not residents of Georgia. See Southern Ry. v. Goodman, 380 S.E.2d 460 (Ga. 1989). This reasoning would not apply to aliens. *Louisiana* rejects the forum non conveniens doctrine on the ground that it is a common-law doctrine and Louisiana is a civil law jurisdiction. Fox v. Board of Supervisors of L.S.U., 576 So. 2d 978 (La. 1991). La. Code Civ. Proc. Ann. Art. 123 provides for dismissal of a claim based solely on a federal cause of action when the act or omission complained of occurs outside Louisiana, but does not permit dismissal of cases brought under the Jones Act (46 U.S.C. §688), or federal maritime law. This leaves primarily cases brought under the Federal Employer Liability Act (45 U.S.C. §51 providing that railroads are liable to employees for negligently inflicted injuries) that can be dismissed. But see McKnett v. St. Louis & S.F. Ry., 292 U.S. 230, 233-34 (1934) (an Alabama court may not dismiss an FELA suit for injury in Tennessee "solely because the suit is brought under a federal law"). Russell v. CSX Transp., Inc., 689 So.2d 1354 (La. 1997), held the Louisiana Code provision that permitted forum non conveniens dismissal of only FELA cases unconstitutional as a violation of the Supremacy Clause, U.S. Const. Art. VI, cl. 2. *Montana* refuses to apply forum non conveniens to FELA cases, but has left open the question whether it will be applied in other circumstances. LaBella v. Burlington Northern R.R., 595 P.2d 1184 (Mont. 1979). *Virginia* does not permit dismissal of actions for asbestos-related injury or disease, but otherwise allows dismissal of actions that arise outside of Virginia and are brought by nonresidents of the state. Va. Code Ann. §8.01-265 (1992).

State courts in states with no or limited forum non conveniens doctrines become magnet forums for foreign plaintiffs injured abroad. *Sibaja* triggers the tactic of preventing removal to federal court. This can be done by suing in a state in which any defendant is domiciled, incorporated, or has its principal place of business. (see note 1 supra.) Another way to prevent removal is to destroy diversity by joining a defendant of the same citizenship as the plaintiff. Strawbridge v. Curtiss, 7 U.S. (3 Cranch) 267 (1806) held that "complete diversity" was required, each defendant being of diverse citizenship from each plaintiff. Chick Kam Choo v. Exxon Corp., 764 F.2d 1148 (5th Cir. 1985), held that for purposes of this complete diversity requirement, all aliens are treated as if they have the same citizenship, so that a citizen of Singapore may not sue a citizen of Liberia under diversity jurisdiction.

In 1988, Congress amended 28 U.S.C. §1332(a), to provide that for purposes of determining diversity jurisdiction, "an alien admitted to the United States for permanent residence shall be deemed a citizen of the State in which such alien is domiciled." Courts are split on the effect of this amendment. Singh v. A.G. Daimler-Benz, 9 F.3d 303 (3rd Cir. 1993), held that 1332(a) permits federal courts to hear suits brought by permanent resident aliens against non-resident aliens). Saadeh v. Farouki, 107 F.3d 52, 60-61 (D.C. Cir. 1997) held that despite the 1988 amendment, there is no "diversity jurisdiction over a lawsuit between an alien on one side, and an alien and a citizen on the other side, regardless of the residence status of the aliens" because the purpose of the amendment was "to contract diversity jurisdiction...not to expand it."

28 U.S.C. §1332(a)(3) permits diversity jurisdiction between "citizens of different states in which citizens or subjects of a foreign state are additional parties." See Charles A. Wright, et al., Federal Practice & Procedure 2d ed. 1984) §3604 at 389 (stating that "the inclusion of a citizen of a state as a party or of citizens of diverse states as parties cannot save jurisdiction of an action in which aliens are the principal adverse parties"). Dresser Industries v. Underwriters at Lloyd's of London, 106 F.3d 494 (3d Cir. 1997),

held that there is diversity jurisdiction when a Delaware corporation with its principal place of business in Texas and its Canadian subsidiary are plaintiffs and alien insurers and a Pennsylvania corporation with its principal place of business in New York are defendants. The court rejected the argument that the alien defendants were not "additional parties" because they had the principal interest in the lawsuit whereas the United States defendant's exposure was for less than 1% of the claim. The court said: "The use of the term 'additional' does not reference the level of involvement of the parties or the interests at stake. Rather it merely indicates that the jurisdictional hook upon which the case hangs is the existence of a legitimate controversy between diverse [United States] citizens." Id. at 500. "[S]ection 1332(a)(3) can best be understood as a congressional abrogation of the complete diversity rule.... [T]he language used by section 1332(a)(3) differs from the language used in both section 1332(a)(1) [providing for jurisdiction of controversies between "citizens of different States"] and section 1332(a)(2) [controversies between "citizens of a State and citizens or subjects of a foreign state"]." The complete diversity requirement applied to 1332(a)1 and (a)(2) but not to (a)(3). Id. at 498.

If the plaintiff attempts to lock the case into state court by joining a defendant resident in that state or of the same citizenship as the plaintiff, the defendant may remove to federal court and contend that the parties thus joined should be dismissed because fraudulently joined for the purpose of preventing diversity jurisdiction. See Cabalceta v. Standard Fruit Co., 883 F.2d 1553 (11th Cir. 1989) (reversing the district court's forum non conveniens dismissal after the district court determined that joinder of a forum defendant was fraudulent and remanding for determination of the fraudulent joinder claim under the applicable Costa Rican law). If the fraudulent joinder contention is successful, federal diversity jurisdiction is established and the case can be dismissed under federal forum non conveniens.

If this fraudulent joinder argument fails, the defendant can comb Title 28 of the United States Code for bases other than diversity of citizenship for removal to federal court. For example, the defendant can implead for contribution and indemnity a "foreign sovereign." The sovereign can then remove the entire action, not just the contribution and indemnity claim, to federal court under the Foreign Sovereign Immunities Act. See Nolan v. Boeing Co., 919 F.2d 1058, 1064 (5th Cir. 1990), cert. denied, 499 U.S. 962 (1991); 28 U.S.C. § 1441(d) (1988). This is not as far-fetched as it may seem because that Act defines as a "sovereign" "a separate legal person, corporate or otherwise a majority of whose shares or other ownership interest is owned by a foreign state or political subdivision thereof." 28 U.S.C. § 1603(b) (1988). The Foreign Sovereign Immunities Act is set out infra at page 281. Even outside of socialist or formerly socialist countries, this includes many manufacturers, airlines, and other commercial entities. In *Nolan*, supra, Boeing, the aircraft manufacturer, impleaded the engine manufacturer, which was owned by the French government.

Title 28 provisions other than those dealing with foreign sovereigns may permit removal. The Second Circuit has held that a federal district court may transfer a case against a bankrupt, involving claims by foreigners for personal injury and death, "from a state court to itself, after the bankrupt announces its intention to move for forum non conveniens dismissal...." In re Pan Am Corp., 16 F.3d 513, 514 (2d Cir. 1994). Transfer was upheld under 28 U.S.C. § 157(b)(5) (providing that a "district court shall order that personal injury tort and wrongful death claims shall be tried in the district court in which the bankruptcy case is pending, or in the district court in the district in which the claim arose").

Federal maritime and Jones Acts claims are not removable to federal court on federal question grounds. See David W. Robertson & Paula K. Speck, Access to State Courts in Transnational Personal Injury Cases: Forum Non Conveniens and Antisuit Injunctions, 68 Tex. L. Rev. 937, 945-47 (1990).

Chick Kam Choo v. Exxon Corp.
486 U.S. 140 (1988)

Justice O'CONNOR delivered the opinion of the Court.

This case concerns the propriety of an injunction entered by the United States District Court for the Southern District of Texas. The injunction prohibited specified parties from litigating a certain matter in the Texas state courts. We must determine whether this injunction is permissible under the Anti-Injunction Act, 28 U.S.C. § 2283, which generally bars federal courts from granting injunctions to stay proceedings in state courts.

I

In 1977 Leong Chong, a resident of the Republic of Singapore, was accidentally killed in that country while performing repair work on a ship owned by respondent Esso Tankers, Inc., a subsidiary of respondent Exxon Corporation. Petitioner Chick Kam Choo, also a resident of Singapore, is Chong's widow. In 1978 she brought suit in the United States District Court for the Southern District of Texas, presenting claims under the Jones Act, 46 U.S.C. § 688, the Death on the High Seas Act (DOHSA), 46 U.S.C. § 761 et seq., the general maritime law of the United States, App. 4, and the Texas Wrongful Death Statute, Tex.Civ.Prac. & Rem.Code Ann. §§ 71.001-71.031 (1986).

Respondents moved for summary judgment on the Jones Act and DOHSA claims, arguing that Chong was not a seaman, which rendered the Jones Act inapplicable, and that Chong had not died on the "high seas" but while the ship was in port, which rendered the DOHSA inapplicable. Respondents also moved for summary judgment on the claim involving the general maritime law of the United States, arguing that due to the lack of substantial contacts with the United States, the maritime law of Singapore, not that of the United States, governed. In addition to seeking summary judgment, respondents moved for dismissal under the doctrine of forum non conveniens, arguing that under the criteria identified in *Gulf Oil Corp. v. Gilbert*, 330 U.S. 501 (1947), the District Court was not a convenient forum.

In 1980, the District Court, adopting the memorandum and recommendations of a Magistrate, granted respondents' motion for summary judgment on the Jones Act and DOHSA claims. The court agreed with respondents that those statutes were inapplicable. With respect to the general maritime law claim, the District Court * * * concluded that the "statutory and maritime law of the United States should not be applied." This conclusion led the court to grant summary judgment on petitioner's general maritime law claim, as well as to consider whether dismissal of the rest of the case was warranted under the doctrine of forum non conveniens. After reviewing the various factors set out in Gilbert, the court concluded that dismissal was appropriate and accordingly granted respondents' motion to dismiss on forum non conveniens grounds, provided respondents submit to the jurisdiction of the Singapore courts. The Court of Appeals for the Fifth Circuit affirmed.

Rather than commence litigation in Singapore, however, petitioner filed suit in the Texas state courts. Although the state complaint initially included all the claims in the federal complaint, as well as a claim based on Singapore law, petitioner later voluntarily dismissed the federal claims. This left only the Texas state law claim and the Singapore law claim. Respondents briefly succeeded in removing the case to the District Court on the basis of diversity of citizenship, but the Court of Appeals for the Fifth Circuit ultimately held that complete diversity did not exist and the case was returned to the District Court with instructions to remand it to state court. 764 F.2d 1148 (1985).

Respondents then initiated a new action in federal court requesting an injunction to prevent petitioner and her attorneys, Benton Musslewhite and Joseph C. Blanks, "from seeking to relitigate in any state forum the issues finally decided" in the federal court's 1980 dismissal. Petitioner moved to dismiss, arguing that the Anti-Injunction Act, 28 U.S.C. § 2283, prohibited the issuance of such an injunction. Respondents, in turn, moved for summary judgment and a final injunction. The District Court granted respondents' motion and permanently enjoined petitioner and her attorneys "from prosecuting or commencing any causes of action or claims against [respondents] in the courts of the State of Texas or any other state...arising out of or related to the alleged wrongful death of Leong Chong."

Petitioner appealed, reiterating her contention that the injunction violated the Anti-Injunction Act. A divided panel of the Court of Appeals for the Fifth Circuit rejected this argument. The panel majority concluded that the injunction here fell within the "relitigation" exception to the Act, which permits a federal court to issue an injunction "to protect or effectuate its judgments." The majority reasoned that an injunction was necessary to prevent relitigation of the forum non conveniens issue because petitioner pointed to no additional factor that made the "Texas court in Houston a more convenient forum for this litigation than a United States District Court in Houston." 817 F.2d 307, 312 (1987). The majority acknowledged that due to an "open courts" provision in the Texas Constitution, Art. I, § 13, which is reflected in the Texas Wrongful Death Statute, Tex.Civ.Prac. & Rem.Code Ann. § 71.031 (1986), the state courts may not apply the same, or indeed, any forum non conveniens analysis to petitioner's case. Rather, as the Court of Appeals noted, it is possible that "Texas has constituted itself the world's forum of final resort, where suit for personal injury or death may always be filed if nowhere else." 817 F.2d, at 314 (footnote omitted). In this maritime context, however, the Court of Appeals majority concluded that the so-called "reverse-Erie" uniformity doctrine, see, e.g., *Offshore Logistics, Inc. v. Tallentire*, 477 U.S. 207, 222-223 (1986), required that federal forum non conveniens determinations pre-empt state law. Because the Court of Appeals found any independent state forum non conveniens inquiry to be pre-empted, it held that the injunction was permissible.

* * *

The Court of Appeals' ruling conflicted with a decision of the Court of Appeals for the Ninth Circuit, *Zipfel v. Halliburton Co.*, 832 F.2d 1477 (1988), cert. pending sub nom. *Crowley Maritime Corp. v. Zipfel*, No. 87-1122, which held that the Anti-Injunction Act precluded an injunction in similar circumstances. We granted certiorari to resolve the conflict, and now reverse and remand.

II

The Anti-Injunction Act generally prohibits the federal courts from interfering with proceedings in the state courts:

> "A court of the United States may not grant an injunction to stay proceedings in a State Court except as expressly authorized by Act of Congress, or where necessary in aid of its jurisdiction, or to protect or effectuate its judgments." 28 U.S.C. § 2283.

The Act, which has existed in some form since 1793, is a necessary concomitant of the Framers' decision to authorize, and Congress' decision to implement, a dual system of federal and state courts. It represents Congress' considered judgment as to how to balance the tensions inherent in such a system. Prevention of frequent federal court intervention is important to make the dual system work effectively. By generally barring such intervention, the Act forestalls "the inevitable friction between the state and federal courts that ensues from the injunction of state judicial proceedings by a federal court." *Vendo Co. v. Lektro-Vend Corp.*, 433 U.S. 623, 630-631 (1977) (plurality opinion). Due in no small part to the fundamental constitutional independence of the States, Congress adopted a general policy under which state proceedings "should normally be allowed to continue unimpaired by intervention of the lower federal courts, with relief from error, if any, through the state appellate courts and ultimately this Court." *Atlantic Coast Line R. Co. v. Locomotive Engineers*, 398 U.S. 281, 287 (1970).

Congress, however, has permitted injunctions in certain, specific circumstances, namely, when expressly authorized by statute, necessary in aid of the court's jurisdiction, or necessary to protect or effectuate the court's judgment. These exceptions are designed to ensure the effectiveness and supremacy of federal law. But as the Court has recognized, the exceptions are narrow and are "not [to] be enlarged by loose statutory construction." Ibid. Because an injunction staying state proceedings is proper only if it falls within one of the statutory exceptions and because the last of the three exceptions is the only one even arguably applicable here, the central question in this case is whether the District Court's injunction was necessary "to protect or effectuate" the District Court's 1980 judgment dismissing petitioner's lawsuit from federal court.

The relitigation exception was designed to permit a federal court to prevent state litigation of an issue that previously was presented to and decided by the federal court. It is founded in the well-recognized concepts of res judicata and collateral estoppel.

* * *

[A]n essential prerequisite for applying the relitigation exception is that the claims or issues which the federal injunction insulates from litigation in state proceedings actually have been decided by the federal court. * * * [T]his prerequisite is strict and narrow.

* * *

First, petitioner asserts a claim under Singapore law. The District Court did not resolve the merits of this claim in its 1980 order. Rather, the only issue decided by the District Court was that petitioner's claims should be dismissed under the federal forum non conveniens doctrine. Federal forum non conveniens principles simply cannot determine whether Texas courts, which operate under a broad "open-courts" mandate, would consider themselves an appropriate forum for petitioner's lawsuit. Respondents' arguments to the District Court in 1980 reflected this distinction, citing federal cases almost exclusively and discussing only federal forum non conveniens principles. Moreover, the Court of Appeals expressly recognized that the Texas courts would apply a significantly different forum non conveniens analysis. 817 F.2d, at 314. Thus, whether the Texas state courts are an appropriate forum for petitioner's Singapore law claims has not yet been litigated, and an injunction to foreclose consideration of that issue is not within the relitigation exception.

Respondents seek to avoid this problem by arguing that any separate state law determination is pre-empted under the "reverse-*Erie*" principle of federal maritime law. See generally *Offshore Logistics, Inc. v. Tallentire*, 477 U.S., at 222-223; *Knickerbocker Ice Co. v. Stewart*, 253 U.S. 149 (1920); *Southern Pacific Co. v. Jensen*, 244 U.S. 205 (1917). Under this view, which was shared by the Court of Appeals, the only permissible forum non conveniens determination in this maritime context is the one made by the District Court, and an injunction may properly issue to prevent the state courts from undertaking any different approach.

The contention that an independent state forum non conveniens determination is pre-empted by federal maritime law, however, does little to help respondents unless that pre-emption question was itself actually litigated and decided by the District Court. Since respondents concede that it was not, the relitigation exception cannot apply. As we have previously recognized, "a federal court does not have inherent power to ignore the limitations of § 2283 and to enjoin state court proceedings merely because those proceedings interfere with a protected federal right or invade an area pre-empted by federal law, even when the interference is unmistakably clear." *Atlantic Coast Line*, 398 U.S., at 294. Rather, when a state proceeding presents a federal issue, even a pre-emption issue, the proper course is to seek resolution of that issue by the state court.

This is the course respondents must follow with respect to the Singapore law claim. It may be that respondents' reading of the pre-emptive force of federal maritime forum non conveniens determinations is correct. This is a question we need not reach and on which we express no opinion. We simply hold that respondents must present their pre-emption argument to the Texas state courts, which are presumed competent to resolve federal issues. Accordingly, insofar as the District Court enjoined the state courts from considering petitioner's Singapore law claim, the injunction exceeded the restrictions of the Anti-Injunction Act.

Finally, petitioner asserts a claim under Texas state law. In contrast to the Singapore law claim, the validity of this claim was adjudicated in the original federal action. Respondents argued to the District Court in 1980 that under applicable choice-of-law principles, the law of Singapore must control petitioner's suit. The District Court expressly agreed, noting that only two of the eight relevant factors "point toward American law," and concluding that the "statutory and maritime law of the United States should not be applied." Petitioner seeks to relitigate this issue in state court by arguing that "there are substantial and/or significant contacts" with the United States such that "the application of American and Texas law is mandated." Because in its 1980 decision the District Court decided that Singapore law must control petitioner's lawsuit, a decision that necessarily precludes the application of Texas law, an injunction preventing relitigation of that issue in state court is within the scope of the relitigation exception to the Anti-Injunction Act.

Accordingly, insofar as the District Court enjoined the state courts from considering petitioner's claim under the substantive law of Texas, the injunction was permissible.

Because the injunction actually entered by the District Court, was broader than the limited injunction we find acceptable, we must reverse the judgment approving a broad injunction and remand for entry of a more narrowly tailored order. Of course, the fact that an injunction may issue under the Anti-Injunction Act does not mean that it must issue. On remand the District Court should decide whether it is appropriate to enter an injunction.

Accordingly, the judgment of the Court of Appeals is reversed, and the case is remanded for further proceedings consistent with this opinion.

It is so ordered.

Justice WHITE, concurring.

* * *

Had the District Court made such a finding here when it dismissed petitioner's case—holding that federal maritime law required that this case be heard in Singapore—then I believe that the relitigation exception found in 28 U.S.C. § 2283 would permit the injunction that the District Court later issued. This is true whether or not a finding of such pre-emption would have been correct: petitioner's remedy for an erroneous preemption decision would have been an appeal of the District Court's dismissal, and not relitigation of the issue in state court. However, the District Court's terse dismissal order in this case lacks any express ruling on uniformity or pre-emption. Absent such a holding, the District Court had no "judgment" on this question which it needed to "protect or effectuate" by enjoining the subsequent state court litigation.

* * *

Notes

1. On February 28, 2000, a Houston jury delivered a $12.7 million verdict in favor of Chick Kam Choo. On April 17, 2000, the trial judge rendered judgment notwithstanding the verdict for Exxon on the ground that plaintiff's claim was barred because in 1977 the deceased worker's widow accepted a Singapore workers' compensation payment of $15,000.

2. American Dredging Co. v. Miller, 510 U.S. 443 (1994) held that a Louisiana state court may refuse to apply the doctrine of forum non conveniens to claims under the Jones Act and general maritime law, even though the doctrine would be available in federal court. The suit was by an American seaman injured on the Delaware River. The majority opinion by Justice Scalia reasoned that forum non conveniens is not "a 'characteristic feature' of admiralty or a doctrine whose uniform application is necessary to maintain the 'proper harmony' of maritime law."

After the decision in *American Dredging*, the Supreme Court of Texas withdrew an opinion in *Choo* that held Texas forum non conveniens doctrine preempted by federal law, concluded instead that federal maritime doctrine did not preempt the application of Texas forum non conveniens law, and affirmed the judgment of the Houston Court of Appeals remanding the case for further proceedings. Exxon Corp. v. Choo, 881 S.W.2d 301 (Tex. 1994).

In *American Dredging* there is no doubt that federal admiralty law applies and the incident and parties are domestic. In *Chick Kam Choo* there is no doubt that federal admiralty law does not apply and the incident and parties are foreign. Is *Chick Kam Choo* a stronger or weaker case for application of reverse-*Erie* to forum non conveniens?

3. In *Chick Kam Choo*, the court cites three cases as examples of the "reverse-*Erie*" doctrine. Offshore Logistics, Inc. v. Tallentire held that recovery under the Death on the High Seas Act could not be supplemented with nonpecuniary elements of damage, including loss of consortium, society, and services, that would be recoverable under state law. Knickerbocker Ice Co. v. Stewart held that it is unconstitutional for Congress to permit recovery under state workers compensation law for death of a seaman. Southern Pacific Co. v. Jensen held that the New York workers compensation act is not applicable to a stevedore killed unloading a ship.

4. Villar v. Crowley Maritime Corp., 990 F.2d 1489 (5th Cir. 1993). Survivors of a Filipino seaman who drowned in Saudi Arabian waters when he fell from on a ship of Panamanian registry, sued a United States company in addition to foreign defendants. Suit was brought in a Texas state court and removed to federal court because of diversity of citizenship. The action against the foreign defendants was dismissed for lack of personal jurisdiction. The action against the United States company was dismissed for forum non conveniens and the plaintiffs were enjoined from suing again on the same claim in any United States court, state or federal. Plaintiffs had previously had their suit dismissed by California state and federal courts. The Fifth Circuit affirmed the dismissal and injunction. The court stated that "*Chick Kam Choo* is not on point because there is no ongoing state court proceeding in this case," and held that the anti-injunction act only bars stays of suits already instituted. Id. at 1499. One judge dissented on the ground that the case should be remanded to permit discovery on the jurisdictional and forum non conveniens issues.

Baris v. Sulpicio Lines, Inc., 101 F.3d 367 (5th Cir. 1996) (en banc), affirms by an equally divided court the district court's ruling that a federal court's dismissal with prejudice on the ground of forum non conveniens did not have res judicata effect on the entire claim, and could not be the basis for invoking the relitigation exception of the Anti-Injunction Act to bar plaintiffs' suit in a Louisiana state court. The Louisiana action had been commenced before the federal dismissal, although process was not served on defendants until after the dismissal.

5. Under a judge-made "strangers" exception to the Anti-Injunction Act, "[o]ne who is not a party to state proceedings, nor in privity with a party, may seek a federal injunction against enforcement of a judgment obtained in those proceedings." Prudential Real Estate Affiliates, Inc. v. PPR Realty, Inc., 204 F.3d 867, 880 (9th Cir. 2000).

Smith Kline & French Laboratories Ltd. v. Bloch
[1983] 2 All ER 72 (Ct. App.)

LORD DENNING MR. As a moth is drawn to the light, so is a litigant drawn to the United States. If he can only get his case into their courts, he stands to win a fortune. At no cost to himself, and at no risk of having to pay anything to the other side. The lawyers there will conduct the case "on spec" as we say, or on a "contingency fee" as they say. The lawyers will charge the litigant nothing for their services but instead they will take 40% of the damages, if they win the case in court, or out of court on a settlement. If they lose, the litigant will have nothing to pay to the other side. The courts in the

United States have no such costs deterrent as we have. There is also in the United States a right to trial by jury. These are prone to award fabulous damages. They are notoriously sympathetic and know that the lawyers will take their 40% before the plaintiff gets anything. All this means that the defendant can be readily forced into a settlement. The plaintiff holds all the cards. If you wish to know how it is all done, you should read *Castanho v Brown & Root (UK) Ltd.* [1981] 1 All ER 143, [1981] AC 557. There a Portuguese sailor was badly injured at Great Yarmouth in England. It was an American ship. He started an action in England but was persuaded by American lawyers to take proceedings in the United States. I was against it (see [1980] 3 All ER 72 at 76-83, [1980] 1 WLR 833 at 849-858). But when it got to the House of Lords they allowed the litigant to go ahead in the United States (see [1981] 1 All ER 143, [1981] AC 557). His American lawyers won a huge settlement to the profit of the litigant and of course for themselves as well. You should also read *Piper Aircraft Co v. Reyno* (1981) 454 U.S. 235 decided on 8 December 1981 by the Supreme Court of the United States. A small commercial aircraft crashed in Scotland, killing all six Scottish people on it. The propellers had been manufactured in the United States. The widows and children were persuaded by lawyers in the United States to bring proceedings there against the manufacturers of the propellers, alleging that they were faulty. No doubt the lawyers had their eyes on the heavy damages and their contingency fees. The Supreme Court of the United States refused to allow the proceedings to continue in the United States. They should have been brought in Scotland, which was the only appropriate forum.

Now we have another case of that ilk. Dr Maurice Bloch lives in England. He has a complaint against an English company. He says that they broke their contract with him. It was an English contract governed by English law. The obvious place where it should be tried is in England. Yet he has gone to American lawyers and they have found an excuse for bringing it in the United States. It is because the English company was a wholly-owned subsidiary of an American corporation. So the American lawyers for Dr Bloch have brought an action in the United States courts against the English subsidiary and its American parent, hoping, no doubt, to get a good settlement out of it, both for themselves and Dr Bloch, at no cost to him.

Now here is the twist in the story. The English company and its American parent wish to stop the proceedings in the United States courts. They want to nip them in the bud. They have applied to the United States courts to stop them. But with no success so far there. An American judge has made an order allowing Dr. Bloch to go ahead with the proceedings in the United States court.

Having been thus rebuffed in America, the English subsidiary (and now its American parent) have applied to the English court. They ask us to issue an injunction against Dr. Bloch to restrain him from proceeding in the United States. They say that he is quite at liberty to sue them in England if he is so advised, in which case they will defend themselves. But he should not be allowed to go on in the United States. I may say that, even in England, Dr. Bloch is "sitting pretty" anyway. He has got legal aid with the result that all his costs here will be paid by the legal aid fund.

At the moment the English High Court has acceded to the request of the English subsidiary and its American parent. It has issued an injunction against Dr. Bloch stopping him from going on with his proceedings in the United States court; he now appeals to this court.

Now there is yet a further twist. Dr. Bloch has asked the United States court to issue a counter-injunction against the American parent to stop it from coming to the English court and an American judge has made the order.

It is apparent from this account of proceedings that there is a conflict of jurisdiction between our courts here in England and the courts in the United States. This is much to be regretted. In the interests of comity, one or other must give way. I wish that we could sit together to discuss it. But, as that is not possible, I propose to put the case forward, as we see it here, in the hope that we may come to an agreed solution.

[Dr. Bloch was hired as a consultant by Smith Kline's English subsidiary to develop compounds for treating stomach disorders. The subsidiary conducted field trials of the compounds, reported to Dr. Bloch that the trials were disappointing, and ended their relationship.]

So here was Dr. Bloch * * * his products discarded by Smith Kline. What was he to do? He had been in touch with English solicitors as far back as 1976, but they foresaw difficulties in litigation in England. So he turned to American lawyers. They advised him to bring an action in the United States, both against the English subsidiary and the American parent. He instituted it on 16 May 1980. He is quite frank about his reasons:

> ...there were financial considerations in that litigation in this Country would undoubtedly involve me in substantial expense on the other hand, if American lawyers agreed to take on my case, they would be prepared to do so in accordance with American legal practice for a contingency fee so that they would be remunerated out of any damages which I might recover.

If Dr. Bloch had attempted to sue the English subsidiary alone in America, the United States courts would not have entertained it for one moment. So he had to bring in the American parent as a defendant to the American proceedings. He alleged that:

(1) The American parent was the principal in his contract with the English subsidiary and liable for a breach of contract by the English subsidiary. For this he claimed damages of $40,000,000.

(2) The American parent and English subsidiary had been guilty of false representation in saying that they intended to market the plaintiff's product whereas they never intended to do so. They intended to keep it out of the market so that it should not be in competition with their own existing product, "Dyazide". For this he claimed another $40,000,000 damages.

(3) The American parent had improperly interfered with the contract by the English subsidiary with Dr Bloch. More damages of $40,000,000.

(4) The American parent and the English subsidiary had intentionally inflicted emotional distress on Dr Bloch for which he was entitled to punitive damages of another $40,000,000.

If you consider each of those four claims, you will see at once that if Dr..Bloch had any cause of action at all he could perfectly well have started it in England against the English subsidiary alone and got all the damages to which he was justly entitled. If he had sought to sue the American parent in England, he would not have got leave to serve it out of the jurisdiction, because he had no semblance of a cause of action against them. At any rate he would not have a good arguable case for these reasons:

(1) The contract was made by Dr. Bloch with the English subsidiary in its own name. That is a factor showing that it was intended that the English subsidiary should be the party to the contract. When that is coupled with the additional factor that "all decisions on registration and marketing of products will be the exclusive responsibility of SK&F" (that is of the English subsidiary), it is plain that only the English subsidiary is liable for the breach, if any, of the contract. The American parent is not liable.

(2) There is nothing to warrant the suggestion that the English subsidiary and the American parent were from 1974 guilty of conspiracy and fraud, or that they intentionally duped Dr. Bloch with the belief that they would develop his project, when they intended never to do so. That is a suggestion made without any evidence to support it. It is decisively refuted by the fact that from 1974 onwards Dr. Bloch was himself in control of the research and development of his product at the many hospitals and so forth. No doubt he developed it to the best of his ability.

(3) and (4) The claims for inducing breach of contract and emotional distress have no substance whatever.

To my mind this claim of Dr. Bloch against the American parent is a device, adopted by American lawyers, so as to get the case into the United States courts, where they will get contingency fees and force a settlement. Such a device ought not to be allowed to succeed. I trust that our courts on both sides of the Atlantic will not allow it.

The Law

It often happens that a plaintiff is entitled to bring proceedings in two or more jurisdictions. Sometimes it is said that the choice is his. He can choose whichever of them suits him best. If he can get more damages in one than he can on the other, then good luck to him. Let him go there. If he will be met by a time bar in one and not in the other, let him go to the one where he is not barred. If it is more convenient for the plaintiff in one than it is for the defendant, then the plaintiff can choose. You need not spin a coin between the two contestants. It always comes down in favour of the plaintiff, so it is said, unless the defendant can prove that it would work an injustice to him. Once a plaintiff institutes an action in accordance with this prior claim of his, then no court in a rival jurisdiction should grant an injunction to prevent the plaintiff from exercising and pursuing his action to its determination. This is the only way, it is said, to avoid unseemly conflict and to ensure comity.

The basis of all this reasoning has now been removed. In England by the House of Lords in *MacShannon v. Rockware Glass Ltd.* [1978] 1 All ER 625, [1978] AC 795. In the United States by the Supreme Court in *Piper Aircraft Co. v. Reyno* (1981) 454 U.S. 235. The plaintiff has no longer an inborn right to choose his own forum. He no longer wins the toss on every throw. The decision rests with the courts. No matter which jurisdiction is invoked, the court must hold the balance between the plaintiff and the defendant. It must take into account the relative advantages and disadvantages to each of them: not only the juridical advantages and disadvantages, but also the personal conveniences and inconveniences: not only the private interests of the parties but also the public interests involved. The court decides according to which way the balance comes down. This was the approach of the House of Lords in *MacShannon v. Rockware Glass Ltd.*, where it was much to the juridical advantage of the plaintiff to bring his action in England, where he would get higher damages, but the natural forum was Scotland. It was in the public interest that a Scottish case should be tried in Scotland. So he was bound to go to Scotland. His action in England was stayed. It was also the approach of the Supreme Court of the United States in *Piper Aircraft Co. v. Reyno*, where it was much to the juridical advantage of the plaintiffs that they should sue in Pennsylvania, where they would get higher damages and the lawyers would get contingency fees.

* * *

By contrast, in *Castanho v. Brown & Root (UK) Ltd.* [1981] 1 All ER 143, [1981] AC 557 the plaintiff had an undisputed claim for damages against a Texan-based group of companies. The only question at issue was quantum. The plaintiff had a legitimate advantage in suing in Texas where he could get such damages as a Texan court thought appropriate. Although I took the other view, the House of Lords held that the balance came down clearly in the plaintiff's favour (see [1981] 1 All ER 143 at 152, [1981] AC 557 at 577).

Holding the Balance

In our present case Dr. Bloch is resident in England. He works in England. He sues on a contract with an English company which was made in England and is governed by English law. The witnesses are mostly in England. The natural forum is England beyond any doubt. The public interest requires that so English a dispute should be tried in England, to which it belongs rather than in the United States.

It would, no doubt, be an advantage to Dr. Bloch to sue in the United States, because he would there get higher damages, trial by jury and lawyers on contingency fees. But that is not a legitimate advantage. It is an illegitimate advantage. Even putting it into the scale, the balance comes down clearly in favour of England.

Injunction

Once the English court decides that the dispute should be tried in England and not in the United States, then it is open to the court to issue an injunction against Dr. Bloch restraining him from continuing his proceedings in the courts of the United States. No doubt this jurisdiction should be exercised with caution, but that it can be done there is no doubt. It was affirmed by the House of Lords in the *Castanho* case.

I have no doubt that this is a case where the court should grant an injunction against Dr. Bloch so as to restrain him from continuing with the proceedings in the United States courts. He will, of course, be able to make his claim in the English courts, either by a fresh action, or by a counterclaim in the present action. He has the benefit of legal aid so he can get justice in this country beyond all doubt. That is the right way of it.

* * *

Conclusion

Seeing that England is the natural and proper forum for any proceedings that Dr. Maurice Bloch is advised to bring, I would grant an injunction against him personally to stop him from going on with any proceedings in the United States. I would grant it at the instance not only of the English subsidiary but also of the American parent. Seeing that both are being harassed in the United States courts, both should be able to come to these courts to stop it.

* * *

I would thus uphold the decision of Sir Douglas Frank and dismiss the appeal.

Notes

1. Lord Denning was a colorful Master of the Rolls, a position that gave him great influence over English intermediate appellate courts. His comments on U.S.-style client acquisition and forum shopping contrast with his earlier remarks in The Atlantic Star, [1972] 3 All E.R. 705, 709 (Ct. App. 1972):

> The right to come here is not confined to Englishmen. It extends to any friendly foreigner. He can seek the aid of our court if he desires to do so. You may call this "forum shopping" if you please, but if the forum is England, it is a good place to shop in, both for the quality of the goods and the speed of service.

In The Atlantic Star, Lord Denning refused to stay an action in England between Dutch parties resulting from a collision on a Belgium river. The House of Lords reversed and commented on the passage quoted above:

> My Lords, with all respect, that [Denning's statement on forum shopping in England] seems to me to recall the good old days, the passing of which many may regret, when inhabitants of this island felt an innate superiority over those unfortunate enough to belong to other races.

The Atlantic Star, [1973] 2 All E.R. 175, 181 (H.L. 1973) (Lord Reid). This opinion began the evolution of a forum non conveniens doctrine in England, much accelerated by the House of Lords opinion in MacShannon v. Rockware Glass Ltd., [1978] 1 All E.R. 625, referred to by Denning in *Smith Kline*.

2. For the United States proceedings in the *Castanho* case, referred to by Lord Denning in the principal case, see Castanho v. Jackson Marine, Inc., 484 F.Supp. 201 (E.D. Tex. 1980) (denies motions for forum non conveniens dismissal and for stay pending outcome of English proceedings), aff'd, 650 F.2d 546 (5th Cir. 1981). In the English Court of Appeal, Lord Denning remarked in *Castanho* that "A Texas-style claim is big business." [1980] 3 All. E.R. 72, 76.

3. Note 1, supra, refers to the development of a forum non conveniens doctrine in England, which closely resembles the doctrine as applied in the United States by federal and many state courts. It may be, however, that as a result of ratifying the EEC Convention on Jurisdiction and the Enforcement of Judgments, supra page 19, the United Kingdom has prevented its courts from granting a forum non conveniens dismissal of an action properly brought under the jurisdictional provisions of that Convention. A leading English treatise on conflict of laws states that the Convention "contains no general discretion to stay actions on the basis of *forum non conveniens*." P.M. North & J.J. Fawcett, Cheshire and North's Private International Law 331 (12th ed. 1992). M. Henri Mayas, as Advocate General before the Court of Justice of the European Communities, has also taken the position that the common-law doctrine of forum non conveniens is inconsistent with the Convention's jurisdictional provisions. Indistrie Tessili Italiana Como v. Dunlop AG (Case 12/76) [1977] 1 C.M.L.R. 26, 39, 44: "It has been stated by authoritative commentators that 'the Convention rejects the theory of the *forum conveniens*.'" (Citing Droz, Compétence Judiciaire et Effects des Jugements dans le Marché Commun 128 (1972). Wolf v. Harry Cox B.V. (Case 42/76) [1977] 2 C.M.L.R. 43, 45, 53: "nobody is entitled to invoke the principles of common law on the subject as a means of escaping the system laid down by the Convention, with which all the Contracting States must comply."

In re Harrods (Buenos Aires) Ltd., [1992] Ch. 72 (C.A.) held that, despite the Convention, a forum non conveniens stay was proper when the defendant was domiciled in England and the alternative forum was in Argentina. North & Fawcett, supra, at 332, note a dispute between "Continental lawyers" and "English lawyers" as to whether the bases of jurisdiction under the Convention are mandatory and do not permit dismissal, even when the alternative forum is not in a Contracting State. The authors conclude "that the decision in Re Harrods is misguided, if not downright wrong." Id. at 334.

For reports on the practice in different countries concerning declining jurisdiction of cases involving foreign elements, see J.J. Fawcett et al., Declining Jurisdiction in Private International Law (1995), containing the Reports to the XIVth Congress of the International Academy of Comparative Law, which convened in Athens in August 1994.

4. SNI Aérospatiale v. Lee Kui Jak, [1987] 3 All. E.R. 510 (Privy Council). A resident of Brunei was killed there in a helicopter crash. The helicopter was manufactured in France by the defendants, a French company, which had a subsidiary in Texas to whom it sold helicopters. Plaintiffs, the widow and administrators of decedent's estate, commenced proceedings in both Brunei and Texas. Overruling the Brunei trial court and court of appeal, the Privy Council granted an injunction restraining the plaintiffs from continuing their Texas proceedings. The court reasoned that Brunei was "the natural forum for the trial of the action"; that this was not changed by the proceedings in Texas including extensive discovery; that continuation of the Texas proceedings would be "oppressive" to the defendants because, if held liable in those proceedings, defendants might not be able to obtain contribution from the Malaysian company that serviced and operated the helicopter.

5. What strategy is suggested by *Smith Kline* and *SNI Aérospatiale* (supra note 4) for a defendant sued in the United States by a foreign plaintiff for injuries incurred abroad, if the defendant has unsuccessfully sought a forum non conveniens dismissal?

Chapter 3

Recognition of Judgments

Section 1: Bases for Non-Recognition

Hilton v. Guyot
159 U.S. 113 (1895)

[Henry Hilton and William Libbey, citizens of the United States and New York, conducted a business in Paris under the name of A.T. Stewart & Co. (Stewart). One of the French firms dealing with Stewart was Charles Fortin & Co. (Fortin). Fortin sued Stewart in the French Tribunal of Commerce and, after a hearing in which Stewart appeared by authorized attorneys, recovered a money judgment. The judgment was affirmed by the Paris Court of Appeals and has not been paid. Guyot, acting as official liquidator of Fortin, brought suit in the Circuit Court of the United States for the Southern District of New York to recovery the amount of the French judgment.

Defendant's answer alleged various irregularities in the French proceedings: the Tribunal of Commerce was composed of merchants and Charles Fortin had been a member until shortly before commencement of the suit against defendants; defendants appeared in the French court only to protect property in France that would have been seized if they did not appear; the French tribunal refused to compel Fortin to produce records; the arbitrator in the French tribunal was deceived by unsworn false testimony and by hearsay evidence including extracts from newspapers and written communications between Fortin and third persons. The New York Federal Circuit Court declined to admit any evidence offered by the defendants to support these allegations and directed a verdict for the plaintiffs for $277,775.44, the amount of the French judgment and interest. The case was brought to the United States Supreme Court by writ of error.]

Elihu Root and James C. Carter, for plaintiffs. Wm. G. Choate, for defendants.

Mr. Justice GRAY, after stating the case, delivered the opinion of the court.

* * *

No law has any effect, of its own force, beyond the limits of the sovereignty from which its authority is derived. The extent to which the law of one nation, as put in force within its territory, whether by executive order, by legislative act, or by judicial decree, shall be allowed to operate within the dominion of another nation, depends upon what our greatest jurists have been content to call "the comity of nations." Although the phrase has been often criticised, no satisfactory substitute has been suggested.

"Comity," in the legal sense, is neither a matter of absolute obligation, on the one hand, nor of mere courtesy and good will, upon the other. But it is the recognition which one nation allows within its territory to the legislative, executive, or judicial acts of another nation, having due regard both to international duty and convenience, and to the rights of its own citizens, or of other persons who are under the protection of its laws.

* * *

In order to appreciate the weight of the various authorities cited at the bar, it is important to distinguish different kinds of judgments. Every foreign judgment, of whatever nature, in order to be entitled to any effect, must have been rendered by a court having jurisdiction of the cause, and upon regular proceedings, and due notice. In alluding to different kinds of judgments, therefore, such jurisdiction, proceedings, and notice will be assumed. It will also be assumed that they are untainted by fraud, the effect of which will be considered later.

A judgment in rem, adjudicating the title to a ship or other movable property within the custody of the court, is treated as valid everywhere.

* * *

A judgment affecting the status of persons, such as a decree confirming or dissolving a marriage, is recognized as valid in every country, unless contrary to the policy of its own law.

* * *

Other judgments, not strictly in rem, under which a person has been compelled to pay money, are so far conclusive that the justice of the payment cannot be impeached in another country, so as to compel him to pay it again. For instance, a judgment in foreign attachment is conclusive, as between the parties, of the right to the property or money attached.

* * *

The extraterritorial effect of judgments in personam, at law, or in equity may differ, according to the parties to the cause. A judgment of that kind between two citizens or residents of the country, and thereby subject to the jurisdiction in which it is rendered, may be held conclusive as between them everywhere. So, if a foreigner invokes the jurisdiction by bringing an action against a citizen, both may be held bound by a judgment in favor of either; and if a citizen sues a foreigner, and judgment is rendered in favor of the latter, both may be held equally bound.

The effect to which a judgment, purely executory, rendered in favor of a citizen or resident of the country, in a suit there brought by him against a foreigner, may be entitled in an action thereon against the latter in his own country, as is the case now before us, presents a more difficult question, upon which there has been some diversity of opinion.

* * *

[W]e are satisfied that where there has been opportunity for a full and fair trial abroad before a court of competent jurisdiction, conducting the trial upon regular proceedings, after due citation or voluntary appearance of the defendant, and under a system of jurisprudence likely to secure an impartial administration of justice between the citizens of its own country and those of other countries, and there is nothing to show either prejudice in the court, or in the system of laws under which it was sitting, or fraud in procuring the judgment, or any other special reason why the comity of this nation should not allow it full effect, the merits of the case should not, in an action brought in this country upon the judgment, be tried afresh, as on a new trial or an appeal, upon the mere assertion of the party that the judgment was erroneous in law or in fact. The defendants, therefore, cannot be permitted, upon that general ground, to contest the validity or the effect of the judgment sued on.

But they have sought to impeach that judgment upon several other grounds, which require separate consideration.

It is objected that the appearance and litigation of the defendants in the French tribunals were not voluntary, but by legal compulsion, and, therefore, that the French courts never acquired such jurisdiction over the defendants that they should be held bound by the judgment.

* * *

The present case is not one of a person traveling through or casually found in a foreign country. The defendants, although they were not citizens or residents of France, but were citizens and residents of the state of New York, and their principal place of business was in the city of New York, yet had a storehouse and an agent in Paris, and were accustomed to purchase large quantities of goods there, although they did not make sales in France. Under such circumstances, evidence that their sole object in appearing and carrying on the litigation in the French courts was to prevent property in their storehouse at Paris, belonging to them, and within the jurisdiction, but not in the custody, of those courts, from being taken in satisfaction of any judgment that might be recovered against them, would not, according to our law, show that those courts did not acquire jurisdiction of the persons of the defendants.

It is next objected that in those courts one of the plaintiffs was permitted to testify not under oath, and was not subjected to cross-examination by the opposite party, and that the defendants were therefore deprived of safeguards which are by our law considered essential to secure honesty and to detect fraud in a witness; and also that documents and papers were admitted in evidence, with which the defendants had no connection, and which would not be admissible under our own system of jurisprudence. But it having been shown by the plaintiffs, and hardly denied by the defendants, that the practice followed and the method of examining witnesses were according to the laws of France, we are not prepared to hold that the fact that the procedure in these respects differed from that of our own courts is, of itself, a sufficient ground for impeaching the foreign judgment.

* * *

There is no doubt that both in this country * * * and in England, a foreign judgment may be impeached for fraud.

* * *

In the case at bar the defendants offered to prove, in much detail, that the plaintiffs presented to the French court of first instance and to the arbitrator appointed by that court, and upon whose report its judgment was largely based, false and fraudulent statements and accounts against the defendants, by which the arbitrator and the French courts were deceived and misled, and their judgments were based upon such false and fraudulent statements and accounts. This offer, if satisfactorily proved, would, according to the decisions of the English court of appeal in *Aboulof v. Oppenheimer* [10 Q.B. 295 (1882) and other cases], be a sufficient ground for impeaching the foreign judgment, and examining into the merits of the original claim.

But whether those decisions can be followed in regard to foreign judgments, consistently with our own decisions as to impeaching domestic judgments for fraud, it is unnecessary in this case to determine, because there is a distinct and independent ground upon which we are satisfied that the comity of our nation does not require us to give conclusive effect to the judgments of the courts of France; and that ground is the want of reciprocity, on the part of France, as to the effect to be given to the judgments of this and other foreign countries.

It appears, therefore, that there is hardly a civilized nation on either continent which, by its general law, allows conclusive effect to an executory foreign judgment for the recovery of money. In France and in a few smaller states—Norway, Portugal, Greece, Monaco, and Hayti—the merits of the controversy are reviewed, as of course, allowing to the foreign judgment, at the most, no more effect than of being prima facie evidence of the justice of the claim. In the great majority of the countries on the continent of Europe,—in Belgium, Holland, Denmark, Sweden, Germany, in many cantons of Switzerland, in Russia and Poland, in Roumania, in Austria and Hungary (perhaps in Italy), and in Spain,—as well as in Egypt, in Mexico, and in a great part of South America, the judgment rendered in a foreign country is allowed the same effect only as the courts of that country allow to the judgments of the country in which the judgment in question is sought to be executed.

* * *

The reasonable, if not the necessary, conclusion appears to us to be that judgments rendered in France, or in any other foreign country, by the laws of which our own judgments are reviewable upon the merits, are not entitled to full credit and conclusive effect when sued upon in this country, but are prima facie evidence only of the justice of the plaintiffs' claim.

In holding such a judgment, for want of reciprocity, not to be conclusive evidence of the merits of the claim, we do not proceed upon any theory of retaliation upon one person by reason of injustice done to another, but upon the broad ground that international law is founded upon mutuality and reciprocity, and that by the principles of international law recognized in most civilized nations, and by the comity of our own country, which it is our judicial duty to known and to declare, the judgment is not entitled to be considered conclusive.

By our law, at the time of the adoption of the constitution, a foreign judgment was considered as prima facie evidence, and not conclusive. There is no statute of the United States, and no treaty of the United States with France, or with any other nation, which has changed that law, or has made any provision upon the subject. It is not to be supposed that, if any statute or treaty had been or should be made, it would recognize as conclusive the judgments of any country, which did not give like effect to our own judgments. In the absence of statute or treaty, it appears to us equally unwarrantable to assume that the comity of the United States requires anything more.

If we should hold this judgment to be conclusive, we should allow it an effect to which, supposing the defendants' offers to be sustained by actual proof, it would, in the absence of a special treaty, be entitled in hardly any other country in Christendom, except the country in which it was rendered. If the judgment had been rendered in this country, or in any other outside of the jurisdiction of France, the French courts would not have executed or enforced it, except after examining into its merits. The very judgment now sued on would be held inconclusive in almost any other country than France. In England, and in the colonies subject to the law of England, the fraud alleged in its procurement would be a sufficient ground for disregarding it. In the courts of nearly every other nation, it would be subject to re-examination, either merely because it was a foreign judgment, or because judgments of that nation would be reexaminable in the courts of France.

For these reasons * * * the Judgment is reversed, and the cause remanded to the circuit court, with directions to set aside the verdict and to order a new trial.

* * *

Mr. Chief Justice FULLER, dissenting.

Plaintiffs brought their action on a judgment recovered by them against the defendants in the courts of France, which courts had jurisdiction over person and subject-matter, and in respect of which judgment no fraud was alleged, except in particulars contested in and considered by the French courts. The question is whether under these circumstances, and in the absence of a treaty or act of congress, the judgment is re-examinable upon the merits. This question I regard as one to be determined by the ordinary and settled rule in respect of allowing a party who has had an opportunity to prove his case in a competent court to retry it on the merits; and it seems to me that the doctrine of res judicata applicable to domestic judgments should be applied to foreign judgments as well, and rests on the same general ground of public policy, that there should be an end of litigation.

I cannot yield my assent to the proposition that, because by legislation and judicial decision in France that effect is not there given to judgments recovered in this country which, according to our jurisprudence, we think should be given to judgments wherever recovered (subject, of course, to the recognized exceptions), therefore we should pursue the same line of conduct as respects the judgments of French tribunals. The application of the doctrine of res judicata does not rest in discretion; and it is for the government, and not for its courts, to adopt the principle of retorsion, if deemed under any circumstances desirable or necessary.

As the court expressly abstains from deciding whether the judgment is impeachable on the ground of fraud, I refrain from any observations on that branch of the case.

Mr. Justice Harlan, Mr. Justice Brewer, and Mr. Justice Jackson concur in this dissent.

Notes

1. Leaders of the bar argued the case. Elihu Root was Theodore Roosevelt's Secretary of State. James Carter was a New York State Commissioner who worked on important codifications. William Choate was a judge and senior partner in a prestigious law firm.

2. As will be apparent from the materials following in this chapter, Justice Fuller's dissenting view disavowing reciprocity as a basis for judgment recognition, has prevailed in most states and is reflected in the Uniform Foreign Money-Judgments Recognition Act.

3. Both the majority and dissent leave open the question whether a foreign judgment can be impeached for "fraud." See the note on the distinction between "intrinsic" and "extrinsic" fraud following the Uniform Foreign Money-Judgments Recognition Act, infra this chapter, page 253.

4. In Munzer v. Munzer-Jacoby, Cass. 1e civ., Jan. 7, 1964, J.C.P. 1964, II, 13,590, obs. Ancel, the French Cour de Cassation disapproved of the doctrine of revision au fond, under which there was re-examination of the merits of foreign judgments.

Somportex Ltd. v. Philadelphia Chewing Gum Corp.
453 F.2d 435 (3rd Cir. 1971), cert. denied, 405 U.S. 1017 (1972)

ALDISERT, Circuit Judge.

Several interesting questions are presented in this appeal from the district court's order granting summary judgment to enforce a default judgment entered by an English court. To resolve them, a complete recitation of the procedural history of this case is necessary.

This case has its genesis in a transaction between appellant, Philadelphia Chewing Gum Corporation, and Somportex Limited, a British corporation, which was to merchandise appellant's wares in Great Britain under the trade name "Tarzan Bubble Gum." * * * For reasons not relevant to our limited inquiry, the transaction never reached fruition.

Somportex filed an action against Philadelphia for breach of contract in the Queen's Bench Division of the High Court of England. Notice of the issuance of a Writ of Summons was served, in accordance with the rules and with the leave of the High Court, upon Philadelphia at its registered address in Havertown, Pennsylvania, on May 15, 1967. The extraterritorial service was based on the English version of long-arm statutes utilized by many American states. Philadelphia then consulted a firm of English solicitors, who, by letter of July 14, 1967, advised its Pennsylvania lawyers:

> I have arranged with the Solicitors for Somportex Limited that they will let me have a copy of their Affidavit and exhibits to that Affidavit which supported their application to serve out of the Jurisdiction. Subject to the contents of the Affidavit, and any further information that can be provided by Philadelphia Chewing Gum Corporation after we have had the opportunity of seeing the Affidavit, it may be possible to make an application to the Court for an Order setting the Writ aside. But for such an application to be successful we will have to show that on the facts the matter does not fall within the provision of (f) and (g) [of the long-arm statute] referred to above.
>
> In the meantime we will enter a conditional Appearance to the Writ in behalf of Philadelphia Chewing Gum Corporation in order to preserve the status quo.

On August 9, 1967, the English solicitors entered a "conditional appearance to the Writ" and filed a motion to set aside the Writ of Summons. At a hearing before a Master on November 13, 1967, the solicitors appeared and disclosed that Philadelphia had elected not to proceed with the summons or to contest the jurisdiction of the English Court, but instead intended to obtain leave of court to withdraw appearance of counsel. The Master then dismissed Philadelphia's summons to set aside plaintiff's Writ of Summons. Four days later, the solicitors sought to withdraw their appearance as counsel for Philadelphia, contending that it was a conditional appearance only. On November 27, 1967, after a Master granted the motion, Somportex appealed. The appeal was denied after hearing before a single judge, but the Court of Appeal, reversing the decision of the Master, held that the appearance was unconditional and that the submission to the jurisdiction by Philadelphia was, therefore, effective.[3] But the court let stand "the origi-

---

3. Somportex v. Philadelphia Chewing Gum [1968], 3 All.E.R. 26, 29, Lord Denning: "In order to decide the point, I think that one has to put oneself in the position of the American company and their advisers when faced with this notice of the writ. They could have not entered an appearance at all, in which case by the law of Pennsylvania they would not be bound by any judgment. Instead of doing that, however, after consultation with a distinguished firm of lawyers in the city of London

nal order which was made by the master on Nov. 13 dismissing the application to set aside. The writ therefore will stand. On the other hand, if the American company would wish to appeal from the order of Nov. 13, I see no reason why the time should not be extended and they can argue that matter out at a later stage if they should so wish."

Thereafter, Philadelphia made a calculated decision: it decided to do nothing. It neither asked for an extension of time nor attempted in any way to proceed with an appeal from the Master's order dismissing its application to set aside the Writ. Instead, it directed its English solicitors to withdraw from the case. There being no appeal, the Master's order became final.

Somportex then filed a Statement of Claim which was duly served in accordance with English Court rules. In addition, by separate letter, it informed Philadelphia of the significance and effect of the pleading, the procedural posture of the case, and its intended course of action.

Philadelphia persisted in its course of inaction; it failed to file a defense. Somportex obtained a default judgment against it in the Queen's Bench Division of the High Court of Justice in England for the sum of pounds sterling 39,562.10.10 (approximately $94,000.00). The award reflected some $45,000.00 for loss of profit; $46,000.00 for loss of good will and $2,500.00 for costs, including attorneys' fees.

Thereafter, Somportex filed a diversity action in the court below, seeking to enforce the foreign judgment, and attached to the complaint a certified transcript of the English proceeding. The district court granted * * * plaintiff's motion for summary judgment.

* * *

Appellant presents a cluster of contentions supporting its major thesis that we should not extend hospitality to the English judgment. First, it contends, and we agree, that because our jurisdiction is based solely on diversity, "the law to be applied...is the law of the state," in this case, Pennsylvania law. *Erie R. Co. v. Tompkins*, 304 U.S. 64 (1938).

* * *

Pennsylvania distinguishes between judgments obtained in the courts of her sister states, which are entitled to full faith and credit, and those of foreign courts, which are

---

they decided to enter a conditional appearance. That was a very important step for them to take (especially if they had assets in England or were likely to bring assets into England) because it was an essential way of defending their own position. After all, if they did not enter an appearance at all, and in consequence the English courts gave judgment against them in default of appearance, that judgment could be executed against them in England in respect of assets in England. In order to guard against that eventuality, they had first to enter a conditional appearance here, then argue whether it was within the jurisdiction of the court or not. If it was outside the jurisdiction, all well and good. The writ would be set aside. They would go away free. If it was within the jurisdiction, however, their appearance became unconditional and they could fight out the case on the merits. In these circumstances it seems to me that they were very wise to enter a conditional appearance. It was a step which would be advised by any competent lawyer if there was a likelihood that assets would then or afterwards come into England. We have, therefore, a wise course of action deliberately decided on by eminent firms in England and the United States after consulation, and I do not think that they should be allowed now to go back on it. It must be remembered that, on the faith of this entry of appearance, the English company have altered their position. They have not gone to the United States, as they might have done, and taken steps there against the American company. They have remained in this country and pursued the action here on the faith that there was a conditional appearance entered which would become unconditional unless it was duly set aside. In the circumstances, I do not think that we should give leave to withdraw the appearance."

subject to principles of comity. *In re Christoff's Estate*, 411 Pa. 419, 192 A.2d 737, cert. denied, 375 U.S. 965 (1964).

* * *

Comity is a recognition which one nation extends within its own territory to the legislative, executive, or judicial acts of another. It is not a rule of law, but one of practice, convenience, and expediency. Although more than mere courtesy and accommodation, comity does not achieve the force of an imperative or obligation. Rather, it is a nation's expression of understanding which demonstrates due regard both to international duty and convenience and to the rights of persons protected by its own laws. Comity should be withheld only when its acceptance would be contrary or prejudicial to the interest of the nation called upon to give it effect.[8]

* * *

Appellant's contention that the district court failed to make an independent examination of the factual and legal basis of the jurisdiction of the English Court at once argues too much and says too little. The reality is that the court did examine the legal basis of asserted jurisdiction and decided the issue adversely to appellant.

Indeed, we do not believe it was necessary for the court below to reach the question of whether the factual complex of the contractual dispute permitted extraterritorial service under the English long-arm statute. In its opinion denying leave of defense counsel to withdraw, the Court of Appeal specifically gave Philadelphia the opportunity to have the factual issue tested before the courts; moreover, Philadelphia was allocated additional time to do just that. Lord Denning said: "They can argue that matter out at a later stage if they should so wish." Three months went by with no activity forthcoming and then, as described by the district court, "[d]uring this three month period, defendant changed its strategy and, not wishing to do anything which might result in its submitting to the English Court's jurisdiction, decided to withdraw its appearance altogether." Under these circumstances, we hold that defendant cannot choose its forum to test the factual basis of jurisdiction. It was given, and it waived, the opportunity of making the adequate presentation in the English Court.[9]

---

8. In *Hilton v. Guyot*, 159 U.S. 113 (1895), the Supreme Court spoke of the likelihood of reciprocity as a condition precedent to the recognition of comity. The doctrine has received no more than desultory acknowledgement. It has been rejected by the courts of New York, *Johnston v. Compagnie Generale Transatlantique*, 242 N.Y. 381, 152 N.E. 121 (N.Y. 1926), and by statute in California. See Reese, "The Status in this Country of Judgments Rendered Abroad," 50 Col.L.Rev. 783, 790-93 (1950).

We agree with the district court that this issue of the enforceability of foreign judgments has not frequently been litigated in Pennsylvania, and the Court has not been cited to, nor has independent examination revealed any Pennsylvania cases which even intimate that a finding of reciprocity is an essential precondition to their enforcing a foreign judgment.

9. In *Baldwin v. Iowa State Traveling Men's Association*, 283 U.S. 522 (1931), a federal district court defendant, who had unsuccessfully conditionally appeared and then, like appellant here, failed either to file a defense or to appeal from the default judgment entered on the merits, was sued in another district court for enforcement of the default judgment. The Court emphasized that "the full faith and credit required by [Article IV, Section 1] is not involved, since neither of the courts was a state court." 283 U.S. at 524. The Court then declared: "The special appearance gives point to the fact that the respondent entered the Missouri court for the very purpose of litigating the question of jurisdiction over its person. It had the election not to appear at all. If, in the absence of appearance, the court had proceeded to judgment, and the present suit had been brought thereon, respondent could have raised and tried out the issue in the present action, because it would never have had its day in court with respect to jurisdiction . It had also the right to appeal from the decision of the Missouri District Court, as is shown by *Harkness v. Hyde*, supra, [98 U.S. 476] and the

Additionally, appellant attacks the English practice wherein a conditional appearance attacking jurisdiction may, by court decision, be converted into an unconditional one. It cannot effectively argue that this practice constitutes "some special ground... for impeaching the judgment," as to render the English judgment unwelcome in Pennsylvania under principles of international law and comity because it was obtained by procedures contrary or prejudicial to the host state. The English practice in this respect is identical to that set forth in both the Federal and Pennsylvania rules of civil procedure. F.R.C.P. 12(b)(2) provides the vehicle for attacking jurisdiction over the person, and, in *Orange Theatre Corp. v. Rayherstz Amusement Corp.*, 139 F.2d 871, 874 (3d Cir. 1944), we said that Rule 12 "has abolished for the federal courts the age-old distinction between general and special appearances." Similarly, a conditional or "de bene esse" appearance no longer exists in Pennsylvania. *Monaco v. Montgomery Cab Co.*, 417 Pa. 135, 208 A.2d 252 (1965), Pa.R.C.P. 1451(a) (7). A challenge to jurisdiction must be asserted there by a preliminary objection raising a question of jurisdiction. Pa.R.C.P. 1017(b) (1).

Thus, we will not disturb the English Court's adjudication. That the English judgment was obtained by appellant's default instead of through an adversary proceeding does not dilute its efficacy. In the absence of fraud or collusion, a default judgment is as conclusive an adjudication between the parties as when rendered after answer and complete contest in the open courtroom. The polestar is whether a reasonable method of notification is employed and reasonable opportunity to be heard is afforded to the person affected.

English law permits recovery, as compensatory damages in breach of contract, of items reflecting loss of good will and costs, including attorneys' fees. These two items formed substantial portions of the English judgment. Because they are not recoverable under Pennsylvania law, appellant would have the foreign judgment declared unenforceable because it constitutes an "...action on the foreign claim [which] could not have been maintained because contrary to the public policy of the forum," citing Restatement, Conflict of Laws, § 445. We are satisfied with the district court's disposition of this argument:

> The Court finds that...while Pennsylvania may not agree that these elements should be included in damages for breach of contract, the variance with Pennsylvania law is not such that the enforcement "tends clearly to injure the public health, the public morals, the public confidence in the purity of the administration of the law, or to undermine that sense of security for individual rights, whether of personal liberty or of private property, which any citizen ought to feel, is against public policy." *Goodyear v. Brown*, 155 Pa. 514, 518, 26 A. 665, 666 (1893).

---

other authorities cited. It elected to follow neither of those courses, but, after having been defeated upon full hearing in its contention as to jurisdiction, it took no further steps, and the judgment in question resulted. "Public policy dictates that there be an end of litigation; that those who have contested an issue shall be bound by the result of the contest, and that matters once tried shall be considered forever settled as between the parties. We see no reason why this doctrine should not apply in every case where one voluntarily appears, presents his case and is fully heard, and why he should not, in the absence of fraud, be thereafter concluded by the judgment of the tribunal to which he has submitted his cause." 283 U.S. at 525-526. The *Baldwin* principle was reaffirmed in *Durfee v. Duke*, 375 U.S. 106 (1963). See also, *American Surety Co. v. Baldwin*, 287 U.S. 156, 166 (1932), in which Mr. Justice Brandeis stated that "the principles of res judicata apply to questions of jurisdiction as well as to other issues."

Somportex Limited v. Philadelphia Chewing Gum Corp. 318 F.Supp. 161, 169 (E.D.Pa.1970).

Finally, appellant contends that since "it maintains no office or employee in England and transacts no business within the country" there were no insufficient contacts there to meet the due process tests of *International Shoe Co. v. Washington*, 326 U.S. 310 (1945). It argues that, at best, "the only contact Philadelphia had with England was the negotiations allegedly conducted by an independent New York exporter by letter, telephone and telegram to sell Philadelphia's products in England." In *Hanson v. Denckla*, 357 U.S. 235, 253 (1958), Chief Justice Warren said: "The application of [the requirement of contact] rule will vary with the quality and nature of the defendant's activity, but it is essential in each case that there be some act by which the defendant purposely avails itself of the privilege of conducting business within the forum State, thus invoking the benefits and protection of its laws." We have concluded that whether the New York exporter was an independent contractor or Philadelphia's agent was a matter to be resolved by the English Court. For the purpose of the constitutional argument, we must assume the proper agency relationship. So construed, we find his activity would constitute the "quality and nature of the defendant's activity" similar to that of the defendant in *McGee v. International Life Ins. Co.*, 355 U.S. 220 (1957), there held to satisfy due process requirements.

For the reasons heretofore rehearsed we will not disturb the English Court's adjudication of jurisdiction; we have deemed as irrelevant the default nature of the judgment; we have concluded that the English compensatory damage items do not offend Pennsylvania public policy; and hold that the English procedure comports with our standards of due process.

In sum, we find that the English proceedings met all the tests enunciated in *Christoff*, supra. We are not persuaded that appellant met its burden of showing that the British "decree is so palpably tainted by fraud or prejudice as to outrage our sense of justice, or [that] the process of the foreign tribunal was invoked to achieve a result contrary to our laws of public policy or to circumvent our laws or public policy." *Christoff*, supra, 192 A.2d at 739.

The judgment of the district court will be affirmed.

Notes

1. The major provisions of the European Economic Community Convention on Jurisdiction and the Enforcement of Judgments in Civil and Commercial Matters, 18 ILM 21 (1979), are set out in chapter 1, page 19. How do the provisions for recognition of judgments from other EEC countries differ from the scope of collateral attack as outlined in *Somportex*? See articles 20, 27 ¶ 2, 28.

The provision in article 20 that when the defendant "does not enter an appearance, the court shall declare of its own motion that is has no jurisdiction unless its jurisdiction is derived from the provisions of this Convention," has special meaning in civil law countries. The civil law maxim, "jura novit curia," "the court knows the law," contemplates a far more active role for the judge in raising and exploring the issues than is true of the common law judge.

Article 27(5) states that if the forum is asked to recognize conflicting judgments, one from another EU court and one from a non-EU court, the earlier judgment prevails. This contrasts with the rule in the United States that as between the conflicting judgments of two states, it is the later judgment that is entitled to full faith and credit. Treinies v. Sunshine Mining Co. 308 U.S. 66 (1939). Ambatielos v. Foundation Co., 116 N.Y.S.2d 641 (N.Y. Sup. Ct. Special Term, N.Y. County 1952) applies this last-in-time rule to inconsistent English and Greek judgments, recognizing the later English judgment.

Article 27(3) gives preference to a judgment of the forum whether earlier of later. There is no provision regarding preference between conflicting judgments from two other EU countries. Articles 22 and 23, which give jurisdiction to the court "first seised," may explain this failure to provide a rule for conflicting EU judgments.

"Towards Greater Efficiency in Obtaining and Enforcing Judgments in the European Union" (A Communication from the EU Commission to the EU Council and the European Parliament), 1998 OJ C 33, ¶ 5, states: "Despite the progress achieved as a result of the Brussels Convention, the implementation of the recognition and enforcement procedures takes far too long and costs too much." The Communication recommends eliminating Brussels Convention Art. 27(1), "public policy," as a ground for refusing to enforce a judgment from another EU country. Id. ¶ 20 The Communication also recommends that if a certificate accompanies the judgment and establishes the conditions required for recognition and enforcement, reception of the judgment "should be virtually automatic" unless the judgment debtor furnishes evidence that establishes one of the Convention grounds for non-recognition. Id. ¶ 19.

2. The EEC convention (see note 1), in article 3, exempts persons domiciled in and companies with their "seat" in EEC countries from jurisdiction under certain bases for jurisdiction that would violate widely recognized international standards. (See chapter 1, note 3 following the Convention.) Persons not domiciled in and companies that do not have their seat in the EEC are not exempt from the exorbitant jurisdictional bases (article 4). Other EEC countries are required to recognize the resulting judgments (articles 26-29). Article 59 permits EEC countries to conclude agreements with non-EEC states prohibiting recognition of EEC judgments utilizing the article 3 bases for jurisdiction.

The United States and the United Kingdom attempted agreement on a bilateral convention on recognition of judgments that would utilize article 59. The bilateral agreement is, however, comatose, if not dead, because of United Kingdom displeasure with huge United States verdicts and the extraterritorial application of United States law, particular antitrust law.

There is no indication that the Article 3 bases for jurisdiction are being widely used in judgments recognized under the EEC convention. See Juenger, "Judicial Jurisdiction in the United States and in the European Communities: A Comparison," 82 Mich. L. Rev. 1195 (1984).

3. Hansen v. American Nat'l Bank, 396 N.W.2d 642 (Minn. App. 1986). Bank sued Hansen in Minnesota and obtained a judgment against him. Hansen had moved to Canada. Bank sued Hansen in British Columbia to enforce the judgment. Hansen defended on the ground that the judgment had been obtained by fraud and that an amended complaint had not been properly served. The British Columbia court held that the Minnesota judgment was res judicata and that Hansen had no defense. Hansen then sued in Minnesota to vacate the prior Minnesota judgment, alleging fraud and improper service of the amended complaint. The Minnesota court held this collateral at-

tack was barred by the British Columbia judgment, which was res judicata on these issues and would be recognized as a matter of comity.

Compare Westend Development Co. v. Westend Amusement Corp., 594 So.2d 553 (La. App. 5th Cir. 1992), writ denied, 596 So.2d 210 (La. 1992). Development Company obtained a Louisiana deficiency judgment against a California resident. When Development Company sued on the judgment in California, the judgment debtor made a collateral attack on the judgment, contending that the Louisiana court did not have personal jurisdiction over him. The California court rejected this attack and made the Louisiana judgment a judgment of the California court. The judgment debtor then sued in Louisiana to nullify the Louisiana judgment for lack of personal jurisdiction. Development Company's exception of res judicata was overruled and the Louisiana Court of Appeal affirmed, holding that the full faith and credit clause of Article IV of the United States Constitution did not prevent Louisiana from determining the validity of its own judgments, and stated that "the common law principle of collateral estoppel or issue preclusion forms no part of our civilian concept of res judicata." 594 So.2d at 556.

4. Eight of the Canadian provinces and territories have legislation permitting registration of judgments of reciprocating jurisdictions from outside Canada. Registration provides a simpler and less expensive method of enforcement than suit on the judgment. These provinces and territories have been slow to declare U.S. states as entitled to utilize registration. In only four provinces has a state official declared one or more American states to be "a reciprocating jurisdiction" whose judgments are entitled to registration. Even in those Canadian provinces and territories that permit registration of judgments from outside Canada, registration is not available unless the defendant is carrying on business or is ordinarily resident in the state whose court rendered the judgment or the defendant has voluntarily submitted to the jurisdiction of that court.

5. Cardenas v. Solis, 570 So.2d 996 (Fla. Ct. App. 3d Dist. 1990), rev. denied, 581 So.2d 163 (Fla. 1991). A Guatemalan wife sued her Guatemalan husband in Guatemala under Guatemalan community property law seeking fifty percent of the property acquired by the parties during their marriage. The wife alleged that her husband deposited business income in Miami and has threatened to dispose of those funds. The Guatemalan court entered an ex parte injunction freezing the husband's bank accounts in Florida and entered a petition to "the Court of the State of Florida" requesting assistance to enforce the injunction. The wife sued in Florida for an injunction to enforce the Guatemalan decree. The Florida circuit court granted a temporary ex parte injunction and, after a hearing, modified the injunction to freeze one half of the Florida deposits. The Court of Appeal affirmed. Compare the English "Mareva" injunction discussed in note 1 following Shaffer v. Heitner in chapter 1.

X v. Y, [1998] H.J. (1647) 107 (Tokyo High Ct., 1998), translation in 42 Japanese Ann. Int'l L 161 (1999), enforced a child support order from a Minnesota court. The Japanese father had impregnated the mother while the father was working in Minnesota. The court held that it had no power to enforce the Minnesota court's order that the father's employer withhold the support payment from the father's pay and forward it to a collection agency in Minnesota. Instead the court ordered the father to pay the support to the mother.

6. In the United Kingdom, leave to serve process outside the jurisdiction must be obtained under Rule of the Supreme Court, Order 11, Rule 1. Rule 1(1) lists the bases for jurisdiction on which a court can base its permission for service and reads much like a detailed long-arm statute. Rule 4 states that an applicant for grant of leave for such ser-

vice must submit an affidavit stating, among other things, "that in the deponent's belief the plaintiff has a good cause of action." Seaconsar Far East Ltd. v. Bank Markazi Jomhouri Islami Iran, [1994] 1 A.C. 438, [1993] 3 W.L.R. 756, [1993] 4 All E.R. 456 (H.L.), held that when service outside the jurisdiction is based upon Rule(1)(d), a contract made within the jurisdiction or a contract made by an agent trading within the jurisdiction, it was sufficient for the applicant to establish that there was "a serious issue to be tried," without further inquiry into the merits of the case.

7. The principal case indicates that when exercising diversity jurisdiction federal courts apply the law of the state in which they are sitting when deciding whether to recognize the judgment of a foreign country. Federal courts apply federal judgment-recognition law in federal question cases. See 18 Charles A. Wright et al, Federal Practice & Procedure § 4473 at 741 (1981). A bare majority of the justices in Hilton v. Guyot, supra page 227, established reciprocity as a requirement for recognition of a foreign judgment. It is unlikely that reciprocity is any longer part of the federal recognition standard, just as it is not part of the standard in most states. See Tahan v. Hodgson, 662 F.2d. 862, 867-68 (D.C. Cir. 1981); Restatement (Third) of the Foreign Relations Law of the United States § 481, cmt. d (1987).

Jet Holdings Inc. v. Patel
[1988] 3 W.L.R. 295, [1989] 2 All E.R. 648 (Ct. App.)

STAUGHTON L.J.:This action is brought to enforce a foreign judgment, that is to say a judgment of the Superior Court of the State of California for Los Angeles County. The defence is, first, that the judgment was obtained by fraud. Alternatively, it is said that the proceedings in which the judgment was obtained were opposed to natural justice. The present proceedings are for summary judgment in the English action. * * * The defendant, Mr Patel, says that he should have leave to defend on those grounds or that * * * there ought for some other reason to be a trial of the action.

[Defendant worked as an accountant in California for three companies that are plaintiffs in this action. Mr. Don Arden is the president of those companies. Mr. Arden accused defendant of wrongfully misappropriating money from the companies and dismissed him. The Defendant denies the misappropriation and alleges three occasions on which Mr. Arden, in California and in England, subjected him to actual or threatened violence and compelled him to make a payment of $100,000. The defendant complained to the police in England. As a result, Mr. Arden's son was prosecuted, convicted of conspiracy to menace defendant and false imprisonment, and sentenced to imprisonment. Later Mr. Arden was also prosecuted, but he was acquitted.]

[O]n 30 May 1984, the plaintiff companies commenced their action in the Californian court against the defendant. Their monetary claim amounted to $168,000, and they also sought punitive damages in the sum of $2m. * * * Then, on 23 July 1984, the defendant entered an appearance in the Californian action, and served an answer to the plaintiffs' complaint. He says that he did this on the advice of his English solicitors and counsel, who were different from those representing him today. That was a most important step, since it acknowledged the jurisdiction of the Californian court. If it had not been taken, I presently do not see any ground on which the Californian judgment could have been enforced in this country. But, as it was, an appearance was entered, an answer was filed and, on 26 November 1984, the defendant filed a cross-claim there against the present plaintiffs, Mr. Arden and a number of others.

In the proceedings that ensued, there are three particular matters to note. First, on 7 November 1984 the California court heard an application that the defendant's deposition be taken in Los Angeles. The application was made on behalf of the plaintiffs. It was opposed, with evidence from the defendant that he did not wish to visit the United States because, if he did so, he would be in fear of his life owing to the violence and threats which he had suffered previously. There was, however, at the same time an assertion by his American lawyer that he would be present later at the trial. It is not altogether easy to reconcile that statement with the defendant's assertion that he was afraid to go to the United States. No doubt he could be cross-examined about that, if it were ever material. On that occasion the judge refused the application. We have no note as such of the judge's reasons, but there is some indication that he did pay regard to the defendant's fears.

Nearly a year later, on 25 October 1985, the Californian court made an order that the defendant attend two doctors in Los Angeles for physical and medical examination on 7 and 8 January 1986. That was no doubt relevant to the assertion in his cross complaint that he had suffered injury which was continuing. The order which the court made on that occasion continued:

> 3. The expense of Bachu Patel's travel to Los Angeles, including air fare, motel and meals, is to be born by plaintiffs and cross-defendants, who shall make the necessary arrangements in advance.
>
> 4. If Bachu Patel desires, he may select a security guard to guard him during his stay in Los Angeles, the expense of which shall be borne by plaintiffs and cross-defendants.

The defendant did not comply with that order. His explanation was:

> On 5 January 1986 I telephoned British Airways in order to verify the existence of a prepaid ticket in my name paid for by Jet Executive Travel for passage from London to Los Angles, California. I was advised that no such prepaid ticket existed. In view of that fact, I did not go to Heathrow Airport on 6 January 1986 as I had previously planned.

There is evidence which suggests that this explanation was untrue. On 10 February 1986 the Californian court made an order excluding evidence that the defendant had suffered any physical or mental injury at the hands of the plaintiffs.

The question of the deposition of the defendant in Los Angeles was raised again before the Californian court by the plaintiffs on 27 February 1986. It was again opposed on his behalf on the ground that he should not be forced to endanger his life by going to Los Angeles. On this occasion an order was made for the deposition to be taken in Los Angeles, on 28 and 29 April 1986. The plaintiffs were again to bear the cost involved, including the cost of a security guard.

Mr. Patel did not attend. He claimed, for the second time, that an air ticket had not be provided. There is again evidence which suggests that this explanation was untrue.

* * *

By that time the defendant's American lawyers had ceased to act for him and had been removed from the record. He says in his affidavit that he did not have the means to instruct them adequately, since the plaintiffs had extorted the sterling equivalent of $100,000 from him by violence and threats. Eventually, on 11 June 1986, the Californian court ordered: (1) the cross-complaint to be dismissed; (2) the answer to be stricken; and (3) default to be entered against the defendant. On that occasion the judge read and considered, as he noted on the document, a declaration by the defendant, in which he again gave brief details of the threats and violence which he had suffered, stated that he had no money left to pay his lawyers, and repeated that airline tickets had not been provided on the two occasions when he had failed to attend in Los Angeles. We have no direct evidence as to whether the judge did or did not accept the truth of what the defendant was saying when he came to make his orders.

On 9 September 1986 the damages were assessed in California. A declaration by Mr. Arden disclosed that he or his companies had received $100,000, and offered to take that into account, but claimed an additional sum of $86,000 in respect of hotel expenses incurred by the defendant. Judgment was entered against the defendant for $168,940, which was the sum originally claimed, without regard to the credit of $100,000 or the additional claim of $86,000. There was also judgment for $2,463.50 costs and punitive damages in the sum of $500,000. It is that judgment which the plaintiffs now seek to enforce here. They have not been able to proceed under any of the statutory provisions relating to the registration of foreign judgments. Instead, they sue on the judgment at common law.

On 3 March 1987 Master Trench gave summary judgment for the plaintiffs * * * in respect of the amount claimed and interest. There was an appeal from that order which was heard by Mr. Patrick Bennett Q.C., sitting as a deputy judge of the Queen's Bench Division, on 23 July 1987. The appeal was dismissed. The defendant now appeals from that order of the deputy judge.

The enforcement of foreign judgments at common law is set out clearly and concisely in Dicey & Morris. The Conflict of Laws, 11th ed (1987), rules 42-46. Those provide:

> 42. A foreign judgment which is final and conclusive on the merits and not impeachable under any of rules 43 to 46 is conclusive as to any matter thereby adjudicated upon, and cannot be impeached for any error either (1) of fact; or (2) of law.
>
> 43. (1) A foreign judgment is impeachable if the courts of the foreign country did not, in the circumstances of the case, have jurisdiction to give that judgment in the view of English law in accordance with the principles set out in rules 37 to 41 inclusive...
>
> 44. A foreign judgment relied upon as such in proceedings in England is impeachable for fraud. Such fraud may be either (1) fraud on the part of the party in whose favour the judgment is given; or (2) fraud on the part of the court pronouncing the judgment.

I need not read rule 45, which deals with public policy.

> 46. A foreign judgment may (semble) be impeached if the proceedings in which the judgment was obtained were opposed to natural justice.

On the threshold of the argument for the defendant is the point that the foreign court's own view as to whether the judgment was obtained by fraud is not conclusive or indeed relevant. The deputy judge seems to have taken the contrary view. In his judgment he said:

> The U.S. court was fully cognizant of the issue as to whether the failure to attend was or might have been because of improper pressures. The services of a bodyguard were offered at the plaintiffs' expense. On the evidence before me I cannot see that the U.S. judgment was obtained by fraud even using the wider meaning of that term. The U.S. court considered the matter. The defendant

was represented and the issue was resolved against him. This was not a case where rule 42 of Dicey & Morris, The Conflict of Laws was avoided by the exception that there was fraud.

The judge then went on to consider the alternative case relating to natural justice and, after referring to *Pemberton v. Hughes* [1899] 1 CH 781 and the comment on rule 46 in Dicey & Morris, he said:

> the objection could have been and was taken before the foreign court. That issue having been raised, argued and adjudicated upon, in my view there was no denial of natural justice.

Where the objection to enforcement is based on jurisdiction—that is rule 43—it is to my mind plain that the foreign court's decision on its own jurisdiction is neither conclusive nor relevant. If the foreign court had no jurisdiction in the eyes of English law, any conclusion it may have reached as to its own jurisdiction is of no value. To put it bluntly, if not vulgarly, the foreign court cannot haul itself up by its own bootstraps. Logically, the same reasoning must apply where enforcement is resisted on the ground of fraud—rule 44. If the rule is that a foreign judgment obtained by fraud is not enforceable, it cannot matter that in the view of the foreign court there was no fraud. But this doctrine makes a great inroad into the objective, which is generally desirable, of enforcing judgments where in the eyes of English law the foreign court had jurisdiction. The defendant may have been served in the foreign country, entered an appearance, given evidence, been disbelieved, and had judgment entered against him. If he asserts that the plaintiff's claim and evidence were fraudulent that issue must be tried all over again in enforcement proceedings. The lesson for the plaintiff is that he should in the first place bring his action where he expects to be able to enforce a judgment.

That doctrine has encountered criticism from academic writers. A possible view which is taken by some is that the fraud relied on must be extraneous or collateral to the dispute which the foreign court determines. But, in my judgment, it is 100 years too late for this court to take that view. The decisions in *Abouloff v Oppenheimer & Co.* [1882] 10 Q.B.D. 295 and *Vadala v. Lawes* [1890] 25 Q.B.D. 310 show that a foreign judgment cannot be enforced if it was obtained by fraud, even though the allegation of fraud was investigated and rejected by the foreign court.

* * *

[I]n the alternative the defendant also relies on rule 46 in Dicey & Morris. The rule itself refers to proceedings opposed to natural justice. In the comment, at p. 474, the authors cite the observations of Lord Lindley M.R. in *Pemberton v. Hughes* [1899] 1 Ch 781, 790:

> If a judgment is pronounced by a foreign court...English courts never investigate the propriety of the proceedings in the foreign court, unless they offend against English views of substantial justice.

* * *

Once again one would expect that the foreign court's views would logically be neither conclusive nor relevant as to the propriety of its own proceedings. If the English court considers that the foreign court did not observe the rules of natural justice—for example, the rule *audi alteram partem* or *nemo judex in rem suam*—why should it make any difference that the foreign court thought that it was observing the rules of natural justice? But Dicey & Morris take the contrary view. * * * But I do not find it necessary to decide this appeal on the basis of rule 46 or on procedural failure to comply with the rules of natural justice or with, as Lord Lindley M.R. puts it, English views of substantial justice. It can be decided in my judgment on rule 44, fraud. It is plain, as I have said, that when considering fraud the English courts have to consider the facts afresh without regard to the decision of the foreign court.

The defendant's case before us was not that there was fraud in the cause of action itself. He does not resist enforcement on the ground that he had misappropriated none of the plaintiffs' money, and that the plaintiffs were fraudulent in asserting that he had misappropriated money. So in sense, his allegation here is of collateral fraud. He asserts that the plaintiffs' conduct was fraudulent in (1) assaulting him with violence and threats, so that he was afraid to go to California; (2) obtaining $100,000 from him by those means, so that he was unable to afford continuing legal representation in California; and (3) failing to invite the Californian court to take that $100,000 into account against the plaintiffs' claim. Factually ground (3) seems to be not supported by the evidence. Alternatively, the defendant says that the Californian court was misled by the plaintiffs as to the true reason for his default.

* * *

[W]e must take the facts to be as deposed to by the defendant in his affidavit, unless what he says is plainly untrue. There are good grounds for questioning the defendant's credibility in relation to the two occasions when he says that no air ticket was available for him. * * *However, there is also independent evidence to support the conclusion that the defendant was subject to mistreatment by the plaintiffs or their associates. * * * I am firmly of the view that the evidence of the defendant cannot * * * be rejected as wholly untruthful.

It is, I think, clear that the plaintiffs' Californian lawyers were asserting to the court implicitly, and even to some extent expressly, that the defendant's account of violence, threats and fear was untrue. If in fact it was true, that assertion, together with the actual incidents relied on, is capable of amounting to fraud in this context

* * *

But [plaintiffs' counsel] submits that the Californian court was not deceived. This is the heart of the matter. He invites us to conclude that the Californian court was prepared to assume the facts on which the defendant relied, but concluded that it was still right to make the orders that it did make, and perhaps also that it had no option but to make those orders.

For my part I would not accept, without express evidence, that a United States or any other judge, believing or assuming on 11 June 1986 that the defendant had on three occasions been subject to threatened and actual violence, that he had been forced to hand over $100,000, that in consequence he had no money left to pay his lawyers, and that he was in genuine fear in going to the United States, would nevertheless have given judgment against him in default for the sum of $168,000 and $500,000 punitive damages. Nor would I accept, without express evidence, that a United States judge, believing or assuming some or all of those facts, would have made the orders for a medical examination or for the defendant's deposition in Los Angeles, relying only on such protection as might be afforded by a security guard. There were other orders that could have been made—for example, an order could have been made for the examination of the defendant in England by a doctor who was qualified to practice medicine in this country; an order could have been made for taking evidence from the defendant in England, though it may well be that in the absence of consent the process which would have had to have been employed might not have been wholly satisfactory. Of course, if the defendant had refused his consent to a process which was the equivalent of what would have happened in the United States the judge would have taken that into account.

In my judgment, there is an issue to be tried in this case as to whether the defendant is entitled to resist enforcement, at any rate on the ground of fraud. Accordingly, this appeal should be allowed, and the judgment set aside. The action must go to trial.

* * *

Appeal allowed with costs.

Notes

1.I Dicey & Morris, Conflict of Laws 487-88, Rule 36 (13th ed. 2000, Lawrence Collins ed.) (stating that that only four bases are recognized for personal jurisdiction in foreign courts for recognition of judgments from countries with which the United Kingdom has not joined in a judgment-recognition treaty: institution of the proceedings while the defendant was present in the foreign country, the defendant sued or counterclaimed in the proceedings, the defendant voluntarily appeared, the defendant consented before suit to submit to the court's jurisdiction).

2. U.K. Civil Jurisdiction and Judgments Act 1982, §33(1):

"For the purposes of determining whether a judgment given by a court of an overseas country should be recognised or enforced in England and Wales or Northern Ireland, the person against whom the judgment was given shall not be regarded as having submitted to the jurisdiction of the court by reason only of the fact that he appeared (conditionally or otherwise) in the proceedings for all or any one or more of the following purposes, namely (a) to contest the jurisdiction of the court; (b) to ask the court to dismiss or stay the proceedings on the ground that the dispute in question should be submitted to arbitration or to the determination of the courts of another country; (c) to protect, or obtain the release of, property seized or threatened with seizure in the proceedings."

3. Adams v. Cape Industries PLC., [1990] 2 W.L.R. 657 (Ct. App.). Recognition of a default judgment by a Texas federal district court for $15.5 million was denied. The judgment was against an English Company which, through subsidiaries, mined and marketed asbestos, and against the English company's worldwide marketing subsidiary, which also was incorporated in England. The bases for non recognition were: (1) the operations of a marketing subsidiary in Illinois was not sufficient to make the English defendants "present" in the United States; (2) the method of determining the amount of the default judgment was contrary to English requirements of substantial justice. To avoid litigating the details of the compensation claims of the 206 workers in a Tyler factory suing for asbestos-related injuries, the trial judge determined that the average award would be $75,000 and let the plaintiffs' lawyer designate which claimants would be put into one of four groups receiving the following amounts for each claimant in the group: $37,000, $60,000, $85,000, and $120,000. It is not evident on what basis the trial judge selected $75,000 as the average award, although the English Court of Appeal speculated that this was the judge's estimate of the settlement value for all the claims divided by the number of claimants. In the course of its opinion, the English Court of Appeal commented as follows on what constitutes a company's "presence" within a jurisdiction.

Id. at 747:

"In relation to trading corporations, we derive the three following propositions from consideration of the many authorities cited to us relating to the 'presence' of an overseas corporation.

"(1) The English courts will be likely to treat a trading corporation incorporated under the law of one country ('an overseas corporation') as present within the jurisdiction of the courts of another country only if either (i) it has established and maintained at its own expense (whether as owner or lessee) a fixed place of business of its own in the other country and for more than a minimal period of time has carried on its own business at or from such premises by its servants or agents (a 'branch office' case), or (ii) a representative of the overseas corporation has for more than a minimal period of time been carrying on the *overseas corporation's* business in the other country at or from some fixed place of business.

"(2) In either of these two cases presence can only be established if it can fairly be said that *the overseas corporation's* business (whether or not together with the representative's own business) has been transacted at or from the fixed place of business. In the first case, this condition is likely to present few problems. In the second, the question whether the representative has been carrying on the overseas corporation's business or has been doing no more than carry on his own business will necessitate an investigation of the functions which he has been performing and all aspects of the relationship between him and the overseas corporation.

"(3) In particular, but without prejudice to the generality of the foregoing, the following questions are likely to be relevant on such investigation: (a) whether or not the fixed place of business from which the representative operates was originally acquired for the purpose of enabling him to act on behalf of the overseas corporation; (b) whether the overseas corporation has directly reimbursed him for (i) the cost of his accommodation at the fixed place of business, (ii) the cost of his staff; (c) what other contributions, if any, the overseas corporation makes to the financing of the business carried on by the representative; (d) whether the representative is remunerated by reference to transactions, e.g. by commission, or by fixed regular payments or in some other way; (e) what degree of control the overseas corporation exercises over the running of the business conducted by the representative; (f) whether the representative reserves (i) part of his accommodation, (ii) part of his staff for conducting business related to the overseas corporation; (g) whether the representative displays the overseas corporation's name at his premises or on his stationery, and if so, whether he does so in such a way as to indicate that he is a representative of the overseas corporation; (h) what business, if any, the representative transacts as principal exclusively on his own behalf, (i) whether the representative makes contracts with customers or other third parties in the name of the overseas corporation, or otherwise in such manner as to bind it; (j) if so, whether the representative requires specific authority in advance before binding the overseas corporation to contractual obligations."

Id. p. 753:

"In deciding whether a company is present in a foreign country by a subsidiary, which is itself present in that country, the court is entitled, indeed bound, to investigate the relationship between the parent and the subsidiary. In particular, that relationship may be relevant in determining whether the subsidiary was acting as the parent's agent and, if so, on what terms. In *Firestone Tyre and Rubber Co., Ltd. v. Lewellin* [1957] 1 W.L.R. 464 (which was referred to by Scott J.) the House of Lords upheld an assessment to tax on the footing that, on the facts, the business both of the parent and subsidiary were carried on by the subsidiary as agent for the parent. However, there is no presumption of any such agency. There is no presumption that the subsidiary is the parent company's alter ego. In the court below the judge refused an invitation to infer that there existed an agency agreement between Cape and N.A.A.C. comparable to that which had previously existed between Cape and Capasco and that refusal is not challenged on this appeal. If a company chooses to arrange the affairs of its group in such a way that the business carried on in a particular foreign country is the business of its subsidiary and not its own, it is, in our judgment, entitled to do so. Neither in this class of case nor in any other class of case is it open to this court to disregard the principle of *Salomon v. A. Salomon & Co. Ltd.* [1897] A.C. 22 merely because it considers it just so to do."

4. The German Supreme Court has refused, on the ground of public policy, to recognize for enforcement in Germany, the punitive damages portion of a California judgment. Judgment of the Bundesgerichtshof, IXth Civil Senate, of June 4, 1992, Docket No. IX ZR 149/91 [1992] Wertpapiermitteilungen 1451. (It is German practice not to identify the parties.) The plaintiff, a fourteen-year old male and an American citizen, sued the defendant, who had dual United States and German citizenship, for sexual abuse. Although the defendant was represented by counsel in the preliminary stages of the litigation, neither the defendant nor his counsel appeared at trial. The plaintiff was awarded $750,260, which included $400,000 in punitive damages. The German Supreme Court held that, notwithstanding the 40% contingent fee to plaintiff's lawyer, the judgment would be enforced in Germany except for the punitive damages. The court stated that it was against German public policy to recognize "a lump-sum award of punitive damages in a not insubstantial amount." [1992] WM at 1460. For comment on the decision, see Peter Hay, "The Recognition and Enforcement of American Money-Judgments in Germany—The 1992 Decision of the German Supreme Court," 40 Amer. J. Comp. L. 729 (1992). For discussion of recognition of judgments abroad, see Enforcing Foreign Judgments in the United States and United States Judgments Abroad (1992, Ronald A. Brand ed.); Martin Bernet & Nicolas C. Ulmer, "Recognition and Enforcement of Foreign Civil Judgments in Switzerland," 27 Int'l Lawyer 317 (1993).

The German Constitutional Court has rejected the argument of a German defendant against service of process in Germany under the procedures of the Hague Service Convention, supra page 96. Service was for suit in a U.S. court. The defendant argued that this exposed it to punitive damages and violated its constitutional right of personality. The court noted that German property was not at risk because a German court would not enforce a judgment for punitive damages. Bundesverfassungsgerict, decision of Dec. 7, 1994, 1995 Nue Juristische Wochenschrift 649.

In Princess Caroline of Monaco v. Publisher of the Magazines "B" and "G", Bundesgerichtshof 1995 Neue Juristische Wochenschrift 861, the German Supreme Court held that damages for violation of the right of privacy should be awarded in an amount sufficient to provide satisfaction to the victim and to deter repetition of the conduct. The court held that the damages awarded by the Court of Appeals were not sufficient to have an impact on the defendant or present a genuine disincentive to such conduct. The case was remanded for a new determination of damages. Does this judgment authorize a form of punitive damages?

The Supreme Court of Japan has held that it is contrary to Japanese public policy to enforce the punitive damages portion of a California judgment. Northon I v. Mansei Kogyo Co., 51 Minshu (6) 2573 (Japan 1997), translation in 41 Japanese Ann. Int'l L. 104 (1998).

O'Gilvie v. United States, 519 U.S. 79 (1996) held that an award of punitive damages in a tort suit is taxable as income because not within an Internal Revenue Code provision excluding from income damages received "on account of personal injuries or sickness." The court stated that punitive damages "do not compensate for any kind of loss." Id. at 86-87. Will this decision have an effect on the recognition abroad of United States judgments for punitive damages?

5. Owens Bank Ltd. v. Bracco, [1992] 2 All E. R. 193, [1992] 2 W.L.R. 621 (H.L. 1992). The House of Lords held that although an English judgment cannot be set aside on the ground that it was obtained by fraud unless the fraud is proven by evidence not available and not discoverable with reasonable diligence before judgment, there is no such limitation on denying recognition to a foreign judgment for fraud. The court stated that the non recognition of foreign judgments for fraud is governed by the Administration of Justice Act 1920 § 9(d) and cannot be changed except by amending that Act.

In *Owens Bank*, the House of Lords referred to the Court of Justice of the European Communities the issue of whether articles 21-23 of the Brussels Convention (supra page xx) applied when the foreign judgment is that of a non-Contracting State and suits to enforce it have been brought in two Contracting States. The plaintiff had obtained a judgment in St. Vincent and then sued to enforce it, first in Italy and then in England. The Court of Justice held that articles 21-23 did not apply and therefore the English court did not have to dismiss an action of which the Italian court was first seized. Case C-129/92, [1994] ECR I-117, [1994] 2 W.L.R. 759. The Court also stated that the Brussels Convention does not require one EU country to enforce a judgment of another EU country if that judgment recognizes a judgment of a non-EU country. For a similar conclusion, see Reading & Bates Construction Co. v. Baker Energy Resources Corp., 976 S.W.2d 702 (Tex. App.-Houston [lst Dist.] 1998, rev. denied), which held that it need not recognize a Louisiana judgment that enforced a Canadian judgment because this would have the effect of giving full faith and credit to the judgment of a foreign country "through the back door." The court stated that the proper method of enforcing the Canadian judgment in Texas was under the Uniform Foreign Money-Judgments Recognition Act.

6. The Matrimonial and Family Provisions Act 1984 permits an English court to make an order for financial relief of a spouse divorced abroad. Hewitson v. Hewitson, [1995] 2 W.L.R. 287 (C.A.) held that such and order should not be made in a case involving a California divorce in which the decree was comprehensive and final and incorporated an agreement negotiated by both spouses and their lawyers.

Society of Lloyd's v. Baker, 673 A.2d 1336 (Me. 1996) enforced an English default judgment against an American "name" (member of a Lloyd's syndicate) who contended that he was induced by fraudulent misrepresentations to contract with Lloyd's. The court held that the fraud was not of a kind that either induced him to consent to an English forum or prevented him from litigating the fraud issue there and therefore was not the kind of "extrinsic" fraud that could be raised in a collateral attack on a foreign judgment. Note that this distinction between intrinsic and extrinsic fraud was rejected by the House of Lords in *Owens Bank* supra. For discussion of intrinsic and extrinsic fraud see infra page 253, Note 2.

Ramirez v. United States, 36 Fed. Cl. 467 (1996) refused to enforce a Honduran judgment against the United States on the ground that the Court of Federal Claims did not have the subject-matter jurisdiction to entertain the suit. The Tucker Act, 50 U.S.C. § 1431, gave the court jurisdiction to decide claims against the United States "for liquidated or unliquidated damages in cases not sounding in tort," but suit on a foreign judgment did not come within the statute even though the underlying claim was for breach of contract.

Concept Generation International, Inc. v. Nippon Design Network, Tokyo Chiho Saibansho (District Court), 1994.1.14, Minji Dai 37 Bu, Hanrei Times No. 864, pp. 269-273, sets out the conditions necessary for a Japanese court to recognize foreign judgments under Article 200 of the Rules of Civil Procedure. The court enforced a New York default judgment against a Japanese defendant. The court found that the jurisdiction of the New York court over the Japanese defendant accorded with Japan's principles for international jurisdiction because New York was the place where the defendant was to perform its contract and was the place of the wrongful act. The court noted that New York recognized foreign judgments under the Uniform Foreign Money-Judgments Recognition Act (infra page 251), that the grounds for non-recognition stated in the Uniform Act were substantially the same as those used by Japanese courts, and that therefore the Japanese requirement of reciprocity was met. For discussion of Japanese practice in recognizing foreign judgments see Takeshi Kojima, Cooperation in International Procedural Conflicts: Prospects and Benefits, 57 Law & Contemp. Probs. 59, 62-74 (Summer 1994).

7. The Hague Conference on Private International law has accepted a United States recommendation to undertake the drafting of a treaty on the recognition and enforcement of judgments. A Special Commission is drafting the convention. One concern of the Commission is whether the convention should contain special provisions excusing or moderating recognition and enforcement of judgments for "excessive" compensatory damages or for multiple or punitive damages. See Preliminary Draft Convention, American Law Institute, International Jurisdiction and Judgments Project, Report 41-65 (April 14, 2000). Article 33 permits a signatory to recognize a foreign judgment only in the amount that its own courts would have awarded. Id. at 60-61.

Section 2: Judgments Enforcing Public Law

United States of America v. Inkley
[1988] 3 All E.R. 144, [1988] 3 W.L.R. 304 (Ct. App.)

PURCHAS L.J. [The defendant was prosecuted for crime in the United States. He was released on bail and was allowed to travel to England to attend his father's funeral. When he did not return, the bail was revoked and the United States obtained a judgment for the bail. A judgment for the bail plus interest was entered below and defendant appeals.]

[T]he judge [below] came to the conclusion that the proceedings were civil proceedings and enforceable by action in the English courts, although he found the question a nicely balanced one. The defendant challenges this decision and asserts that on the authorities the judge should have come to the conclusion that the substance of this action was the enforcement of a public law remedy in the nature of a penal proceeding and, therefore, would not be enforceable in the English courts.

It is necessary to turn shortly to the authorities and the textbooks. The starting point is the dictum of Gray J. in *Wisconsin v Pelican Insurance Co.* (1887) 127 U.S. 265 approved by the Privy Council in *Huntington v. Attrill* [1893] A.C. 150, 157, per Lord Watson:

In delivering the judgment of the bench, Gray J, after referring to the text books, and the dictum by Marshall C.J. already cited, went on to say: "The rule that the courts of no country execute the law of another applies not only to prosecutions and sentences for crimes and misdemeanors, but to all suits in favour of the state for the recovery of pecuniary penalties for any violation of statutes for the protection of its revenue or other municipal laws, and to all judgments for such penalties." Their Lordships do not hesitate to accept that exposition of the law, which, in their opinion, discloses the proper test for ascertaining whether an action is penal within the meaning of the rule. A proceeding, in order to come within the scope of the rule, must be in the nature of a suit in favour of the state whose law has been infringed.

Earlier Lord Watson had defined the role of the court in which the proceedings were brought and the foreign court whose jurisdiction was invoked, at p. 155:

> Their Lordships cannot assent to the proposition that, in considering whether the present action was penal in such sense as to oust their jurisdiction, the courts of Ontario were bound to pay absolute deference to any interpretation which might have been put upon the Statute of 1875 in the State of New York. They had to construe and apply an international rule, which is a matter of law entirely within the cognizance of the foreign court whose jurisdiction is invoked. Judicial decisions in the state where the cause of action arose are not precedents which must be followed, although the reasoning upon which they are founded must always receive careful consideration, and may be conclusive. The court appealed to must determine for itself, in the first place, the substance of the right sought to be enforced; and, in the second place, whether its enforcement would, either directly or indirectly, involve the execution of the penal law of another state.

In *Attorney-General of New Zealand v. Ortiz* [1984] A.C. 1 the Court of Appeal recognised *Huntington v. Attrill* as correctly stating the law; although the House of Lords in dealing with the matter decided the appeal on an alternative ground. However, Ackner L.J. said, at p. 33:

> Huntington's case makes it clear that the first part of Mr. Gray's definition of foreign penal law, namely that it must be part of the criminal code of a foreign country, is not sustainable. The right which it is sought to enforce may be a right which arises under legislation which is essentially designed to regulate commercial activities such as company legislation which may well contain a penal provision. I agree with the judge that it cannot be right simply to categorise the statute sought to be enforced as a whole. The court must pay regard to the particular provision of the foreign law which it is sought to enforce... In the instant submission, the claim is made by the Attorney-General on behalf of the state. It is not a claim by a private individual. Further, the cause of action does not concern a private right which demands reparation or compensation. It concerns a public right—the preservation of historic articles within New Zealand—which right the state seeks to vindicate.

In Ort's case the issue arose out of a statute passed in New Zealand which enabled customs officers to impound an artifact of historic importance being exported without a certificate. The claim was brought in the English courts, the artifact in question having been successfully, if illegally, exported. In these circumstances the Court of Appeal and, on other grounds, the House of Lords held that no action lay in the English courts. This is to be compared with Huntington's case where the New York statute, although penal in shape and form, in fact provided a right to be enjoyed by an investor to claim compensation from the directors of a company who had issued a fraudulently inaccurate document. In that case the Privy Council held that the claim arising in New York was in fact enforceable in the courts of Ontario.

The court was referred to the treatment of this topic in Dicey & Morris, The Conflict of Laws, vol 1, pp 100-107. The two areas where the question of jurisdiction to entertain a foreign suit normally arise are where enforcement is sought either directly or indirectly of a "penal" or "revenue" law. Dicey & Morris, however, clearly recognises a third category described as "other public law." The proposition is put forward that the enforcement of public law may be the general umbrella under which both penal and revenue suits are embraced. In our judgment, the extracts from Lord Watson's judgment and the judgment of Ackner L.J. demonstrate this proposition. * * * The proposition also received support from the speech of Lord Keith of *Avonholm in Government of India v. Taylor* [1955] A.C. 491, 511:

> One explanation of the rule thus illustrated may be thought to be that enforcement of a claim for taxes is but an extension of the sovereign power which imposed the taxes, and that an assertion of sovereign authority by one state within the territory of another, as distinct from a patrimonial claim by a foreign sovereign, is (treaty or convention apart) contrary to all concepts of independent sovereignties.

From these authorities the following propositions seem to emerge which are relevant to the present appeal: (1) the consideration of whether the claim sought to be enforced in the English courts is one which involves the assertion of foreign sovereignty, whether it be penal, revenue or other public law, is to be determined according to the criteria of English law; (2) that regard will be had to the attitude adopted by the courts in the foreign jurisdiction which will always receive serious attention and may on occasions be decisive; (3) that the category of the right of action, i.e. whether public or private, will depend on the party in whose favour it is created, on the purpose of the law or enactment in the foreign state on which it is based and on the general context of the case as a whole; (4) that the fact that the right, statutory or otherwise, is penal in nature will not deprive a person, who asserts a personal claim depending thereon, from having recourse to the courts of this country; on the other hand, by whatever description it may be known if the purpose of the action is the enforcement of a sanction, power or right at the instance of the state in its sovereign capacity, it will not be entertained; (5) that the fact that in the foreign jurisdiction recourse may be had in a civil forum to enforce the right will not necessarily affect the true nature of the right being enforced in this country.

Applying the above criteria to the facts of this case we have come firmly to the conclusion that the general context and background against which the appearance bond was executed was criminal or penal. The power to require the execution of the bond arose from section 3146 et seq of the United States Code for Crimes and Criminal Procedure. The circumstances in which it came into existence were clearly criminal in nature and breaches of the conditions incorporated in it could give rise to further criminal process. Finally, the whole purpose of the bond was to ensure, so far as it was possible, the presence of the executor of the bond to meet justice at the hands of the state in a criminal prosecution. The fact that the obligations under the bond were the subject matter of the declaratory judgment in a civil court does not affect, in our judgment, the basic characteristic of the right which that judgment itself enforced, namely the right of the state as the administrator of public law and justice to ensure the due observance of the criminal law or the exaction of pecuniary penalties if that course was frustrated. Notwithstanding its civil clothing, the purpose of the action initiated by the writ issued in this case was the due execution by the United State of America of a public law process aimed to ensure the attendance of persons accused of crime before the criminal courts.

For these reasons we have come to the conclusion that [it is] right in this case to set aside the judgment in default and to strike out the proceedings. We would, therefore, allow this appeal.

* * *

Notes

1. Her Majesty v. Gilbertson, 597 F.2d 1161 (9th Cir. 1979) dismissed a suit to enforce a British Columbia certificate of tax assessment. The tax was on income that the defendants, Oregon citizens, received from logging in British Columbia. The filing of the assessment in British Columbia had the effect of a judgment. The court noted that British Columbia courts refuse to enforce tax judgments of United States courts.

2. Nicol v. Tanner, 310 Minn. 68, 256 N.W.2d 796 (1976). A German default judgment for child support is entitled to res judicata effect if on remand the trial court determines that the German court was a fair and convenient forum in which to litigate the issues. The reciprocity requirement of Hilton v. Guyot is rejected.

3. Note that the Uniform Foreign Money-Judgments Recognition Act, §1(2), which follows, excludes "a judgment for taxes, a fine or other penalty." It also excludes "a judgment for support in matrimonial or family matters." The Revised Reciprocal Enforcement of Support Act, however, includes in its definition of a "state" (§2(m)) whose decrees are entitled to enforcement, "any foreign jurisdiction in which this or a substantially similar reciprocal law is in effect." URESA therefore codifies a reciprocity requirement, which the Uniform Foreign Money-Judgments Recognition Act does not. The Uniform Interstate Family Support Act, promulgated in 1992 and intended to supersede URESA, defines "state" to include "a foreign jurisdiction that has established procedures for issuance and enforcement of support orders which are substantially similar to the procedures under this Act." (§101(19)).

Section 3: The Uniform Act

Uniform Foreign Money-Judgments Recognition Act, 13 ULA 263

§ 1. [Definitions].

As used in this Act:

(1) "foreign state" means any governmental unit other than the United States, or any state, district, commonwealth, territory, insular possession thereof, or the Panama Canal Zone, the Trust Territory of the Pacific Islands, or the Ryukyu Islands;

(2) "foreign judgment" means any judgment of a foreign state granting or denying recovery of a sum of money, other than a judgment for taxes, a fine or other penalty, or a judgment for support in matrimonial or family matters.

§ 2. [Applicability].

This Act applies to any foreign judgment that is final and conclusive and enforceable where rendered even though an appeal therefrom is pending or it is subject to appeal.

§ 3. [Recognition and Enforcement].

Except as provided in section 4, a foreign judgment meeting the requirements of section 2 is conclusive between the parties to the extent that it grants or denies recovery of a sum of money. The foreign judgment is enforceable in the same manner as the judgment of a sister state which is entitled to full faith and credit.

§ 4. [Grounds for Non-recognition].

(a) A foreign judgment is not conclusive if

(1) the judgment was rendered under a system which does not provide impartial tribunals or procedures compatible with the requirements of due process of law;

(2) the foreign court did not have personal jurisdiction over the defendant; or

(3) the foreign court did not have jurisdiction over the subject matter.

(b) A foreign judgment need not be recognized if

(1) the defendant in the proceedings in the foreign court did not receive notice of the proceedings in sufficient time to enable him to defend;

(2) the judgment was obtained by fraud;

(3) the [cause of action] [claim for relief] on which the judgment is based is repugnant to the public policy of this state;

(4) the judgment conflicts with another final and conclusive judgment;

(5) the proceeding in the foreign court was contrary to an agreement between the parties under which the dispute in question was to be settled otherwise than by proceedings in that court; or

(6) in the case of jurisdiction based only on personal service, the foreign court was a seriously inconvenient forum for the trial of the action.

§ 5. [Personal Jurisdiction].

(a) The foreign judgment shall not be refused recognition for lack of personal jurisdiction if

(1) the defendant was served personally in the foreign state;

(2) the defendant voluntarily appeared in the proceedings, other than for the purpose of protecting property seized or threatened with seizure in the proceedings or of contesting the jurisdiction of the court over him;

(3) the defendant prior to the commencement of the proceedings had agreed to submit to the jurisdiction of the foreign court with respect to the subject matter involved;

(4) the defendant was domiciled in the foreign state when the proceedings were instituted, or, being a body corporate had its principal place of business, was incorporated, or had otherwise acquired corporate status, in the foreign state;

(5) the defendant had a business office in the foreign state and the proceedings in the foreign court involved a [cause of action] [claim for relief] arising out of business done by the defendant through that office in the foreign state; or

(6) the defendant operated a motor vehicle or airplane in the foreign state and the proceedings involved a [cause of action] [claim for relief] arising out of such operation.

(b) The courts of this state may recognize other bases of jurisdiction.

§ 6. [Stay in Case of Appeal].

If the defendant satisfies the court either that an appeal is pending or that he is entitled and intends to appeal from the foreign judgment, the court may stay the proceedings until the appeal has been determined or until the expiration of a period of time sufficient to enable the defendant to prosecute the appeal.

§ 7. [Savings Clause].

This Act does not prevent the recognition of a foreign judgment in situations not covered by this Act.

Notes

1. As of January 1, 2000, 29 states, the District of Columbia, and the Virgin Islands had enacted the Uniform Act.

2. In the United States, with regard to relief from a domestic judgment "obtained by fraud," there is a supposed distinction in many jurisdictions between "extrinsic" and "intrinsic" fraud. In jurisdictions drawing this distinction, only extrinsic fraud is said to permit relief from a judgment. "Extrinsic" fraud is fraud that induced a party to default or consent to judgment against him, or otherwise prevented presentation of the party's case, while "intrinsic" fraud refers to the knowing use of perjured or fabricated evidence.

California's version of the Uniform Act inserts "extrinsic" before "fraud" in § 4(b)(2). Wests Ann. Cal. C.C.P. § 1713.4(b)(2).

Fairchild, Arabatzis & Smith, Inc. v. Prometco Co., Ltd. 470 F. Supp. 610, 615 ((S.D.N.Y. 1979) holds that "fraud" in the New York Uniform Act refers to fraud on the court and not to an issue that could have been litigated.Federal Rule of Civil Procedure 60 provides: "On motion and upon such terms as are just, the court may relieve a party or a party's legal representative from a final judgment, order, or proceeding for the following reasons * * * (3) fraud (whether heretofore denominated intrinsic or extrinsic), misrepresentation, or other misconduct of an adverse party."

Restatement (Second) of Judgments § 70(1) (b) (1982) provides that "a judgment in a contested action may be avoided if the judgment * * * Was based on a claim that the party obtaining the judgment knew to be fraudulent." § 70(2)(c) requires that a party whose claim for relief from a judgment "is based on falsity of the evidence on which the judgment was based, show that he had made a reasonable effort in the original action to ascertain the truth of the matter." Comment c to this section states that distinctions between intrinsic and extrinsic fraud "[a]side form not being very persuasive * * * are not consistently applied."

3. Bachchan v. India Abroad Publications Inc., 585 N.Y.S.2d 661 (S. Ct. 1992) refuses, on the "public policy" ground in § 4 on the Uniform Act, to enforce an English libel judgment. The court notes the constitutional limits that the United States Supreme

Court has placed on libel recoveries in the United States. Matusevitch v. Telnikoff, 877 F. Supp. 1 (D.D.C. 1995), aff'd in unpublished opinion, 159 F.3d 636 (D.C. Cir. 1998), also refused on public policy grounds to recognize an English libel judgment. For the unpublished opinion affirming *Matusevitch* see 1998 W.L. 388800 (D.C. Cir. 1998) (after certifying to the Maryland Court of Appeals the question of whether enforcement of the English libel judgment would violate Maryland public policy and receiving an affirmative answer).

Bank Melli Iran v. Pahlavi, 58 F.3d 1406 (9th Cir.), cert. denied, 516 U.S. 989 (1995), refused to enforce Iranian default judgments against the sister of the former Shah because defendant could not have obtained due process in an Iranian court at the time of the judgments.

Jaffe v. Snow, 610 So.2d 482 (Fla. Ct. App., 5th Dist., 1993), review denied, 621 So.2d 432 (Fla. 1993), cert. denied, 512 U.S. 1227 (1994), refused on public policy grounds to recognize a wife's Canadian judgment against a Florida bail bond company for loss of consortium. Agents of the company had apprehended her husband in Canada and returned him to Florida to face criminal charges after he had jumped bail in Florida and fled to Canada. The capture and return were privileged under Florida law but not under Canadian law.

Tonga Air Service, Ltd. v. Fowler, 826 P.2d 204 (Wash. 1992), reversed a trial court's refusal to recognize a Tonga judgment. The court held that the lack of a verbatim transcript for appeal of the judgment in Tonga did not violate due process. The court also held that review of a trial court's refusal to recognize a foreign judgment under § 4 of the Uniform Foreign Money-Judgments Recognition Act was de novo and not for abuse of discretion. Id. at 208.

Royal Bank of Canada v. Trentham Corp.,
665 F.2d 515 (5th Cir. 1981)

Before RUBIN, RANDALL and TATE, Circuit Judges.

RANDALL, Circuit Judge:

This suit was brought by the Royal Bank of Canada ("Royal Bank") for recognition and enforcement in the United States of a default judgment of $250,000 plus interest entered in the Court of the Trial Division of the Supreme Court of Alberta, Judicial District of Calgary, on October 11, 1978. The Alberta suit concerned a contract of guaranty by which Defendant Trentham Corporation agreed to guarantee payment of all liabilities up to $250,000 owed to Royal Bank by Trentham Canada. The present suit was brought in the United States District Court for the Southern District of Texas. The trial court, in a thorough opinion excellent in all respects, granted summary judgment to Royal Bank. *Royal Bank of Canada v. Trentham Corp.*, 491 F.Supp. 404 (S.D.Tex.1980). However, because of an intervening change in Texas law, we vacate the district court's judgment and remand for further proceedings.

Because the litigation was based on diversity of citizenship, the federal district court considered whether the Canadian judgment would be recognized under Texas law. In deciding that the foreign judgment would be recognized, the court considered the argument that because an Alberta court would not have recognized a default judgment entered by a United States court under the circumstances presented in this case, a Texas court would not recognize the Alberta judgment based on the doctrine of reciprocity. Unfortunately, there was a dearth of Texas law on this question. In a well-reasoned and scholarly discussion of the issue, the district court concluded on the basis of the modern trend of the common law in the state courts that Texas would not apply the doctrine of reciprocity, a doctrine which has come under increasing criticism from courts and commentators. It thus saw no bar to recognition of the Canadian judgment and entered summary judgment for Royal Bank on June 2, 1980.

Defendant Trentham Corporation appealed to this court, and after oral argument had been completed, brought to this court's attention a recent change in the applicable Texas state law. As luck would have it, the State of Texas adopted the Uniform Foreign Country Money-Judgment Recognition Act on June 17, 1981. The Act as originally drafted does not employ the doctrine of reciprocity as a reason for non-recognition of a foreign judgment. However, the Texas Legislature specifically included the requirement of reciprocity in its version of the Act:

SECTION 5. GROUNDS FOR NONRECOGNITION. (b) A foreign country judgment need not be recognized if: ...

(7) it is established that the foreign country in which the judgment was rendered does not recognize judgments rendered in this state that, but for the fact that they are rendered in Texas, conform to the definition of "foreign country judgment" in Section 2(2) of this Act.

* * *

It is doubtful that the Texas courts, faced with what is really a case of first impression, would create a common law of recognition of foreign judgments for cases involving judgments rendered before June 17, 1981, and then apply different rules for later judgments. Instead, it is more likely that, given that the issue of reciprocity had never been squarely addressed in recent years by the Texas judiciary, a Texas court in our position would look to the new statute in the interests of uniformity. It would do so not because it was compelled by the statutory language; rather, it would do so because no purpose would be served in carving out a new and different rule for an arbitrary set of cases. In our opinion, the new Act has changed the legal climate in Texas with respect to this question, and thus we think that the provisions of the Act would be applied by the Texas state courts.

Royal Bank argues that even if this is so, the Act does not preclude summary judgment against Trentham. It points out that while section 5(a) of the Act lists grounds under which a foreign judgment is "not conclusive," the reciprocity provision falls under section 5(b), which lists grounds under which a foreign judgment "need not be recognized." Royal Bank thus argues that the decision whether or not to grant recognition under section 5(b) is a matter of discretion for the trial judge. This interpretation of the difference between Sections 5(a) and 5(b) is consistent with the language of the Act and is the view expressed by various commentators.

Even though section 5(b)(7) might give the trial court discretion to recognize the judgment despite nonreciprocity by the foreign forum, in the present case the trial court granted recognition because it thought reciprocity was irrelevant. Thus we cannot affirm the trial court's judgment since it was based on a view of the law which, while correct when the judgment was rendered, has ceased to be so. We therefore remand to the district court for a determination of whether the judgment should be recognized under the new Act. Unfortunately, the Act itself does not make clear under what conditions a court's discretion to permit recognition of a judgment under section 5(b) should be exercised, and we are unaided by any state court constructions of the meaning of the Act in Texas. We remind the trial court that although it possesses some discretion, the clear message of the Texas Legislature's amendment to the Uniform Act is that foreign judgments which would not be reciprocally recognized if made in Texas are not favored. Given the views of the Texas Legislature and the complete absence of criteria for guidance fashioned by the state courts, the trial court should proceed cautiously in the use of its discretion. Nevertheless, we think that the state courts would permit some inquiry into equitable considerations weighing in favor of recognizing the judgment. In particular, we note that Royal Bank could scarcely have foreseen that the Texas Legislature would adopt a variant from the Uniform Act recognizing the principle of reciprocity. In view of the peculiar facts of this case, therefore, the trial court should determine whether Royal Bank would now be prevented from pursuing a new action in the Texas courts because of the applicable statute of limitations or for any other reason. If a trial on the merits cannot be had in Texas, this may weigh in favor of enforcing the present Canadian judgment.

* * *

VACATED and REMANDED.

Note

Colorado, Florida, Georgia, Idaho, Massachusetts, North Carolina, and Ohio have also added reciprocity provisions to their versions of the Uniform Act.

Col. Rev. Stat. Ann. § 13-62-102(1) in effect nullifies the Act by defining "foreign state" in § 1(1) as a "governmental unit [that] has entered into a reciprocal agreement with the United States recognizing any judgment of a court of record of the United States..." There is no such foreign state.

Fla.Stat. Ann. § 55.605(2)(g) provides for discretionary nonrecognition if foreign country "would not give recognition to a similar judgment rendered in this state" and directs the Florida Secretary of State to maintain a list of such countries.

O.C.Ga. Ann. § 9-12-114(10) states that a foreign judgment "shall not be recognized if...the party seeking to enforce the judgment fails to demonstrate that judgments of courts of the United States and of states thereof of the same type and based on substantially similar jurisdictional grounds are recognized and enforced in the courts of the foreign state."

Idaho Code § 10-1404(2)(g) states that "a foreign country judgment need not be recognized if...Judgments of this state are not recognized in the courts of the foreign state."

N.C. Gen. Stat. § 1C-1804(b)(7) provides for discretionary nonrecognition if "[t]he foreign court...would not recognize a comparable judgment of this State."

Mass. G.L. Ann. c. 235 § 23A states that a foreign judgment "shall not be recognized if...judgments of this state are not recognized in the courts of the foreign state."

Ohio Rev. Code Ann. § 2329.92(B) provides that if the foreign country does not have a procedure for recognizing judgments of other countries "substantially similar" to the Uniform Foreign Money-Judgments Act, its judgments "may be recognized and enforced...in the discretion of the court."

Assuming that it were politically necessary to add a non-uniform reciprocity requirement to a state's version of the Act, which provision would you prefer, that of Colorado, Florida, Georgia, Idaho, Massachusetts, North Carolina, Ohio, or Texas?

New Hampshire has not enacted the Uniform Act but has a reciprocity provision for Canadian judgments. N.H. Stat. Ann. § 524:11: "In suits on judgments rendered in the courts of the Dominion of Canada or any province thereof, said judgments shall be give such faith and credit as is given in the courts of the Dominion of Canada or any province thereof to the judgments rendered in the courts of New Hampshire."

Detamore v. Sullivan,
731 S.W.2d 122 (Tex. Civ. App.—Houston [14th Dist.], 1987, no writ)

Before J. CURTISS BROWN, C.J., and ROBERTSON and CANNON, JJ.

ORIGINAL PROCEEDING WRIT OF MANDAMUS

CANNON, Justice.

This is an original petition for writ of mandamus to require the Honorable Tom Sullivan, Judge of the County Civil Court at Law Number Two of Harris County, to vacate his order for turnover of stock and to nullify recognition of the foreign country money judgment. On April 2, 1987, we granted relator leave to file the mandamus. We conditionally grant the petition.

On January 2, 1986, the Court of Queen's Bench of Alberta, Judicial District of Edmonton, granted a default judgment for $16,079.12 (Canadian dollars) plus costs of $498.58 (Canadian dollars) in favor of Continental Bank of Canada (Continental) against relator, Loren A. Detamore.

On June 24, 1986, Continental filed its Canadian default judgment and an affidavit of last known address in the Harris County Clerk's Office, requesting issuance of an abstract of judgment and a writ of execution. On July 2, 1986, the Harris County Clerk's Office issued a Corrected Abstract of Judgment and a Corrected Execution. In response to Continental's application for turnover order, on March 12, 1987, the trial court judge signed an order for turnover of relator's stock to Constable Rankin for sale under the writ of execution.

Relator contends that the foreign judgment has not been properly recognized as a Texas judgment pursuant to [the Texas Uniform Foreign Money-Judgments Act] because a plenary suit was not filed and a plenary hearing held. In support of this proposition, he relies on *Hennessy v. Marshall*, 682 S.W.2d 340 (Tex.App.—Dallas 1984, no writ). In *Hennessy*, the Dallas Court of Appeals interpreted the provisions of the Texas Uniform Foreign Money-Judgments Act as requiring a plenary suit to be filed and a plenary hearing held prior to recognition and enforcement of a foreign country money judgment in order to satisfy due process.

While we agree with the rationale behind the *Hennessy* opinion, we cannot find any procedures within [the Act] providing for a plenary hearing on recognition. To incorporate procedures for a hearing into [the Act], where none are provided, places us in the position of judicially legislating. Thus, we cannot agree with relator's contention that [the Act] requires that a plenary suit be filed and a hearing be held before a foreign country money judgment is entitled to recognition and enforcement.

Alternatively, relator maintains that [the Act] is unconstitutional. He argues that his right to due process is violated because [the Act] does not provide that he be given notice and an opportunity to be heard on the conclusiveness of the foreign country judgment.

The real party in interest argues that a foreign country money judgment debtor is given an opportunity to show any grounds for nonrecognition or inconclusiveness at the time the judgment creditor seeks to register the judgment pursuant to the provisions of Tex.Civ.Prac. & Rem.Code Ann. §§ 35.001-.008 (Vernon 1986) (Chapter 35). Thus, the real party in interest argues, a judgment debtor is not denied due process. We disagree.

Registration of a foreign judgment pursuant to Chapter 35 pertains to the enforcement of the judgment. However, recognition of a foreign country money judgment is a prerequisite to its enforcement. Thus the registration and enforcement provisions of Chapter 35 do not come into play until a foreign country judgment is recognized pursuant to [the Foreign Money-Judgments Act].

* * *

Section [4 of the Foreign Money-Judgments Act] provides the grounds upon which a judgment debtor may rely in order to show that a foreign country money judgment is not entitled to recognition. Section [5] provides a series of affirmative defenses for the judgment creditor to assert if the judgment debtor alleges lack of personal jurisdiction as a ground for nonrecognition.

Clearly, by drafting section [4], the legislature recognized that grounds exist for determining that a foreign country money judgment is not entitled to recognition and enforcement in Texas. For example, a foreign country judgment is not entitled to recognition if the foreign country court did not have personal jurisdiction over the defendant. However, the legislature has failed to create a procedure whereby a judgment debtor could assert those grounds for nonrecognition. Thus a judgment debtor could find himself in the procedural quandary of having a valid defense to recognition and enforcement of a foreign country judgment but being unable to assert that defense. This results in a denial of due process.

Thus we hold that [the Foreign Money-Judgments Act] is unconstitutional because it has no provisions for a judgment debtor to receive notice and to have an opportunity to assert grounds for nonrecognition of a foreign country money judgment. Consequently, any enforcement of the foreign country money judgment is void.

Accordingly, we assume the respondent will vacate his turnover order and stay any proceedings connected therewith in accordance with this opinion.

The petition is conditionally granted.

Note

Chapter 35 of the Texas Civil Practice & Remedies Code, referred to in the principal case, is the Texas enactment of the Uniform Enforcement of Foreign Judgments Act, which, despite its title, refers to filing of sister-state judgments. The drafters' Comment to § 3 of the Foreign Money-Judgments Act (Foreign-country judgments) states: "The method of enforcement will be that of the Uniform Enforcement of Foreign Judgments Act... [sister-state judgments] in a state having enacted that Act." Section 3 of the sister-state judgments Act provides:

"§ 3. Notice of Filing

"(a) At the time of the filing of the foreign judgment, the judgment creditor or his lawyer shall make and file with the Clerk of Court an affidavit setting forth the name and last known post office address of the judgment debtor, and the judgment creditor.

"(b) Promptly upon the filing of the foreign judgment and the affidavit, the Clerk shall mail notice of the filing of the foreign judgment to the judgment debtor at the address given and shall make a note of the mailing in the docket. The notice shall include the name and post office address of the judgment creditor and the judgment creditor's lawyer, if any, in this state. In addition, the judgment creditor may mail a notice of the filing of the judgment to the judgment debtor and may file proof of mailing with the Clerk. Lack of mailing notice of filing by the Clerk shall not affect the enforcement proceedings if proof of mailing by the judgment creditor has been filed.

"(c) No execution or other process for enforcement of a foreign judgment filed hereunder shall issue until [ ] days after the date the judgment is filed.]"

Should a similar provision have been inserted in the Foreign Money-Judgments Act?

Effective June 14, 1989, the Texas version of the Foreign Money-Judgments Act was amended to require that notice be sent to the judgment debtor either by the clerk of court or by the party seeking recognition of the foreign judgment. The time given the judgment debtor to file a motion for non recognition of the foreign judgment is 30 days (or if the debtor is domiciled in a foreign country, 60 days) after service of the notice that the judgment has been filed for recognition.

Don Docksteader Motors, Ltd. v. Patal Enterprises, Ltd., 794 S.W.2d 760 (Tex. 1990) held that the Foreign Money-Judgments Act did not prevent a common-law suit for recognition of a foreign judgment, the procedure followed in *Docksteader*, and that this procedure provided for notice and hearing that satisfied due process. The court remarked that to the extent Detamore v. Sullivan conflicts with *Docksteader*, it is disapproved. 794 S.W.2d at 761 n.2.

See Richard J. Graving & Jon H. Sylvester, "Is the Uniform Foreign Money-Judgments Act Potentially Unconstitutional: If So, Should the Texas Cure Be Adopted Elsewhere?," 25 Geo. Wash. J. Int'l L. & Econ. 737 (1992).

Chapter 4

The Act of State Doctrine

Section 1: Application and Exceptions

Banco Nacional de Cuba v. Sabbatino
376 U.S. 398 (1964)

Mr. Justice HARLAN delivered the opinion of the Court.

The question which brought this case here, and is now found to be the dispositive issue, is whether the so-called act of state doctrine serves to sustain petitioner's claims in this litigation. Such claims are ultimately founded on a decree of the Government of Cuba expropriating certain property, the right to the proceeds of which is here in controversy. The act of state doctrine in its traditional formulation precludes the courts of this country from inquiring into the validity of the public acts a recognized foreign sovereign power committed within its own territory.

I

In February and July of 1960, respondent Farr, Whitlock & Co., an American commodity broker, contracted to purchase Cuban sugar, free alongside the steamer, from a wholly owned subsidiary of Compania Azucarera Vertientes-Camaguey de Cuba (C.A.V.), a corporation organized under Cuban law whose capital stock was owned principally by United States residents. Farr, Whitlock agreed to pay for the sugar in New York upon presentation of the shipping documents and a sight draft.

On July 6, 1960, the Congress of the United States amended the Sugar Act of 1948 to permit a presidentially directed reduction of the sugar quota for Cuba. On the same day President Eisenhower exercised the granted power. The day of the congressional enactment, the Cuban Council of Ministers adopted "Law No. 851," which characterized this reduction in the Cuban sugar quota as an act of "aggression, for political purposes" on the part of the United States, justifying the taking of countermeasures by Cuba. The law gave the Cuban President and Prime Minister discretionary power to nationalize by forced expropriation property or enterprises in which American nationals had an interest.

Although a system of compensation was formally provided, the possibility of payment under it may well be deemed illusory. Our State Department has described the Cuban law as "manifestly in violation of those principles of international law which have long been accepted by the free countries of the West. It is in its essence discriminatory, arbitrary and confiscatory."

Between August 6 and August 9, 1960, the sugar covered by the contract between Farr, Whitlock and C.A.V. was loaded, destined for Morocco, onto the S.S. Hornfels, which was standing offshore at the Cuban port of Jucaro (Santa Maria). On the day loading commenced, the Cuban President and Prime Minister, acting pursuant to Law No. 851, issued Executive Power Resolution No. 1. It provided for the compulsory expropriation of all property and enterprises, and of rights and interests arising therefrom, of certain listed companies, including C.A.V., wholly or principally owned by American nationals. * * * In consequence of the resolution, the consent of the Cuban Government was necessary before a ship carrying sugar of a named company could leave Cuban waters. In order to obtain this consent, Farr, Whitlock, on August 11, entered into contracts, identical to those it had made with C.A.V., with the Banco Para el Comercio Exterior de Cuba, an instrumentality of the Cuban Government. The S.S. Hornfels sailed for Morocco on August 12.

Banco Exterior assigned the bills of lading to petitioner, also an instrumentality of the Cuban Government, which instructed its agent in New York, Societe Generale, to deliver the bills and a sight draft in the sum of $175,250.69 to Farr, Whitlock in return for payment. Societe Generale's initial tender of the documents was refused by Farr, Whitlock, which on the same day was notified of C.A.V.'s claim that as rightful owner of the sugar it was entitled to the proceeds. In return for a promise not to turn the funds over to petitioner or its agent, C.A.V. agreed to indemnify Farr, Whitlock for any loss. Farr, Whitlock subsequently accepted the shipping documents, negotiated the bills of lading to its customer, and received payment for the sugar. It refused, however, to hand over the proceeds to Societe Generale. Shortly thereafter, Farr, Whitlock was served with an order of the New York Supreme Court, which had appointed Sabbatino as Temporary Receiver of C.A.V.'s New York assets, enjoining it from taking any action in regard to the money claimed by C.A.V. that might result in its removal from the State. Following this, Farr, Whitlock, pursuant to court order, transferred the funds to Sabbatino, to abide the event of a judicial determination as to their ownership.

Petitioner then instituted this action in the Federal District Court for the Southern District of New York. Alleging conversion of the bills of lading it sought to recover the proceeds thereof from Farr, Whitlock and to enjoin the receiver from exercising any dominion over such proceeds. Upon motions to dismiss and for summary judgment, the District Court sustained federal in personam jurisdiction despite state control of the funds. It found that the sugar was located within Cuban territory at the time of expropriation and determined that under merchant law common to civilized countries Farr, Whitlock could not have asserted ownership of the sugar against C.A.V. before making payment. It concluded that C.A.V. had a property interest in the sugar subject to the territorial jurisdiction of Cuba. The court then dealt with the question of Cuba's title to the sugar, on which rested petitioner's claim of conversion. While acknowledging the continuing vitality of the act of state doctrine, the court believed it inapplicable when the questioned foreign act is in violation of international law. Proceeding on the basis that a taking invalid under international law does not convey good title, the District Court found the Cuban expropriation decree to violate such law in three separate respects: it was motivated by a retaliatory and not a public purpose; it discriminated against American nationals; and it failed to provide adequate compensation. Summary judgment against petitioner was accordingly granted.

The Court of Appeals, affirming the decision on similar grounds, relied on two letters (not before the District Court) written by State Department officers which it took as evidence that the Executive Branch had no objection to a judicial testing of the

Cuban decree's validity. The court was unwilling to declare that any one of the infirmities found by the District Court rendered the taking invalid under international law, but was satisfied that in combination they had that effect. We granted certiorari because the issues involved bear importantly on the conduct of the country's foreign relations and more particularly on the proper role of the Judicial Branch in this sensitive area. For reasons to follow we decide that the judgment below must be reversed.

* * *

IV

The classic American statement of the act of state doctrine, which appears to have taken root in England as early as 1674, *Blad v. Bamfield*, 3 Swans. 604, 36 Eng.Rep. 992, and began to emerge in the jurisprudence of this country in the late eighteenth and early nineteenth centuries, see e.g., *Ware v. Hylton*, 3 Dall. 199, 230; *Hudson v. Guestier*, 4 Cranch 293, 294; *The Schooner Exchange v. M'Faddon*, 7 Cranch 116, 135, 136, *L'Invincible*, 1 Wheat. 238, 253, *The Santissima Trinidad*, 7 Wheat. 283, 336, is found in *Underhill v. Hernandez*, 168 U.S. 250, p. 252, where Chief Justice Fuller said for a unanimous Court:

> Every sovereign state is bound to respect the independence of every other sovereign state, and the courts of one country will not sit in judgment on the acts of the government of another, done within its own territory. Redress of grievances by reason of such acts must be obtained through the means open to be availed of by sovereign powers as between themselves.

Following this precept the Court in that case refused to inquire into acts of Hernandez, a revolutionary Venezuelan military commander whose government had been later recognized by the United States, which were made the basis of a damage action in this country by Underhill, an American citizen, who claimed that he had had unlawfully assaulted, coerced, and detained in Venezuela by Hernandez.

None of this Court's subsequent cases in which the act of state doctrine was directly or peripherally involved manifest any retreat from Underhill. See *American Banana Co. v. United Fruit Co.*, 213 U.S. 347; *Oetjen v. Central Leather Co.*, 246 U.S. 297; *Ricaud v. American Metal Co.*, 246 U.S. 304; *Shapleigh v. Mier*, 299 U.S. 468; *United States v. Belmont*, 301 U.S. 324; *United States v. Pink*, 315 U.S. 203. On the contrary in two of these cases, *Oetjen* and *Ricaud*, the doctrine as announced in Underhill was reaffirmed in unequivocal terms.

Oetjen involved a seizure of hides from a Mexican citizen as a military levy by General Villa, acting for the forces of General Carranza, whose government was recognized by this country subsequent to the trial but prior to decision by this Court. The hides were sold to a Texas corporation which shipped them to the United States and assigned them to defendant. As assignee of the original owner, plaintiff replevied the hides, claiming that they had been seized in violation of the Hague Conventions. In affirming a judgment for defendant, the Court suggested that the rules of the Conventions did not apply to civil war and that, even if they did, the relevant seizure was not in violation of them. Nevertheless, it chose to rest its decision on other grounds. It described the designation of the sovereign as a political question to be determined by the legislative and executive departments rather than the judicial department, invoked the established rule that such recognition operates retroactively to validate past acts, and found the basic tenet of *Underhill* to be applicable to the case before it. "The principle that the conduct of one independent government cannot be successfully questioned in the courts of another is as applicable to a case involving the title to property brought within the custody of a court, such as we have here, as it was held to be to the cases cited, in which claims for damages were based upon acts done in a foreign country, for it rests at last upon the highest considerations of international comity and expediency. To permit the validity of the acts of one sovereign state to be reexamined and perhaps condemned by the courts of another would very certainly 'imperil the amicable relations between governments and vex the peace of nations.'" Id., 246 U.S. at 303-304.

* * *

In deciding the present case the Court of Appeals relied in part upon an exception to the unqualified teachings of *Underhill, Oetjen,* and *Ricaud* which that court had earlier indicated. In *Bernstein v. Van Heyghen Freres Societe Anonyme*, 2 Cir., 163 F.2d 246, suit was brought to recover from an assignee property allegedly taken, in effect, by the Nazi Government because plaintiff was Jewish. Recognizing the odious nature of this act of state, the court, through Judge Learned Hand, nonetheless refused to consider it invalid on that ground. Rather, it looked to see if the Executive had acted in any manner that would indicate that United States Courts should refuse to give effect to such a foreign decree. Finding no such evidence, the court sustained dismissal of the complaint. In a later case involving similar facts the same court again assumed examination of the German acts improper, *Bernstein v. N.V. Nederlandsche-Amerikaansche Stoomvaart-Maatschappij,* 2 Cir., 173 F.2d 71, but, quite evidently following the implications of Judge Hand's opinion in the earlier case, amended its mandate to permit evidence of alleged invalidity, 2 Cir., 210 F.2d 375, subsequent to receipt by plaintiff's attorney of a letter from the Acting Legal Adviser to the State Department written for the purpose of relieving the court from any constraint upon the exercise of its jurisdiction to pass on that question.

This Court has never had occasion to pass upon the so-called *Bernstein* exception, nor need it do so now. For whatever ambiguity may be thought to exist in the two letters from State Department officials on which the Court of Appeals relied, is now removed by the position which the Executive has taken in this Court on the act of state claim; respondents do not indeed contest the view that these letters were intended to reflect no more than the Department's then wish not to make any statement bearing on this litigation.

The outcome of this case, therefore, turns upon whether any of the contentions urged by respondents against the application of the act of state doctrine in the premises is acceptable: (1) that the doctrine does not apply to acts of state which violate international law, as is claimed to be the case here; (2) that the doctrine is inapplicable unless the Executive specifically interposes it in a particular case; and (3) that, in any event, the doctrine may not be invoked by a foreign government plaintiff in our courts.

V

Preliminarily, we discuss the foundations on which we deem the act of state doctrine to rest, and more particularly the question of whether state or federal law governs its application in a federal diversity case.

We do not believe that this doctrine is compelled either by the inherent nature of sovereign authority, as some of the earlier decisions seem to imply, see *Underhill,* supra; *American Banana,* supra; *Oetjen,* supra, 246 U.S. at 303, or by some principle of international law. If a transaction takes place in one jurisdiction and the forum is in another, the forum does not by dismissing an action or by applying its own law purport to divest the first jurisdiction of its territorial sovereignty; it merely declines to adjudicate or makes applicable its own law to parties or property before it. The refusal of one country to enforce the penal laws of another is a typical example of an instance when a court will not entertain a cause of action arising in another jurisdiction. While historic notions of sovereign authority do bear upon the wisdom or employing the act of state doctrine, they do not dictate its existence.

That international law does not require application of the doctrine is evidenced by the practice of nations. Most of the countries rendering decisions on the subject fail to follow the rule rigidly. No international arbitral or judicial decision discovered suggests that international law prescribes recognition of sovereign acts of foreign governments, and apparently no claim has ever been raised before an international tribunal that failure to apply the act of state doctrine constitutes a breach of international obligation. If international law does not prescribe use of the doctrine, neither does it forbid application of the rule even if it is claimed that the act of state in question violated international law. The traditional view of international law is that it establishes substantive principles for determining whether one country has wronged another. Because of its peculiar nation-to-nation character the usual method for an individual to seek relief is to exhaust local remedies and then repair to the executive authorities of his own state to persuade them to champion his claim in diplomacy or before an international tribunal. Although it is, of course, true that United States courts apply international law as a part of our own in appropriate circumstances, the public law of nations can hardly dictate to a country which is in theory wronged how to treat that wrong within its domestic borders.

Despite the broad statement in *Oetjen* that "The conduct of the foreign relations of our government is committed by the Constitution to the executive and legislative * * * departments," 246 U.S. at 302, it cannot of course be thought that "every case or controversy which touches foreign relations lies beyond judicial cognizance." *Baker v. Carr*, 369 U.S. 186, 211. The text of the Constitution does not require the act of state doctrine; it does not irrevocably remove from the judiciary the capacity to review the validity of foreign acts of state.

The act of state doctrine does, however, have "constitutional" underpinnings. It arises out of the basic relationships between branches of government in a system of separation of powers. It concerns the competency of dissimilar institutions to make and implement particular kinds of decisions in the area of international relations. The doctrine as formulated in past decisions expresses the strong sense of the Judicial Branch that its engagement in the task of passing on the validity of foreign acts of state may hinder rather than further this country's pursuit of goals both for itself and for the community of nations as a whole in the international sphere. Many commentators disagree with this view; they have striven by means of distinguishing and limiting past decisions and by advancing various considerations of policy to stimulate a narrowing of the apparent scope of the rule. Whatever considerations are thought to predominate, it is plain that the problems involved are uniquely federal in nature. If federal authority, in this instance this Court, orders the field of judicial competence in this area for the federal courts, and the state courts are left free to formulate their own rules, the purposes behind the doctrine could be as effectively undermined as if there had been no federal pronouncement on the subject.

We could perhaps in this diversity action avoid the question of deciding whether federal or state law is applicable to this aspect of the litigation. New York has enunciated the act of state doctrine in terms that echo those of federal decisions.

* * *

However, we are constrained to make it clear that an issue concerned with a basic choice regarding the competence and function of the Judiciary and the National Executive in ordering our relationships with other members of the international community must be treated exclusively as an aspect of federal law.[23] It seems fair to assume that the Court did not have rules like the act of state doctrine in mind when it decided *Erie R. Co. v. Tompkins* [304 U.S. 64 (1938)]. Soon thereafter, Professor Philip C. Jessup, now a judge of the International Court of Justice, recognized the potential dangers were *Erie* extended to legal problems affecting international relations. He cautioned that rules of international law should not be left to divergent and perhaps parochial state interpretations. His basic rationale is equally applicable to the act of state doctrine.

* * *

VI

If the act of state doctrine is a principle of decision binding on federal and state courts alike but compelled by neither international law nor the Constitution, its continuing vitality depends on its capacity to reflect the proper distribution of functions between the judicial and political branches of the Government on matters bearing upon foreign affairs. It should be apparent that the greater the degree of codification or consensus concerning a particular area of international law, the more appropriate it is for the judiciary to render decisions regarding it, since the courts can then focus on the application of an agreed principle to circumstances of fact rather than on the sensitive task of establishing a principle not inconsistent with the national interest or with international justice. It is also evident that some aspects of international law touch much more sharply on national nerves than do others; the less important the implications of an issue are for our foreign relations, the weaker the justification for exclusivity in the political branches. The balance of relevant considerations may also be shifted if the government which perpetrated the challenged act of state is no longer in existence, as in the *Bernstein* case, for the political interest of this country may, as a result, be measurably altered. Therefore, rather than laying down or reaffirming an inflexible and all encompassing rule in this case, we decide only that the Judicial Branch will not examine the validity of a taking of property within its own territory by a foreign sovereign government, extant and recognized by this country at the time of suit, in the absence of a treaty or other unambiguous agreement regarding controlling legal principles, even if the complaint alleges that the taking violates customary international law.

There are few if any issues in international law today on which opinion seems to be so divided as the limitations on a state's power to expropriate the property of aliens. There is, of course, authority, in international judicial and arbitral decisions, in the expressions of national governments, and among commentators for the view that a taking is improper under international law if it is not for a public purpose, is discriminatory, or is without provision for prompt, adequate, and effective compensation. However, Communist countries, although they have in fact provided a degree of compensation after diplomatic efforts, commonly recognize no obligation on the part of the taking country. Certain representatives of the newly independent and underdeveloped countries have questioned whether rules of state responsibility toward aliens can bind na-

---

23. At least this is true when the Court limits the scope of judicial inquiry. We need not now consider whether a state court might, in certain circumstances, adhere to a more restrictive view concerning the scope of examination of foreign acts than that required by this Court.

tions that have not consented to them and it is argued that the traditionally articulated standards governing expropriation of property reflect "imperialist" interests and are inappropriate to the circumstances of emergent states.

The disagreement as to relevant international law standards reflects an even more basic divergence between the national interests of capital importing and capital exporting nations and between the social ideologies of those countries that favor state control of a considerable portion of the means of production and those that adhere to a free enterprise system. It is difficult to imagine the courts of this country embarking on adjudication in an area which touches more sensitively the practical and ideological goals of the various members of the community of nations.

When we consider the prospect of the courts characterizing foreign expropriations, however justifiably, as invalid under international law and ineffective to pass title, the wisdom of the precedents is confirmed. While each of the leading cases in this Court may be argued to be distinguishable in its facts from this one—*Underhill* because sovereign immunity provided an independent ground and *Oetjen, Ricaud,* and *Shapleigh* because there was actually no violation of international law—the plain implication of all these opinions, and the import of express statements in *Oetjen,* 246 U.S. at 304, and *Shapleigh,* 299 U.S. at 471, is that the act of state doctrine is applicable even if international law has been violated. In *Ricaud,* [in which a Mexican general seized lead bullion belonging to an American citizen,] the one case of the three most plausibly involving an international law violation, the possibility of an exception to the act of state doctrine was not discussed. Some commentators have concluded that it was not brought to the Court's attention but Justice Clarke delivered both the *Oetjen* and *Ricaud* opinions, on the same day, so we can assume that principles stated in the former were applicable to the latter case.

The possible adverse consequences of a conclusion to the contrary of that implicit in these cases in highlighted by contrasting the practices of the political branch with the limitations of the judicial process in matters of this kind. Following an expropriation of any significance, the Executive engages in diplomacy aimed to assure that United States citizens who are harmed are compensated fairly. Representing all claimants of this country, it will often be able, either by bilateral or multilateral talks, by submission to the United Nations, or by the employment of economic and political sanctions, to achieve some degree of general redress. Judicial determinations of invalidity of title can, on the other hand, have only an occasional impact, since they depend on the fortuitous circumstance of the property in question being brought into this country. Such decisions would, if the acts involved were declared invalid, often be likely to give offense to the expropriating country; since the concept of territorial sovereignty is so deep seated, any state may resent the refusal of the courts of another sovereign to accord validity to acts within its territorial borders. Piecemeal dispositions of this sort involving the probability of affront to another state could seriously interfere with negotiations being carried on by the Executive Branch and might prevent or render less favorable the terms of an agreement that could otherwise be reached. Relations with third countries which have engaged in similar expropriations would not be immune from effect.

The dangers of such adjudication are present regardless of whether the State Department has, as it did in this case, asserted that the relevant act violated international law. If the Executive Branch has undertaken negotiations with an expropriating country, but has refrained from claims of violation of the law of nations, a determination to that effect by a court might be regarded as a serious insult, while a finding of compliance with international law would greatly strengthen the bargaining hand of the other state with consequent detriment to American interests.

Even if the State Department has proclaimed the impropriety of the expropriation, the stamp of approval of its view by a judicial tribunal, however, impartial, might increase any affront and the judicial decision might occur at a time, almost always well after the taking, when such an impact would be contrary to our national interest. Considerably more serious and far- reaching consequences would flow from a judicial finding that international law standards had been met if that determination flew in the face of a State Department proclamation to the contrary. When articulating principles of international law in its relations with other states, the Executive Branch speaks not only as an interpreter of generally accepted and traditional rules, as would the courts, but also as an advocate of standards it believes desirable for the community of nations and protective of national concerns. In short, whatever way the matter is cut, the possibility of conflict between the Judicial and Executive Branches could hardly be avoided.

Respondents contend that, even if there is not agreement regarding general standards for determining the validity of expropriations, the alleged combination of retaliation, discrimination, and inadequate compensation makes it patently clear that this particular expropriation was in violation of international law. If this view is accurate, it would still be unwise for the courts so to determine. Such a decision now would require the drawing of more difficult lines in subsequent cases and these would involve the possibility of conflict with the Executive view. Even if the courts avoided this course, either by presuming the validity of an act of state whenever the international law standard was thought unclear or by following the State Department declaration in such a situation, the very expression of judicial uncertainty might provide embarrassment to the Executive Branch.

Another serious consequence of the exception pressed by respondents would be to render uncertain titles in foreign commerce, with the possible consequence of altering the flow of international trade. If the attitude of the United States courts were unclear, one buying expropriated goods would not know if he could safely import them into this country. Even were takings known to be invalid, one would have difficulty determining after goods had changed hands several times whether the particular articles in question were the product of an ineffective state act.

Against the force of such considerations, we find respondents' countervailing arguments quite unpersuasive. Their basic contention is that United States courts could make a significant contribution to the growth of international law, a contribution whose importance, it is said, would be magnified by the relative paucity of decisional law by international bodies. But given the fluidity of present world conditions, the effectiveness of such a patchwork approach toward the formulation of an acceptable body of law concerning state responsibility for expropriations is, to say the least, highly conjectural. Moreover, it rests upon the sanguine presupposition that the decisions of the courts of the world's major capital exporting country and principal exponent of the free enterprise system would be accepted as disinterested expressions of sound legal principle by those adhering to widely different ideologies.

It is contended that regardless of the fortuitous circumstances necessary for United States jurisdiction over a case involving a foreign act of state and the resultant isolated application to any expropriation program taken as a whole, it is the function of the courts to justly decide individual disputes before them. Perhaps the most typical act of state case involves the original owner or his assignee suing one not in association with the expropriating state who has had "title" transferred to him. But it is difficult to regard the claim of the original owner, who otherwise may be recompensed through diplomatic channels, as more demanding of judicial cognizance than the claim of title by the innocent third party purchaser, who, if the property is taken from him, is without any remedy.

Respondents claim that the economic pressure resulting from the proposed exception to the act of state doctrine will materially add to the protection of United States investors. We are not convinced, even assuming the relevance of this contention. Expropriations take place for a variety of reasons, political and ideological as well as economic. When one considers the variety of means possessed by this country to make secure foreign investment, the persuasive or coercive effect of judicial invalidation of acts of expropriation dwindles in comparison. The newly independent states are in need of continuing foreign investment; the creation of a climate unfavorable to such investment by wholesale confiscations may well work to their long-run economic disadvantage. Foreign aid given to many of these countries provides a powerful lever in the hands of the political branches to ensure fair treatment of United States nationals. Ultimately the sanctions of economic embargo and the freezing of assets in this country may be employed. Any country willing to brave any or all of these consequences is unlikely to be deterred by sporadic judicial decisions directly affecting only property brought to our shores. If the political branches are unwilling to exercise their ample powers to effect compensation, this reflects a judgment of the national interest which the judiciary would be ill-advised to undermine indirectly.

It is suggested that if the act of state doctrine is applicable to violations of international law, it should only be so when the Executive Breach expressly stipulates that it does not wish the courts to pass on the question of validity. We should be slow to reject the representations of the Government that such a reversal of the *Bernstein* principle would work serious inroads on the maximum effectiveness of United States diplomacy. Often the State Department will wish to refrain from taking an official position, particularly at a moment that would be dictated by the development of private litigation but might be inopportune diplomatically. * * * We do not now pass on the *Bernstein* exception, but even if it were deemed valid, its suggested extension is unwarranted.

However offensive to the public policy of this country and its constituent States an expropriation of this kind may be, we conclude that both the national interest and progress toward the goal of establishing the rule of law among nations are best served by maintaining intact the act of state doctrine in this realm of its application.

VII

Finally, we must determine whether Cuba's status as a plaintiff in this case dictates a result at variance with the conclusions reached above. If the Court were to distinguish between suits brought by sovereign states and those of assignees, the rule would have little effect unless a careful examination were made in each case to determine if the private party suing had taken property in good faith. Such an inquiry would be exceptionally difficult, since the relevant transaction would almost invariably have occurred outside our borders. If such an investigation were deemed irrelevant, a state could always assign its claim.

It is true that the problem of security of title is not directly presented in the instance of a sovereign plaintiff, although were such a plaintiff denied relief, it would ship its goods elsewhere, thereby creating an alteration in the flow of trade. The sensitivity in regard to foreign relations and the possibility of embarrassment of the Executive are, of course, heightened by the presence of a sovereign plaintiff. The rebuke to a recognized power would be more pointed were it a suitor in our courts. In discussing the rule against enforcement of foreign penal and revenue laws, the Eire High Court of Justice, in *Peter Buchanan Ltd. v. McVey*, (1955) A.C. 516, 529-530, aff'd, id., at 530, emphasized that its justification was in large degree the desire to avoid embarrassing another state by scrutinizing its penal and revenue laws. Although that rule presumes invalidity in the forum whereas the act of state principle presumes the contrary, the doctrines have a common rationale, a rationale that negates the wisdom of discarding the act of state rule when the plaintiff is a state which is not seeking enforcement of a public act.

Certainly the distinction proposed would sanction self-help remedies, something hardly conducive to a peaceful international order. Had Farr, Whitlock not converted the bills of lading, or alternatively breached its contract, Cuba could have relied on the act of state doctrine in defense of a claim brought by C.A.V. for the proceeds. It would be anomalous to preclude reliance on the act of state doctrine because of Farr, Whitlock's unilateral action, however justified such action may have been under the circumstances.

Respondents offer another theory for treating the case differently because of Cuba's participation. It is claimed that the forum should simply apply its own law to all the relevant transactions. An analogy is drawn to the area of sovereign immunity, *National City Bank v. Republic of China*, 348 U.S. 356, in which, if a foreign country seeks redress in our courts, counterclaims are permissible. But immunity relates to the prerogative right not to have sovereign property subject to suit; fairness has been thought to require that when the sovereign seeks recovery, it be subject to legitimate counterclaims against it. The act of state doctrine, however, although it shares with the immunity doctrine a respect for sovereign states, concerns the limits for determining the validity of an otherwise applicable rule of law. It is plain that if a recognized government sued on a contract with a United States citizen, concededly legitimate by the locus of its making, performance, and most significant contacts, the forum would not apply its own substantive law of contracts. Since the act of state doctrine reflects the desirability of presuming the relevant transaction valid, the same result follows; the forum may not apply its local law regarding foreign expropriations.

Since the act of state doctrine proscribes a challenge to the validity of the Cuban expropriation decree in this case, any counterclaim based on asserted invalidity must fail. Whether a theory of conversion or breach of contract is the proper cause of action under New York law, the presumed validity of the expropriation is unaffected. Although we discern no remaining litigable issues of fact in this case, the District Court may hear and decide them if they develop.

The judgment of the Court of Appeals is reversed and the case is remanded to the District Court for proceedings consistent with this opinion. It is so ordered.

Judgment of Court of Appeals reversed and case remanded to the District Court.

Mr. Justice WHITE, dissenting.

I am dismayed that the Court has, with one broad stroke, declared the ascertainment and application of international law beyond the competence of the courts of the United States in a large and important category of cases. * * * No other civilized country has found such a rigid rule necessary for the survival of the executive branch of its government; the executive of no other government seems to require such insulation from international law adjudications in its courts; and no other judiciary is apparently so incompetent to ascertain and apply international law.

* * *

If my view had prevailed I would have stayed further resolution of the issues in this Court to afford the Department of State reasonable time to clarify its views in light of the opinion. In the absence of a specific objection to an examination of the validity of Cuba's law under international law, I would have proceeded to determine the issue and resolve this litigation on the merits.

Notes

1. Why does Justice Harlan say that Farr, Whitlock "converted the bills of lading"? The delivery term was "free alongside the steamer." On the meaning of "F.A.S.", see note 3 following In re Good Hope Chemical Corp., supra page 170.

2. The "Sabbatino" or "Hickenlooper" amendment to the Foreign Relations Act (22 U.S.C. §2370(e)(2)), was enacted in 1964 after the decision in the principal case: "Notwithstanding any other provisions of law, no court in the United States shall decline on the ground of the federal act of state doctrine to make a determination on the merits giving effect to the principles of international law in a case in which a claim of title or other right to property is asserted by a party including a foreign state (or a party claiming through such state) based upon (or traced through) a confiscation or other taking after January 1, 1959, by an act of that state in violation of the principles of international law, including the principles of compensation and the other standards set out in this subsection [§2370(e)(1) suspends assistance to any country that expropriates or imposes discriminatory exactions on the property of United States citizens or on companies in which United States citizens own at least 50% of the stock, if such country fails to make "speedy compensation for such property in convertible foreign exchange, equivalent to the full value thereof, as required by international law, or fails to take steps designed to provide relief from such taxes, exactions or conditions"]: Provided, that this subparagraph shall not be applicable (1) in any case in which an act of a foreign state is not contrary to international law or with respect to a claim of title or other right to property acquired pursuant to an irrevocable letter of credit of not more than 180 days duration, issued in good faith prior to the time of the confiscation or other taking, or (2) in any case with respect to which the President determines that application of the act of state doctrine is required in that particular case by the foreign policy interests of the United States and a suggestion to this effect is filed on his behalf in that case with the court."

On remand of the principal case, when the executive department failed to request application of the act of state doctrine, the Cuban bank's complaint was dismissed. This judgment was based on findings that the Hickenlooper amendment was retroactive and constitutional and that the expropriation by the Cuban government violated international law. Banco Nacional de Cuba v. Farr, 383 F.2d 166 (2d Cir. 1967), cert. denied, 390 U.S. 956 (1968).

The first proviso to the Hickenlooper amendment, concerning a letter of credit, is intended to protect United States banks if a bank issues a letter of credit and a foreign state confiscates the funds that have been deposited in a foreign branch of the bank as security for the letter of credit. Under the proviso, the bank may invoke the act of state doctrine as a defense to paying on the letter of credit.

The Hickenlooper amendment discussed in this Note is sometimes referred to as the "Second Hickenlooper Amendment" to distinguish it from the amendment of the Foreign Relations Act the previous year that suspended aid to countries that expropriate property of U.S. citizens.

3. Hunt v. Coastal States Gas Producing Co., 583 S.W.2d 322 (Tex.), cert. denied, 444 U.S. 992 (1979). The Libyan government granted Hunt a concession to explore for oil. Six years later, the Libyan government nationalized all Hunt's rights in the concession agreement. Coastal States purchased some oil from a field in which Hunt had exploration rights. Hunt sued Coastal States for conversion. Held: for Coastal States. The Act of State doctrine bars inquiry into the validity of Libyan nationalization. The Hickenlooper Amendment applies only to "a claim of title or other right to property" and does not apply when, as here, only a contract right is expropriated.

4. Galu v. Swissair, 873 F.2d 650 (2d Cir. 1989). A United States citizen permanently residing in France, but commuting to work in Switzerland, was ordered expelled from Switzerland. Swiss police forcibly placed her on a Swissair flight to the United States. She claimed that under Swiss law, she was entitled to return to France and sued Swissair for its role in her removal. The District Court dismissed the claim as barred by the act of state doctrine. Held: Reversed and remanded. The court states that in applying the doctrine, courts "have rarely had to consider the threshold issue of whether the challenged action was the act of a foreign state, since the action has usually been taken by an official of sufficient rank to eliminate any doubt that the official was exercising the sovereign power of his government." (Id. at 653). The court finds the "threshold issue" present in this case because it was not clear from the record whether placing the plaintiff on a flight to the United States "was an action that had been ordered in the exercise of the sovereign authority of Switzerland, or whether it was simply an *ad hoc* decision of the local police." (Id. at 654). The court remands for determination of this issue stating that "[t]he burden is on the defendant to establish foreign law to the extent necessary to demonstrate its entitlement to the act of state defense." (Id. at 654).

A similar issue arose in Alfred Dunhill of London, Inc. v. Republic of Cuba, 425 U.S. 682 (1976). Cuba nationalized Cuban cigar manufacturing companies. United States companies continued to import cigars from the nationalized companies and paid the entities designated by Cuba to run the companies. The former Cuban owners fled to the United States and sued the United States importers for the price of cigars imported before and after the nationalization. Cuba and the managers of the nationalized companies intervened. The trial judge held that under the act of state doctrine, the former owners could not recover for cigars imported after nationalization, but were entitled to payment for pre-nationalization sales. The court also held that the United States importers could recover from Cuba the full amount of the money they had paid for these prior sales. On appeal, the court of appeals limited recovery by the United States importers to an offset against amounts owed for post-nationalization sales. Dunhill, one of the importers, had paid more for pre-nationalization sales than it owed for post-nationalization sales and obtained certiorari. The Supreme Court reversed finding insufficient proof of an act of state: "[T]he mere refusal of the [managers of the nationalized factories] to repay funds followed by a failure to prove that [the managers] 'were not acting within the scope of their authority as agents of the Cuban government' [did not satisfy the managers'] burden of establishing their act of state defense... No statute, decree, order, or resolution of the Cuban Government itself was offered in evidence indicating that Cuba had repudiated its obligations in general or any class thereof or that it had as a sovereign matter determined to confiscate the amounts due... foreign importers." 425 U.S. at 694-95. In addition, the opinion stated that "an act of state should not be extended to include the repudiation of a purely commercial obligation owed by a foreign sovereign or by one of its commercial instrumentalities." Id. at 695.

With regard to this "commercial" exception to the act of state doctrine, see the Foreign Sovereign Immunities Act, set out at the beginning of chapter 5. The Act was enacted five months after the decision in *Dunhill* and took effect eight months after *Dunhill*. The issue of whether a "commercial" exception exists may arise even after passage of the Act. See Callejo v. Bancomer, S.A. 764 F.2d 1101 (5th Cir. 1985). Americans purchased dollar certificates of deposits in a privately owned Mexican bank which was subsequently nationalized. The Mexican government issued a regulation requiring that all deposits in Mexican banks, including dollar deposits, be repaid in pesos at specified rates of exchange, which were below market rates. *Callejo* held that although suit against the Mexican bank was permitted under the exception in § 1605(a)(2) of the Act, it was barred by the act of state doctrine.

Honduras Aircraft Registry, Ltd. v. Government of Honduras, 129 F.3d 543 (11th Cir. 1997), cert. denied, 524 U.S. 952 (1998), held that there was jurisdiction under the commercial exception of the Foreign Sovereign Immunities Act for a suit by Honduran and Bahamian corporations against the Government of Honduras, but remanded for determination of whether the district court should decline to hear the claim under the act of state doctrine. The court stated that "there is no commercial exception to the act of state doctrine as there is under the FSIA. The factors to be considered...may sometimes overlap with the FSIA commercial exception, but a commercial exception alone is not enough." Id. at 550.

5. United States v. Pink, 315 U.S. 203 (1942). Funds deposited in New York by a Russian insurance company became vested in the Soviet Government when the company was nationalized. Under the Litvinov Assignment, these funds were passed to the United States. The United States was held entitled to the property as against the insurance company and foreign creditors.

6. Grupo Portexa, S.A. v. All American Marine Slip, a Division of Marine Office of America Corp., 20 F.3d 1224 (3rd Cir.), cert. denied, 513 U.S. 986 (1994), held that the act of state doctrine did not prevent a United States court from inquiring into the validity under Mexican law of a Mexican port captain's order to remove a sunken vessel from a bay off the coast of Mexico. The ship owner sued its insurers for recovery of the costs of removal. The policy covered these costs if the removal was "compulsory by law." The court found that under Mexican law the port captain's order was not valid and that the insured was not entitled to recover the removal expenses from the insurance companies.

Republic of Philippines v. Westinghouse Electric Corp., 43 F.3d 65 (3rd Cir. 1995). The Republic of the Philippines sued United States companies concerning the construction of a nuclear power plant in the Philippines. There was evidence that Philippine authorities in the Philippines harassed Philippine citizens who gave evidence in the case. The district court enjoined the Philippines from continuing with this harassment. The Third Circuit held that although the act of state doctrine did not apply, in the light of international comity, the district court had abused its discretion in enjoining a sovereign's conduct on its own territory. The court stated that other sanctions were available, including monetary sanctions or dismissal, and remanded the case.

For discussion of the origin and purposes of the act of state doctrine see Hans W. Baade, The Operation of Foreign Public Law, 30 Texas Int'l L.J. 429, 439, 452 (1995). For discussion of the circumstances in which a taking of property owned by aliens violates international law, see George H. Aldrich, What Constitutes A Compensable Taking of Property? The Decisions of the Iran-United States Claims Tribunal, 88 Am. J. Int'l L. 585 (1994).

7. The Cuban Liberty and Democratic Solidarity (Libertad) Act of 1996 (Helms-Burton Act), PL 104-114, 110 Stat 785, reprinted in Note following 22 U.S.C.A. §6021, amends the Cuban Democracy Act of 1992. PL 202-484, reprinted in Note following 22 U.S.C.A. §6001. The new Act enables any United States national who owns property confiscated by Cuba to sue anyone who "traffics" in the property. "Traffics" includes purchase. Section 302(a)(6) provides that "[n]o court of the United States shall decline, based upon the act of state doctrine, to make a determination on the merits in an action brought under [the Act]."

8. As amended in 1988, the Foreign Sovereign Immunities Act (infra page 281) and the Federal Arbitration Act (FAA) provide incentives to use arbitration agreements in commercial dealings with foreign sovereigns. 28 U.S.C. §1605(a)(6) (infra page 283) provides that a foreign state is not immune from the jurisdiction of U.S. courts to enforce an agreement to submit to arbitration or to confirm an arbitration award..28 U.S.C. §1610(a)(6) (infra page 288) permits execution of a judgment confirming an arbitral award on any property of a foreign state used for commercial activity in the U.S. even if the property is not used for the commercial activity on which the claim is based. The FAA, in 9 U.S.C. §15, provides: "Enforcement of arbitration agreements, confirmation of arbitral awards, and execution upon judgments based on orders confirming such awards shall not be refused on the basis of the Act of State Doctrine." Thus arbitration agreements are now probably preferable to conciliation or arbitration under the Convention on the Settlement of Investment Disputes Between States and Nationals of Other States (infra page 516), which was promulgated in 1965 by the Executive Directors of the International Bank for Reconstruction and Development to encourage private investment abroad. Moreover, the Convention has what arbitrators refer to as the "Article 52 problem." This article of the Convention (infra page xxx), creates an appeals process within the International Centre for Settlement of Investment Disputes in which the parties do not pick the panel members.

9. For the view that federal courts should not develop a common law of foreign relations but should leave "redressing state intrusions on federal foreign relations prerogatives" to the "federal political branches," see Jack L. Goldsmith, Federal Courts, Foreign Affairs, and Federalism, 83 Va. L. Rev. 1617, 1623 (1997).

Section 2: Intangible Property

Allied Bank International v. Banco Credito Agricola de Cartago
757 F.2d 516, (2d Cir.), cert, dismissed, 473 U.S. 934 (1985)

Before MESKILL and PIERCE, Circuit Judges, and METZNER, District Judge.

MESKILL, Circuit Judge:

This matter is before us on rehearing. We vacate our previous decision dated April 23, 1984. We reverse the dismissal of the cause by the United States District Court for the Southern District of New York, Griesa, J. We also reverse the district court's denial of plaintiff-appellant Allied Bank International's (Allied) motion for summary judgment. Both district court rulings were predicated solely on the act of state doctrine. Because that doctrine is not applicable, we remand to the district court for entry of summary judgment for Allied.

I

Allied is the agent for a syndicate of thirty-nine creditor banks. Defendants-appellees are three Costa Rican banks that are wholly owned by the Republic of Costa Rica and subject to the direct control of the Central Bank of Costa Rica (Central Bank). Allied brought this action in February 1982 to recover on promissory notes issued by the Costa Rican banks. The notes, which were in default, were payable in United States dollars in New York City. The parties' agreements acknowledged that the obligations were registered with Central Bank which was supposed to provide the necessary dollars for payment.

The defaults were due solely to actions of the Costa Rican government. In July 1981, in response to escalating national economic problems, Central Bank issued regulations which essentially suspended all external debt payments. In November 1981, the government issued an executive decree which conditioned all payments of external debt on express approval from Central Bank. Central Bank subsequently refused to authorize any foreign debt payments in United States dollars, thus precluding payment on the notes here at issue. In accordance with the provisions of the agreements, Allied accelerated the debt and sued for the full amount of principal and interest outstanding.

* * *

Allied moved for summary judgment. The sole defense raised by appellees in response was the act of state doctrine.

The district court denied all of the motions. Reasoning that a judicial determination contrary to the Costa Rican directives could embarrass the United States government in its relations with the Costa Rican government, the court held that the act of state doctrine barred entry of summary judgment for Allied.

* * *

II

In our previous decision, we affirmed the district court's dismissal. We did not address the question of whether the act of state doctrine applied because we determined that the actions of the Costa Rican government which precipitated the default of the Costa Rican banks were fully consistent with the law and policy of the United States. We therefore concluded that principles of comity compelled us to recognize as valid the Costa Rican directives.

Our interpretation of United States policy, however, arose primarily from our belief that the legislative and executive branches of our government fully supported Costa Rica's actions and all of the economic ramifications. On rehearing, the Executive Branch of the United States joined this litigation as amicus curiae and respectfully disputed our reasoning. The Justice Department brief gave the following explanation of our government's support for the debt resolution procedure that operates through the auspices of the International Monetary Fund (IMF). Guided by the IMF, this long established approach encourages the cooperative adjustment of international debt problems. The entire strategy is grounded in the understanding that, while parties may agree to renegotiate conditions of payment, the underlying obligations to pay nevertheless remain valid and enforceable. Costa Rica's attempted unilateral restructuring of private obligations, the United States contends, was inconsistent with this system of international cooperation and negotiation and thus inconsistent with United States policy.

The United States government further explains that its position on private international debt is not inconsistent with either its own willingness to restructure Costa Rica's intergovernmental obligations or with continued United States aid to the economically distressed Central American country. Our previous conclusion that the Costa Rican decrees were consistent with United States policy was premised on these two circumstances.

In light of the government's elucidation of its position, we believe that our earlier interpretation of United States policy was wrong. Nevertheless, if, as Judge Griesa held, the act of state doctrine applies, it precludes judicial examination of the Costa Rican decrees. Thus we must first consider that question.

* * *

The Supreme Court has been quite careful to avoid the creation of "an inflexible and all-encompassing rule" to govern the application of the doctrine; "the less important the implications of an issue are for our foreign relations, the weaker the justification for exclusivity in the political branches." *Sabbatino*, 376 U.S. at 428. The doctrine demands a case-by-case analysis of the extent to which in the context of a particular dispute separation of powers concerns are implicated.

This analysis must always be tempered by common sense. See *Tabacalera Severiano Jorge, S.A. v. Standard Cigar Co.*, 392 F.2d 706, 715 (5th Cir.), cert. denied, 393 U.S. 924 (1968). The doctrine does not necessarily "preclude judicial resolution of all commercial consequences" that result from acts of foreign sovereigns performed within their own borders. *Arango v. Guzman Travel Advisors Corp.*, 621 F.2d 1371, 1380-81 (5th Cir.1980). But, obviously, where the taking is wholly accomplished within the foreign sovereign's territory, "it would be an affront to such foreign government for courts of the United States to hold that such act was a nullity." *Tabacalera*, 392 F.2d at 715. Furthermore, under such circumstances, the court's decision would almost surely be disregarded within the borders of the foreign state.

The extraterritorial limitation, an inevitable conjunct of the foreign policy concerns underlying the doctrine, dictates that our decision herein depends on the situs of the property at the time of the purported taking. The property, of course, is Allied's right to receive repayment from the Costa Rican banks in accordance with the agreements. The act of state doctrine is applicable to this dispute only if, when the decrees were promulgated, the situs of the debts was in Costa Rica. Because we conclude that the situs of the property was in the United States, the doctrine is not applicable.

As the Fifth Circuit explained in *Tabacalera*, the concept of the situs of a debt for act of state purposes differs from the ordinary concept. It depends in large part on whether the purported taking can be said to have "come to complete fruition within the dominion of the [foreign] government." *Tabacalera*, 392 F.2d at 715-16. In this case, Costa Rica could not wholly extinguish the Costa Rican banks' obligation to timely pay United States dollars to Allied in New York. Thus the situs of the debt was not Costa Rica.

The same result obtains under ordinary situs analysis. The Costa Rican banks conceded jurisdiction in New York and they agreed to pay the debt in New York City in United States dollars. Allied, the designated syndicate agent, is located in the United States, specifically in New York; some of the negotiations between the parties took place in the United States. The United States has an interest in maintaining New York's status as one of the foremost commercial centers in the world. Further, New York is the international clearing center for United States dollars. In addition to other international activities, United States banks lend billions of dollars to foreign debtors each year. The United States has an interest in ensuring that creditors entitled to payment in the United States in United States dollars under contracts subject to the jurisdiction of United States courts may assume that, except under the most extraordinary circumstances, their rights will be determined in accordance with recognized principles of contract law.

In contrast, while Costa Rica has a legitimate concern in overseeing the debt situation of state-owned banks and in maintaining a stable economy, its interest in the contracts at issue is essentially limited to the extent to which it can unilaterally alter the payment terms. Costa Rica's potential jurisdiction over the debt is not sufficient to locate the debt there for the purposes of act of state doctrine analysis.

Thus, under either analysis, our result is the same: the situs of the debt was in the United States, not in Costa Rica. Consequently, this was not "a taking of property within its own territory by [Costa Rica]." *Sabbatino*, 376 U.S. at 428. The act of state doctrine is, therefore, inapplicable.

IV

Acts of foreign governments purporting to have extraterritorial effect—and consequently, by definition, falling outside the scope of the act of state doctrine—should be recognized by the courts only if they are consistent with the law and policy of the United States. Thus, we have come full circle to reassess whether we should give effect to the Costa Rican directives. We now conclude that we should not.

* * *

The Costa Rican directives are inconsistent with the law and policy of the United States. We refuse, therefore, to hold that the directives excuse the obligations of the Costa Rican banks. The appellees' inability to pay United States dollars relates only to the potential enforceability of the judgment; it does not determine whether judgment should enter.

* * *

We vacate our previous decision, reverse the district court's denial of Allied's motion for summary judgment and its dismissal of the action and direct the district court to enter judgment for Allied.

Notes

1. The court indicates that "[t]he same result obtains under ordinary situs analysis." For at least some purposes, a debt not embodied in a document is deemed located where the debtor is found. See Restatement (Second) Conflict of Laws § 68 (1969) (a court having personal jurisdiction over a debtor, may apply the debt to the satisfaction of a claim asserted against another person over whom the court does not have jurisdiction).

Situs of a debt at the location of the debtor, was the basis for the district court's opinion in *Alfred Dunhill*. (See note 4 supra, page 272.) The Second Circuit disagreed, placing the situs of the debt in Cuba.

In *Alfred Dunhill*, the Second Circuit's allowance of a set off relied on First National City Bank v. Banco Nacional de Cuba, 406 U.S. 759 (1972), in which a plurality agreed that Banco, an instrumentality of the Cuban government, could not sue for funds due to it without submitting to a decision on the merits of a counterclaim. Bank had made a loan to Banco's predecessor. Bank had sold the collateral when the loan was in default and retained a surplus from this sale. When Banco sued for this surplus, Bank counterclaimed to offset against Banco's claim, the value of Bank's Cuban properties that had been expropriated.

2. Pravin Banker Associates, Ltd. v. Banco Popular Del Peru, 109 F.3d 850 (2d Cir. 1997), affirmed summary judgment for a creditor suing a Peruvian Bank and the Republic of Peru, which had guaranteed the bank's debt. The creditor sued to recover proceeds of a loan to the bank that was in default. The court concluded that staying the action on the ground of international comity would be contrary to United States. policy.

Credit Suisse v. United States District Court, 130 F.3d 1342 (9th Cir. 1997), ordered the district court to dismiss an action. The action requested the court to enjoin Swiss banks from transferring assets, order the Swiss banks to hold the assets subject to the court's further orders, and declare that an assignment of claims to the clerk of the federal court in Hawaii for the benefit of the plaintiffs was valid. The banks held the accounts on behalf of the estate of Ferdinand Marcos, former Philippine head of state. Victims of human rights violations under the Marcos regime had won a judgment in the federal district court in Hawaii of over $1.9 billion against the estate. In an attempt to collect on the judgment, the plaintiffs registered the judgment in federal court in California and served writs of execution on the Swiss banks' offices in California although none of the accounts were maintained there. Swiss government officials had issued orders freezing all assets belonging to Marcos or his family. The Ninth Circuit held that ordering the Swiss banks to hold the assets subject to the federal district court's orders or declaring valid the assignment "would be in direct contravention of the Swiss freeze orders" and would violate the act of state doctrine. Id. at 1347-48.

Riggs National Corp. v. Commissioner of Internal Revenue Service, 163 F.3d 1363 (D.C. Cir. 1999), held that under the act of state doctrine the Commissioner could not challenge the ruling of the Brazilian Minister of Finance that Brazilian law required the Central Bank of Brazil to pay taxes on interest from loans that the Bank had made to the government of Brazil.

John Doe I v. Unocal Corp., 963 F. Supp. 880 (C.D. Cal. 1997), held that the act of state doctrine did not bar suit against an American oil company that had constructed a gas pipeline in Burma. The plaintiffs contended that the oil company was liable for acts of torture and slavery by the Burmese government in connection with the construction. The court held, however, that the act of state doctrine barred claims against the oil company based on expropriation of property by the Burmese government.

3. F & H.R. Farman-Farmaian Consulting Engineers Firm v. Harza Engineering Co., 882 F.2d 281 (7th Cir. 1989), cert. denied, 497 U.S. 1038 (1990). A United States company performed work in Iran before the revolution. The Iran-United States Claims Tribunal ordered the successor regime to pay the company for this work. (With regard to the Tribunal, see Ministry of Defense of Islamic Republic of Iran v. Gould, Inc., a principal case in chapter 11.) The owners of an expropriated Iranian company sued the United States company claiming that the expropriated company had not been paid for consulting work done for the United States company and that the Tribunal award included payment for this consulting work. Held: the act of state doctrine bars the claim. "[T]o describe the Consulting Firm's claim for payment of [the United States company's] debt to it as an asset located in Iran, as we have done, may be thought to beg the question. A debt (like a word, a number, an idea) has no space-time location; it is not a

physical object, and efforts to treat it as such...seem bound to fail....What is at issue in this case is not the rights or interests of an American company...but the propriety of dealings between the Iranian government and an Iranian corporation. With the American interest so attenuated, considerations of comity...come to the fore; and it is those considerations and the resulting concern with the judiciary's stepping on the State Department's toes, that inform the modern understanding of the act of state doctrine." Id. at 286-87.

4. Trinh v. Citibank, N.A., 850 F.2d 1164 (6th Cir. 1988), cert. denied, 496 U.S. 912 (1990). Plaintiff's father had deposited funds in Citibank's (CB) branch in South Vietnam (SV). As required by SV law, CB operated the SV bank as a branch, not as a separately incorporated subsidiary. The deposit agreement provided that the only method of withdrawal was at the Saigon branch in SV currency and that CB was not responsible for any loss suffered as a result of government orders or causes beyond its control. The SV branch was abandoned when Saigon fell to North Vietnam, which took possession of the branch and all funds. Plaintiff's father, upon his release from a reeducation camp, sent the passbook to his son in Michigan. The son sued CB for recovery of the funds deposited in CB's former Saigon branch. Held: judgment for plaintiff affirmed. Under general banking principles, the home office is liable for payment of its foreign branch deposits. This expectation was reinforced by SV law requiring operation as a branch, not as an independent entity, and was not adequately dispelled by the manner in which the deposit agreement was drafted. "[A] person who had signed [the] deposit agreement would not have been aware that he had" assumed the "sovereign risk" that the branch's assets would be seized by a successor political regime. Id. at 1170.

Citibank N.A. v. Wells Fargo Asia Ltd., 495 U.S. 660 (1990). A Wells Fargo (WF) bank deposited funds in CB's Manila branch. The Philippine government issued an order preventing repayment from Philippine assets. WF sued CB in New York and prevailed. The district court decided that the deposit agreement did not cover the method of collection and WF would prevail under either Philippine or New York law. The Second Circuit affirmed on the ground that the deposit agreement permitted collection in New York. Held: reversed and remanded. The trial court was not clearly erroneous in finding that the deposit agreement did not cover whether WF could collect in New York from CB's general assets. The case was remanded to determine what law (New York, federal common law, or Philippine) governs WF's collection rights in the absence of agreement, and what the content of that law is. On remand, it was held that New York law applied and that under that law, absent an agreement to the contrary, the depositor may collect the account in New York from the bank's world-wide assets. Wells Fargo Asia Ltd. v. Citibank N.A., 936 F.2d 723 (2d Cir. 1991) cert. denied, 505 U.S. 1204 (1992).

What could Citibank have done to prevent the results in *Trinh* and *Wells Fargo*?

In 1994 Congress enacted 12 U.S.C. §633, which provides that any bank that is a member of the Federal Reserve System (covered by Federal deposit insurance) "shall not be required to repay any deposit made at a foreign branch of the bank if the bank cannot repay the deposit due to (1) an act of war, insurrection or civil strife; or (2) an action by a foreign government or instrumentality (whether de jure or de facto) in the country in which the branch is located; unless the member bank has expressly agreed in writing to repay the deposit under those circumstances." Will this statute prevent courts from construing poorly drafted deposit agreements in favor of depositors?

5. W.S. Kirkpatrick & Co., Inc. v. Environmental Tectonics Corp., Int'l, 493 U.S. 400 (1990). Kirkpatrick allegedly obtained a construction contract from the Nigerian gov-

ernment by bribing Nigerian officials. Nigerian law prohibits the payment and receipt of such bribes. Environmental, an unsuccessful bidder for the contract, sued Kirkpatrick under various federal and state statutes. The district court dismissed on the ground that the suit was barred by the act of state doctrine. The third circuit reversed and cert. was granted. Held: affirmed, Justice Scalia writing for a unanimous court:

> The act of state doctrine does not establish an exception [to the rule that United States courts have the obligation to decide cases properly before them] for cases...that may embarrass foreign governments, but merely requires that, in the process of deciding, the acts of foreign sovereigns taken within their own jurisdictions shall be deemed valid. That doctrine has no application to the present case because the validity of no foreign sovereign act is at issue. (Id. at 409-10).

Chapter 5

Foreign Sovereign Immunity

Section 1: The Foreign Sovereign Immunities Act

Foreign Sovereign Immunities Act, 28 U.S.C.

§ 1330. Actions against foreign states

(a) The district courts shall have original jurisdiction without regard to amount in controversy of any nonjury civil action against a foreign state as defined in section 1603(a) of this title as to any claim for relief in personam with respect to which the foreign state is not entitled to immunity either under sections 1605-1607 of this title or under any applicable international agreement.

(b) Personal jurisdiction over a foreign state shall exist as to every claim for relief over which the district courts have jurisdiction under subsection (a) where service has been made under section 1608 of this title.

(c) For purposes of subsection (b), an appearance by a foreign state does not confer personal jurisdiction with respect to any claim for relief not arising out of any transaction or occurrence enumerated in sections 1605-1607 of this title.

§ 1602. Findings and declaration of purpose

The Congress finds that the determination by United States courts of the claims of foreign states to immunity from the jurisdiction of such courts would serve the interests of justice and would protect the rights of both foreign states and litigants in United States courts. Under international law, states are not immune from the jurisdiction of foreign courts insofar as their commercial activities are concerned, and their commercial property may be levied upon for the satisfaction of judgments rendered against them in connection with their commercial activities. Claims of foreign states to immunity should henceforth be decided by courts of the United States and of the States in conformity with the principles set forth in this chapter.

§ 1603. Definitions

For purposes of this chapter—

(a) A "foreign state", except as used in section 1608 of this title, includes a political subdivision of a foreign state or an agency or instrumentality of a foreign state as defined in subsection (b).

(b) An "agency or instrumentality of a foreign state" means any entity—(1) which is a separate legal person, corporate or otherwise, and(2) which is an organ of a foreign state or political subdivision thereof, or a majority of whose shares or other ownership interest is owned by a foreign state or political subdivision thereof, and(3) which is neither a citizen of a State of the United States as defined in section 1332(c) and (d) of this title, nor created under the laws of any third country.

(c) The "United States" includes all territory and waters, continental or insular, subject to the jurisdiction of the United States.

(d) A "commercial activity" means either a regular course of commercial conduct or a particular commercial transaction or act. The commercial character of an activity shall be determined by reference to the nature of the course of conduct or particular transaction or act, rather than by reference to its purpose.

(e) A "commercial activity carried on in the United States by a foreign state" means commercial activity carried on by such state and having substantial contact with the United States.

§ 1604. Immunity of a foreign state from jurisdiction

Subject to existing international agreements to which the United States is a party at the time of enactment of this Act a foreign state shall be immune from the jurisdiction of the courts of the United States and of the States except as provided in sections 1605 to 1607 of this chapter.

§ 1605. General exceptions to the jurisdictional immunity of a foreign state

(a) A foreign state shall not be immune from the jurisdiction of courts of the United States or of the States in any case—

(1) in which the foreign state has waived its immunity either explicitly or by implication, notwithstanding any withdrawal of the waiver which the foreign state may purport to effect except in accordance with the terms of the waiver;

(2) in which the action is based upon a commercial activity carried on in the United States by the foreign state; or upon an act performed in the United States in connection with a commercial activity of the foreign state elsewhere; or upon an act outside the territory of the United States in connection with a commercial activity of the foreign state elsewhere and that act causes a direct effect in the United States;

(3) in which rights in property taken in violation of international law are in issue and that property or any property exchanged for such property is present in the United States in connection with a commercial activity carried on in the United States by the foreign state; or that property or any property exchanged for such property is owned or operated by an agency or instrumentality of the foreign state and that agency or instrumentality is engaged in a commercial activity in the United States;

(4) in which rights in property in the United States acquired by succession or gift or rights in immovable property situated in the United States are in issue;

(5) not otherwise encompassed in paragraph (2) above, in which money damages are sought against a foreign state for personal injury or death, or damage to or loss of property, occurring in the United States and caused by the tortious act or omission of that foreign state or of any official or employee of that foreign state while acting within the scope of his office or employment; except this paragraph shall not apply to—

(A) any claim based upon the exercise or performance or the failure to exercise or perform a discretionary function regardless of whether the discretion be abused, or

(B) any claim arising out of malicious prosecution, abuse of process, libel, slander, misrepresentation, deceit, or interference with contract rights; or

(6) in which the action is brought, either to enforce an agreement made by the foreign state with or for the benefit of a private party to submit to arbitration all or any differences which have arisen or which may arise between the parties with respect to a defined legal relationship, whether contractual or not, concerning a subject matter capable of settlement by arbitration under the laws of the United States, or to confirm an award made pursuant to such an agreement to arbitrate, if (A) the arbitration takes place or is intended to take place in the United States, (B) the agreement or award is or may be governed by a treaty or other international agreement in force for the United States calling for the recognition and enforcement of arbitral awards, (C) the underlying claim, save for the agreement to arbitrate, could have been brought in a United States court under this section or section 1607, or (D) paragraph (1) of this subsection is otherwise applicable; or

(7) not otherwise covered by paragraph (2), in which money damages are sought against a foreign state for personal injury or death that was caused by an act of torture, extrajudicial killing, aircraft sabotage, hostage taking, or the provision of material support or resources (as defined in section 2339A of title 18 [proscribing crime of "providing material support to terrorists"]) for such an act if such act or provision of material support is engaged in by an official, employee, or agent of such foreign state while acting within the scope of his or her office, employment, or agency, except that the court shall decline to hear a claim under this paragraph—

(A) if the foreign state was not designated as a state sponsor of terrorism under section 6(j) of the Export Administration Act of 1979 (50 U.S.C. App. 2405(j)) or section 620A of the Foreign Assistance Act of 1961 (22 U.S.C. 2371) at the time the act occurred, unless later so designated as a result of such act; and

(B) even if the foreign state is or was so designated, if—

(i) the act occurred in the foreign state against which the claim has been brought and the claimant has not afforded the foreign state a reasonable opportunity to arbitrate the claim in accordance with accepted international rules of arbitration; or

(ii) the claimant or victim was not a national of the United States (as that term is defined in section 101(a)(22) of the Immigration and Nationality Act) when the act upon which the claim is based occurred.

(b) A foreign state shall not be immune from the jurisdiction of the courts of the United States in any case in which a suit in admiralty is brought to enforce a maritime lien against a vessel or cargo of the foreign state, which maritime lien is based upon a commercial activity of the foreign state: Provided, That—

(1) notice of the suit is given by delivery of a copy of the summons and of the complaint to the person, or his agent, having possession of the vessel or cargo against which the maritime lien is asserted; and if the vessel or cargo is arrested pursuant to process obtained on behalf of the party bringing the suit, the service of process of arrest shall be deemed to constitute valid delivery of such notice, but the party bringing the suit shall be liable for any damages sustained by the foreign state as a result of the arrest if the party bringing the suit had actual or constructive knowledge that the vessel or cargo of a foreign state was involved; and

(2) notice to the foreign state of the commencement of suit as provided in section 1608 of this title is initiated within ten days either of the delivery of notice as provided in paragraph (1) of this subsection or, in the case of a party who was unaware that the vessel or cargo of a foreign state was involved, of the date such party determined the existence of the foreign state's interest.

(c) Whenever notice is delivered under subsection (b)(1), the suit to enforce a maritime lien shall thereafter proceed and shall be heard and determined according to the principles of law and rules of practice of suits in rem whenever it appears that, had the vessel been privately owned and possessed, a suit in rem might have been maintained. A decree against the foreign state may include costs of the suit and, if the decree is for a money judgment, interest as ordered by the court, except that the court may not award judgment against the foreign state in an amount greater than the value of the vessel or cargo upon which the maritime lien arose. Such value shall be determined as of the time notice is served under subsection (b)(1). Decrees shall be subject to appeal and revision as provided in other cases of admiralty and maritime jurisdiction. Nothing shall preclude the plaintiff in any proper case from seeking relief in personam in the same action brought to enforce a maritime lien as provided in this section.

(d) A foreign state shall not be immune from the jurisdiction of the courts of the United States in any action brought to foreclose a preferred mortgage, as defined in the Ship Mortgage Act, 1920 (46 U.S.C. 911 and following). Such action shall be brought, heard, and determined in accordance with the provisions of that Act and in accordance with the principles of law and rules of practice of suits in rem, whenever it appears that had the vessel been privately owned and possessed a suit in rem might have been maintained.

(e) For purposes of paragraph (7) of subsection (a)—

(1) the terms "torture" and "extrajudicial killing" have the meaning given those terms in section 3 of the Torture Victim Protection Act of 1991 [see infra page 414];

(2) the term "hostage taking" has the meaning given that term in Article 1 of the International Convention Against the Taking of Hostages; and

(3) the term "aircraft sabotage" has the meaning given that term in Article 1 of the Convention for the Suppression of Unlawful Acts Against the Safety of Civil Aviation.

(f) No action shall be maintained under subsection (a)(7) unless the action is commenced not later than 10 years after the date on which the cause of action arose. All principles of equitable tolling, including the period during which the foreign state was immune from suit, shall apply in calculating this limitation period. [The amendments to the FSIA adding (a)(7) and related provisions were enacted April 24, 1996, PL 104-132, 110 Stat 1214, 1241. Subsection c of the enactment provides: "The amendments made by this subtitle shall apply to any cause of action arising before on, or after the date of the enactment of this Act."]

(g) Limitation on Discovery—

(1) In general.—

(A) Subject to paragraph (2), if an action is filed that would otherwise be barred by section 1604, but for subsection (a)(7), the court, upon request of the Attorney General, shall stay any request, demand, or order for discovery on the United States that the Attorney General certifies would significantly interfere with a criminal investigation or prosecution, or a national security operation, related to the incident that gave rise to the cause of action, until such time as the Attorney General advises the court that such request, demand, or order will no longer so interfere.

(B) A stay under this paragraph shall be in effect during the 12-month period beginning on the date on which the court issues the order to stay discovery. The court shall renew the order to stay discovery for additional 12-month periods upon motion by the United States if the Attorney General certifies that discovery would significantly interfere with a criminal investigation or prosecution, or a national security operation, related to the incident that gave rise to the cause of action.

(2) Sunset—

(A) Subject to subparagraph (B), no stay shall be granted or continued in effect under paragraph (1) after the date that is 10 years after the date on which the incident that gave rise to the cause of action occurred.

(B) After the period referred to in subparagraph (A), the court, upon request of the Attorney General, may stay any request, demand, or order for discovery on the United States that the court finds a substantial likelihood would—

(i) create a serious threat of death or serious bodily injury to any person;

(ii) adversely affect the ability of the United States to work in cooperation with foreign and international law enforcement agencies in investigating violations of United States law; or

(iii) obstruct the criminal case related to the incident that gave rise to the cause of action or undermine the potential for a conviction in such case.

(3) Evaluation of evidence.—

The court's evaluation of any request for a stay under this subsection filed by the Attorney General shall be conducted ex parte and in camera.

(4) Bar on motions to dismiss.—A stay of discovery under this subsection shall constitute a bar to the granting of a motion to dismiss under rules 12 (b) (6) and 56 of the Federal Rules of Civil Procedure.

(5) Construction.—Nothing in this subsection shall prevent the United States from seeking protective orders or asserting privileges ordinarily available to the United States.

§ 1606. Extent of liability

As to any claim for relief with respect to which a foreign state is not entitled to immunity under section 1605 or 1607 of this chapter, the foreign state shall be liable in the same manner and to the same extent as a private individual under like circumstances; but a foreign state except for an agency or instrumentality thereof shall not be liable for punitive damages, except any action under section 1605(a)(7) or 1610(f); if, however, in any case wherein death was caused, the law of the place where the action or omission occurred provides, or has been construed to provide, for damages only punitive in nature, the foreign state shall be liable for actual or compensatory damages measured by the pecuniary injuries resulting from such death which were incurred by the persons for whose benefit the action was brought.

§ 1607. Counterclaims

In any action brought by a foreign state, or in which a foreign state intervenes, in a court of the United States or of a State, the foreign state shall not be accorded immunity with respect to any counterclaim—

(a) for which a foreign state would not be entitled to immunity under section 1605 of this chapter had such claim been brought in a separate action against the foreign state; or

(b) arising out of the transaction or occurrence that is the subject matter of the claim of the foreign state; or

(c) to the extent that the counterclaim does not seek relief exceeding in amount or differing in kind from that sought by the foreign state.

§ 1608. Service; time to answer; default

(a) Service in the courts of the United States and of the States shall be made upon a foreign state or political subdivision of a foreign state:

(1) by delivery of a copy of the summons and complaint in accordance with any special arrangement for service between the plaintiff and the foreign state or political subdivision; or

(2) if no special arrangement exists, by delivery of a copy of the summons and complaint in accordance with an applicable international convention on service of judicial documents; or

(3) if service cannot be made under paragraphs (1) or (2), by sending a copy of the summons and complaint and a notice of suit, together with a translation of each into the official language of the foreign state, by any form of mail requiring a signed receipt, to be addressed and dispatched by the clerk of the court to the head of the ministry of foreign affairs of the foreign state concerned, or

(4) if service cannot be made within 30 days under paragraph (3), by sending two copies of the summons and complaint and a notice of suit, together with a translation of each into the official language of the foreign state, by any form of mail requiring a signed receipt, to be addressed and dispatched by the clerk of the court to the Secretary of State in Washington, District of Columbia, to the attention of the Director of Special Consular Services—and the Secretary shall transmit one copy of the papers through diplomatic channels to the foreign state and shall send to the clerk of the court a certified copy of the diplomatic note indicating when the papers were transmitted.

As used in this subsection, a "notice of suit" shall mean a notice addressed to a foreign state and in a form prescribed by the Secretary of State by regulation.

(b) Service in the courts of the United States and of the States shall be made upon an agency or instrumentality of a foreign state:

(1) by delivery of a copy of the summons and complaint in accordance with any special arrangement for service between the plaintiff and the agency or instrumentality; or

(2) if no special arrangement exists, by delivery of a copy of the summons and complaint either to an officer, a managing or general agent, or to any other agent authorized by appointment or by law to receive service of process in the United States; or in accordance with an applicable international convention on service of judicial documents; or

(3) if service cannot be made under paragraphs (1) or (2), and if reasonably calculated to give actual notice, by delivery of a copy of the summons and complaint, together with a translation of each into the official language of the foreign state—

(A) as directed by an authority of the foreign state or political subdivision in response to a letter rogatory or request or

(B) by any form of mail requiring a signed receipt, to be addressed and dispatched by the clerk of the court to the agency or instrumentality to be served, or

(C) as directed by order of the court consistent with the law of the place where service is to be made.

(c) Service shall be deemed to have been made—

(1) in the case of service under subsection (a) (4), as of the date of transmittal indicated in the certified copy of the diplomatic note; and

(2) in any other case under this section, as of the date of receipt indicated in the certification, signed and returned postal receipt, or other proof of service applicable to the method of service employed.

(d) In any action brought in a court of the United States or of a State, a foreign state, a political subdivision thereof, or an agency or instrumentality of a foreign state shall serve an answer or other responsive pleading to the complaint within sixty days after service has been made under this section.

(e) No judgment by default shall be entered by a court of the United States or of a State against a foreign state, a political subdivision thereof, or an agency or instrumentality of a foreign state, unless the claimant establishes his claim or right to relief by evidence satisfactory to the court. A copy of any such default judgment shall be sent to the foreign state or political subdivision in the manner prescribed for service in this section.

§ 1609. *Immunity from attachment and execution of property of a foreign state*

Subject to existing international agreements to which the United States is a party at the time of enactment of this Act the property in the United States of a foreign state shall be immune from attachment arrest and execution except as provided in sections 1610 and 1611 of this chapter.

§ 1610. *Exceptions to the immunity from attachment or execution*

(a) The property in the United States of a foreign state, as defined in section 1603(a) of this chapter, used for a commercial activity in the United States, shall not be immune from attachment in aid of execution, or from execution, upon a judgment entered by a court of the United States or of a State after the effective date of this Act, if—

(1) the foreign state has waived its immunity from attachment in aid of execution or from execution either explicitly or by implication, notwithstanding any withdrawal of the waiver the foreign state may purport to effect except in accordance with the terms of the waiver, or

(2) the property is or was used for the commercial activity upon which the claim is based, or

(3) the execution relates to a judgment establishing rights in property which has been taken in violation of international law or which has been exchanged for property taken in violation of international law, or

(4) the execution relates to a judgment establishing rights in property—

(A) which is acquired by succession or gift, or

(B) which is immovable and situated in the United States: Provided, That such property is not used for purposes of maintaining a diplomatic or consular mission or the residence of the Chief of such mission, or

(5) the property consists of any contractual obligation or any proceeds from such a contractual obligation to indemnify or hold harmless the foreign state or its employees

under a policy of automobile or other liability or casualty insurance covering the claim which merged into the judgment, or

(6) the judgment is based on an order confirming an arbitral award rendered against the foreign state, provided that attachment in aid of execution, or execution, would not be inconsistent with any provision in the arbitral agreement; or

(7) the judgment relates to a claim for which the foreign state is not immune under section 1605(a)(7), regardless of whether the property is or was involved with the act upon which the claim is based.

(b) In addition to subsection (a), any property in the United States of an agency or instrumentality of a foreign state engaged in commercial activity in the United States shall not be immune from attachment in aid of execution, or from execution, upon a judgment entered by a court of the United States or of a State after the effective date of this Act if—

(1) the agency or instrumentality has waived its immunity from attachment in aid of execution or from execution either explicitly or implicitly, notwithstanding any withdrawal of the waiver the agency or instrumentality may purport to effect except in accordance with the terms of the waiver, or

(2) the judgment relates to a claim for which the agency or instrumentality is not immune by virtue of section 1605(a) (2), (3), (5), or (7), or 1605(b) of this chapter, regardless of whether the property is or was involved in the act upon which the claim is based.

(c) No attachment or execution referred to in subsections (a) and (b) of this section shall be permitted until the court has ordered such attachment and execution after having determined that a reasonable period of time has elapsed following the entry of judgment and the giving of any notice required under section 1608(e) of this chapter.

(d) The property of a foreign state, as defined in section 1603(a) of this chapter, used for a commercial activity in the United States, shall not be immune from attachment prior to the entry of judgment in any action brought in a court of the United States or of a State, or prior to the elapse of the period of time provided in subsection (c) of this section, if—

(1) the foreign state has explicitly waived its immunity from attachment prior to judgment, notwithstanding any withdrawal of the waiver the foreign state may purport to effect except in accordance with the terms of the waiver, and

(2) the purpose of the attachment is to secure satisfaction of a judgment that has been or may ultimately be entered against the foreign state, and not to obtain jurisdiction.

(e) The vessels of a foreign state shall not be immune from arrest in rem, interlocutory sale, and execution in actions brought to foreclose a preferred mortgage as provided in section 1605(d).

(f)(1)(A) Notwithstanding any other provision of law, including but not limited to section 208(f) of the Foreign Missions Act (22 U.S.C. 4308(f)), and except as provided in subparagraph (B), any property with respect to which financial transactions are prohibited or regulated pursuant to section 5(b) of the Trading with the Enemy Act (50 U.S.C. App. 5(b)), section 620(a) of the Foreign Assistance Act of 1961 ($22 U.S.C. 2370(a)), sections 202 and 203 of the International Emergency Economic Powers Act (50 U.S.C. 1701-1702), or any other proclamation, order, regulation, or license issued pursuant thereto, shall be subject to execution or attachment in aid of execution of any judgment relating to a claim for which a foreign state (including any agency or instrumentality or such state) claiming such property is not immune under section 1605(a)(7).

(B) Subparagraph (A) shall not apply if, at the time the property is expropriated or seized by the foreign state, the property has been held in title by a natural person or, if held in trust, has been held for the benefit of a natural person or persons.

(2)(A) At the request of any party in whose favor a judgment has been issued with respect to a claim for which the foreign state is not immune under section 1605(a)(7), the Secretary of the Treasury and the Secretary of State shall fully, promptly, and effectively assist any judgment creditor or any court that has issued any such judgment in identifying, locating, and executing against the property of that foreign state or any agency or instrumentality of such state.

(B) In providing such assistance, the Secretaries—

(i) may provide such information to the court under seal; and

(ii) shall provide the information in a manner sufficient to allow the court to direct the United States Marshall's office to promptly and effectively execute against that property.

§ 1611. Certain types of property immune from execution

(a) Notwithstanding the provisions of section 1610 of this chapter, the property of those organizations designated by the President as being entitled to enjoy the privileges, exemptions, and immunities provided by the International Organizations Immunities Act shall not be subject to attachment or any other judicial process impeding the disbursement of funds to, or on the order of, a foreign state as the result of an action brought in the courts of the United States or of the States.

(b) Notwithstanding the provisions of section 1610 of this chapter, the property of a foreign state shall be immune from attachment and from execution, if—

(1) the property is that of a foreign central bank or monetary authority held for its own account, unless such bank or authority, or its parent foreign government, has explicitly waived its immunity from attachment in aid of execution, or from execution, notwithstanding any withdrawal of the waiver which the bank, authority or government may purport to effect except in accordance with the terms of the waiver; or

(2) the property is, or is intended to be, used in connection with a military activity and

(A) is of a military character, or

(B) is under the control of a military authority or defense agency.

(c) Notwithstanding the provisions of section 1610 of this chapter, the property of a foreign state shall be immune from attachment and from execution in an action brought under section 302 of the Cuban Liberty and Democratic Solidarity (LIBERTAD) Act of 1996 to the extent that the property is a facility or installation used by an accredited diplomatic mission for official purposes.

Notes

1. Three additional sections affecting suits in which foreign states are parties are: 28 U.S.C. §§:

1332(a)(4), providing diversity jurisdiction in suits between "a foreign state...as plaintiff and citizens of a State or of different States";

1391(f), setting venue in any judicial district where "a substantial part of the events or omissions giving rise to the claim occurred, or a substantial part of property that is the subject of the action is situated"; if the claim is under 1605(b), where "the vessel or cargo of a foreign state is situated"; or, if against an agency or instrumentality of a foreign state, where "the agency or instrumentality is licensed to do business or is doing business"; if "against a foreign state or political subdivision thereof," in the District of Columbia;

1441(d), permitting a foreign state, if sued in a state court, to remove to federal court for trial without a jury. In re Air Crash Disaster Near Roselawn, Indiana on October 31, 1994, 96 F.3d 932 (7th Cir. 1996) held that although the action against all defendants, not just the sovereign defendant, could be removed, actions against the non-sovereign defendants would be tried to a jury.

The 1998 legislation amending § 1606 to insert after "punitive damages" the words "except any action under section 1605(a)(7) or 1610(f)" and amending § 1610 to add § 1610(f) provided: "The President may waive the requirements of this section in the interest of national security" (Pub. L. 105-277, Div. A, § 101(h), 112 Stat. 2681-491.) On October 21, 1998, President Clinton issued a "Determination to Waive Requirements Relating to Blocked Property of Terrorist-List States" that waived the requirements of the section. Presidential Determination No. 99-1, 63 F.R. 59201.

In 1996, Congress enacted the Civil Liability for Acts of State Sponsored Terrorism bill (PL 104-208, 110 Stat. 3009-172:

(a) an official, employee, or agent of a foreign state designated as a state sponsor of terrorism designated under section 6(j) of the Export Administration Act of 1979 while acting within the scope of his or her office, employment, or agency shall be liable to a United States national or the national's legal representative for personal injury or death caused by acts of that official, employee, or agent for which the courts of the United States may maintain jurisdiction under section 1605(a)(7) of title 28, United States Code, for money damages which may include economic damages, solatium, pain, and suffering, and punitive damages if the acts were among those described in section 1605(a)(7).

(b) Provisions related to statute of limitations and limitations on discovery that would apply to an action brought under 28 U.S.C. 1605(f) and (g) shall also apply to actions brought under this section.

No action shall be maintained under this [act] if an official, employee, or agent of the United States, while acting within the scope of his or her office, employment, or agency would not be liable for such acts if carried out within the United States.

2. Section 1603(a)(3) denies "foreign state" status to an "agency or instrumentality of a foreign state" that is "a citizen of the United States as defined in section 1332(c) and (d)." Under 28 U.S.C. § 1332(c), a corporation is "deemed to be a citizen of any State by which it has been incorporated and of the State where it has its principal place of business..." Section 1332(d) defines "states" to include "Territories, the District of Columbia, and the Commonwealth of Puerto Rico."

3. Despite the use of the present tense "is" in § 1603(b), courts have held that, in the case of a formerly state-owned business that has been sold to private interests before suit, the time when the acts complained of occurred is the time to determine sovereignty status. General Electric Capital Corp. v. Grossman, 991 F.2d 1376, 1380 (8th Cir. 1993) (disapproving of Ocasek v. Flintkote Co., 796 F. Supp. 362, 365 (N.D. Ill., 1992); Gould, Inc. v. Pechiney Ugine Kuhlmann, 853 F.2d 445 (6th Cir. 1988). Peré v. Nuovo Pigone, Inc., 150 F.3d 477 (5th Cir. 1998), held that the FSIA applies to a company that was state owned when plaintiff was injured, but not when suit was filed. The court dis-

agreed with *Straub*, infra this Note, and indicated that the time of injury, not the time of suit, is the time to determine state ownership. The court did not cite *Callejo*, infra this Note, from its own circuit.

When, however, a bank that was privately owned when deposits were made has been nationalized at the time suit is brought, it has been held that the bank is an "agency or instrumentality of a foreign state." Callejo v. Bancomer, S.A., 764 F.2d 1101, 1106 (5th Cir. 1985). Accord, Straub v. A. P. Green, Inc., 38 F.3d 448 (9th Cir. 1994) (applying the FSIA to a company that was state owned at the time of suit, but not when plaintiff was injured).

If the defendant makes a prima facie showing of its "foreign state" status, the burden shifts to the plaintiff to raise an exception to sovereign immunity under the Act, although the defendant retains the "ultimate burden of persuasion" on the issue. Gerding v. Republic of France, 943 F.2d 521, 526 (4th Cir. 1991), cert. denied, 507 U.S. 1017 (1993).

The defendant whose motion to dismiss because of sovereign immunity is denied, may take an interlocutory appeal. United States v. Moats, 961 F.2d 1198, 1201 (5th Cir. 1992); Compania Mexicana de Aviacion, S.A. v. United States District Court, 859 F.2d 1354, 1356 (9th Cir. 1988).

4. A split of authority has occurred as to what choice-of-law rule governs the law applicable under the FSIA. Liu v. Republic of China, 892 F.2d 1419 (9th Cir. 1989), cert. dism'd, 497 U.S. 1058 (1990) applied a federal choice-of-law rule, modeled on the "most significant relationship" rule of the Restatement (Second) of Conflict of laws. Barkanic v. General Administration of Civil Aviation of People's Republic of China, 923 F.2d 957 (2d Cir. 1991) applied the choice-of-law rule of the state in which the federal court is sitting, finding that this is the meaning of the § 1606 provision that "the foreign state shall be liable in the same manner and to the same extent as a private individual under like circumstances." The court also held that the language in 1606, "the law of the place where the action or omission occurred," applies only to punitive damages and not to the general issue of choice of law. The court distinguished Richards v. United States, 369 U.S. 1 (1962), in which similar language in the Federal Tort Claims Act was held to refer to the whole law of the place of act or omission, including the choice-of-law rules of that place. The court stated that the provision in the Federal Tort Claims Act (28 U.S.C. § 1346(b)) was expressly a choice-of-law rule, unlike the passage in § 1606 of the FSIA.

5. Section 1603(a) flags § 1608, method of service, as an instance in which it makes a difference whether the "foreign state" is, on the one hand, the foreign state or a political subdivision of that state, or on the other hand, an agency or instrumentality of a foreign state, such as a state-owned manufacturing company. There are other instances in which it makes a difference. See §§ 1605(a)(3), 1606, and 1610.

6. Federal circuits have split as to whether "foreign state" in the last sentence of FSIA § 1608(e), requiring service of a default judgment, includes "an agency or instrumentality of a foreign state." Antoine v. Atlas Turner, Inc., 66 F.3d 105 (6th Cir. 1995) holds that it does, despite the exception of § 1608 in § 1603 (a). The court notes that "agency or instrumentality" is expressly referred to in the first sentence of § 1608(e) and the second sentence refers to "such default." The court holds, however, that failure to serve a copy of the default judgment makes the judgment voidable, not void, and remands to determine if the defendant received actual notice. Straub v. A.P. Green, Inc., 38 F.3d 448 (9th Cir. 1994) holds that in this context, "foreign state" does not include an agency or instrumentality.

7. Courts have disagreed on the relationship between the commercial activity exception in 1605(a)(2) and the tortious act or omission exception in 1605(a)(5). Export Group v. Reef Industries, 54 F.3d 1466 (9th Cir. 1995) holds that a claim for interference with contract, although barred under 1605(a)(5)(B), can be brought under 1605(a)(2). The court states that "the commercial activities exception in section 1605(a)(2) encompasses tortious activities for which immunity is retained in section 1605(a)(5)(B) for foreign states when acting in their noncommercial, sovereign capacity." Id. at 1477. Accord, El-Hadad v. United Arab Emirates, 216 F.3d 29 (D.C. Cir. 2000) (holding that a claim based on commercial activity is not subject to the libel and slander exception of 1605(a)(5)(B); Southway v. Central Bank of Nigeria, 198 F.3d 1210 (10th Cir. 1999) (same with regard to misrepresentation and deceit exceptions). Bryks v. Canadian Broadcasting Corp., 906 F. Supp. 204 (S.D.N.Y. 1995) disagrees and holds that the exception for defamation in 1605(a)(5)(B) cannot be avoided by suing "a foreign state for defamation under the 'commercial activity' exception." Id. at 209. Aldy v. Valmet Paper Machinery, 74 F.3d 72 (5th Cir.), cert. denied, 519 U.S. 817 (1996), holds that suit may be brought under the third clause of 1605(a)(2) (commercial activity outside the United States that causes a direct effect in the United States) in a wrongful death product-liability suit. A machine designed and manufactured in Finland caused fatal injuries to workers in Louisiana. The court did not mention 1605(a)(5). Vermeulen v. Renault, U.S.A., Inc., 985 F.2d 1534 (11th Cir.), cert. denied, 508 U.S. 907 (1993), reached the same result in a suit for personal injuries allegedly caused by design and manufacturing defects in an automobile manufactured by a company wholly owned by France.

The Report of the House Judiciary Committee on the FSIA states: "*Noncommercial torts.*—Section 1605(a)(5) is directed primarily at the problem of traffic accidents but is cast in general terms as apply to all tort actions for money damages, not otherwise encompassed by section 1605(a)(2) relating to commercial activities." H.R. Rep. No. 94-1487, 94th Cong. 2d Sess. (1976), U.S.C.C.A.N. 6604, 6619 (italics in original).

Section 1605(a)(5) states that the injury must occur in the United States. Courts have stated that the tortious act or omission must also occur in the United States. Wolf v. Federal Republic of Germany, 95 F.3d 536, 542 (7th Cir. 1996) cert. denied, 520 U.S. 1106 (1997); Frolova v. Union of Soviet Socialist Republics, 761 F.2d 370 (7th Cir. 1985) (dictum, neither act nor injury occurred in the United States); Persinger v. Islamic Republic of Iran, 729 F.2d 835) (D.C. Cir.), cert. denied, 469 U.S. 881 (1984) (dictum, neither occurred in the United States); Olsen by Sheldon v. Government of Mexico, 729 F.2d 641 (9th Cir.), cert. denied, 469 U.S. 917 (1984) (finding jurisdiction when pilot error that caused the crash occurred in the United States, although other acts that contributed to the crash did not occur in the United States). But cf. Letelier v. Republic of Chile, 488 F. Supp. 665, 674 (D.D.C. 1980) (stating, in the context of an act-of-state defense that the fact acts of Chile occurred in that country will not permit it to absolve itself of liability under that doctrine "if actions of its alleged agents [in the United States] resulted in tortious injury in this country").

8. When a company is owned by several foreign countries, their interest may be "pooled" to determine whether a "majority" of the ownership interest is in a foreign state. In re Air Crash Disaster Near Roselawn, supra Note 1; Mangattu v. M/V Ibn Hayyan, 35 F.3d 205 (5th Cir. 1994). Most courts have held that the ownership interest of a foreign state in a subsidiary can be "tiered" through state ownership of the parent company. In re Air Crash Disaster Near Roselawn, supra Note 1 (holding that the subsidiary is "an agency or instrumentality of a foreign state"); Corporacion Mexicana de

Servicios Maritimos, S.A. de C.V. v. M/T Respect, 89 F.3d 650 (9th Cir. 1996) (holding that the subsidiary is an "organ" of the foreign state). Linton v. Airbus Industrie, 934 S.W.2d 754 (Tex. App.—Houston [14th Dist.] 1996), writ of error denied, cert. denied, 525 U.S. 1145 (1999), held that a court can pool and tier to determine sovereign ownership but that it cannot tier through a company that is not majority owned by a foreign state. But see Gates v. Victor Fine Foods, 54 F.3d 1457 (9th Cir.), cert. denied, 516 U.S. 869 (1995) (disallowing tiering on ground that the subsidiary is not "an agency or instrumentality of a foreign state").

Federal Insurance Co. v. Richard I. Rubin & Co., 12 F.3d 1270 (3rd Cir.), cert. denied, 511 U.S. 1107 (1994), held that the acts of the subsidiary in the United States could not be attributed to the foreign parents for the purpose of exercising jurisdiction over the parents under the commercial activity exception, 1605(a)(2).

9. Is an individual entitled to immunity under the FSIA? Foreign heads of state (see Lafontant v. Aristide, 844 F. Supp. 128 (E.D.N.Y. 1994) (holding President of Haiti immune from suit under Alien Tort Claims Act (ATCA) or Torture Victim Protection Act (TVPA), both Acts are the focus of Chapter 7) and, to a lesser extent, diplomatic and consular agents of foreign governments (see Restatement of Foreign Relations Law (Third) §§ 464 (stating immunity of foreign diplomatic agents), 465 (stating immunity of foreign consular personnel)), are immune from civil suit.

United States v. Noriega, 117 F.3d 1206 (11th Cir. 1997), cert. denied, 523 U.S. 1060 (1998), denies immunity to Manuel Noriega for drug-related offenses committed while he was head of state in Panama. The court states: "The Executive Branch has not merely refrained from taking a position on [immunity]; to the contrary, by pursuing Noriega's capture and this prosecution, the Executive Branch has manifested its clear sentiment that Noriega should be denied head-of-state immunity." Id. at 1212. The court also noted that "Noriega never served as the constitutional leader of Panama, that Panama has not sought immunity for Noriega, and that the charged acts relate to Noriega's private pursuit of personal enrichment...." Id.

Regina v. Bow Street Metropolitan Stipendiary Magistrate, Ex parte Pinochet Ugarte, 2 W.L.R. 827 (House of Lords, 1999), denied immunity from arrest and extradition to General Pinochet, the former President of Chile, for the crimes of torture and conspiracy to commit torture, committed while he was head of state. Spain had requested Pinochet's extradition to prosecute him for his treatment of Spanish citizens in Chile. The Lords ruled that the crimes were extraditable offenses under the UK Extradition Act so long as they occurred after September 29, 1988, when torture by a public official performing official duties became a crime in the UK. The court ruled that Pinochet could not invoke as "official acts" under the UK State Immunity Act those acts such as torture that are regarded as criminal under international law. On March 2, 2000, British Home Secretary of State Jack Straw released Pinochet from house arrest for reasons of the general's mental and physical disabilities. Pinochet returned to Chile. On August 8, 2000, the Chilean Supreme Court affirmed the order of the Santiago Appeals Court that removed the immunity from prosecution that Pinochet had as a "senator for life."

Are officials of foreign governments who are not heads of state entitled to cloak themselves with the sovereign immunity of their states? The FSIA defines a "foreign state" to include "a political subdivision of a foreign state or an agency or instrumentality of a foreign state." 1603(a). "Agency or instrumentality" is defined as "any entity (1) which is a separate legal person, corporate or otherwise, and (2) which is an organ of a foreign state or political subdivision thereof or a majority of whose shares or other ownership interest is owned by a foreign state or political subdivision thereof." § 1603(b). This language does not appear to be applicable to an individual. In Argentine Republic v. Amerada Hess Shipping Corp., 488 U.S. 428 (1989), which held that the FSIA barred suit against Argentina, the Court remarked that Filartiga v. Pena-Irala, 630 F.2d 876 (2d Cir. 1980) (infra page 403), which permitted suit under the ATCA, was a suit "against a Paraguayan police official for torture; the Paraguayan Government was not joined as a defendant." 488 U.S. at 436 n.4. This observation suggests that the Court does not consider the FSIA applicable to individuals. See also H.Rep. No. 367, 102d Cong., 1st Sess. pt. 1, at 5 (stating that "[w]hile sovereign immunity would not generally be an available defense, nothing in the TVPA overrides the doctrines of diplomatic and head of state immunity"); Jeffrey M. Blum & Ralph G. Steinhardt, 22 Harv. Int'l L.J. 53, 107 (1981) (stating that "[t]here is no indication in the legislative history of the FSIA that individuals would be entitled to sovereign immunity"); Tom Lininger, Overcoming Immunity Defenses to Human Rights Suits in U.S. Courts, 7 Harv. Hum. Rts. J., 177, 186 (1994) (stating that the language of the FSIA "does not contemplate the inclusion of human beings under the rubric of 'foreign state'").

In Chuidian v. Philippine National Bank, 912 F.2d 1095 (9th Cir. 1990), however, the Ninth Circuit affirmed dismissal of a suit against a member of a Philippine presidential commission. The court held that the defendant was entitled to sovereign immunity for acts in his capacity as a member of the commission, finding that the FSIA is "ambiguous as to its extension to individual foreign officials." Id. at 1101. The opinion stated that the FSIA should cover individuals operating in their official capacity, because otherwise it would omit the common law immunity of officials that existed before the Act took effect. See also El-Fadl v. Central Bank of Jordan, 75 F.3d 668 (D.C. Cir. 1996) (holding that "[a]n individual can qualify as an 'agency or instrumentality of a foreign state' and citing *Chuidian* with approval); Jungquist v. Sheikh Sultan Bin Khalifa Al Nahyan, 115 F.3d 1020, 1027 (D.C. Cir. 1997) (holding that a medical attaché at the United Arab Emirates office in D.C. and his employee were entitled to immunity under the FSIA when they were sued for terminating payments for medical treatment in the U.S. of a U.S. citizen injured in Abu Dhabi and stating that "[i]ndividuals acting in their official capacities are considered 'agencies or instrumentalities of a foreign state'");.cf. Estate of Marcos v. Hilao, 25 F.3d 1467 (9th Cir. 1994), cert. denied, 513 U.S. 1126 (1995) (holding that a foreign official accused of ordering acts of torture and execution is not entitled to immunity under the FSIA because the acts were outside the scope of his official authority).

Does *Chuidian* misunderstand the pre-FSIA law concerning immunity of foreign officials? The Second Restatement of Foreign Relations states that: "The immunity of a foreign state...extends to...(b) its head of state and any person designated by him as a member of his official party[and] (f) any other public minister, official, or agent of the state with respect to acts performed in his official capacity *if the effect of exercising jurisdiction would be to enforce a rule of law against the state.* Restatement (Second) of the Foreign Relations Law of the United States § 66 (1962) (emphasis added). The Restatement further provides that: "Public ministers, officials, or agents of a state do not have immunity from personal liability even for acts carried out in their official capacity, unless the effect of exercising jurisdiction would be to enforce a rule against the foreign state or unless they have one of the specialized immunities referred to above [diplomatic and consular officials, and representatives to international organizations]. Id. cmt. b. As an illustration of when permitting suit against a foreign official "would be to enforce a rule against the foreign state," the Restatement provides the following: "X, an official of the defense ministry of state A, enters into a contract in state B with Y for the purchase of supplies for the armed forces of A. A disagreement arises under the contract and Y brings suit in B against X as an individual, seeking to compel him to apply certain funds of A in his possession to satisfy obligations of A under the contract. X is entitled to the immunity of A." Id. illus. 2.

Thus, before the FSIA, foreign officials could cloak themselves in the immunity of their state only if the suit would have the effect of enforcing liability against the state itself.

10. Transaero Inc. v. La Fuerza Aerea Boliviana, 30 F.3d 148 (D.C. Cir. 1994), cert. denied, 513 U.S. 1150 (1995), held that the Bolivian Air Force is a "foreign state or political subdivision of a foreign state" that must be served under 1608(a), rather than an "agency or instrumentality" of a foreign state that can be served under 1608(b).

11. Kelly v. Syria Shell Petroleum Development B.V., 213 F.3d 841 (5th Cir. 2000), holds that even if a foreign sovereign did not have a majority interest in the defendant company, the company is entitled to immunity under the FSIA because the company is an "organ of a foreign state." The state created the company for a national purpose and controlled its activities.

Kelly also notes "the well-established principle that, although a party claiming FSIA immunity retains the ultimate burden of persuasion on immunity, it need only present a prima facie case that it is a foreign state; and if it does, the burden shifts to the party opposing immunity to present evidence that one of the exceptions to immunity applies." Id. at 847. Although the plaintiff is entitled to discovery on the jurisdictional facts, "discovery should be ordered circumspectly and only to verify allegations of specific facts crucial to an immunity determinations." Arriba Ltd. v. Petroleos Mexicanos, 962 F.2d 528, 534 (5th Cir.), cert. denied, 506 U.S. 956 (1992).See Steven R. Swanson, Jurisdictional Discovery under the Foreign Sovereign Immunities Act, .13 Emory Int'l L. Rev. 445 (1999). If the trial court denies the defendant's sovereign immunity defense, the defendant can appeal immediately. See Transatlantic Shiffahrtskontor GmbH v. Shanghai Foreign Trade Corp. 204 F.3d 384 (2d Cir. 2000); Byrd v. Corporacion Forestal y Industrial de Olancho, 182 F.3d 380 (5th Cir. 1999).

12. 11 U.S.C. § 106 provides that "sovereign immunity is abrogated as to a governmental unit" for claims under numerous sections of the Bankruptcy Act. See In re Tuli, 172 F.3d 707 (9th Cir. 1999) (holding that Iraq did not have immunity in a proceeding under § 542 of the Bankruptcy Act to recover property for the bankruptcy estate).

13. For comparative treatment of sovereign immunity in various countries, see Joan E. Donoghue, The Public Face of Private International Law: Prospects for a Convention on Foreign Sovereign Immunity, 57 Law & Contemp. Probs. 305 (Summer 1994).

Verlinden B.V. v. Central Bank of Nigeria.
461 U.S. 480 (1983)

Chief Justice BURGER delivered the opinion of the Court.

We granted certiorari to consider whether the Foreign Sovereign Immunities Act of 1976, by authorizing a foreign plaintiff to sue a foreign state in a United States District Court on a non-federal cause of action, violates Article III of the Constitution.

I

On April 21, 1975, the Federal Republic of Nigeria and petitioner Verlinden B.V., a Dutch corporation with its principal offices in Amsterdam, The Netherlands, entered into a contract providing for the purchase of 240,000 metric tons of cement by Nigeria. The parties agreed that the contract would be governed by the laws of the Netherlands and that disputes would be resolved by arbitration before the International Chamber of Commerce, Paris, France.

The contract provided that the Nigerian government was to establish an irrevocable, confirmed letter of credit for the total purchase price through Slavenburg's Bank in Amsterdam. According to petitioner's amended complaint, however, respondent Central Bank of Nigeria, an instrumentality of Nigeria, improperly established an unconfirmed letter of credit payable through Morgan Guaranty Trust Company in New York. [Nigeria defaulted, Morgan refused to pay, and Verlinden sued.]

* * *

The District Court first held that a federal court may exercise subject matter jurisdiction over a suit brought by a foreign corporation against a foreign sovereign. Although the legislative history of the Foreign Sovereign Immunities Act does not clearly reveal whether Congress intended the Act to extend to actions brought by foreign plaintiffs, Judge Weinfeld reasoned that the language of the Act is "broad and embracing. It confers jurisdiction over 'any nonjury civil action' against a foreign state." 488 F.Supp. 1284, 1292 (S.D.N.Y.1980). Moreover, in the District Court's view, allowing all actions against foreign sovereigns, including those initiated by foreign plaintiffs, to be brought in federal court was necessary to effectuate "the Congressional purpose of concentrating litigation against sovereign states in the federal courts in order to aid the development of a uniform body of federal law governing assertions of sovereign immunity." Ibid. The District Court also held that Article III subject matter jurisdiction extends to suits by foreign corporations against foreign sovereigns, stating: "[The Act] imposes a single, federal standard to be applied uniformly by both state and federal courts hearing claims brought against foreign states. In consequence, even though the plaintiff's claim is one grounded upon common law, the case is one that 'arises under' a federal law because the complaint compels the application of the uniform federal standard governing assertions of sovereign immunity. In short, the Immunities Act injects an essential federal element into all suits brought against foreign states." Ibid.

The District Court nevertheless dismissed the complaint, holding that a foreign instrumentality is entitled to sovereign immunity unless one of the exceptions specified in the Act applies. After carefully considering each of the exceptions upon which petitioner relied, the District Court concluded that none applied, and accordingly dismissed the action.[5]

---

5. The District Court dismissed "for lack of personal jurisdiction." Under the Act, however, both statutory subject matter jurisdiction (otherwise known as "competence") and personal jurisdiction turn on application of the substantive provisions of the Act. Under § 1330(a), federal district courts are provided subject matter jurisdiction if a foreign state is "not entitled to immunity either under sections 1605-1607...or under any applicable international agreement;" § 1330(b) provides personal jurisdiction wherever subject matter jurisdiction exists under subsection (a) and service of process has been made under § 1608 of the Act. Thus, if none of the exceptions to sovereign immunity set forth in the Act applies, the District Court lacks both statutory subject matter jurisdiction and personal jurisdiction. The District Court's conclusion that none of the exceptions to the Act applied therefore signified an absence of both competence and personal jurisdiction.

The Court of Appeals for the Second Circuit affirmed, but on different grounds. The court agreed with the District Court that the Act was properly construed to permit actions brought by foreign plaintiffs. The court held, however, that the Act exceeded the scope of Article III of the Constitution. In the view of the Court of Appeals, neither the diversity clause[6] nor the "arising under" clause[7] of Article III is broad enough to support jurisdiction over actions by foreign plaintiffs against foreign sovereigns; accordingly it concluded that Congress was without power to grant federal courts jurisdiction in this case, and affirmed the District Court's dismissal of the action.

We granted certiorari, and we reverse and remand.

II

For more than a century and a half, the United States generally granted foreign sovereigns complete immunity from suit in the courts of this country. In *The Schooner Exchange v. M'Faddon*, 7 Cranch 116 (1812), Chief Justice Marshall concluded that, while the jurisdiction of a nation within its own territory "is susceptible of no limitation not imposed by itself," id., at 136, the United States had impliedly waived jurisdiction over certain activities of foreign sovereigns. Although the narrow holding of *The Schooner Exchange* was only that the courts of the United States lack jurisdiction over an armed ship of a foreign state found in our port, that opinion came to be regarded as extending virtually absolute immunity to foreign sovereigns.

As *The Schooner Exchange* made clear, however, foreign sovereign immunity is a matter of grace and comity on the part of the United States, and not a restriction imposed by the Constitution. Accordingly, this Court consistently has deferred to the decisions of the political branches—in particular, those of the Executive Branch—on whether to take jurisdiction over actions against foreign sovereigns and their instrumentalities.

Until 1952, the State Department ordinarily requested immunity in all actions against friendly foreign sovereigns. But in the so-called Tate Letter,[9] the State Department announced its adoption of the "restrictive" theory of foreign sovereign immunity. Under this theory, immunity is confined to suits involving the foreign sovereign's public acts, and does not extend to cases arising out of a foreign state's strictly commercial acts.

The restrictive theory was not initially enacted into law, however, and its application proved troublesome. As in the past, initial responsibility for deciding questions of sovereign immunity fell primarily upon the Executive acting through the State Department, and the courts abided by "suggestions of immunity" from the State Department. As a consequence, foreign nations often placed diplomatic pressure on the State Department in seeking immunity. On occasion, political considerations led to suggestions of immunity in cases where immunity would not have been available under the restrictive theory.

---

6. The foreign diversity clause provides that the judicial power extends "to Controversies...between a State, or the Citizens thereof, and foreign States, Citizens or Subjects." U.S. Const., Art. III, §2, cl. 1.

7. The so-called "arising under" clause provides: "The judicial Power [of the United States] shall extend to all Cases...arising under this Constitution, the Laws of the United States, and Treaties made, or which shall be made, under their Authority." U.S. Const., Art. III, §2, cl. 1.

9. Letter from Jack B. Tate, Acting Legal Adviser, Department of State, to Acting Attorney General Philip B. Perlman (May 19, 1952), reprinted in 26 Dep't of State Bull. 984-985 (1952), and in *Alfred Dunhill of London, Inc. v. Cuba*, 425 U.S. 682, 711 (1976) (Appendix 2 to opinion of WHITE, J.).

An additional complication was posed by the fact that foreign nations did not always make requests to the State Department. In such cases, the responsibility fell to the courts to determine whether sovereign immunity existed, generally by reference to prior State Department decisions. Thus, sovereign immunity determinations were made in two different branches, subject to a variety of factors, sometimes including diplomatic considerations. Not surprisingly, the governing standards were neither clear nor uniformly applied.

In 1976, Congress passed the Foreign Sovereign Immunities Act in order to free the Government from the case-by-case diplomatic pressures, to clarify the governing standards, and to "assur[e] litigants that...decisions are made on purely legal grounds and under procedures that insure due process," H.R.Rep. No. 94-1487, p. 7 (1976), reprinted in [1976] U.S.Code Cong. & Ad.News 6604. To accomplish these objectives, the Act contains a comprehensive set of legal standards governing claims of immunity in every civil action against a foreign state or its political subdivisions, agencies or instrumentalities.

For the most part, the Act codifies, as a matter of federal law, the restrictive theory of sovereign immunity. A foreign state is normally immune from the jurisdiction of federal and state courts, 28 U.S.C. § 1604, subject to a set of exceptions specified in §§ 1605 and 1607. Those exceptions include actions in which the foreign state has explicitly or impliedly waived its immunity, § 1605(a)(1), and actions based upon commercial activities of the foreign sovereign carried on in the United States or causing a direct effect in the United States, § 1605(a)(2). When one of these or the other specified exceptions applies, "the foreign state shall be liable in the same manner and to the same extent as a private individual under like circumstances," 28 U.S.C. § 1606.

The Act expressly provides that its standards control in "the courts of the United States and of the States," id. § 1604, and thus clearly contemplates that such suits may be brought in either federal or state courts. However, "[i]n view of the potential sensitivity of actions against foreign states and the importance of developing a uniform body of law in this area," H.R.Rep. No. 94-1487, at 32, the Act guarantees foreign states the right to remove any civil action from a state court to a federal court, id. § 1441(d). The Act also provides that any claim permitted under the Act may be brought from the outset in federal court, id. § 1330(a). If one of the specified exceptions to sovereign immunity applies, a federal district court may exercise subject matter jurisdiction under § 1330(a); but if the claim does not fall within one of the exceptions, federal courts lack subject matter jurisdiction. In such a case, the foreign state is also ensured immunity from the jurisdiction of state courts by § 1604.

III

The District Court and the Court of Appeals both held that the Foreign Sovereign Immunities Act purports to allow a foreign plaintiff to sue a foreign sovereign in the courts of the United States, provided the substantive requirements of the Act are satisfied. We agree.

On its face, the language of the statute is unambiguous. The statute grants jurisdiction over "any non-jury civil action against a foreign state...with respect to which the foreign state is not entitled to immunity," 28 U.S.C. § 1330(a). The Act contains no indication of any limitation based on the citizenship of the plaintiff.

The legislative history is less clear in this regard. The House Report recites that the Act would provide jurisdiction for "*any* claim with respect to which the foreign state is not entitled to immunity under sections 1605-1607," H.R.Rep. No. 94-1487, at 13 (emphasis added), and also states that its purpose was "to provide when and how *parties* can maintain a lawsuit against a foreign state or its entities," id., at p. 6 (emphasis added). At another point, however, the Report refers to the growing number of disputes between "American citizens" and foreign states, id., at 6-7, and expresses the desire to ensure "*our citizens*...access to the courts," id., at 6 (emphasis added).

Notwithstanding this reference to "our citizens," we conclude that, when considered as a whole, the legislative history reveals an intent not to limit jurisdiction under the Act to actions brought by American citizens. Congress was aware of concern that "our courts [might be] turned into small 'international courts of claims[,]'...open...to all comers to litigate any dispute which any private party may have with a foreign state anywhere in the world." Testimony of Bruno A. Ristau, Hearings on H.R. 11315, at 31. As the language of the statute reveals, Congress protected against this danger not by restricting the class of potential plaintiffs, but rather by enacting substantive provisions requiring some form of substantial contact with the United States. See 28 U.S.C. § 1605.[15] If an action satisfies the substantive standards of the Act, it may be brought in federal court regardless of the citizenship of the plaintiff.

IV

We now turn to the core question presented by this case: whether Congress exceeded the scope of Article III of the Constitution by granting federal courts subject matter jurisdiction over certain civil actions by foreign plaintiffs against foreign sovereigns where the rule of decision may be provided by state law.

* * *

Congress, pursuant to its unquestioned Article I powers, has enacted a broad statutory framework governing assertions of foreign sovereign immunity. In so doing, Congress deliberately sought to channel cases against foreign sovereigns away from the state courts and into federal courts, thereby reducing the potential for a multiplicity of conflicting results among the courts of the 50 states. The resulting jurisdictional grant is within the bounds of Article III, since every action against a foreign sovereign necessarily involves application of a body of substantive federal law, and accordingly "arises under" federal law, within the meaning of Article III.

V

A conclusion that the grant of jurisdiction in the Foreign Sovereign Immunities Act is consistent with the Constitution does not end the case. An action must not only satisfy Article III but must also be supported by a statutory grant of subject matter jurisdiction. As we have made clear, deciding whether statutory subject matter jurisdiction exists under the Foreign Sovereign Immunities Act entails an application of the substantive terms of the Act to determine whether one of the specified exceptions to immunity applies.

---

15. Section 1605(a)(1), which provides that sovereign immunity shall not apply if waived, may be seen as an exception to the normal pattern of the Act, which generally requires some form of contact with the United States. We need not decide whether, by waiving its immunity, a foreign state could consent to suit based on activities wholly unrelated to the United States. The Act does not appear to affect the traditional doctrine of forum non conveniens. See generally Kane, *Suing Foreign Sovereigns: A Procedural Compass*, 34 Stanford L.Rev. 385, 411-412 (1982); Note, *Suits by Foreigners Against Foreign States in United States Courts: A Selective Expansion of Jurisdiction*, 90 Yale L.J. 1861, 1871-1873 (1981).

In the present case, the District Court, after satisfying itself as to the constitutionality of the Act, held that the present action does not fall within any specified exception. The Court of Appeals, reaching a contrary conclusion as to jurisdiction under the Constitution, did not find it necessary to address this statutory question. Accordingly, on remand the Court of Appeals must consider whether jurisdiction exists under the Act itself. If the Court of Appeals agrees with the District Court on that issue, the case will be at an end. If, on the other hand, the Court of Appeals concludes that jurisdiction does exist under the statute, the action may then be remanded to the District Court for further proceedings.

It is so ordered.

Notes

1. The grounds argued below for jurisdiction under the Foreign Sovereign Immunities Act were the commercial activity provision § 1605(a)(2) in the light of the letter of credit payable by Morgan bank, and the waiver provision, § 1605(a)(1), in the light of Nigeria's agreement that the contract was governed by the law of the Netherlands and that disputes would be resolved by arbitration before the International Chamber of Commerce in Paris. There were no further proceedings. If the only applicable exception under the FSIA were the waiver provision of § 1605(a)(1), would application of the Act violate Article III of the Constitution?

2. The opinion provides useful background on the FSIA. Until the 20th century, states were considered immune from jurisdiction in the courts of another state. As states began to engage more in commercial activities, this changed. Even before World War II, Belgium and Italy had adopted a "restrictive" theory denying immunity in cases arising out of commercial transactions or the operation of state-owned vessels for trade.

Section 2: Commercial or Governmental

Republic of Argentina v. Weltover, Inc.
504 U.S. 607 (1992)

[Argentina issued bonds, called "Bonods," to foreign creditors of Argentine businesses. The Bonods, which refinanced an existing debt, provided for payment of principal and interest in United States dollars in either London, Frankfurt, or New York, at the election of the creditor. When the Bonods matured, Argentina unilaterally extended the time for payment. Two Panamanian corporations and a Swiss bank, which held $1.3 million of Bonods, refused to accept the rescheduling and insisted on full payment in New York. Argentina did not pay and the creditors brought a breach-of-contract action in New York federal court under the Foreign Sovereign Immunities Act. The Supreme Court of the United States affirmed the lower courts' denial of Argentina's motion to dismiss for lack of subject-matter jurisdiction, lack of personal jurisdiction, and forum non conveniens.]

Justice SCALIA delivered the opinion of the Court.

This case requires us to decide whether the Republic of Argentina's default on certain bonds issued as part of a plan to stabilize its currency was an act taken "in connection with a commercial activity" that had a "direct effect in the United States" so as to subject Argentina to suit in an American court under the Foreign Sovereign Immunities Act of 1976, 28 U.S.C. § 1602 et seq.

* * *

II

* * *

In the proceedings below, respondents relied only on the third clause of § 1605(a)(2) to establish jurisdiction, and our analysis is therefore limited to considering whether this lawsuit is (1) "based...upon an act outside the territory of the United States"; (2) that was taken "in connection with a commercial activity" of Argentina outside this country; and (3) that "cause[d] a direct effect in the United States." * * * The dispute pertains to whether the unilateral refinancing of the Bonods was taken "in connection with a commercial activity" of Argentina, and whether it had a "direct effect in the United States." We address these issues in turn.

A

Respondents and their amicus, the United States, contend that Argentina's issuance of, and continued liability under, the Bonods constitute a "commercial activity" and that the extension of the payment schedules was taken "in connection with" that activity. The latter point is obvious enough, and Argentina does not contest it; the key question is whether the activity is "commercial" under the FSIA.

The FSIA defines "commercial activity" to mean:

> [E]ither a regular course of commercial conduct or a particular commercial transaction or act. The commercial character of an activity shall be determined by reference to the nature of the course of conduct or particular transaction or act, rather than by reference to its purpose. 28 U.S.C. § 1603(d).

This definition, however, leaves the critical term "commercial" largely undefined: The first sentence simply establishes that the commercial nature of an activity does not depend upon whether it is a single act or a regular course of conduct; and the second sentence merely specifies what element of the conduct determines commerciality (i.e., nature rather than purpose), but still without saying what "commercial" means. * * *

[W]e conclude that when a foreign government acts, not as regulator of a market, but in the manner of a private player within it, the foreign sovereign's actions are "commercial" within the meaning of the FSIA. Moreover, because the Act provides that the commercial character of an act is to be determined by reference to its "nature" rather than its "purpose," 28 U.S.C. § 1603(d), the question is not whether the foreign government is acting with a profit motive or instead with the aim of fulfilling uniquely sovereign objectives. Rather, the issue is whether the particular actions that the foreign state performs (whatever the motive behind them) are the type of actions by which a private party engages in "trade and traffic or commerce," Black's Law Dictionary 270 (6th ed. 1990). Thus, a foreign government's issuance of regulations limiting foreign currency exchange is a sovereign activity, because such authoritative control of commerce cannot be exercised by a private party; whereas a contract to buy army boots or even bullets is a "commercial" activity, because private companies can similarly use sales contracts to acquire goods.

The commercial character of the Bonods is confirmed by the fact that they are in almost all respects garden-variety debt instruments: They may be held by private parties; they are negotiable and may be traded on the international market (except in Argentina); and they promise a future stream of cash income. * * *

Argentina contends that, although the FSIA bars consideration of "purpose," a court must nonetheless fully consider the context of a transaction in order to determine whether it is "commercial." Accordingly, Argentina claims that the Court of Appeals erred by defining the relevant conduct in what Argentina considers an overly generalized, acontextual manner and by essentially adopting a per se rule that all "issuance of debt instruments" is "commercial." * * * We have no occasion to consider such a per se rule, because it seems to us that even in full context, there is nothing about the issuance of these Bonods (except perhaps its purpose) that is not analogous to a private commercial transaction.

Argentina points to the fact that the transactions in which the Bonods were issued did not have the ordinary commercial consequence of raising capital or financing acquisitions. Assuming for the sake of argument that this is not an example of judging the commerciality of a transaction by its purpose, the ready answer is that private parties regularly issue bonds, not just to raise capital or to finance purchases, but also to refinance debt. That is what Argentina did here:* * *

Argentina argues that the Bonods differ from ordinary debt instruments in that they "were created by the Argentine Government to fulfill its obligations under a foreign exchange program designed to address a domestic credit crisis, and as a component of a program designed to control that nation's critical shortage of foreign exchange." * * * We think this line of argument is squarely foreclosed by the language of the FSIA. However difficult it may be in some cases to separate "purpose" (i.e., the reason why the foreign state engages in the activity) from "nature" (i.e., the outward form of the conduct that the foreign state performs or agrees to perform), the statute unmistakably commands that to be done, 28 U.S.C. § 1603(d). * * *

B

The remaining question is whether Argentina's unilateral rescheduling of the Bonods had a "direct effect" in the United States, 28 U.S.C. § 1605(a)(2). In addressing this issue, the Court of Appeals rejected the suggestion in the legislative history of the FSIA that an effect is not "direct" unless it is both "substantial" and "foreseeable." That suggestion is found in the House Report, which states that conduct covered by the third clause of § 1605(a)(2) would be subject to the jurisdiction of American courts "consistent with principles set forth in section 18, Restatement of the Law, Second, Foreign Relations Law of the United States (1965)." Section 18 states that American laws are not given extraterritorial application except with respect to conduct that has, as a "direct and foreseeable result," a "substantial" effect within the United States. Since this obviously deals with jurisdiction to legislate rather than jurisdiction to adjudicate, this passage of the House Report has been charitably described as "a bit of a non sequitur," Texas Trading & Milling Corp. v. Federal Republic of Nigeria, 647 F.2d 300, 311 (CA2 1981), cert. denied, 454 U.S. 1148 (1982). Of course the generally applicable principle de minimis non curat lex ensures that jurisdiction may not be predicated on purely trivial effects in the United States. But we reject the suggestion that § 1605(a)(2) contains any unexpressed requirement of "substantiality" or "foreseeability." As the Court of Appeals recognized, an effect is "direct" if it follows "as an immediate consequence of the defendant's...activity." * * *

We * * * have little difficulty concluding that Argentina's unilateral rescheduling of the maturity dates on the Bonods had a "direct effect" in the United States. Respondents had designated their accounts in New York as the place of payment, and Argentina made some interest payments into those accounts before announcing that it was rescheduling the payments. Because New York was thus the place of performance for Argentina's ultimate contractual obligations, the rescheduling of those obligations necessarily had a "direct effect" in the United States: Money that was supposed to have been delivered to a New York bank for deposit was not forthcoming. We reject Argentina's suggestion that the "direct effect" requirement cannot be satisfied where the plaintiffs are all foreign corporations with no other connections to the United States. We expressly stated in *Verlinden* [supra page xxx] that the FSIA permits "a foreign plaintiff to sue a foreign sovereign in the courts of the United States, provided the substantive requirements of the Act are satisfied."

Finally, Argentina argues that a finding of jurisdiction in this case would violate the Due Process Clause of the Fifth Amendment, and that, in order to avoid this difficulty, we must construe the "direct effect" requirement as embodying the "minimum contacts" test of International Shoe Co. v. Washington, 326 U.S. 310 (1945). Assuming, without deciding, that a foreign state is a "person" for purposes of the Due Process Clause, cf. South Carolina v. Katzenbach, 383 U.S. 301, 323- 324, (1966) (States of the Union are not "persons" for purposes of the Due Process Clause), we find that Argentina possessed "minimum contacts" that would satisfy the constitutional test. By issuing negotiable debt instruments denominated in United States dollars and payable in New York and by appointing a financial agent in that city, Argentina "'purposefully avail[ed] itself of the privilege of conducting activities within the [United States].'" Burger King Corp. v. Rudzewicz, 471 U.S. 462, 475, (1985), quoting Hanson v. Denckla, 357 U.S. 235, 253, (1958).

We conclude that Argentina's issuance of the Bonods was a "commercial activity" under the FSIA; that its rescheduling of the maturity dates on those instruments was taken in connection with that commercial activity and had a "direct effect" in the United States; and that the District Court therefore properly asserted jurisdiction, under the FSIA, over the breach-of-contract claim based on that rescheduling. Accordingly, the judgment of the Court of Appeals is

Affirmed.

Notes

1. The principal case holds that Argentina has sufficient "minimum contacts" with the United States to make exercise of personal jurisdiction over that country under the FSIA consistent with the Due Process Clause of the Fifth Amendment. For the argument that a similar objection may prevent jurisdiction over state sponsors of terrorism under FSIA § 1605(a)(7), see Keith E. Sealing, "State Sponsors of Terrorism" Are Entitled to Due Process Too: The Amended Sovereign Immunities Act is Unconstitutional, 15 Am. U. Int'l L. Rev. 395, 397-98 (2000) (stating that "giving the court personal jurisdiction over a foreign sovereign simply because the Executive Branch has concluded that it is a 'state sponsor of terrorism' or because an offshore terrorist act has some 'effect' in the United States would violate the Due Process Clause of the Fifth Amendment

absent the performance of traditional 'minimum contacts' analysis under both the specific and general personal jurisdiction tests").

For comment on *Weltover*, see Georges R. Delaume, The Foreign Sovereign Immunities Act and Public Debt Litigation: Some Fifteen Years Later, 88 Am. J. Int'l L. 257 (1994).

2. Holland v. Lampden-Wolfe, [2000] 1 W.L.R. 1573 (House of Lords, 2000), affirmed dismissal of a libel complaint brought by a civilian instructor at a United States airforce base in England. A memorandum from the instructor's supervisor to the program's director adversely criticized the instructor's performance. The United States invoked sovereign immunity on behalf of the supervisor. The United Kingdom State Immunity Act 1978 codified the restrictive theory of sovereign immunity and excepted from its coverage "anything done by or in relation to the armed forces of a state whilst present in the United Kingdom." The Court held that this provision excluded coverage by the State Immunity Act and left liability to be determined by common law. At common law, the issue was whether the supervisor's communication concerning the instructor constituted commercial or governmental activity. Lord Hope of Craighead wrote:

> [I]t is the nature of the act that determines whether it is to be characterised as iure imperii [governmental] or iure gestionis [commercial]. The process of characterisation requires that the act must be considered in its context.
>
> In the present case the context is all important. The overall context was that of the provision of educational services to military personnel and their families stationed on a U.S. base overseas. The maintenance of the base itself was plainly a sovereign activity. As Hoffmann L.J. (now Lord Hoffmann) said in Littrell v. United States of America (No.2) [1995] 1 W.L.R. 82, 95A-B, this looks about as imperial an activity as could be imagined. But that is not enough to determine the issue. At first sight, the writing of a memorandum by a civilian educational services officer in relation to an educational programme provided by civilian staff employed by a university seems far removed from the kind of act that would ordinarily be characterised as something done iure imperii. But regard must be had to the place where the programme was being provided and to the persons by whom it was being provided and who it was designed to benefit—where did it happen and whom did it involve? The provision of the programme on the base * * * was designed to serve the needs of U.S. personnel on the base, and it was provided by U.S. citizens who were working there on behalf of a U.S. university. The whole activity was designed as part of the process of maintaining forces and associated civilians on the base by U.S. personnel to serve the needs of the U.S. military authorities. The memorandum was written on the base in response to complaints which are alleged to have been made by U.S. servicemen about the behaviour of the appellant, who is also a U.S. citizen, while she was working there. On these facts the acts of the respondent seem to me to fall well within the area of sovereign activity.

3. For other cases dealing with whether breach of contract causes a "direct effect" in the United States, see United World Trade Inc. v. Mangyshlakneft Oil Production Assoc., 33 F.3d 1232 (10th Cir. 1994), cert. denied, 513 U.S. 1112 (1995) (holding that loss of profits to Colorado corporation did not have a direct effect in the United States although contract required payment "in U.S. dollars"); Goodman Holdings v. Rafidain Bank, 26 F.3d 1143 (D.C. Cir. 1994), cert. denied, 513 U.S. 1079 (1995) (holding that Iraqi bank's failure to pay Irish companies on letters of credit did not have a "direct ef-

fect" in the United States because there was no contractual requirement that the payment be made from United States accounts). See also Princz v. Federal Republic of Germany, 26 F.3d 1166 (D.C. Cir. 1994) cert. denied, 513 U.S. 1121 (1995) (holding that Germany's leasing of prisoners as slave labor during World War II did not have a direct effect in the United States).

4. Stephens v. National Distillers & Chem. Corp., 69 F.3d 1226 (2d Cir. 1996) holds that requiring a pre-answer bond from a foreign sovereign insurance company is an "attachment" within the meaning of FSIA § 1609 that is not authorized by § 1610. The court also holds that the McCarran-Ferguson Act provision, 15 U.S.C. § 1012(b), exempting state regulation of insurance from invalidation by acts of Congress, did not prevent application of the FSIA to the state bond requirement.

Weston Compagnie de Finance et d'Investissement, S.A. v. La Republica del Ecuador, 823 F. Supp. 1106 (S.D.N.Y. 1993), held that the waiver exception of 1610(d)(1) referring to pre-judgment attachment, did not apply to a foreign central bank. 1611(b)(1), which does not refer to waiver of pre-judgment attachment, covers Central banks. Therefore the bank's waiver of pre-judgment attachment was not effective.

Saudi Arabia v. Nelson
507 U.S. 349 (1993)

Justice SOUTER delivered the opinion of the Court.

The Foreign Sovereign Immunities Act of 1976 entitles foreign states to immunity from the jurisdiction of courts in the United States, subject to certain enumerated exceptions. One is that a foreign state shall not be immune in any case "in which the action is based upon a commercial activity carried on in the United States by the foreign state." § 1605(a)(2). We hold that respondents' action alleging personal injury resulting from unlawful detention and torture by the Saudi Government is not "based upon a commercial activity" within the meaning of the Act, which consequently confers no jurisdiction over respondents' suit.

I

Because this case comes to us on a motion to dismiss the complaint, we assume that we have truthful factual allegations before us, though many of those allegations are subject to dispute. Petitioner Kingdom of Saudi Arabia owns and operates petitioner King Faisal Specialist Hospital in Riyadh, as well as petitioner Royspec Purchasing Services, the Hospital's corporate purchasing agent in the United States. The Hospital Corporation of America, Ltd. (HCA), an independent corporation existing under the laws of the Cayman Islands, recruits Americans for employment at the Hospital under an agreement signed with Saudi Arabia in 1973.

In its recruitment effort, HCA placed an advertisement in a trade periodical seeking applications for a position as a monitoring systems engineer at the Hospital. The advertisement drew the attention of respondent Scott Nelson in September 1983, while Nelson was in the United States. After interviewing for the position in Saudi Arabia, Nelson returned to the United States, where he signed an employment contract with the Hospital, satisfied personnel processing requirements, and attended an orientation session that HCA conducted for Hospital employees. In the course of that program, HCA identified Royspec as the point of contact in the United States for family members who might wish to reach Nelson in an emergency.

In December 1983, Nelson went to Saudi Arabia and began work at the Hospital, monitoring all "facilities, equipment, utilities and maintenance systems to insure the safety of patients, hospital staff, and others." He did his job without significant incident until March 1984, when he discovered safety defects in the Hospital's oxygen and nitrous oxide lines that posed fire hazards and otherwise endangered patients' lives. Over a period of several months, Nelson repeatedly advised Hospital officials of the safety defects and reported the defects to a Saudi Government commission as well. Hospital officials instructed Nelson to ignore the problems.

The Hospital's response to Nelson's reports changed, however, on September 27, 1984, when certain Hospital employees summoned him to the Hospital's security office where agents of the Saudi Government arrested him. The agents transported Nelson to a jail cell, in which they "shackled, tortured and bea[t]" him, and kept him four days without food. Although Nelson did not understand Arabic, Government agents forced him to sign a statement written in that language, the content of which he did not know; a Hospital employee who was supposed to act as Nelson's interpreter advised him to sign "anything" the agents gave him to avoid further beatings. Two days later, Government agents transferred Nelson to the Al Sijan Prison "to await trial on unknown charges."

* * *

It was only at the personal request of a United States Senator that the Saudi Government released Nelson, 39 days after his arrest, on November 5, 1984. Seven days later, after failing to convince him to return to work at the Hospital, the Saudi Government allowed Nelson to leave the country.

In 1988, Nelson and his wife filed this action against petitioners in the United States District Court for the Southern District of Florida seeking damages for personal injury. The Nelsons' complaint sets out 16 causes of action, which fall into three categories. Counts II through VII and counts X, XI, XIV, and XV allege that petitioners committed various intentional torts, including battery, unlawful detainment, wrongful arrest and imprisonment, false imprisonment, inhuman torture, disruption of normal family life, and infliction of mental anguish. Counts I, IX, and XIII charge petitioners with negligently failing to warn Nelson of otherwise undisclosed dangers of his employment, namely, that if he attempted to report safety hazards the Hospital would likely retaliate against him and the Saudi Government might detain and physically abuse him without legal cause. Finally, counts VIII, XII, and XVI allege that Vivian Nelson sustained derivative injury resulting from petitioners' actions. Presumably because the employment contract provided that Saudi courts would have exclusive jurisdiction over claims for breach of contract, the Nelsons raised no such matters.

The District Court dismissed for lack of subject-matter jurisdiction under the Foreign Sovereign Immunities Act of 1976. It rejected the Nelsons' argument that jurisdiction existed, under the first clause of §1605(a)(2), because the action was one "based upon a commercial activity" that petitioners had "carried on in the United States." Although HCA's recruitment of Nelson in the United States might properly be attributed to Saudi Arabia and the Hospital, the District Court reasoned, it did not amount to commercial activity "carried on the United States" for purposes of the Act. The court explained that there was no sufficient "nexus" between Nelson's recruitment and the injuries alleged. "Although [the Nelsons] argu[e] that but for [Scott Nelson's] recruitment in the United States, he would not have taken the job, been arrested, and suffered the personal injuries," the court said, "this 'connection' [is] far too tenuous to support jurisdiction" under the Act. Likewise, the court concluded that Royspec's commercial activity in the United States, purchasing supplies and equipment for the Hospital, had no nexus with the personal injuries alleged in the complaint; Royspec had simply provided a way for Nelson's family to reach him in an emergency.

The Court of Appeals reversed. 923 F.2d 1528 (CA11 1991). It concluded that Nelson's recruitment and hiring were commercial activities of Saudi Arabia and the Hospital, carried on in the United States for purposes of the Act, and that the Nelsons' action was "based upon" these activities within the meaning of the statute. Id., at 1533-1536. There was, the court reasoned, a sufficient nexus between those commercial activities and the wrongful acts that had allegedly injured the Nelsons: "the detention and torture of Nelson are so intertwined with his employment at the Hospital," the court explained, "that they are 'based upon' his recruitment and hiring" in the United States. Id., at 1535. The court also found jurisdiction to hear the claims against Royspec. After the Court of Appeals denied petitioners' suggestion for rehearing en banc, we granted certiorari. We now reverse.

II

The Foreign Sovereign Immunities Act "provides the sole basis for obtaining jurisdiction over a foreign state in the courts of this country." *Argentine Republic v. Amerada Hess Shipping Corp.*, 488 U.S. 428, 443 (1989). Under the Act, a foreign state is presumptively immune from the jurisdiction of United States courts; unless a specified exception applies, a federal court lacks subject-matter jurisdiction over a claim against a foreign state.

Only one such exception is said to apply here. The first clause of § 1605(a)(2) of the Act provides that a foreign state shall not be immune from the jurisdiction of United States courts in any case "in which the action is based upon a commercial activity carried on in the United States by the foreign state."

* * *

There is no dispute here that Saudi Arabia, the Hospital, and Royspec all qualify as "foreign state[s]" within the meaning of the Act. For there to be jurisdiction in this case, therefore, the Nelsons' action must be "based upon" some "commercial activity" by petitioners that had "substantial contact" with the United States within the meaning of the Act. Because we conclude that the suit is not based upon any commercial activity by petitioners, we need not reach the issue of substantial contact with the United States.

* * *

In this case, the Nelsons have alleged that petitioners recruited Scott Nelson for work at the Hospital, signed an employment contract with him, and subsequently employed him. While these activities led to the conduct that eventually injured the Nelsons, they are not the basis for the Nelsons' suit. Even taking each of the Nelsons' allegations about Scott Nelson's recruitment and employment as true, those facts alone entitle the Nelsons to nothing under their theory of the case. The Nelsons have not, after all, alleged breach of contract, but personal injuries caused by petitioners' intentional wrongs and by petitioners' negligent failure to warn Scott Nelson that they might commit those wrongs. Those torts, and not the arguably commercial activities that preceded their commission, form the basis for the Nelsons' suit.

Petitioners' tortious conduct itself fails to qualify as "commercial activity" within the meaning of the Act, although the Act is too "obtuse" to be of much help in reaching that conclusion. Callejo [v. Bancomer., S.A., 764 F2d 1101 (5th Cir. 1985)] at 1107 (citation omitted). We have seen already that the Act defines "commercial activity" as "either a regular course of commercial conduct or a particular commercial transaction or act," and provides that "[t]he commercial character of an activity shall be determined by reference to the nature of the course of conduct or particular transaction or act, rather than by reference to its purpose." 28 U.S.C. § 1603(d). If this is a definition, it is one distinguished only by its diffidence; as we observed in our most recent case on the subject, it "leaves the critical term 'commercial' largely undefined." Republic of Argentina v. Weltover, Inc., 112 S.Ct. 2160, 2165 (1992). We do not, however, have the option to throw up our hands. The term has to be given some interpretation, and congressional diffidence necessarily results in judicial responsibility to determine what a "commercial activity" is for purposes of the Act.

We took up the task just last Term in *Weltover*, supra, which involved Argentina's unilateral refinancing of bonds it had issued under a plan to stabilize its currency. Bondholders sued Argentina in federal court, asserting jurisdiction under the third clause of § 1605(a)(2). In the course of holding the refinancing to be a commercial activity for purposes of the Act, we observed that the statute "largely codifies the so-called 'restrictive' theory of foreign sovereign immunity first endorsed by the State Department in 1952." 112 S.Ct., at 2165. We accordingly held that the meaning of "commercial" for purposes of the Act must be the meaning Congress understood the restrictive theory to require at the time it passed the statute.

Under the restrictive, as opposed to the "absolute," theory of foreign sovereign immunity, a state is immune from the jurisdiction of foreign courts as to its sovereign or public acts (*jure imperii*), but not as to those that are private or commercial in character (*jure gestionis*). We explained in Weltover, supra, 112 S.Ct., at 2166 (quoting [*Alfred Dunhill of London Inc., v. Republic of Cuba*, 425 U.S. 682 (1976)], at 704, that a state engages in commercial activity under the restrictive theory where it exercises "'only those powers that can also be exercised by private citizens,'" as distinct from those "'powers peculiar to sovereigns.'" Put differently, a foreign state engages in commercial activity for purposes of the restrictive theory only where it acts "in the manner of a private player within" the market. 112 S.Ct., at 2166; see Restatement (Third) of the Foreign Relations Law of the United States § 451 (1987) ("Under international law, a state or state instrumentality is immune from the jurisdiction of the courts of another state, except with respect to claims arising out of activities of the kind that may be carried on by private persons").

* * *

[T]he intentional conduct alleged here (the Saudi Government's wrongful arrest, imprisonment, and torture of Nelson) could not qualify as commercial under the restrictive theory. The conduct boils down to abuse of the power of its police by the Saudi Government, and however monstrous such abuse undoubtedly may be, a foreign state's exercise of the power of its police has long been understood for purposes of the restrictive theory as peculiarly sovereign in nature.

* * *

In addition to the intentionally tortious conduct, the Nelsons claim a separate basis for recovery in petitioners' failure to warn Scott Nelson of the hidden dangers associated with his employment. The Nelsons allege that, at the time petitioners recruited

Scott Nelson and thereafter, they failed to warn him of the possibility of severe retaliatory action if he attempted to disclose any safety hazards he might discover on the job. In other words, petitioners bore a duty to warn of their own propensity for tortious conduct. But this is merely a semantic ploy. For aught we can see, a plaintiff could recast virtually any claim of intentional tort committed by sovereign act as a claim of failure to warn, simply by charging the defendant with an obligation to announce its own tortious propensity before indulging it. To give jurisdictional significance to this feint of language would effectively thwart the Act's manifest purpose to codify the restrictive theory of foreign sovereign immunity.

III

The Nelsons' action is not "based upon a commercial activity" within the meaning of the first clause of § 1605(a)(2) of the Act, and the judgment of the Court of Appeals is accordingly reversed.

It is so ordered.

Justice WHITE, with whom Justice BLACKMUN joins, concurring in the judgment.

* * *

The majority concludes that petitioners enjoy sovereign immunity because respondents' action is not "based upon a commercial activity." I disagree. I nonetheless concur in the judgment because in my view the commercial conduct upon which respondents base their complaint was not "carried on in the United States."

* * *

Indeed, I am somewhat at a loss as to what exactly the majority believes petitioners have done that a private employer could not. As countless cases attest, retaliation for whistleblowing is not a practice foreign to the marketplace. Congress passed a statute in response to such behavior, see Whistleblower Protection Act of 1989, 5 U.S.C. § 1213 et seq. (1988 ed., Supp. III), as have numerous States. On occasion, private employers also have been known to retaliate by enlisting the help of police officers to falsely arrest employees. More generally, private parties have been held liable for conspiring with public authorities to effectuate an arrest, and for using private security personnel for the same purposes. Therefore, had the hospital retaliated against Nelson by hiring thugs to do the job, I assume the majority—no longer able to describe this conduct as "a foreign state's exercise of the power of its police,"—would consent to calling it "commercial." For, in such circumstances, the state-run hospital would be operating as any private participant in the marketplace and respondents' action would be based on the operation by Saudi Arabia's agents of a commercial business.

* * *

Nevertheless, I reach the same conclusion as the majority because petitioners' commercial activity was not "carried on in the United States." The Act defines such conduct as "commercial activity...having substantial contact with the United States." 28 U.S.C. § 1603(e). Respondents point to the hospital's recruitment efforts in the United States, including advertising in the American media, and the signing of the employment contract in Miami. As I earlier noted, while these may very well qualify as commercial activity in the United States, they do not constitute the commercial activity upon which respondents' action is based. Conversely, petitioners' commercial conduct in Saudi Arabia, though constituting the basis of the Nelsons' suit, lacks a sufficient nexus to the United States. Neither the hospital's employment practices, nor its disciplinary procedures, has any apparent connection to this country. On that basis, I agree that the Act does not grant the Nelsons access to our courts.

Justice BLACKMUN, concurring in part and dissenting in part.

I join Justice White's opinion because it finds that respondents' intentional tort claims are "based upon a commercial activity" and that the commercial activity at issue in those claims was not "carried on in the United States." I join Justice Kennedy's opinion insofar as it concludes that the "failure to warn" claims should be remanded.

Justice KENNEDY, with whom Justice BLACKMUN and Justice STEVENS join as to Parts I-B and II, concurring in part and dissenting in part.

I join all of the Court's opinion except the last paragraph of Part II, where, with almost no explanation, the Court rules that, like the intentional tort claim, the claims based on negligent failure to warn are outside the subject-matter jurisdiction of the federal courts. These claims stand on a much different footing from the intentional tort claims for purposes of the Foreign Sovereign Immunities Act (FSIA). In my view, they ought to be remanded to the District Court for further consideration.

I

A

I agree with the Court's holding that the Nelsons' claims of intentional wrongdoing by the Hospital and the Kingdom of Saudi Arabia are based on sovereign, not commercial, activity, and so fall outside the commercial activity exception to the grant of foreign sovereign immunity contained in 28 U.S.C. § 1604. The intentional tort counts of the Nelsons' complaint recite the alleged unlawful arrest, imprisonment, and torture of Mr. Nelson by the Saudi police acting in their official capacities. These are not the sort of activities by which a private party conducts its business affairs; if we classified them as commercial, the commercial activity exception would in large measure swallow the rule of foreign sovereign immunity Congress enacted in the FSIA.

B

By the same token, however, the Nelsons' claims alleging that the Hospital, the Kingdom, and Royspec were negligent in failing during their recruitment of Nelson to warn him of foreseeable dangers are based upon commercial activity having substantial contact with the United States. As such, they are within the commercial activity exception and the jurisdiction of the federal courts. Unlike the intentional tort counts of the complaint, the failure to warn counts do not complain of a police beating in Saudi Arabia; rather, they complain of a negligent omission made during the recruiting of a hospital employee in the United States. To obtain relief, the Nelsons would be obliged to prove that the Hospital's recruiting agent did not tell Nelson about the foreseeable hazards of his prospective employment in Saudi Arabia.

* * *

In my view, the FSIA conferred subject-matter jurisdiction on the District Court to entertain the failure to warn claims, and with all respect, I dissent from the Court's refusal to remand them.

Justice STEVENS, dissenting.

* * *

In this case, as Justice White has demonstrated, petitioner's operation of the hospital and its employment practices and disciplinary procedures are "commercial activities" within the meaning of the statute, and respondent's claim that he was punished for acts performed in the course of his employment was unquestionably "based upon" those activities. Thus, the first statutory condition is satisfied; petitioner is not entitled to immunity from the claims asserted by respondent.

Unlike Justice White, however, I am also convinced that petitioner's commercial activities—whether defined as the regular course of conduct of operating a hospital or, more specifically, as the commercial transaction of engaging respondent "as an employee with specific responsibilities in that enterprise," Brief for Respondents 25—have sufficient contact with the United States to justify the exercise of federal jurisdiction. Petitioner Royspec maintains an office in Maryland and purchases hospital supplies and equipment in this country. For nearly two decades the Hospital's American agent has maintained an office in the United States and regularly engaged in the recruitment of personnel in this country. Respondent himself was recruited in the United States and entered into his employment contract with the hospital in the United States. Before traveling to Saudi Arabia to assume his position at the hospital, respondent attended an orientation program in Tennessee. The position for which respondent was recruited and ultimately hired was that of a monitoring systems manager, a troubleshooter, and, taking respondent's allegations as true, it was precisely respondent's performance of those responsibilities that led to the hospital's retaliatory actions against him.

Whether the first clause of § 1605(a)(2) broadly authorizes "general" jurisdiction over foreign entities that engage in substantial commercial activity in this country, or, more narrowly, authorizes only "specific" jurisdiction over particular commercial claims that have a substantial contact with the United States, petitioners' contacts with the United States in this case are, in my view, plainly sufficient to subject petitioners to suit in this country on a claim arising out of its nonimmune commercial activity relating to respondent. If the same activities had been performed by a private business, I have no doubt jurisdiction would be upheld. And that, of course, should be a touchstone of our inquiry; for * * * when a foreign nation sheds its uniquely sovereign status and seeks out the benefits of the private marketplace, it must, like any private party, bear the burdens and responsibilities imposed by that marketplace. I would therefore affirm the judgment of the Court of Appeals.

Notes

1. The objection in *Nelson*, that the commercial activity of running the hospital was not carried out in the United States, might be eliminated by use of the last clause of 1605(a) (2), commercial activity outside the United States that "causes a direct effect in the United States." Martin v. Republic of South Africa, 836 F.2d 91 (2d Cir. 1987), held that injuries caused when an African-American on a privately sponsored dance tour in South Africa was refused admission to a government hospital reserved for Caucasians, did not have a "direct effect" in the United States. How can *Martin* be distinguished from *Nelson*?

2. Sun v. Taiwan, 201 F.3d 1105 (9th Cir. 2000). Parents of an American student who drowned while participating in a cultural tour in Taiwan that was sponsored by the government of Taiwan. A wrongful death suit against Taiwan, the student's parents, in

order to establish "the nexus between their action and Taiwan's commercial activity in the United States * * * argue that, like other tour organizers, Taiwan was under an affirmative duty to exercise reasonable care by disclosing know information concerning prospective dangers on the tour and not misleading prospective participants." Id. at 1110. The court remanded the case to determine whether in the light of this argument, whether the parents claim "is based on commercial activity that took place in the United States." Id. The court stated: "This is not the same as the attempt by the plaintiffs in *Nelson* * * * to turn their intentional torts claim into a failure to war claim. The Suns' point is not that tour organizers have a duty to warn, but rather that there is a duty to take reasonable care in arranging a tour itinerary." Id. 1110 n.2.

International Association of Machinists v. Organization of Petroleum Exporting Countries (OPEC)
649 F.2d 1354 (9th Cir. 1981), cert. denied, 454 U.S. 1163 (1982)

Before Choy and Nelson, Circuit Judges, and Spears, District Judge.

Choy, Circuit Judge:

I: Introduction

The members of the International Association of Machinists and Aerospace Workers (IAM) were disturbed by the high price of oil and petroleum-derived products in the United States. They believed the actions of the Organization of the Petroleum Exporting Countries, popularly known as OPEC, were the cause of this burden on the American public. Accordingly, IAM sued OPEC and its member nations in December of 1978, alleging that their price-setting activities violated United States anti-trust laws. IAM sought injunctive relief and damages. The district court entered a final judgment in favor of the defendants, holding that it lacked jurisdiction and that IAM had no valid anti-trust claim. We affirm the judgment of the district court on the alternate ground that, under the act of state doctrine, exercise of federal court jurisdiction in this case would be improper.

II: Factual Background

* * *

OPEC is an organization of the petroleum-producing and exporting nations of what is sometimes referred to as the Third World. The OPEC nations have organized to obtain the greatest possible economic returns for a special resource which they hope will remove them from the ranks of the underdeveloped and the poverty-plagued.

* * *

OPEC achieves its goals by a system of production limits and royalties which its members unanimously adopt. There is no enforcement arm of OPEC. The force behind OPEC decrees is the collective self-interest of the 13 nations.

* * *

In December 1978, IAM brought suit against OPEC and its member nations. IAM's complaint alleged price fixing in violation of the Sherman Act, 15 U.S.C. §1, and requested treble damages and injunctive relief under the Clayton Act, 15 U.S.C. §§15, 16. IAM claimed a deliberate targeting and victimization of the United States market, directly resulting in higher prices for Americans.

The defendants refused to recognize the jurisdiction of the district court, and they did not appear in the proceedings below. Their cause was argued by various amici, with additional information provided by court-appointed experts. The district court ordered a full hearing, noting that the Foreign Sovereign Immunities Act (FSIA) prohibits the entry of a default judgment against a foreign sovereignty "unless the claimant establishes his claim or right to relief by evidence satisfactory to the court." 28 U.S.C. §1608(e).

* * *

At the close of the trial, the district judge granted judgment in favor of the defendants. The court held, first, that it lacked jurisdiction over the defendant nations under the Foreign Sovereign Immunities Act.

* * *

III: Discussion

A: Sovereign Immunity

* * *

A critical step in characterizing the nature of a given activity is defining exactly what that activity is. The immunity question may be determined by how broadly or narrowly that activity is defined. In this case, IAM insists on a very narrow focus on the specific activity of "price fixing." IAM argues that the FSIA does not give immunity to this activity. Under the FSIA a commercial activity is one which an individual might "customarily carr(y) on for profit." H.R.Rep.No.94-1487, 94th Cong., 2d Sess. 16, reprinted in (1976) U.S.Code Cong. & Ad.News 6604, 6615. OPEC's activity, characterized by IAM as making agreements to fix prices, is one which is presumably done for profit; it is thus commercial and immunity does not apply.

The court below defined OPEC's activity in a different way: "[I]t is clear that the nature of the activity engaged in by each of these OPEC member countries is the establishment by a sovereign state of the terms and conditions for the removal of a prime natural resource to wit, crude oil from its territory." 477 F.Supp. at 567. The trial judge reasoned that, according to international law, the development and control of natural resources is a prime governmental function. Id. at 567-78. The opinion cites several resolutions of the United Nations' General Assembly, which the United States supported, and the United States Constitution, Art. 4, §3, cl. 2, which treat the control of natural resources as governmental acts.

* * *

The district court was understandably troubled by the broader implications of an anti-trust action against the OPEC nations. The importance of the alleged price-fixing activity to the OPEC nations cannot be ignored. Oil revenues represent their only significant source of income. Consideration of their sovereignty cannot be separated from their near total dependence upon oil. We find that these concerns are appropriately addressed by application of the act of state doctrine. While we do not apply the doctrine of sovereign immunity, its elements remain relevant to our discussion of the act of state doctrine.

B: The Act of State Doctrine

The act of state doctrine declares that a United States court will not adjudicate a politically sensitive dispute which would require the court to judge the legality of the sovereign act of a foreign state.

* * *

The doctrine of sovereign immunity is similar to the act of state doctrine in that it also represents the need to respect the sovereignty of foreign states. The two doctrines differ, however, in significant respects. The law of sovereign immunity goes to the jurisdiction of the court. The act of state doctrine is not jurisdictional. Rather, it is a prudential doctrine designed to avoid judicial action in sensitive areas. Sovereign immunity is a principle of international law, recognized in the United States by statute. It is the states themselves, as defendants, who may claim sovereign immunity. The act of state doctrine is a domestic legal principle, arising from the peculiar role of American courts. It recognizes not only the sovereignty of foreign states, but also the spheres of power of the co-equal branches of our government. Thus a private litigant may raise the act of state doctrine, even when no sovereign state is a party to the action. The act of state doctrine is apposite whenever the federal courts must question the legality of the sovereign acts of foreign states.

It has been suggested that the FSIA supersedes the act of state doctrine, or that the amorphous doctrine is limited by modern jurisprudence. We disagree.

Congress in enacting the FSIA recognized the distinction between sovereign immunity and the act of state doctrine. See, e. g., H.R.Rep.No.94-1487, 94th Cong., 2d Sess. 20 n.1, reprinted in (1976) U.S.Code Cong. & Ad.News 6619 n.1 ("The Committee has found it unnecessary to address the act of state doctrine in this legislation"); see generally Jurisdiction of U.S. Courts in Suits Against Foreign States: Hearings on H.R.11315 Before the Subcomm. on Admin.Law and Governmental Relations of the House Comm. on the Judiciary, 94th Cong., 2d Sess. 29-57 (1976); Immunities of Foreign States: Hearings on H.R.3493 Before the Subcomm. on Claims & Governmental Relations of the Committee on the Judiciary, 93d Cong., 1st Sess. 20 (1973) (the FSIA "in no way affects existing law concerning the extent to which the 'act of state' doctrine may be applicable in similar circumstances"). Indeed, because the act of state doctrine addresses concerns central to our system of government, the doctrine must necessarily remain a part of our jurisprudence unless and until such time as a radical change in the role of the courts occurs.

The act of state doctrine is not diluted by the commercial activity exception which limits the doctrine of sovereign immunity. While purely commercial activity may not rise to the level of an act of state, certain seemingly commercial activity will trigger act of state considerations. As the district court noted, OPEC's "price-fixing" activity has a significant sovereign component. While the FSIA ignores the underlying purpose of a state's action, the act of state doctrine does not. * * * When the state qua state acts in the public interest, its sovereignty is asserted. The courts must proceed cautiously to avoid an affront to that sovereignty. Because the act of state doctrine and the doctrine of sovereign immunity address different concerns and apply in different circumstances, we find that the act of state doctrine remains available when such caution is appropriate, regardless of any commercial component of the activity involved.

* * *

The remedy IAM seeks is an injunction against the OPEC nations. The possibility of insult to the OPEC states and of interference with the efforts of the political branches to seek favorable relations with them is apparent from the very nature of this action and the remedy sought. While the case is formulated as an anti-trust action, the granting of any relief would in effect amount to an order from a domestic court instructing a foreign sovereign to alter its chosen means of allocating and profiting from its own valuable natural resources. On the other hand, should the court hold that OPEC's actions are legal, this "would greatly strengthen the bargaining hand" of the OPEC nations in the event that Congress or the executive chooses to condemn OPEC's actions. [*Banco Nacional de Cuba v.*] *Sabbatino*, 376 U.S. [398 (1964)] at 432.

A further consideration is the availability of internationally-accepted legal principles which would render the issues appropriate for judicial disposition.

* * *

While conspiracies in restraint of trade are clearly illegal under domestic law, the record reveals no international consensus condemning cartels, royalties, and production agreements. The United States and other nations have supported the principle of supreme state sovereignty over natural resources. The OPEC nations themselves obviously will not agree that their actions are illegal. We are reluctant to allow judicial interference in an area so void of international consensus. An injunction against OPEC's alleged price-fixing activity would require condemnation of a cartel system which the community of nations has thus far been unwilling to denounce. The admonition in *Sabbatino* that the courts should consider the degree of codification and consensus in the area of law is another indication that judicial action is inappropriate here.

The district court was understandably reluctant to proceed on the complaint below and the act of state doctrine provides sound jurisprudential support for such reluctance. While the act of state doctrine does not compel dismissal as a matter of course, in a case such as this where the controlling issue is the legality of a sovereign act and where the only remedy sought is barred by act of state considerations dismissal is appropriate.

IV: Conclusion

The act of state doctrine is applicable in this case. The courts should not enter at the will of litigants into a delicate area of foreign policy which the executive and legislative branches have chosen to approach with restraint. The issue of whether the FSIA allows jurisdiction in this case need not be decided, since a judicial remedy is inappropriate regardless of whether jurisdiction exists.

* * *

The decision of the district court dismissing this action is AFFIRMED.

Note

Argentine Republic v. Amerada Hess Shipping Corp., 488 U.S. 428 (1989). Plaintiff's tanker was damaged by Argentine military aircraft in international waters during the Falkland war. The Second Circuit permitted plaintiff to sue Argentina under the Alien Tort Statute (infra Chapter 7), which confers jurisdiction over civil actions by an alien for a tort committed in violation of the law of nations. The Supreme Court reversed holding (p. 443) that "the FSIA provides the sole basis for obtaining jurisdiction over a foreign state in the courts of this country, and...none of the enumerated exceptions to the Act applies to the facts of this case" [including 1605(a)(5) because damage to property "occurring in the United States" does not include the high seas, which are not, under 1603(c), "waters, continental or insular, subject to the jurisdiction of the United States"].

MOL, Inc. v. The Peoples Republic of Bangladesh
736 F.2d 1326 (9th Cir.), cert. denied, 469 U.S. 1037 (1984)

Before Wright, Hug, and Nelson, Circuit Judges.

Eugene A. Wright, Circuit Judge:

MOL, Inc. sues Bangladesh for termination of a licensing agreement for the export of rhesus monkeys from Bangladesh. Because the granting and revocation of a license to export a natural resource are sovereign acts, we have no jurisdiction over this claim. Foreign Sovereign Immunities Act of 1976, 28 U.S.C. § 1604.

FACTS

In 1977, a division of the Bangladesh Ministry of Agriculture granted MOL, Inc., an Oregon corporation, a ten-year license to capture and export rhesus monkeys. The licensing agreement specified quantities and prices and required MOL to build in Bangladesh in 1978 a breeding farm for rhesus monkeys.

By its terms, the agreement was granted "on the grounds and sole condition that the primates exported by [MOL] from Bangladesh shall be used exclusively for the purposes of medical and other scientific research by highly skilled and competent personnel for the general benefit of all peoples of the world." To enable Bangladesh to monitor uses of the monkeys, it required MOL to keep available records on each monkey and arrange for duplicate records in Bangladesh.

The agreement provided for arbitration of disputes, each party selecting one arbitrator. Bangladesh reserved the right to terminate the agreement "without notice if [MOL] has failed to fulfill its obligations under this Agreement."

In November 1977, India banned the export of its rhesus monkeys. As India had been the major exporter of these animals, which are valuable for research because of their anatomical and behavioral similarity to humans, Bangladesh became an important supplier. Although world monkey prices rose while MOL's payments to Bangladesh remained fixed, Bangladesh complied with the licensing agreement through the spring of 1978.

Bangladesh threatened to cancel the agreement in May 1978 because MOL had not built the breeding farm or exported agreed quantities. MOL denied any departure from the agreement. In September 1978, it delivered some Bangladesh monkeys to the United States armed services for radiobiological research.

Bangladesh announced on January 3, 1979, that it was terminating the agreement because MOL had not constructed the breeding farm in 1978 and had breached the requirement that the monkeys be used only for humanitarian purposes. It claimed that MOL sold the monkeys to the armed services for "neutron bomb radiation experiments."

When MOL sought arbitration, Bangladesh refused, asserting its right to terminate for breach by MOL. Apparently MOL asked the State Department to intervene. Despite these efforts and MOL's reassurances that monkeys would not be used for radiation experiments, Bangladesh did not reinstate the licensing agreement.

In 1982, MOL sued Bangladesh for $15 million. Bangladesh did not appear, and MOL moved for default. Amicus curiae, Attorneys for Animal Rights, moved to dismiss for lack of jurisdiction under the Foreign Sovereign Immunities Act of 1976 (FSIA), 28 U.S.C. § 1604. The district court, 572 F.Supp. 79, denied the default judgment and dismissed the action, holding it barred both by the FSIA and by the act of state doctrine.

Because we decide that the district court lacked jurisdiction under the FSIA, we do not reach the issue whether the act of state doctrine prevented the district court from exercising its jurisdiction.

SOVEREIGN IMMUNITY

MOL argues that Bangladesh does not enjoy sovereign immunity because its acts fall under the commercial activity exception of the FSIA. That Act denies immunity in any case in which the action is based "upon an act outside the territory of the United States in connection with a commercial activity of the foreign state elsewhere and that act causes a direct effect in the United States." 28 U.S.C. § 1605(a)(2). The exception turns on whether the act is commercial: * * * 28 U.S.C. § 1603(d).

* * *

A crucial step in determining whether the basis of this suit was a commercial activity is defining the "act complained of here." *IAM v. OPEC*, 649 F.2d 1354, at 1357-58. The court must then decide whether that act is commercial or sovereign.

MOL asserts that the activity here relates to Bangladesh's contracting to sell monkeys. It admits that licensing the exploitation of natural resources is a sovereign activity. It argues, however, that this suit arises not from license revocation but from termination of a contract. In essence, Bangladesh lost its sovereign status when it contracted and then terminated pursuant to contract terms.

The argument seems persuasive because, in breaking the agreement, Bangladesh itself spoke in commercial terms, basing its termination on MOL's alleged breaches. The true nature of the action, however, does not depend on terminology.

Bangladesh was terminating an agreement that only a sovereign could have made. This was not just a contract for trade of monkeys. It concerned Bangladesh's right to regulate imports and exports, a sovereign prerogative. It concerned Bangladesh's right to regulate its natural resources, also a uniquely sovereign function. See *IAM v. OPEC*, 477 F.Supp. 553, 567-68 (C.D.Cal.1979) (citing United States and international authority), aff'd on other grounds, 649 F.2d 1354 (9th Cir.1981). A private party could not have made such an agreement.

MOL complains that this conclusion relies on the purpose of the agreement, in contradiction of the FSIA. See 28 U.S.C. § 1603(d). But consideration of the special elements of export license and natural resource looks only to the nature of the agreement and does not require examination of the government's motives.

In short, the licensing agreement was a sovereign act, not just a commercial transaction. Its revocation was sovereign by nature, not commercial. Bangladesh has sovereign immunity from this suit.

C: Direct Effect

Because the act complained of was not a commercial activity and Bangladesh has sovereign immunity, effect in the United States is irrelevant. See 28 U.S.C. § 1605(a)(2).

AFFIRMED.

Notes

1. This case is decided by a different panel (Judge Nelson was on both panels) of the same circuit that decided the previous case, but on FSIA rather than act-of-state grounds. The opinion cites the district court opinion in the prior case, which was decided under the FSIA.

2. For other cases drawing the commercial-governmental distinction see MCI Telecommunications Corp. v. Alhadhood, 82 F.3d 658 (5th Cir.), cert denied, 519 U.S. 1007 (1996) (holding that long-distance telephone calls made by military trainees training in the United States under an agreement between the United Arab Emirates and the United States did not constitute commercial activity nor did promises by pay for the calls made by the Emirates' ambassador); Wolf v. Federal Republic of Germany, 95 F.3d 536 (7th Cir. 1996) cert. denied, 520 U.S. 1106 (1997), (holding that wrongful failure to pay reparations is not commercial). See also Richard Wydeven, The Foreign Sovereign Immunities Act of 1976: A Contemporary Look at Jurisdiction Under the Commercial Activity Exception, 13 Rev. Litig. 143 (1993).

In Kuwait Airways Corp. v. Iraqi Airways Co., [1995] 1 W.L.R. 1147, [1995] 3 All E.R. 694 (H.L.), the House of Lords held that the seizure of Kuwait Airways' airplanes and their removal to Iraq by Iraqi Airways was an exercise of sovereign authority entitled to state immunity, but Iraqi Airways' retention and use of the aircraft as its own were "commercial transactions" not entitled to immunity under the State Immunity Act 1978. The case was remanded for consideration, among other issues, of whether the case is justiciable under act of state and related doctrines. For comment on the case see Hazel Fox, States in the Market Place, 110 Law Quarterly Rev. 199 (1994). See also Littrell v. United States of America, [1995] 1 W.L.R. 82 (C.A.), [1994] 4 All E.R. 203 (C.A.) (holding that medical treatment of a member of the U.S. armed forces at a U.S. military hospital in England was an exercise of sovereign immune authority and not a commercial transaction).

Section 3: Enforcing a Judgment

Letelier v. Republic of Chile
748 F.2d 790 (2d Cir. 1984), cert. denied, 471 U.S. 1125 (1985)

Before Cardamone and Pratt, Circuit Judges and Bonsal, District Judge.

Cardamone, Circuit Judge:

The critical question posed on this appeal is whether the assets of a foreign state's wholly owned airline are subject to execution to satisfy a default judgment obtained against the foreign state. The district court, believing that Congress under the Foreign Sovereign Immunities Act of 1976, (FSIA or the Act), would not have established a right to jurisdiction over the foreign state without also providing a remedy, ordered execution. We reverse although we recognize that our decision may preclude the plaintiffs from collecting on their judgment. How one wishes to decide a case comes lightly to mind, on a wing; but often how one must decide it comes arduously, weighed down by somber thought. To rule otherwise here would only illustrate once again that hard cases make bad law.

FACTS

Orlando Letelier, the former Chilean Ambassador to the United States, his aide, Michael Moffitt, and Moffitt's wife, Ronni, were riding to work in Washington, D.C. in September, 1976 when an explosive device planted under the driver's seat in their car was detonated killing both Letelier and Ronni Moffitt and seriously injuring Michael Moffitt. That assassination gives rise to the present appeal.

Investigation by agencies of the United States government into these murders revealed the identity of nine assassins and their alleged connection to the government of Chile.

* * *

In August 1978 the personal representatives of Letelier and Moffitt instituted a civil tort action in the United States District Court for the District of Columbia against the indicted individuals [implicated in the assassination] and the Republic of Chile. * * * The complaint alleged that the noncommercial tort exception of § 1605(a)(5) of the FSIA applied and that Chile was not entitled to sovereign immunity in the tort action.

All defendants defaulted, although Chile sent two Diplomatic Notes to the United States Department of State asserting its sovereign immunity and that the allegations against it were false. The State Department forwarded these Notes to the clerk of the district court. In August 1978 the trial court granted default judgments against the individual defendants. During 1979 and 1980 the district court heard plaintiffs' motion for a default judgment against Chile, see *Letelier v. Republic of Chile*, 488 F.Supp. 665 (D.D.C.1980), and finally resolved that motion. See *Letelier v. Republic of Chile*, 502 F.Supp. 259 (D.D.C.1980). In the former case, the court ruled that it had subject matter jurisdiction pursuant to the exception to immunity found in § 1605(a)(5) of the Act. In the latter case the trial court * * * granted a default judgment against the Republic of Chile and awarded plaintiffs over five million dollars including interest, compensatory and punitive damages, counsel fees and out of pocket expenses. The Republic of Chile did not take an appeal from either of these judgments.

The resulting judgment against the Republic of Chile was entered in the United States District Court for the District of Columbia. Plaintiffs subsequently filed the judgment in the United States District Court for the Southern District of New York for the purpose of executing on the property interests that The Republic of Chile has in the Chilean national airline, Linea Aerea Nacional-Chile or LAN, which is located in New York, and for the appointment of Michael Moffitt as a receiver of those interests to satisfy the judgment against Chile. * * * The application for execution against LAN's assets came before District Court Judge Morris E. Lasker. LAN moved to dismiss claiming that it should not be held to answer for Chilean debts and that its assets were immune from execution. Relying upon a recent decision of the United States Supreme Court, *First National City Bank v. Banco Para El Comercio Exterior de Cuba (Bancec)*, 462 U.S. 611 (1983), which based a decision to disregard separate corporation identities on "international equitable principles," Judge Lasker first held in an opinion and order dated July 28, 1983 that, were the facts as asserted, LAN's role in the assassination was commercial activity under the Act. He further held that to adhere to LAN's separate corporate identity would, as in Bancec, violate equitable principles. *Letelier v. Republic of Chile*, 567 F.Supp. 1490, 1496 (S.D.N.Y.1983).

Having concluded that LAN's assets were subject to execution to satisfy a judgment against Chile, the district court concluded that the language of § 1610(a)(2) did not limit execution only to commercial assets used for commercial purposes, as LAN claimed, but also permitted execution to satisfy tort judgments "so long as the assets on which the judgment creditor seeks to execute were also used commercially in the activity giving rise to the claim." Id. at 1499. The rationale for this reading of the statute was that a statute should not be interpreted to create a right without a remedy. The court reasoned that if jurisdictional immunity is lifted, the presumption is that there will be a right to execute. Id. at 1500 & n. 7.

Plaintiffs later sought discovery against The Republic of Chile by serving it with interrogatories and requests to produce documents and admit facts. Chile refused to comply and again filed Diplomatic Notes asserting its refusal to recognize either the validity of the default judgment or the district court's jurisdiction in the supplementary proceedings for enforcement. Judge Lasker in an order dated December 20, 1983 granted plaintiff's motions for Rule 37 sanctions against LAN consisting of adverse findings of fact that provided a basis to disregard LAN's juridical separateness, and appointed Moffitt as a receiver of LAN's assets in the United States. 575 F.Supp. 1217 (S.D.N.Y.1983). From the rulings of July 28 and December 20, 1983 LAN has appealed and raised a number of issues.

DISCUSSION

The principal issue is whether LAN's assets may be executed upon to satisfy the judgment obtained in the District of Columbia against Chile. This discussion necessarily focuses on the Foreign Sovereign Immunities Act of 1976, which is the exclusive source of subject matter jurisdiction over all suits involving foreign states or their instrumentalities.

* * *

The judgment creditors claim that § 1610(a)(2) allows them to execute upon LAN's assets in this case. Section 1610(a)(2) provides:

> The property in the United States of a foreign state...used for a commercial activity in the United States, shall not be immune from attachment in aid of execution, or from execution...if...the property is or was used for the commercial activity upon which the claim is based...

We consider first whether LAN's separate juridical existence may be ignored, thereby making its assets "[t]he property in the United States of a foreign state."

I: Separate Juridical Existence

In *Bancec* the Supreme Court determined whether a claim of a foreign agency plaintiff was subject to a set-off for the debts of its parent government. *Bancec* deserves close scrutiny because it provides a conceptual framework for resolving plaintiff's assertion that LAN's assets should be treated as assets of Chile and because the district court relied on it to reach that conclusion.

In *Bancec*, the Cuban bank of the same name brought suit against Citibank to collect on a letter of credit issued in its favor in 1960. Citibank counterclaimed arguing that it was entitled to set-off amounts as compensation due it for the Cuban government's expropriation of Citibank's assets in Cuba. We ruled that as *Bancec* was not the alter ego of the Cuban government, it could not be held to account for Cuban debts. The Supreme Court reversed. Relying on the Act's legislative history, the Court noted that it was not intended to affect the substantive law of liability of a foreign state or the attribution of liability among its entities and proceeded to resolve the appeal on "equitable principles." The *Bancec* Court recognized that "government instrumentalities established as juridical entities distinct and independent from their sovereign should normally be treated as such." 103 S.Ct. at 2600. * * * The Supreme Court concluded in *Bancec* that the presumption of separateness had been overcome. It reasoned that the real beneficiary of any recovery would be the Cuban government, and that Cuba should not be permitted to obtain relief in American courts without answering for its seizure of Citibank's assets. The Court commented that "Cuba cannot escape liability for acts in violation of international law simply by retransferring the assets to separate juridical entities." 103 S.Ct. at 2603.

Thus, *Bancec* rests primarily on two propositions. First, Courts may use set-off as a unique, equitable remedy to prevent a foreign government from eluding liability for its own acts when it affirmatively seeks recovery in an American judicial proceeding. The broader message is that foreign states cannot avoid their obligations by engaging in abuses of corporate form. The *Bancec* Court held that a foreign state instrumentality is answerable just as its sovereign parent would be if the foreign state has abused the corporate form, or where recognizing the instrumentality's separate status works a fraud or an injustice.

The district court analyzed the present case in light of *Bancec* and ruled that Chile's alleged use of LAN to transport [an assassin] and explosives to the United States were "significant steps in the conspiracy" that if proven "would constitute a gross abuse of the corporate form." 567 F.Supp. at 1496. Accordingly, it held, "If Chile ignored LAN's separate existence in accomplishing the wrong, it may not invoke that separate existence in order to deny the injured a remedy." Id. at 1496.

The district judge "found" the following facts based "on the record" and "established" by evidentiary sanctions imposed pursuant to Rule 37(b)(2)(A): From January 1975 through January 1979 LAN's assets and facilities were under the direct control of Chile, which had the power to use them; Chile could have decreed LAN's dissolution and taken over property interests held in LAN's name; Chile, through its agencies, officers, and employees, intentionally used facilities and personnel of LAN to plan and carry out its conspiracy to assassinate Orlando Letelier by (a) transporting [an assassin] between Chile and the United States, (b) transporting explosives on several occasions, (c) assisting with currency transactions involved in paying off the co-conspirators in the assassination, (d) providing a meeting place for the co-conspirators, (e) arranging for [an assassin] to exit the United States under an alias after the assassination. By using LAN in these endeavors, the district court found, Chile ignored LAN's separate existence and abused the corporate form.

In our view this is not the sort of "abuse" that overcomes the presumption of separateness established by *Bancec*. Joint participation in a tort is not the "classic" abuse of corporate form to which the Supreme Court referred. In *Bancec* the Court relied by analogy on the domestic law of private corporations that ignores separate juridical status "where a corporate entity is so extensively controlled by its owner that a relationship of principal and agent is created," where "the corporate form...is interposed to defeat legislative policies," or where recognition of corporate form "'would work fraud or injustice.'" 103 S.Ct. at 2601. The facts that the district court "found" here do not add up to anything that resembles the abuses in the decisions cited in *Bancec*. None of these facts shows that Chile ignored LAN's separate status. Instead, they simply demonstrate that [the assassin] was able to enlist the cooperation of certain LAN pilots and officials with whom he had a pre-existing social relationship in pursuing his sinister goal. There was no finding that LAN's separate status was established to shield its owners from liability for their torts or that Chile ignored ordinary corporate formalities.

Plaintiffs had the burden of proving that LAN was not entitled to separate recognition. * * * The evidence submitted by the judgment creditors does not reveal abuse of corporate form of the nature or degree that *Bancec* found sufficient to overcome the presumption of separate existence. As both *Bancec* and the FSIA legislative history caution against too easily overcoming the presumption of separateness, we decline to extend the *Bancec* holding to do so in this case.

II: Commercial Activity

Even assuming the district court was correct in disregarding LAN's corporate form and finding that LAN's assets were Chile's property in the United States, § 1610(a)(2) also requires that the property be "used for the commercial activity upon which the claim is based." In permitting execution against LAN's assets the court below essentially concluded that LAN's activities aided * * * in the assassination and constituted the "commercial activities" that § 1610(a)(2) requires. We cannot agree because a consistent application of the Act, analysis of the background of its enactment, its language and legislative history, and the case law construing it compel the opposite conclusion.

We first note that the district court for the District of Columbia found that Chile lost its immunity from jurisdiction pursuant to § 1605(a)(5), the "tortious activity" exception to jurisdictional immunity. Section 1605(a)(5) specifically states that it applies to situations "not otherwise encompassed in paragraph (2)." Section 1605(a)(2) is the commercial activity exception. This language suggests that the commercial activity exception to jurisdictional immunity under (2) and the tort exception under (5) are mutually exclusive. If the district court in the District of Columbia lifted jurisdictional immunity based on its finding that the activities complained of were tortious, not commercial, it is inconsistent for this court to lift execution immunity based on a finding that the activities were commercial.

Our disagreement with the finding that LAN's activities were commercial rests on more than the resulting lack of symmetry in application of the FSIA. If LAN, as the trial court found, acted in complicity with the Chilean secret police in the assassination, its activities had nothing to do with its place in commerce. The nature of its course of conduct could not have been as a merchant in the marketplace. Its activities would have been those of the foreign state: governmental, not private or commercial.

* * *

Congress intended the "essential nature" of given behavior to determine its status for purposes of the commercial activities exception, and gave the courts a "great deal of latitude" to decide this issue. Id. at 6615. The legislative history makes clear that courts should not deem activity "commercial" as a whole simply because certain aspects of it are commercial. The example given is that the AID programs remain governmental even though they involve behavior traditionally performed by private persons.

* * *

A private person cannot lawfully engage in murder any more than he can in kidnapping or criminal assault. Carriage of passengers and packages is an activity in which a private person could engage. But it is not for those activities that LAN's assets are being executed against. Rather, plaintiffs assert that LAN itself participated in the assassination and essentially accuse LAN of being a co-conspirator or joint tortfeasor. In other words, LAN is accused of engaging in state-sponsored terrorism the purpose of which, irrelevant under the FSIA, was to assassinate an opponent of the Chilean government. Politically motivated assassinations are not traditionally the function of private individuals. They can scarcely be considered commercial activity. Viewed in this light, LAN's participation, if any, in the assassination is not commercial activity that falls within the § 1610(a)(2) exception and its assets therefore are not stripped of immunity.

* * *

The FSIA distinguishes between execution against property of an agency or instrumentality of a foreign state, which may be executed against regardless of whether the property was used for the activity on which the claim is based under § 1610(b)(2), and the property of the foreign state itself, which may be executed against only when the property was used for the commercial activity on which the claim is based under § 1610(a)(2). In so distinguishing, Congress sharply restricted immunity from execution against agencies and instrumentalities, but was more cautious when lifting immunity from execution against property owned by the State itself.

* * *

CONCLUSION

We hold therefore that the Foreign Sovereign Immunities Act does not allow execution against the assets of LAN, the Chilean National Airlines.[4] The court below improperly ignored defendant LAN's separate juridical status from the Republic of Chile. Ordi-

---

4. Although tenuous, other remedies may still be possible. Chile itself may decide as an act of international good-will to honor the judgment of the United States District Court for the District of Columbia. Alternatively, the United States may be persuaded to bring this claim before some international tribunal as it did in Z & F Assets Realization Corp. v. Hull, 311 U.S. 470, 487 (1941).

narily, we would remand for further evidentiary hearings on the separateness issue, but we are further persuaded, even were LAN and Chile found to be alter egos, that Congress did not provide for execution against a foreign state's property under the circumstances of this case. Congress provided for execution against property used in commercial activity upon which the claim is based. An act of political terrorism is not the kind of commercial activity that Congress contemplated.

Accordingly, we reverse the orders appealed from and dismiss the supplementary proceedings.

Notes

1. Pursuant to a 1914 Treaty between the United States and Chile for the settlement of disputes, an international Commission (1 Chilean, 1 U.S. citizen, 1 Briton, and 2 from Latin American countries other than Chile) was established to determine the amount of compensation appropriate for the deaths and injuries. The payments were to be made "ex gratia," without admission of Chilean government liability. In January, 1992, the Commission ordered Chile to pay $2.6 million to the United States for the families of Letelier and Moffitt. In September, 1991, two commanders of the secret police under the Pinochet regime were arrested and ordered to be tried for plotting the assassination of Orlando Letelier. In May, 1995, Chile's highest court upheld their prison sentences, seven years for one, six years for the other. Their sentences will be served in a new prison just north of Santiago built at the request of the army specifically for officers convicted of atrocities. An elite army unit will serve as guards.

2. Plaintiffs did not sue LAN because sufficient evidence against LAN was not available at the time pleadings were filed. There was a chance that a motion to amend would not have been granted at a late date and even if granted, would trigger a new round of delays in already very lengthy proceedings. Memorandum from Michael E. Tigar, attorney for plaintiffs, to the author, June 6, 1989.

The award of punitive damages was only against the individual defendants and not against Chile. 502 F.Supp. at 266-67.

3. Liu v. Republic of China, 892 F.2d 1419 (9th Cir. 1989), cert. dism'd, 497 U.S. 1058 (1990) permitted suit against the Republic of China under the FSIA for damages resulting from the assassination of plaintiff's husband in California under orders of the Director of the Republic's Defense Intelligence Bureau. The court held that under California law, the Director acted "within the scope of his employment" under § 1605(a)(5) and that the "discretionary function" exception of 1605(a)(5)(A) does not apply "when an employee of a foreign government violates its own internal law." The court also rejected an act-of-state defense. The dismissal of the petition for certiorari was by agreement of the parties. The Republic of China agreed to make an ex gratia payment to the plaintiff. Brent E. Christopher, "State Responsibility and Noncommercial Torts Under the Foreign Sovereign Immunities Act," 27 Tex. Int'l L. J. 137, 145 n.45 (1992).

4. Siderman de Blake v. Republic of Argentina, 965 F.2d 699 (9th Cir. 1992), cert. denied, 507 U.S. 1017 (1993). Plaintiffs claimed that their property in Argentina was expropriated by a military junta that took over the Argentine government and that Mr. de Blake was tortured by government officials. The court held that the claim for compensation for the expropriated property, a hotel, might be brought under the first two clauses of the "commercial activity" exception in § 1605(a)(2). Guests for the hotel were solicited by ad-

vertisements in the United States, United States citizens patronized the hotel, and Argentina accepts payment in the United States for reservations. The provision covering taking of property in violation of international law, 1605(a)(3), was held available on behalf of a United States citizen who was a member of the family, but not on behalf of Argentine citizens. The fact that torture is a "jus cogens" violation of international law (see the note on jus cogens, supra page 118) is not sufficient to create a waiver of sovereign immunity to this claim, but waiver was found by the fact that Argentina sought to prosecute one of the Sidermans and enlisted the aid of a California court by means of a letter rogatory to serve process in the prosecution. Smith v. Socialist People's Libyan Arab Jamahiriya, 101 F.3d 239 (2d Cir. 1996) also holds that violation of a jus cogens standard does not constitute an implied waiver of sovereign immunity and collects authority in accord.

The 1996 amendments to FSIA adding §§ 1605(a)(7),(e), (f), and (g), and 1610(a)(7) and amending 1610(b) (supra pages 283-288) provided recovery under some circumstances against a foreign sovereign for "torture, extrajudicial killing, aircraft sabotage, [and] hostage taking." These are some of the acts on which plaintiffs have based the argument for a jus cogens implied waiver. See Andreas Zimmermann, Sovereign Immunity and Violations of International Jus Cogens—Some Critical Remarks, 16 Mich. J. Int'l L. 433 (1995) (stating that "denial of immunity through an amendment to U.S. statutes eliminating the grant of sovereign immunity in cases of purported violations of international human rights would be both illegal under current public international law and politically unwise").

Civil Liability for Acts of State Sponsored Terrorism, Pub. L. 104-208, 110 Stat. 3009-172 (1996) created civil liability, including punitive damages, of an official, employee, or agent of a foreign state for acts that would subject a foreign state to suit under FSIA § 1605(a)(7). Pub. L. 105-277, 112 Stat. 2681-491, § 117(b), amended FSIA § 1606 to permit punitive damages against a foreign state that is not immune under §1605(a)(7).

For judgments against foreign states under FSIA § 1605(a)(7) see Anderson v. Islamic Republic of Iran, 90 F. Supp.2d 107 (D.C. 2000) ($24.5 million compensatory and $300 million punitive); Cicippio v. Islamic Republic of Iran, 18 F. Supp.2d 62 (D.D.C. 1998) ($65 million); Flatow v. Islamic Republic of Iran, 999 F. Supp. 1 (1998) ($22.5 million in compensatory damages and $225 million in punitive damages against both Iran and various Iranian officials); Alejandre v. The Republic of Cuba, 996 F. Supp. 1239 (S.D. Fla. 1997) ($49.9 million compensatory damages against Cuba and the Cuban Air Force and $137.7 million punitive damages against the Cuban Air Force); Rein v. Socialist People's Libyan Arab Jamahiriya, 995 F. Supp. 325 (E.D.N.Y. 1998) (dismissing defendants' motions to dismiss for lack of subject-matter and personal jurisdiction and for failure to state claims), aff'd, 162 F.3d 748 (2d Cir. 1998) (FSIA § 1605(a)(7) constitutional as applied to Libya because Libya already on list of state sponsors of terrorism when Congress passed this amendment; therefore issue of whether Congress unconstitutionally delegated to State Department power to control jurisdiction of federal courts does not arise), cert. denied, 525 U.S. 1003 (1999). The Cicippio case demonstrates the effect of the addition of 1605(a)(7). Before this amendment, the plaintiffs' suit against Iran had been dismissed for lack of subject matter jurisdiction. 30 F.3d 164 (D.C. Cir. 1994), cert. denied, 513 U.S. 1078 (1995).

Daliberti v. Republic of Iraq, 97 F. Supp.2d 38 (D.C. 2000), held that the act of state doctrine does not require dismissal of a claim under 1605(a)(7).

Joseph v. Office of the Consulate General of Nigeria
830 F.2d 1018, (9th Cir. 1987), cert. denied 485 U.S. 905 (1988)

Before Choy, Senior Circuit Judge, Tang and Nelson, Circuit Judges.

Choy, Senior Circuit Judge:

This appeal primarily requires us to decide whether the district court has subject matter jurisdiction over a landlord-tenant dispute between a landlord and a foreign state, its consulate, and its consular officials. We conclude that the district court has jurisdiction over the landlord's breach of contract and tort claims. The district court's order finding jurisdiction over only the tort claims is affirmed in part and reversed in part.

BACKGROUND

The sovereign defendants in this case are the Federal Republic of Nigeria ("Nigeria") and the Consulate General of Nigeria (the "Consulate"). According to the defendants, the basic function of the Consulate is to protect the interests of Nigerians residing in its consular district, and to encourage cultural exchanges between Nigerian and American organizations.

In 1978, Catherine Joseph ("Joseph") leased a house in San Francisco to the Consulate. O. Effiong, a former consular officer, signed the standard form lease on behalf of the Consulate. The house was used as a residence by employees of the Consulate and their families. One of those consular employees was defendant A.A. Olalandu ("Olalandu"), a finance officer for the Consulate, who began residence at the Joseph property in 1982.

Shortly after the end of the five-year lease period, Joseph allegedly discovered that the tenants had removed property from the house and had left the premises severely damaged. Joseph brought suit in federal district court, seeking, inter alia, compensation for damages to fixtures, landscaping, and appliances. Joseph asserts four causes of action against both Nigeria and the Consulate. The first is for breach of contract; the other three are tort claims for conversion, trespass, and waste. In addition, Joseph asserts three tort claims against Olalandu for conversion, trespass, and waste.

Joseph filed her complaint in district court in August 1984.

* * *

On August 12, 1986, the court issued an opinion and order. The court determined that it had jurisdiction over Nigeria and the Consulate pursuant to the Foreign Sovereign Immunities Act ("FSIA"). Specifically, the court found jurisdiction over Joseph's tort claims under the FSIA's "tortious activity" exception to immunity. However, the court concluded that jurisdiction over Nigeria and the Consulate was not conferred by the FSIA's "waiver," "commercial activity," and "immovable property," exceptions. Because the district court found jurisdiction only pursuant to the tortious activity exception, the court's decision immunized Nigeria and the Consulate from Joseph's breach of contract claims.

The court found jurisdiction over Olalandu pursuant to 28 U.S.C. § 1351 (1982). The court determined that Olalandu was not protected by consular immunity under the Vienna Convention on Consular Relations, April 24, 1963, 21 U.S.T. 77, T.I.A.S. No. 6820, 596 U.N.T.S. 261 (the "Vienna Convention"), which provides immunity to consular officials for actions which are performed in the exercise of the officials' consular functions.

* * *

Both Joseph and the defendants have brought interlocutory appeals in regard to the district court's decision. The defendants appeal the district court's determination that it had jurisdiction over Joseph's tort claims against Nigeria and the Consulate pursuant to the tortious activity exception. Olalandu apparently appeals the district court's determination that he is not protected by consular immunity.

Joseph * * * argues that the district court incorrectly determined that jurisdiction over Nigeria and the Consulate is not conferred by the waiver, commercial activity, and immovable property exceptions to the FSIA.

DISCUSSION

Our evaluation of the defendants' claims of immunity involves two independent doctrines. The doctrine of sovereign immunity is applicable only to states and their instrumentalities—here, Nigeria and the Consulate. The doctrine of consular immunity is applicable only to consular officials and employees—here, Olalandu.

I: Sovereign Immunity

* * *

A: Waiver Exception

The FSIA's waiver exception denies immunity in any case "in which the foreign state has waived its immunity either explicitly or by implication..." 28 U.S.C. § 1605(a)(1). The waiver exception is narrowly construed. See *Frolova v. Union of Soviet Socialist Republics*, 761 F.2d 370, 377 (7th Cir.1985). Implicit waivers are ordinarily found only where: "(1) a foreign state has agreed to arbitration in another country; (2) a foreign state has agreed that a contract is governed by the law of a particular country; and (3) a foreign state has filed a responsive pleading in a case without raising the defense of sovereign immunity." Id.

At issue in this case is whether the lease agreement between Joseph and the Consulate implicitly waives sovereign immunity. The relevant lease provision states:

> In the event that any action shall be commenced by either party hereto arising out of, or concerning this lease or any right or obligation derived therefrom, then in addition to all other relief at law or equity, the prevailing party shall be entitled to recover attorney's fees as fixed by the court.

We conclude that this provision constitutes a waiver of sovereign immunity as to all of Joseph's claims against Nigeria and the Consulate.

A foreign state does not waive its sovereign immunity merely by entering into a contract with another party. Nevertheless, at the very least it is clear that a sovereign party has waived immunity where a contract specifically states that the laws of a jurisdiction within the United States are to govern the transaction. On the other hand, where a contract specifies that the laws of a jurisdiction outside of the United States are to govern, a waiver of sovereign immunity has not been made for the purposes of the FSIA.

In the instant case, the lease agreement does not specify which jurisdiction's laws will govern disputes under the lease. Joseph argues that it is not necessary for a contract to specify which law will govern a contract in order for the waiver exception to apply. Indeed, there appears to be no justification for requiring a contract to specifically state the governing law in order for there to be a waiver of immunity. Waiver by contract is premised on an agreement by the parties that the United States courts may become involved in disputes arising pursuant to the contract. Where an agreement contemplates adjudication of a dispute by the United States courts, the waiver exception should be applied, regardless of whether the governing law is explicitly identified.

Because the lease at issue provides for adjudication of landlord-tenant disputes in court, we conclude that the lease contemplates participation of the United States courts in disputes between Joseph and her tenants. In light of the wholly local nature of the transaction, it is virtually inconceivable that the Consulate contemplated that adjudication of disputes would occur in a court outside of the United States. Therefore, we believe that the waiver exception is applicable to Joseph's breach of contract and tort claims. Nevertheless, because of the vagueness of the waiver provision at issue, and because the waiver exception should be narrowly construed, we deem it advisable to refer to other FSIA exceptions to immunity to support our finding of jurisdiction.

B: The Commercial Activity Exception

The commercial activity exception denies immunity in any case "in which the action is based upon a commercial activity carried on in the United States by the foreign state." 28 U.S.C. § 1605(a)(2). In determining whether the commercial activity exception applies, the courts focus only on those specific acts that form the basis of the suit. *De Sanchez v. Banco Central de Nicaragua*, 770 F.2d 1385, 1391 (5th Cir.1985). That is, the courts examine "whether the particular conduct giving rise to the claim in question actually constitutes or is in connection with commercial activity, regardless of the defendant's generally commercial or governmental character." *Arango v. Guzman Travel Advisors Corp.*, 621 F.2d 1371, 1379 (5th Cir.1980). Our discussion of the commercial activity exception will focus on Joseph's breach of contract claim. Thus, we must determine whether the lease agreement, and the alleged breach of that agreement, constituted commercial activities.

The FSIA, somewhat tautologically, defines "commercial activity" as "either a regular course of commercial conduct or a particular commercial transaction or act." 28 U.S.C. § 1603(d). The FSIA directs the courts to evaluate the nature rather than the purpose of the activity in question. Id. Thus, a contract to purchase military supplies, although clearly undertaken for public use, is commercial in nature and therefore subject to the commercial activity exception. *McDonnell Douglas Corp. v. Islamic Republic of Iran*, 758 F.2d 341, 349 (8th Cir.), cert. denied, 474 U.S. 948 (1985). Nevertheless, the purpose of an act may be relevant in defining its nature: "[o]ften, the essence of an act is defined by its purpose." *De Sanchez*, 770 F.2d at 1393.

In the instant case, the district court stated that "[c]ommercial activity is defined as the type of act an individual would customarily carry on for profit." The district court concluded that the commercial activity exception did not apply because the Consulate did not contract to be a lessee of the Joseph residential property for profit.

This reasoning is flawed. Some courts have indeed indicated that the commercial activity exception will ordinarily be applied where a sovereign engages in a transaction for profit. * * * However, there is no indication that Congress intended the presence of a profit motive on the part of the sovereign to be a *threshold requirement* for applying the commercial activity exception. In this regard the Legislative History merely states that "[c]ertainly, if an activity is customarily carried on for profit, its commercial nature could readily be assumed." H. R. Rep. No. 1487, 94th Cong., 2d Sess. 16, reprinted in 1976 U.S.Code Cong. & Admin.News 6604, 6615. Moreover, the use of profit motive as a threshold requirement for applying the commercial activity exception would be inconsistent with the FSIA's focus on the nature of the transaction at issue rather than its purpose. See *De Sanchez*, 770 F.2d at 1393.

In addition, a transaction need not be made in connection with a business or commercial enterprise operated by the sovereign in order to be "commercial" for the purposes of the FSIA. Transactions between strictly governmental entities and commercial enterprises are covered by the commercial activity exception if the role of the sovereign is one which might be played by a private actor.

* * *

Applying the principles articulated above, we conclude that, although the lease agreement at issue was not undertaken by the Consulate for profit, it nevertheless was a commercial transaction. See H. R. Rep. No. 1487, 94th Cong., 2d Sess. 16, reprinted in 1976 U.S.Code Cong. & Admin.News 6604, 6615 (government's leasing of property is commercial; contracts to construct a government building and to make repairs on an embassy building are commercial). In renting the Joseph property, the Consulate entered the marketplace as a commercial actor. Compare *De Sanchez*, 770 F.2d at 1394. There is nothing about the lease agreement, or the alleged breach of that agreement, which distinguishes the transaction from an ordinary private commercial transaction, aside from the fact that the Consulate General of Nigeria was the tenant. Neither the Consulate's rental agreement, nor its alleged breach of that agreement, constitute sovereign activities. Therefore, contrary to the district court's decision, Joseph's *breach of contract* claim against Nigeria may be heard pursuant to the commercial activity exception. See id. at 1394 & n. 11.

C: Tortious Activity Exception

We find it unnecessary to determine the applicability of the commercial activity exception to Joseph's tort claims, in light of our determination that the district court correctly concluded that the FSIA's tortious activity exception applies to these claims.

The tortious activity exception provides jurisdiction over tort actions not encompassed in the commercial activity exception "in which money damages are sought against a foreign state for...damage to or loss of property, occurring in the United States and caused by the tortious act or omission of that foreign state." 28 U.S.C. § 1605(a)(5). In order to find that a foreign sovereign can be sued under the tortious activity exception, the court must find: (1) that the tortious acts of individual employees of the sovereign were undertaken within the scope of employment, and (2) that the claim is not based upon the exercise or failure to exercise a discretionary function. Id. Both requirements are met in the instant case.

1: Scope of Employment

The "scope of employment" provision of the tortious activity exception essentially requires a finding that the doctrine of respondeat superior applies to the tortious acts of individuals. See *Skeen v. Federative Republic of Brazil*, 566 F.Supp. 1414, 1417-18

(D.D.C.1983). This determination is governed by state law. Id. at 1417. In this case, the law of California applies.

Under California respondeat superior doctrine, the determination of whether an employee has committed a tort during the course of employment turns on whether: (1) the act performed was either required or incident to his or her duties, or (2) the employee's misconduct could be reasonably foreseen by the employer. *Clark Equipment Co. v. Wheat*, 92 Cal.App.3d 503, 154 Cal.Rptr. 874, 882 (1979). Joseph contends that the second "foreseeability" approach is applicable here. We agree.

* * *

In light of California's expansive approach to respondeat superior, we conclude that the individual tortious acts alleged by Joseph were within the scope of employment of the residents of the Joseph house. The damage allegedly caused by the consular employees was a risk inherent in the consular enterprise, under the defendants' broad definition of that enterprise. The defendants cannot avoid responsibility for damage done by its employees in the Joseph house.

2: Discretionary Function

In order for the tortious activity exception to be applied to this case, the torts alleged by Joseph must not involve the exercise of discretionary functions. See 28 U.S.C. § 1605(a)(5)(A). The existence of a discretionary function under the FSIA is generally analyzed under the principles developed pursuant to the Federal Tort Claims Act's ("FTCA") discretionary function exception. *Olsen v. Government of Mexico*, 729 F.2d 641, 646-47 (9th Cir.), cert. denied, 469 U.S. 917 (1984). At one time, this circuit distinguished between two types of governmental acts: those at the "planning" level and those at the "operational" level. The former qualified for the discretionary function exception; the latter did not. See Olsen, 729 F.2d at 647. This approach was utilized by the district court in finding that the acts in question were not discretionary. However, we have abandoned this approach in FTCA cases, pursuant to the Supreme Court's decision in *United States v. S.A. Empresa de Viacao Aerea Rio Grandense (Varig Airlines)*, 467 U.S. 797, 104 S.Ct. 2755, 81 L.Ed.2d 660 (1984). *See, e.g., Mitchell v. United States*, 787 F.2d 466, 468 (9th Cir.1986) (planning-operational distinction has been abandoned); *Chamberlin v. Isen*, 779 F.2d 522, 524 (9th Cir.1985) (same); *Begay v. United States*, 768 F.2d 1059, 1062-63 n. 2 (9th Cir.1985) (same).

Pursuant to *Varig*, a two-pronged test has been developed for determining whether the discretionary function exception applies in FTCA cases. First, the court must examine "'the nature of the conduct, rather than the status of the actor.'" *Begay*, 768 F.2d at 1064 (quoting Varig, 467 U.S. at 813). Second, the court must inquire whether the governmental acts at issue were "'grounded in social, economic, and political policy.'" Id. In other words, the court should avoid second-guessing policy decisions through the medium of a tort action. Id. The execution of policy decisions by subordinates, even those subordinates at the operational level, comes under the discretionary function exception if the acts involved the exercise of policy judgment. *Red Lake Band of Chippewa Indians v. United States*, 800 F.2d 1187, 1196 (D.C.Cir.1986).

The application of the *Varig* approach to FSIA cases is ably discussed in *MacArthur Area Citizens Association v. Republic of Peru*, 809 F.2d 918 (D.C.Cir.), amended on other grounds, 823 F.2d 606 (D.C.Cir.1987). The factual situation in *MacArthur* is somewhat similar to the case at issue. Peru purchased a building in an area zoned for residential use, and proceeded to convert the property into a chancery. Primarily for security reasons, Peru put bricks and bars over various parts of the building, established an elaborate alarm system, and installed harsh fluorescent lights. Id. at 919. Because of the unsightly nature of the results, a neighborhood association sued for damages. The district court dismissed the suit on the ground of sovereign immunity, and the court of appeals affirmed pursuant to, inter alia, the FSIA's discretionary function exception.

The court stated that "establishing a chancery...to conduct foreign relations is a discretionary public policy decision and...this decision undergirds the specific acts which the Association bewails." Id. at 922. The court found that the decisions to purchase and modify the chancery building were made in order to implement the determination to establish the chancery. The court concluded that these implementing decisions involved a measure of policy judgment and were thereby protected by the discretionary function exception. Id. at 922-23. Specifically, the court stated that the implementing decisions at issue: "(1) [were] grounded in an economic judgment regarding which property represents the best value; or (2) embodie[d] a political decision regarding the image that the Peruvian Government seeks to project through the offices it occupies; or (3) reflect[ed] security considerations..." Id. at 923. In sum, the actions taken by Peru were intimately connected with policy decisions made by a sovereign, and were therefore discretionary.

MacArthur indicates that the *acquisition and operation* of the Joseph residence by the Consulate was a discretionary policy decision. However, *MacArthur* does not indicate that the purely destructive acts which give rise to Joseph's tort claims were discretionary. Destruction of property can hardly be considered as part of a policy decision to establish a consular residence. Nor will the exercise of jurisdiction over the instant lawsuit encroach on the ability of foreign sovereigns to make policy decisions regarding their consular buildings. We therefore conclude that the discretionary function exception does not apply to Joseph's tort claims.

In sum, all of the requirements of the tortious activity exception are met in this case. The district court has jurisdiction over Joseph's tort claims against Nigeria and the Consulate.

D: Immovable Property Exception

Because we have already determined that the district court has jurisdiction over Joseph's breach of contract and tort claims against Nigeria and the Consulate, we find it unnecessary to decide whether the FSIA's immovable property exception is applicable to this case.

II: Consular Immunity

Jurisdiction by the district court over consular official Olalandu is premised on 28 U.S.C. § 1351, which states that "[t]he district courts shall have original jurisdiction... of all civil actions and proceedings against—(1) consuls or vice consuls of foreign states." However, the district court does not have jurisdiction over Olalandu if he is protected by consular immunity. We review de novo the district court's conclusion that it does have subject matter jurisdiction over Joseph's tort claims against Olalandu.

The consular immunity of Olalandu is governed by the Vienna Convention. Under article 43 of the Vienna Convention, consular officials are subject to the jurisdiction of the receiving state except "in respect of acts performed in the exercise of consular functions." 21 U.S.T. at 104. Article 5 of the Vienna Convention defines the term "consular function." Articles 5(a)-5(1) list twelve specific consular functions. Article 5(m), a "catch-all" provision, defines "consular function" to include "any other functions entrusted to a consular post by the sending State which are not prohibited by the laws and regulations of the receiving State." 21 U.S.T. at 82-85.

We conclude that the tortious acts alleged by Joseph were not "performed in the exercise of" Olalandu's consular function as a resident of the Joseph house, or of any of Olalandu's other consular functions.

* * *

CONCLUSION

The district court has jurisdiction under the FSIA over Joseph's breach of contract and tort claims against Nigeria and the Consulate. We REVERSE the district court's determination that Joseph's breach of contract claims cannot be heard pursuant to the waiver or commercial activity exceptions. We AFFIRM the district court's determination that Joseph's tort claims can be heard pursuant to the tortious activity exception. We also conclude that the waiver exception is applicable to Joseph's tort claims.

In addition, the district court is not precluded by the Vienna Convention from hearing Joseph's tort claims against Olalandu. The district court's decision to that effect is AFFIRMED.

* * *

AFFIRMED in part, REVERSED in part, and REMANDED for further proceedings.

Notes

1. The opinion states that "the standard form lease" was used. Would you advise a landlord to do this when renting to a foreign consulate?

2. The opinion holds that "the law of California" determines the meaning of "scope of...employment" under § 1605(a)(5). Is this desirable when dealing with a basic issue of subject matter jurisdiction under FSIA? Is the court's conclusion supported by the language in § 1606 that "the foreign state shall be liable in the same manner and to the same extent as a private individual under like circumstances"? Williams v. United States, 380 U.S. 857 (1955) held that for suits against the federal government under the Federal Tort Claims Act, state law determined scope of employment. Is *Williams* distinguishable? Randolph v. Budget Rent-A-Car, 97 F.3d 319 (9th Cir. 1996), holds that whether a student is an employee of a foreign sovereign for purposes of § 1605(a)(5) is governed by state law.

The principal case also discusses the "discretionary function" exception to 1605(a)(5) by analogy to decisions under the FTCA. For a subsequent FTCA decision, see United States v. Gaubert, 499 U.S. 315, 323 (1991), which holds that the Federal Home Loan Bank Board was performing a discretionary function while involved in the day-to-day operations of a savings and loan institution that became insolvent. The Court states: "A discretionary act is one that involves choice or judgment; there is nothing in that description that refers exclusively to policymaking or planning functions."

3. The court applies the Vienna Convention on Consular Relations to determine Olalandu's liability as a consular official. The liability of a diplomatic, as distinguished from a consular official, is determined by the Vienna Convention on Diplomatic Relations, 23

U.S.T. 3227, T.I.A.S. No. 7502, 500 U.N.T.S. 95, to which the United States became a party in 1972. Diplomats are given immunity from arrest, detention, criminal process, and with few exceptions, civil process, even though their actions were not in the scope of their employment. The few exceptions relate to determination of succession rights to realty or to suits relating to personal professional or commercial activities. The United States does not permit foreign diplomats to engage in such activities. The almost complete immunity of diplomatic officials from civil suit is remedied in part by 28 U.S.C. §1364, which confers the right of direct action against the officials' liability insurer, and 22 U.S.C. §254(e), which requires that members of diplomatic missions and their families have insurance to cover liability resulting from the operation of motor vehicles, vessels, and aircraft. By contrast, the immunity of a consular officials is limited to acts performed in the exercise of consular functions and even this immunity is not applicable to damage caused by motor vehicle, vessel, or aircraft. The key distinction between consular and diplomatic officials is set out in Article 3 of the Diplomatic Convention providing for functions missing from Article 5 of the Consular Convention. The chief distinguishing diplomatic functions are representing the sending state in the receiving state and negotiating with the government of the receiving state. A diplomatic officer may perform consular functions, but not vice versa.

Tabion v. Mufti, 73 F.3d 535 (4th Cir. 1996), holds that the hiring of a domestic servant is not a "commercial activity" within the meaning of the Vienna Convention on Diplomatic Relations and that the diplomat retains immunity from suit arising from that employment relationship. The court states that "commercial activity" in the Convention "relates only to trade or business activity engaged in for personal profit." Id. at 537. In Holden v. Canadian Consulate, 92 F.3d 918, (9th Cir. 1996), cert. denied, 519 U.S. 1091 (1997), a former commercial officer brought a wrongful termination action against the Consulate. The court held that the Consulate was not immune because the hiring was a "commercial activity" and stated that "employment of diplomatic, civil service or military personnel is governmental and the employment of other personnel is commercial." Id. at 921.

Annually Congress enacts legislation withholding from a country's funds under the Foreign Assistance Act any amount of fully adjudicated and unpaid parking fines owed to the District of Columbia by that country. See, e.g., PL 104-107, 110 Stat. 704, 741 (1996).

On rare occasions a country will waive their diplomat's immunity from criminal prosecution. On February 15, 1997, the Republic of Georgia waived the immunity of a high-ranking embassy official, so that he could be prosecuted for allegedly causing a death in a traffic accident in the District of Columbia while speeding and intoxicated. The Republic of Georgia receives hundreds of millions of dollars in foreign aid from the United States.

On December 19, 1997, a District of Columbia judge sentenced the embassy official referred to in the last paragraph of the note to seven to twenty-one years in prison for involuntary manslaughter and aggravated assault. With regard to the same incident, Knab v. Republic of Georgia, Civ. No. 97-3118 (TFH), 1998 U.S. Dist. LEXIS 8820 (D.D.C. 1998), dismissed a civil suit against the official on the ground that "he enjoys residual immunity for actions taken in performance of his former duties."

In 1989 Belgium waived diplomatic immunity for a 25-year-old embassy driver who admitted killing two men in Florida.

4. The court states that waiver of sovereign immunity will be implied if "a foreign state has filed a responsive pleading...without raising the defense...." Drexel Burnham Lambert Group Inc. v. Committee of Receivers for A.W. Galadari, 12 F.3d 317 (2d Cir.

1993), cert. denied, 511 U.S. 1069 (1994), held that there was no waiver when the Emirate of Dubai answered the complaint without asserting the immunity defense, but followed this almost immediately with a motion to dismiss that did assert the defense. Eckert International Inc. v. Government of the Sovereign Democratic Republic of Fiji, 32 F.3d 77 (4th Cir. 1994), held that an implied waiver occurred when, in a contract with a U.S. consulting firm, Fiji agreed that in the event of a dispute, the contract would be "construed and interpreted" under Virginia law.

5. Under the International Organizations Immunities Act, 22 U.S.C. §288a(b) "[i]nternational organizations, their property and their assets, wherever located, and by whomsoever held, shall enjoy the same immunity from suit and every form of judicial process as is enjoyed by foreign governments." Under 22 U.S.C. §288d(b) the officers and employees of such organizations "shall be immune from suit and legal process relating to acts performed by them in their official capacity and falling within their functions.... except insofar as such immunity may be waived by the foreign government or international organization concerned." Rendall-Speranza v. Nassim, 107 F.3d 913 (D.C. Cir. 1997) held a supervisor at the International Finance Corporation, a subsidiary of the World Bank, immune from suit for an assault that the plaintiff admitted was committed in the supervisor's official capacity.

Chapter 6

Extraterritorial Application of United States Law

Section 1: Antitrust Law

Restatement (Third) The Foreign Relations Law of the United States (1986)

Copyright 1987 by the American Law Institute. Reprinted with the permission of the American Law Institute.

§ 401. Categories Of Jurisdiction

Under international law, a state is subject to limitations on

(a) jurisdiction to prescribe, i.e., to make its law applicable to the activities, relations, or status of persons, or the interests of persons in things, whether by legislation, by executive act or order, by administrative rule or regulation, or by determination of a court;

(b) jurisdiction to adjudicate, i.e., to subject persons or things to the process of its courts or administrative tribunals, whether in civil or in criminal proceedings, whether or not the state is a party to the proceedings;

(c) jurisdiction to enforce, i.e., to induce or compel compliance or to punish noncompliance with its laws or regulations, whether through the courts or by use of executive, administrative, police, or other nonjudicial action.

§ 402. Bases Of Jurisdiction To Prescribe

Subject to § 403, a state has jurisdiction to prescribe law with respect to

(1) (a) conduct that, wholly or in substantial part, takes place within its territory;

(b) the status of persons, or interests in things, present within its territory;

(c) conduct outside its territory that has or is intended to have substantial effect within its territory;

(2) the activities, interests, status, or relations of its nationals outside as well as within its territory; and

(3) certain conduct outside its territory by persons not its nationals that is directed against the security of the state or against a limited class of other state interests.

§ 403. Limitations On Jurisdiction To Prescribe

1) Even when one of the bases for jurisdiction under § 402 is present, a state may not exercise jurisdiction to prescribe law with respect to a person or activity having connections with another state when the exercise of such jurisdiction is unreasonable.

2) Whether exercise of jurisdiction over a person or activity is unreasonable is determined by evaluating all relevant factors, including, where appropriate:

a) the link of the activity to the territory of the regulating state, i.e., the extent to which the activity takes place within the territory, or has substantial, direct, and foreseeable effect upon or in the territory;

b) the connections, such as nationality, residence, or economic activity, between the regulating state and the person principally responsible for the activity to be regulated, or between that state and those whom the regulation is designed to protect;

c) the character of the activity to be regulated, the importance of regulation to the regulating state, the extent to which other states regulate such activities, and the degree to which the desirability of such regulation is generally accepted.

d) the existence of justified expectations that might be protected or hurt by the regulation;

e) the importance of the regulation to the international political, legal, or economic system;

f) the extent to which the regulation is consistent with the traditions of the international system;

g) the extent to which another state may have an interest in regulating the activity; and

h) the likelihood of conflict with regulation by another state.

3) When it would not be unreasonable for each of two states to exercise jurisdiction over a person or activity, but the prescriptions by the two states are in conflict, each state has an obligation to evaluate its own as well as the other state's interest in exercising jurisdiction, in light of all the relevant factors, including those set out in Subsection (2); a state should defer to the other state if that state's interest is clearly greater.

[Two sections of the Restatement apply the general principles of 402 and 403 to antitrust and securities regulation:]

§ 415. Jurisdiction To Regulate Anti-Competitive Activities

(1) Any agreement in restraint of United States trade that is made in the United States, and any conduct or agreement in restraint of such trade that is carried out in significant measure in the United States, are subject to the jurisdiction to prescribe of the United States, regardless of the nationality or place of business of the parties to the agreement or of the participants in the conduct.

(2) Any agreement in restraint of United States trade that is made outside of the United States, and any conduct or agreement in restraint of such trade that is carried out predominantly outside of the United States, are subject to the jurisdiction to prescribe of the United States, if a principal purpose of the conduct or agreement is to interfere with the commerce of the United States, and the agreement or conduct has some effect on that commerce.

(3) Other agreements or conduct in restraint of United States trade are subject to the jurisdiction to prescribe of the United States if such agreements or conduct have sub-

stantial effect on the commerce of the United States and the exercise of jurisdiction is not unreasonable.

§ 416. Jurisdiction To Regulate Activities Related To Securities

(1) The United States may generally exercise jurisdiction to prescribe with respect to

(a) (i) any transaction in securities carried out in the United States to which a national or resident of the United States is a party, or

(ii) any offer to enter into a securities transaction, made in the United States by or to a national or resident of the United States;

(b) any transaction in securities

(i) carried out, or intended to be carried out, on an organized securities market in the United States, or

(ii) carried out, or intended to be carried out, predominantly in the United States, although not on an organized securities market;

(c) conduct, regardless of where it occurs, significantly related to a transaction described in Subsection (1)(b), if the conduct has, or is intended to have, a substantial effect in the United States;

(d) conduct occurring predominantly in the United States that is related to a transaction in securities, even if the transaction takes place outside the United States; or

(e) investment advice or solicitation of proxies or of consents with respect to securities, carried out predominantly in the United States.

(2) Whether the United States may exercise jurisdiction to prescribe with respect to transactions or conduct other than those addressed in Subsection (1) depends on whether such exercise of jurisdiction is reasonable in the light of § 403, in particular

(a) whether the transaction or conduct has, or can reasonably be expected to have, a substantial effect on a securities market in the United States for securities of the same issuer or on holdings in such securities by United States nationals or residents;

(b) whether representations are made or negotiations are conducted in the United States;

(c) whether the party sought to be subjected to the jurisdiction of the United States is a United States national or resident, or the persons sought to be protected are United States nationals or residents.

Notes

1. Section 401 adds "jurisdiction to enforce" to the classic categories of "jurisdiction to prescribe" and "jurisdiction to adjudicate." The purpose of this addition is to recognize that "[e]nforcement is often carried out through executive or administrative rather than judicial action…" Restatement (Third) Part IV, Introductory Note.

2. Subsection 402(1) states the "territorial" basis for jurisdiction to prescribe. As the materials in this chapter illustrate, it is the "effect within its territory," (1)(c), that, when utilized, produces the most controversy, particularly in the application of United States antitrust law.

Subsection 402(3) could be viewed as an example of the "effect" doctrine writ large. It is often discussed separately in international literature as the "protective" principle.

An example of conduct abroad by aliens that may make application of an affected nation's laws reasonable, is counterfeiting of currency with the purpose of disrupting the nation's financial system.

Not listed as a basis for jurisdiction to prescribe, and not generally recognized as proper, is the "passive personality principle." Under this principle, a nation would apply its law to conduct abroad by non-citizens if the conduct affected a citizen, even though this effect occurred abroad. 18 U.S.C. §2332(b) is an example of the invocation of the passive personality principle. The section applies criminal penalties to "[w]hoever outside the United States attempts to kill, or engages in a conspiracy to kill, a national of the United States..." 18 U.S.C. §2332(d) provides that there shall be no prosecution under the section "except on written certification of the Attorney General, or the highest ranking subordinate of the Attorney General with responsibility for criminal prosecutions that, in the judgment of the certifying official, such offense was intended to coerce, intimidate, or retaliate against a government or a civilian population." For expression of doubt as to the constitutionality of the combination in this statute of passive personality and prosecution certification by a prosecutor, see Andreas F. Lowenfeld, U.S. Law Enforcement Abroad: The Constitution and International Law, 83 Am. J. Int'l L. 880, 891-92 (1989). In 1996 the Foreign Sovereign Immunities Act was amended to add §1605(a)(7) [supra page 283], which permits suits by United States nationals against foreign states for torture, extrajudicial killing, aircraft sabotage, and hostage taking. For doubts as to the constitutionality of the passive personality principle itself, see Lea Brilmayer and Charles Norchi, "Federal Extraterritoriality and Fifth Amendment Due Process," 105 Harv. L. Rev. 1217, 1261 (1992).

In the S. S. Lotus, 1927 P.C.I.J. (Ser. A) No. 9 (Sept. 7), a French Ship and a Turkish ship collided on the high seas resulting in the death of eight Turkish citizens. Turkey prosecuted the French officer of the watch at the time of the collision for involuntary manslaughter. France objected to the Turkish criminal proceedings against the French officer and the two countries submitted their dispute to the Permanent Court of International Justice. Turkey claimed two bases for jurisdiction—injury to Turkish nationals and injury inflicted aboard a Turkish vessel, which should be treated as Turkish territory for this purpose. A majority of the judges declined to pass on the legitimacy under international law of harm to citizens as a basis for criminal jurisdiction finding a sufficient basis for Turkish jurisdiction on the second ground urged by Turkey. The dissenters thought even infliction of harm aboard a Turkish ship was not sufficient to support jurisdiction. The basis for jurisdiction approved by the majority in S.S. Lotus is excluded by Article 11 of the Convention on the High Seas, April 29, 1958, 13 U.S.T. 2312, 450 U.N.T.S. 82, which limits penal or disciplinary proceedings against ship's personnel to "the judicial or administrative authorities either of the flag state or of the state of which such person is a national."

Sometimes what appears to be use of the passive personality principle can be explained as invocation of a more recognized basis for jurisdiction to prescribe, "universal jurisdiction." This jurisdiction extends to punishment of offenses internationally recognized as concerning all states. The classic example is piracy. See United States v. Yunis, 924 F.2d 1086 (D.C. Cir. 1991) (affirming conviction of person who hijacked a Jordanian airplane in Beirut on which two Americans were passengers).

3. Section 403 provides a multi-factor reasonableness standard for limiting §402. The list of factors in 403(2) is not intended to be exclusive ("including"). For prescriptions by two states to be "in conflict" within the meaning of 403(3), compliance with the laws of both countries must be "impossible." The subsection "is addressed primarily

to the political departments of government, but it may be relevant also in judicial proceedings." Id. comment e.

One factor that might have been expected in the 403(2) list but is missing, is "reciprocity"—whether the other state would apply its law under similar circumstances. Reporters' Note 5 to the section explains its absence on the ground that "a determination as to whether an exercise of jurisdiction is reasonable must take account of the interests of the persons affected as well as the interests or practices of other states." Is this explanation satisfactory?

4. Section 415, comment a, states that if a principal purpose of conduct is to interfere with United States commerce, "some" in 415(2) means "not insignificant" although it may be "insubstantial." Comment a further states that "any exercise of jurisdiction under this section is subject to the requirement of reasonableness." Comment d "takes no position on the question whether intended or threatened effect (without actual effect)...satisfies the requirement of effect under Subsection (2)." The Comment states that a potential effect is sufficient for injunctive relief.

Timberlane Lumber Co. v. Bank of America
549 F.2d 597 (9th Cir., 1976)

Before Browning and Choy, Circuit Judges, and Gray, District Judge.

Choy, Circuit Judge:

[Timberlane brought antitrust actions against the Bank, several of its employees in the United States and Central America, Honduran corporations and a Honduran citizen, alleging that "officials of the Bank of America and others located in both the United States and Honduras conspired to prevent Timberlane, through its Honduras subsidiaries, from milling lumber in Honduras and exporting it to the United States, thus maintaining control of the Honduras lumber export business in the hands of a few select individuals financed and controlled by the Bank." Timberlane also alleged that the operation of its Honduran subsidiary was disrupted by the defendants who refused to settle their claims against the business, obtained a Honduran court-ordered attachment of the business, and caused Timberlane's Honduran manager to be falsely imprisoned. The district court dismissed the antitrust suits under the "act of state" doctrine and, because no direct and substantial effect on United States commerce was alleged, for lack of subject matter jurisdiction. The Ninth Circuit vacated the dismissal and remanded the action.]

Act of State

* * *

A corollary to the act of state doctrine in the foreign trade antitrust field is the often-recognized principle that corporate conduct which is compelled by a foreign sovereign is also protected from antitrust liability, as if it were an act of the state itself. Thus, in *Interamerican Refining Corp. v. Texaco Maracaibo, Inc.*, 307 F.Supp. 1291 (D.Del.1970), a refusal by defendants to sell Venezuelan crude oil to plaintiff was held not to be an illegal restraint of trade because it was a complete defense that the Venezuelan government had imposed a boycott forbidding such sales. The court there observed that "[w]hen a nation compels a trade practice, firms there have no choice but to obey. Acts of business become effectively acts of the sovereign." Id. at 1298.

On the other hand, mere governmental approval or foreign governmental involvement which the defendants had arranged does not necessarily provide a defense. In *United States v. Sisal Sales Corp.*, 274 U.S. 268 (1927), the defendants were accused of conspiring to monopolize sales of sisal, a material used in making rope, from Mexico to the United States by inducing Mexican officials to recognize the conspirators as the exclusive traders and to impose discriminatory taxes on rival sellers. The Court rejected the defendants' claim to act of state protection, ruling that a conspiracy formed in the United States for the purpose of monopolizing sales to the United States was not protected simply because one element of the conspiracy involved securing favorable action by foreign officials.

* * *

The distinction was recognized and relied upon in *United States v. The Watchmakers of Switzerland Information Center, Inc.*, 1963 Trade Cases ¶ 70,600 (S.D.N.Y.1962), order modified, 1965 Trade Cases ¶ 70,352 (S.D.N.Y.1965), the "*Swiss Watch*" case:

> If, of course, the defendants' activities had been required by Swiss law, this court could indeed do nothing. An American court would have under such circumstances no right to condemn the governmental activity of another sovereign nation. In the present case, however, the defendants' activities were not required by the laws of Switzerland. They were agreements formulated privately without compulsion on the part of the Swiss Government. It is clear that these private agreements were then recognized as facts of economic and industrial life by that nation's government. Nonetheless, the fact that the Swiss Government may, as a practical matter, approve of the effects of this private activity cannot convert what is essentially a vulnerable private conspiracy into an unassailable system resulting from foreign governmental mandate.

The touchstone of *Sabbatino*—the potential for interference with our foreign relations—is the crucial element in determining whether deference should be accorded in any given case. We wish to avoid "passing on the validity" of foreign acts. *Sabbatino*, 376 U.S. at 423. Similarly, we do not wish to challenge the sovereignty of another nation, the wisdom of its policy, or the integrity and motivation of its action. On the other hand, repeating the terms of *Sabbatino*, at 428, "the less important the implications of an issue are for our foreign relations, the weaker the justification for exclusivity in the political branches."

* * *

On the basis of the foregoing analysis, we conclude that the court below erred in dismissing the instant suit on the authority of *Occidental Petroleum Corp. v. Buttes Gas & Oil Co.*, 331 F.Supp. 92, 108-13 (C.D.Cal. 1971), aff'd, 461 F.2d 1261 (9th Cir.), cert. denied, 409 U.S. 950 (1972). The actions of the Honduran government that are involved here including the application by its courts and their agents of the Honduran laws concerning security interests and the protection of the underlying property against diminution are clearly distinguishable from the sovereign decrees laying claim to off-shore waters that were at issue in *Occidental Petroleum*. Here, the allegedly "sovereign" acts of Honduras consisted of judicial proceedings which were initiated by Caminals, a private party and one of the alleged co-conspirators, not by the Honduran government itself. Unlike the *Occidental Petroleum* plaintiffs, Timberlane does not seek to name Honduras or any Honduran officer as a defendant or co-conspirator, nor does it challenge Honduran policy or sovereignty in any fashion that appears on its face to hold any threat to relations between Honduras and the United States. In fact, there is no indication that the actions of the Honduran court and authorities reflected a sovereign decision that Timberlane's efforts should be crippled or that trade with the United States should be restrained. Moreover, and once again unlike the situation in *Occidental Petroleum*, see 331 F.Supp. at 109-10 n. 28, plaintiffs here apparently complain of additional agreements and actions which are totally unrelated to the Honduran government. These separate activities would clearly be unprotected even if procurement of a Honduran act of state were one part of defendants' overall scheme.

Under these circumstances, it is clear that the "act of state" doctrine does not require dismissal of the Timberlane action.

Extraterritorial Reach of the United States Antitrust Laws

There is no doubt that American antitrust laws extend over some conduct in other nations. There was language in the first Supreme Court case in point, *American Banana Co. v. United Fruit Co.*, 213 U.S. 347 (1909), casting doubt on the extension of the Sherman Act to acts outside United States territory. But subsequent cases have limited *American Banana* to its particular facts, and the Sherman Act and with it other antitrust laws has been applied to extraterritorial conduct. See, e. g., *Continental Ore Co. v. Union Carbide & Carbon Corp.*, 370 U.S. 690 (1962); *United States v. Sisal Sales Corp.*, 274 U.S. 268, 47 S.Ct. 592, 71 L.Ed. 1042 (1927); *United States v. Aluminum Co. of America*, 148 F.2d 416, (2d Cir. 1945) (the "Alcoa" case). The act may encompass the foreign activities of aliens as well as American citizens.

That American law covers some conduct beyond this nation's borders does not mean that it embraces all, however. Extraterritorial application is understandably a matter of concern for the other countries involved. Those nations have sometimes resented and protested, as excessive intrusions into their own spheres, broad assertions of authority by American courts. Our courts have recognized this concern and have, at times, responded to it, even if not always enough to satisfy all the foreign critics. In any event, it is evident that at some point the interests of the United States are too weak and the foreign harmony incentive for restraint too strong to justify an extraterritorial assertion of jurisdiction.

What that point is or how it is determined is not defined by international law. Nor does the Sherman Act limit itself.[14] In the domestic field the Sherman Act extends to the full reach of the commerce power. To define it somewhat more modestly in the foreign commerce area courts have generally, and logically, fallen back on a narrower construction of congressional intent, such as expressed in Judge Learned Hand's oft-cited opinion in *Alcoa*, 148 F.2d at 443:

---

14. The tendency seems to be for federal regulatory statutes to contain sweeping jurisdictional language. Sections 1 and 2 of the Sherman Act, 15 U.S.C. §§ 1, 2, reach, respectively "[e]very contract...in restraint of..." and "[e]very person who shall monopolize, or attempt to monopolize any part of" "the trade or commerce among the several States, or with foreign nations." Although it may be "evident from the text of the antitrust statutes" that "*some* [actual or intended] effect on our foreign commerce is a prerequisite to jurisdiction." Occidental Petroleum, 331 F.Supp. at 102 (emphasis in original), the statutory terms themselves are not precise or limited enough to provide additional guidance to the courts.

> [T]he only question open is whether Congress intended to impose the liability and whether our own Constitution permitted it to do so: as a court of the United States we cannot look beyond our own law. Nevertheless, it is quite true that we are not to read general words, such as those in this Act, without regard to the limitations customarily observed by nations upon the exercise of their powers: limitations which generally correspond to those fixed by the "Conflict of Laws." We should not impute to Congress an intent to punish all whom its courts can catch, for conduct which has no consequences within the United States.

It is the effect on American foreign commerce which is usually cited to support extraterritorial jurisdiction. *Alcoa* set the course, when Judge Hand declared, id.:

> [I]t is settled law...that any state may impose liabilities, even upon persons not within its allegiance, for conduct outside its borders that has consequences within its borders which the state reprehends; and these liabilities other states will ordinarily recognize.

Despite its description as "settled law," *Alcoa*'s assertion has been roundly disputed by many foreign commentators as being in conflict with international law, comity, and good judgment. Nonetheless, American courts have firmly concluded that there is some extraterritorial jurisdiction under the Sherman Act.

Even among American courts and commentators, however, there is no consensus on how far the jurisdiction should extend. The district court here concluded that a "direct and substantial effect" on United States foreign commerce was a prerequisite, without stating whether other factors were relevant or considered. The same formula was employed, to some extent, by the district courts in the *Swiss Watch* case, 1963 Trade Cases ¶ 70,600, in *United States v. R. P. Oldham Co.*, 152 F.Supp. 818, 822 (N.D.Cal.1957), and in [*United States v.*] *General Electric*, 82 F.Supp. [753] at 891 [D.N.J. 1949]. It has been identified and advocated by several commentators. See, e.g., W. Fugate, Foreign Commerce and the Antitrust Laws 30, 174 (2d ed. 1973); J. Van Cise, Understanding the Antitrust Laws 204 (1973 ed.). See also Report of the Attorney General's National Committee to Study the Antitrust Laws 76 (1955) ("substantial anticompetitive effects"); Restatement (Second) of Foreign Relations Law of the United States § 18.

Other courts have used different expressions, however. See, e. g., *Thomsen v. Cayser*, 243 U.S. 66, 88 (1917) ("the combination affected the foreign commerce of this country"); *Alcoa*, 148 F.2d at 444 ("intended to affect imports and exports (and)...is shown actually to have had some effect on them"); *United States v. Imperial Chemical Industries, Ltd.*, 100 F.Supp. 504, 592 (S.D.N.Y.1951) ("a conspiracy...which affects American commerce"); *United States v. Timken Roller Bearing Co.*, 83 F.Supp. 284, 309 (N.D.Ohio 1949), modified and affirmed, 341 U.S. 593 (1951) ("a direct and influencing effect on trade"). * * *.

Few cases have discussed the nature of the effect required for jurisdiction, perhaps because most of the litigated cases have involved relatively obvious offenses and rather significant and apparent effects on competition within the United States. It is probably in part because the standard has not often been put to a real test that it seems so poorly defined. * * *

The effects test by itself is incomplete because it fails to consider other nations' interests. Nor does it expressly take into account the full nature of the relationship between the actors and this country. Whether the alleged offender is an American citizen, for instance, may make a big difference; applying American laws to American citizens raises fewer problems than application to foreigners. * * *

American courts have, in fact, often displayed a regard for comity and the prerogatives of other nations and considered their interests as well as other parts of the factual circumstances, even when professing to apply an effects test. To some degree, the requirement for a "substantial" effect may silently incorporate these additional considerations, with "substantial" as a flexible standard that varies with other factors. The intent requirement suggested by *Alcoa*, 148 F.2d at 443-44, is one example of an attempt to broaden the court's perspective, as is drawing a distinction between American citizens and non-citizens.

The failure to articulate these other elements in addition to the standard effects analysis is costly, however, for it is more likely that they will be overlooked or slighted in interpreting past decisions and reaching new ones. Placing emphasis on the qualification that effects be "substantial" is also risky, for the term has a meaning in the interstate antitrust context which does not encompass all the factors relevant to the foreign trade case.

Indeed, that "substantial effects" element of interstate antitrust analysis may well be responsible for the use of an effects test for foreign commerce. The Sherman Act reaches restraints directly intended to limit the flow of interstate trade or whose sole impact is on interstate commerce, but it also reaches "wholly local business restraints" if the particular restraint "substantially and adversely affects interstate commerce." *Gulf Oil Corp. v. Copp Paving Co.*, 419 U.S. 186, 195 (1974). Such a test is necessary in the interstate context to separate the restraints which fall within the federal ambit under the interstate commerce clause from those which, as purely intrastate burdens, remain the province of the states. Since, however, no comparable constitutional problem exists in defining the scope of congressional power to regulate foreign commerce, it may be unwise blindly to apply the "substantiality" test to the international setting. Only respect for the role of the executive and for international notions of comity and fairness limit that constitutional grant.

A tripartite analysis seems to be indicated. As acknowledged above, the antitrust laws require in the first instance that there be some effect actual or intended on American foreign commerce before the federal courts may legitimately exercise subject matter jurisdiction under those statutes. Second, a greater showing of burden or restraint may be necessary to demonstrate that the effect is sufficiently large to present a cognizable injury to the plaintiffs and, therefore, a civil violation of the antitrust laws. Third, there is the additional question which is unique to the international setting of whether the interests of, and links to, the United States including the magnitude of the effect on American foreign commerce are sufficiently strong, vis-à-vis those of other nations, to justify an assertion of extraterritorial authority.

It is this final issue which is both obscured by undue reliance on the "substantiality" test and complicated to resolve. An effect on United States commerce, although necessary to the exercise of jurisdiction under the antitrust laws, is alone not a sufficient basis on which to determine whether American authority should be asserted in a given case as a matter of international comity and fairness. In some cases, the application of the direct and substantial test in the international context might open the door too widely by sanctioning jurisdiction over an action when these considerations would indicate dismissal. At other times, it may fail in the other direction, dismissing a case for which comity and fairness do not require forbearance, thus closing the jurisdictional door too tightly for the Sherman Act does reach some restraints which do not have both a direct and substantial effect on the foreign commerce of the United States. A more comprehensive inquiry is necessary. We believe that the field of conflict of laws presents the proper approach. * * *

The act of state doctrine discussed earlier demonstrates that the judiciary is sometimes cognizant of the possible foreign implications of its action. Similar awareness should be extended to the general problems of extraterritoriality. Such acuity is especially required in private suits, like this one, for in these cases there is no opportunity for the executive branch to weigh the foreign relations impact, nor any statement implicit in the filing of the suit that that consideration has been outweighed.

What we prefer is an evaluation and balancing of the relevant considerations in each case in the words of Kingman Brewster, a "jurisdictional rule of reason." Balancing of the foreign interests involved was the approach taken by the Supreme Court in *Continental Ore Co. v. Union Carbide & Carbon Corp.*, 370 U.S. 690 (1962), where the involvement of the Canadian government in the alleged monopolization was held not to require dismissal. The Court stressed that there was no indication that the Canadian authorities approved or would have approved of the monopolization, meaning that the Canadian interest, if any, was slight and was outweighed by the American interest in condemning the restraint. Similarly, in *Lauritzen v. Larsen*, 345 U.S. 571 (1953), the Court used a like approach in declining to apply the Jones Act to a Danish seaman, injured in Havana on a Danish ship, although he had signed on to the ship in New York.

The elements to be weighed include the degree of conflict with foreign law or policy, the nationality or allegiance of the parties and the locations or principal places of businesses or corporations, the extent to which enforcement by either state can be expected to achieve compliance, the relative significance of effects on the United States as compared with those elsewhere, the extent to which there is explicit purpose to harm or affect American commerce, the foreseeability of such effect, and the relative importance to the violations charged of conduct within the United States as compared with conduct abroad. A court evaluating these factors should identify the potential degree of conflict if American authority is asserted. A difference in law or policy is one likely sore spot, though one which may not always be present. Nationality is another; though foreign governments may have some concern for the treatment of American citizens and business residing there, they primarily care about their own nationals. Having assessed the conflict, the court should then determine whether in the face of it the contacts and interests of the United States are sufficient to support the exercise of extraterritorial jurisdiction.

We conclude, then, that the problem should be approached in three parts: Does the alleged restraint affect, or was it intended to affect, the foreign commerce of the United States? Is it of such a type and magnitude so as to be cognizable as a violation of the Sherman Act? As a matter of international comity and fairness, should the extraterritorial jurisdiction of the United States be asserted to cover it? The district court's judgment found only that the restraint involved in the instant suit did not produce a direct and substantial effect on American foreign commerce. That holding does not satisfy any of these inquiries.

The Sherman Act is not limited to trade restraints which have both a direct and substantial effect on our foreign commerce. Timberlane has alleged that the complained of activities were intended to, and did, affect the export of lumber from Honduras to the United States—the flow of United States foreign commerce, and as such they are within the jurisdiction of the federal courts under the Sherman Act. Moreover, the magnitude of the effect alleged would appear to be sufficient to state a claim.

The comity question is more complicated. From Timberlane's complaint it is evident that there are grounds for concern as to at least a few of the defendants, for some are identified as foreign citizens * * *. Moreover, it is clear that most of the activity took place in Honduras, though the conspiracy may have been directed from San Francisco, and that the most direct economic effect was probably on Honduras. However, there has been no indication of any conflict with the law or policy of the Honduran government, nor any comprehensive analysis of the relative connections and interests of Honduras and the United States. Under these circumstances, the dismissal by the district court cannot be sustained on jurisdictional grounds. We, therefore, vacate the dismissal and remand the Timberlane action * * *

Notes

1. On remand in Timberlane, the trial judge reached the same result under the 9th Circuit's "tripartite analysis" and this time the 9th Circuit affirmed, noting: "the potential for conflict with Honduran economic policy and commercial law is great. The effect on the foreign commerce of the United States is minimal." 749 F. 2d 1378, 1386 (9th Cir. 1984).

2. Discussion of the territorial reach of United States antitrust law typically begins with the Holmes opinion cited in the principal case, which rejected any extraterritorial application. American Banana Co. v. United Fruit Co., 213 U.S. 347 (1909), was a suit under the Sherman Act by an Alabama corporation against a New Jersey corporation. The plaintiff alleged that the giant United Fruit Company had caused the government of Costa Rica to interfere with the operation of plaintiff's banana plantation in that country and had prevented the plaintiff from buying bananas from others for export and sale. Justice Holmes was heavily influenced by the rigid territorial choice-of-law dogma of the time. See id. at 356, citing three classic conflicts decisions (Slater v. Mexican Nat'l R.R., 194 U.S. 120 (1904); Milliken v. Pratt, 125 Mass. 374 (1878); Phillips v. Eyre, [1870] 6 Q.B. 1), and the leading English conflict-of-laws treatise (A. V. Dicey, Conflict of Laws (2d ed. 1908)). One of the cases cited, his own opinion in *Slater*, determines the law applicable to the wrongful death of a railroad employee. The employee was a Texas resident fatally injured in the course of his employment in Nuevo Laredo. The railroad that employed him was incorporated in Colorado and ran trains from Texas into Mexico. Holmes held that Mexican law controlled and that suit could not be maintained in an American court, because the Mexican law provided a recovery for wrongful death damages in modifiable installments. He concluded that no United States court had the "power to make a decree of this kind..." Id. at 128. The suit was ordered dismissed and the plaintiffs advised to sue "in Mexico, on the other side of the river." Id. at 129. The rationale for this result was a classic statement of the "vested rights" theory of conflict of laws, which prevailed in United States courts for the first half of this century:

> The theory of the...suit is that although the act complained of was subject to no law having force in the forum, it gave rise to an obligation, an *obligatio*, which, like other obligations, follows the person, and may be enforced wherever the person may be found. But as the only source of this obligation is the law of the place of the act, it follows that that law determines not merely the existence of the obligation, but equally determines its extent. Id. at 126 (citations omitted).

Just as this choice-of-law reasoning is now largely displaced by a method that attempts to give maximum accommodation to the relevant policies of the states having contacts with the parties and the transaction (see Restatement (Second) of Conflict of Laws § 6 (1969)) the American Banana denial of any extraterritorial application to our antitrust laws has been superseded. See W.S. Kirkpatrick & Co., Inc. v. Environmental Tectonics Corp., Int'l, 493 U.S. 400, 407 (1990) ("American Banana was squarely decided on the ground (later substantially overruled) that the antitrust laws had no extraterritorial application") (citation omitted). Learned Hand's opinion in United States v. Aluminum Co. of America, also cited in the principal case, held the Sherman Act applicable to agreements abroad if they were intended to and did have consequences in the United States. The *Alcoa* case was decided under unusual procedural circumstances. 15 U.S.C. § 29 provided for a direct appeal from the district court to the Supreme Court. Four justices disqualified themselves from hearing the case, thus preventing a quorum in the Supreme Court. Congress then authorized the Court to transfer the case to the Second Circuit, and this was done. See 320 U.S. 708 (1943); 322 U.S. 716 (1944); 58 Stat. 272 (June 9, 1944, c. 239).

Now the debate over extraterritorial application is focused on when United States antitrust law should apply if foreign conduct has effects in the United States. The spectrum of views, ranging from very limited to expansive application, include the following: (1) There is a presumption against extraterritorial application of United States public law, which can be rebutted only by express statutory language. This is the position taken by Justice Holmes in a Sherman Act decision, American Banana Co. v. United Fruit Co., 213 U.S. 347 (1909). In Hartford Fire Ins. Co. v. California (infra page 362), Justice Scalia says that this approach would be "worth considering" if it were not foreclosed by precedent. (2) The application of United States public law should be treated as other choice-of-law problems, and United States law applied only if our country has the "most significant relationship" to the parties and the transaction. For this position, see Born, A Reappraisal of the Extraterritorial Reach of U.S. Law, 24 Law & Policy in Int'l Business 1, 88 (1992). (3) Even though conduct abroad causes effects in the United States, United States public law should be applied to that conduct only if this is reasonable under considerations of international comity. This is the position of Restatement (Third) of Foreign Relations Law § 403. See also Lowenfeld, Public Law in the International Arena: Conflict of Laws, International Law, and Some Suggestions for Their Interaction, 163 Collected Courses [Recueil des cours] Academy of International Law 311 (1979). Professor Lowenfeld was Associate Reporter for the Restatement (Third). (4) Presume that United States public law applies whenever conduct abroad produces substantial and foreseeable effects here that it is the purpose of our law to prevent. This presumption is rebutted if the effects in the United States are slight when compared with the reasonable interest of the foreign country in permitting the conduct centered there. For this position, see Weintraub, The Extraterritorial Application of Antitrust and Security Laws: An Inquiry into the Utility of a "Choice-of-Law" Approach, 70 Texas L. Rev. 1799 (1992). Consolidated Gold Field PLC v. Minorco, S.A. 871 F.2d 252, modified, 890 F.2d 569 (2d Cir.), cert. dismissed, 492 U.S. 39 (1989), infra page 395, Note 2, is an example of a case in which it is arguable that the presumption in favor of application of United States public law should have been rebutted. (5) Apply United States antitrust law whenever conduct abroad was meant to produce and did in fact produce some substantial effect in the United States. For this position, see Kramer, Extraterritorial Application of American Law after the Insurance Antitrust Case: A Reply to Professors Lowenfeld and Trimble, 89 Am. J. Int'l L. 750, 751 (1995). (6) Make a purely unilateral analysis of the relevant United States public law and apply it to conduct abroad whenever the policies underlying the law will be advanced. Under this approach, United States law would be applied whenever conduct abroad causes substantial and foreseeable effects here that it is the purpose of the law to prevent. For this position, see

William S. Dodge, Extraterritoriality and Conflict-of-Laws Theory: An Argument for Judicial Unilateralism, 39 Harv. Int'l L.J. 101 (1988); Scharf, Case 2, Conference on Jurisdiction, Justice and Choice of Law for the 21st Century, 29 New Eng.L. Rev. 618 (1995).

3. Capital Currency Exchange, N.V. v. National Westminster Bank PLC, 155 F.3d 603 (2d Cir. 1998), cert. denied, 526 U.S. 1067 (1999), affirmed a forum non conveniens dismissal of Sherman Act claims by a Netherlands Antilles corporation against English banks and their officers.

Laker Airways Ltd. v. Sabena, Belgian World Airlines
731 F.2d 909 (D.C. Cir. 1984)

Before Wilkey and Starr, Circuit Judges, and MacKinnon, Senior Circuit Judge.

Opinion for the Court filed by Circuit Judge Wilkey.

[This is an antitrust suit by the bankrupt Laker Airways against domestic, British, and other foreign airlines. Laker, for a time, operated very successful cut rate flights between London and New York, but claimed that it was driven out of business by an antitrust conspiracy engaged in by the defendants. The alleged conspiracy consisted of charging predatory low prices for airfare over the same routes flown by Laker, paying secret commissions to travel agents to divert business from Laker, and putting pressure on Laker's lenders not to refinance loans. Although some of these alleged actions took place in the United States, they mostly occurred abroad. These acts drove Laker into liquidation resulting in higher prices for American international air passengers. Laker's principal creditors were American and any recovery would be to their benefit. The British and some foreign airlines had obtained decrees in the United Kingdom enjoining Laker from prosecuting the antitrust action in the United States. The district court had granted Laker an injunction ordering other foreign airlines not to obtain anti-suit injunctions in England.]

Although the flash point of the controversy has been the antisuit injunctions, the real powder keg is the strongly mandated legislative policies which each national court is bound to implement. Thus, it is unlikely that the underlying controversy would be defused regardless of the action we take today.

Because the principles of comity and concurrent jurisdiction clearly authorize the use of a defensive preliminary injunction designed to permit the United States claim to go forward free of foreign interference, we affirm the decision of the district court. * * *

This appeal is the direct result of a clash between two governments asserting jurisdiction to prescribe law over a single series of transactions. The district court's injunction is defended by Laker as necessary to protect the court's jurisdiction. If there is no justification for the court's exercise of jurisdiction, the injunctive relief should necessarily fail. Similarly, if the United Kingdom courts would lack jurisdiction over a claim filed by Sabena and KLM, the district court should be under no obligation to defer to the actions of those foreign tribunals. A true conflict arises only if the national jurisdictions overlap. We must therefore begin our analysis with a review of the recognized bases supporting prescriptive jurisdiction, and then examine whether the alleged facts of this case satisfy those requirements. * * *

Because two or more states may have legitimate interests in prescribing governing law over a particular controversy, these jurisdictional bases are not mutually exclusive.

For example, when the national of one state causes substantial effects in another state, both states may potentially have jurisdiction to prescribe governing law. Thus, under international law, territoriality and nationality often give rise to concurrent jurisdiction. A court faced with assertions of conflicting or inconsistent prescriptive power under facially concurrent jurisdiction must first examine the sufficiency of jurisdictional contacts under each base of jurisdiction to determine whether either claim of jurisdiction is unfounded. If both claims to jurisdiction are legitimately exercised, avenues of conflict resolution must be considered before jurisdiction to prescribe can go forward.

2. United States Jurisdictional Base

The prescriptive application of United States antitrust law to the alleged conspiracies between KLM, Sabena, and the other antitrust defendants is founded upon the harmful effects occurring within the territory of the United States as a direct result of the alleged wrongdoing. * * * [W]e wish to make it clear that this aspect of territorial jurisdiction is entirely consistent with nationally and internationally recognized limits on sovereign authority. * * *

In addition to the protection of American consumers' and creditors' interests, the United States has a substantial interest in regulating the conduct of business within the United States. The landing rights granted to appellants are permits to do business in this country. Foreign airlines fly in the United States on the prerequisite of obeying United States law. They have offices and employees within the United States, and conduct substantial operations here. By engaging in this commercial business they subject themselves to the in personam jurisdiction of the host country's courts. They waive either expressly or implicitly other objections that might otherwise be raised in defense. A major reason for this subjection to business regulation is to place foreign corporations generally in the same position as domestic businesses. Thus, United States creditors are entitled to, and do, rely on their ability to enforce their claims against foreign corporations like the appellants.

This equivalency works in both directions. Foreign corporations are privileged to, and do, rely on United States law. Consequently, creditors rely on the ability of foreign corporations, not only to be sued, but to sue in courts. Creditors expect to recover claims derivatively when foreign corporations possess a claim. Foreign corporations thus have the same obligation as domestic corporations—to sue for benefit of creditors when they are financially troubled and need money for satisfaction of creditors' claims.

The United States has an interest in maintaining open forums for resolution of creditors' claims. Just as the appellants are expected to abide by the United States laws governing those who do business here, so is Laker entitled to the protection of those laws. Permitting Laker to maintain its antitrust suit satisfies the legitimate expectations of Laker and its creditors.

B: Adequacy of United States Territorial Interests

It is beyond dispute that these contacts support an exercise of jurisdiction under the Sherman and Clayton Acts. Jurisdiction exists under United States antitrust laws whenever conduct is intended to, and results in, substantial effects within the United States. Under the conspiracy alleged by Laker, the intent to affect American commerce is obvious. The asserted predatory pricing of fares and interference with refinancing attempts were designed specifically to drive Laker out of business and eventually to raise the fares paid by transatlantic passengers, the bulk of whom are American.

Substantial realization of those intended effects has also been alleged by Laker. Laker was forced into liquidation shortly after its refinancing attempts collapsed. Its creditors have not yet been satisfied. The downward pressure on fares induced by Laker's competition, which previously benefited transatlantic passengers, has been eliminated. Moreover, providing a forum for Laker's suit would also respect domestic creditors' reliance on the ability of foreign corporations to sue and be sued under the United States laws which ordinarily govern the business operations of foreign corporations within the United States. Thus, significant and long standing American economic interests would be vindicated through a successful antitrust action by Laker.

3: *British Jurisdictional Base*

Some of the British jurisdictional contacts are territorial. The plaintiff did business on routes between the United States and United Kingdom. A number of the purported conspiratorial acts took place in Great Britain. The conspiracy allegedly caused bankruptcy of a corporation operating in Great Britain.

However, the primary base of jurisdiction is the British nationality of the parties involved in the transactions cited in Laker's complaint. Laker itself is incorporated under Jersey law, and is thus a British national for purposes of this litigation. Two of the named defendants, British Airways and British Caledonian, are also incorporated under British law. In addition, the conspiracy may also tangentially implicate the activities of other British entities such as the Bank of England and the Civil Aviation Authority.

Regulating the activities of businesses incorporated within a state is one of the oldest and most established examples of prescriptive jurisdiction. We cannot say that these nationality-based jurisdictional contacts would be insufficient to support British jurisdiction over a claim filed by KLM or Sabena, especially when the conspiracy charged does have territorial contacts with the United Kingdom. Thus, existence of British jurisdiction to prescribe is not seriously challenged by Laker.

4: *Concurrent Jurisdiction*

The sufficiency of jurisdictional contacts with both the United States and England results in concurrent jurisdiction to prescribe. Both forums may legitimately exercise this power to regulate the events that allegedly transpired as a result of the asserted conspiracy. * * *

B: Propriety of the Antisuit Injunction

It is well settled that English and American courts have power to control the conduct of persons subject to their jurisdiction to the extent of forbidding them from suing in foreign jurisdictions. However, the fundamental corollary to concurrent jurisdiction must ordinarily be respected: parallel proceedings on the same in personam claim should ordinarily be allowed to proceed simultaneously, at least until a judgment is reached in one which can be pled as res judicata in the other. The mere filing of a suit in one forum does not cut off the preexisting right of an independent forum to regulate matters subject to its prescriptive jurisdiction. For this reason, injunctions restraining litigants from proceeding in courts of independent countries are rarely issued. * * *

Whatever the merits of the British defendants' claims based upon the Bermuda II Treaty, KLM and Sabena have no claim to antitrust immunity under their air service treaties. In fact, far from conferring any immunity, their treaties contain express language subjecting them to the jurisdiction of the United States over predatory pricing and abuse of monopoly power. * * *

C: Paramount Nationality

We turn now to the appellants' argument that Laker's nationality requires the United States District Court to defer to the injunctions issued by the courts of the United Kingdom. * * *

We are asked to recognize an entirely novel rule. Although a court has power to enjoin its nationals from suing in foreign jurisdictions, it does not follow that the United States courts must recognize an absolute right of the British government to regulate the remedies that the United States may wish to create for British nationals in United States courts. The purported principle of paramount nationality is entirely unknown in national and international law. Territoriality, not nationality, is the customary and preferred base of jurisdiction.[90] Moreover, no rule of international law or national law precludes an exercise of jurisdiction solely because another state has jurisdiction. In fact, international law recognizes that a state with a territorial basis for its prescriptive jurisdiction may establish laws intended to prevent compliance with legislation established under authority of nationality-based jurisdiction. * * *

D. International Comity

Appellants and amici curiae argue strenuously that the district court's injunction violates the crucial principles of comity that regulate and moderate the social and economic intercourse between independent nations. We approach their claims seriously, recognizing that comity serves our international system like the mortar which cements together a brick house. No one would willingly permit the mortar to crumble or be chipped away for fear of compromising the entire structure. * * *

Under the position advanced by appellants, the United States District Court would no longer be free to rule that comity prevented the United States from exercising prescriptive jurisdiction over the defendants, since that determination would be made as of right by a separate forum.

In this latter context we cannot rule that the district court abused its discretion to protect its jurisdiction. Between the state courts, the Full Faith and Credit Clause has not been held to compel recognition of an antisuit injunction. A fortiori, the principles of comity do not prevent proceeding in the face of a foreign injunction.

Comity ordinarily requires that courts of a separate sovereign not interfere with concurrent proceedings based on the same transitory claim, at least until a judgment is reached in one action, allowing res judicata to be pled in defense. The appeal to the recognition of comity by the American court in order to permit the critical issues to be adjudicated in England, which is the plea made by appellants here, thus comes based on a very strange predicate. Since the action seeking to determine Laker's right to recover for anticompetitive injuries was first instituted in the United States, the initial opportunity to exercise comity, if this were called for, was put to the United Kingdom courts.

---

90. See Restatement (Revised) [of the Foreign Relations Law of the United States] §402 Comment b (Tentative Draft No. 2) [(1981)]; Restatement (Second) [of the Foreign Relations Law of the United States] §30 Comment b [(1965)].

No recognition or acceptance of comity was made in those courts. The appellants' claims of comity now asserted in United States courts come burdened with the failure of the British to recognize comity. * * *

E: Judicial Reconciliation of Conflicting Assertions of Jurisdiction

We recognize that the district court's injunction, precipitated as it was by preemptive interim injunctions in the High Court of Justice, unfortunately will not resolve the deadlock currently facing the parties to this litigation. We have searched for some satisfactory avenue, open to an American court, which would permit the frictionless vindication of the interests of both Britain and the United States. However, there is none, for the British legislation defines the British interest solely in terms of preventing realization of United States interests. The laws are therefore contradictory and mutually inconsistent.

1. *Nature of the Conflict*

The conflict faced here is not caused by the courts of the two countries. Rather, its sources are the fundamentally opposed national policies toward prohibition of anti-competitive business activity. These policies originate in the legislative and executive decisions of the respective counties. * * *

2. *Judicial Interest Balancing*

Even as the political branches of the respective countries have set in motion the legislative policies which have collided in this litigation, they have deprived courts of the ability meaningfully to resolve the problem. The American and English courts are obligated to attempt to reconcile two contradictory laws, each supported by recognized prescriptive jurisdiction, one of which is specifically designed to cancel out the other.

The suggestion has been made that this court should engage in some form of interest balancing, permitting only a "reasonable" assertion of prescriptive jurisdiction to be implemented. However, this approach is unsuitable when courts are forced to choose between a domestic law which is designed to protect domestic interests, and a foreign law which is calculated to thwart the implementation of the domestic law in order to protect foreign interests allegedly threatened by the objectives of the domestic law. Interest balancing in this context is hobbled by two primary problems: (1) there are substantial limitations on the court's ability to conduct a neutral balancing of the competing interests, and (2) the adoption of interest balancing is unlikely to achieve its goal of promoting international comity.

A: Defects in the Balancing Process

Most proposals for interest balancing consist of a long list of national contacts to be evaluated and weighed against those of the foreign country. These interests may be relevant to the desirability of allocating jurisdiction to a particular national forum. However, their usefulness breaks down when a court is faced with the task of selecting one forum's prescriptive jurisdiction over that of another. * * *

The inherent noncorrelation between the interest balancing formula and the economic realities of modern commerce is an additional reason which may underlie the reluctance of most courts to strike a balance in favor of nonapplication of domestic law.

An assertion of prescriptive jurisdiction should ultimately be based on shared assessments that jurisdiction is reasonable. Thus, international law prohibits the assertion of prescriptive jurisdiction unsupported by reasonable links between the forum and the controversy.

However, it does not necessarily follow, as the use of interest balancing as a method of choosing between competing jurisdictions assumes, that there is a line of reasonableness which separates jurisdiction to prescribe into neatly adjoining compartments of national jurisdiction. There is no principle of international law which abolishes concurrent jurisdiction. Since prescriptive jurisdiction is based on well recognized state contacts with controversies, the reality of our interlocked international economic network guarantees that overlapping, concurrent jurisdiction will often be present. There is, therefore, no rule of international law holding that a "more reasonable" assertion of jurisdiction mandatorily displaces a "less reasonable" assertion of jurisdiction as long as both are, in fact, consistent with the limitations on jurisdiction imposed by international law. That is the situation faced in this case: the territoriality and nationality bases of jurisdiction of the United Kingdom and the United States are both unimpeached. * * *

We unhesitatingly conclude that United States jurisdiction to prescribe its antitrust laws must go forward and was therefore properly protected by the district court. Despite the contrary assertions of the British government, there is no indication in this case that the limits of international law are exceeded by either country's exercise of prescriptive jurisdiction. But even so, application of national law may go forward despite a conflict with international law. Both Britain and the United States recognize this rule. It follows a fortiori that national laws do not evaporate when counteracted by the legislation of another sovereign.

Although, in the interest of amicable relations, we might be tempted to defuse unilaterally the confrontation by jettisoning our jurisdiction, we could not, for this is not our proper judicial role. The problem in this case is essentially a political one, arising from the vast difference in the political- economic theories of the two governments which has existed for many years. Both nations have jurisdiction to prescribe and adjudicate. Both have asserted that jurisdiction. However, this conflict alone does not place the court in a position to initiate a political compromise based on its decision that United States laws should not be enforced when a foreign jurisdiction, contrary to the domestic court's statutory duty, attempts to eradicate the domestic jurisdiction. Judges are not politicians. The courts are not organs of political compromise. It is impossible in this case, with all the good will manifested by the English Justices and ourselves, to negotiate an extraordinarily long arms-length agreement on the respective impact of our countries' policies regulating anti-competitive business practices. * * *

In contrast, diplomatic and executive channels are, by definition, designed to exchange, negotiate, and reconcile the problems which accompany the realization of national interests within the sphere of international association. These forums should and, we hope, will be utilized to avoid or resolve conflicts caused by contradictory assertions of concurrent prescriptive jurisdiction.

However, in the absence of some emanation from the Executive Branch,[178] Laker's suit may go forward against appellants.

---

178. If the United States Executive interpreted the Bermuda II Treaty to waive both the obligation of United Kingdom air carriers to comply with antitrust laws, and the right of those carriers to rely on the protection of those laws, then Laker's claim against the foreign airlines would probably

The decision of the district court is therefore

Affirmed.

STARR, Circuit Judge, dissenting: * * *

A tempest has been brewing for some time among the nations as to the reach of this country's antitrust laws, and today's decision strikes a strong blow in favor of what will be viewed by many of our friends and allies as a rather parochial American outlook. But whether that blow is well conceived, it is, with all respect, at tension with the orderly operation of our two nations' respective judicial systems. As both the majority and the District Court recognize, it is serious business to issue an injunction against proceedings in a sister nation. This is most keenly true with respect to a nation from which we inherited so much of our legal system. Inasmuch as only extraordinary reasons justify the issuance of such an injunction, I would remand the case to the District Court for further proceedings aimed at narrowing the injunction, consistent with the principles of comity that inform the seemly accommodation of sharply divergent and competing national interests.

Note

The majority states that "[t]erritoriality, not nationality, is the customary and preferred base of jurisdiction." Neither of the Restatement provisions cited for this proposition in note 90 support the statement. Restatement (Revised) of the Foreign Relations Law of the United States §402 comment b (Tentative Draft No. 2) (1981) states: "In general, territoriality is considered the normal, and nationality the exceptional, basis for the exercise of jurisdiction, though no state (and certainly not international law) rejects nationality as a basis for jurisdiction to prescribe." Restatement (Second) of the Foreign Relations Law of the United States §30 comment b (1965) states: "The fact that a state has [nationality as a basis for jurisdiction to prescribe] does not mean that it is permitted by international law to direct a national to engage in activities without regard to harmful consequences in another state." The only illustration to this comment is that state A violates state B's rights under international law if state A orders a national of A to assassinate the prime minister of state B.

"Revised" was the working title for the Restatement (Third). Restatement (Third) §402 comment b states that when there are conflicting prescriptions on the basis of nationality and territoriality, the conflict requires "evaluation of the competing interests by a standard of reasonableness, as set forth in §403(3) and Comment e to that section." Comment e contains no suggestion that one internationally recognized basis for jurisdiction to prescribe is superior to another. "Normal" and "exceptional," the terms used in §402 comment b, appear to refer to the empirical fact of frequency of use, and to make no judgment as to the legitimacy of that use.

Agreement Between the United States and the United Kingdom Concerning Air Services ["Bermuda II"]
28 U.S.T. 5367 (1977)

ARTICLE II

---

fail. Of course, if only the British airlines' duty of compliance were ceded by the treaty, then nothing would prevent Laker from continuing its suit against KLM and Sabena.

Fair Competition

(1) The designated airline or airlines of one Contracting Party shall have a fair and equal opportunity to compete with the designated airline or airlines of the other Contracting Party.

(2) The designated airline or airlines of one Contracting Party shall take into consideration the interests of the designated airline or airlines of the other Contracting Party so as not to affect unduly that airline's or those airlines' services on all or part of the same routes. In particular, when a designated airline of one Contracting Party proposes to inaugurate services on a gateway route segment already served by a designated airline or airlines of the other Contracting Party, the incumbent airline or airlines shall each refrain from increasing the frequency of their services to the extent and for the time necessary to ensure that the airline inaugurating service may fairly exercise its rights under paragraph (1) of this Article. Such obligation to refrain from increasing frequency shall not last longer than two years or beyond the point when the inaugurating airline matches the frequencies of any incumbent airline, whichever occurs first, and shall not apply if the services to be inaugurated are limited as to their capacity by the license or certificate granted by the designating Contracting Party.

(3) Services provided by a designated airline under this Agreement shall retain as their primary objective the provision of capacity adequate to the traffic demands between the country of which such airline is a national and the country of ultimate destination of the traffic. The right to embark or disembark on such services international traffic destined for and coming from third countries at a point or points on the routes specified in this Agreement shall be exercised in accordance with the general principles of orderly development of international air transport to which both Contracting Parties subscribe and shall be subject to the general principle that capacity should be related to:

(a) the traffic requirements between the country of origin and the countries of ultimate destination of the traffic;

(b) the requirements of through airline operations; and

(c) the traffic requirements of the area through which the airline passes, after taking account of local and regional services.

(4) The frequency and capacity of services to be provided by the designated airlines of the Contracting Parties shall be closely related to the requirements of all categories of public demand for the carriage of passengers and cargo including mail in such a way as to provide adequate service to the public and to permit the reasonable development of routes and viable airline operations. Due regard shall be paid to efficiency of operation so that frequency and capacity are provided at levels appropriate to accommodate the traffic at load factors consistent with tariffs based on the criteria set forth in paragraph (2) of Article 12 (Tariffs).

(5) The Contracting Parties recognize that airline actions leading to excess capacity or to the under provision of capacity can both run counter to the interests of the travelling public. * * *

Note

What provisions of the treaty might support the defendants' allegations in Laker Airways that the United States has agreed not to prosecute United Kingdom airlines for antitrust violations?

British Airways Board v. Laker Airways Ltd.
[1984] 3 All ER 39; [1984] 3 W.L.R. 413; [1985] 1 A.C. 58 (1984) (House of Lords)

[The airlines sued by Laker applied to Parker, J. for injunctions restraining Laker from pursuing the action in the United States. Parker refused and the antitrust defendants appealed. While the appeal was pending, the United Kingdom Secretary of State for Trade and Industry took the action referred to in this opinion. The Court of Appeal reversed the denial of the injunctions, but dismissed Laker's application to review the action of the Secretary of State.]

Lord Diplock. My Lords, of these conjoined appeals, two are brought in civil actions in which the British Airways Board (B.A.) and British Caledonian Airways Ltd. (B.C.) respectively are plaintiffs. With these I propose to deal first; the third appeal is brought in an application for judicial review. All three appeals form part of the aftermath of the relatively brief incursion into the ranks of airlines operating scheduled services between the United Kingdom and the United States of America, that was made by Sir Freddie Laker operating through a company, Laker Airways Ltd., incorporated in Jersey but with its principal office in London and transacting business there and elsewhere in the United Kingdom and in the United States. To this company, and the other companies through which Sir Freddie operated scheduled air services across the North Atlantic and the liquidators of those companies, I shall refer, collectively and individually, as "Laker."

The civil actions in the High Court

Laker's attempts to break into the market for the provision of scheduled air services between places in the United Kingdom and places in the United States of America (which, under the Chicago Convention of 1944, required the consent of the governments, of both countries) achieved success in 1977 when it became an airline designated by the United Kingdom to operate a scheduled service on the New York-London route. This was done under the bipartite treaty between the United Kingdom and the United States known as "Bermuda 2" (Agreement between the Government of the United Kingdom of Great Britain and Northern Ireland and the Government of the United States of America concerning Air Services (1977) (Cmnd. 7016)), which entitled each country to designate two of its airlines to operate on that route. The other designated British airline was B.A. * * *

My Lords, one of the characteristics of the rules of civil procedure in the federal courts of the United States (as well as in most state courts), which seems to any English lawyer strange and, indeed, oppressive upon defendants, is that a "complaint," the document by which an action is begun, while it alleges that the complainant has a cause of action against the defendant or defendants, does not disclose, or discloses only in a most exiguous form, the facts which the plaintiff will eventually rely upon at the trial as giving rise to that cause of action. Instead, the complaint is accompanied, or immediately followed, by a request to the defendants for pre-trial discovery which bears little resemblance to the kind of discovery that is available in English civil actions. Its breadth, the variety of methods, oral and written, that it makes available for a wide-roving search for any information that might be helpful to the case of the party seeking discovery, the enormous expense, irrecoverable in any award of costs to a successful defendant, in which it may involve parties from whom discovery is sought, and its potentiality for oppressive use by plaintiffs, particularly in antitrust actions, receive sufficient mention in the various speeches in this House in *Rio Tinto Zinc Corp. v. Re Westinghouse Electric Corporation* [1978] A.C. 547. What for present purposes is important particularly as respects the civil action by B.C. is that if the American action ever reaches the stage of trial, what evidence in support of its complaint Laker will by that time have unearthed by the process of pre-trial discovery it is as yet impossible to foretell; but, again, for the purpose of disposing of the instant appeal it is, I think, enough to say that the aim of the antitrust combination and conspiracy (and intentional tort) alleged in the complaint was to drive Laker out of the scheduled airline business as a competitor of the I.A.T.A. [International Air Transport Association] airline defendants; and that the principal means by which this was to be accomplished were first to attract potential passengers away from Laker's airline by offering to carry them at what in antitrust jargon are described as "predatory fares," i.e. loss-making fares which while they matched Laker's fares (which in conformity with its Skytrain policy covered carriage alone) included, as well as actual carriage but free of any extra charge, those in-flight services and other advantages available to passengers by I.A.T.A. airlines to which reference has been made above and to provide which involved those airlines in substantial expense which could not be met out of the fares they charged. The second means, to which B.C., Lufthansa and Swissair, among the I.A.T.A. airlines, and McDonnell [Douglas Corp., the aircraft manufacturers] are alleged to have played an active part after Laker had been reduced to the financial straits in which it found itself at the beginning of 1982 in consequence of the above-mentioned predatory fares, was to put pressure upon potential participants in the financial rescue scheme for Laker at the beginning of 1982 to withdraw their support and so to prevent Laker's survival as a competitor of the I.A.T.A. airline defendants in the provision of scheduled services across the North Atlantic.

My Lords, there are two propositions, one of American law and thus of fact, the other of English law, which, if correct, are in my view decisive of the appeals in both the civil actions without its being necessary for your Lordships to make detailed reference to the multitudinous documents which this litigation has already generated.

Upon the first proposition, that of American law, not only is the expert evidence all one way but it is also common ground between the parties, that if the allegations made against B.A. and B.C. in the complaint in the American action can be proved at the trial they disclose a cause of action by Laker against B.A. and B.C. under the antitrust law of the United States (viz. the Sherman Act and the Clayton Act) which falls within the jurisdiction of the Federal District Court for the District of Columbia within whose territorial area both B.A. and B.C. have premises at which they carry on business. Indeed, Judge Greene, the judge of the District Court who has been in charge of the pre-trial proceedings in the American action, regards the complaint as being of a kind so commonplace that he describes it as an antitrust action of "the garden variety," a description which embraces the alternative way of pleading the antitrust cause of action as a count for "intentional tort."

The second proposition, that of English law, was understood by your Lordships to have been common ground between the parties, at any rate throughout the lengthy hearing of the appeal; no argument casting any doubt upon it was advanced. The proposition is that, even if the allegations against B.A. and B.C. in the complaint in the American action can be proved, they disclose no cause of action on the part of Laker against B.A. or B.C. that is justiciable in an English court. The Clayton Act which creates the civil remedy with threefold damages for criminal offences under the Sherman Act is, under English rules of conflict of laws, purely territorial in its application, while because the predominant purpose of acts of B.A. and B.C. that are complained of was the defence of their own business interests as providers of scheduled airline services on routes on which Laker was seeking to attract customers from them by operating its Skytrain policy, any English cause of action for conspiracy would be ruled out under the now well-established principle of English (as well as Scots) law laid down in a series of cases in this House spanning 50 years.

In the result your Lordships are confronted in the civil actions with a case in which there is a single forum only that is of competent jurisdiction to determine the merits of the claim; and the single forum is a foreign court. For an English court to enjoin the claimant from having access to that foreign court is, in effect, to take upon itself a one-sided jurisdiction to determine the claim upon the merits against the claimant but also to prevent its being decided upon the merits in his favour. This poses a novel problem, different in kind from that involved where there are alternative fora in which a particular civil claim can be pursued: an English court and a court of some foreign country both of which are recognised under English rules of conflict of laws as having jurisdiction to entertain proceedings against a defendant for a remedy for acts or omissions which constitute an actionable wrong under the substantive law of both England and that foreign country. * * *

The statement of the attitude taken by the executive government towards the American action by Laker was that in failing to see to it that steps were taken (presumably by C.A.B. [the United States Civil Aeronautics Board] under the Federal Aviation Act) in relation to B.A. and B.C.'s operations in the United States that would make those British Airlines immune from suit under the Clayton Act and from prosecution under the Sherman Act (which is concurrently the subject of investigation by a grand jury) the U.S. Government was in breach of its treaty obligations under Bermuda 2. This is disputed by the U.S. Government; and that treaty itself contains provision, to which neither government has so far had recourse, for the resolution of this dispute by arbitration between the two states. Nevertheless, Parker J. was beguiled into construing Bermuda 2 for himself as a result of which he reached the conclusion that the U.S. Government had committed no such breach. The interpretation of treaties to which the United Kingdom is a party but the terms of which have not either expressly or by reference been incorporated in English domestic law by legislation is not a matter that falls within the interpretative jurisdiction of an English court of law. In this House the contrary has not been contended and no arguments have been addressed to your Lordships directed to the construction of the language of Bermuda 2. In the United States, where Bermuda 2 is part of the domestic law, it may be that B.A. and B.C. will be able to rely upon its provisions as providing one or both of them with a defence in the American action; but that is not a matter upon which your Lordships can relevantly indulge in speculation. * * *

My Lords, I can now turn to the steps taken by the Secretary of State under the 1980 Act in the interval between the judgment of Parker J. and the hearing of the appeal in the Court of Appeal. These steps, in the view of Sir John Donaldson M.R., who delivered the judgment of that court, produced "a wholly different situation." (see [1983] 3 All E.R. 375 at 396, [1984] Q.B. 142 at 184).

The relevant provisions of the Act of 1980 are to be found in sections 1 to 6. The attack made in the application for judicial review of an order and two directions of the Secretary of State will make it necessary to set out the actual words of sections 1 and 2:

"1—(1) If it appears to the Secretary of State—(a) that measures have been or are proposed to be taken by or under the law of any overseas country for regulating or controlling international trade; and (b) that those measures, in so far as they apply or would apply to things done or to be done outside the territorial jurisdiction of that country by persons carrying on business in the United Kingdom, are damaging or threaten to damage the trading interests of the United Kingdom, the Secretary of State may by order direct that this section shall apply to those measures either generally or in their application to such cases as may be specified in the order.

"(2) The Secretary of State may by order make provision for requiring, or enabling the Secretary of State to require, a person in the United Kingdom who carries on business there to give notice to the Secretary of State of any requirement or prohibition imposed or threatened to be imposed on that person pursuant to any measures in far as this section applies to them by virtue of an order under subsection (1) above.

"(3) the Secretary of State may give to any person in the United Kingdom who carries on business there such directions for prohibiting compliance with any such requirement or prohibition as aforesaid as he considers appropriate for avoiding damage to the trading interests of the United Kingdom. * * *

"2—(1) If it appears to the Secretary of State—(a) that a requirement has been or may be imposed on a person or persons in the United Kingdom to produce to any court, tribunal or authority of an overseas Country any commercial document which is not within the territorial jurisdiction of that country or to furnish any commercial information to any such court, tribunal or authority; or (b) that any such authority has imposed or may impose a requirement on a person or persons in the United Kingdom to publish any such document or information, the Secretary of State may, if it appears to him that the requirement is inadmissible by virtue of subsection (2) or (3) below, give directions for prohibiting compliance with the requirement.

"(2) A requirement such as is mentioned in subsection (1)(a) or (b) above is inadmissible—(a) if it infringes the jurisdiction of the United Kingdom or is otherwise prejudicial to the sovereignty of the United Kingdom; or (b) if compliance with the requirement would be prejudicial to the security of the United Kingdom or to the relations of the government of the United Kingdom with the government of any other country.

"(3) A requirement such as is mentioned in subsection (1)(a) above is also inadmissible—(a) if it is made otherwise than for the purposes of civil or criminal proceedings which have been instituted in the overseas country; or (b) if it requires a person to state what documents relevant to any such proceedings are or have been in his possession, custody or power or to produce for the purposes of any such proceedings any documents other than particular documents specified in the requirement." * * *

In the instant cases, the Secretary of State made an order under section 1(1) of the Act of 1980 entitled the Protection of Trading Interests (U.S. Antitrust Measures) Order 1983 that came into operation on 27 June 1983 and was in the following terms:

> Whereas it appears to the Secretary of State that the measures to which this Order relates have been taken by or under the law of the United States of America ("the United States") for regulating or controlling international trade and that those measures, in so far as they apply to things done or to be done outside the territorial jurisdiction of the United States by persons carrying on business in the United Kingdom, are damaging or threaten to damage the trading interests of the United Kingdom: Now therefore the Secretary of State, in exercise of his powers under section 1(1) of the Protection of Trading Interests Act 1980 ("the 1980 Act") and of all other powers enabling him in that behalf, hereby makes the following Order—

* * *

2—(1) The Secretary of State hereby directs that section 1 of the 1980 Act shall apply to sections 1 and 2 of the United States' Sherman Act and sections 4 and 4A of the United States' Clayton Act in their application to the cases described in the following paragraph.

(2) The cases mentioned in paragraph (1) of this article are: (i) an agreement or arrangement (whether legally enforceable or not) to which a U.K. designated airline is a party, (ii) a discussion or communication to which a U.K. designated airline is a party, (iii) any act done by a U.K. designated airline, which, in respect of each case, concerns the tariffs charged or to be charged by any such airline or otherwise relates to the operation by it of an air service authorised pursuant to the Bermuda 2 Agreement.

He also gave general directions under section 1(5) and section 2(1) of the Act to come into operation on the same date as the Order. That two directions were in the following terms respectively. The § 1 direction states:

PROTECTION OF TRADING INTERESTS ACT 1980 GENERAL
DIRECTION BY THE SECRETARY OF STATE (UNDER SECTION 1)

Whereas the Secretary of State: (1) has directed that section 1 of the Protection of Trading Interests Act 1980 ('the 1980 Act') shall apply, in the circumstances specified by him, to sections 1 and 2 of the United States' Sherman Act and sections 4 and 4A of the United States' Clayton Act ('the U.S. antitrust measures'); (2) has considered the effect of the U.S. antitrust measures on United Kingdom designated airlines and in particular on their ability freely to participate in discussions or agreements relating to tariffs or other matters relating to the operation of air services authorised pursuant to the Bermuda 2 Agreement; (3) has considered the effect of the U.S. Measures on the trading interests of the United Kingdom; (4) considers that the following direction is appropriate for avoiding damage to the trading interests of the United Kingdom: Now, therefore, the Secretary of State, in exercise of his powers under section 1(3) of the 1980 Act, hereby gives the following direction—

1. Except with the consent of the Secretary of State no person in the United Kingdom who carries on business there shall comply, or cause or permit compliance, with any requirement or prohibition imposed on that person pursuant to the U.S. antitrust measures in so far as such requirement or prohibition relates to or arises out of any of the cases described in article 2(2) of the Protection of Trading Interests (U.S. Antitrust Measures) Order 1983.

* * *

PROTECTION OF TRADING INTERESTS ACT 1980 GENERAL
DIRECTION BY THE SECRETARY OF STATE (UNDER SECTION 2)

* * *

1. Except with the consent of the Secretary of State no person or persons in the United Kingdom shall comply, or cause or permit compliance, whether by themselves, their officers, servants or agents, with any requirement to produce or furnish to the United States' Department of Justice, the grand jury or the District Court any document in the United Kingdom or any commercial information which relates to the said Department of Justice investigation or the grand jury or District Court proceedings. * * *

The judicial review application

Since Laker alleged that the Order and both directions were ultra vires and its application for judicial review of them was disposed of by the Court of Appeal at the same time as the appeals in the civil actions, an excursus on the validity of the Order and directions seems appropriate at this point though it need only be short.

* * *

It was next submitted that the Secretary of State ought to have given reasons for making the order and each of the directions that were more explicit than those contained in the actual recitals to them, which do no more than state the conclusions that the Secretary of State has reached. This submission on behalf of Laker was based upon the minatory dictum of Lord Upjohn in *Padfield v. Minister of Agriculture Fisheries, and Food* [1968] 1 All ER 694 at 719, [1968] A.C. 997 at 1061-1062 that:

> if [a minister] does not give any reason for his decision it may be, *if circumstances warrant it*, that a court may be at liberty to come to the conclusion that he had no good reason for reaching that conclusion...

The qualification made in the words that I have italicised in Lord Upjohn's dictum have the effect of equating it with, and adding nothing to, a recognition of the *Wednesbury* principle (*Associated Provincial Picture Houses Ltd. v. Wednesbury Corporation* [1948] 1 K.B. 223) that a decision reached by a person upon whom a statute confers a discretion to exercise coercive powers over individuals may be held by a court of law to be ultra vires if it be established to the satisfaction of the court upon an application for judicial review that the decision is one that no reasonable person holding the office of minister upon whom the discretion is conferred could have reached. Where the decision is one which concerns international relations between the United Kingdom and a foreign sovereign state a very strong case needs to be made out to justify a court of law in holding the decision to be ultra vires under the *Wednesbury* principle. In the instant case, I agree with the Court of Appeal that Laker does not come anywhere near doing so.

The civil actions in the Court of Appeal

* * *

[T]he Court of Appeal in its judgment dealt first with the disadvantages to Laker of being forced to abandon the American action as against B.A. and B.C. These cannot be other than all one way, as the Court of Appeal appears to recognise. The judgment then went on to refer to the burden that the U.S. system for the administration of justice, in antitrust civil actions in particular, imposed upon defendants: threefold damages, burdensome and ruinously expensive pre-trial discovery, the contingency basis on which such actions were undertaken by plaintiffs' attorneys, a costs system under which a successful defendant was entitled to recover a sum for costs that represented no more than an infinitesimal part of those that he had actually incurred. While expressly disclaiming any criticism of the American system of procedure in civil actions, the court considered that the existence of such burdens was a factor in B.A.'s and B.C.'s favour that ought to be taken into account on its side of the critical equation.* * *

The Court of Appeal, however, do not state how they would have solved "the critical equation" if there had not been present in that equation by the time that the appeal reached them what they described as the "decisive factor" in favour of B.A. and B.C., viz. the effect of the Order and directions.

Two reasons are relied on by the court for treating the Order and the two directions as the decisive factor. With respect, I think that both these reasons are fallacious.

The first reason is that the direction under section 1(3) of the Act would prohibit B.A. and B.C. from satisfying any judgment given against them in the American action and thus render their aircraft liable to seizure in execution in the United States. This is based upon what, in my opinion, is a misconstruction of the Act which draws a clear distinction between "requirements" and "prohibitions" on the one hand and "judgments" on the other. The distinction between the former which are referred to as being "imposed" and the latter which are referred to as being "given" first appears in the long title of the Act itself. Sections 1 and 3 deal with requirements and prohibitions, which so far as is relevant to the instant appeal in the civil actions would be limited to pretrial, i.e. interlocutory, orders made in the American action by the U.S. District Court. Judgments are dealt with not in sections 1 to 3 but in sections 5 and 6; section 6 is drafted upon the assumption that a person carrying on business in the United Kingdom and a United Kingdom company or citizen commits no breach of English law by paying a foreign judgment for multiple damages in the country in which the judgment was given. It gives such person a remedy in the United Kingdom for recovering such sum included in the foreign judgment that he has paid as was not purely compensatory. The direction given under section 1(3) would not prohibit B.A. or B.C. paying in the United States any judgment for threefold damages given against them in the American action.

The second reason relied upon by the Court of Appeal is that the direction given under section 2 disables B.A. and B.C. from giving discovery of information and documents that would assist their defence in the American action. To this the short and realistic answer is that if the two companies think, as is claimed in an affidavit filed on behalf of B.A. in its civil action, that disclosure of particular documents or information would help their own defence rather than hinder Laker's ability to establish its complaint in the American action when it comes to trial, the direction enables them to apply to the Secretary of State for his consent to such disclosure, and since, to put it colloquially, the Secretary of State is "on their side," such consent would appear more likely than not to be forthcoming. So the Order and directions, if they make any difference, operate to the disadvantage of Laker in the American action rather than that of B.A. and B.C. who, to the extent that they do not seek or are refused the Secretary of State's consent to disclosure of particular information or documents, will be saved the irrecoverable costs of pretrial discovery on the American pattern of documents in their possession or control in the United Kingdom and of information known to their officers and employees in the United Kingdom who do not pay regular visits to the United States. * * *

For my part I should allow Laker's appeals in both civil actions and discharge the injunctions granted by the Court of Appeal. I should dismiss Laker's appeal in the application for judicial review against the Secretary of State. * * *

Appeals in civil actions allowed. Appeals in judicial review proceedings dismissed.

Notes

1. Section 6 of the Protection of Trading Interests Act, described in the opinion as giving an English business "a remedy in the United Kingdom for recovering such sum included in the foreign judgment that he has paid as was not purely compensatory," is

often referred to as the "Clawback Act." An Australian statute goes a step beyond this. The Foreign Proceedings (Excess of Jurisdiction) Act 1984, Acts of Parliament, Australia, empowers the Attorney General to declare that a foreign court's assumption of jurisdiction in an antitrust proceeding is "contrary to international law or inconsistent with international comity or international practice." (§9(1)(b)(ii)). If the Attorney General so declares, an Australian citizen or corporation, not resident in or having its principal place of business in the foreign country, who has paid a judgment in the foreign proceedings, may recover from the party paid, the entire amount of the judgment. (§10).

2. Midland Bank v. Laker Airways, [1986] 1 All E. R. 526 (Ct. of Appeal) enjoined Laker's English liquidator from filing an antitrust action in the United States against an English bank, which had a United States subsidiary. The court reasoned that the bank had not submitted to United States law because its transactions with Laker had taken place in England and the bank's United States subsidiary had a separate existence and no connection with the activities litigated in the antitrust suit; that the bank had acted only in England to defend the bank's own legitimate interests; that the bank's acts were intended to be governed by English law, under which the liquidator had no claim against the bank.

3. In 1985, Sir Freddie Laker settled the antitrust claims for 8 million pounds.

Hartford Fire Insurance Co. v. California
509 U.S. 764 (1993)

Justice SOUTER announced the judgment of the Court and delivered the opinion of the Court with respect to Parts I, II(A), III, and IV, and an opinion with respect to Part II(B) [concerning the definition of "boycott"] in which Justice WHITE, Justice BLACKMUN and Justice STEVENS join.

The Sherman Act makes every contract, combination, or conspiracy in unreasonable restraint of interstate or foreign commerce illegal. 26 Stat. 209, as amended, 15 U.S.C. §1. These consolidated cases present questions about the application of that Act to the insurance industry, both here and abroad. The plaintiffs (respondents here) allege that both domestic and foreign defendants (petitioners here) violated the Sherman Act by engaging in various conspiracies to affect the American insurance market. A group of domestic defendants argues that the McCarran-Ferguson Act, 59 Stat. 33, as amended, 15 U.S.C. §1011 et seq., precludes application of the Sherman Act to the conduct alleged; a group of foreign defendants argues that the principle of international comity requires the District Court to refrain from exercising jurisdiction over certain claims against it. We hold that most of the domestic defendants' alleged conduct is not immunized from antitrust liability by the McCarran-Ferguson Act, and that, even assuming it applies, the principle of international comity does not preclude District Court jurisdiction over the foreign conduct alleged.

I

The two petitions before us stem from consolidated litigation comprising the complaints of 19 States and many private plaintiffs alleging that the defendants, members of the insurance industry, conspired in violation of §1 of the Sherman Act to restrict the terms of coverage of commercial general liability (CGL) insurance available in the

United States. Because the cases come to us on motions to dismiss, we take the allegations of the complaints as true.

A

According to the complaints, the object of the conspiracies was to force certain primary insurers (insurers who sell insurance directly to consumers) to change the terms of their standard CGL insurance policies to conform with the policies the defendant insurers wanted to sell. The defendants wanted four changes.

First, CGL insurance has traditionally been sold in the United States on an "occurrence" basis, through a policy obligating the insurer "to pay or defend claims, whenever made, resulting from an accident or 'injurious exposure to conditions' that occurred during the [specific time] period the policy was in effect." In place of this traditional "occurrence" trigger of coverage, the defendants wanted a "claims-made" trigger, obligating the insurer to pay or defend only those claims made during the policy period. Such a policy has the distinct advantage for the insurer that when the policy period ends without a claim having been made, the insurer can be certain that the policy will not expose it to any further liability. Second, the defendants wanted the "claims-made" policy to have a "retroactive date" provision, which would further restrict coverage to claims based on incidents that occurred after a certain date. Such a provision eliminates the risk that an insurer, by issuing a claims-made policy, would assume liability arising from incidents that occurred before the policy's effective date, but remained undiscovered or caused no immediate harm. Third, CGL insurance has traditionally covered "sudden and accidental" pollution; the defendants wanted to eliminate that coverage. Finally, CGL insurance has traditionally provided that the insurer would bear the legal costs of defending covered claims against the insured without regard to the policy's stated limits of coverage; the defendants wanted legal defense costs to be counted against the stated limits (providing a "legal defense cost cap").

To understand how the defendants are alleged to have pressured the targeted primary insurers to make these changes, one must be aware of two important features of the insurance industry. First, most primary insurers rely on certain outside support services for the type of insurance coverage they wish to sell. Defendant Insurance Services Office, Inc. (ISO), an association of approximately 1,400 domestic property and casualty insurers (including the primary insurer defendants, Hartford Fire Insurance Company, Allstate Insurance Company, CIGNA Corporation, and Aetna Casualty and Surety Company), is the almost exclusive source of support services in this country for CGL insurance. ISO develops standard policy forms and files or lodges them with each State's insurance regulators; most CGL insurance written in the United States is written on these forms. All of the "traditional" features of CGL insurance relevant to this case were embodied in the ISO standard CGL insurance form that had been in use since 1973 (1973 ISO CGL form). For each of its standard policy forms, ISO also supplies actuarial and rating information: it collects, aggregates, interprets, and distributes data on the premiums charged, claims filed and paid, and defense costs expended with respect to each form and on the basis of this data it predicts future loss trends and calculates advisory premium rates. Most ISO members cannot afford to continue to use a form if ISO withdraws these support services.

Second, primary insurers themselves usually purchase insurance to cover a portion of the risk they assume from the consumer. This so-called "reinsurance" may serve at least two purposes, protecting the primary insurer from catastrophic loss, and allowing the primary insurer to sell more insurance than its own financial capacity might otherwise permit. * * *

B

* * *

Dissatisfied with [the ISO's retention of coverage the defendants did not desire] the defendants began to take other steps to force a change in the terms of coverage of CGL insurance generally available, steps that, the plaintiffs allege, implemented a series of conspiracies in violation of § 1 of the Sherman Act.

* * *

The [claims for relief] charge the four domestic primary insurer defendants and varying groups of domestic and foreign reinsurers, brokers, and associations with conspiracies to manipulate the ISO CGL forms. * * * Hartford and General Re enlisted a domestic reinsurance broker to give a speech to the ISO Board of Directors, in which he stated that no reinsurers would "break ranks" to reinsure the 1984 ISO CGL forms.

The four primary insurer defendants (Hartford, Aetna, CIGNA, and Allstate) also encouraged key actors in the London reinsurance market, an important provider of reinsurance for North American risks, to withhold reinsurance for coverages written on the 1984 ISO CGL forms. As a consequence, many London-based underwriters, syndicates, brokers, and reinsurance companies informed ISO of their intention to withhold reinsurance on the 1984 forms and at least some of them told ISO that they would withhold reinsurance until ISO incorporated all four desired changes into the ISO CGL forms.

* * *

C

Nineteen States and a number of private plaintiffs filed 36 complaints against the insurers involved in this course of events, charging that the conspiracies described above violated § 1 of the Sherman Act, 15 U.S.C. § 1. After the actions had been consolidated for litigation in the Northern District of California, the defendants moved to dismiss for failure to state a cause of action, or, in the alternative, for summary judgment. The District Court granted the motions to dismiss. It held that the conduct alleged fell within the grant of antitrust immunity contained in § 2(b) of the McCarran-Ferguson Act, 15 U.S.C. § 1012(b), because it amounted to "the business of insurance" and was "regulated by State law" within the meaning of that section; none of the conduct, in the District Court's view, amounted to a "boycott" within the meaning of the § 3(b) exception to that grant of immunity. 15 U.S.C. § 1013(b). The District Court also dismissed the three claims that named only certain London-based defendants, invoking international comity and applying the Ninth Circuit's decision in *Timberlane Lumber Co. v. Bank of America, N.T. & S.A.*, 549 F.2d 597 (CA9 1976).

The Court of Appeals reversed. Although it held the conduct involved to be "the business of insurance" within the meaning of § 2(b), it concluded that the defendants could not claim McCarran-Ferguson Act antitrust immunity for two independent reasons. First, it held, the foreign reinsurers were beyond the regulatory jurisdiction of the States; because their activities could not be "regulated by State law" within the meaning of § 2(b), they did not fall within that section's grant of immunity. Although the domestic insurers were "regulated by State law," the court held, they forfeited their § 2(b) exemption when they conspired with the nonexempt foreign reinsurers. Second, the Court of Appeals held that, even if the conduct alleged fell within the scope of §2(b), it also fell within the §3(b) exception for "act[s] of boycott, coercion, or intimidation." Finally, as to the three claims brought solely against foreign defendants, the court applied its *Timberlane* analysis, but concluded that the principle of international comity was no bar to exercising Sherman Act jurisdiction.

We granted certiorari to address two narrow questions about the scope of McCarran-Ferguson Act antitrust immunity, and to address the application of the Sherman Act to the foreign conduct at issue. We now affirm in part, reverse in part, and remand.

[On the boycott issue, Justice Scalia, in an opinion joined by Rehnquist, C.J. and O'Connor, Kennedy, and Thomas, JJ., wrote the opinion for the court holding that on remand, in order to prevail under the "boycott" exception to McCarran-Ferguson, the plaintiffs would have to show that the defendants' refusal to deal involved refusal to reinsure forms of insurance other than GCL unless changes were made in the GCL forms. Justice Souter, in an opinion joined by White, Blackmun, and Stevens, JJ., would permit a finding of "boycott" if the United States insurers solicited refusals to deal from reinsurers, to compel agreement from other insurers, even though the refusals to deal concerned only the CGL forms. The Court unanimously agreed that the United States defendants did not lose their McCarran-Ferguson defense by conspiring with foreign reinsurers. Only the opinions dealing with the extraterritorial application of the Sherman Act and comity follow, first Justice Souter's majority opinion then Justice Scalia's dissent.]

* * *

III

Finally, we take up the question whether certain claims against the London reinsurers should have been dismissed as improper applications of the Sherman Act to foreign conduct.

* * *

At the outset, we note that the District Court undoubtedly had jurisdiction of these Sherman Act claims, as the London reinsurers apparently concede. See Tr. of Oral Arg. 37 ("Our position is not that the Sherman Act does not apply in the sense that a minimal basis for the exercise of jurisdiction doesn't exist here. Our position is that there are certain circumstances, and that this is one of them, in which the interests of another State are sufficient that the exercise of that jurisdiction should be restrained"). Although the proposition was perhaps not always free from doubt, see *American Banana Co. v. United Fruit Co.*, 213 U.S. 347 (1909), it is well established by now that the Sherman Act applies to foreign conduct that was meant to produce and did in fact produce some substantial effect in the United States. Such is the conduct alleged here: that the London reinsurers engaged in unlawful conspiracies to affect the market for insurance in the United States and that their conduct in fact produced substantial effect.

According to the London reinsurers, the District Court should have declined to exercise such jurisdiction under the principle of international comity. The Court of Appeals agreed that courts should look to that principle in deciding whether to exercise jurisdiction under the Sherman Act. This availed the London reinsurers nothing, however. To be sure, the Court of Appeals believed that "application of [American] antitrust laws to the London reinsurance market 'would lead to significant conflict with English law and policy,'" and that "[s]uch a conflict, unless outweighed by other factors, would by itself be reason to decline exercise of jurisdiction." [938 F.2d] at 933 (citation omitted). But other factors, in the court's view, including the London reinsurers' express purpose to affect United States commerce and the substantial nature of the effect produced, outweighed the supposed conflict and required the exercise of jurisdiction in this case. Id., at 934.

When it enacted the Foreign Trade Antitrust Improvements Act of 1982 (FTAIA), 96 Stat. 1246, 15 U.S.C. §6a, Congress expressed no view on the question whether a court with Sherman Act jurisdiction should ever decline to exercise such jurisdiction on grounds of international comity. See H.R.Rep. No. 97-686, p. 13 (1982) ("If a court determines that the requirements for subject matter jurisdiction are met, [the FTAIA] would have no effect on the court['s] ability to employ notions of comity... or otherwise to take account of the international character of the transaction") (citing *Timberlane*). We need not decide that question here, however, for even assuming that in a proper case a court may decline to exercise Sherman Act jurisdiction over foreign conduct (or, as Justice SCALIA would put it, may conclude by the employment of comity analysis in the first instance that there is no jurisdiction), international comity would not counsel against exercising jurisdiction in the circumstances alleged here.

The only substantial question in this case is whether "there is in fact a true conflict between domestic and foreign law." *Société Nationale Industrielle Aérospatiale v. United States District Court*, 482 U.S. 522, 555 (1987) (BLACKMUN, J., concurring in part and dissenting in part). The London reinsurers contend that applying the Act to their conduct would conflict significantly with British law, and the British Government, appearing before us as amicus curiae, concurs. They assert that Parliament has established a comprehensive regulatory regime over the London reinsurance market and that the conduct alleged here was perfectly consistent with British law and policy. But this is not to state a conflict. "[T]he fact that conduct is lawful in the state in which it took place will not, of itself, bar application of the United States antitrust laws," even where the foreign state has a strong policy to permit or encourage such conduct. Restatement (Third) Foreign Relations Law §415, Comment j. No conflict exists, for these purposes, "where a person subject to regulation by two states can comply with the laws of both." Restatement (Third) Foreign Relations Law §403, Comment e. Since the London reinsurers do not argue that British law requires them to act in some fashion prohibited by the law of the United States, or claim that their compliance with the laws of both countries is otherwise impossible, we see no conflict with British law. We have no need in this case to address other considerations that might inform a decision to refrain from the exercise of jurisdiction on grounds of international comity.

IV

The judgment of the Court of Appeals is affirmed in part and reversed in part, and the case is remanded for further proceedings consistent with this opinion.

It is so ordered.

Justice SCALIA delivered the opinion of the Court with respect to Part I, and delivered a dissenting opinion with respect to Part II, in which Justice O'CONNOR, Justice KENNEDY, and Justice THOMAS have joined.

* * *

II

The petitioners, various British corporations and other British subjects, argue that certain of the claims against them constitute an inappropriate extraterritorial application of the Sherman Act. It is important to distinguish two distinct questions raised by this petition: whether the District Court had jurisdiction, and whether the Sherman Act reaches the extraterritorial conduct alleged here. On the first question, I believe that the District Court had subject-matter jurisdiction over the Sherman Act claims against all the defendants (personal jurisdiction is not contested). The respondents asserted non-frivolous claims under the Sherman Act, and 28 U.S.C. § 1331 vests district courts with subject-matter jurisdiction over cases "arising under" federal statutes. As precedents such as *Lauritzen v. Larsen*, 345 U.S. 571 (1953), make clear, that is sufficient to establish the District Court's jurisdiction over these claims. *Lauritzen* involved a Jones Act claim brought by a foreign sailor against a foreign shipowner. The shipowner contested the District Court's jurisdiction, apparently on the grounds that the Jones Act did not govern the dispute between the foreign parties to the action. Though ultimately agreeing with the shipowner that the Jones Act did not apply, the Court held that the District Court had jurisdiction.

* * *

The second question—the extraterritorial reach of the Sherman Act—has nothing to do with the jurisdiction of the courts. It is a question of substantive law turning on whether, in enacting the Sherman Act, Congress asserted regulatory power over the challenged conduct. If a plaintiff fails to prevail on this issue, the court does not dismiss the claim for want of subject-matter jurisdiction—want of power to adjudicate; rather, it decides the claim, ruling on the merits that the plaintiff has failed to state a cause of action under the relevant statute.

There is, however, a type of "jurisdiction" relevant to determining the extraterritorial reach of a statute; it is known as "legislative jurisdiction," or "jurisdiction to prescribe," 1 Restatement (Third) of Foreign Relations Law of the United States 235 (1987) (hereinafter Restatement (Third)). This refers to "the authority of a state to make its law applicable to persons or activities," and is quite a separate matter from "jurisdiction to adjudicate," see id., at 231. There is no doubt, of course, that Congress possesses legislative jurisdiction over the acts alleged in this complaint: Congress has broad power under Article I, § 8, cl. 3 "[t]o regulate Commerce with foreign Nations," and this Court has repeatedly upheld its power to make laws applicable to persons or activities beyond our territorial boundaries where United States interests are affected. But the question in this case is whether, and to what extent, Congress has exercised that undoubted legislative jurisdiction in enacting the Sherman Act.

Two canons of statutory construction are relevant in this inquiry. The first is the "long-standing principle of American law 'that legislation of Congress, unless a contrary intent appears, is meant to apply only within the territorial jurisdiction of the United States.'" [*EEOC v. Arabian American Oil Co. (Aramco)*], 111 S.Ct. [1227] at 1230 (quoting *Foley Bros., Inc. v. Filardo*, 336 U.S. 281, 285 (1949)). Applying that canon in *Aramco*, we held that the version of Title VII of the Civil Rights Act of 1964 then in force, 42 U.S.C. §§ 2000e-2000e-17 (1988 ed.), did not extend outside the territory of the United States even though the statute contained broad provisions extending its prohibitions to, for example, "'any activity, business, or industry in commerce.'" 111 S.Ct., at 1231 (quoting 42 U.S.C. § 2000e(h)). We held such "boilerplate language" to be an insufficient indication to override the presumption against extraterritoriality. 111 S.Ct., at 1232. The Sherman Act contains similar "boilerplate language," and if the question were not governed by precedent, it would be worth considering whether that presumption controls the outcome here. We have, however, found the presumption to be overcome with respect to our antitrust laws; it is now well established that the Sherman Act applies extraterritorially. But if the presumption against extraterritoriality has been overcome or is otherwise inapplicable, a second canon of statutory construction becomes relevant: "[A]n act of congress ought never to be construed to violate the law of nations if any other possible construction remains." *Murray v. The Charming Betsy*, 2 Cranch 64, 118 (1804) (Marshall, C.J.). This canon is "wholly independent" of the presumption against extraterritoriality. *Aramco*, 111 S.Ct., at 1239. It is relevant to determining the substantive reach of a statute because "the law of nations," or customary international law, includes limitations on a nation's exercise of its jurisdiction to prescribe. Though it clearly has constitutional authority to do so, Congress is generally presumed not to have exceeded those customary international-law limits on jurisdiction to prescribe.

* * *

In sum, the practice of using international law to limit the extraterritorial reach of statutes is firmly established in our jurisprudence. In proceeding to apply that practice to the present case, I shall rely on the Restatement (Third) of Foreign Relations Law for the relevant principles of international law. Its standards appear fairly supported in the decisions of this Court construing international choice-of-law principles and in the decisions of other federal courts, especially *Timberlane*. Whether the Restatement precisely reflects international law in every detail matters little here, as I believe this case would be resolved the same way under virtually any conceivable test that takes account of foreign regulatory interests.

Under the Restatement, a nation having some "basis" for jurisdiction to prescribe law should nonetheless refrain from exercising that jurisdiction "with respect to a person or activity having connections with another state when the exercise of such jurisdiction is unreasonable." Restatement (Third) §403(1). The "reasonableness" inquiry turns on a number of factors including, but not limited to: "the extent to which the activity takes place within the territory [of the regulating state]* ," id., §403(2)(a); "the connections, such as nationality, residence, or economic activity, between the regulating state and the person principally responsible for the activity to be regulated," id., §403(2)(b); "the character of the activity to be regulated, the importance of regulation to the regulating state, the extent to which other states regulate such activities, and the degree to which the desirability of such regulation is generally accepted," id., §403(2)(c); "the extent to which another state may have an interest in regulating the activity," id., §403(2)(g); and "the likelihood of conflict with regulation by another state," id., §403(2)(h). Rarely would these factors point more clearly against application of United States law. The activity relevant to the counts at issue here took place primarily in the United Kingdom, and the defendants in these counts are British corporations and British subjects having their principal place of business or residence outside the United States. Great Britain has established a comprehensive regulatory scheme governing the London reinsurance markets, and clearly has a heavy "interest in regulating the activity," id., §403(2)(g). Finally, §2(b) of the McCarran-Ferguson Act allows state regulatory statutes to override the Sherman Act in the insurance field, subject only to the narrow "boycott" exception set forth in §3(b)—suggesting that "the importance of

---

* Brackets in original. Ed.

regulation to the [United States]," id., § 403(2)(c), is slight. Considering these factors, I think it unimaginable that an assertion of legislative jurisdiction by the United States would be considered reasonable, and therefore it is inappropriate to assume, in the absence of statutory indication to the contrary, that Congress has made such an assertion.

It is evident from what I have said that the Court's comity analysis, which proceeds as though the issue is whether the courts should "decline to exercise...jurisdiction," ante, at 2910, rather than whether the Sherman Act covers this conduct, is simply misdirected. * * * It concludes that no "true conflict" counseling nonapplication of United States law (or rather, as it thinks, United States judicial jurisdiction) exists unless compliance with United States law would constitute a violation of another country's law. That breathtakingly broad proposition, which contradicts the many cases discussed earlier, will bring the Sherman Act and other laws into sharp and unnecessary conflict with the legitimate interests of other countries—particularly our closest trading partners.

In the sense in which the term "conflic[t]" was used in *Lauritzen*, 345 U.S., at 582, 592 and is generally understood in the field of conflicts of laws, there is clearly a conflict in this case. The petitioners here, like the defendant in *Lauritzen*, were not compelled by any foreign law to take their allegedly wrongful actions, but that no more precludes a conflict-of-laws analysis here than it did there. Where applicable foreign and domestic law provide different substantive rules of decision to govern the parties' dispute, a conflict-of-laws analysis is necessary. See generally R. Weintraub, Commentary on Conflict of Laws 2-3 (1980); Restatement (First) of Conflict of Laws § 1, Comment c and Illustrations (1934).

Literally the only support that the Court adduces for its position is § 403 of the Restatement (Third) of Foreign Relations Law—or more precisely Comment e to that provision, which states: "Subsection (3) [which says that a state should defer to another state if that state's interest is clearly greater] applies only when one state requires what another prohibits, or where compliance with the regulations of two states exercising jurisdiction consistently with this section is otherwise impossible. It does not apply where a person subject to regulation by two states can comply with the laws of both...." The Court has completely misinterpreted this provision. Subsection (3) of § 403 (requiring one State to defer to another in the limited circumstances just described) comes into play only after subsection (1) of § 403 has been complied with—i.e., after it has been determined that the exercise of jurisdiction by both of the two states is not "unreasonable." That prior question is answered by applying the factors (inter alia) set forth in subsection (2) of § 403, that is, precisely the factors that I have discussed in text and that the Court rejects. * * *

I would reverse the judgment of the Court of Appeals on this issue, and remand to the District Court with instructions to dismiss for failure to state a claim on the three counts at issue.

Notes

1. Justice Scalia is correct that according to the Restatement (Third) of The Foreign Relations Law of the United States, the factors set out in § 403(2) are applied to determine whether application of law under the "effects" doctrine is reasonable, even though different sovereigns do not compel inconsistent conduct. Is Justice Souter misreading § 403 or is the following a proper interpretation of his opinion? Under any comity analysis, including that of § 403(2), it is clear that the Sherman Act properly applies to

the foreign defendants' conduct, which was intended to and did cause effects in the United States that the Sherman Act forbids. Therefore the only defense available to the English defendants would be that their conduct was compelled by a foreign sovereign, and such a defense is not available on the facts of this case.

For adverse criticism of Justice Souter's opinion by commentators that agree with Justice Scalia's reading of the opinion, see Andreas F. Lowenfeld, International Litigation and the Quest for Reasonableness 27-28 (1996); Roger P. Alford, The Extraterritorial Application of Antitrust Laws: A Postscript on Hartford Fire Insurance Co. v. California, 34 Va. J. Int'l Law 216, 226-29 (1993); Robert C. Reuland, Hartford Fire Insurance Co., Comity, and the Extraterritorial Reach of United States Antitrust Laws, 29 Tex. Int'l L.J. 159, 161 (1994). For approval of Justice Souter's opinion although in agreement with Justice Scalia's reading, see Larry Kramer, Extraterritorial Application of American Law after the Insurance Antitrust Case: A Reply to Professors Lowenfeld and Trimble, 89 Am. J. Int'l L. 750, 755 (1995). See also Joseph P. Griffin, EC and U.S. Extraterritoriality: Activism and Cooperation, 17 Fordham Int'l L.J. 353, 387 (1994) (quoting "[a]n official of the British Embassy in Washington" as stating "[o]ne perverse result of the [*Hartford Fire Insurance*] judgment may be to reduce the incentive of other foreign states to cooperate with the U.S. Regulatory authorities, and in certain circumstances, to give them no option but to make use of blocking statutes").

2. In quoting from § 403(2)(a), supra page 336, what words does Justice Scalia omit? Considering these words, is Justice Scalia correct in stating "[r]arely would [the § 403(2)] factors point more clearly against application of United States law"?

3. Justice Scalia states that the McCarran-Ferguson Act exemption from the Sherman Act of the business of insurance "regulated by State law" indicates that the importance to the United States of regulating the conduct of the English defendants "is slight." Is this true if English regulation, unlike state regulation, does not protect the American public from anticompetitive conduct by insurers?

4. In Metro Industries, Inc. v. Sammi Corp., 82 F.3d 839 (9th Cir.), cert. denied, 519 U.S. 868 (1996), the Ninth Circuit applied the tripartite analysis it used in Timberlane Lumber Co. v. Bank of America [Timberlane I], 549 F.2d 597 (9th Cir. 1976), supra page 339, to deny recovery under the Sherman act. The court states that even if the conduct of the defendant would constitute a per se violation in a domestic context, "application of the per se rule is not appropriate where the conduct in question occurred in another country." Id. at 844. Applying, then, a "rule of reason," to the substantive antitrust issue, the court found that the plaintiff had not presented evidence of an antitrust violation. With regard to *Hartford*, the court said: "While *Hartford Fire Ins.* overruled our holding in Timberlane II [supra page 345, Note 1] that a foreign government's encouragement of conduct which the United States prohibits would amount to a conflict of law, it did not question the propriety of the jurisdictional rule of reason or the seven comity factors set forth in Timberlane I."

5. In a case of first impression, United States v. Nippon Paper Industries Co., 109 F.3d 1 (1st Cir. 1997), cert. denied 522 U.S. 1044 (1998), held that the United States may bring a criminal prosecution under the Sherman Act even though the defendant acted only in Japan when it conspired to fix prices of thermal fax paper in the United States. The court noted that "in both criminal and civil cases, the claim that Section One [of the Sherman Act] applies extraterritorially is based on the same language in the same section of the same statute" and that "common sense suggests that courts should

interpret the same language...uniformly, regardless of whether the impetus for interpretation is criminal or civil." Id. at 4.

British Nylon Spinners, Ltd. v. Imperial Chemical Industries
[1953] 1 Ch. 19

[The defendant, Imperial Chemical, contracted to assign to the plaintiffs, British Nylon Spinners, the exclusive right to manufacture and market nylon in England. The contract was made pursuant to an assignment to Imperial Chemical by du Pont of du Pont's nylon patent. After this contract was made, a United States judge, Sylvester Ryan, ordered du Pont not to grant exclusive rights, of the sort it had granted to Imperial Chemical, so that United States manufacturers, operating under du Pont licenses, could manufacture nylon and export it to England and other countries. Du Pont was ordered by Judge Ryan to grant manufacturing licenses for a reasonable royalty and Imperial Chemical was ordered not to grant exclusive licenses, such as the one it had granted to British Nylon Spinners.]

In June, 1952, the plaintiffs asked the defendants' solicitors to execute formal licences under the assigned patents to enable the plaintiffs to register them, and were informed that, owing to the existence of legal proceedings in the United States, the defendants could not execute any documents relating to the patents in question. * * *

The plaintiffs thereupon issued a writ, claiming declarations as to their rights to licences, and asking for an order that the defendants should execute formal grants of those licences, and for specific performance of the contract [in which defendant granted them the exclusive English rights.] They also asked for an injunction to restrain the defendants from assigning or dealing with or parting with any of the patent rights in question in obedience to the order of the United States court.

On August 13, 1952, Upjohn J. granted an interlocutory injunction to restrain the defendants from assigning the patents until judgment or further order.

The defendants appealed. * * *

EVERSHED M.R. stated the facts and continued: * * * It is plain * * * that there is here a question of what is sometimes called the comity which subsists between civilised nations. In other words, it involves the extent to which the courts of one country will pay regard and give effect to the decisions and orders of another country. I certainly should be the last to indicate any lack of respect for any decision of the district courts of the United States, but I think that in this case there is raised a somewhat serious question whether the order, in the form that it takes, does not assert an extraterritorial jurisdiction which the courts of this country cannot recognise, notwithstanding any such comity. Applied conversely, I conceive that the American courts would likewise be slow (to say the least) to recognise an assertion on the part of the British courts of jurisdiction extending, in effect, to the business affairs of persons and corporations in the United States.

Having said that much, I must make one reference to a passage in the second of the opinions which his Honour delivered, dated May, 1952. It is plain that the judge [Ryan] considered this matter most carefully and, indeed, as UPJOHN, J., pointed out, expressed his own doubts whether, in giving effect, as he felt it his duty to do, to the implications of the Sherman Act, he might not be going beyond the normally recognised limits of territorial jurisdiction. He said: "It is not an intrusion on the authority of a foreign sovereign for this court to direct that steps be taken to remove the harmful effects on the trade of the United States." If by that passage the judge intended to say (as it seems to me that he did) that it was not an intrusion on the authority of a foreign sovereign to make directions addressed to that foreign sovereign, or to its courts, or to nationals of that foreign power, effective to remove (as he says) "harmful effects on the trade of the United States", I am bound to say that, as at present advised, I find myself unable to agree with it.

Questions affecting the trade of one country may well be matters proper to be considered by the government of another country. Tariffs are sometimes imposed by one country which obviously affect the trade of another country, and the imposition of such tariffs, as it seems to me, is a matter for the government of the particular country which imposes them. And if that observation of the learned judge were conversely applied to directions designed to remove harmful effects on the trade, say, of Great Britain or British nationals in America, I should be surprised to find that it was accepted as not being an intrusion on the rights and sovereign authority of the United States. On the other hand, there is no doubt that it is competent for the courts of a particular country, in a suit between persons who are either nationals or subjects of that country or are otherwise subject to its jurisdiction, to make orders in personam against one such party, directing it, for example, to do something or to refrain from doing something in another country affecting the other party to the action. As a general proposition, that would not be open to doubt, but the plaintiff in this case is neither a subject nor a national of the United States, nor (unlike the defendant company) was it a party to the proceedings before the district judge, nor is it otherwise subject to his jurisdiction.

What the precise relationship, commercially or otherwise, is between the plaintiff company and the defendant company we have not at this stage of the proceedings considered, and I proceed on the assumption (and I am not to be taken as hinting that the contrary is the fact) that the plaintiff is an independent trade corporation and entitled to be treated as independent of the defendant company. Being so independent, it has beyond question, according to the laws of England, certain rights, certain choses in action, by virtue of the contract [granting exclusive rights] which the courts of this country, in exercise of the laws which they claim to be entitled to administer, will in this country protect and enforce. Broadly speaking, the contract * * * being an English contract, made between English nationals and to be performed in England, the right which the plaintiff company has may be described as its right, under the contract, to have it performed and, if necessary, to have an order made by the courts of this country for its specific performance. That is a right, or, in other words, a species of property (seeing, particularly, that it is related to patents) which is English in character and is subject to the jurisdiction of the English courts, and it seems to me that the plaintiff company has, at least, established a prima facie case for saying that it is not competent for the courts of the United States, or of any other country, to interfere with those rights or to make orders, the observance of which by our courts would require that our courts should not exercise the jurisdiction which they have and which it is their duty to exercise in regard to those rights.

But I think that the matter goes somewhat further. The subject-matter of the contract [between Du Pont and Imperial Chemical] is a number of English and Commonwealth patents. An English patent is a species of English property of the nature of a chose in action and peculiar in character. By English law it confers on its proprietor certain monopoly rights, exercisable in England. A person who has an enforceable right to a licence under an English patent appears, therefore, to me to have, at least, some kind of proprietary interest which it is the duty of our courts to protect. And, certainly, so far as the English patents are concerned, it seems to me, with all deference to the judgment of the district judge, to be an assertion of an extra-territorial jurisdiction which we do not recognise for the American courts to make orders which would destroy or qualify those statutory rights belonging to an English national who is not subject to the jurisdiction of the American courts.

* * *

I think it undesirable that I should say more, except to re-affirm the proposition that the courts of this country will, in the natural course, pay great respect and attention to the superior courts of the United States of America, but I conceive that it is none the less the proper province of English courts, when their jurisdiction is invoked, not to refrain from exercising that jurisdiction if they think that it is their duty so to do for the protection of rights which are peculiarly subject to their protection. In so saying, I do not conceive that I am offending in any way against the principles of comity which apply between the two countries, and, like UPJOHN, J., I take some comfort from the doubts which the district judge himself entertained about the extent to which his order might go, if carried to its logical conclusion, go.

One final word: I suggested to Mr. Winn [defendant's counsel] that it might be right to include in the order some express reservation of the defendants' right to apply to discharge the injuction if some change took place in the circumstances, particularly if some steps of a penal character were taken against the defendants in the American courts. But, on reflection, it seems unnecessary to make any addition to the order to that effect, for the order is (as all interlocutory orders of this kind are expressed to be) only "until judgment or further order." It will therefore, I think, suffice to say that in dismissing this appeal (an in my judgment we should) we do not in any way prejudice the right of the defendants, if any of the events that I have indicated should occur—and there is no evidence before us as to what might happen—to apply to the judge for a discharge of the injunction, either as to the whole of the subject-matter of the agreement [between Du Port and defendants] or as to some of the patents—for example, the non-English patents—or otherwise as they may be advised.

DENNING, L.J.: I agree. It would be a serious matter if there was a conflict between the orders of the courts of the United States and the orders of these courts. The writ of the United States does not run in this country, and, if due regard is had to the comity of nations, it will not seek to run here. But, as I read this judgment of the United States court, there is a saving clause which prevents any conflict, because, although Imperial Chemical Industries has been ordered to do certain acts by the United States court, nevertheless there is a provision which says that nothing in the judgment shall operate against the company for action taken in complying with the law of any foreign government or instrumentality thereof to which the company is for the time being subject. With that saving clause I hope that there will be no conflict between the orders.

* * *

Appeal dismissed.

Notes

1. Subsequent proceedings in *British Nylon Spinners* granted specific performance of the contract between British Nylon Spinners and Imperial Chemical. Imperial Chemical was ordered to execute licenses and restrained from any acts that would interfere with

the licenses until the licenses were registered. [1955] ch. 37 (1954). No further proceedings are reported.

2. In the United States proceedings, Judge Ryan found that British Nylon Spinners, "knew exactly what it was receiving" when it purchased the hotly disputed rights from Imperial Chemical. United States v. Imperial Chem. Indus., Ltd., 105 F. Supp. 215, 231 (S.D.N.Y. 1952).

McGlinchy v. Shell Chemical Co.
845 F.2d 802 (9th Cir. 1988)

Before Choy, Goodwin and Beezer, Circuit Judges.

Beezer, Circuit Judge:

Appellants William McGlinchy and Dan-de Products Corporation filed claims against various defendants for antitrust violations, breach of contract, and related torts. They appeal from the district court's * * * (3) grant of judgment on the pleadings for failure to state an antitrust claim concerning the polybutylene market; (4) dismissal of the antitrust claims for lack of subject matter jurisdiction * * *. We affirm.

I

In 1977 Shell Chemical Company purchased all the patents, rights, and commercial production facilities for polybutylene (PB) from Whetco Company. PB resin is used to manufacture various products, including piping designed to carry water.

In 1978 William McGlinchy entered into an oral agreement with Shell Chemical to promote the sale of PB pipe grade resin in Southeast Asia. On January 25, 1979, Dan-de Products Corporation, owned and operated by McGlinchy, entered into a written contract with Shell Chemical for the same purpose. The written contract designated Dan-de as Shell Chemical's representative for the promotion and solicitation of orders for PB pipe resin in designated countries throughout Southeast Asia. The contract expressly provided that it would remain in force for one year, ending December 31, 1979, with year-to-year renewal subject to termination at year-end upon 30 days prior notice. The written contract was extended in May 1979 to include Saudi Arabia.

On April 6, 1981 McGlinchy entered into a written contract with Shell Chemical to promote PB resin in South America. In June 1980 Dan-de and Shell International Chemical Company (SICC) entered into a similar written contract covering sale and promotion of PB resin in Africa and the Middle East.

On November 5, 1982 Shell Chemical notified McGlinchy and Dan-de in writing that the contract for promotion and sale of PB resin in Southeast Asia and Saudi Arabia would be terminated. The contract remained in force through December 31, 1982, and Shell Chemical continued to pay Dan-de commissions on actual sales through the end of 1983 as the contract required. The contract between Shell Chemical and McGlinchy covering PB resin sales and promotion in South America and the contract between SICC and Dan-de covering Middle Eastern and African PB resin sales were also terminated in 1982 by Shell Chemical and SICC, respectively, pursuant to the terms of those contracts.

In February 1984 McGlinchy and Dan-de (collectively, appellants) instituted this action against Shell Oil Company, Shell Chemical Co. and Pecten Chemicals, Inc. (collectively, Shell Oil defendants), SICC, and other Shell-related entities. The original complaint alleged federal and state antitrust violations, as well as breach of contract and related torts. Appellants filed a first amended complaint on May 29, 1984. * * *

Shell Oil defendants moved for judgment on the pleadings with respect to the federal and state antitrust claims relating to PB pipe fittings. The PB pipe fitting defendants joined in the motion, which the district court granted on June 7, 1985. * * *

V

Appellants appeal the district court's dismissal of their Sherman Act claims—alleging concerted and unilateral refusal to deal in various foreign markets—against SICC and the Shell Oil defendants. Because appellants pleaded only injury to customers or potential customers located in Southeast Asia and to plaintiffs themselves, we affirm the district court's holding that 15 U.S.C. §6a precluded subject matter jurisdiction. * * *

Appellants argue that their antitrust claims do not relate exclusively to foreign commerce and that their allegations meet the requirements of section 6a. Moreover, they contend that their complaint has alleged injury to competition in the United States in the relevant market.

SICC responds that appellants have not met the requirements of subsections 1(A) and 1(B) by showing that any effect on United States commerce was "direct, substantial, and reasonably foreseeable." 15 U.S.C. §6a. In addition, SICC maintains that appellants have not sufficiently alleged an antitrust violation as required by subsection 2 of section 6(a). Shell Oil defendants argue that because all of the purportedly illegal conduct by defendants lacks the requisite domestic effect, the district court properly dismissed the antitrust claims alleging concerted and unilateral refusal to deal in various foreign markets for lack of subject matter jurisdiction under section 6a.

Section 6a was added by the Foreign Trade Antitrust Improvements Act of 1982, Pub.L. No. 97-290, 96 Stat. 1246. It provides:

> Sections 1 to 7 of this title shall not apply to conduct involving trade or commerce (other than import trade or import commerce) with foreign nations unless—
>
> (1) such conduct has a direct, substantial, and reasonably foreseeable effect—
>
> (A) on trade or commerce which is not trade or commerce with foreign nations, or on import trade or import commerce with foreign nations; or
>
> (B) on export trade or export commerce with foreign nations, of a person engaged in such trade or commerce in the United States; and
>
> (2) such effect gives rise to a claim under the provisions of sections 1 to 7 of this title, other than this section.
>
> If sections 1 to 7 of this title apply to such conduct only because of the operation of paragraph (1)(B), then sections 1 to 7 of this title shall apply to such conduct only for injury to export business in the United States.

15 U.S.C. §6a.[8] There is little case law interpreting this section. In *Eurim-Pharm GmbH v. Pfizer*, Inc., 593 F.Supp. 1102 (S.D.N.Y.1984), the district court granted defen-

---

8. Prior to enactment of section 6a. the extraterritorial reach of the antitrust laws was governed in this circuit by a tripartite test: (1) the effect or intended effect on the foreign commerce of the United States; (2) the type and magnitude of the alleged illegal behavior; and (3) the appropriateness of exercising extraterritorial jurisdiction in light of considerations of international comity and fairness. *Timberlane Lumber Co. v. Bank of America*, 549 F.2d 597, 613, 615 (9th Cir. 1976) (Timber-

dants' motion to dismiss for lack of subject matter jurisdiction because the plaintiff had failed to establish that defendants' alleged conduct resulted in an anticompetitive effect on United States domestic or import commerce. Id. at 1107. The court reasoned that section 6a "was intended to exempt from United States antitrust law conduct that lacks the requisite domestic effect, even where such conduct originates in the United States or involved American-owned entities operating abroad." Id. at 1106. * * *

In their first amended complaint appellants alleged that their agreement with Shell Chemical involved "the promotion and solicitation of orders for PB resin in Hong Kong, India, Indonesia, Malaysia, the Philippines, Singapore, Taiwan, and Thailand," including attempts "to locate, develop and promote local manufacturers or extruders of PB pipe in South East Asia." Because appellants challenge conduct in their antitrust claim that involves trade or commerce (other than import trade or import commerce) with foreign nations, they must satisfy either subsection (1)(A) or (1)(B), and subsection 2 of section 6a.

Appellants draw our attention to their allegations that "Dan-de was and is now engaged in the domestic and overseas business of selling and promoting pipe," and that the defendants' conspiracy resulted "in the termination of plaintiffs' agreement with Shell Chemical to be its exclusive representative in the sale, promotion, and distribution of PB resin and products in South East Asia and other areas."

As to subsection (1)(A), appellants have failed to allege that the defendants' conduct has a "direct, substantial, and reasonably foreseeable effect" on domestic commerce or import trade. 15 U.S.C. §6a(1)(A). As to subsection (1)(B), appellants have not sufficiently alleged a direct, substantial, and reasonably foreseeable effect on export trade or commerce. 15 U.S.C. §6a(1)(B). Indeed, in their first amended complaint appellants never maintained that they were exporters.

Finally, appellants have failed to allege an antitrust claim under subsection 2 of section 6a. Appellants must allege antitrust injury to the market or to competition in general, not merely injury to individuals or individual firms. Appellants' first amended complaint only alleges injury to themselves, rather than to the relevant market.

After a careful review of the first amended complaint, we conclude that appellants' claims relate only to foreign commerce without the requisite domestic anti-competitive effect. The district court properly dismissed the antitrust claims concerning refusal to deal in foreign trade and commerce on the ground that the court lacked subject matter jurisdiction. * * *

---

lane I). Upon remand of *Timberlane I*, the district court applied the tripartite test. See *Timberlane Lumber Co. v. Bank of America*, 574 F.Supp. 1453, 1463-67 (N.D.Cal. 1983), aff'd, 749 F.2d 1378 (9th Cir. 1984), cert. denied, 472 U.S. 1032 (1985)(Timberlane II). On subsequent appeal, this Court reviewed the district court's analysis under the *Timberlane I* standard without mentioning section 6a. See *Timberlane II*, 749 F.2d at 1383-86. Other circuits had expressly rejected the *Timberlane I* test. See, e.g. *National Bank of Canada v. International Card Ass'n*, 666 F.2d 6, 8-9 (2d Cir. 1981)(holding that there must be an appreciable anti-competitive effect on this country's commerce of a type sufficient to justify assertion of jurisdiction); see also *Liamuige Tours v. Travel Impressions, Ltd.* 617 F.Supp. 920, 923 (E.D.N.Y. 1985).

In an effort to provide a single standard for the issue of extraterritorial application of the Sherman Act, Congress enacted section 6a. Despite the peculiar procedural history of *Timberlane*—section 6a was enacted between the remand and subsequent appeal—we are bound to apply section 6a.

We note that in passing the Foreign Trade Antitrust Improvements Act, Congress did not change the ability of the courts to exercise principles of international comity. See H.R.Rep. 686, 97th Cong.; 2d Sess. 13 (1982), U.S.Code Cong. & Admin.News 1982, p. 2431: see also *Laker Airways v. Sabena, Belgian World Airways*, 731 F.2d 909, 946 n. 137 (D.C.Cir. 1984).

Notes

1. Could the result in *Timberlane I*, supra page 339, be reached under 15 U.S.C. §6a? As footnote 8 to the opinion in the principal case indicates, §6a was enacted between the time of *Timberlane I* and the review of the trial court's decision after remand in *Timberlane II*, but was not discussed in *Timberlane II*. Hartford Fire Ins. v. California (supra page 362) affirmed the extraterritorial application of the Sherman Act by In re Insurance Antitrust Litigation, 938 F.2d 919 (9th Cir. 1991). That Ninth Circuit opinion had this to say about its circuit's comity analysis in *Timberlane*:

> We do not believe a *Timberlane* analysis can be unaffected by the statute. If a complaint survives the new bar of 15 U.S.C. §6a because the conduct has "a direct, substantial, and reasonable foreseeably effect" on American commerce, it is only in an unusual case that comity will require abstention from the exercise of jurisdiction. But as the legislation does not eliminate comity, a court should look to see if the case before it is one in which comity still has a role to play.

Id. at 932. The court then goes on to apply its *Timberlane* analysis and decide that comity was no bar to exercising Sherman Act jurisdiction over the English defendants.

2. It is sometimes stated that one purpose of §6a was to exempt from Sherman Act prosecution actions of United States firms in the United States that affect only foreign consumers. See Eurim-Pharm GmbH v. Pfizer, Inc., 593 F. Supp. 1102, 1106 (S.D.N.Y. 1984). If this is so, that purpose was largely achieved in 1918 with the passage of the Webb-Pomerene Act, 15 U.S.C. §§61-65. Foreign countries may apply their antitrust law to such conduct under the "effects" basis for jurisdiction to prescribe.

Antitrust Enforcement Guidelines for International Operations—1995

On April 5, 1995, The Department of Justice and the Federal Trade Commission issued Antitrust Enforcement Guidelines for International Operations—1995, superseding the 1988 version. The new Guidelines are published in 4 CCH Trade Regulation Reporter ¶ 13,107.

The 1988 Guidelines caused considerable controversy by taking the position, in notorious "footnote 159," that the Justice Department was concerned only with adverse effects on competition that would harm U.S. Consumers, thus seeming inconsistent with 15 U.S.C. §6a's protection of export commerce. Under the new Guidelines, there is no question that jurisdiction is asserted over acts abroad that affect United States export commerce. Jurisdiction is broadly asserted under the "effects" doctrine. "Anticompetitive conduct that affects U.S. domestic or foreign commerce may violate the U.S. antitrust laws regardless of where such conduct occurs or the nationality of the parties involved." (Section 3.1). Referring to §1(B) of the Foreign Trade Antitrust Improvement Act (FTAIA), quoted supra page 375, the Guidelines state: "Agencies may, in appropriate cases, take enforcement action against anticompetitive conduct, wherever occurring, that restrains U.S. exports, if (1) the conduct has a direct, substantial, and reasonably foreseeable effect on exports of goods or services from the United States, and (2) the U.S. courts can obtain jurisdiction over persons or corporations engaged in such conduct." (Section 3.122). Illustration D is of two foreign producers that successfully conspire to prevent a competing U.S. producer from entering the market in their country. The discussion of the illustration states: "[T]he virtually total foreclosure from [the foreign market] would almost certainly qualify as a substantial effect for jurisdictional purposes. However, if the Agencies [the Department of Justice and the FTC] believe that they may encounter difficulties in establishing personal jurisdiction or in obtaining effective relief, the case may be one in which the Agencies would seek to resolve their concerns by working with other authorities who are examining the transaction."

Section 3.121, Example B, illustrates the application of FTAIA 1(A). A foreign cartel conspires to raise the price of a product. Rather than selling the product directly into the U.S., "the cartel sells to an intermediary outside the United States, which they know will resell the product in the United States. The intermediary is not part of the cartel." In deciding whether to assert jurisdiction in this case, the Guidelines state "the Agencies would focus on the potential harm that would ensue if the conspiracy were successful, not on whether the actual conduct in furtherance of the conspiracy had in fact the prohibited effect upon interstate or foreign commerce."

Section 3.2, on "Comity," states: "In enforcing the antitrust laws, the Agencies consider international comity.... In performing a comity analysis, the Agencies take into account all relevant factors. Among others, these may include (1) the relative significance to the alleged violation of conduct within the United States, as compared to conduct abroad; (2) the nationality of the persons involved in or affected by the conduct; (3) the presence or absence of a purpose to affect U.S. consumers, markets, or exporters; (4) the relative significance and foreseeability of the effects of the conduct on the United States as compared to the effects abroad; (5) the existence of reasonable expectations that would be furthered or defeated by the action; (6) the degree of conflict with foreign law or articulated foreign economic policies; (7) the extent to which the enforcement activities of another country with respect to the same persons, including remedies resulting from those activities, may be affected; and (8) the effectiveness of foreign enforcement as compared to U.S. enforcement.... The Agencies take full account of comity factors beyond whether there is a conflict with foreign law."

The section goes on to state that when the Department of Justice decides to prosecute an antitrust action, "[t]he Department does not believe that it is the role of the courts to 'second-guess the executive branch's judgment as to the proper role of comity concerns under these circumstances.'" (Quoting United States v. Baker Hughes, Inc., 431 F. Supp. 3, 6 n.5 (D.D.C. 1990), aff'd, 908 F.2d 981 (D.C. Cir. 1990)).

Section 3.32 covers "Foreign Sovereign Compulsion" and states: "[T]he Agencies will refrain from enforcement actions on the ground of foreign sovereign compulsion only when certain criteria are satisfied. First, the foreign government must have compelled the anticompetitive conduct under circumstances in which a refusal to comply with the foreign government's command would give rise to the imposition of penal or other severe sanctions.... Foreign government measures short of compulsion do not suffice for this defense, although they can be relevant in a comity analysis.

"Second, although there can be no strict territorial test for this defense, the defense normally applies only when the foreign government compels conduct which can be accomplished entirely within its own territory. If the compelled conduct occurs in the United States, the Agencies will not recognize the defense.* * *

"Third, * * * the order must come from the foreign government acting in its governmental capacity. The defense does not arise from conduct that would fall within the FSIA commercial activity exception." For the "commercial activity exception" of the Foreign Sovereign Immunities Act, see 28 U.S.C. § 1605(a)(2), supra page 282.

Notes

1. See Matsushita Elec. Indus. Co. v. Zenith Radio Corp., 475 U.S. 574, 578, 589-91, 598 (1986) (noting the allegation that Japan encourages its enterprises to form cartels, resulting in high prices for Japanese consumers and low prices for Japanese products in foreign markets, but holding that the defendants were entitled to summary judgment on the charge of violating United States antitrust laws because of insufficient evidence of a predatory pricing conspiracy, and declaring it not necessary to reach the sovereign compulsion issue).

2. As of January 1, 2000, The United States and 28 other countries have ratified the Convention on the Organization for Economic Cooperation and Development (OECD), opened for signature Dec. 14, 1960, 12 U.S.T. 1729, T.I.A.S. No. 4891 (entered into force Jan. 1, 1961). The OECD objectives are to achieve economic growth while maintaining financial stability, and to contribute to the expansion of world trade. OECD Guidelines for Multinational Enterprises 2 (1986).

The Council of the OECD has adopted a Recommendation Concerning Co-Operation Between Member Countries On Anticompetitive Practices Affecting International Trade, Doc. C(95)130, 35 I.L.M. 1313 (1996). Action recommended includes notification, exchange of information, and co-ordination of actions concerning anticompetitive activity that may affect the interests of other members. The preamble to the Recommendation recognizes "the need for Member countries to give effect to the principles of international law and comity and to use moderation and self-restraint in the interest of co-operation on the field of anticompetitive practices." If members cannot resolve a dispute concerning extraterritorial application of antitrust law, they are urged to use the OECD's Competition Law and Policy Committee to assist conciliation. The 1995 Antitrust Enforcement Guidelines for International Operations, issued by the Department of Justice and the Federal Trade Commission, states that those agencies "have agreed with respect to member countries of the OECD to consider the legitimate interests of other nations in accordance with relevant OECD recommendations."

Lucchino v. Foreign Countries of Brazil, et al,
476 A.2d 1369 (Pa. Cmwlth. Ct. 1984)

CRUMLISH, President Judge.

Frank J. Lucchino, Controller of Allegheny County, has filed a petition for determination of discrimination against the foreign countries of Brazil, South Korea, Spain, Mexico and Argentina pursuant to the Pennsylvania Trade Practices Act, 71 P.S. § 773.101. Respondent Mexico has filed a motion to dismiss, asserting that it is immune from this Court's jurisdiction under the federal Foreign Sovereign Immunities Act of 1976 and under the judicially-determined Act of State Doctrine. There has been no response, to date, from the countries of Brazil, South Korea, Spain and Argentina. We deny Mexico's motion to dismiss. After reviewing the evidence presented by Lucchino in support of his petition, we hold that the respondent foreign countries have discriminated against the steel and aluminum industries of Pennsylvania.

A hearing was held on the petition for determination of discrimination on February 1, 1984. Various exhibits were admitted into evidence and the record remained open for the submission of additional evidence. The evidence was admitted on February 15, 1984, following which the record was closed. based upon this evidence, the Court has made the following findings of fact:

* * *

3. That notwithstanding proper service of the petition upon the respondent foreign countries, Brazil, South Korea, Spain, Mexico and Argentina, the respondent foreign countries Brazil, South Korea, Spain and Argentina did not appear or present any testimony during the hearing seeking a determination of discrimination.

4. That only respondent foreign country, Mexico, attended the hearing, but only to the extent of submitting a document seeking dismissal of the petition as it pertained to the respondent, Mexico.* * *

11. That the International Trade Administration has determined that the benefits conferred by Brazil to manufacturers of steel, iron and aluminum products within Brazil pertain to the products identified in Finding of Fact No. 10, include the following: Industrial Products Tax (IPI) export credit premium; preferential working capital financing for exports; income tax exemptions for export earnings; long-term loans; IPI rebates for capital investment; Industrial Development Council (CDI) program; accelerated depreciation for capital goods manufactured in Brazil; government provision of equity capital; government assistance in repaying foreign loans; short-term financing (Resolution 674); funding for expansion through IPI tax rebates; Resolution 68 (FINEX); and raw materials (iron ore) supplied at government controlled rates. * * *

19. That the International Trade Administration has determined that the benefits conferred by Spain to manufacturers of steel, iron and aluminum products within Spain pertaining to the products identified in Finding of Fact No. 17, include the following: medium and long-term preferential loans; short-term preferential loans; Privileged Circuit Exporter Credits (a form of working capital loans); cash grants and capital infusion. * * *

33. That the International Trade Administration has determined that the benefits conferred by Mexico to manufacturers of steel, iron and aluminum products within Mexico, pertaining to the products identified in Finding of Fact No. 32, include the following: Fund for Promotion of Exports of Mexican manufactured products (FOMEX); Fund for Industrial Development (FONEI); Guarantee and Development Fund for medium and small industries (FOGAIN); state tax incentives, Nacional Financiera, S.A. (NAFINSA); preferential federal tax incentives (CEPROFI); Article 94 loans; and accelerated depreciated allowances.

34. That the International Trade Administration has determined that the benefits conferred by Mexico enumerated in Finding of Fact No. 33, pertaining to the products identified in Finding of Fact No. 32, constitute subsidization by Mexico of said products and the manufacturing thereof. * * *

At the February 1st hearing, respondent Mexico submitted a motion to dismiss on the grounds that it enjoyed sovereign immunity under the Foreign Sovereign Immunities Act of 1976 and the Act of State Doctrine. We disagree.

Section 1605 of the Immunities Act lists the general exceptions to jurisdictional immunity of a foreign state. Section 1605(a)(2) states that there is jurisdiction when

> the action is based upon a commercial activity carried on in the United States by the foreign state; or upon an act performed in the United States in connection with a commercial activity of the foreign state elsewhere; *or upon an act outside the territory of the United States in connection with a commercial activity of the foreign state elsewhere and that act causes a direct effect in the United States.* (Emphasis added.)

Mexico contends that the discriminatory acts alleged by Lucchino were public governmental acts and therefore were not commercial activities. Mexico further alleges that jurisdiction is lacking under the Act of State Doctrine. The Act of State Doctrine was judicially established so as to preclude the courts of the United States from questioning the power and sovereignty of foreign states in sensitive areas. However, the Fifth Circuit Court of Appeals, in Arango v. Guzman Travel Advisors Corp., 621 F.2d 1371 (5th Cir.1980), declared that the Act of State Doctrine does not preclude judicial resolution of all commercial consequences stemming from the occurrence of such public acts.

On review of the evidence, we hold that the discriminatory acts are commercial in nature. * * *

2. The sovereign immunity defense to this Court's subject matter jurisdiction is unavailable to the respondent foreign countries Brazil, South Korea, Spain, Mexico and Argentina due to the commercial nature of the activities engaged in, as set forth in the Findings of Fact, by said respondent foreign countries. See 28 U.S.C. § 1605(a)(2).

3. The "act of state" defense to this Court's subject matter jurisdiction is unavailable to the respondent foreign countries Brazil, South Korea, Spain, Mexico and Argentina due to the commercial nature of the activities engaged in, as set forth in the Findings of Fact, by said respondent foreign countries. * * *

11. The violations of the Pennsylvania Trade Practices Act by each of the respondent foreign countries Brazil, South Korea, Spain, Mexico and Argentina entitles petitioner to the relief he seeks and thereby makes it unlawful for any public agency to specify, purchase, or permit to be furnished or used, in any public works, steel, iron and aluminum products made in any of the respondent foreign countries which have been determined by this Court to discriminate pursuant to the Act.

ORDER

The foreign countries of Brazil, South Korea, Spain, Mexico and Argentina have been found to be discriminating against certain aluminum and steel products made in the Commonwealth of Pennsylvania under the Trade Practices Act, Act of July 23, 1968, P.L. 686, 71 P.S. §773.101. Pursuant to 71 P.S. §773.108, the Prothonotary of the Commonwealth Court shall place on the Foreign Registry Docket the name of the respondent foreign countries and the specific products of each country whose purchase or use shall be prohibited by the Act. * * *

ORDER

Respondent Mexico's motion to dismiss is hereby denied.

Note

71 Pa. Stat. Ann. §773.104, first enacted in 1968, provides: "If all considerations in or affecting a bid or a bidder are equal, each public agency shall give preference to aluminum and steel made in the United States."

The Treaty of Friendship, Commerce, and Navigation between the United States of America and the Federal Republic of Germany, signed at Washington, D.C., October 29, 1954, entered into force July 14, 1956, 7 U.S.T. 1839, TIAS 3593, in Article XVII, provides that "Each Party undertakes (a) that enterprises owned or controlled by its Government, and that monopolies or agencies granted exclusive or special privileges within its territories, shall make their purchases and sales involving either imports or exports affecting the commerce of the other Party solely in accordance with commercial considerations, including price, quality, availability, marketability, transportation and other conditions of purchase or sale; and (b) that the nationals, companies and commerce of such other Party shall be afforded adequate opportunity, in accordance with customary business practice, to compete for participation in such purchases and sales."

Zschernig v. Miller, 389 U.S. 429 (1968), struck down an Oregon reciprocity statute as it was applied to block the inheritance of an East German citizen. The court assumed that Oregon could properly condition a foreign citizen's right to inherit Oregon property on a reciprocal right of a United States citizen to take property in the foreign country. The court, however, found unconstitutional as applied Oregon's requirement that the foreign heirs receive the proceeds of Oregon estates "without confiscation," which resulted in Oregon courts undertaking a detailed criticism of the authoritarian nature of the East German government. The opinion concludes:

> Where [state] laws conflict with a treaty, they must bow to the superior federal policy. Yet, even in absence of a treaty, a State's policy may disturb foreign relations.* * *. Certainly a State could not deny admission to a traveler from East Germany nor bar its citizens from going there. If there are to be such restraints, they must be provided by the Federal Government. The present Oregon law is not as gross an intrusion in the federal domain as those others might be. Yet, as we have said, it has a direct impact upon foreign relations and may well adversely affect the power of the central government to deal with those problems." Id. at 441

See Daniel M. Price & John P. Hannah, The Constitutionality of United States State and Local Sanctions, 39 Harv. Int'l L.J. 443, 447-48 (1998) (stating that sanctions such as those enacted by Massachusetts against Burma "necessarily infringe upon governmental powers which the Framers reserved exclusively to the national authority and should, therefore, be deemed unconstitutional").

In order to sanction Burma (renamed Myanmar) for human rights violations and to change Burma's domestic policies, Massachusetts enacted a statute that prohibited the State and its agents from purchasing goods or services from anyone doing business with Burma. Crosby v. National Foreign Trade Council, 120 S.Ct. 2288 (2000), held that the Massachusetts statute was preempted by a federal statute that imposed sanctions on Burma, and authorized the President to impose additional sanctions, to waive sanctions, and to develop a strategy for improving human rights practices and the quality of life in Burma.

Japan-United States: Agreement on Semiconductor Trade
25 ILM 1408 (1986)

I. Market Access

1. The Governments of Japan and the United States of American are desirous of enhancing free trade in semiconductors on the basis of market principles and the competitive positions of their respective industries. Both Governments have exchanged views

regarding the future size and shape of the global semiconductor market, including, *inter alia*, the present and prospective situation in their respective domestic markets. These exchanges have been based upon detailed analysis of the economics of various markets, competitiveness of their respective industries, and independent, non-governmental forecasts of anticipated growth in these markets. Their semiconductor industries anticipate substantial market growth both domestically and internationally, and the two Governments strongly support and encourage expanded trade in these products. The Japanese producers and users of semiconductors anticipate substantially increased supply by and usage of foreign-based semiconductors. The United States of America anticipates substantially improved opportunities for foreign semiconductor sales in the Japanese market more reflective of the competitiveness of the U.S. industry.

Based upon such recognitions, the Government of Japan will impress upon the Japanese producers and users of semiconductors the need to aggressively take advantage of increased market access opportunities in Japan for foreign-based firms which wish to improve their actual sales performance and position. In turn, the Government of the United States of America will impress upon the U.S. semiconductor producers the need to aggressively pursue every sales opportunity in the Japanese market.

2. Both Governments agree that the expected improvement in access should be gradual and steady over the period of this Arrangement.

3. (1) The Government of Japan will provide further support for expanded sales of foreign-produced semiconductors in Japan through:

a. establishment of an organization which will provide sales assistance for foreign semiconductor producers as they attempt to penetrate the Japanese market. This organization will also make quality assessments of foreign semiconductor products, upon request, and will organize a research fellowship program, seminars, exhibitions, etc., for foreign firms; and

b. promotion of long-term relationships between Japanese semiconductor purchasers and foreign producers, including joint product development with Japanese customers.

(2) The Government of the United States of American will also provide support for the above activities, to the extent possible.

4. The Government of Japan and the Government of the United States of America reaffirm their determination that there should be full and equitable access for foreign companies to patents resulting from government-sponsored research and development in this area, and both Governments have every intention to refrain from policies or programs which stimulate inordinate increases in semiconductor production capacity.

II: Prevention of Dumping

1. Suspension of Antidumping Cases

Present antidumping cases on EPROMs and 256k and above DRAMs will be suspended upon mutually agreed completion of the Suspension Agreements between the Department of Commerce of the United States of America (hereinafter called "the Department of Commerce") and the Japanese companies concerned on those products (hereinafter called "the Suspension Agreements").

2. Monitoring (U.S. Market)

(1) Both Governments recognize the need to prevent dumping in accordance with relevant provisions of the General Agreement on Tariffs and Trade (hereinafter called "the GATT")

(2) In order to prevent dumping, the Government of Japan will monitor costs and prices on the products exported from Japan to the United States of America. * * *

(5) If the Government of the United States of America believes that exports or sales of any monitored product are being made by one or more Japanese firms in the U.S. market at prices less than company-specific fair value and the Government of the United States of America provides the Government of Japan with information to support that belief, immediate consultations may be requested. Consultations shall have a maximum 14 day limit, unless both Governments mutually agree to a longer period.

(6) Based upon monitoring and/or consultation, the Government of Japan will take appropriate actions available under laws and regulations in Japan to prevent exports at prices less than company-specific fair value.

(7) Based upon consultation and with concurrence of the Government of the United States of America, the Government of Japan will take appropriate action through Japanese semiconductor exporters so that their related party in the United States of America will not sell to the first unrelated party in the United States of America at prices less than company-specific fair value.

(8) The Government of the United States of America, either by self-initiation or in response to petition, retains full rights to initiate antidumping cases based on any information available to it. Prior consultation shall be made in the case of self-initiation. * * *

3. Monitoring (Third Country Markets)

(1) Both Governments recognize the need to prevent dumping in accordance with relevant provisions of the GATT and will encourage respective industries to conform with the above principles.

(2) In order to prevent dumping, the Government of Japan will monitor, as appropriate, costs and export prices on the products exported by Japanese semiconductor firms from Japan. * * *

It is understood by the Government of Japan that should the U.S. capital-affiliated semiconductor companies established in Japan believe they are not being accorded national treatment, the Government of the United States of America will request immediate consultations with the Government of Japan. Such consultations will be held within 14 days of the request.

13. The duration of this Arrangement will be five years, ending on July 31, 1991.

European Community Declaration Concerning Japanese-United States Agreement on Semiconductor Trade
25 ILM 1621 (1986)

The E.C. Commission, confirming the fears it expressed on August 1, 1986, believes that the agreement concluded July 30 between the United States and Japan on semiconductors contains elements that jeopardize the international trading rules and threaten the legitimate interests of the European Community.

We have therefore asked that a formal consultation procedure be opened under the General Agreement on Tariffs and Trade, both of a general nature and under the international antidumping code.

From an economic standpoint, our fears essentially center on two aspects of this arrangement:

—The arbitrary increase of semiconductor prices on Community markets;

—The privileged access of American firms to the Japanese market.

One objective of the Japanese-American accord is indeed a considerable increase in the price of semiconductors—affecting not only the American market, but also the markets of third countries, including the Community's.

Meanwhile, it has been noted that substantial price increases have occurred on the American market.

The European industry is highly dependent on semiconductor imports, the true raw material for new technologies. It is not normal for the prices in the sector to be fixed arbitrarily by the United States and Japan.

Moreover, it would be unacceptable for this agreement to have the effect of improving access to the Japanese market only for American manufacturers, to the detriment of competing firms in the Community.

This would constitute on the part of the two most important international trading partners a flagrant contradiction—with potentially serious consequences—of the determination, expressed again recently at Punta del Este, to liberalize trade to benefit the entire international community.

Notes

1. A new five-year Japan-U.S. Semiconductor Agreement was signed in June, 1991, under which Japan agrees to assist the U.S. in obtaining 20% of the Japanese market and the U.S. agrees to lift $165 million in trade sanctions. Arrangement Between the Government of Japan and the Government of the United States of America concerning Trade in Semiconductor Products, June 4, 1991. Under the 1986 agreement, the U.S. had achieved 12% of the Japanese chip market. "Nippon Notes," Economist, June 8, 1991, at 63; "Semiconductor Trade: Son of a Deal," id, at 68-69. In the last quarter of 1992, foreign companies supplied 20.2% of the Japanese chip market. Economist, "A Target for Protection," March 27, 1993, at 65. In August 1996 the United States and Japan agreed to a new three-year semiconductor trade pact. The new agreement does not set targets for U.S. Sales in Japan. A separate agreement between U.S. and Japanese semiconductor trade associations establishes a Semiconductor Council to collect market share and other data in each country to be periodically reviewed by the two governments.

On September 23, 1991, the U.S. and the EEC signed an agreement "On Antitrust Cooperation and Coordination." 30 I.L.M. 1491. The agreement provides for notification of enforcement activities that may affect interests of the other party (Art. II), cooperation in enforcement activities (Art. IV), and recognizes that activities in the territory of one party may "adversely affect important interests of the other Party" (Art. V(1)). The agreement seeks "avoidance of conflicts over enforcement activities" and to this end states criteria similar to those in §403 of the Restatement (Third) for balancing the interests of the respective parties (Art. VI(3)). (A new agreement retroactive to the date of the original agreement cured a procedural defect in the EEC adoption of this agreement; OJ L95/45, 34 I.L.M. 850 (1995)).

On June 4, 1998, an Agreement on the Application of Positive Comity Principles in the Enforcement of Their Competition Law entered into force between the U.S. and the European Communities. 37 I.L.M. 1070 (1998). The Agreement supplements the 1991 Agreement discussed in the previous paragraph. The Agreement provides that one party may request the other "to remedy anticompetitive activities in accordance with the Requested Party's competition law." (Art. III). Further the "Requesting Party will normally defer or suspend [its] own enforcement activities in favor of enforcement activities by...the Requested Party when...[t]he anticompetitive activities at issue (i) do not have a direct, substantial and reasonably foreseeable impact on consumers in the Requesting Party's territory, or (ii)...they occur principally in and are directed principally towards the other Party's territory." (Art. IV(2)). With regard to i supra, compare 15 U.S.C. §6a(1)(B), supra page 375.

The United States and Australia have agreed to a modest degree of cooperation in antitrust enforcement. Agreement between the Government of the United States and the Government of Australia Relating to Cooperation in Antitrust Matters, June 28, 1982, 22 I.L.M. 702 (1982). The United States promises to inform Australia when the Department of Justice or the Federal Trade Commission decides to undertake an antitrust investigation that may affect Australian interests (Art. 1 (2-5)). Australia agrees that it "may" notify the United States when Australia adopts "a policy that it considers may have antitrust implications for the United States" (Art. 1 (1)). Perhaps the most important concession to United States interests is the agreement that discovery procedures alone "shall not...be regarded by either Party as affecting adversely its significant national interests" (Art. 5(2)).

The United States has also entered bilateral agreements concerning antitrust cooperation with France, Germany, and Canada. See Diane P. Wood, The Impossible Dream: Real International Antitrust, 1992 U. Chicago Legal Forum 277, 293-94. In 1994 Congress enacted the International Antitrust Enforcement Assistance Act, 15 U.S.C. §§ 6201-12. The Act allows the Department of Justice and the Federal Trade Commission to enter into mutual assistance agreements with foreign antitrust authorities and, pursuant to such agreements, share information developed in antitrust investigations.

For an indication that the aspect of United States antitrust law that is most offensive to other nations is treble damages in private civil actions under 15 U.S.C. § 15 and that effective bilateral agreements between the United States and other countries may be feasible if the agreements eliminate the treble damage remedy in extraterritorial application, see Seung Wha Chang, Extraterritorial Application of U.S. Antitrust Laws to Other Pacific Countries: Proposed Bilateral Agreements for Resolving International Conflicts with the Pacific Community, 16 Hastings Int'l & Comp. L. Rev. 295, 312, 316-17 (1993).

2. Several western European countries, including both members and non-members of the EEC, have included the effects principle in their antitrust doctrine. See David J. Gerber, Beyond Balancing: International Law Restraints on the Reach of National Laws, 10 Yale J. Int'l L. 185, 201 (1984) (reporting developments in France, Germany, Denmark, Sweden, and Switzerland). In A. Ahlstrom Osakeyhtio v. Commission of the European Communities, [1988] E.C.R. 5193, (the "Wood Pulp Case"), the Court of Justice of the European Communities held that the law established by the EEC Antitrust Treaty applies to agreements between non-EEC producers, including U.S. producers of

wood pulp (used to manufacture paper and cardboard). The Court affirmed, with one minor exception, a decision of the EEC Commission holding that the foreign producers had violated Article 85 of the EEC Treaty and imposing fines. The Advocate General, Mr. Darmon had urged affirmance based on the "direct, substantial and foreseeable effect" of agreements abroad in the Common Market, and distinguished this "effect" doctrine from the territorial basis for jurisdiction to prescribe. Id. at 5214-15, 5227. The Court, however, while not rejecting the effects doctrine, stated: "The decisive factor is the place where [the price-fixing agreement] is implemented.... It is immaterial in that respect whether or not [the conspirators] had recourse to subsidiaries, agents, sub-agents, or branches within the Community in order to make their contracts with purchasers within the Community. Accordingly the Community jurisdiction to apply its competition rules to such conduct is covered by the territorial principle as universally recognized in public international law." Id. at 5243.

Actions of the Commission of the European Union reflect use of the effects principle. The Federal Trade Commission approved Boeing's acquisition of McDonnell Douglas but the Commission objected because the merger of the two U.S. airplane manufacturers would have an anticompetitive effect on Airbus Industrie, Boeing's only competitor in the global market for commercial airline sales. Airbus Industrie, located in Toulouse, France, is a consortium consisting of British, German, French, and Spanish airplane manufacturers. The Commission approved the acquisition only after Boeing agreed not to enforce agreements with airlines that made Boeing the airlines' exclusive vendor of planes, not to enter into new exclusive contracts, to maintain McDonnell Douglas as a separate legal entity for ten years, to supply the E.U. with an annual report on Boeing's business activities, and to make some of its aviation technology available to competitors for a fee. Commission Decision 97/816/EC in Case IV/M.877 [1997] OJ L 336/16.

U.S. companies have found the European Commission offers quicker resolution of their antitrust complaints against other U.S. companies than does the U.S. Justice Department. Santa Cruz Operation, Inc., (SCO) a California company, wished Microsoft Corp. to release SCO from a SCO's 1987 agreement to include Microsoft code in future versions of an operating system and pay royalties whether or not SCO used that code. SCO complained to the U.S. Justice Department, but before the Department acted, SCO obtained an order from the European Commission objecting to the agreement on grounds that it violated E.U. competition laws. Microsoft then released SCO from the agreement.

On August 3, 2000, The EU Competition Commissioner announced that the E.U. Commission had sent a statement of objections to Microsoft giving Microsoft two months to reply to the objections. The Commissioner stated that the Commission had evidence that Microsoft has used its dominant Windows operating system to prevent rivals from developing software to run computer servers.

3. In 1989 the EEC promulgated merger control rules, making a 180 degree change from the former policy which regarded concentrations of industry as a desirable means of strengthening national economies. Commission Regulation 4064/89, 1990 O.J. (L 257) 13; Common Mkt. Rep. (CCH) ¶ 2839 (1989).

4. For discussion of the antitrust law of countries other than the United States, see: European Community: Jacques H.J. Bourgeois, EC Competition Law and Member State Courts, 17 Fordham Int'l L.J. 331 (1994); Andre Fiebig, The Extraterritorial Application of the European Merger Control Regulation, 5 Colum. J. Int'l L. 79 (1998); Joseph P.

Griffin, EC and U.S. Extraterritoriality: Activism and Cooperation, 17 Fordham Int'l L.J. 353 (1994); Spencer Weber Waller & Noel J. Byrne, Changing View of Intellectual Property and Competition Law in the European Community and the United States of America, 20 Brook. J. Int'l L. 1 (1993). Japan: Yoichiro Hamabe, Changing Antimonopoly Policy in the Japanese Legal System—An International Perspective, 28 Int'l Law. 903 (1994); Spencer Weber Waller, Neo-Realism and the International Harmonization of Law: Lessons from Antitrust, 42 Kansas L. Rev. 557 (1994); cf. Joel Davidow, Application of U.S. Antitrust Laws to Keiretsu Practices, 18 World Competition L. & Econ. Rev. 5 (1994).

Section 2: Securities Law

Zoelsch v. Arthur Andersen & Co.,
824 F.2d 27 (D.C. Cir. 1987)

Before WALD, Chief Judge, and BORK and SILBERMAN, Circuit Judges.

Opinion for the Court filed by Circuit Judge BORK.

Opinion concurring in the judgment filed by Chief Judge WALD.

BORK, Circuit Judge:

Klaus Zoelsch brought this action against Arthur Andersen & Co. in federal court in the District of Columbia on behalf of himself and at least thirty-one others, all citizens of the Federal Republic of Germany. In the complaint, he stated two claims under the United States securities laws and four common law claims. He alleged federal court jurisdiction on the basis of the federal claims and diversity of citizenship. The district court dismissed the action for want of subject matter jurisdiction. Zoelsch appeals only the district court's refusal of jurisdiction over the federal claims. We affirm.

I

The transactions that led to this lawsuit involved four principal participants. Dr. Loescher und Co. KG ("Loescher") is a West German limited partnership. First American International Real Estate Limited Partnership ("FAIR") is an American limited partnership based in Miami, Florida. Arthur Andersen & Co. GmbH ("GmbH") is a West German limited liability corporation. Arthur Andersen & Co. ("AA-USA"), the sole defendant in this case, is an American general partnership organized under the laws of Illinois.

Zoelsch and the other West Germans invested in an intricate investment and tax shelter plan. Under the plan, their funds were placed either directly with Loescher, or indirectly with another West German entity that is a limited partner of Loescher. In either case, the investors understood that their funds would be channeled through these entities to FAIR. FAIR, in turn, would invest the funds in property and condominium conversions in Memphis, Tennessee, and Atlanta, Georgia.

In April of 1981, Loescher and FAIR entered into an investment agreement. In September of 1981, Loescher commissioned GmbH to prepare an audit report on the entire plan, including an analysis of FAIR's written description of the American investments. Within the month, GmbH issued its report. Loescher then solicited investors by distributing a package of materials to them, which included GmbH's audit report and FAIR's materials. It is undisputed that FAIR's materials were prepared in the United States, that the audit report was prepared in West Germany, and that the package of materials was distributed only in West Germany to West German investors. The investments were not successful, and Zoelsch's complaint alleges that he and the other investors detrimentally relied on a number of false representations and material omissions in the audit report.

Zoelsch has brought a separate suit against GmbH in Munich, West Germany. He brings this suit, however, only against AA-USA, which was not directly involved in the solicitation of these investors or in the preparation of any of the documents that induced these purchases of securities. The sole link between AA-USA and the package of materials distributed by Loescher is one reference to AA-USA in the audit report prepared by GmbH. The reference is in German, and plaintiff's translation reads: "With respect to a number of data and particulars in the prospectus in conjunction with the economic fundamentals we have made inquiries thereabout by way of our branch-establishment Arthur Andersen & Co., Memphis." * * *

Zoelsch's complaint alleged that AA-USA provided false and misleading information to GmbH with ample reason to know that this information would be incorporated in GmbH's audit report and would be relied on by investors such as Zoelsch. Zoelsch alleged fraud in connection with the sale of securities and the aiding and abetting of securities fraud in violation of section 10(b) of the Securities Exchange Act of 1934 and its attendant Rule 10b-5. See 15 U.S.C. § 78j(b) (1982); 17 C.F.R. § 240.10b-5 (1985). The district court granted defendant's motion to dismiss for lack of subject matter jurisdiction.

II

A

The issue, not previously addressed in this circuit, is American court jurisdiction over securities law claims against a defendant who acted in the United States when the securities transaction occurred abroad and there was no effect felt in this country.

Congress can, of course, prescribe the extent of federal jurisdiction over actions to enforce the federal securities laws, so long as it does not overstep the broad limits set by the due process clause. See, e.g., *Leasco Data Processing Equip. Corp. v. Maxwell*, 468 F.2d 1326, 1334 (2d Cir.1972). But in the Securities Exchange Act of 1934, Congress said little that bears on this issue. The explicit purposes of the Act are:

> to remove impediments to and perfect the mechanisms of a national market system for securities and a national system for the clearance and settlement of securities transactions and the safeguarding of securities and funds related thereto, and to impose requirements necessary to make such regulation and control reasonably complete and effective, in order to protect interstate commerce, the national credit, the Federal taxing power, to protect and make more effective the national banking system and Federal Reserve System, and to insure the maintenance of fair and honest markets in such transactions.

15 U.S.C. § 78b (1982). The relevant language of section 10(b) prohibits "any person, directly or indirectly, by the use of any means or instrumentality of interstate commerce or of the mails" from using "in connection with the purchase or sale of any security…

any manipulative or deceptive device or contrivance" proscribed by the SEC. Id. §78j(b). "Interstate commerce" is broadly defined to include "trade, commerce, transportation, or communication...between any foreign country and any State." Id. §78c(a)(17). And the federal district courts are given exclusive jurisdiction of suits brought to enforce the securities laws. See id. §78aa. These provisions frame a fairly broad grant of jurisdiction, but they furnish no specific indications of when American federal courts have jurisdiction over securities law claims arising from extraterritorial transactions.

A single passage in the statute addresses this issue explicitly. Section 30(b) states that the 1934 Act "shall not apply to any person insofar as he transacts a business in securities without the jurisdiction of the United States, unless he transacts such business in contravention of such rules and regulations as the Commission may prescribe as necessary or appropriate to prevent the evasion of this chapter." 15 U.S.C. §78dd(b) (1982). But AA-USA is not alleged to have transacted a business in securities anywhere. Nevertheless, as will be seen, section 30(b) gives some reinforcement to the conclusion that there is no jurisdiction to entertain Zoelsch's claims.

If the text of the 1934 Act is relatively barren, even more so is the legislative history. Fifty years ago, Congress did not consider how far American courts should have jurisdiction to decide cases involving predominantly foreign securities transactions with some link to the United States. The web of international connections in the securities market was then not nearly as extensive or complex as it has become. In this state of affairs, our inquiry becomes the dubious but apparently unavoidable task of discerning a purely hypothetical legislative intent. As Judge Friendly candidly put it in a very similar case: "We freely acknowledge that if we were asked to point to language in the statutes, or even in the legislative history, that compelled these conclusions, we would be unable to respond. The Congress that passed these extraordinary pieces of legislation in the midst of the depression could hardly have been expected to foresee the development of offshore funds thirty years later.... Our conclusions rest on...our best judgment as to what Congress would have wished if these problems had occurred to it." *Bersch v. Drexel Firestone, Inc.*, 519 F.2d 974, 993 (2d Cir.), cert. denied, 423 U.S. 1018 (1975).

B

The courts have not confined federal jurisdiction to securities transactions consummated in the United States. They have deviated from this position in two respects. First, they have asserted jurisdiction over extraterritorial conduct that produces substantial effects within the United States, such as effects on domestic markets or domestic investors. Second, they have asserted jurisdiction in some cases over acts done in the United States that "directly caused" the losses suffered by investors outside this country. See, e.g., *Bersch*, 519 F.2d at 991-93.

Zoelsch concedes that jurisdiction in this case cannot be premised on domestic "effects" of predominantly foreign conduct, and "[j]urisdiction may not be sustained on a theory that the plaintiff has not advanced." *Merrell Dow Pharmaceuticals Inc. v. Thompson*, 106 S.Ct. 3229, 3233 n. 6 (1986). Zoelsch relies on AA-USA's domestic conduct as the basis for jurisdiction.

Several tests have been devised for determining when American courts have jurisdiction over domestic conduct that is alleged to have played some part in the perpetration of a securities fraud on investors outside this country. The Second Circuit has set the most restrictive standard. It has declined jurisdiction over alleged violations of the securities laws based on conduct in the United States when the conduct here was "merely preparatory" to the alleged fraud, that is, when the conduct here did not "directly cause" the losses elsewhere. See, e.g., *Bersch*, 519 F.2d at 992-93. In later cases, the line between domestic conduct that is "merely preparatory" and conduct that "directly causes" the losses elsewhere has been significantly clarified. The Second Circuit's rule seems to be that jurisdiction will lie in American courts where the domestic conduct comprises all the elements of a defendant's conduct necessary to establish a violation of section 10(b) and Rule 10b-5: the fraudulent statements or misrepresentations must originate in the United States, must be made with scienter and in connection with the sale or purchase of securities, and must cause the harm to those who claim to be defrauded, even though the actual reliance and damages may occur elsewhere.

The Third, Eighth, and Ninth Circuits appear to have relaxed the Second Circuit's test. They too have asserted jurisdiction only when the conduct in this country "directly causes" the losses elsewhere. See *SEC v. Kasser*, 548 F.2d 109, 115 (3d Cir.), cert. denied, 431 U.S. 938 (1977); *Continental Grain (Australia) Pty. Ltd. v. Pacific Oilseeds, Inc.*, 592 F.2d 409, 418-20 (8th Cir.1979); *Grunenthal GmbH v. Hotz*, 712 F.2d 421, 424 (9th Cir.1983). But in *Continental Grain* the court explicitly repudiated the Second Circuit's requirement that "domestic conduct constitute the elements of a rule 10b-5 violation," 592 F.2d at 418, in favor of a test that would find jurisdiction whenever the domestic conduct "was in furtherance of a fraudulent scheme and was significant with respect to its accomplishment." Id. at 421. The Third Circuit's formulation seems more permissive, allowing subject matter jurisdiction "where at least some activity designed to further a fraudulent scheme occurs within this country." *Kasser*, 548 F.2d at 114. The consequence of these approaches has been a loosening of the jurisdictional requirements: any significant activity undertaken in this country—or perhaps any activity at all—that furthers a fraudulent scheme can provide the basis of American jurisdiction over the domestic actor.

C

We believe that a more restrictive test, such as the Second Circuit's, provides the better approach to determining when American courts should assert jurisdiction in a case such as this. There is no doubt, of course, that Congress could confer jurisdiction over activity like that alleged to have been engaged in by AA-USA. Moreover, considerations of comity, which will often cause a court to stay its hand, appear to be minimal or nonexistent here. Appellants do not seek to have us assert jurisdiction over West German parties, nor would a judgment about AA-USA's conduct in the United States necessarily or even probably require a pronouncement on the propriety of the behavior of the West German parties. The case going forward in the Federal Republic would likely be unaffected by this case. Nevertheless, we think we should not assert jurisdiction.

We begin from the established canon of construction that "legislation of Congress, unless a contrary intent appears, is meant to apply only within the territorial jurisdiction of the United States," which "is based on the assumption that Congress is primarily concerned with domestic conditions." *Foley Bros. v. Filardo*, 336 U.S. 281, 285 (1949). And even aside from this presumption, it is quite clear that the Securities Exchange Act of 1934 had as its purpose the protection of American investors and markets. See, e.g., H.R.Rep. No. 1383, 73d Cong., 2d Sess. 1-16 (1934); S.Rep. No. 792, 73d Cong., 2d Sess. 1- 13 (1934). That is the inference to be drawn from section 30(b) as well, for it states that the statute does not apply to persons transacting business in securities abroad unless the Securities and Exchange Commission issues rules and regulations making the statute applicable to such persons because that is "necessary or appropriate to prevent the evasion" of the statute. That rather clearly implies that Congress was concerned with extraterritorial transactions only if they were part of a plan to harm American investors or markets. The Commission has never issued such rules or regulations and there is no allegation in this case that AA-USA's conduct was engaged in to evade American law.

Courts have also been concerned to preserve American judicial resources for the adjudication of domestic disputes and the enforcement of domestic law. *Bersch*, 519 F.2d at 985 ("When, as here, a court is confronted with transactions that on any view are predominantly foreign, it must seek to determine whether Congress would have wished the precious resources of the United States courts and law enforcement agencies to be devoted to them rather than leave the problem to foreign countries."). It is far from clear that these resources would be well spent on all the potential disputes in which domestic conduct makes a relatively small contribution to securities fraud that occurs elsewhere.[2]

Were it not for the Second Circuit's preeminence in the field of securities law, and our desire to avoid a multiplicity of jurisdictional tests, we might be inclined to doubt that an American court should ever assert jurisdiction over domestic conduct that causes loss to foreign investors. It is somewhat odd to say, as *Bersch* and some other opinions do, that courts must determine their jurisdiction by divining what "Congress would have wished" if it had addressed the problem. A more natural inquiry might be what jurisdiction Congress in fact thought about and conferred. Congress did not think about conduct here that contributes to losses abroad in enacting the Securities Exchange Act of 1934; it could easily provide such jurisdiction if that seemed desirable today. But, for the reasons just given, we defer to *Bersch* and the later Second Circuit cases and adopt the Second Circuit's approach. We are not persuaded by the reasoning of those circuits that have broadened federal court jurisdiction for reasons that are essentially legislative. In *Continental Grain*, the court said, "[w]e frankly admit that the finding of subject matter jurisdiction in the present case is largely a policy decision." 592 F.2d at 421. Yet Congress is available to make any policy decisions that are required. In *Kasser*, similarly, the court justified its approach in part because "[f]rom a policy perspective, and it should be recognized that this case in a large measure calls for a policy decision, we believe that there are sound rationales for asserting jurisdiction." 548 F.2d at 116 (footnote omitted). Three rationales were offered. "First, to deny such jurisdiction may embolden those who wish to defraud foreign securities purchasers or sellers to use the United States as a base of operations." Id. Second, "[b]y finding jurisdiction here, we may encourage other nations to take appropriate steps against parties who seek to perpetrate frauds in the United States." Id. Finally, the court's action "will enhance the ability of the SEC to police vigorously the conduct of securities dealings within the United States." Id. *Kasser* concluded: "We are reluctant to conclude that Congress in-

---

2. Given this concern, it would also seem counterproductive to adopt a balancing test, or any test that makes jurisdiction turn on a welter of specific facts. See, e.g., Restatement [Revised] of the Foreign Relations Law of the United States § 403(2) (2d draft 1981). As we know from our experience in the extraterritorial application of antitrust law, such tests are difficult to apply and are inherently unpredictable. See, e.g., *Laker Airways Ltd. v. Sabena, Belgian World Airlines*, 731 F.2d 909, 948-53 (D.C.Cir.1984). They thus present powerful incentives for increased litigation on the jurisdictional issue itself, which inevitably tends to defeat efforts to protect limited American judicial resources. A strong argument has also been made that balancing tests "are not faithful to the principle of comity among nations," for in practice they tend to deemphasize foreign sovereign interests and almost never lead a court to decline jurisdiction. See Note, Predictability and Comity: Toward Common Principles of Extraterritorial Jurisdiction, 98 Harv.L.Rev. 1310, 1323- 25 (1985).

tended to allow the United States to become a 'Barbary Coast,' as it were, harboring international securities 'pirates.'" 548 F.2d at 116.

We, too, are reluctant to conclude that Congress intended any such thing, but we are less reluctant to conclude that Congress in 1934 had no intention at all on the subject because it was concerned with United States investors and markets. That being so, *Kasser*'s policy arguments may provide very good reasons why Congress should amend the statute but are less adequate as reasons why courts should do so. As the Supreme Court has said in another context, "[t]he responsibilities for assessing the wisdom of such policy choices and resolving the struggle between competing views of the public interest are not judicial ones: 'Our Constitution vests such responsibilities in the political branches.'" *Chevron U.S.A. Inc. v. Natural Resources Defense Council*, Inc., 467 U.S. 837, 866 (1984) (quoting *TVA v. Hill*, 437 U.S. 153, 195 (1978)). This is particularly the case since such an amendment providing jurisdiction over aspects of predominantly foreign transactions should take into account considerations of comity and foreign affairs. Those factors do not weigh heavily in this case but they may in others.[3]

For these reasons we adopt what we understand to be the Second Circuit's test for finding jurisdiction based on domestic conduct: jurisdiction is appropriate when the fraudulent statements or misrepresentations originate in the United States, are made with scienter and in connection with the purchase or sale of securities, and "directly cause" the harm to those who claim to be defrauded, even if reliance and damages occur elsewhere. Indeed, we believe this test is only a slight recasting, if at all, of the traditional view that jurisdiction will lie in American courts only over proscribed acts done in this country. * * *

These allegations, even if true, are insufficient to support jurisdiction under the test we have enunciated. At the most, they establish that AA-USA made misrepresentations to GmbH that GmbH credited in drawing up its audit report. AA-USA's statements were not themselves made for distribution to the public, and were not transmitted to the public. AA-USA was merely one of the sources GmbH consulted in conducting the investigations which culminated in its audit report. That report, which was circulated to investors as part of the larger package of materials distributed by Loescher, was prepared and certified by GmbH alone. * * *

To put the matter in the Second Circuit's terminology, AA-USA's alleged misrepresentations to GmbH were "merely preparatory" to any fraud perpetrated on West German investors, and did not "directly cause" their losses. *Bersch*, 519 F.2d at 992-93. * * *

WALD, Chief Judge, concurring in the judgment:

I agree with the majority that the District Court properly dismissed this action for lack of subject matter jurisdiction. In reaching that result, I find it unnecessary, however, to adopt the Second Circuit's restrictive test for determining the extent of federal

---

3. In this connection, there may be more reason to find jurisdiction in a case like *Kasser*, which was brought by the SEC, than in a case like the present one, brought by foreign private individuals. The SEC, while an independent agency, is a responsible governmental agency and will surely take into account in framing its enforcement actions any foreign policy concerns communicated to it by the Department of State. A private individual need not and often will not. A court can feel more comfortable asserting jurisdiction if it knows that foreign policy concerns can be accommodated by the plaintiff and are not left entirely to the court's untutored evaluation. Whether or not that consideration should be sufficient to allow jurisdiction in an SEC action that would not lie in a private action we need not decide.

jurisdiction over securities law claims involving international transactions. It seems clear that, even under the less strict approach adopted by the Third, Eighth, and Ninth Circuits, AA-USA's alleged misrepresentations or omissions of material fact were so insignificant and so indirectly related to the overall fraudulent scheme as set out in the complaint that no federal jurisdiction would exist over Zoelsch's claims.

Notes

1. Kauthar SDN BHD v. Sternberg, 149 F.3d 659 (7th Cir. 1998), cert. denied, 525 U.S. 1114 (1999), held that there is subject matter jurisdiction over a securities fraud claim by a foreign shareholder against U.S. defendants. The court stated that it has jurisdiction for violations of U.S. securities laws "when the conduct occurring in the United States directly causes the plaintiff's alleged loss in that the conduct forms a substantial part of the alleged fraud and is material to its success. This conduct must be more than merely preparatory in nature; however, we do not go so far as to require that the conduct occurring domestically must itself satisfy the elements of a securities violation."

Robinson v. TCI/US West Communications Inc., 117 F.3d 900, 905 n.10 (5th Cir. 1997), adopts the Second Circuit's test for application of the Securities Exchange Act to protect investors abroad, but states that test to be "whether material domestic conduct directly caused the complained-of loss." The court characterizes the view that the Second Circuit test requires that "domestic conduct comprises all the elements...necessary to establish a violation * * * a bit of an overstatement."

The provision of Restatement (Third) that would apply to cases like Zoelsch is §416(1)(d) set out at the beginning of this chapter. What result would be reached in Zoelsch under this provision? Reporters' Note 2 following this section gives the only guidance as to what "related" means: "if a national of state X and a national of state Y meet in New York for convenience and one fraudulently induces the other to make purchases of Japanese securities on the Tokyo Stock Exchange, it might not be reasonable to apply the United States securities laws..."

Central Bank of Denver v. First Interstate Bank of Denver, N.A., 511 U.S. 164 (1994), held that a private plaintiff may not maintain an action under the Securities Exchange Act of 1934 § 10(b) against a defendant alleged to be "secondarily liable under § 10B for its conduct in aiding and abetting the [other defendant's] fraud." 511 U.S. at 191. This holding with regard to domestic enforcement, reinforces the view of the Second Circuit concerning the narrow scope of extraterritorial application, which Judge Bork adopted in the principal case. United States Securities & Exchange Commission v. Fehn, 97 F.3d 1276 (9th Cir. 1996), holds that § 104 of the Private Securities Litigation Reform Act of 1995, PL 104-67, 109 Stat. 737, bars extending *Central Bank of Denver* to SEC injunctive actions. Section 104 amended 15 U.S.C. § 78t as follows: "Authority of Commission to Prosecute Aiding and Abetting. For purpose of any action brought by the Commission...any person that knowingly provides substantial assistance to another person in violation of a provision of [the Securities Exchange Act of 1934] or of any rule or regulation issued under [the Act], shall be deemed in violation of such provision to the same extent as the person to whom such assistance is provided."

2. Schoenbaum v. Firstbrook, 405 F.2d 200 (2d Cir. 1968), modified en banc, 405 F.2d 215 (2d Cir. 1968) (finding liability as well as jurisdiction), cert. denied, 395 U.S. 906 (1969), found subject matter jurisdiction in a derivative action under § 10(b) of the Securities Act of 1934 and Rule 10b-5. An American shareholder sued for harm to a

Canadian corporation, alleging that its treasury stock was sold to other foreign corporations at a price that the defendant directors knew was too low. The court found that the resulting reduction of the shareholders' equity was "a sufficiently serious effect upon United States commerce to warrant assertion of jurisdiction for the protection of American investors." Id. at 209.

Leasco Data Processing Equipment Corp. v. Maxwell, 468 F.2d 1326 (2d Cir. 1972), illustrates the limited utility of a distinction between acts abroad causing harm here and acts here causing harm abroad. Leasco and its United Kingdom subsidiary alleged that the subsidiary was fraudulently induced by the late Robert Maxwell and others to buy shares in a British company on the London Stock Exchange. Misrepresentations were alleged to have taken place in the United States as well as abroad. Judge Friendly found that "it tips the scales in favor of applicability when substantial misrepresentations were made in the United States," (id. at 1337) although he expressed doubt that there would be jurisdiction based solely on the effects on the United States parent company "[i]f all the misrepresentations here alleged had occurred in England." (Id. at 1334).

Bersch v. Drexel Firestone, Inc., 519 F.2d 974 (2d Cir.), cert. denied, 423 U.S. 1018 (1975), demonstrates the importance of harmful effects to United States interests when the fraudulent acts occur abroad. The suit was a class action under the Securities Exchange Act for fraud committed abroad in the sale of the stock of a Canadian corporation. The court ordered the district court to "eliminate from the class action all purchasers other than persons who were residents or citizens of the United States." Id. at 997. Judge Friendly stated that where, as here, all the significant fraudulent acts occurred abroad, there was United States prescriptive jurisdiction "only when [the foreign act] results in injury to purchasers or sellers...in whom the United States has an interest, not where acts simply have an adverse [e]ffect on the American economy or American investors generally." Id. at 989.

Consolidated Gold Fields PLC v. Minorco, S.A., 871 F.2d 252, modified, 890 F.2d 569 (2d Cir.), cert. dismissed, 492 U.S. 939 (1989), finds the Second Circuit asserting jurisdiction even though American residents held only 2.5% of the shares in a company that was the target of a hostile takeover by a Luxembourg Company that was controlled by South African Companies. The target, a British company, and its United States subsidiary brought suit under both section 7 of the Clayton Act (15 U.S.C. § 18) contending that the "acquisition may be substantially to lessen competition" and under Rule 10b-5 alleging fraudulent representations in connection with the tender offer. Tender offers were forwarded to the United States shareholders through British nominees rather than directly. The court found that the effect on the American residents, representing 2.5% of the target's shareholders, who owned 5.3 million shares with a market value of about 120 million dollars, was "substantial" and supported jurisdiction over both the Clayton Act and 10b-5 claims. The court declared that "the antifraud provisions of American securities laws have broader extraterritorial reach than American filing requirements" (871 F.2d at 262) and enjoined the tender offer worldwide pending corrective disclosure. This order overrode a Securities and Exchange Commission recommendation that the court "abstain, for reasons of international comity, from enjoining the tender offer worldwide pending corrective disclosure." 890 F.2d at 569. The SEC took no position on whether corrective disclosure itself should be ordered, but the court rejected the SEC's distinction, based on degree of extraterritorial effect, between enjoining tender and ordering disclosure. Id. at 569 n. 7. The British Monopolies and Mergers Commission had declared the proposed acquisition consistent with British public interests. 871 F.2d at 254 n. 1.

Howe v. Goldcorp Investments, Ltd., 946 F.2d 944 (1st Cir. 1991), cert. denied, 502 U.S. 1995 (1992), affirmed dismissal on forum non conveniens grounds of an action under federal securities laws by an American shareholder against a Canadian company and its Canadian officers, investment advisors, and lawyers. Plaintiff claimed that the defendants had failed to disclose adequately plans to take over two other Canadian companies.

Allen v. Lloyd's of London, 94 F.3d 923 (4th Cir. 1996), held that Lloyd's settlement offer to United States "Names," under which a Name waived any claim against Lloyd's or its agents in exchange for Lloyd's partial funding of the Name's obligation to a restructured Lloyd's, was not subject to the disclosure requirements of U.S. securities laws.

Itoba, Ltd. v. Lep Group PLC, 54 F.3d 118 (2d Cir. 1995), cert. denied, 516 U.S. 1044 (1996), upheld jurisdiction under the Securities Exchange Act of 1934 over a London-based holding company that had allegedly filed false information with the Securities and Exchange Commission. The court analyzed extraterritorial jurisdiction under both "conduct" and "effects" tests, stating that "an admixture or combination of the two often gives a better picture of whether there is sufficient United States involvement to justify exercise of jurisdiction by an American court." Id. at 122. The "conduct test" focuses on whether the defendant's activities in the United States were "more than 'merely preparatory' to a securities fraud conducted elsewhere [and whether] these activities or culpable failure to act within the United states 'directly caused' the claimed losses." Id. The court found sufficient effects in the United States "[i]n view of the deleterious effect this continued nondisclosure had on the thousands of [the defrauded company's] shareholders in the United States." Id. at 124.

See Lewis D Lowenfels & Alan R. Bromberg, U.S. Securites Fraud Across the Border: Unpredictable Jurisdiction, 55 The Business Lawyer 975 (May 2000).

3. One difference between extraterritorial application of United States securities law and antitrust law, is that there is far less substantive disagreement abroad concerning securities regulation. The EEC has taken a step not taken by the United States Congress or the SEC and has defined what constitutes "insider trading." Council Directive Coordinating Regulations on Insider Trading, Directive 89/592, art. 32, 1989 OJ (L 334), 1 Common Mkt. Rep. (CCH) ¶ 1761. See also Roberta S. Karmel, Securities Law in the European Community: Harmony or Cacophony?, 1 Tulane J. Int'l & Comp. L. 3 (1993); Eugenio Ruggiero, The Regulation of Insider Trading in Italy, 22 Brook. J. Int'l L. 157 (1996); Daniel James Standen, Insider Trading Reforms Sweep Across Germany: Bracing for the Cold Winds of Change, 36 Harv. Int'l L.J. 177 (1995).

Switzerland agreed to modify its bank secrecy requirements to assist the Securities and Exchange Commission in investigations of insider trading, and an annexed "Private Agreement Among Members of the Swiss Bankers' Association" set out a procedure to implement this cooperation. Switzerland-United States, Memorandum of Understanding to Establish Mutually Acceptable Means for Improving International Law Enforcement Cooperation in the Field of Insider Trading, 22 I.L.M. 1 (1983). This agreement does contain some limitations on cooperation. For example, the banks agree to remit funds deposited by inside traders only up to the amount of the unlawful profit (Agreement of the Swiss Bankers' Assoc. Art. 9(2)(a)) and the only sanction that the Association agrees to impose on one of its members is to "exclude the bank from the Agreement, and... inform the Federal Banking Commission and the SEC accordingly." (Art. 10(b)). One reason why the Memorandum of Understanding was needed is that a 1977

U.S.-Swiss Treaty for cooperation between law enforcement authorities required that an offense be a crime under the law of each country before cooperation was required under the Treaty. Many acts that would constitute illegal insider trading under U.S. law would not violate Swiss law at that time. In 1988 Switzerland enacted a provision of its Penal Code criminalizing insider trading in a manner that makes it less likely that its law will differ from that of the United States on this issue. Schweizerisches Strafegesetzbuch (StGB), Swiss Penal Code art. 161.

See also Memorandum of the United States Securities and Exchange Commission and the Securities Bureau of the Japanese Ministry of Finance on the Sharing of Information, 25 I.L.M. 1429 (1986).

4. The Tokyo stock exchange now has a high percentage of the equity market and other foreign exchanges are increasing their market share. U.S. investors were often excluded from opportunities to participate in foreign equity offerings (particularly rights, exchange, and tender offers) because foreign issuers wished to avoid the expense of registering their securities in the U.S. As a result, the Securities and Exchange Commission has, in a 1991 rule covering Canadian issuers (56 Fed. Reg. 30036) and in Regulation S (17 C.F.R. §§ 230,901-904 (1991)), ended in many cases the requirement of U.S. registration for foreign securities offered to U.S. investors. In January 1995, the Commission's Division of Market Regulation granted exemptions from certain Trading Practice Rules to facilitate distribution in the U.S. of securities of certain U.K. insurers that were highly capitalized or insurers whose securities traded on Stock Exchange Automated Quotation International system. Securities Act Release No. 7127, Fed. Sec. L. Rep. (CCH) ¶ 76,960. See also Marc I. Steinberg & Daryl L. Lansdale, Jr., Regulation S and Rule 144A: Creating a Workable Fiction in an Expanding Global Securities Market, 29 Int'l Law. 43 (1995).

Section 3: Other Problems

Restatement (Third) The Foreign Relations Law of the United States (1986)

Copyright 1987 by the American Law Institute. Reprinted with the permission of the American Law Institute.

§ 414. *Jurisdiction with Respect to Activities of Foreign Branches and Subsidiaries*

(1) Subject to §§ 403 and 441, a state may exercise jurisdiction to prescribe for limited purposes with respect to activities of foreign branches of corporations organized under its laws.

(2) A state may not ordinarily regulate activities of corporations organized under the laws of a foreign state on the basis that they are owned or controlled by nationals of the regulating state. However, under § 403 and subject to § 441, it may not be unreasonable for a state to exercise jurisdiction for limited purposes with respect to activities of affiliated foreign entities

(a) by direction to the parent corporation in respect of such matters as uniform accounting, disclosure to investors, or preparation of consolidated tax returns of multinational enterprises; or

(b) by direction to either the parent or the subsidiary in exceptional cases, depending on all relevant factors, including the extent to which

(i) the regulation is essential to implementation of a program to further a major national interest of the state exercising jurisdiction;

(ii) the national program of which the regulation is a part can be carried out effectively only if it is applied also to foreign subsidiaries;

(iii) the regulation conflicts or is likely to conflict with the law or policy of the state where the subsidiary is established.

(c) In the exceptional cases referred to in paragraph (b), the burden of establishing reasonableness is heavier when the direction is issued to the foreign subsidiary than when it is issued to the parent corporation.

Notes

1. Section 441, referred to in §414, covers "Foreign State Compulsion" and provides that "[i]n general" a state may not require the doing of an act in another state prohibited by that state or prohibit an act in another state required by that state.

Is the distinction in §414 between foreign branches and subsidiaries justified? There may be no functional distinction between the ability to control branches and subsidiaries and the choice of the subsidiary form may be for tax and liability purposes. See Stanley J. Marcuss, "Jurisdiction with Respect to Foreign Branches and Subsidiaries: Judicial Power in the Foreign Affairs Context Under Section 414 of the Foreign Relations Restatement," 26 Int'l Lawyer 1, 6 (1992).

2. The U.S.S.R.-Western Europe Pipeline Caper: A natural gas pipeline was planned to bring natural gas from the Soviet Union to Western Europe. The United States wished to discourage construction of the pipeline. One of the articulated reasons for the United States position was displeasure over the imposition of martial law in Poland. In 1982, the United States prohibited furnishing of goods and technology for use on the pipeline. The prohibition purported to apply not only to exports from the United States, but also to foreign subsidiaries of United States countries, and, most far reaching of all, to foreign companies with no United States contacts except that they were using retroactively prohibited goods or technology under contract with United States companies. The European response was prompt and predictable. "The U.S. measures as they apply in the present case are unacceptable under international law because of their extra-territorial aspects.... Furthermore, its is reprehensible that present U.S. Regulations encourage non-US companies to submit 'voluntarily' [under threat of trade sanctions] to this kind of mobilization for U.S. purposes.... [T]hey constitute an unacceptable interference in the independent commercial policy of the E.C.... [T]he European Community calls upon the U.S. Authorities to withdraw these measures." European Communities: Comments on the U.S. Regulations Concerning Trade with the U.S.S.R., 21 ILM 891, 893, 895, 904 (1982). After some attempts to enforce the regulations through administrative sanctions, the controls were withdrawn before their validity could be tested in the courts.

In 1989, the Commodity Futures Trading Commission attempted to compel members of the London Metal Exchange to keep the cash of their American clients in segregated accounts, contrary to practice on the Exchange. The CFTC in Britain, Economist, Sept. 2, 1989, at 75-6.

That same year, the Securities and Exchange Commission recovered a judgment against one Fred Lee for $12.5 million that he had allegedly obtained by insider trading. Mr. Lee had an account in the Hongkong branch of Standard Chartered, a bank with its main office in London. Instead of applying to a Hongkong court for assistance, the SEC obtained a court order that Standard Chartered pay the money. Standard Chartered paid the money into court in New York and was supported in its appeal by the British government, the Federal Reserve Bank of New York, and the New York Clearing House Association. Economist, June 10, 1989, at 16.

In a grand jury investigation of Marc Rich AG, a Swiss company, Marc Rich was ordered to produce documents located in Switzerland. Production would violate the Swiss Penal Code. Only after the highest Swiss executive body, the Federal Council, took action to block production of the documents, did the United States make a formal request to Switzerland for judicial assistance. This request resulted in production of the documents. Kurt H. Hoechner, A Swiss Perspective on Conflicts of Jurisdiction, 50 Law & Contemp. Probs. 271, 277-78 (Summer 1987).

The Iran and Libya Sanctions Act of 1996 (D'Amato-Kennedy Act), PL 104-172, 110 Stat 1541, reprinted in Note following 50 U.S.C.A. 1701, imposes sanctions on entities making investments that contribute to the enhancement of the ability of Iran or Libya to develop their petroleum resources, or on entities exporting items that enhance Libya's weapons or aviation capabilities or its ability to develop its petroleum resources. "Investment" is defined to exclude "the entry into, performance, or financing of a contract to sell or purchase goods, services, or technology." Id. § 14(9)(C). France has threatened to impose sanctions on U.S. companies if French companies are sanctioned under the Act.

The Cuban Liberty and Democratic Solidarity (Libertad) Act of 1996 (Helms-Burton Act), PL 104-114, 110 Stat 785, reprinted in Note following 22 U.S.C.A. § 6021, amends the Cuban Democracy Act of 1992. PL 202-484, reprinted in Note following 22 U.S.C.A. § 6001. The new Act enables any United States national who owns property confiscated by Cuba to sue anyone who "traffics" in the property. "Traffics" includes purchase. No United States court may decline to entertain such an action on the basis of the act of state doctrine. Id. § 302. If a financial institution such as the International Monetary Fund or the Inter-American Development Bank makes a loan to Cuba over United States opposition, the United States will withhold equal amounts in payments to that institution. Id. § 104. The European Union foreign ministers adopted a regulation that authorizes EU companies sued under Helms-Burton to bring "clawback" suits against the European subsidiaries of companies that have used the act. The EU brought a complaint against the U.S. before the World Trade Organization (WTO). When the parties could not agree on appointment of a hearing panel, the WTO appointed a panel of three. The U.S. announced that it would boycott the panel on the ground that the dispute "is essentially a disagreement over foreign policy." Canada has enacted legislation punishing Canadian companies, including subsidiaries of U.S. companies, that refuse to trade with Cuba in compliance with Helms-Burton. The Act authorizes the President to suspend the rights of U.S. nationals to sue under § 302 for periods of six months. President Clinton has suspended the right to sue and has renewed this suspension every six months.

3. Equal Employment Opportunity Cmm'n v. Arabian Amer. Oil Co., 499 U.S. 244 (1991). held (5-4) that Title VII of the Civil Rights Act of 1964 does not apply extraterritorially to prohibit discrimination in Saudi Arabia against a United States citizen by a Delaware corporation. The majority relied upon a canon of construction that "legisla-

tion of Congress, unless a contrary intent appears, is meant to apply only within the territorial jurisdiction of the United States." This is the same canon that Justice Holmes used in American Banana Co. v. United Fruit Co., 213 U.S. 347 (1909), to deny extraterritorial application to U.S. antitrust laws. As the materials in this chapter indicate, this view with regard to antitrust has been long superseded under the "effects" basis for prescriptive jurisdiction. Congress has already abrogated EEOC v. Aramco in the Civil Rights Act of 1991 by including in the definition of "employee," a U.S. citizen employed abroad. S. 1745, 102nd Cong., 1st Sess. § 109(a) (1991). See Michael Starr, Who's the Boss? The Globalization of U.S. Employment Law, 51 Bus. Law. 635 (1996).

Smith v. United States, 507 U.S. 197 (1993) held that the Federal Tort Claims Act (FTCA) does not apply to tortious acts or omissions occurring in Antarctica. The Court construed several provisions of that Act to reach this result and also stated: "Lastly, the presumption against extraterritorial application of United States statutes requires that any lingering doubt regarding the reach of the FTCA be resolved against its encompassing torts committed in Antarctica." Id. at 1183.

Couzado v. United States, 105 F.3d 1389 (11th Cir. 1997), held that a claim is not barred under the FTCA if the tortious conduct occurs in the United States even though the injury is sustained in a foreign country. U.S. government agents had placed cocaine on a commercial airline as part of a sting operation, resulting in the incarceration of the passengers and crew in Honduras.

For cases refusing to give extraterritorial effect to the Racketeer Influenced and Corrupt Organizations Act (RICO), 18 U.S.C. §§ 1961-68, see North South Finance Corporation v. Al-Turki, 100 F.3d 1046 (2d Cir. 1996) (finding that the conduct alleged in the United States is insufficient to support subject matter jurisdiction under the civil penalties provisions of RICO); Butte Mining PLC v. Smith, 76 F.3d 287, 291 (9th Cir. 1996) (holding that under either conduct or effects tests there was no basis for a civil action under United States securities laws and "[o]nce the securities fraud claim was dismissed the...RICO claims that related to this fraud had to be dismissed as well"); United States v. Vasquez-Velasco, 15 F.3d 833 (9th Cir. 1994) (holding that 18 U.S.C. § 1959, which punishes violent crimes in aid of racketeering activity, as defined in § 1961, did not apply to the murders of two U.S. tourists in Mexico for the purpose of maintaining and increasing defendant's position in a drug trafficking cartel).

Kollias v. D & G Marine Maintenance, 29 F.3d 67 (2d Cir. 1994), cert. denied, 513 U.S. 1146 (1995), held that the Longshore and Harbor Workers' Compensation Act applied to longshore workers injured while working on vessels on the high seas because "the LHWCA contains a sufficiently clear indication of Congressional intent to apply the statute extraterritorially." Id. at 73.

Totalplan Corp. of America v. Colborne, 14 F.3d 824 (2d Cir. 1994), refused to apply the Trademark Act of 1946 (the "Lanham Act") extraterritorially, finding that affixing trademarks to cameras in the United States for sale in Japan by alien defendants had no substantial effect on U.S. commerce. Sterling Drug, Inc. v. Bayer AG, 14 F.3d 733 (2d Cir. 1994), stated that three factors determined the extraterritorial application of the Lanham Act: (1) whether the defendant's conduct has a substantial effect on United States Commerce; (2) whether the defendant is a citizen of the United States; and (3) whether there exists a conflict between defendant's trademark rights established under foreign law, and plaintiff's trademark rights established under domestic law." Id. at 745-46. The court vacated the extraterritorial provisions of the district court's injunction of defendant's activities and remanded for reconsideration under theses factors. See James W. Dabney, The Territorial Reach of the Lanham Act, 83 Trademark Rep. 465 (1993).

Subafilms Ltd. v. MGM-Pathe Communications Co., 24 F.3d 1088 (9th Cir.) (en banc), cert. denied, 513U.S. 1001 (1994), refused to apply the Copyright Act, 17 U.S.C. §§ 106-120, to authorization within the United States of acts abroad. The court states that the Act does not apply extraterritorially and imposes liability for acts of authorization only when the authorized activity itself would amount to infringement, overruling Peter Starr Prod. Co. v. Twin Continental Films, Inc., 783 F.2d 1440 (9th Cir. 1986).

Nieman v. Dryclean U.S.A. Franchise Co., 178 F.3d 1126 (11th Cir. 1999), cert. denied, 120 S.Ct. 938 (2000), held that the Federal Trade Commission's Franchise Rule, which requires specified disclosures, did not apply extraterritorially to a franchisee in Argentina.

Denty v. Smithkline Beecham Corp., 109 F.3d 147, (3rd Cir.), cert. denied, 522 U.S. 820 (1997), held that neither the federal Age Discrimination in Employment Act nor the Pennsylvania Human Relations Act applied to an employee in a Pennsylvania subsidiary of a U.K. company when the promotional opportunity allegedly denied because of age was in the U.K.

Chapter 7

Civil Suits for Atrocities That Violate International Law

Section 1: The Alien Tort Claims Act

Filartiga v. Pena-Irala
630 F.2d 876 (2d Cir. 1980)

Before FEINBERG, Chief Judge, KAUFMAN and KEARSE, Circuit Judges.

Irving R. KAUFMAN, Circuit Judge:

Upon ratification of the Constitution, the thirteen former colonies were fused into a single nation, one which, in its relations with foreign states, is bound both to observe and construe the accepted norms of international law, formerly known as the law of nations. Under the Articles of Confederation, the several states had interpreted and applied this body of doctrine as a part of their common law, but with the founding of the "more perfect Union" of 1789, the law of nations became preeminently a federal concern.

Implementing the constitutional mandate for national control over foreign relations, the First Congress established original district court jurisdiction over "all causes where an alien sues for a tort only (committed) in violation of the law of nations." Judiciary Act of 1789, ch. 20, § 9(b), 1 Stat. 73, 77 (1789), codified at 28 U.S.C. § 1350. Construing this rarely-invoked provision, we hold that deliberate torture perpetrated under color of official authority violates universally accepted norms of the international law of human rights, regardless of the nationality of the parties. Thus, whenever an alleged torturer is found and served with process by an alien within our borders, § 1350 provides federal jurisdiction. Accordingly, we reverse the judgment of the district court dismissing the complaint for want of federal jurisdiction.

I

The appellants, plaintiffs below, are citizens of the Republic of Paraguay. Dr. Joel Filartiga, a physician, describes himself as a longstanding opponent of the government of President Alfredo Stroessner, which has held power in Paraguay since 1954. His daughter, Dolly Filartiga, arrived in the United States in 1978 under a visitor's visa, and has since applied for permanent political asylum. The Filartigas brought this action in the Eastern District of New York against Americo Norberto Pena-Irala (Pena), also a citizen of Paraguay, for wrongfully causing the death of Dr. Filartiga's seventeen-year old son, Joelito. Because the district court dismissed the action for want of subject matter jurisdiction, we must accept as true the allegations contained in the Filartigas' complaint and affidavits for purposes of this appeal.

The appellants contend that on March 29, 1976, Joelito Filartiga was kidnapped and tortured to death by Pena, who was then Inspector General of Police in Asuncion, Paraguay.

* * *

In July of 1978, Pena sold his house in Paraguay and entered the United States under a visitor's visa. He was accompanied by Juana Bautista Fernandez Villalba, who had lived with him in Paraguay. The couple remained in the United States beyond the term of their visas, and were living in Brooklyn, New York, when Dolly Filartiga, who was then living in Washington, D. C., learned of their presence. Acting on information provided by Dolly the Immigration and Naturalization Service arrested Pena and his companion, both of whom were subsequently ordered deported on April 5, 1979 following a hearing. They had then resided in the United States for more than nine months.

Almost immediately, Dolly caused Pena to be served with a summons and civil complaint at the Brooklyn Navy Yard, where he was being held pending deportation. The complaint alleged that Pena had wrongfully caused Joelito's death by torture and sought compensatory and punitive damages of $10,000,000. The Filartigas also sought to enjoin Pena's deportation to ensure his availability for testimony at trial. * * * Jurisdiction is claimed under the general federal question provision, 28 U.S.C. § 1331 and, principally on this appeal, under the Alien Tort Statute, 28 U.S.C. § 1350.

Judge Nickerson stayed the order of deportation, and Pena immediately moved to dismiss the complaint on the grounds that subject matter jurisdiction was absent and for forum non conveniens. On the jurisdictional issue, there has been no suggestion that Pena claims diplomatic immunity from suit. The Filartigas submitted the affidavits of a number of distinguished international legal scholars, who stated unanimously that the law of nations prohibits absolutely the use of torture as alleged in the complaint. Pena, in support of his motion to dismiss on the ground of forum non conveniens, submitted the affidavit of his Paraguayan counsel, Jose Emilio Gorostiaga, who averred that Paraguayan law provides a full and adequate civil remedy for the wrong alleged. Dr. Filartiga has not commenced such an action, however, believing that further resort to the courts of his own country would be futile.

Judge Nickerson heard argument on the motion to dismiss on May 14, 1979, and on May 15 dismissed the complaint on jurisdictional grounds.[6] The district judge recognized the strength of appellants' argument that official torture violates an emerging norm of customary international law. Nonetheless, he felt constrained by dicta contained in two recent opinions of this Court, *Dreyfus v. von Finck*, 534 F.2d 24 (2d Cir.), cert. denied, 429 U.S. 835 (1976); *IIT v. Vencap, Ltd.*, 519 F.2d 1001 (2d Cir. 1975), to construe narrowly "the law of nations," as employed in § 1350, as excluding that law which governs a state's treatment of its own citizens.

---

6. The court below accordingly did not consider the motion to dismiss on forum non conveniens grounds, which is not before us on this appeal.

The district court continued the stay of deportation for forty-eight hours while appellants applied for further stays. These applications were denied by a panel of this Court on May 22, 1979, and by the Supreme Court two days later. Shortly thereafter, Pena and his companion returned to Paraguay.

II

Appellants rest their principal argument in support of federal jurisdiction upon the Alien Tort Statute, 28 U.S.C. § 1350, which provides: "The district courts shall have original jurisdiction of any civil action by an alien for a tort only, committed in violation of the law of nations or a treaty of the United States." Since appellants do not contend that their action arises directly under a treaty of the United States, a threshold question on the jurisdictional issue is whether the conduct alleged violates the law of nations. In light of the universal condemnation of torture in numerous international agreements, and the renunciation of torture as an instrument of official policy by virtually all of the nations of the world (in principle if not in practice), we find that an act of torture committed by a state official against one held in detention violates established norms of the international law of human rights, and hence the law of nations.

The Supreme Court has enumerated the appropriate sources of international law. The law of nations "may be ascertained by consulting the works of jurists, writing professedly on public law; or by the general usage and practice of nations; or by judicial decisions recognizing and enforcing that law." *United States v. Smith*, 18 U.S. (5 Wheat.) 153, 160-61 (1820). In *Smith*, a statute proscribing "the crime of piracy (on the high seas) as defined by the law of nations," 3 Stat. 510(a) (1819), was held sufficiently determinate in meaning to afford the basis for a death sentence. The *Smith* Court discovered among the works of Lord Bacon, Grotius, Bochard and other commentators a genuine consensus that rendered the crime "sufficiently and constitutionally defined." *Smith*, supra, 18 U.S. (5 Wheat.) at 162.

> *The Paquete Habana*, 175 U.S. 677 (1900), reaffirmed that where there is no treaty, and no controlling executive or legislative act or judicial decision, resort must be had to the customs and usages of civilized nations; and, as evidence of these, to the works of jurists and commentators, who by years of labor, research and experience, have made themselves peculiarly well acquainted with the subjects of which they treat. Such works are resorted to by judicial tribunals, not for the speculations of their authors concerning what the law ought to be, but for trustworthy evidence of what the law really is.

Id. at 700. Modern international sources confirm the propriety of this approach.[8]

---

8. The Statute of the International Court of Justice, Arts. 38 ¶ 59, June 26, 1945, 59 Stat. 1055, 1060 (1945) provides:

Art. 38

1. The Court, whose function is to decide in accordance with international law such disputes as are submitted to it, shall apply: (a) international conventions, whether general or particular, establishing rules expressly recognized by the contesting states; (b) international custom, as evidence of a general practice accepted as law; (c) the general principles of law recognized by civilized nations; (d) subject to the provisions of Article 59, judicial decisions and the teachings of the most highly qualified publicists of the various nations, as subsidiary means for the determination of the rules of law.

2. This provision shall not prejudice the power of the Court to decide a case ex aequo et bono, if the parties agree thereto.

Art. 59

* * *

Having examined the sources from which customary international law is derived-the usage of nations, judicial opinions and the works of jurists-we conclude that official torture is now prohibited by the law of nations. The prohibition is clear and unambiguous, and admits of no distinction between treatment of aliens and citizens. Accordingly, we must conclude that the dictum in *Dreyfus v. von Finck*, supra, 534 F.2d at 31, to the effect that "violations of international law do not occur when the aggrieved parties are nationals of the acting state," is clearly out of tune with the current usage and practice of international law. The treaties and accords cited above, as well as the express foreign policy of our own government, all make it clear that international law confers fundamental rights upon all people vis-a-vis their own governments. While the ultimate scope of those rights will be a subject for continuing refinement and elaboration, we hold that the right to be free from torture is now among them. We therefore turn to the question whether the other requirements for jurisdiction are met.

III

Appellee submits that even if the tort alleged is a violation of modern international law, federal jurisdiction may not be exercised consistent with the dictates of Article III of the Constitution. The claim is without merit. Common law courts of general jurisdiction regularly adjudicate transitory tort claims between individuals over whom they exercise personal jurisdiction, wherever the tort occurred. Moreover, as part of an articulated scheme of federal control over external affairs, Congress provided, in the first Judiciary Act, §9(b), 1 Stat. 73, 77 (1789), for federal jurisdiction over suits by aliens where principles of international law are in issue. The constitutional basis for the Alien Tort Statute is the law of nations, which has always been part of the federal common law.

It is not extraordinary for a court to adjudicate a tort claim arising outside of its territorial jurisdiction. A state or nation has a legitimate interest in the orderly resolution of disputes among those within its borders, and where the lex loci delicti commissi is applied, it is an expression of comity to give effect to the laws of the state where the wrong occurred. Thus, Lord Mansfield in *Mostyn v. Fabrigas*, 1 Cowp. 161 (1774), quoted in McKenna v. Fisk, 42 U.S. (1 How.) 241, 248 said:

> [I]f A becomes indebted to B, or commits a tort upon his person or upon his personal property in Paris, an action in either case may be maintained against A in England, if he is there found...[A]s to transitory actions, there is not a colour of doubt but that any action which is transitory may be laid in any county in England, though the matter arises beyond the seas.

Mostyn came into our law as the original basis for state court jurisdiction over out-of-state torts and it has not lost its force in suits to recover for a wrongful death occurring upon foreign soil, *Slater v. Mexican National Railroad Co.*, 194 U.S. 120 (1904), as long as the conduct complained of was unlawful where performed. Here, where in personam jurisdiction has been obtained over the defendant, the parties agree that the acts alleged would violate Paraguayan law, and the policies of the forum are consistent with the foreign law, state court jurisdiction would be proper. Indeed, appellees conceded as much at oral argument.

The decision of the Court has no binding force except between the parties and in respect of that particular case.

Recalling that *Mostyn* was freshly decided at the time the Constitution was ratified, we proceed to consider whether the First Congress acted constitutionally in vesting jurisdiction over "foreign suits," *Slater*, supra, 194 U.S. at 124, alleging torts committed in violation of the law of nations. A case properly "aris(es) under the...laws of the United States" for Article III purposes if grounded upon statutes enacted by Congress or upon the common law of the United States. The law of nations forms an integral part of the common law, and a review of the history surrounding the adoption of the Constitution demonstrates that it became a part of the common law of the United States upon the adoption of the Constitution. Therefore, the enactment of the Alien Tort Statute was authorized by Article III.

* * *

As ratified, the judiciary article contained no express reference to cases arising under the law of nations. Indeed, the only express reference to that body of law is contained in Article I, sec. 8, cl. 10, which grants to the Congress the power to "define and punish... offenses against the law of nations." Appellees seize upon this circumstance and advance the proposition that the law of nations forms a part of the laws of the United States only to the extent that Congress has acted to define it. This extravagant claim is amply refuted by the numerous decisions applying rules of international law uncodified in any act of Congress. * * * As John Jay wrote in The Federalist No. 3, at 22 (1 Bourne ed. 1901), "Under the national government, treaties and articles of treaties, as well as the laws of nations, will always be expounded in one sense and executed in the same manner, whereas adjudications on the same points and questions in the thirteen states will not always accord or be consistent." Federal jurisdiction over cases involving international law is clear.

* * *

Although the Alien Tort Statute has rarely been the basis for jurisdiction during its long history, in light of the foregoing discussion, there can be little doubt that this action is properly brought in federal court. This is undeniably an action by an alien, for a tort only, committed in violation of the law of nations. The paucity of suits successfully maintained under the section is readily attributable to the statute's requirement of alleging a "*violation* of the law of nations" (emphasis supplied) at the jurisdictional threshold. Courts have, accordingly, engaged in a more searching preliminary review of the merits than is required, for example, under the more flexible "arising under" formulation.

* * *

Thus, the narrowing construction that the Alien Tort Statute has previously received reflects the fact that earlier cases did not involve such well-established, universally recognized norms of international law that are here at issue.

* * *

Since federal jurisdiction may properly be exercised over the Filartigas' claim, the action must be remanded for further proceedings. Appellee Pena, however, advances several additional points that lie beyond the scope of our holding on jurisdiction. Both to emphasize the boundaries of our holding, and to clarify some of the issues reserved for the district court on remand, we will address these contentions briefly.

IV

Pena argues that the customary law of nations, as reflected in treaties and declarations that are not self-executing, should not be applied as rules of decision in this case.

In doing so, he confuses the question of federal jurisdiction under the Alien Tort Statute, which requires consideration of the law of nations, with the issue of the choice of law to be applied, which will be addressed at a later stage in the proceedings. The two issues are distinct. Our holding on subject matter jurisdiction decides only whether Congress intended to confer judicial power, and whether it is authorized to do so by Article III. The choice of law inquiry is a much broader one, primarily concerned with fairness; consequently, it looks to wholly different considerations. Should the district court decide that [choice-of-law] analysis requires it to apply Paraguayan law, our courts will not have occasion to consider what law would govern a suit under the Alien Tort Statute where the challenged conduct is actionable under the law of the forum and the law of nations, but not the law of the jurisdiction in which the tort occurred.[25]

Pena also argues that "[i]f the conduct complained of is alleged to be the act of the Paraguayan government, the suit is barred by the Act of State doctrine." This argument was not advanced below, and is therefore not before us on this appeal. We note in passing, however, that we doubt whether action by a state official in violation of the Constitution and laws of the Republic of Paraguay, and wholly unratified by that nation's government, could properly be characterized as an act of state. Paraguay's renunciation of torture as a legitimate instrument of state policy, however, does not strip the tort of its character as an international law violation, if it in fact occurred under color of government authority.

Finally, we have already stated that we do not reach the critical question of forum non conveniens, since it was not considered below. In closing, however, we note that the foreign relations implications of this and other issues the district court will be required to adjudicate on remand underscores the wisdom of the First Congress in vesting jurisdiction over such claims in the federal district courts through the Alien Tort Statute. Questions of this nature are fraught with implications for the nation as a whole, and therefore should not be left to the potentially varying adjudications of the courts of the fifty states.

* * *

Notes

1. The court finds Pena's actions violate international law even though it rejects in dictum an "act of state" defense because his actions were "wholly unratified" by Paraguay. The court explains this on the ground that Pena's tort occurred "under color of government authority." When the actions of an individual that are unlawful under the law of the country where they occur are nevertheless attributable to that country is a recurrent problem. The Restatement (Third) §702 provides that "[a] state violates in-

---

25. In taking that broad range of factors into account, the district court may well decide that fairness requires it to apply Paraguayan law to the instant case. See *Slater v. Mexican National Railway Co.*, 194 U.S. 120 (1904). Such a decision would not retroactively oust the federal court of subject matter jurisdiction, even though plaintiff's cause of action would no longer properly be "created" by a law of the United States. See *American Well Works Co. v. Layne & Bowler Co.*, 241 U.S. 257, 260 (1916) (Holmes, J.). Once federal jurisdiction is established by a colorable claim under federal law at a preliminary stage of the proceeding, subsequent dismissal of that claim (here, the claim under the general international proscription of torture) does not deprive the court of jurisdiction previously established.

ternational law if, as a matter of state policy, it practices, encourages, or condones" various acts, including torture.

On remand, there was a default judgment for the plaintiffs for $10,385,364, 10 million of which was for punitive damages. 577 F. Supp. 860 (E.D. N.Y. 1984).

2. Tel-Oren v. Libyan Arab Republic, 726 F.2d 774 (D.C. Cir. 1984), cert. denied, 470 U.S. 1003 (1985). Survivors of an attack on a civilian bus in Israel and representatives of persons killed in the attack, mostly Israeli citizens, sued under the Alien Tort Statute, as well as under federal question and diversity jurisdiction, for compensatory and punitive damages. Defendants were Libya, the Palestine Liberation Organization, and several other Arab organizations. In a per curiam opinion, the court affirmed the district court's dismissal. Each judge wrote a concurring opinion. Judge Edwards distinguished *Filartiga* on the grounds that the law of nations does not impose "the same responsibility or liability on nonstate actors, such as the PLO, as it does on states and persons acting under color of state law" and that the law of nations does not outlaw "politically motivated terrorism." Judge Bork disagreed with *Filartiga* on the ground that Congress' grant of jurisdiction in the Alien Tort Statute did not create a cause of action and "it is essential that there be an explicit grant of a cause of action before a private plaintiff be allowed to enforce principles of international law in a federal tribunal." Otherwise, courts would risk interfering with the conduct of foreign relations. Judge Bork did write that, to avoid draining § 1350 of all meaning, suits might be allowed for violations of international law that might have been in the mind of Congress in 1789 when it passed the statute, such as violation of safeconduct, infringement of the rights of ambassadors, and piracy. Judge Bork wrote that in 1789, there was no concept of international human rights. Judge Robb also disagreed with *Filartiga* and thought the "political question doctrine" precluded entry "into so sensitive an area of foreign policy."

Klinghoffer v. S.N.C. Achille Lauro, 937 F.2d 44 (2d Cir. 1991) held that the PLO could be sued for tort committed when hijacking a cruise ship; that the PLO was not a "state" entitled to sovereign immunity; and that suit was not barred by the political question doctrine.

In re Estate of Marcos Human Rights Litigation, 978 F.2d 493 (9th Cir. 1992), cert. denied, 508 U.S. 972 (1993), upheld a default judgment against the daughter of Ferdinand Marcos under the Alien Tort Statute for the death by torture in the Philippines of plaintiff's son. The court found that there was no problem of sovereign immunity because the defendant admitted acting on her own authority.

Goldstar (Panama) S.A. v. United States, 967 F.2d 965 (4th Cir. 1992), cert. denied, 506 U.S. 955 (1992), affirmed the dismissal of a suit against the United States under the Alien Tort Statute. The plaintiffs were Panamanian businesses that suffered losses from civil disorder because of lack of police protection during the United States invasion of Panama in 1989. The court held that the United States could not be sued under the Alien Tort Statute unless it had waived sovereign immunity under the Federal Tort Claims Act (FTCA), but the Act barred suit for a claim "based upon the exercise or performance or the failure to exercise or perform a discretionary function or duty." 28 U.S.C. § 2680(a). (Although the court did not mention it, the FTCA bars claims "arising in a foreign country." 28 U.S.C. § 2680(k). Perhaps the plaintiffs could allege that the negligent decisions not to provide police protection were made in the United States.) For the holding that suit against a sovereign under the Alien Tort Statute must first overcome the defense of sovereign immunity, see also Argentine Republic v. Amerada Hess Shipping Corp., 488 U.S. 428 (1989), holding that suit cannot be brought against Argentina under the Statute because no exception to sovereign immunity under the Foreign Sovereign Immunities Act applies (see note following IAM v. OPEC in chapter 5).

In re Estate of Ferdinand Marcos, Human Rights Litigation, 25 F.3d 1467 (9th Cir. 1994), cert. denied, 513 U.S. 1126 (1995). The Ninth Circuit affirmed an order of the United States District Court for the District of Hawaii preliminarily enjoining the former President's estate from transferring or otherwise disposing of assets during the litigation. The court held: the President was not immune under the Foreign Sovereign Immunities Act (FSIA) because the acts of torture and execution he is accused of ordering were outside the scope of his official authority and therefore were not the acts of an agency or instrumentality of a foreign state within the meaning of FSIA; "[a]n official acting under color of authority, but not within an official mandate, can violate international law and not be entitled to immunity under FSIA" (id. at 1472 n.8); the Alien Tort Claims Act (ATCA) creates a cause of action for violation of the law of nations; the claims did not abate upon the former President's death.

Hilao v. Estate of Marcos, 103 F.3d 767 (9th Cir. 1996), a class action, affirmed a judgment against the estate for $1.2 billion in exemplary damages and $766 million in compensatory damages, applying Philippine law. The court held that the former president could be held liable for human rights abuses committed by the military under his command if he either directed the atrocities or knew of such conduct and failed to use his power to prevent it. The class consisted of "all civilian citizens of the Philippines who, between 1972 and 1986, were tortured, summarily executed, or 'disappeared' by Philippine military or paramilitary groups [including] survivors of deceased class members." Id. at 771. The victims concluded a settlement agreement with the estate and the government of the Philippines for a payment of $150 million in exchange for releasing claims against Marcos' wife and children. In August 2000 the settlement had not yet been paid. The victims elected to terminate the settlement and proceed with attempts to recover the full amount of the judgment.

Doe v. Unocal Corp., 110 F. Supp. 2d 1294 (C.D. Cal. 2000), is a class action by Burmese citizens under the Alien Tort Claims Act (ATCA), the Racketeer Influenced and Corrupt Organizations Act (RICO), and federal question jurisdiction, against Unocal, a U.S. oil company. Plaintiffs alleged that the oil company, with knowledge of a Burmese military junta's practice of forced labor, continued to pay the junta to provide labor and security for a pipeline project in Burma. The court granted Unocal's motion for summary judgment as to plaintiffs' federal claims and declined to exercise supplemental jurisdiction over the pendent state law claims. The court held that Unocal had not acted under color of law and that there was no showing that the defendant sought to employ forced or slave labor.

Beanal v. Freeport-McMoran, Inc., 197 F.3d 161 (5th Cir. 1999), affirmed dismissal of a suite by Indonesian citizens against U.S. companies conducting mining activities in Indonesia. Plaintiffs' sued under the ATCA and the Torture Victim Protection Act (TVPA) alleging environmental abuses, human rights violations , and genocide. The court held that there was an insufficient showing that environmental depredation was a violation of international law. The allegation that defendants' activities caused plaintiffs, members of a native tribe, to be displaced and relocated was not sufficient because "cultural genocide" is not recognized as a violation of international law.

Wiwa v. Royal Dutch Petroleum Co., 226 F.3d 88 (2d Cir. 2000), reversed the forum non conveniens dismissal of a suit under the ATCA against foreign corporations alleged to have participated with the Nigerian government in human rights violations committed in Nigeria. The court stated that the trial judge had failed to give proper consideration to the choice of a U.S. forum by the plaintiffs, who now resided in the U.S., and to the interest of the U.S. in providing a forum for adjudication of claims alleging international human rights abuses.

See Richard L. Herz, Litigating Environmental Abuses Under the Alien Tort Claims Act: A Practical Assessment, 40 Va. J. Int'l L. 545 (2000); Saman Zia-Zarifi, Suing Multinational Corporations in the U.S. for Violating International Law, 4 UCLA J. Int'l L. & For. Aff. 81 (1999).

Iwanowa v. Ford Motor Company, 67 F.Supp.2d 424 (1999), dismissed a class action against a German manufacturer of motor vehicles and its American parent. The suit sought compensation and damages for forced labor in the German company's factory during World War II. The court held that limitations had run and that the claim was barred under the political question doctrine and principles of comity. The court found that it was the intent of treaties and agreements between the U.S. and Germany that individual claims be resolved as part of reparations agreements between the two governments.

3. Was *Filartiga* correct in construing the ATCA to provide a civil cause of action in federal court to any alien who was tortiously injured abroad by any act that violated international law, as that law has evolved to the present? The legislative history of the First Judiciary Act casts no light on the ATCA's purposes. Judge Friendly has famously said of the ATCA: "This old but little used section is a kind of legal Lohengrin; although it has been with us since the first Judiciary Act, no one seems to know whence it came." IIT v. Vencap, Ltd., 519 F.2d 1001, 1015 (2d Cir. 1975) (holding that fraud, although universally condemned, does not violate international law). (Lohengrin is the eponymous hero of an opera by Richard Wagner, which was first performed in 1850. When a Duke's daughter is accused of murder, a mysterious stranger, Lohengrin, appears to defend her in trial by combat.)

Before *Filartiga* opened the floodgates, only twice in the preceding almost two hundred years had jurisdiction under the Act been upheld. Adra v. Clift, 195 F. Supp. 857, 863 (D. Md. 1961) (upholding jurisdiction in suit over custody of child on ground that the mother's movement of the child under an improper passport violated international law and noting that "[d]espite its age, only six cases and one opinion of Attorney General Bonaparte are cited in the annotations [to the Act]"); Bolchos v. Darrel, 3 F. Cas. 810 (D.S.C. 1795) (using the Act, along with admiralty, as a basis for jurisdiction in a suit for restitution of cargo on board a Spanish ship seized as a prize of war). Since *Filartiga*, the Act's jurisdiction has been invoked successfully in a large and growing number of suits. In addition to the cases cited supra in Note 2, see Abebe-Jira v. Negewo, 72 F.3d 844 (11th Cir.), cert. denied, 519 U.S. 830 (1996) (affirming award of compensatory and punitive damages against former Ethiopian official); Mushikiwabo v. Barayagwiza, No. 94 CIV. 3627 (JSM), 1996 WL 164496 (S.D.N.Y. Apr. 9, 1996) (awarding compensatory and punitive damages against Rwandan political leader); Paul v. Avril, 901 F. Supp. 330 (S.D. Fla. 1994) (awarding compensatory and punitive damages against former Haitian military ruler); Xuncax v. Gramajo, 886 F. Sup. 162 (D. Mass. 1995) (awarding compensatory and punitive damages against former Guatemalan Minister of Defense); Forti v. Suarez-Mason, 672 F. Supp. 1531, 1539 (N.D. Cal. 1987), modified, 694 F. Supp. 707 (N.D. Cal. 1988) (denying in part former Argentine general's motion to dismiss).

Some judges, however, have limited the Act to a narrow compass. See Judge Bork's concurring opinion in *Tel-Oren*, supra Note 2. Before becoming a Justice of the

Supreme Court, Judge Scalia wrote that the Act "may conceivably have been meant to cover only private, nongovernmental acts that are contrary to treaty or the law of nations-the prominent examples being piracy and assaults on ambassadors." Sanchez-Espinoza v. Reagan, 770 F.2d 202, 206 (D.C. Cir. 1985) (dismissing a suit by citizens of Nicaragua and two Florida residents against President Reagan and others for claims arising out of United States support of anti-government guerrillas in Nicaragua). Some law review articles have also urged restricting jurisdiction under the Act. See Jean-Marie Simon, The Alien Tort Claims Act: Justice or Show Trials?, 11 B.U. Int'l L.J. 1, 34 (stating that "Congress intended the statute to give foreigners the ability to sue U.S. citizens, not fellow aliens, for law of nations violations").Other articles and comments have applauded *Filartiga*'s broad interpretation. See, e.g., Anne-Marie Burley, The Alien Tort Statute and the Judiciary Act of 1789: A Badge of Honor, 83 Am. J. Int'l L. 461, 488 (1989) (stating that "understanding the Statute as fulfilling a more general duty under the law of nations evokes a positive spirit supporting an expansive reading of its letter").

Professor Sweeney has advocated the narrowest construction of the Act. In time of war, under the law of prize, United States warships and authorized private vessels could stop apparently neutral vessels to determine whether an intercepted ship was in fact neutral, or was attempting to aid the enemy. Professor Sweeney contends that "tort" applies only to wrongs done to person or property on neutral vessels stopped under the law of prize. Joseph Modeste Sweeney, A Tort Only in Violation of the Law of Nations, 18 Hastings Int'l & Comp. L. Rev. 445, 447, 453-67 (1995). After Professor Sweeney's article was published, the defendant in the next principal case, Kadic v. Karadzic, moved for a rehearing seeking to give the Act Sweeney's restrictive interpretation. The motion was denied on the ground that "Professor Sweeney's argument is interesting but far from conclusive." *Kadic*, 74 F.3d 377, 378 (2d Cir. 1996). Is an argument for a restrictive interpretation of the Alien Tort Claims Act weakened by passage of the Torture Victim Protection Act, set out at the beginning of the next section?

4. In footnote 25 of the principal case, the court discusses choice of law under the ATCA. There are four major possibilities for choice of law under the Act: (1) use a choice-of-law rule to select the proper domestic tort law; (2) use choice-of-law analysis to select proper domestic law, but reject that law when incompatible with international law; (3) fashion new tort law from standards of international law; (4) fashion new tort law as a matter of federal common law. Would the last possibility deny the defendant due process?

On remand in *Filartiga*, the district court applied the law of Paraguay, but rejected Paraguay's failure to provide for punitive damages on the ground that this was contrary to international law. 577 F. Supp. 860, 864 (E.D.N.Y. 1984). See also Paul v. Avril, 901 F. Supp. 330, 335 (S.D. Fla. 1994) (citing favorably this *Filartiga* opinion and awarding compensatory and punitive damages, but not referring to the law of Haiti, where the offenses occurred). Is it likely that recovery of punitive damages can be justified under the aegis of international law when such damages are rejected by most legal systems? For a survey of countries that permit recovery of only compensatory damages and countries that permit awards of punitive damages, see John Y. Gotanda, Awarding Punitive Damages in International Commercial Arbitrations in the Wake of *Mastrobuono v. Shearson Lehman, Inc.*, 38 Harv. Int'l. L.J. 59, 106-112 (1997) (listing Brazil, Israel, Norway, Philippines, and Poland as the only "civil law countries permitting awards of punitive damages").

Also in footnote 25 of the principal case, the court invokes the "colorable claim" doctrine, which applies to pendent jurisdiction over non-federal claims after a federal court has dismissed all federal claims. Was this necessary? For the view that "arising under" jurisdiction permits Congress to channel to federal courts an issue in which there is a compelling federal interest, even though state or foreign law determines rights and remedies, see Henry M. Hart, Jr. & Herbert Wechsler, The Federal Courts and the Federal System 744-45 (1953) (discussing "protective jurisdiction"); Paul J. Mishkin, The Federal "Question" in the District Courts, 53 Colum. L. Rev. 157, 192 (1953) (stating that "[w]here there is an articulated and active federal policy regulating a field, the 'arising under' clause of Article III apparently permits the conferring of jurisdiction on the national courts of all cases in the area—including those substantively governed by state law").

5. On October 2, 2000, the Human Rights Act 1998 (c 42) entered into force in the United Kingdom. The Act codifies the provisions of the European Convention on Human Rights. The Act authorizes U.K. courts to declare that legislation is incompatible with the Convention. (Sec. 4). Although this declaration theoretically does not affect the validity of the legislation (sec. 4(6)(a)), the Act declares it "unlawful for a public authority to act in a way which is incompatible with a Convention right" (sec. 6(1)) and authorizes persons aggrieved by such an unlawful act to sue the public authority (sec. 7). The Act permits Courts to give remedies in such suits, including awarding damages. (Sec.8). The Convention prohibits torture, slavery, forced labor, discrimination because of status, and provides for fair trials in civil and criminal proceedings. The Convention guarantees rights to privacy, freedom of thought, conscience, religion, and expression. A protocol to the Convention abolishes the death penalty except "in respect of acts committed in time of war or of imminent threat of war." (Sixth Protocol).

Section 2: The Torture Victim Protection Act

Torture Victim Protection Act
Pub. L. No. 102-256, 106 Stat. 73 (1992), codified at 28 U.S.C. § 1350 (Supp. V 1993)

An Act to carry out obligations of the United States under the United Nations Charter and other international agreements pertaining to the protection of human rights by establishing a civil action for recovery of damages from an individual who engages in torture or extrajudicial killing. * * *

2. Establishment of civil action.

(a) Liability.-An individual who, under actual or apparent authority, or color of law, of any foreign nation-

(1) subjects an individual to torture shall, in a civil action, be liable for damages to that individual; or

(2) subjects an individual to extrajudicial killing

shall, in a civil action, be liable for damages to the individual's legal representative, or to any person who may be a claimant in an action for wrongful death.

(b) Exhaustion of remedies.-A court shall decline to hear a claim under this section if the claimant has not exhausted adequate and available remedies in the place in which the conduct giving rise to the claim occurred.

(c) Statute of limitations.-No action shall be maintained under this section unless it is commenced within 10 years after the cause of action arose.

3. Definitions.

(a) Extrajudicial killing.-For the purposes of this Act, the term "extrajudicial killing" means a deliberated killing not authorized by a previous judgment pronounced by a regularly constituted court affording all the judicial guarantees which are recognized as indispensable by civilized peoples. Such term, however, does not include any such killing that, under international law, is lawfully carried out under the authority of a foreign nation.

(b) Torture.-For the purposes of this Act-

(1) the term "torture" means any act, directed against an individual in the offender's custody or physical control, by which severe pain or suffering (other than pain or suffering arising only from or inherent in, or incidental to, lawful sanctions), whether physical or mental, is intentionally inflicted on that individual for such purposes as obtaining from that individual or a third person information or a confession, punishing that individual for an act that individual or a third person has committed or is suspected of having committed, intimidating or coercing that individual or a third person, or for any reason based on discrimination of any kind; and

(2) mental pain or suffering refers to prolonged mental harm caused by or resulting from-

(A) the intentional infliction or threatened infliction of severe physical pain or suffering;

(B) the administration or application, or threatened administration or application, of mind altering substances or other procedures calculated to disrupt profoundly the senses or the personality;

(C) the threat of imminent death; or

(D) the threat that another individual will imminently be subjected to death, severe physical pain or suffering, or the administration or application of mind altering substances or other procedures calculated to disrupt profoundly the senses or personality.

Note

Hilao v. Estate of Marcos, 103 F.3d 767, 773 (9th Cir. 1996), held that the 10-year statute of limitations in §2(c) "is subject to equitable tolling, including for periods in which the defendant is absent from the jurisdiction or immune from lawsuits and for periods in which the plaintiff is imprisoned or incapacitated." The court declined to consider whether the TVPA was properly applied retroactively because the issue was not sufficiently raised on appeal. Id. at 778, n.4.

Alvarez-Machain v. United States, 107 F.3d 696 (9th Cir. 1996), cert. denied, 522 U.S. 814 (1997), held that the TVPA could be applied to acts prior to its effective date without improper retroactive effect.

Kadic v. Karadzic
70 F.3d 232 (2d Cir. 1995), cert. denied, 518 U.S. 1005 (1996)

[The plaintiffs in these suits "allege that they are victims, and representatives of victims, of various atrocities, including brutal acts of rape, forced prostitution, forced impregnation, torture, and summary execution, carried out by Bosnian-Serb military forces as part of a genocidal campaign conducted in the course of the Bosnian civil war." The scene for these events is the former Yugoslavia. In 1992 the Croats and Muslims of Bosnia-Herzegovina voted to form an independent nation. Serbs living in this area boycotted the referendum and claimed two-thirds of the territory as their country. Radovan Karadzic is the self-proclaimed president of this entity, called "Srpska." Srpska is not recognized by other nations or by the United Nations. Karadzic is alleged to have ordered and directed a campaign of "ethnic cleansing" designed to eliminate Croat and Muslim residents from Srpska by killing them or driving them into exile. Tactics included massacres, murders, torture, and, as integral part of the scheme, rape. Approximately 20,000 Muslim and Croat women were raped by Serb soldiers. Many of these women were subjected to repeated gang rapes, and forced to give birth to children thus conceived.

Two actions were brought against Karadzic in the United States District Court for the Southern District of New York to recover compensatory and punitive damages. One action was brought by "Jane Doe" plaintiffs on behalf of themselves and members of their class. The other action was brought by Kadic "on her own behalf and on behalf of her infant sons." Jurisdiction was founded primarily on the Alien Tort Claims Act and the Torture Victim Protection Act. The district court dismissed the actions on the ground that Karadzic did not act under color of law of any state and therefore his actions did not violate international law. The Second Circuit reversed and remanded for further proceedings.]

Before: NEWMAN, Chief Judge, FEINBERG and WALKER, Circuit Judges.

JON O. NEWMAN, Chief Judge: * * *

In early 1993, Karadzic was admitted to the United States on three separate occasions as an invitee of the United Nations. According to affidavits submitted by the plaintiffs, Karadzic was personally served with the summons and complaint in each action during two of these visits while he was physically present in Manhattan. Karadzic admits that he received the summons and complaint in the *Kadic* action, but disputes whether the attempt to serve him personally in the *Doe* action was effective.

In the District Court, Karadzic moved for dismissal of both actions on the grounds of insufficient service of process, lack of personal jurisdiction, lack of subject-matter jurisdiction, and nonjusticiability of plaintiffs' claims. * * *

Turning to the issue of subject-matter jurisdiction under the Alien Tort Act, the [District] Court concluded that "acts committed by non-state actors do not violate the law of nations." Finding that "[t]he current Bosnian-Serb warring military faction does not constitute a recognized state," and that "the members of Karadzic's faction do not act under the color of any recognized state law," the Court concluded that "the acts alleged in the instant action[s], while grossly repugnant, cannot be remedied through [the Alien Tort Act]." The Court did not consider the plaintiffs' alternative claim that Karadzic acted under color of law by acting in concert with the Serbian Republic of the former Yugoslavia, a recognized nation.

The District Judge also found that the apparent absence of state action barred plaintiffs' claims under the Torture Victim Act, which expressly requires that an individual defendant act "under actual or apparent authority, or color of law, of any foreign nation," Torture Victim Act § 2(a). With respect to plaintiffs' further claims that the law of nations, as incorporated into federal common law, gives rise to an implied cause of action over which the Court would have jurisdiction pursuant to [28 U.S.C.] section 1331 [federal question jurisdiction], the Judge found that the law of nations does not give rise to implied rights of action absent specific Congressional authorization, and that, in any event, such an implied right of action would not lie in the absence of state action. Finally, having dismissed all of plaintiffs' federal claims, the Court declined to exercise supplemental jurisdiction over their state-law claims.

Discussion

Though the District Court dismissed for lack of subject-matter jurisdiction, the parties have briefed not only that issue but also the threshold issues of personal jurisdiction and justiciability under the political question doctrine. * * * We consider each in turn.

I. Subject-Matter Jurisdiction

Appellants allege three statutory bases for the subject-matter jurisdiction of the District Court-the Alien Tort Act, the Torture Victim Act, and the general federal-question jurisdictional statute.

A. The Alien Tort Act

1. General Application to Appellants' Claims * * *

Our decision in Filartiga [v. Pena-Irala, 630 F.2d 876 (2d Cir. 1980), supra page xxx] established that this statute confers federal subject-matter jurisdiction when the following three conditions are satisfied: (1) an alien sues (2) for a tort (3) committed in violation of the law of nations (i.e., international law). The first two requirements are plainly satisfied here, and the only disputed issue is whether plaintiffs have pleaded violations of international law.

Because the Alien Tort Act requires that plaintiffs plead a "violation of the law of nations" at the jurisdictional threshold, this statute requires a more searching review of the merits to establish jurisdiction than is required under the more flexible "arising under" formula of section 1331. Thus, it is not a sufficient basis for jurisdiction to plead merely a colorable violation of the law of nations. There is no federal subject-matter jurisdiction under the Alien Tort Act unless the complaint adequately pleads a violation of the law of nations (or treaty of the United States).

Filartiga established that courts ascertaining the content of the law of nations "must interpret international law not as it was in 1789, but as it has evolved and exists among the nations of the world today." Id. at 881. * * *

Karadzic contends that appellants have not alleged violations of the norms of international law because such norms bind only states and persons acting under color of a state's law, not private individuals. In making this contention, Karadzic advances the contradictory positions that he is not a state actor, even as he asserts that he is the President of the self-proclaimed Republic of Srpska. For their part, the *Kadic* appellants also take somewhat inconsistent positions in pleading defendant's role as President of Srpska, and also contending that "Karadzic is not an official of any government." * * *

We do not agree that the law of nations, as understood in the modern era, confines its reach to state action. Instead, we hold that certain forms of conduct violate the law of nations whether undertaken by those acting under the auspices of a state or only as private individuals. An early example of the application of the law of nations to the acts of private individuals is the prohibition against piracy. In The Brig Malek Adhel, 43 U.S. (2 How.) 210, 232 (1844), the Supreme Court observed that pirates were "hostis humani generis" (an enemy of all mankind) in part because they acted "without any pretense of public authority." Later examples are prohibitions against the slave trade and certain war crimes.

The liability of private persons for certain violations of customary international law and the availability of the Alien Tort Act to remedy such violations was early recognized by the Executive Branch in an opinion of Attorney General Bradford in reference to acts of American citizens aiding the French fleet to plunder British property off the coast of Sierra Leone in 1795. See Breach of Neutrality, 1 Op. Att'y Gen. 57, 59 (1795). The Executive Branch has emphatically restated in this litigation its position that private persons may be found liable under the Alien Tort Act for acts of genocide, war crimes, and other violations of international humanitarian law. See Statement of Interest of the United States at 5-13.

The Restatement (Third) of the Foreign Relations Law of the United States (1986) ("Restatement (Third) ") proclaims: "Individuals may be held liable for offenses against international law, such as piracy, war crimes, and genocide." Restatement (Third) pt. II, introductory note. The Restatement is careful to identify those violations that are actionable when committed by a state, Restatement (Third) § 702, and a more limited category of violations of "universal concern," id. § 404, partially overlapping with those listed in section 702. Though the immediate focus of section 404 is to identify those offenses for which a state has jurisdiction to punish without regard to territoriality or the nationality of the offenders, cf. id. § 402(1)(a), (2), the inclusion of piracy and slave trade from an earlier era and aircraft hijacking from the modern era demonstrates that the offenses of "universal concern" include those capable of being committed by non-state actors. Although the jurisdiction authorized by section 404 is usually exercised by application of criminal law, international law also permits states to establish appropriate civil remedies, id. § 404 cmt. b, such as the tort actions authorized by the Alien Tort Act.* * *

Karadzic disputes the application of the law of nations to any violations committed by private individuals.* * * Karadzic also contends that Congress intended the state-action requirement of the Torture Victim Act to apply to actions under the Alien Tort Act. We disagree. Congress enacted the Torture Victim Act to codify the cause of action recognized by this Circuit in *Filartiga*, and to further extend that cause of action to plaintiffs who are U.S. citizens. See H.R.Rep. No. 367, 102d Cong., 2d Sess., at 4 (1991), reprinted in 1992 U.S.C.C.A.N. 84, 86 (explaining that codification of *Filartiga* was necessary in light of skepticism expressed by Judge Bork's concurring opinion in *Tel-Oren*). At the same time, Congress indicated that the Alien Tort Act "has other important uses and should not be replaced," because

> Claims based on torture and summary executions do not exhaust the list of actions that may appropriately be covered [by the Alien Tort Act]. That statute should remain intact to permit suits based on other norms that already exist or may ripen in the future into rules of customary international law.

Id. The scope of the Alien Tort Act remains undiminished by enactment of the Torture Victim Act.

2. Specific Application of Alien Tort Act to Appellants' Claims

In order to determine whether the offenses alleged by the appellants in this litigation are violations of the law of nations that may be the subject of Alien Tort Act claims against a private individual, we must make a particularized examination of these offenses, mindful of the important precept that "evolving standards of international law govern who is within the [Alien Tort Act's] jurisdictional grant." Amerada Hess [Shipping Corp. v. Argentine Republic], 830 F.2d [421] at 425[2d Cir. 1987), rev'd on other grounds, 488 U.S. 428 (1989)]. In making that inquiry, it will be helpful to group the appellants' claims into three categories: (a) genocide, (b) war crimes, and (c) other instances of inflicting death, torture, and degrading treatment.

(a) Genocide. In the aftermath of the atrocities committed during the Second World War, the condemnation of genocide as contrary to international law quickly achieved broad acceptance by the community of nations. In 1946, the General Assembly of the United Nations declared that genocide is a crime under international law that is condemned by the civilized world, whether the perpetrators are "private individuals, public officials or statesmen." G.A.Res. 96(I), 1 U.N.GAOR, U.N. Doc. A/64/Add.1, at 188-89 (1946). * * * The Convention on the Prevention and Punishment of the Crime of Genocide, 78 U.N.T.S. 277, entered into force Jan. 12, 1951, for the United States Feb. 23, 1989 (hereinafter "Convention on Genocide"), provides a more specific articulation of the prohibition of genocide in international law. The Convention has been ratified by more than 120 nations, including the United States. * * * Especially pertinent to the pending appeal, the Convention makes clear that "[p]ersons committing genocide shall be punished, *whether they are constitutionally responsible rulers, public officials or private individuals.*" Id. art. IV (emphasis added).* * *

Appellants' allegations that Karadzic personally planned and ordered a campaign of murder, rape, forced impregnation, and other forms of torture designed to destroy the religious and ethnic groups of Bosnian Muslims and Bosnian Croats clearly state a violation of the international law norm proscribing genocide, regardless of whether Karadzic acted under color of law or as a private individual. The District Court has subject-matter jurisdiction over these claims pursuant to the Alien Tort Act.

(b) War crimes. Plaintiffs also contend that the acts of murder, rape, torture, and arbitrary detention of civilians, committed in the course of hostilities, violate the law of war. Atrocities of the types alleged here have long been recognized in international law as violations of the law of war. Moreover, international law imposes an affirmative duty on military commanders to take appropriate measures within their power to control troops under their command for the prevention of such atrocities. * * *

The offenses alleged by the appellants, if proved, would violate the most fundamental norms of the law of war * * * which [bind] parties to internal conflicts regardless of whether they are recognized nations or roving hordes of insurgents. The liability of private individuals for committing war crimes has been recognized since World War I and was confirmed at Nuremberg after World War II. * * * The District Court has jurisdiction pursuant to the Alien Tort Act over appellants' claims of war crimes and other violations of international humanitarian law.

(c) Torture and summary execution. In *Filartiga*, we held that official torture is prohibited by universally accepted norms of international law and the Torture Victim Act confirms this holding and extends it to cover summary execution. Torture Victim Act §§ 2(a), 3(a). However, torture and summary execution-when not perpetrated in the course of genocide or war crimes-are proscribed by international law only when committed by state officials or under color of law. * * *

In the present case, appellants allege that acts of rape, torture, and summary execution were committed during hostilities by troops under Karadzic's command and with the specific intent of destroying appellants' ethnic-religious groups. Thus, many of the alleged atrocities are already encompassed within the appellants' claims of genocide and war crimes. Of course, at this threshold stage in the proceedings it cannot be known whether appellants will be able to prove the specific intent that is an element of genocide, or prove that each of the alleged torts were committed in the course of an armed conflict, as required to establish war crimes. It suffices to hold at this stage that the alleged atrocities are actionable under the Alien Tort Act, without regard to state action, to the extent that they were committed in pursuit of genocide or war crimes, and otherwise may be pursued against Karadzic to the extent that he is shown to be a state actor. Since the meaning of the state action requirement for purposes of international law violations will likely arise on remand and has already been considered by the District Court, we turn next to that requirement.

3. The State Action Requirement for International Law Violations

In dismissing plaintiffs' complaints for lack of subject-matter jurisdiction, the District Court concluded that the alleged violations required state action and that the "Bosnian-Serb entity" headed by Karadzic does not meet the definition of a state. Appellants contend that they are entitled to prove that Srpska satisfies the definition of a state for purposes of international law violations and, alternatively, that Karadzic acted in concert with the recognized state of the former Yugoslavia and its constituent republic, Serbia.

(a) Definition of a state in international law. The definition of a state is well established in international law:

Under international law, a state is an entity that has a defined territory and a permanent population, under the control of its own government, and that engages in, or has the capacity to engage in, formal relations with other such entities.

Restatement (Third) §201.

Although the Restatement's definition of statehood requires the capacity to engage in formal relations with other states, it does not require recognition by other states. Recognized states enjoy certain privileges and immunities relevant to judicial proceedings, but an unrecognized state is not a juridical nullity. Our courts have regularly given effect to the "state" action of unrecognized states. See, e.g., United States v. Insurance Cos., 89 U.S. (22 Wall.) 99, 101-03 (1875) (seceding states in Civil War).

The customary international law of human rights, such as the proscription of official torture, applies to states without distinction between recognized and unrecognized states. It would be anomalous indeed if non-recognition by the United States, which typically reflects disfavor with a foreign regime-sometimes due to human rights abuses-had the perverse effect of shielding officials of the unrecognized regime from liability for those violations of international law norms that apply only to state actors.

Appellants' allegations entitle them to prove that Karadzic's regime satisfies the criteria for a state, for purposes of those international law violations requiring state action. * * * Moreover, it is likely that the state action concept, where applicable for some violations like "official" torture, requires merely the semblance of official authority. The inquiry, after all, is whether a person purporting to wield official power has exceeded internationally recognized standards of civilized conduct, not whether statehood in all its formal aspects exists.

(b) Acting in concert with a foreign state. Appellants also sufficiently alleged that Karadzic acted under color of law insofar as they claimed that he acted in concert with the former Yugoslavia, the statehood of which is not disputed. * * * The appellants are entitled to prove their allegations that Karadzic acted under color of law of Yugoslavia by acting in concert with Yugoslav officials or with significant Yugoslavian aid.

B. The Torture Victim Protection Act * * *

By its plain language, the Torture Victim Act renders liable only those individuals who have committed torture or extrajudicial killing "under actual or apparent authority, or color of law, of any foreign nation." Legislative history confirms that this language was intended to "make clear that the plaintiff must establish some governmental involvement in the torture or killing to prove a claim," and that the statute "does not attempt to deal with torture or killing by purely private groups." H.R.Rep. No. 367, 102d Cong., 2d Sess., at 5 (1991), reprinted in 1992 U.S.C.C.A.N. 84, 87. * * *

Though the Torture Victim Act creates a cause of action for official torture, this statute, unlike the Alien Tort Act, is not itself a jurisdictional statute. The Torture Victim Act permits the appellants to pursue their claims of official torture under the jurisdiction conferred by the Alien Tort Act and also under the general federal question jurisdiction of section 1331, to which we now turn.

C. Section 1331

The appellants contend that section 1331 provides an independent basis for subject-matter jurisdiction over all claims alleging violations of international law. Relying on the settled proposition that federal common law incorporates international law, they reason that causes of action for violations of international law "arise under" the laws of the United States for purposes of jurisdiction under section 1331. Whether that is so is an issue of some uncertainty that need not be decided in this case. * * * We recognized the possibility of section 1331 jurisdiction in *Filartiga*, 630 F.2d at 887 n. 22, but rested jurisdiction solely on the applicable Alien Tort Act. Since that Act appears to provide a remedy for the appellants' allegations of violations related to genocide, war crimes, and official torture, and the Torture Victim Act also appears to provide a remedy for their allegations of official torture, their causes of action are statutorily authorized, and, as in *Filartiga*, we need not rule definitively on whether any causes of action not specifically authorized by statute may be implied by international law standards as incorporated into United States law and grounded on section 1331 jurisdiction.

II. Service of Process and Personal Jurisdiction

Appellants aver that Karadzic was personally served with process while he was physically present in the Southern District of New York. In the *Doe* action, the affidavits detail that on February 11, 1993, process servers approached Karadzic in the lobby of the Hotel Intercontinental at 111 East 48th St. in Manhattan, called his name and identified their purpose, and attempted to hand him the complaint from a distance of two feet, that security guards seized the complaint papers, and that the papers fell to the floor. Karadzic submitted an affidavit of a State Department security officer, who generally confirmed the episode, but stated that the process server did not come closer than six feet of the defendant. In the *Kadic* action, the plaintiffs obtained from Judge Owen an order for alternate means of service, directing service by delivering the complaint to a member of defendant's State Department security detail, who was ordered to hand the complaint to the defendant. The security officer's affidavit states that he received the complaint and handed it to Karadzic outside the Russian Embassy in Manhattan. Karadzic's statement confirms that this occurred. * * * Appellants also allege that during his visits to New York City, Karadzic stayed at hotels outside the "headquarters district" of the United Nations and engaged in non-United Nations-related activities such as fund-raising. Fed.R.Civ.P. 4(e)(2) specifically authorizes personal service of a summons and complaint upon an individual physically present within a judicial district of the United States, and such personal service comports with the requirements of due process for the assertion of personal jurisdiction. See Burnham v. Superior Court of California, 495 U.S. 604 (1990). Nevertheless, Karadzic maintains that his status as an invitee of the United Nations during his visits to the United States rendered him immune from service of process. He relies on both the Agreement Between the United Nations and the United States of America Regarding the Headquarters of the United Nations, reprinted at 22 U.S.C. §287 note (1988) ("Headquarters Agreement"), and a claimed federal common law immunity. We reject both bases for immunity from service.

A. Headquarters Agreement

The Headquarters Agreement provides for immunity from suit only in narrowly defined circumstances. First, "service of legal process may take place within the headquarters district only with the consent of and under conditions approved by the Secretary-General." Id. §9(a). This provision is of no benefit to Karadzic, because he was not served within the well-defined confines of the "headquarters district," which is bounded by Franklin D. Roosevelt Drive, 1st Avenue, 42nd Street, and 48th Street. Second, certain representatives of members of the United Nations, whether residing inside or outside of the "headquarters district," shall be entitled to the same privileges and immunities as the United States extends to accredited diplomatic envoys. Id. §15. This provision is also of no benefit to Karadzic, since he is not a designated representative of any member of the United Nations.

A third provision of the Headquarters Agreement prohibits federal, state, and local authorities of the United States from "impos[ing] any impediments to transit to or from the headquarters district of...persons invited to the headquarters district by the United Nations...on official business." Id. §11. Karadzic maintains that allowing service of process upon a United Nations invitee who is on official business would violate this section, presumably because it would impose a potential burden-exposure to suit-on the invitee's transit to and from the headquarters district. However, this Court has previously refused "to extend the immunities provided by the Headquarters Agreement beyond those explicitly stated." See Klinghoffer v. S.N.C. Achille Lauro, 937 F.2d 44, 48 (2d Cir.1991). We therefore reject Karadzic's proposed construction of section 11, because it would effectively create an immunity from suit for United Nations invitees where none is provided by the express terms of the Headquarters Agreement. * * *

B. Federal common law immunity

Karadzic nonetheless invites us to fashion a federal common law immunity for those within a judicial district as a United Nations invitee. He contends that such a rule is necessary to prevent private litigants from inhibiting the United Nations in its ability to consult with invited visitors. * * * [W]e decline the invitation to create a federal common law immunity as an extension of the precise terms of a carefully crafted treaty that struck the balance between the interests of the United Nations and those of the United States.

Finally, we note that the mere possibility that Karadzic might at some future date be recognized by the United States as the head of state of a friendly nation and might thereby acquire head-of-state immunity does not transform the appellants' claims into a nonjusticiable request for an advisory opinion, as the District Court intimated. Even if such future recognition, determined by the Executive Branch, it would be entirely inappropriate for a court to create the functional equivalent of such an immunity based on speculation about what the Executive Branch might do in the future. In sum, if appellants personally served Karadzic with the summons and complaint while he was in New York but outside of the U.N. headquarters district, as they are prepared to prove, he is subject to the personal jurisdiction of the District Court.

III. Justiciability

We recognize that cases of this nature might pose special questions concerning the judiciary's proper role when adjudication might have implications in the conduct of this nation's foreign relations. We do not read *Filartiga* to mean that the federal judiciary must always act in ways that risk significant interference with United States foreign relations. To the contrary, we recognize that suits of this nature can present difficulties that implicate sensitive matters of diplomacy historically reserved to the jurisdiction of the political branches. See First National Bank v. Banco Nacional de Cuba, 406 U.S. 759, 767 (1972) [supra page 277 Note 1]. We therefore proceed to consider whether, even though the jurisdictional threshold is satisfied in the pending cases, other considerations relevant to justiciability weigh against permitting the suits to proceed.

Two nonjurisdictional, prudential doctrines reflect the judiciary's concerns regarding separation of powers: the political question doctrine and the act of state doctrine. It is the "'constitutional' underpinnings" of these doctrines that influenced the concurring opinions of Judge Robb and Judge Bork in *Tel-Oren* [supra page 409 Note 2]. Although we too recognize the potentially detrimental effects of judicial action in cases of this nature, we do not embrace the rather categorical views as to the inappropriateness of judicial action urged by Judges Robb and Bork. Not every case "touching foreign relations" is nonjusticiable, see Baker v. Carr, 369 U.S. 186, 211 (1962), and judges should not reflexively invoke these doctrines to avoid difficult and somewhat sensitive decisions in the context of human rights. We believe a preferable approach is to weigh carefully the relevant considerations on a case-by-case basis. This will permit the judiciary to act where appropriate in light of the express legislative mandate of the Congress in section 1350, without compromising the primacy of the political branches in foreign affairs.

Karadzic maintains that these suits were properly dismissed because they present nonjusticiable political questions. We disagree. Although these cases present issues that arise in a politically charged context, that does not transform them into cases involving nonjusticiable political questions. * * *

A nonjusticiable political question would ordinarily involve one or more of the following factors:

> [1] a textually demonstrable constitutional commitment of the issue to a coordinate political department; or [2] a lack of judicially discoverable and manageable standards for resolving it; or [3] the impossibility of deciding without an initial policy determination of a kind clearly for nonjudicial discretion; or [4] the impossibility of a court's undertaking independent resolution without expressing lack of the respect due coordinate branches of government; or [5] an unusual need for unquestioning adherence to a political decision already made; or [6] the potentiality of embarrassment from multifarious pronouncements by various departments on one question.

Baker v. Carr, 369 U.S. at 217. With respect to the first three factors, we have noted in a similar context involving a tort suit against the PLO that "[t]he department to whom this issue has been 'constitutionally committed' is none other than our own-the Judiciary." *Klinghoffer*, 937 F.2d at 49. Although the present actions are not based on the common law of torts, as was *Klinghoffer*, our decision in *Filartiga* established that universally recognized norms of international law provide judicially discoverable and manageable standards for adjudicating suits brought under the Alien Tort Act, which obviates any need to make initial policy decisions of the kind normally reserved for nonjudicial discretion. Moreover, the existence of judicially discoverable and manageable standards further undermines the claim that such suits relate to matters that are constitutionally committed to another branch.

The fourth through sixth *Baker* factors appear to be relevant only if judicial resolution of a question would contradict prior decisions taken by a political branch in those limited contexts where such contradiction would seriously interfere with important governmental interests. Disputes implicating foreign policy concerns have the potential to raise political question issues, although, as the Supreme Court has wisely cautioned, "it is 'error to suppose that every case or controversy which touches foreign relations lies beyond judicial cognizance.'" *Japan Whaling Ass'n v. American Cetacean Society*, 478 U.S. 221, 229-30, (1986) (quoting *Baker*, 369 U.S. at 211).

The act of state doctrine, under which courts generally refrain from judging the acts of a foreign state within its territory, might be implicated in some cases arising under section 1350. However, as in *Filartiga*, we doubt that the acts of even a state official, taken in violation of a nation's fundamental law and wholly unratified by that nation's government, could properly be characterized as an act of state.

In the pending appeal, we need have no concern that interference with important governmental interests warrants rejection of appellants' claims. After commencing their action against Karadzic, attorneys for the plaintiffs in *Doe* wrote to the Secretary of State to oppose reported attempts by Karadzic to be granted immunity from suit in the United States; a copy of plaintiffs' complaint was attached to the letter. Far from intervening in the case to urge rejection of the suit on the ground that it presented political questions, the Department responded with a letter indicating that Karadzic was not immune from suit as an invitee of the United Nations. After oral argument in the pending appeals, this Court wrote to the Attorney General to inquire whether the United States wished to offer any further views concerning any of the issues raised. In a "Statement of Interest," signed by the Solicitor General and the State Department's Legal Adviser, the United States has expressly disclaimed any concern that the political question doctrine should be invoked to prevent the litigation of these lawsuits: "Although there might be instances in which federal courts are asked to issue rulings under the Alien Tort Statute or the Torture Victim Protection Act that might raise a political question, this is not one of them." Statement of Interest of the United States at 3. Though even an assertion of the political question doctrine by the Executive Branch, entitled to respectful consideration, would not necessarily preclude adjudication, the Government's reply to our inquiry reinforces our view that adjudication may properly proceed. * * *

As to the act of state doctrine, the doctrine was not asserted in the District Court and is not before us on this appeal. Moreover, the appellee has not had the temerity to assert in this Court that the acts he allegedly committed are the officially approved policy of a state. Finally, as noted, we think it would be a rare case in which the act of state doctrine precluded suit under section 1350. *Banco Nacional* [de Cuba v. Sabbatino, 376 U.S. 398 (1964), supra page 261] was careful to recognize the doctrine "in the absence of . . . unambiguous agreement regarding controlling legal principles," 376 U.S. at 428, such as exist in the pending litigation, and applied the doctrine only in a context-expropriation of an alien's property-in which world opinion was sharply divided.

Finally, we note that at this stage of the litigation no party has identified a more suitable forum, and we are aware of none. Though the Statement of the United States suggests the general importance of considering the doctrine of forum non conveniens, it seems evident that the courts of the former Yugoslavia, either in Serbia or war-torn Bosnia, are not now available to entertain plaintiffs' claims, even if circumstances concerning the location of witnesses and documents were presented that were sufficient to overcome the plaintiffs' preference for a United States forum.

Conclusion

The judgment of the District Court dismissing appellants' complaints for lack of subject-matter jurisdiction is reversed, and the cases are remanded for further proceedings in accordance with this opinion.

Notes

1. The court upholds personal jurisdiction over Karadzic based on service while he was present in New York, citing Burnham v. Superior Court, 495 U.S. 604 (1990), supra page 30 Note 4. In *Burnham*, the defendant was a resident of New Jersey served in California. Is *Karadzic* distinguishable? See Restatement (Third) The Foreign Relations Law of the United States § 421(2)(a): "In general, a state's exercise of jurisdiction to adjudicate with respect to a person is reasonable if, at the time jurisdiction is asserted the person is present in the territory of the state, other than transitorily."

On March 27, 2000, the District Court granted a motion for decertification of the class action against Karadzic. A group of class members filed the motion and pursued relief as plaintiffs in a separate action. Doe I v. Karadzic, 2000 W.L 763851 (S.D.N.Y. 2000). On August 10, 2000, in one of the two actions against Karadzic, the jury returned a verdict against him of $745 million, $265 million in compensatory damages and $480 million in punitive damages. On September 25, 2000, the jury in the other action returned a verdict against Karadzic of $4.5 billion, $619 million in compensatory damages and $3.9 billion in punitive damages.

2. Two international criminal tribunals are indicting and trying persons accused of "serious violations of international humanitarian law" committed in Rwanda and neighboring states and in the former Yugoslavia. One of the persons indicted by the International Criminal Tribunal for the former Yugoslavia, sitting in The Hague, is Radovan Karadzic. The tribunals were created by resolutions of the United Nations Security Council. For the argument that in creating these tribunals the Security Council exceeded its powers under the United Nations Charter, see Tara Sapra, Into the Heart of Darkness: The Case Against the Foray of the Security Council Tribunal into the Rwandan Crisis, 32 Tex. Int'l L.J. 329 (1997).

On July 17, 1998, a UN diplomatic conference in Rome opened for signature a treaty to establish a permanent international criminal court. See Rome Statute of the International Criminal Court, UN Doc. A/CONF. 183/9*, 37 ILM 999 (1998). The court operates only when national courts fail to act. The court, which will sit permanently in The Hague, has jurisdiction over crimes worldwide if the state in which the conduct occurred or of which the person accused of crime is a national has ratified the treaty. The treaty will enter in force the first day of the month following ratification by the sixtieth country and apply only to crimes committed after that date. As of September 7, 2000, 101 countries had signed the Treaty and seventeen had ratified it. The United States has not signed the treaty because the U.S. wishes an exception for U.S. troops deployed in foreign countries and because of opposition in Congress. The U.S. did receive permission to continue its participation in negotiations on the form and functions of the court. The current status of the Treaty is available at its Web site: <http://www.un.org/icc/statute/status/htm>.

The competence of the International Tribunal for the Former Yugoslavia is limited to "the power to prosecute persons responsible for serious violations of international humanitarian law" and does not include civil compensation. Statute of the Yugoslavian Tribunal art. 1, contained in the Report of the Secretary-General pursuant to Paragraph 2 of Security Council Resolution 808, U.N. SCOR, 48th Sess., U.N. Doc. S/25704 (1993), reprinted in 32 I.L.M. 1159, 1170. Would civil actions before an international tribunal be preferable to suits under the ATCA or TVPA?

3. Are individuals who are not heads of state or diplomatic or consular agents entitled to sovereign immunity under the Foreign Sovereign Immunities Act? See supra page 293 Note 9. If the FSIA did apply to individuals, it would all but foreclose suit against foreign officials under the ATCA or the TVPA, if the officials' acts were authorized. Argentine Republic v. Amerada Hess Shipping Corp., 488 U.S. 428 (1989), held that suit could be brought under the ATCA against a foreign government only if one of the FSIA exceptions to sovereign immunity applied. The Report of the Senate Committee on the Judiciary, S. Rep. No. 249, 102d Cong. 1st Sess., states that the TVPA is also subject to the FSIA. Id. at 7. Section 1605(a)(5) of the FSIA permits suits for torts only if the harm occurs "in the United States." Moreover, abuse of police power, if authorized, would likely be considered performance of "a discretionary function" and thus another exception to tort liability under the FSIA § 1605(a)(5)(A). See Saudi Arabia v. Nelson, 507 U.S. 349 (1993), supra page 305.

If the FSIA applies to individuals and therefore there is ATCA or TVPA liability only if the acts are not authorized, an outlaw state could cloak its officials with immunity. The April 1996 amendment to the FSIA, which added § 1605(a)(7), supra page 283, provides a limited exception to this immunity for some atrocities if the foreign state is designated as a state sponsor of terrorism and if the victim is a United States citizen. This would permit some actions under the TVPA but not the ATCA. The ATCA is limited to claims by aliens.

4. The principal case holds that Karadzic can be sued for some violations of international law even if he did not act under color of law of any state, but that other claims do require state agency. See Claire Finkelstein, Changing Notions of State Agency in International Law: The Case of Paul Touvier, 30 Texas Int'l L.J. 261, 262 (1995) (suggesting "that the correct test for state agency would focus on the *status* of the offender and whether there is an expectation of accountability between the offender and the relevant state").

5. The principal case leaves open the question "whether any causes of action not specifically authorized by statute may be implied by international law standards as incorporated into United States law and grounded on section 1331 [federal question] jurisdiction." See Curtis A. Bradley & Jack L. Goldsmith, Customary International Law as Federal Common Law: A Critique of the Modern Position, 110 Harv. L. Rev. 815 (1997). The authors note that "[t]he proposition that customary international law is part of this country's federal common law has become a well-entrenched component of U.S. foreign relations law." Id. at 816. They conclude, however, that "in the absence of federal political branch authorization [customary international law] is not a source of federal law [and therefore] a case arising under [customary international law] would not by that fact alone establish federal question jurisdiction." Id. at 870.

6. Lafontant v. Aristide, 844 F. Supp. 128 (E.D. N.Y. 1994). Judge Weinstein held that a head of a recognized state who has violated the civil rights of a person by having him

killed is, because of his status as head of state, immune from civil prosecution in this country, and this immunity is not affected by the FSIA or the TVPA. Plaintiff, the wife of a person allegedly killed by Haitian soldiers acting on the specific orders of President of Haiti Aristide, sued Aristide under, among other provisions, the ATCA and the TVPA. At the time of suit, Aristide was living in the United States after his exile following a military coup and before his return to Haiti.

Chapter 8

Damages Resulting from International Flights: The Warsaw Convention

Section 1: Current and Proposed Recovery Rules

Convention for the Unification of Certain Rules Relating to International Transportation by Air (Warsaw Convention), opened for signature Oct. 12, 1929, 49 Stat. 3000, 137 L.N.T.S. 11, reprinted in note following 49 U.S.C. § 40105, as amended by Montreal Protocol No. 4,* reprinted in S. Exec. Rep. No. 105-20, pp. 21-32 (1998).

Chapter I. Scope: Definitions

Article 1

(1) This convention shall apply to all international transportation of persons, baggage, or goods performed by aircraft for hire. It shall apply equally to gratuitous transportation by aircraft performed by an air transportation enterprise.

(2) For the purposes of this convention the expression "international transportation" shall mean any transportation in which, according to the contract made by the parties, the place of departure and the place of destination, whether or not there be a break in the transportation or a transshipment, are situated either within the territories of two High Contracting Parties, or within the territory of a single High Contracting Party, if there is an agreed stopping place within a territory subject to the sovereignty, suzerainty, mandate or authority of another power, even though that power is not a

---

* The United States ratified Montreal Protocol No. 4 in September 1998. The Protocol went into force in the United States on March 4, 1999. The Protocol was promulgated in 1955.

party to this convention. Transportation without such an agreed stopping place between territories subject to the sovereignty, suzerainty, mandate, or authority of the same High Contracting Party shall not be deemed to be international for the purposes of this convention.

(3) Transportation to be performed by several successive air carriers shall be deemed, for the purposes of this convention, to be one undivided transportation, if it has been regarded by the parties as a single operation, whether it has been agreed upon under the form of a single contract or of a series of contracts, and it shall not lose its international character merely because one contract or a series of contracts is to be performed entirely within a territory subject to the sovereignty, suzerainty, mandate, or authority of the same High Contracting Party.

Article 2

(1) This convention shall apply to transportation Performed by the state or by legal entities constituted under public law provided it falls within the conditions laid down in article 1. * * *

Chapter II. Transportation Documents

Section I: Passenger Ticket

Article 3

(1) For the transportation of passengers the carrier must deliver a passenger ticket which shall contain the following particulars:

(a) The place and date of issue;

(b) The place of departure and of destination;

(c) The agreed stopping places, provided that the carrier may reserve the right to alter the stopping places in case of necessity, and that if he exercises that right, the alteration shall not have the effect of depriving the transportation of its international character;

(d) The name and address of the carrier or carriers;

(e) A statement that the transportation is subject to the rules relating to liability established by this convention.

(2) The absence, irregularity, or loss of the passenger ticket shall not affect the existence or the validity of the contract of transportation, which shall none the less be subject to the rules of this convention. Nevertheless, if the carrier accepts a passenger without a passenger ticket having been delivered he shall not be entitled to avail himself of those provisions of this convention which exclude or limit his liability.

Section II: Baggage Check

Article 4

(l) For the transportation of baggage, other than small personal objects of which the passenger takes charge himself, the carrier must deliver a baggage check.

(2) The baggage check shall be made out in duplicate, one part for the passenger and the other part for the carrier.

(3) The baggage check shall contain the following particulars

(a) The place and date of issue;

(b) The place of departure and of destination;

(c) The name and address of the carrier or carriers;

(d) The number of the passenger ticket;

(e) A statement that delivery of the baggage will be made to the bearer of the baggage check;

(f) The number and weight of the packages;

(g) The amount of the value declared in accordance with article 22(2);

(h) A statement that the transportation is subject to the rules relating to liability established by this convention.

(4) The absence, irregularity, or loss of the baggage check shall not affect the existence or the validity of the contract of transportation which shall none the less be subject to the rules of this convention. Nevertheless, if the carrier accepts baggage without a baggage check having been delivered, or if the baggage check does not contain the particulars set out at (d), (f), and (h) above, the carrier shall not be entitled to avail himself of those provisions of the convention which exclude or limit his liability.

Section III: Air Waybill

Article 5

(1) In respect of the carriage of cargo an air waybill shall be delivered.

(2) Any other means which would preserve a record of the carriage to be performed may, with the consent of the consignor, be substituted for the delivery of the air waybill. * * *

* * *

Article 8

The air waybill and the receipt for the cargo shall contain:

(a) an indication of the places of departure and destination;

(b) if the places of departure and destination are within the territory of a single High Contracting Party, one or more agreed stopping places being within the territory of another State, an indication of at least one such stopping place; and

(c) an indication of the weight of the consignment.

Article 9

Non-compliance with the provisions of Articles 5 to 8 shall not affect the existence or the validity of the contract of carriage, which shall, nonetheless, be subject to the rules of this Convention including those relating to limitation of liability.

* * *

Chapter III. Liability of the Carrier

Article 17

The carrier shall be liable for damage sustained in the event, of the death or wounding of a passenger or any other bodily injury suffered by a passenger, if the accident which caused the damage so sustained took place on board the aircraft or in the course of any of the operations of embarking or disembarking.

Article 18

(1) The carrier is liable for damage sustained in the event of the destruction or loss of, or of damage to, any checked baggage or any goods, if the occurrence which caused the damage so sustained took place during the carriage by air.

* * *

(3) However, the carrier is not liable if he proves that the destruction, loss of, or damage to the cargo resulted solely from [inherent defect, defective packaging performed by a person other than the carrier, an act of war, or an act of public authority].

(4) The carriage by air within the meaning of the preceding paragraphs of this Article comprises the period during which the baggage or cargo is in charge of the carrier, whether in an airport or on board an aircraft, or, in the case of a landing outside an airport, in any place whatsoever.

(5) The period of carriage by air shall not extend to any carriage by land, by sea, or by river performed outside an airport. If, however, such carriage takes place in the performance of a contract for carriage by air, for the purpose of loading, delivery or transshipment, any damage is presumed, subject to proof to the contrary, to have been the result of an event which took place during the carriage by air.

Article 19

The carrier shall be liable for damage occasioned by delay in the transportation by air of passengers, baggage, or goods.

Article 20

In the carriage of passengers and baggage, and in the case of damage occasioned by delay in the carriage of cargo, the carrier shall not be liable if he proves that he and his servants and agents have taken all necessary measure to avoid the damage or that it was impossible for them to take such measures.

Article 21

(1) In the case of passengers and baggage, if the carrier proves that the damage was caused by or contributed to by the negligence of the person suffering the damage the Court may, in accordance with the provisions of its own law, exonerate the carrier wholly or partly from his liability.

(2) In the carriage of cargo, if the carrier proves that the damage was caused by or contributed to by the negligence or other wrongful act or omission of the person claiming compensation, or the person from whom he derives his rights, the carrier shall be

wholly or partly exonerated from his liability to the claimant to the extent that such negligence or wrongful act or omission caused or contributed to the damage.

Article 22

(1) In the transportation of passengers the liability of the carrier for each passenger shall be limited to the sum of 125,000 francs. Where, in accordance with the law of the court to which the case is submitted, damages may be awarded in the form of periodical payments, the equivalent capital value of the said payments shall not exceed 125,000 francs. Nevertheless, by special contract, the carrier and the passenger may agree to a higher limit of liability.

(2)(a) In the transportation of checked baggage, the liability of the carrier shall be limited to a sum of 250 francs per kilogram, unless the consignor has made, at the time when the package was handed over to the carrier, a special declaration of the value at delivery and has paid a supplementary sum if the case so requires. In that case the carrier will be able to pay a sum not exceeding the declared sum, unless he proves that that sum is greater than the actual value to the consignor at delivery.

(b) In the carriage of cargo, the liability of the carrier is limited to a sum of 17 Special Drawing Rights per kilogram, unless the consignor has made, at the time when the package was handed over to the carrier, a special declaration of interest in delivery at destination and has paid a supplementary sum if the case so requires. In that case the carrier will be able to pay a sum not exceeding the declared sum, unless he proves that that sum is greater than the consignor's actual interest in delivery at destination.

(3) As regards objects of which the passenger takes charge himself the liability of the carrier shall be limited to 5,000 francs per Passenger.

(4) The sums mentioned above shall be deemed to refer to the French franc consisting of 65 1/2 milligrams of gold at the standard of fineness of nine hundred thousandths. These sums may be converted into any national currency in round figures. * * *

(6) The sums mentioned in the terms of the Special Drawing Right in this Article shall be deemed to refer to the Special Drawing Right as defined by the International Monetary Fund. * * *

Article 23

Any provision tending to relieve the carrier of liability or to fix a lower limit than that which is laid down in this convention shall be null and void, but the nullity of any such provision shall not involve the nullity of the whole contract, which shall remain subject to the provisions of this convention.

Article 24

(1) In the carriage of passengers and baggage, any action for damages, however founded, can only be brought subject to the conditions and limits set out in this convention, without prejudice to the question as to who are the persons who have the right to bring suit and what are their respective rights.

(2) In the carriage of cargo, any action for damages, however founded * * * can only be brought subject to the conditions and limits * * * set out in this convention, without prejudice to the question as to who are the persons who have the right to bring suit and what are their respective rights. Such limits of liability constitute maximum limits and may not be exceeded whatever the circumstances which gave rise to the liability.

Article 25

In the carriage of passengers and baggage, the limits of liability specified in Article 22 shall not apply if it is proved that the damage resulted from an act or omission of the carrier, his servants or agents, done with intent to cause damage or recklessly and with knowledge that damage would probably result; provided that, in the case of such act or omission of a servant or agent, it is also proved that he was acting within the scope of his employment.

* * *

Article 28

(1) An action for damages must be brought, at the option of the plaintiff, in the territory of one of the High Contracting Parties, either before the court of the domicile of the carrier or of his principal place of business, or where he has a place of business through which the contract has been made, or before the court at the place of destination.

(2) Questions of procedure shall be governed by the law of the court to which the case is submitted.

Article 29

(1) The right to damages shall be extinguished if an action is not brought within 2 years, reckoned from the date of arrival at the destination, or from the date on which the aircraft ought to have arrived, or from the date on which the transportation stopped.

(2) The method of calculating the period of limitation shall be determined by the law of the court to which the case is submitted.

Article 30

(1) In the case of transportation to be performed by various successive carriers and falling within the definition set out in the third paragraph of article 1, each carrier who accepts passengers, baggage or goods shall be subject to the rules set out in this convention, and shall be deemed to be one of the contracting parties to the contract of transportation insofar as the contract deals with that part of the transportation which is performed under his supervision

(2) In the case of transportation of this nature, the passenger or his representative can take action only against the carrier who performed the transportation during which the accident or the delay occurred, save in the case where, by express agreement, the first carrier has assumed liability for the whole journey.

(3) As regards baggage or goods, the passenger or consignor shall have a right of action against the first carrier, and the passenger or consignee who is entitled to delivery shall have a right of action against the last carrier, and further, each may take action against the carrier who performed the transportation during which the destruction, loss, damage, or delay took place. These carriers shall be jointly and severally liable to the passenger or to the consignor or consignee.

* * *

Chapter IV. Provisions Relating to Combined Transportation

Article 31

(1) In the case of combined transportation performed partly by air and partly by any other mode of transportation, the, provisions of this convention shall apply only to the transportation by air, provided that the transportation by air falls, within the terms of article 1

(2) Nothing in this convention shall prevent the parties in the case of combined transportation from inserting in the document of air transportation conditions relating to other modes of transportation provided that the provisions of this convention are observed as regards the transportation by air.

Chapter V. General and Final Provisions

Article 32

Any clause contained in the contract and all special agreements entered into before the damage occurred by which the parties purport to infringe the rules laid down by this convention, whether by deciding the law to be applied, or by altering the rules as to jurisdiction, shall be null and void. Nevertheless for the transportation of goods arbitration clauses shall be allowed, subject to this convention, if the arbitration is to take place within one of the jurisdictions referred to in the first paragraph of article 28.

* * *

Article 36

This convention is drawn up in French in a single copy which shall remain deposited in the archives of the Ministry for Foreign Affairs of Poland and of which one duly certified copy shall be sent by the Polish Government to the Government of each of the High Contracting Parties.

* * *

Article 39

(1) Any one of the High Contracting Parties may denounce this convention by a notification addressed to the Government of the Republic of Poland, which shall at once inform the Government of each of the High Contracting Parties.

(2) Denunciation shall take effect six months after the notification of denunciation, and shall operate only as regards the party which shall have proceeded to denunciation.

Civil Aeronautics Board Order Concerning Hague Protocol and Montreal Agreement,
31 Fed. Reg. 7302

The Convention for the Unification of Certain Rules Relating to International Transportation by Air, generally known as the Warsaw Convention, creates a uniform body of law with respect to the rights and responsibilities of passenger, shippers, and air carriers in international air transportation. The United States became a party to the Convention in 1934, and eventually over 90 countries likewise became parties to the Convention. [The Convention was amended by the Protocol signed at Hague in 1955 which has never been ratified by the United States. The Convention (subject to certain provisions limits carriers' liability for death or injury to passengers in international transportation to 125,000 gold francs, or approximately $8,300. The Protocol, subject to certain provisions, provides for liability limitations of approximately $16,600.] On November 15, 1965, the U.S. Government gave notice of denunciation of the Convention, emphasizing that such action was solely because of the Convention's low limits of liability for personal injury or death to passengers. Pursuant to Article 39 of the Convention this notice would become effective upon 6 months' notice, in this case, May 15, 1966. Subsequently, the International Air Transport Association (IATA) made efforts to effect an arrangement among air carriers, foreign air carriers, and other carriers (including carriers not members of IATA) providing the major portions of international air carriage to and from the United States to increase the limitations of liability now applicable to claims for personal injury and death under the Convention and the Protocol. The purpose of such action is to provide a basis upon which the United States could withdraw its notice of denunciation.

The arrangement proposed has been embodied in an agreement (Agreement CAB 18900) between various air carriers, foreign air carriers, and other carriers which has been filed with the Board pursuant to section 412(a) of the Federal Aviation Act of 1958 [section 1382(a) of this title] and Part 261 of the Board's economic regulations and assigned the above-designated CAB number.

By this agreement, the parties thereto bind themselves to include in their tariffs, effective May 16, 1966, a special contract in accordance with Article 22(1) of the Convention or the Protocol providing for a limit of liability for each passenger for death, wounding, or other bodily injury of $75,000 inclusive of legal fees, and, in case of a claim brought in a State where provision is made for separate award of legal fees and costs, a limit of $58,000 exclusive of legal fees and costs. These limitations shall be applicable to international transportation by the carrier as defined in the Convention or Protocol which includes a point in the United States as a point of origin, point of destination, or agreed stopping place. The parties further agree to provide in their tariffs that the Carrier shall not, with respect to any claim arising out of the death, wounding, or other bodily injury of a passenger, avail itself of any defense under Article 20(1) of the Convention or the Convention as amended by the Protocol. The tariff provisions would stipulate, however, that nothing therein shall be deemed to affect the rights and liabilities of the Carrier with regard to any claim brought by, on behalf of, or in respect of any person who has willfully caused damage which results in death, wounding, or other bodily injury of a passenger.

The carriers by the agreement further stipulate that they will, at time of delivery of the tickets, furnish to each passenger governed by the Convention or the Protocol and by the special contract described above a notice in 10 point type advising international passengers of the limitations of liability established by the Convention or the Protocol, or the higher liability agreed to by the special contracts pursuant to the Convention or Protocol as described above.

* * *

The agreement will result in a salut[a]ry increase in the protection given to passengers from the increased liability amounts and the waiver of defenses under Article 20(1) of the Convention or Protocol. The U.S. Government has concluded that such arrangements warrant withdrawal of the Notice of Denunciation of the Warsaw Convention. Implementation of the agreement will permit continued adherence to the Convention with the benefits to be derived therefrom, but without the imposition of the low liability limits therein contained upon most international travel involving travel to or from the United States. The stipulation that no tariff provision shall be deemed to affect the rights and liabilities of the carrier with regard to any claim brought by, on behalf of, on in respect of any person who has willfully caused damage which results in death, wounding or other bodily injury of a passenger operates to diminish any incentive for sabotage.

Upon consideration of the agreement, and of matters relating thereto of which the Board takes notice, the Board does not find that the agreement is adverse to the public interest or in violation of the Act and it will be approved.

* * *

Note

The wrong way to unify liability law so as to simplify litigation of mass torts is to set the liability limit so low that no compensation issues remain. This is the effect of the Warsaw Convention, which dates from the early days of commercial aviation, when it was an acceptable idea to subsidize the infant industry with the blood of its customers. Moreover, low liability limits are likely to have more of an impact in the United States than in other countries where the safety net of social services is higher and wider.

There have been several amendments of the Convention to increase recovery. The Hague Protocol of 1955, 478 U.N.T.S. 371, referred to in the CAB Order approving the Montreal Agreement, doubled the liability limit to $16,600. The Guatemala City Protocol of 1971, ICAO Doc. No. 8932, 10 I.L.M. 613 (1971), raised the recovery limit to $100,000 and made recovery easier by eliminating the requirement of an "accident" under Article 17 and substituting the word "event." Montreal Protocols 3 and 4, opened for signature September 25, 1975, Civ. Av. Org. Doc. Nos. 9147, 9148, 22 I.L.M. 13 (1982) (Protocols and Report of the Senate Committee on Foreign Relations analyzing the Protocols), use "Special Drawing Rights" (SDR) as the unit of compensation for both personal injury or death and property damage. A SDR is an international reserve asset created by the International Monetary Fund (IMF). The value of a SDR is the value of a specified basket of major Western currencies. The IMF reviews the content of the basket every five years. On July 31, 2000, the currencies in the basket were the Euro, Japanese yen, pound sterling, and U.S. dollar. On that date, each SDR was worth $1.31. For the current status of a SDR visit the IMF Web Site: <http://www.imf.org/external/np/exr/facts/sdr.htm>

The Montreal Protocols raise the liability limit for personal injury or death to approximately $130,000, eliminate the possibility of avoiding this limit, but more significantly, permit contracting states to provide a supplementary compensation system to be funded by a surcharge on tickets for international flights. The Montreal Protocols with progressively more generous supplementary compensation systems have been before the United States Senate on several occasions and have even won the support of some personal injury lawyers, but were successfully opposed by others until the U.S. ratified Protocol 4 in 1998. The opponents wish to see the entire Warsaw Convention system consigned to the scrap heap and damages resulting from international air flights subjected to the normal tort regime. As a result, for over 30 years United States passengers continued to be subject to the original Convention alleviated only by the unilateral Montreal Agreement of the airlines, resulting in a liability limit for personal injury or death of $75,000.

In 1995, the airlines agreed to remove liability limits for United States passengers. In October 1995, at the annual meeting of the International Air Transport Association (IATA) in Kuala Lampur, international airlines noted that "[t]he Convention's limits of liability are now grossly inadequate" and agreed "[t]o take action to waive the limitation of liability on recoverable compensatory damages in Article 22 paragraph 1 of the Warsaw Convention as to claims for death, wounding or other bodily injury of a passenger within the meaning of Article 17 of the Convention, so that recoverable compensatory damages may be determined and awarded by reference to the law of the domicile of the passenger." As approved by the United States Department of Transportation on November 26, 1996, the agreement removes the Warsaw Convention limits for damages caused by carrier fault and provides for strict liability in the absence of fault up to 100,000 Special Drawing Rights. The Agreement took effect January 1, 1997. On January 8, 1997 (Order 97-1-2) the U.S. Department of Transportation permitted airlines to substitute the IATA Intercarrier Agreement for the 1966 Montreal Agreement.

In May, 1999, the Contracting States of the International Civil Aviation Organization, meeting in Montreal opened for signature a new convention intended to supersede the Warsaw Convention and the various amendments to that Convention.

CONVENTION FOR THE UNIFICATION OF CERTAIN RULES FOR INTERNATIONAL CARRIAGE BY AIR (MONTREAL CONVENTION)

* * *

Chapter III Liability of the Carrier and Extent of Compensation for Damage

Article 17—Death and Injury of Passengers—Damage to Baggage

1.   The carrier is liable for damage sustained in case of death or bodily injury of a passenger upon condition only that the accident which caused the death or injury took place on board the aircraft or in the course of any of the operations of embarking or disembarking.

2.   The carrier is liable for damage sustained in case of destruction or loss of, or of damage to, checked baggage upon condition only that the event which caused the destruction, loss or damage took place on board the aircraft or during any period within which the checked baggage was in the charge of the carrier. However, the carrier is not liable if and to the extent that the damage resulted from the inherent defect, quality or vice of the baggage. In the case of unchecked baggage, including personal items, the carrier is liable if the damage resulted from its fault or that of its servants or agents.

3.   If the carrier admits the loss of the checked baggage, or if the checked baggage has not arrived at the expiration of twenty-one days after the date on which it ought to

have arrived, the passenger is entitled to enforce against the carrier the rights which flow from the contract of carriage.

4. Unless otherwise specified, in this Convention the term "baggage" means both checked baggage and unchecked baggage.

Article 18—Damage to Cargo

1. The carrier is liable for damage sustained in the event of the destruction or loss of, or damage to, cargo upon condition only that the event which caused the damage so sustained took place during the carriage by air.

2. However, the carrier is not liable if and to the extent it proves that the destruction, or loss of, or damage to, the cargo resulted from one or more of the following:

   (a) inherent defect, quality or vice of that cargo;

   (b) defective packing of that cargo performed by a person other than the carrier or its servants or agents;

   (c) an act of war or an armed conflict;

   (d) an act of public authority carried out in connection with the entry, exit or transit of the cargo.

3. The carriage by air within the meaning of paragraph 1 of this Article comprises the period during which the cargo is in the charge of the carrier.

4. The period of the carriage by air does not extend to any carriage by land, by sea or by inland waterway performed outside an airport. If, however, such carriage takes place in the performance of a contract for carriage by air, for the purpose of loading, delivery or transshipment, any damage is presumed, subject to proof to the contrary, to have been the result of an event which took place during the carriage by air. If a carrier, without the consent of the consignor, substitutes carriage by another mode of transport for the whole or part of a carriage intended by the agreement between the parties to be carriage by air, such carriage by another mode of transport is deemed to be within the period of carriage by air.

Article 19—Delay

The carrier is liable for damage occasioned by delay in the carriage by air of passengers, baggage or cargo. Nevertheless, the carrier shall not be liable for damage occasioned by delay if it proves that it and its servants and agents took all measures that could reasonably be required to avoid the damage or that it was impossible for it or them to take such measures.

Article 20—Exoneration

If the carrier proves that the damage was caused or contributed to by the negligence or other wrongful act or omission of the person claiming compensation, or the person from whom he or she derives his or her rights, the carrier shall be wholly or partly exonerated from its liability to the claimant to the extent that such negligence or wrongful act or omission caused or contributed to the damage. When by reason of death or injury of a passenger compensation is claimed by a person other than the passenger, the carrier shall likewise be wholly or partly exonerated from its liability to the extent that it proves that the damage was caused or contributed to by the negligence or other wrongful act or omission of that passenger. This Article applies to all the liability provisions in this Convention, including paragraph 1 of Article 21.

Article 21—Compensation in Case of Death or Injury of Passengers

1. For damages arising under paragraph 1 of Article 17 not exceeding 100,000 Special Drawing Rights for each passenger, the carrier shall not be able to exclude or limit its liability.

2. The carrier shall not be liable for damages arising under paragraph 1 of Article 17 to the extent that they exceed for each passenger 100,000 Special Drawing Rights if the carrier proves that:

   (a) such damage was not due to the negligence or other wrongful act or omission of the carrier or its servants or agents; or

   (b) such damage was solely due to the negligence or other wrongful act or omission of a third party.

Article 22—Limits of Liability in Relation to Delay, Baggage and Cargo

1. In the case of damage caused by delay as specified in Article 19 in the carriage of persons, the liability of the carrier for each passenger is limited to 4,150 Special Drawing Rights.

2. In the carriage of baggage, the liability of the carrier in the case of destruction, loss, damage or delay is limited to 1,000 Special Drawing Rights for each passenger unless the passenger has made, at the time when the checked baggage was handed over to the carrier, a special declaration of interest in delivery at destination and has paid a supplementary sum if the case so requires. In that case the carrier will be liable to pay a sum not exceeding the declared sum, unless it proves that the sum is greater than the passenger's actual Interest in delivery at destination.

3. In the carriage of cargo, the liability of the carrier in the case of destruction, loss, damage or delay is limited to a sum of 17 Special Drawing Rights per kilogram, unless the consignor has made, at the time when the package was handed over to the carrier, a special declaration of interest in delivery at destination and has paid a supplementary sum if the case so requires. In that case the carrier will be liable to pay a sum not exceeding the declared sum, unless it proves that the sum is greater than the consignor's actual interest in delivery at destination.

* * *

5. The foregoing provisions of paragraphs I and 2 of this Article shall not apply if it is proved that the damage resulted from an act or omission of the carrier, its servants or agents, done with intent to cause damage or recklessly and with knowledge that damage would probably result; provided that, in the case of such act or omission of a servant or agent, it is also proved that such servant or agent was acting within the scope of its employment.

6. The limits prescribed in Article 21 and in this Article shall not prevent the court from awarding, in accordance with its own law, in addition, the whole or part of the court costs and of the other expenses of the litigation incurred by the plaintiff, including interest. The foregoing provision shall not apply if the amount of the damages awarded, excluding court costs and other expenses of the litigation, does not exceed the sum which the carrier has offered in writing to the plaintiff within a period of six months from the date of the occurrence causing the damage, or before the commencement of the action, if that is later.

Article 23—Conversion of Monetary Units

1.   The sums mentioned in terms of Special Drawing Right in this Convention shall be deemed to refer to the Special Drawing Right as defined by the International Monetary Fund. Conversion of the sums into national currencies shall, in case of judicial proceedings, be made according to the value of such currencies in terms of the Special Drawing Right at the date of the judgement. The value of a national currency, in terms of the Special Drawing Right, of a State Party which is a Member of the International Monetary Fund, shall be calculated in accordance with the method of valuation applied by the International Monetary Fund, in effect at the date of the judgement, for its operations and transactions. The value of a national currency, in terms of the Special Drawing Right, of a State Party which is not a Member of the International Monetary Fund, shall be calculated in a manner determined by that State.

* * *

Article 24—Review of Limits

1.   Without prejudice to the provisions of Article 25 of this Convention and subject to paragraph 2 below, the limits of liability prescribed in Articles 21, 22 and 23 shall be reviewed by the Depositary at five-year intervals, the first such review to take place at the end of the fifth year following the date of entry into force of this Convention, or if the Convention does not enter into force within five years of the date it is first open for signature, within the first year of its entry into force, by reference to an inflation factor which corresponds to the accumulated rate of inflation since the previous revision or in the first instance since the date of entry into force of the Convention. The measure of the rate of inflation to be used in determining the inflation factor shall be the weighted average of the annual rates of increase or decrease in the Consumer Price Indices of the States whose currencies comprise the Special Drawing Right mentioned in paragraph 1 of Article 23.

2.   If the review referred to in the preceding paragraph concludes that the inflation factor has exceeded 10 percent, the Depositary shall notify States Parties of a revision of the limits of liability. Any such revision shall become effective six months after its notification to the States Parties. If within three months after its notification to the States Parties a majority of the States Parties register their disapproval, the revision shall not become effective and the Depositary shall refer the matter to a meeting of the States Parties. The Depositary shall immediately notify all States Parties of the coming into force of any revision.

3.   Notwithstanding paragraph 1 of this Article, the procedure referred to in paragraph 2 of this Article shall be applied at any time pr6vided that one-third of the States Parties express a desire to that effect and upon condition that the inflation factor referred to in paragraph 1 has exceeded 30 per cent since the previous revision or since the date of entry into force of this Convention if there has been no previous revision. Subsequent reviews using the procedure described in paragraph 1 of this Article will take place at five-year intervals starting at the end of the fifth year following the date of the reviews under the present paragraph.

Article 25—Stipulation on Limits

A carrier may stipulate that the contract of carriage shall be subject to higher limits of liability than those provided for in this Convention or to no limits of liability whatsoever.

Article 26—Invalidity of Contractual Provisions

Any provision tending to relieve the carrier of liability or to fix a lower limit than that which is laid down in this Convention shall be null and void, but the nullity of any such provision does not involve the nullity of the whole contract, which shall remain subject to the provisions of this Convention.

Article 27—Freedom to Contract

Nothing contained in this Convention shall prevent the carrier from refusing to enter into any contract of carriage, from waiving any defenses available under the Convention, or from laying down conditions which do not conflict with the provisions of this Convention.

Article 28—Advance Payments

In the case of aircraft accidents resulting in death or injury of passengers, the carrier shall, if required by its national law, make advance payments without delay to a natural person or persons who are entitled to claim compensation in order to meet the immediate economic needs of such persons. Such advance payments shall not constitute a recognition of liability and may be offset against any amounts subsequently paid as damages by the carrier.

Article 29—Basis of Claims

In the carriage of passengers, baggage and cargo, any action for damages, however founded, whether under this Convention or in contract or in tort or otherwise, can only be brought subject to the conditions and such limits of liability as are set out in this Convention without prejudice to the question as to who are the persons who have the fight to bring suit and what are their respective rights. In any such action, punitive, exemplary or any other non-compensatory damages shall not be recoverable.

* * *

Article 33—Jurisdiction

1. An action for damages must be brought, at the option of the plaintiff, in the territory of one of the States Parties, either before the court of the domicile of the carrier or of its principal place of business, or where it has a place of business through which the contract has been made or before the court at the place of destination.

2. In respect of damage resulting from the death or injury of a passenger, an action may be brought before one of the courts mentioned in paragraph 1 of this Article, or in the territory of a State Party in which at the time of the accident the passenger has his or her principal and permanent residence and to or from which the carrier operates services for the carriage of passengers by air, either on its own aircraft, or on another carrier's aircraft pursuant to a commercial agreement, and in which that carrier conducts its business of carriage of passengers by air from premises leased or owned by the carrier itself or by another carrier with which it has a commercial agreement.

3. For the purposes of paragraph 2,
    (a) "commercial agreement" means an agreement, other than an agency agreement, made between carriers and relating to the provision of their joint services for carriage of passengers by air;

(b) "principal and permanent residence" means the one fixed and permanent abode of the passenger at the time of the accident. The nationality of the passenger shall not be the determining factor in this regard.

4. Questions of procedure shall be governed by the law of the court seized of the case.

Article 34—Arbitration

1. Subject to the provisions of this Article, the parties to the contract of carriage for cargo may stipulate that any dispute relating to the liability of the carrier under this Convention shall be settled by arbitration. Such agreement shall be in writing.

2. The arbitration proceedings shall, at the option of the claimant, take place within one of the jurisdictions referred to in Article 33.

3. The arbitrator or arbitration tribunal shall apply the provisions of this Convention.

4. The provisions of paragraphs 2 and 3 of this Article shall be deemed to be part of every arbitration clause or agreement, and any term of such clause or agreement which is inconsistent therewith shall be null and void.

Article 35—Limitation of Actions

1. The right to damages shall be extinguished if an action is not brought within a period of two years, reckoned from the date of arrival at the destination, or from the date on which the aircraft ought to have arrived, or from the date on which the carriage stopped.

2. The method of calculating that period shall be determined by the law of the court seized of the case.

Article 36—Successive Carriage

1. In the case of carriage to be performed by various successive carriers and falling within the definition set out in paragraph 3 of Article 1, each carrier which accepts passengers, baggage or cargo is subject to the rules set out in this Convention and is deemed to be one of the parties to the contract of carriage in so far as the contract deals with that part of the carriage which is performed under its supervision.

2. In the case of carriage of this nature, the passenger or any person entitled to compensation in respect of him or her can take action only against the carrier which performed the carriage during which the accident or the delay occurred, save in the case where, by express agreement, the first carrier has assumed liability for the whole journey.

3. As regards baggage or cargo, the passenger or consignor will have a right of action against the first carrier, and the passenger or consignee who is entitled to delivery will have a right of action against the last carrier, and further, each may take action against the carrier which performed the carriage during which the destruction, loss, damage or delay took place. These carriers will be jointly and severally liable to the passenger or to the consignor or consignee.

Article 37—Right of Recourse against Third Parties

Nothing in this Convention shall prejudice the question whether a person liable for damage in accordance with its provisions has a right of recourse against any other person.

* * *

Chapter VI Other Provisions

Article 49—Mandatory Application

Any clause contained in the contract of carriage and all special agreements entered into before the damage occurred by which the parties purport to infringe the rules laid down by this Convention, whether by deciding the law to be applied, or by altering the rules as to jurisdiction, shall be null and void.

Article 50—Insurance

States Parties shall require their carriers to maintain adequate insurance covering their liability under this Convention. A carrier may be required by the State Party into which it operates to furnish evidence that it maintains adequate insurance covering its liability under this Convention.

* * *

Final Clauses

Article 53—Signature, Ratification and Entry into Force

1. This Convention shall be open for signature in Montreal on 28 May 1999 by States participating in the International Conference on Air Law held at Montreal from 10 to 28 May 1999. After 28 May 1999, the Convention shall be open to all States for signature at the Headquarters of the International Civil Aviation Organization in Montreal until it enters into force in accordance with paragraph 6 of this Article.

2. This Convention shall similarly be open for signature by Regional Economic Integration Organizations. For the purpose of this Convention, a "Regional Economic Integration Organization" means any organization which is constituted by sovereign States of a given region which has competence in respect of certain matters governed by this Convention and has been duly authorized to sign and to ratify, accept, approve or accede to this Convention. * * *

6. This Convention shall enter into force on the sixtieth day following the date of deposit of the thirtieth instrument of ratification, acceptance, approval or accession with the Depositary between the States which have deposited such instrument. An instrument deposited by a Regional Economic Integration Organization shall not be counted for the purpose of this paragraph.

* * *

Article 55—Relationship with other Warsaw Convention Instruments

This Convention shall prevail over any rules which apply to international carriage by air [under the Warsaw Convention as amended by any of its protocols].

Note

On September 6, 2000, President Clinton transmitted the Montreal Convention to the Senate with his recommendation that the Senate give the Convention "early and favorable consideration... and that the Senate give its advice and consent to ratification." The Senate's presiding officer referred the Convention to the Committee on Foreign Relations.

The Montreal Convention removes limits on compensation for personal injury and death. Article 21 creates a two-tier system for compensation in the case of death or injury. The carrier is liable without fault up to 100,000 Special Drawing Rights. The carrier is liable for compensatory damages in an additional amount without limit unless the carrier can prove that the carrier's fault did not cause the harm. Article 29 preempts all other causes of action against a carrier and excludes recovery of punitive damages.

On October 17, 1998, a European Union Council Regulation on air carrier liability went into force. Council Regulation 2027/97 of Oct. 1997, O.J. (L285) 1. Like the Montreal Convention, the Regulation creates a two-tier system of absolute liability up to SDR 100,000 and presumed liability over this amount unless the carrier can prove that it was without fault.

Before the 1995 IATA Intercarrier Agreement removed monetary limits on recovery for personal injury and death, basic plaintiff strategy was to avoid the Convention's limits by invoking the intentional or reckless injury exception in Article 25** or by suing third parties not covered by the Convention, such as airplane manufacturers and governments vicariously liable for the negligence of air traffic controllers. Under the IATA agreement, and, if ratified, the Montreal Convention, these tactics will be of less importance. A reason for seeking recovery not controlled by Warsaw, IATA, or Montreal is that Article 29 of the Montreal Convention continues the exclusion of punitive damages that exists under the Warsaw Convention. See In Re Korean Air Lines Disaster of September 1, 1983, 932 F.2d 1475 (D.C. Cir.), cert. denied, 502 U.S. 994 (1991) (holding that a carrier guilty of "willful misconduct" is not liable for punitive damages). With the removal of limits on compensatory damages, plaintiffs will sometimes seek to bring their claims under the Warsaw or Montreal conventions when the carrier was not a fault and there is no other route to recovery. For example, Husserl v. Swiss Air Transport Co., 351 F. Supp. 7802 (S.D.N.Y. 1972), aff'd w.o. opinion, 485 F.2d 1240 (2d Cir. 1973), held that the 1966 Montreal Agreement eliminated the carrier's due care defense under Warsaw article 20(1) and permitted recovery for injuries suffered when members of the Popular Front for the Liberation of Palestine hijacked an airplane. The Montreal Convention continues this no fault recovery up to 100,000 Special Drawing Rights under article 21(1).

The most important issues under the IATA agreement and the Montreal Convention will be the meanings of "accident" (Warsaw and Montreal article 17) and "injury" (id.). Other issues are the meanings of "embarking" and "disembarking" (id.) and the extent to which the Warsaw or Montreal conventions preempt other causes of action.

** Before its amendment by Montreal Protocol Number 4, the Article 25 exception referred to "willful misconduct." Protocol 4 had the effect of unifying the definition of "willful misconduct." Under the Warsaw Convention, the "the law of the court to which the case is submitted" determined whether the carrier's fault amounted to willful misconduct.

Section 2: Defining Convention Terms and Determining Preemption

Air France v. Saks
470 U.S. 392 (1985)

Justice O'Connor delivered the opinion of the Court.

Article 17 of the Warsaw Convention makes air carriers liable for injuries sustained by a passenger "if the accident which caused the damage so sustained took place on board the aircraft or in the course of any of the operations of embarking or disembarking." We granted certiorari to resolve a conflict among the Courts of Appeals as to the proper definition of the word "accident" as used in this international air carriage treaty.

I

On November 16, 1980, respondent Valerie Saks boarded an Air France jetliner in Paris for a 12-hour flight to Los Angeles. The flight went smoothly in all respects until, as the aircraft descended to Los Angeles, Saks felt severe pressure and pain in her left ear. The pain continued after the plane landed, but Saks disembarked without informing any Air France crew member or employee of her ailment. Five days later, Saks consulted a doctor who concluded that she had become permanently deaf in her left ear.

Saks filed suit against Air France in California state court, alleging that her hearing loss was caused by negligent maintenance and operation of the jetliner's pressurization system. The case was removed to the United States District Court for the Central District of California. After extensive discovery, Air France moved for summary judgment on the ground that respondent could not prove that her injury was caused by an "accident" within the meaning of the Warsaw Convention. The term "accident," according to Air France, means an "abnormal, unusual or unexpected occurrence aboard the aircraft." All the available evidence, including the postflight reports, pilot's affidavit, and passenger testimony, indicated that the aircraft's pressurization system had operated in the usual manner. Accordingly, the airline contended that the suit should be dismissed because the only alleged cause of respondent's injury-normal operation of a pressurization system-could not qualify as an "accident." In her opposition to the summary judgment motion, Saks acknowledged that "[t]he sole question of law presented...by the parties is whether a loss of hearing proximately caused by normal operation of the aircraft's pressurization system is an 'accident' within the meaning of Article 17 of the Warsaw Convention..." She argued that "accident" should be defined as a "hazard of air travel," and that her injury had indeed been caused by such a hazard.

Relying on precedent which defines the term "accident" in Article 17 as an "unusual or unexpected" happening, see *DeMarines v. KLM Royal Dutch Airlines*, 580 F.2d 1193, 1196 (CA3 1978), the District Court granted summary judgment to Air France. See also *Warshaw v. Trans World Airlines, Inc.*, 442 F.Supp. 400, 412-413 (ED Pa.1977) (normal cabin pressure changes are not "accidents" within the meaning of Article 17). A divided panel of the Court of Appeals for the Ninth Circuit reversed. 724 F.2d 1383 (1984). The appellate court reviewed the history of the Warsaw Convention and its modification by the 1966 Montreal Agreement, a private agreement among airlines that has been approved by the United States Government. The court concluded that the language, history, and policy of the Warsaw Convention and the Montreal Agreement impose absolute liability on airlines for injuries proximately caused by the risks inherent in air travel. The court found a definition of "accident" consistent with this history and policy in Annex 13 to the Convention on International Civil Aviation, Dec. 7, 1944, 61 Stat. 1180, T.I.A.S. No. 1591, 15 U.N.T.S. 295; conformed to in 49 CFR § 830.2 (1984): "an occurrence associated with the operation of an aircraft which takes place between the time any person boards the aircraft with the intention of flight and all such persons have disembarked..." 724 F.2d, at 1385. Normal cabin pressure changes qualify as an "accident" under this definition. A dissent agreed with the District Court that "accident" should be defined as an unusual or unexpected occurrence. Id., at 1388 (Wallace, J.). We disagree with the definition of "accident" adopted by the Court of Appeals, and we reverse.

II

Air France is liable to a passenger under the terms of the Warsaw Convention only if the passenger proves that an "accident" was the cause of her injury. The narrow issue presented is whether respondent can meet this burden by showing that her injury was caused by the normal operation of the aircraft's pressurization system. The proper answer turns on interpretation of a clause in an international treaty to which the United States is a party.

* * *

A

Article 17 of the Warsaw Convention establishes the liability of international air carriers for harm to passengers. Article 18 contains parallel provisions regarding liability for damage to baggage. The governing text of the Convention is in the French language * * *. The official American translation of this portion of the text, which was before the Senate when it ratified the Convention in 1934, reads as follows:

"Article 17

"The carrier shall be liable for damage sustained in the event of the death or wounding of a passenger or any other bodily injury suffered by a passenger, if the accident which caused the damage [lorsque l'accident qui a causé le dommage] so sustained took place on board the aircraft or in the course of any of the operations of embarking or disembarking.

"Article 18

"(1) The carrier shall be liable for damage sustained in the event of the destruction or loss of, or of damage to, any checked baggage or any goods, *if the occurrence which caused the damage* [lorsque l'événement qui a causé le dommage] so sustained took place during the transportation by air." 49 Stat. 3018-3019.

Two significant features of these provisions stand out in both the French and the English texts. First, Article 17 imposes liability for injuries to passengers caused by an "accident," whereas Article 18 imposes liability for destruction or loss of baggage caused by an "occurrence." This difference in the parallel language of Articles 17 and 18 implies that the drafters of the Convention understood the word "accident" to mean something different than the word "occurrence," for they otherwise logically would have used the same word in each article. The language of the Convention accordingly renders suspect the opinion of the Court of Appeals that "accident" means "occurrence."

Second, the text of Article 17 refers to an accident which caused the passenger's injury, and not to an accident which is the passenger's injury. In light of the many senses in which the word "accident" can be used, this distinction is significant. As Lord Lindley observed in 1903: "The word 'accident' is not a technical legal term with a clearly defined meaning. Speaking generally, but with reference to legal liabilities, an accident means any unintended and unexpected occurrence which produces hurt or loss. But it is often used to denote any unintended and unexpected loss or hurt apart from its cause; and if the cause is not known the loss or hurt itself would certainly be called an accident. The word 'accident' is also often used to denote both the cause and the effect, no attempt being made to discriminate between them." *Fenton v. J. Thorley & Co.*, [1903] A.C. 443, 453.

In Article 17, the drafters of the Warsaw Convention apparently did make an attempt to discriminate between "the cause and the effect"; they specified that air carriers would be liable if an accident caused the passenger's injury. The text of the Convention thus implies that, however we define "accident," it is the cause of the injury that must satisfy the definition rather than the occurrence of the injury alone. American jurisprudence has long recognized this distinction between an accident that is the cause of an injury and an injury that is itself an accident. See *Landress v. Phoenix Mutual Life Ins. Co.*, 291 U.S. 491 (1934).

While the text of the Convention gives these two clues to the meaning of "accident," it does not define the term. Nor is the context in which the term is used illuminating. To determine the meaning of the term "accident" in Article 17 we must consider its French legal meaning. This is true not because "we are forever chained to French law" by the Convention, see *Rosman v. Trans World Airlines, Inc.*, 34 N.Y.2d 385, 394, 358 N.Y.S.2d 97, 102, 314 N.E.2d 848, 853 (1974), but because it is our responsibility to give the specific words of the treaty a meaning consistent with the shared expectations of the contracting parties. We look to the French legal meaning for guidance as to these expectations because the Warsaw Convention was drafted in French by continental jurists.

A survey of French cases and dictionaries indicates that the French legal meaning of the term "accident" differs little from the meaning of the term in Great Britain, Germany, or the United States. Thus, while the word "accident" is often used to refer to the event of a person's injury, it is also sometimes used to describe a cause of injury, and when the word is used in this latter sense, it is usually defined as a fortuitous, unexpected, unusual, or unintended event. See 1 Grand Larousse de La Langue Francaise 29 (1971) (defining "accident" as "Evénement fortuit et fâcheux, causant des dommages corporels ou matériels"); *Air France v. Haddad*, Judgment of June 19, 1979, Cour d'appel de Paris, Premiere Chambre Civile, 1979 Revue Francaise de Droit Aerien 327, 328, appeal rejected, Judgment of February 16, 1982, Cour de Cassation, 1982 Bull.Civ. I 63. This parallels British and American jurisprudence. The text of the Convention consequently suggests that the passenger's injury must be caused by an unexpected or unusual event.

B

This interpretation of Article 17 is consistent with the negotiating history of the Convention, the conduct of the parties to the Convention, and the weight of precedent in foreign and American courts. In interpreting a treaty it is proper, of course, to refer to the records of its drafting and negotiation. In part because the "travaux preparatoires" of the Warsaw Convention are published and generally available to litigants, courts frequently refer to these materials to resolve ambiguities in the text.

The treaty that became the Warsaw Convention was first drafted at an international conference in Paris in 1925. The protocol resulting from the Parish Conference contained an article specifying: "The carrier is liable for accidents, losses, breakdowns, and delays. It is not liable if it can prove that it has taken reasonable measures designed to pre-empt damage..." The protocol drafted at Paris was revised several times by a committee of experts on air law, and then submitted to a second international conference that convened in Warsaw in 1929. The draft submitted to the conference stated:

The carrier shall be liable for damage sustained during carriage:

(a) in the case of death, wounding, or any other bodily injury suffered by a traveler;

(b) in the case of destruction, loss, or damage to goods or baggage;

(c) in the case of delay suffered by a traveler, goods, or baggage.

International Conference on Air Law Affecting Air Questions, Minutes, Second International Conference on Private Aeronautical Law, October 4-12, 1929, Warsaw 264-265 (R. Horner & D. Legrez trans. 1975).

Article 22 of this draft, like the original Paris draft, permitted the carrier to avoid liability by proving it had taken reasonable measures to avoid the damage. Id., at 265. None of the early drafts required that an accident cause the passenger's injury.

At Warsaw, delegates from several nations objected to the application of identical liability rules to both passenger injuries and damage to baggage, and the German delegation proposed separate liability rules for passengers and baggage. Id., at 36. The need for separate rules arose primarily because delegates thought that liability for baggage should commence upon delivery to the carrier, whereas liability for passengers should commence when the passengers later embark upon the aircraft. Id., at 72-74 (statements of French, Swiss, and Italian delegates). The Reporter on the Preliminary Draft of the Convention argued it would be too difficult to draft language specifying this distinction, and that such a distinction would be unnecessary because "Article 22 establishes a very mitigated system of liability for the carrier, and from the moment that the carrier has taken the reasonable measures, he does not answer for the risks, nor for the accidents occur[r]ing to people by the fault of third parties, nor for accidents occur[r]ing for any other cause." Id., at 77-78 (statement of Reporter De Vos). The delegates were unpersuaded, and a majority voted to have a drafting committee rework the liability provisions for passengers and baggage. Id., at 83.

A few days later, the drafting committee proposed the liability provisions that became Articles 17 and 18 of the Convention. Article 20(1) of the final draft contains the "necessary measures" language which the Reporter believed would shield the carrier from liability for "the accidents occur[r]ing to people by the fault of third parties" and for "accidents occur[r]ing for any other cause." Nevertheless, the redrafted Article 17 also required as a prerequisite to liability that an accident cause the passenger's injury, whereas the redrafted Article 18 required only that an occurrence cause the damage to baggage. Although Article 17 and Article 18 as redrafted were approved with little discussion, the President of the drafting committee observed that "given that there are *entirely different* liability cases: death or wounding, disappearance of goods, delay, we have deemed that it would be better to begin by setting out *the causes* of liability for persons, then for goods and baggage, and finally liability in the case of delay." Id., at 205 (statement of Delegate Giannini) (emphasis added). This comment at least implies that the addition of language of causation to Articles 17 and 18 had a broader purpose than specification of the time at which liability commenced. It further suggests that the causes of liability for persons were intended to be different from the causes of liability for baggage. The records of the negotiation of the Convention accordingly support what is evident from its text: A passenger's injury must be caused by an accident, and an accident must mean something different than an "occurrence" on the plane. Like the text of the Convention, however, the records of its negotiation offer no precise definition of "accident."

Reference to the conduct of the parties to the Convention and the subsequent interpretations of the signatories helps clarify the meaning of the term. At a Guatemala City International Conference on Air Law in 1971, representatives of many of the Warsaw signatories approved an amendment to Article 17 which would impose liability on the carrier for an "event which caused the death or injury" rather than for an "accident which caused" the passenger's injury, but would exempt the carrier from liability if the death or injury resulted "solely from the state of health of the passenger." The Guatemala City Protocol of 1971 and the Montreal Protocols Nos. 3 and 4 of 1975 include this amendment, but have yet to be ratified by the Senate, and therefore do not govern the disposition of this case. The statements of the delegates at Guatemala City indicate that they viewed the switch from "accident" to "event" as expanding the scope of carrier liability to passengers. The Swedish Delegate, for example, in referring to the choice between the words "accident" and "event," emphasized that the word "accident" is too narrow because a carrier might be found liable for "other acts which could not be considered as accidents." See International Civil Aviation Organization, 1 Minutes of the International Conference on Air Law, ICAO Doc. 9040-LC/167-1, p. 34 (1972). See also Mankiewicz, Warsaw Convention: The 1971 Protocol of Guatemala City, 20 Am.J.Comp.L. 335, 337 (1972) (noting that changes in Article 17 were intended to establish "strict liability").

In determining precisely what causes can be considered accidents, we "find the opinions of our sister signatories to be entitled to considerable weight." *Benjamins v. British European Airways*, 572 F.2d 913, 919 (CA2 1978), cert. denied, 439 U.S. 1114 (1979). While few decisions are precisely on point, we note that, in *Air France v. Haddad*, Judgment of June 19, 1979, Cour d'appel de Paris, Premiere Chambre Civile, 1979 Revue Francaise de Droit Aerien, at 328, a French court observed that the term "accident" in Article 17 of the Warsaw Convention embraces causes of injuries that are fortuitous or unpredictable. European legal scholars have generally construed the word "accident" in Article 17 to require that the passenger's injury be caused by a sudden or unexpected event other than the normal operation of the plane. See, e.g., O. Riese & J. Lacour, Precis de Droit Aerien 264 (1951) (noting that Swiss and German law require that the damage be caused by an accident, and arguing that an accident should be construed as an event which is sudden and independent of the will of the carrier); 1 C. Shawcross & K. Beaumont, Air Law P VII(148) (4th ed. 1984) (noting that the Court of Appeals for the Third Circuit's definition of accident accords with some English definitions and "might well commend itself to an English court"). These observations are in accord with American decisions which, while interpreting the term "accident" broadly nevertheless refuse to extend the term to cover routine travel procedures that produce an injury due to the peculiar internal condition of a passenger. See, e.g. *Abramson v. Japan Airlines Co.*, 739 F.2d 130 (CA3 1984) (sitting in airline seat during normal flight which aggravated hernia not an "accident"), cert. pending, No. 84-939 [cert. denied, 470 U.S. 1059 (1985)]; *MacDonald v. Air Canada*, 439 F.2d 1402 (CA5 1971) (fainting while waiting in the terminal for one's baggage not shown to be caused by an "accident"); *Scherer v. Pan Amer-*

ican World Airways, Inc., 54 App.Div.2d 636, 387 N.Y.S.2d 580 (1976) (sitting in airline seat during normal flight which aggravated thrombophlebitis not an "accident").

III

We conclude that liability under Article 17 of the Warsaw Convention arises only if a passenger's injury is caused by an unexpected or unusual event or happening that is external to the passenger. This definition should be flexibly applied after assessment of all the circumstances surrounding a passenger's injuries. For example, lower courts in this country have interpreted Article 17 broadly enough to encompass torts committed by terrorists or fellow passengers. In cases where there is contradictory evidence, it is for the trier of fact to decide whether an "accident" as here defined caused the passenger's injury. See *DeMarines v. KLM Royal Dutch Airlines*, 580 F.2d 1193 (CA3 1978) (contradictory evidence on whether pressurization was normal). See also *Weintraub v. Capital International Airways, Inc.*, 16 CCH Av.Cas. 18,058 (N.Y.Sup.Ct., 1st Dept., 1981) (plaintiff's testimony that "sudden dive" led to pressure change causing hearing loss indicates injury was caused by an "accident"). But when the injury indisputably results from the passenger's own internal reaction to the usual, normal, and expected operation of the aircraft, it has not been caused by an accident, and Article 17 of the Warsaw Convention cannot apply. The judgment of the Court of Appeals in this case must accordingly be reversed.

* * *

Our duty to enforce the "accident" requirement of Article 17 cannot be circumvented by reference to the Montreal Agreement of 1966. It is true that in most American cases the Montreal Agreement expands carrier liability by requiring airlines to waive their right under Article 20(1) of the Warsaw Convention to defend claims on the grounds that they took all necessary measures to avoid the passenger's injury or that it was impossible to take such measures. Because these "due care" defenses are waived by the Montreal Agreement, the Court of Appeals and some commentators have characterized the Agreement as imposing "absolute" liability on air carriers. As this case demonstrates, the characterization is not entirely accurate.

* * *

Finally, respondent suggests an independent ground supporting the Court of Appeals' reversal of the summary judgment against her. She argues that her original complaint alleged a state cause of action for negligence independent of the liability provisions of the Warsaw Convention, and that her state negligence action can go forward if the Warsaw liability rules do not apply. Expressing no view on the merits of this contention, we note that it is unclear from the record whether the issue was raised in the Court of Appeals. We leave the disposition of this claim to the Court of Appeals in the first instance.

The judgment of the Court of Appeals is reversed, and the case is remanded for further proceedings consistent with this opinion.

It is so ordered.

Justice Powell took no part in the consideration or decision of this case.

Note

Other cases continue to struggle with the meaning of "accident." Krys v. Lufthansa German Airlines, 119 F.3d 1515 (11th Cir. 1997), cert denied, 522 U.S. 1111 (1998), held that aggravation of injury to a passenger's heart during flight by the crew's negligent failure to make an unscheduled landing for medical treatment of a heart attack was not an "accident." The court reasoned: "Having provided for a defense turning on the absence of negligence [Warsaw Convention article 20(1)], we think it unlikely that the drafters intended that the initial 'accident' inquiry be resolved by reference to negligence.... [L]ooking solely to the factual description of the aggravating event in this case—i.e., the continuation of the flight to its scheduled point of arrival—compels a conclusion that the aggravation injury was not caused by an 'unusual or unexpected event or happening that is external to the [plaintiff].'" Id. at 1522 (quoting from Air France v. Saks, 470 U.S. 392, 405 1985)). The court affirmed damages awards under Florida law for the passenger and his wife in amounts exceeding Convention limits and held that Lufthansa had waived its arguments that Florida law was pre-empted by the Convention or by maritime law because these arguments were not timely asserted.

Fishman v. Delta Air Line, Inc., 132 F.3d 138 (2d Cir. 1998), held that a stewardess' negligent application of a scalding compress to a passenger was an "accident" that resulted in injury covered by the Warsaw Convention and that the passenger's and her mother's state-law claims were pre-empted by the Convention.

Wallace v. Korean Air, 214 F.3d 293 (2d Cir. 2000), held that a sexual assault by a fellow passenger was an "accident" because "the characteristics of air travel increased [the victim's] vulnerability to [the] assault." The court found it unnecessary to decide whether it was necessary for the risk to be characteristic of air travel or "whether all co-passenger torts are necessarily accidents for purposes of the Convention." Id. at 299

El Al Israel Airlines v. Tseng, 525 U.S. 155 (1999), infra page 457, answered the pre-emption question left open in the last paragraph of the principal case. The Court held that the Warsaw Convention preempts all causes of action for claims arising from on board an international flight or in the course of embarking or disembarking. The Court noted that it was assuming that the circumstances did not amount to an "accident" only because the parties so stipulated and stated that this stipulation was "questionable." The Court indicated that courts should apply the definition of "accident" set out in Air France v. Saks "flexibly." Do the cases noted in the preceding paragraphs of this note properly determine the meaning of "accident."

Eastern Airlines, Inc. v. Floyd.
499 U.S. 530 (1991)

Justice MARSHALL delivered the opinion of the Court.

Article 17 of the Warsaw Convention sets forth conditions under which an international air carrier can be held liable for injuries to passengers. This case presents the question whether Article 17 allows recovery for mental or psychic injuries unaccompanied by physical injury or physical manifestation of injury.

I

On May 5, 1983, an Eastern Airlines flight departed from Miami, bound for the Bahamas. Shortly after takeoff, one of the plane's three jet engines lost oil pressure. The flight crew shut down the failing engine and turned the plane around to return to Miami. Soon thereafter, the second and third engines failed due to loss of oil pressure. The plane began losing altitude rapidly, and the passengers were informed that the plane would be ditched in the Atlantic Ocean. Fortunately, after a period of descending flight without power, the crew managed to restart an engine and land the plane safely at Miami International Airport. Respondents, a group of passengers on the flight, brought separate complaints against petitioner, Eastern Airlines, Inc. (Eastern), each claiming damages solely for mental distress arising out of the incident. [The District Court held that mental anguish alone is not compensable under Article 17. The 11th Circuit reversed holding that Article 17 permits recovery for emotional distress. The Supreme Court reversed, holding "that Article 17 does not allow recovery for purely mental injuries."]

II

* * *

A

Because the only authentic text of the Warsaw Convention is in French, the French text must guide our analysis. The text reads as follows:

> Le transporteur est responsable du dommage survenu *en cas de mort, de blessure ou de toute autre lesion corporelle* subie par un voyageur lorsque l'accident qui a cause le dommage s'est produit a bord de l'aeronef ou au cours de toutes operations d'embarquement et de debarquement. 49 Stat. 3005 (emphasis added).

The American translation of this text, employed by the Senate when it ratified the Convention in 1934, reads:

> The carrier shall be liable for damage sustained *in the event of the death or wounding of a passenger or any other bodily injury* suffered by a passenger, if the accident which caused the damage so sustained took place on board the aircraft or in the course of any of the operations of embarking or disembarking. 49 Stat. 3018 (emphasis added).

Thus, under Article 17, an air carrier is liable for passenger injury only when three conditions are satisfied: (1) there has been an accident, in which (2) the passenger suffered "mort," "blessure," "ou...toute autre lesion corporelle," and (3) the accident took place on board the aircraft or in the course of operations of embarking or disembarking. As petitioner concedes, the incident here took place on board the aircraft and was an "accident" for purposes of Article 17. Moreover, respondents concede that they suffered neither "mort" nor "blessure" from the mishap. Therefore, the narrow issue presented here is whether, under the proper interpretation of "lesion corporelle," condition (2) is satisfied when a passenger has suffered only a mental or psychic injury.

We must consider the "French legal meaning" of "lesion corporelle" for guidance as to the shared expectations of the parties to the Convention because the Convention was drafted in French by continental jurists. Perhaps the simplest method of determining the meaning of a phrase appearing in a foreign legal text would be to consult a bilingual dictionary. Such dictionaries suggest that a proper translation of "lesion corporelle" is "bodily injury." These translations, if correct, clearly suggest that Article 17 does not permit recovery for purely psychic injuries. Although we have previously relied on such French dictionaries as a primary method for defining terms in the Warsaw Convention, we recognize that dictionary definitions may be too general for purposes of treaty interpretation. Our concerns are partly allayed when, as here, the dictionary translation accords with the wording used in the "two main translations of the 1929 Convention in English." Mankiewicz, [The Liability Regime of the International Air Carrier] 197 [1981]. As we noted earlier, the translation used by the United States Senate when ratifying the Warsaw Convention equated "lesion corporelle" with "bodily injury." The same wording appears in the translation used in the United Kingdom Carriage by Air Act of 1932. We turn, then, to French legal materials, to determine whether French jurists' contemporary understanding of the term "lesion corporelle" differed from its translated meaning.

In 1929, as in the present day, lawyers trained in French civil law would rely on the following principal sources of French law: Our review of these materials indicates neither that "lesion corporelle" was a widely used legal term in French law nor that the term specifically encompassed psychic injuries. * * *

Subsequent to the adoption of the Warsaw Convention, some scholars have argued that "lesion corporelle" as used in Article 17 should be interpreted to encompass such injury. These scholars draw on the fact that, by 1929, France—unlike many other countries, permitted tort recovery for mental distress. However, this general proposition of French tort law does not demonstrate that the specific phrase chosen by the contracting parties—"lesion corporelle"—covers purely psychic injury.

We find it noteworthy, moreover, that scholars who read "lesion corporelle" as encompassing psychic injury do not base their argument on explanations of this term in French cases or French treatises or even in the French Civil Code; rather, they chiefly rely on the principle of French tort law that any damage can "giv[e] rise to reparation when it is real and has been verified." We do not dispute this principle of French law. However, we have been directed to no French case prior to 1929 that allowed recovery based on that principle for the type of mental injury claimed here—injury caused by fright or shock— absent an incident in which someone sustained physical injury. Since our task is to "give the specific words of the treaty a meaning consistent with the shared expectations of the contracting parties," *Saks*, 470 U.S., at 399, we find it unlikely that those parties' apparent understanding of the term "lesion corporelle" as "bodily injury" would have been displaced by a meaning abstracted from the French law of damages. Particularly is this so when the cause of action for psychic injury that evidently was possible under French law in 1929 would not have been recognized in many other countries represented at the Warsaw Convention.

Nor is this conclusion altered by our examination of Article 17's structure. In the decision below, the Court of Appeals found that the Article's wording "suggests that the drafters did not intend to exclude any particular category of damages," because if they had intended "to refer only to injury caused by physical impact," they "would not have singled out and specifically referred to a particular case of physical impact such as blessure ('wounding')." This argument, which has much the same force as the surplusage canon of domestic statutory construction, is plausible. * * * However, because none of the other sources of French legal meaning noted above support the Court of Appeals' construction, we are reluctant to give this argument dispositive weight. * * *

In sum, neither the Warsaw Convention itself nor any of the applicable French legal sources demonstrates that "lesion corporelle" should be translated other than as "bodily injury"—a narrow meaning excluding purely mental injuries. However, because a broader interpretation of "lesion corporelle" reaching purely mental injuries is plausible, and the term is both ambiguous and difficult, we turn to additional aids to construction.

B

Translating "lesion corporelle" as "bodily injury" is consistent, we think, with the negotiating history of the Convention. * * *

Our review of the documentary record for the Warsaw Conference confirms— and courts and commentators appear universally to agree—that there is no evidence that the drafters or signatories of the Warsaw Convention specifically considered liability for psychic injury or the meaning of "lesion corporelle." Two explanations commonly are offered for why the subject of mental injuries never arose during the Convention proceedings: (1) many jurisdictions did not recognize recovery for mental injury at that time, or (2) the drafters simply could not contemplate a psychic injury unaccompanied by a physical injury. Indeed, the unavailability of compensation for purely psychic injury in many common and civil law countries at the time of the Warsaw Conference persuades us that the signatories had no specific intent to include such a remedy in the Convention. Because such a remedy was unknown in many, if not most, jurisdictions in 1929, the drafters most likely would have felt compelled to make an unequivocal reference to purely mental injury if they had specifically intended to allow such recovery.

In this sense, we find it significant that, when the parties to a different international transport treaty wanted to make it clear that rail passengers could recover for purely psychic harms, the drafters made a specific modification to this effect. The liability provision of the Berne Convention on International Rail, drafted in 1952, originally conditioned liability on "la mort, les blessures et toute autre atteinte, a l'integrite corporelle." The drafters subsequently modified this provision to read "l'integrite physique ou mentale."

The narrower reading of "lesion corporelle" also is consistent with the primary purpose of the contracting parties to the Convention: limiting the liability of air carriers in order to foster the growth of the fledgling commercial aviation industry. * * *

C

We also conclude that, on balance, the evidence of the post-1929 "conduct" and "interpretations of the signatories," Saks, 470 U.S. at 403, supports the narrow translation of "lesion corporelle." * * * In 1951, a committee composed of 20 Warsaw Convention signatories met in Madrid and adopted a proposal to substitute "affection corporelle" for "lesion corporelle" in Article 17. Although the committee's proposed amendment was never subsequently implemented, its discussion and vote in Madrid suggest that, in the view of the 20 signatories on the committee, "lesion corporelle" in Article 17 had a distinctly physical scope. * * *

We must also consult the opinions of our sister signatories in searching for the meaning of a "lesion corporelle." The only apparent judicial decision from a sister signatory addressing recovery for purely mental injuries under Article 17 is that of the Supreme Court of Israel. That court held that Article 17 does allow recovery for purely psychic injuries. See Cie Air France v. Teichner, 39 Revue Francaise de Droit Aerien, at 243, 23 Eur.Tr.L., at 102.[14]

Teichner arose from the hijacking in 1976 of an Air France flight to Entebbe, Uganda. Passengers sought compensation for psychic injuries caused by the ordeal of the hijacking and detention at the Entebbe Airport. While acknowledging that the negotiating history of the Warsaw Convention was silent as to the availability of such compensation, the court determined that "desirable jurisprudential policy" favored an expansive reading of Article 17 to reach purely psychic injuries. In reaching this conclusion, the court emphasized the post-1929 development of the aviation industry and the evolution of

---

14. In the only published versions that we could find, the Israeli opinion is reported in French.

Anglo-American and Israeli law to allow recovery for psychic injury in certain circumstances. * * *

Although we recognize the deference owed to the Israeli court's interpretation of Article 17, we are not persuaded by that court's reasoning. Even if we were to agree that allowing recovery for purely psychic injury is desirable as a policy goal, we cannot give effect to such policy without convincing evidence that the signatories' intent with respect to Article 17 would allow such recovery. As discussed, neither the language, negotiating history, nor postenactment interpretations of Article 17 clearly evidences such intent. * * *

Moreover, we believe our construction of Article 17 better accords with the Warsaw Convention's stated purpose of achieving uniformity of rules governing claims arising from international air transportation. As noted, the Montreal Agreement subjects international carriers to strict liability for Article 17 injuries sustained on flights connected with the United States. * * * We have no doubt that subjecting international air carriers to strict liability for purely mental distress would be controversial for most signatory countries. Our construction avoids this potential source of divergence.

III

We conclude that an air carrier cannot be held liable under Article 17 when an accident has not caused a passenger to suffer death, physical injury, or physical manifestation of injury. Although Article 17 renders air carriers liable for "damage sustained in the event of" ("dommage survenu en cas de") such injuries, we express no view as to whether passengers can recover for mental injuries that are accompanied by physical injuries. That issue is not presented here because respondents do not allege physical injury or physical manifestation of injury. Eastern urges us to hold that the Warsaw Convention provides the exclusive cause of action for injuries sustained during international air transportation. The Court of Appeals did not address this question, and we did not grant certiorari to consider it. We therefore decline to reach it here. * * *

The judgment of the Court of Appeals is reversed.

Zicherman v. Korean Air Lines Co., Ltd.
516 U.S. 217 (1996)

Justice SCALIA delivered the opinion of the Court.

This action presents the question whether, in a suit brought under Article 17 of the Warsaw Convention governing international air transportation, a plaintiff may recover damages for loss of society resulting from the death of a relative in a plane crash on the high seas.

I

On September 1, 1983, Korean Air Lines Flight KE007, en route from Anchorage, Alaska, to Seoul, South Korea, strayed into air space of the Soviet Union and was shot down over the Sea of Japan. All 269 persons on board were killed, including Muriel Kole. Petitioners Marjorie Zicherman and Muriel Mahalek, (Kole's sister and mother, respectively, sued respondent Korean Air Lines Co., Ltd. (KAL), in the United States District Court for the Southern District of New York.* * *

At petitioners' damages trial in the Southern District of New York, KAL moved for determination that the Death on the High Seas Act (DOHSA), 41 Stat. 537, 46 U.S.C.App. § 761 et seq. (1988 ed.), prescribed the proper claimants and the recoverable damages, and that it did not permit damages for loss of society. The District Court denied the motion and held, inter alia, that petitioners could recover for loss of "love, affection, and companionship." The jury awarded loss-of-society damages in the amount of $70,000 to Zicherman and $28,000 to Mahalek.

The Court of Appeals for the Second Circuit set aside this award * * * We granted certiorari.

II

* * *

The first and principal question before us is whether loss of society of a relative is made recoverable by [Article 17 of the Warsaw Convention].

It is obvious that the English word "damage" or "harm"—or in the official text of the Convention, the French word "dommage " can be applied to an extremely wide range of phenomena, from the medical expenses incurred as a result Kole's injuries (for which every legal system would provide tort compensation) to the mental distress of some stranger who reads about Kole's death in the paper (for which no legal system would provide tort compensation). It cannot seriously be maintained that Article 17 uses the term in this broadest sense, thus exploding tort liability beyond what any legal system in the world allows, to the farthest reaches of what could be denominated "harm." We therefore reject petitioners' initial proposal that we simply look to English dictionary definitions of "damage" and apply that term's "plain meaning."

* * *The nicer question, and the critical one here, is whether the word "dommage " establishes as the content of the concept "legally cognizable harm" what French law accepted as such in 1929. No case of ours provides precedent for the adoption of French law in such detail. In *Floyd*, we looked to French law to determine whether "lesion corporelle " indeed meant (as it had been translated) "bodily injury"—not to determine the subsequent question (equivalent to the question at issue here) whether "bodily injury" encompassed psychic injury. And in *Saks*, once we had determined that in French legal terminology the word "accident " referred to an unforeseen event, we did not further inquire whether French courts would consider the event at issue in the case unforeseen; we made that judgment for ourselves.

It is particularly implausible that "the shared expectations of the contracting parties" were that their mere use of the French language would effect adoption of the precise rule applied in France as to what constitutes legally cognizable harm. Those involved in the negotiation and adoption of the Convention could not have been ignorant of the fact that the law on this point varies widely from jurisdiction to jurisdiction, and even from statute to statute within a single jurisdiction. Just as we found it "unlikely" in Floyd that Convention signatories would have understood the general term "lesion corporelle" to confer a cause of action available under French law but unrecognized in many other nations, so also in the present case we find it unlikely that they would have understood Article 17's use of the general term "dommage" to require compensation for elements of harm recognized in France but unrecognized elsewhere, or to forbid compensation for elements of harm unrecognized in France but recognized elsewhere. * * *

The other alternative, and the only one we think realistic, is to believe that "dommage" means (as it does in French legal usage) "legally cognizable harm," but that Article 17 leaves it to adjudicating courts to specify what harm is cognizable. * * *

Because a treaty ratified by the United States is not only the law of this land, but also an agreement among sovereign powers, we have traditionally considered as aids to its interpretation the negotiating and drafting history (travaux preparatoires) and the postratification understanding of the contracting parties. Both of these sources confirm that the compensable injury is to be determined by domestic law. * * *

The postratification conduct of the contracting parties displays the same understanding that the damages recoverable—so long as they consist of compensation for harm incurred (dommage survenu)—are to be determined by domestic law. Some countries, including England, Germany and the Netherlands, have adopted domestic legislation to govern the types of damages recoverable in a Convention case. The Court of Appeals of Quebec has rejected the argument that Article 17 permits damages unrecoverable under domestic Quebec law. Dame Surprenant v. Air Canada, [1973] C.A. 107, 117-118, 126-127 (opinion of Deschenes, J.). But see Preston v. Hunting Air Transport Ltd., [1956] 1 Q.B. 454, 461-462 (granting damages under Convention, but without considering Article 24). Finally, the expert commentators are virtually unanimous that the type of harm compensable is to be determined by domestic law.

III

Having concluded that compensable harm is to be determined by domestic law, the next question to which we would logically turn is that of which sovereign's domestic law. * * * Choice of law is, of course, determined by the forum jurisdiction, and would normally be a question confronting us here. We have been spared that inquiry, however, because both parties agree that if the issue of compensable harm is (as we have determined) unresolved by the Convention itself, it is governed in the present case by the law of the United States.

That leaves a final question unresolved: Which particular law of the United States provides the governing rule? The Second Circuit, moved by the need to "maintain a uniform law under the Warsaw Convention," held that general maritime law governs causes of action under the Convention, whether the accident out of which they arise occurs on land or on the high seas. We think not. As we have discussed, the Convention itself contains no rule of law governing the present question; nor does it empower us to develop some common-law rule—under cover of general admiralty law or otherwise—that will supersede the normal federal disposition. Congress may choose to enact special provisions applicable to Warsaw Convention cases, as some countries have done. Absent such legislation, however, Articles 17 and 24(2) provide nothing more than a passthrough, authorizing us to apply the law that would govern in absence of the Warsaw Convention. There is little doubt what that law is in this case.

[The Court holds that the Death on the High Seas Act (DOHSA) governs recovery.] Section 762 of DOHSA provides that the recovery in a suit under §761 "shall be a fair and just compensation for the pecuniary loss sustained by the persons for whose benefit the suit is brought." 46 U.S.C.App. §762. Thus, petitioners cannot recover loss-of-society damages under DOHSA. Moreover, where DOHSA applies, neither state law, nor general maritime law, can provide a basis for recovery of loss-of-society damages. * * *

Finally, petitioners contend that DOHSA cannot supply the substantive law of damages, because this would result in an unintended "double cap." They argue that the Warsaw Convention's $75,000 per passenger limit on liability (except in cases of willful misconduct), when combined with a DOHSA rule prohibiting compensation for nonpecuniary harm, will not sufficiently deter willful misconduct. We are unpersuaded. The Convention unquestionably envisions the application of domestic law; it is the function of Congress, and not of this Court, to decide that domestic law, alone or in combination with the Convention, provides inadequate deterrence. * * *

Accordingly, that portion of the Second Circuit judgment * * * vacating the award of loss-of-society damages to Mahalek is affirmed.

Notes

1. Because the parties' stipulation of United States law made a choice-of-law analysis unnecessary in *Zicherman*, that case does not discuss the issue of whether its reference to the conflicts rules of the forum means the rules of the state in which the federal district court is sitting or a federal common law choice law rule. Pescatore v. Pan American World Airways, Inc., 97 F.3d 1 (2d Cir. 1996) discusses this issue and holds that the choice-of-law law rules that apply in Warsaw Convention cases are those of the state in which the district court is sitting.

Note that the Intercarrier Agreement on Passenger Liability, supra page 436, states that the airlines waive limitations on damages "so that recoverable compensatory damages may be determined and awarded by reference to the law of the domicile of the passenger." How will this agreement on choice of law operate? Will a plaintiff wishing to take advantage of the Agreement's waiver of damage restrictions be limited to the law of the passenger's domicile or is the law of this jurisdiction available at the plaintiff's option in addition to the law selected by the forum's choice-of-law rules?

2. The Death on the High Seas Act has been amended to permit recovery of "nonpecuniary damages" resulting "from a commercial aviation accident." PL 106-18, 200 HR 1000, 114 Stat. 131 (amending 46 U.S.C. § 762).

El Al Israel Airlines, Ltd. v. Tseng
525 U.S. 155 (1999)

Justice GINSBURG delivered the opinion of the Court.

Plaintiff-respondent Tsui Yuan Tseng was subjected to an intrusive security search at John F. Kennedy International Airport in New York before she boarded an El Al Israel Airlines May 22, 1993 flight to Tel Aviv. Tseng seeks tort damages from El Al for this occurrence. The episode-in-suit, both parties now submit, does not qualify as an "accident" within the meaning of the treaty popularly known as the Warsaw Convention, which governs air carrier liability for "all international transportation." Tseng alleges psychic or psychosomatic injuries, but no "bodily injury," as that term is used in the Convention. Her case presents a question of the Convention's exclusivity: When the Convention allows no recovery for the episode-in-suit, does it correspondingly preclude the passenger from maintaining an action for damages under another source of law, in this case, New York tort law?

The exclusivity question before us has been settled prospectively in a Warsaw Convention protocol (Montreal Protocol No. 4) recently ratified by the Senate. In accord with the protocol, Tseng concedes, a passenger whose injury is not compensable under the Convention (because it entails no "bodily injury" or was not the result of an "accident") will have no recourse to an alternate remedy. We conclude that the protocol, to which the United States has now subscribed, clarifies, but does not change, the Convention's exclusivity domain. We therefore hold that recovery for a personal injury suffered "on board [an] aircraft or in the course of any of the operations of embarking or disembarking," Art. 17, 49 Stat. 3018, if not allowed under the Convention, is not available at all.

The Court of Appeals for the Second Circuit ruled otherwise. In that court's view, a plaintiff who did not qualify for relief under the Convention could seek relief under local law for an injury sustained in the course of international air travel. We granted certiorari, and now reverse the Second Circuit's judgment. Recourse to local law, we are persuaded, would undermine the uniform regulation of international air carrier liability that the Warsaw Convention was designed to foster. * * *

The Second Circuit concluded first that no "accident" within Article 17's compass had occurred * * *.[9]

Our inquiry begins with the text of Article 24, which prescribes the exclusivity of the Convention's provisions for air carrier liability. * * *

Article 24 provides that "cases covered by article 17" * * * may "only be brought subject to the conditions and limits set out in th[e] [C]onvention." That prescription is not a model of the clear drafter's art. We recognize that the words lend themselves to divergent interpretation. * * *

The cardinal purpose of the Warsaw Convention, we have observed, is to "achieve uniformity of rules governing claims arising from international air transportation." Floyd, 499 U.S., at 552. * * * Given the Convention's comprehensive scheme of liability rules and its textual emphasis on uniformity, we would be hard put to conclude that the delegates at Warsaw meant to subject air carriers to the distinct, nonuniform liability rules of the individual signatory nations. * * *

A complementary purpose of the Convention is to accommodate or balance the interests of passengers seeking recovery for personal injuries, and the interests of air carriers seeking to limit potential liability. * * *

Construing the Convention, as did the Court of Appeals, to allow passengers to pursue claims under local law when the Convention does not permit recovery could produce several anomalies. Carriers might be exposed to unlimited liability under diverse legal regimes, but would be prevented, under the treaty, from contracting out of such liability. * * *

The Second Circuit feared that if Article 17 were read to exclude relief outside the Convention for Tseng, then a passenger injured by a malfunctioning escalator in the airline's terminal would have no recourse against the airline, even if the airline recklessly disregarded its duty to keep the escalator in proper repair. As the United States pointed out in its amicus curiae submission, however, the Convention addresses and concerns, only and exclusively, the airline's liability for passenger injuries occurring "on board the

---

9. An "accident" under Article 17 is "an unexpected or unusual event or happening that is external to the passenger." *Saks*, 470 U.S., at 405. That definition, we have cautioned, should "be flexibly applied after assessment of all the circumstances surrounding a passenger's injuries." Ibid. * * * It is questionable whether the Court of Appeals "flexibly applied" the definition of "accident" we set forth in *Saks*. Both parties, however, now accept the Court of Appeals' disposition of that issue. In any event, even if El Al's search of Tseng was an "accident," the core question of the Convention's exclusivity would remain [because under Eastern Airlines, Inc. v. Floyd, supra page 450, Tseng could not recover for emotional harm not accompanied by physical harm].

aircraft or in the course of any of the operations of embarking or disembarking." Art. 17. A carrier, therefore, "is indisputably subject to liability under local law for injuries arising outside of that scope: e.g., for passenger injuries occurring before 'any of the operations of embarking or disembarking.'" [Brief for United States as Amicus Curiae].* * *

Montreal Protocol No. 4, ratified by the Senate on September 28, 1998, amends Article 24 to read, in relevant part: "In the carriage of passengers and baggage, any action for damages, however founded, can only be brought subject to the conditions and limits set out in this Convention....." Both parties agree that, under the amended Article the Convention's preemptive effect is clear: The treaty precludes passengers from bringing actions under local law when they cannot establish air carrier liability under the treaty. Revised Article 24, El Al urges and we agree, merely clarifies, it does not alter, the Convention's rule of exclusivity. * * *

Decisions of the courts of other Convention signatories corroborate our understanding of the Convention's preemptive effect. In Sidhu [v. British Airways Plc, [1997] 1 All E.R. 193], the British House of Lords considered and decided the very question we now face concerning the Convention's exclusivity when a passenger alleges psychological damages, but no physical injury, resulting from an occurrence that is not an "accident" under Article 17. Reviewing the text, structure, and drafting history of the Convention, the Lords concluded that the Convention was designed to "ensure that, in all questions relating to the carrier's liability, it is the provisions of the [C]onvention which apply and that the passenger does not have access to any other remedies, whether under the common law or otherwise, which may be available within the particular country where he chooses to raise his action." Courts of other nations bound by the Convention have also recognized the treaty's encompassing preemptive effect. The "opinions of our sister signatories," we have observed, are "entitled to considerable weight." *Saks*, 470 U.S., at 404. The text, drafting history, and underlying purpose of the Convention, in sum, counsel us to adhere to a view of the treaty's exclusivity shared by our treaty partners. * * *

Justice STEVENS, dissenting.

My disagreement with the Court's holding today has limited practical significance, not just because the issue has been conclusively determined for future cases by the recent amendment to the Warsaw Convention, but also because it affects only a narrow category of past cases. The decision is nevertheless significant because, in the end, it rests on the novel premise that preemption analysis should be applied differently to treaties than to other kinds of federal law. Because I disagree with that premise, I shall briefly explain why I believe the Court has erred. * * *

Everyone agrees that the literal text of the treaty does not preempt claims of personal injury that do not arise out of an accident. It is equally clear that nothing in the drafting history requires that result. * * I firmly believe that a treaty, like an Act of Congress, should not be construed to preempt state law unless its intent to do so is clear.* * *

Notes

1. Hernandez v. Air France, 545 F.2d 279 (1st Cir. 1976), cert. denied, 430 U.S. 950 (1977), held that passengers were no longer "disembarking" within the meaning of Article 17 of the Warsaw Convention when they were killed and injured by Japanese terrorists in the baggage retrieval area of the terminal building a Lod International Airport in Israel. Therefore the passengers could not recover against the airline under the no-

fault provisions of the 1966 Montreal Agreement. Previously the court had held that disembarking has been completed when the passengers reach "a safe point inside of the terminal." MacDonald v. Air Canada, 439 F.2d 1402, 1405 (1st Cir. 1971). In Hernandez the court held that the passengers had completed disembarking when attacked even if the court substituted a tripartite test, referring to plaintiffs' activity, carrier's control, and location, for the simple location test of MacDonald.

McCarthy v. Northwest Airlines, Inc., 56 F.3d 313 (1st Cir. 1995) held that a passenger who fell in a public area of the airport while being led by an airline employee "at a fast trot" to her gate was not "embarking" within the meaning of article 17. The court viewed the three elements of activity, location, and control, used in Hernandez, not as "separate legs of a stool, but, rather, as forming a single unitary base." Id. at 317. The court required "a close temporal and spatial relationship with the flight itself" (id. at 317) and rejected a suggestion that the elements of activity and location were not needed if the passenger was under the carrier's control (id. at 318).

2. In re Air Crash Disaster Near New Orleans, 821 F.2d 1147 (5th Cir. 1987), (cert. granted and judgment vacated for reconsideration in light of Chan v. Korean Air Lines [490 U.S. 122], 490 U.S. 1032, remanded for reconsideration of damages, otherwise reinstated, 883 F.2d 17 (5th Cir. 1989)), stated that despite proper venue under Article 28(1), a federal may grant a forum non conveniens dismissal, which is one of the "[q]uestions of procedure" referred to in Article 28(2). The court affirmed the trial court's denial of the forum non conveniens motion on the ground that this denial was not an abuse of discretion. Srl v. British Airways, [1996] 3 W.L.R. 642, [1996] 3 All E.R. 537 (C.A), expressly disagreed with In re Air Crash Disaster Near New Orleans and held that a forum non conveniens dismissal is not available if the plaintiff's suit is brought within a venue that is proper under Article 28.

Mabud v. Pakistan International Airlines, 717 P.2d 1350 (Utah 1986), held that although plaintiff's suit in Utah complied with the venue requirements of Warsaw Convention article 28(1), there was no jurisdiction over the airline because of its lack of "minimum contacts" with the forum.

3. Convention Article 17 provides for liability to a "passenger." Article 3(2) provides that "if the carrier accepts a passenger without a passenger ticket having been delivered he shall not be entitled to avail himself of those provisions of this convention which exclude or limit his liability." These provisions have been invoked on behalf of airline employees who were traveling without a ticket contending that they were not on duty and therefore were passengers.

In re Mexico City Aircrash of October 31, 1979, 708 F.2d 400 (9th Cir. 1983). An action was brought for the wrongful death of three stewardesses on board the airplane when it crashed. Two were working on the flight and actions for their death were held properly dismissed on the ground that their recovery was under state worker's compensation law. The third stewardess was not working on the flight, but was en route to Mexico City where she was scheduled to work on a flight departing from that location. The dismissal of the claim for her death was reversed and the case remanded for determination of the fact issue of whether she was free to choose any method of transportation that would get her to Mexico City on time to assume her duty assignment. If so, she was a passenger and recovery for her death was available under the Convention without the limits of Article 22. Even if recovery for her death was also available under state worker's compensation law, "[t]he Warsaw Convention...preempts the exclusivity of the California worker's compensation statute." Id. at 418.

Sulewski v. Federal Express Corp., 933 F.2d 180 (2d Cir. 1991). A mechanic was killed in the crash of his employer's airplane. When the airplane landed, he was to have serviced it. The court held that he was not a passenger because, even if he had no in flight duties, he was required to be on that airplane so that he could service it when it landed.

4. Wolgel v. Mexicana Airlines, 821 F.2d 442 (7th Cir.), cert. denied, 484 U.S. 927 (1987). A passenger who was bumped from a flight that was overbooked brought suit against the airline more than two years later. The court held that the action was not barred by Article 29(1) because the Convention did not cover the claim. The provision in Article 19 for "damage occasioned by delay" does not apply to bumping, which constitutes nonperformance rather than delayed performance.

5. Several cases have dealt with the meaning of "destination" under Warsaw Convention articles1(2) and 28(1) and with the meaning of "one undivided transportation" in article 1(3). Petrire v. Spantax, S.A., 756 F.2d 263 (2d Cir.), cert. denied, 474 U.S. 846 (1995), held that when a carrier issues two ticket booklets for a round-trip journey, the "destination" for the purposes of the venue provisions of 28(1) is the designated ending point of the round-trip and not the ending point of the travel covered by the first booklet. Haldimann v. Delta Airlines, Inc., 168 F.3d 1324 (D.C. Cir. 1999), held a passenger's recovery subject to the Convention limits although she was injured on a flight from Pensacola to Gainesville within the state of Florida. The flight was part of "international transportation" (article 1(1)) because booked at the same time as the passenger booked a Swisssair flight for a round trip between Switzerland and Washington D.C. At the same time she booked flights on Delta Airlines for a round trip between Washington D.C. and Gainesville. The court followed *Petrire* and other decisions that it characterized as finding "simultaneous issue of ticket booklets at a single place sufficient to establish the 'single operation' required by Article 1(3)." Id. at 1325.

Chapter 9

International Child Abduction

Section 1: Duty to Return the Child

Hague Convention on the Civil Aspects of International Child Abduction
51 Fed. Reg. 10498 (1986), 19 ILM 1501 (1980)

The States signatory to the present Convention.

Firmly convinced that the interests of children are of paramount importance in matters relating to their custody.

Desiring to protect children internationally from the harmful effects of their wrongful removal or retention and to establish procedures to ensure their prompt return to the State of their habitual residence, as well as to secure protection for rights of access.

Have resolved to conclude a Convention to this effect, and have agreed upon the following provisions-

Chapter I: Scope of the Convention

Article 1

The objects of the present Convention are-

a. to secure the prompt return of children wrongfully removed to or retained in any Contracting State: and

b. to ensure that rights of custody and of access under the law of one Contracting State are effectively respected in the other Contracting States.

Article 2

Contracting States shall take all appropriate measures to secure within their territories the implementation of the objects of the Convention. For this purpose they shall use the most expeditious procedures available.

Article 3

The removal or the retention of a child is to be considered wrongful where-

a. it is in breach of rights of custody attributed to a person, an institution or any other body, either jointly or alone, under the law of the State in which the child was habitually resident immediately before the removal or retention: and

b. at the time of removal or retention those rights were actually exercised, either jointly or alone, or would have been so exercised but for the removal or retention.

The rights of custody mentioned in sub-paragraph a above, may arise in particular by operation of law or by reason of a judicial or administrative decision, or by reason of an agreement having legal effect under the law of that State.

Article 4

The Convention shall apply to any child who was habitually resident in a Contracting State immediately before any breach of custody or access rights. The Convention shall cease to apply when the child attains the age of 16 years.

Article 5

For the purposes of this Convention-

a. "rights of custody" shall include rights relating to the care of the person of the child and, in particular, the right to determine the child's place of residence;

b. "rights of access" shall include the right to take a child for a limited period of time to a place other than the child's habitual residence.

Chapter II: Central Authorities

Article 6

A Contracting State shall designate a Central Authority to discharge the duties which are imposed by the Convention upon such authorities.

Federal States, States with more than one system of law or States having autonomous territorial organizations shall be free to appoint more than one Central Authority and to specify the territorial extent of their powers. Where a State has appointed more than one Central Authority, it shall designate the Central Authority to which applications may be addressed for transmission to the appropriate Central Authority within that State.

Article 7

Central Authorities shall co-operate with each other and promote co-operation amongst the competent authorities in their respective States to secure the prompt return of children and to achieve the other objects of this Convention.

In particular, either directly or through any intermediary, they shall take all appropriate measures-

a. to discover the whereabouts of a child who has been wrongfully removed or retained;

b. to prevent further harm to the child or prejudice to interested parties by taking or causing to be taken provisional measures;

c. to secure the voluntary return of the child or to bring about an amicable resolution of the issues;

d. to exchange, where desirable, information relating to the social background of the child;

e. to provide information of a general character as to the law of their State in connection with the application of the Convention;

f. to initiate or facilitate the institution of judicial or administrative proceedings with a view to obtaining the return of the child and, in a proper case, to make arrangements for organizing or securing the effective exercise of rights of access;

g. where the circumstances so require, to provide or facilitate the provision of legal aid and advice, including the participation of legal counsel and advisers;

h. to provide such administrative arrangements as may be necessary and appropriate to secure the safe return of the child;

i. to keep each other informed with respect to the operation of this Convention and, as far as possible, to eliminate any obstacles to its application.

Chapter III: Return of Children

Article 8

Any person, institution or other body claiming that a child has been removed or retained in breach of custody rights may apply either to the Central Authority of the child's habitual residence or to the Central Authority of any other Contracting State for assistance in securing the return of the child.

The application shall contain-

a. information concerning the identity of the applicant, of the child and of the person alleged to have removed or retained the child;

b. where available, the date of birth of the child;

c. the grounds on which the applicant's claim for return of the child is based;

d. all available information relating to the whereabouts of the child and the identity of the person with whom the child is presumed to be.

The application may be accompanied or supplemented by-

e. an authenticated copy of any relevant decision or agreement;

f. a certificate or an affidavit emanating from a Central Authority, or other competent authority of the State of the child's habitual residence, or from a qualified person, concerning the relevant law of that State;

g. any other relevant document.

Article 9

If the Central Authority which receives an application referred to in Article 8 has reason to believe that the child is in another Contracting State, it shall directly and without delay transmit the application to the Central Authority of that Contracting State and inform the requesting Central Authority, or the applicant, as the case may be.

Article 10

The Central Authority of the State where the child is shall take or cause to be taken all appropriate measures in order to obtain the voluntary return of the child.

Article 11

The judicial or administrative authorities of Contracting States shall act expeditiously in proceedings for the return of children.

If the judicial or administrative authority concerned has not reached a decision within six weeks from the date of commencement of the proceedings, the applicant or the Central Authority of the requested State, on its own initiative or if asked by the Central Authority of the requesting State, shall have the right to request a statement of the reasons for the delay. If a reply is received by the Central Authority of the requested State, that Authority shall transmit the reply to the Central Authority of the requesting State, or to the applicant, as the case may be.

Article 12

Where a child has been wrongfully removed or retained in terms of Article 3 and, at the date of the commencement of the proceedings before the judicial or administrative authority of the Contracting State where the child is, a period of less than one year has elapsed from the date of the wrongful removal or retention, the authority concerned shall order the return of the child forthwith. The judicial or administrative authority, even where the proceedings have been commenced after the expiration of the period of one year referred to in the preceding paragraph, shall also order the return of the child, unless it is demonstrated that the child is now settled in its new environment.

Where the judicial or administrative authority in the requested State has reason to believe that the child has been taken to another State, it may stay the proceedings or dismiss the application for the return of the child.

Article 13

Notwithstanding the provisions of the preceding Article, the judicial or administrative authority of the requested State is not bound to order the return of the child if the person, institution or other body which opposes its return establishes that-

a. the person, institution or other body having the care of the person of the child was not actually exercising the custody rights at the time of removal or retention, or had consented to or subsequently acquiesced in the removal or retention; or

b. there is a grave risk that his or her return would expose the child to physical or psychological harm or other wise place the child in an intolerable situation.

The judicial or administrative authority may also refuse to order the return of the child if it finds that the child objects to being returned and has attained an age and degree of maturity at which it is appropriate to take account of its views.

In considering the circumstances referred to in this Article, the judicial and administrative authorities shall take into account the information relating to the social background of the child provided by the Central Authority or other competent authority of the child's habitual residence.

Article 14

In ascertaining whether there has been a wrongful removal or retention within the meaning of Article 3, the judicial or administrative authorities of the requested State may take notice directly of the law of, and of judicial or administrative decisions, formally recognized or not in the State of the habitual residence of the child, without recourse to the specific procedures for the proof of that law or for the recognition of foreign decisions which would otherwise be applicable.

Article 15

The judicial or administrative authorities of a Contracting State may, prior to the making of an order for the return of the child, request that the applicant obtain from the authorities of the State of the habitual residence of the child a decision or other determination that the removal or retention was wrongful within the meaning of Article 3 of the Convention, where such a decision or determination may be obtained in that State. The Central Authorities of the Contracting States shall so far as practicable assist applicants to obtain such a decision or determination.

Article 16

After receiving notice of a wrongful removal or retention of a child in the sense of Article 3, the judicial or administrative authorities of the Contracting State to which the child has been removed or in which it has been retained shall not decide on the merits of rights of custody until it has been determined that the child is not to be returned under this Convention or unless an application under this Convention is not lodged within a reasonable time following receipt of the notice.

Article 17

The sole fact that a decision relating to custody has been given in or is entitled to recognition in the requested State shall not be a ground for refusing to return a child under this Convention, but the judicial or administrative authorities of the requested State may take account of the reasons for that decision in applying this Convention.

Article 18

The provisions of this Chapter do not limit the power of a judicial or administrative authority to order the return of the child at any time.

Article 19

A decision under this Convention concerning the return of the child shall not be taken to be a determination on the merits of any custody issue.

Article 20

The return of the child under the provisions of Article 12 may be refused if this would not be permitted by the fundamental principles of the requested State relating to the protection of human rights and fundamental freedoms.

Chapter IV: Rights of Access

Article 21

An application to make arrangements for organizing or securing the effective exercise of rights of access may be presented to the Central Authorities of the Contracting States in the same way as an application for the return of a child.

The Central Authorities are bound by the obligations of co-operation which are set forth in Article 7 to promote the peaceful enjoyment of access rights and the fulfillment of any conditions to which the exercise of those rights may be subject. The central Authorities shall take steps to remove, as far as possible, all obstacles to the exercise of such rights. The Central Authorities, either directly or through intermediaries, may initiate or assist in the institution of proceedings with a view to organizing or protecting these rights and securing respect for the conditions to which the exercise of these rights may be subject.

Chapter V: General Provisions

* * *

Article 24

Any application, communication or other document sent to the Central Authority of the requested State shall be in the original language, and shall be accompanied by a translation into the official language or one of the official languages of the requested State or, where that is not feasible, a translation into French or English.

However, a Contracting State may, by making a reservation in accordance with Article 42, object to the use of either French or English, but not both, in any application, communication or other document sent to its Central Authority.

Article 25

Nationals of the Contracting States and persons who are habitually resident within those States shall be entitled in matters concerned with the application of this Convention to legal aid and advice in any other Contracting State on the same conditions as if they themselves were nationals of and habitually resident in that State.

Article 26

Each Central Authority shall bear its own costs in applying this Convention.

Central Authorities and other public services of Contracting States shall not impose any charges in relation to applications submitted under this Convention. In particular, they may not require any payment from the applicant towards the costs and expenses of the proceedings or, where applicable, those arising from the participation of legal counsel or advisers. However, they may require the payment of the expenses incurred or to be incurred in implementing the return of the child.

However, a Contracting State may, by making a reservation in accordance with Article 42, declare that it shall not be bound to assume any costs referred to in the preceding paragraph resulting from the participation of legal counsel or advisers or from court proceedings, except insofar as those costs may be covered by its system of legal aid and advice.

Upon ordering the return of a child or issuing an order concerning rights of access under this Convention, the judicial or administrative authorities may, where appropriate, direct the person who removed or retained the child, or who prevented the exercise of rights of access, to pay necessary expenses incurred by or on behalf of the applicant including travel expenses, any costs incurred or payments made for locating the child, the costs of legal representation of the applicant, and those of returning the child.

* * *

Article 29

This Convention shall not preclude any person, institution or body who claims that there has been a breach of custody or access rights within the meaning of Article 3 or 21 from applying directly to the judicial or administrative authorities of a Contracting State, whether or not under the provisions of this Convention.

* * *

Article 31

In relation to a State which in matters of custody of children has two or more systems of law applicable in different territorial units-

a. any reference to habitual residence in that State shall be construed as referring to habitual residence in a territorial unit of that State;

b. any reference to the law of the State of habitual residence shall be construed as referring to the law of the territorial unit in that State where the child habitually resides.

* * *

Article 36

Nothing in this Convention shall prevent two or more Contracting States, in order to limit the restrictions to which the return of the child may be subject, from agreeing among themselves to derogate from any provisions of this Convention which may imply such a restriction.

Chapter VI: Final Clauses

* * *

Article 42

Any State may, not later than the time of ratification, acceptance, approval or accession * * * make one or both of the reservations provided for in Article 24 and Article 26, third paragraph. No other reservation shall be permitted.

* * *

Done at The Hague, on the 25th day of October, 1980, in the English and French languages, both texts being equally authentic, in a single copy which shall be deposited in the archives of the Government of the Kingdom of the Netherlands, and of which a certified copy shall be sent, through diplomatic channels, to each of the States Members of the Hague Conference on Private International Law at the date of its Fourteenth Session.

Notes

1. The United States has ratified the Child Abduction Convention and has enacted, as implementing legislation, the International Child Abduction Remedies Act (ICARA), 42 U.S.C. §§ 11601-11610. Section 11601(b)(2) declares that "[t]he provisions of this chapter are in addition to and not in lieu of the provisions of the Convention"; § 11603(a) provides concurrent jurisdiction under the Convention to state and federal courts. Section 11603(e) covers "burdens of proof." The petitioner has the burden of

proving by a preponderance of the evidence that the child has been wrongfully removed or retained and, in the case of rights of access, that the petitioner has such rights. The party opposing return of the child has the burden of establishing by clear and convincing evidence the exceptions in articles 13(b) or 20 and the burden of establishing by a preponderance of the evidence that any other exception in articles 12 or 13 applies. Section 11603(h) provides that "[t]he remedies established by the Convention and this chapter shall be in addition to remedies available under other laws or international agreements."

The International Parental Kidnapping Act, 18 U.S.C. § 1204, provides for fines and imprisonment up to 3 years of a person "who removes a child from the United States or retains a child (who has been in the United States) outside the United States with intent to obstruct the lawful exercise of parental rights." (1204(a)). The Act provides defenses if the defendant acted within the provisions of a valid court order, was fleeing domestic violence, or had physical custody abroad pursuant to a court order and failed to return the child because of circumstances beyond the defendant's control. (1204(c)). The Act declares that it "does not detract from The Hague Convention." (1204(d)). Nevertheless, United States v. Amer, 110 F.3d 873 (2d Cir.), cert. denied, 522 U.S. 904 (1997), held that a defendant convicted under the Act could not raise a defense under Article 13 of the Convention that return would place the children in "an intolerable situation." This is not one of the defenses listed in the Act and Egypt, where the children were taken, had not ratified the Convention. The court left open the question "whether a defendant should be permitted to raise Hague Convention defense when... there is a parallel or ongoing civil proceeding under the Convention." Id. at 882.

By Executive Order No. 12648, Aug. 11, 1988, 53 F.R. 30637, President Reagan designated the Department of State as the Central Authority of the United States. The Office of Children's Issues is the State Department agency that assists with Convention issues; telephone number (202) 736-7000; Fax (202) 647-2835. For discussion of use of the Central Authority in the parent's home country, see Carol S. Bruch, The Central Authority's Role Under the Hague Child Abduction Convention, 28 Family L.Q. 35, 41-42 (1994) (urging use of the local Central Authority before abduction for help with preventive measures and after abduction for assistance in reaching a foreign Central Authority).

The Hague Conference on Private International Law web site for the Child Abduction Convention containing a list of countries that are parties, the date the Convention entered into force in each country, and indicating when the list was last updated is: <http://www.hcch.net/e/status/stat28e.html>.

Regulations governing the Convention are in 22 CFR Part 94. A Legal Analysis of the Convention including a model form is in 51 Fed. Reg. 10503 (1986). The Legal Analysis contains frequent references to the report of the official Hague Conference reporter for the Convention, Elisa Perez-Vera, Actes et documents de la Quatorziem Session (1980) Vol. III, Child Abduction, which may be obtained from the Netherlands Government Printing and Publishing Office, 1 Christoffel Plantijnstraat, P. O. Box 20014, 2500 EA The Hague, Netherlands. Also obtainable from this source is the report of the Special Commission which met in The Hague on January 18-21, 1993 to study the operation of the Convention. The Report states that at the January 18 session "[a] number of speakers remarked that, despite a few speedy return cases, the excessive time periods for return proceedings remains a major problem to be resolved." A summary of the Report is at 33 I.L.M. 225 (1994). For discussion of experience with the Convention see Linda Silberman, Hague International Child Abduction Convention: A Progress Report, 57 Law

& Contemp. Probs. 209 (Summer 1994); Linda Silberman, Hague Convention on International Child Abduction: A Brief Overview and Case Law Analysis, 28 Family L.Q. 9 (1994).

Convention Article 29 and 42 U.S.C. § 11603(h) permit an action for return of the child under law other than the Convention. The primary United States legislation under which such an action would be brought is the Uniform Child Custody Jurisdiction Act (UCCJA), 9 ULA Part I, or the statute that has superseded it some states, the Uniform Child Custody Jurisdiction and Enforcement Act (UCCJEA), id.

Section 23 of the UCCJA provides that the Act's "general policies...extend to the international area" and that the Act's provisions "relating to the recognition and enforcement of custody decrees...apply to custody decrees...rendered by appropriate authorities of other nations if reasonable notice and opportunity to be heard were given to all affected persons." Section 8(a) gives a court discretion to decline to exercise jurisdiction to enter an initial custody decree if the petitioner "has wrongfully taken the child from another state or has engaged in similar reprehensible conduct." Section 8(b) provides that "[u]nless required in the interest of the child, the court shall not exercise its jurisdiction to modify a custody decree of another state if the petitioner, without consent of the person entitled to custody, has improperly removed the child from the physical custody of the person entitled to custody or has improperly retained the child after a visit..." "State" does not include a foreign country (§ 2(10)), but the comment to § 23 states that the "general principles" referred to in that section include "the principles underlying provisions like sectio[n]...8..."

Section 105 of the UCCJEA provides that "[a] court of this State shall treat a foreign country as if it were a State of the United States for the purpose of applying [the Act's provisions on jurisdiction to make and modify custody determinations]. Further, foreign decrees are entitled to enforcement if made "in substantial conformity with the jurisdictional standards of [the UCCJEA]." Section 302 provides for enforcement of orders "for the return of the child made under the Hague Convention." Sections 305-308 provide for registration and expedited enforcement of the child-custody determinations of other jurisdictions.

There may be advantages to utilizing the UCCJA or UCCJEA even when Convention procedures are available and, under Convention Article 4, the Uniform Acts must be used if the child was not "habitually resident in a Contracting State immediately before any breach of custody or access rights."

The fact that another country has not ratified the Convention may affect a court's determination of custody and visitation. Al-Zouhayli v. Al-Zouhayli, 486 N.W.2d 10 (Minn. App. 1992) affirmed the trial judge's order permitting unsupervised visitation by the father with the child. The father was a naturalized United States citizen but retained his Syrian citizenship. A majority thought that the trial judge's discounting the risk of abduction to Syria was not an abuse of discretion, but one of the three judges dissented on this issue. Both majority and dissent noted that Syria is not a party to the Convention, that its courts would not honor a United States custody decree, and that a Syrian court would "be compelled by local law and custody to award custody of the child to" the father. Id. at 13.

That the child has been taken from a non-Convention country may also affect the standard applied to the decision to order return. See In re P, [1997] 2 W.L.R. 223, 233 (C.A.) (stating that "one does not proceed upon a basis that it is necessary that the child

would be in some obvious moral or physical danger if returned [see article 13(b)]....
[W]elfare [of the child], wide ranging a concept as it is, is the only criterion").

2. The Fourth Inter-American Specialized Conference on Private International Law was attended by 19 members of the Organization of American States, including the United States. On July 15, 1989, the Conference approved for submission to the OAS countries the Inter-American Convention on International Repatriation of Children. The I-A Convention is similar to the Hague Convention. Nevertheless, some states opposed Article 33 of the I-A Convention, which permits signatories to agree bilaterally among themselves to give priority to the Hague Convention.

The European Convention on Recognition and Enforcement of Decisions Concerning Custody of Children and on Restoration of Custody of Children, opened for Signature May 20, 1980, 19 I.L.M. 273 (1981), unlike the Hague Convention, is premised on the existence of a prior custody determination and is designed to facilitate reciprocal recognition and enforcement of custody decisions, rather than provide for immediate return of an abducted child. Article 1(d) defines "improper removal" as "the removal of a child across an international frontier in breach of a decision relating to his custody which has been given in a Contracting State" and also includes failure to return the child after a visit. The European Convention is open to ratification only by member States of the Council of Europe. If a state has ratified both the Hague and European Conventions, a court in the Netherlands has held "that the application of the Convention which is most likely to bring about the return of the child should take precedence." Judgment given by R.H.M. Hooymans-van Oerle, Vice-President and Children's Judge, at the public sitting of 's-Hertogenbosch District Court, 13 February 1991 (applying the Hague Convention to order return of a child removed from England to the Netherlands; the Netherlands and the United Kingdom had ratified both Conventions).

In April 1999 the International Centre for Missing and Exploited Children opened in London. The Centre's objective is to provide technology to help track missing children, establish adequate law enforcement, and raise awareness of problems.

Friedrich v. Friedrich
983 F.2d 1396 (6th Cir. 1993)

BOGGS, Circuit Judge.

This is a case of first impression, requiring us to determine when the removal of a child from one country to another by one parent, without the consent of the other, is "wrongful" as defined by the Hague Convention on the Civil Aspects of International Child Abduction ("the Convention") as implemented by the United States Congress in the International Child Abduction Remedies Act ("the Act"), 42 U.S.C. §§ 11601-11610. Emanuel Friedrich appeals from the denial of his petition for the return of his son, Thomas, to Germany. Thomas was removed from Germany to the United States by his mother, Jeana Friedrich, a few days after the Friedrichs informally separated. The district court found that Mrs. Friedrich did not wrongfully remove Thomas from Germany within the meaning of the Convention because at the time of removal Thomas was a "habitual resident" of the United States and Mr. Friedrich was not exercising his parental custody rights. For the reasons that follow, we reverse the district court's ruling and remand the case for a determination of whether, under German law, Mr. Friedrich had custody rights at the time of the removal that he was exercising or would have exercised but for the removal, and for consideration of any affirmative defenses that Mrs. Friedrich might raise.

I

In December 1989, Emanuel Friedrich married Jeana Friedrich in the Federal Republic of Germany. Mrs. Friedrich, a citizen of the United States, was a member of the United States Army stationed in Bad Aibling, Germany. Mr. Friedrich, a citizen of Germany, was employed on the military base as a bartender and club manager.

On December 29, 1989, the Friedrichs' only child, Thomas David Friedrich, was born in Bad Aibling. During 1990 and early 1991, Thomas lived with both of his parents in Bad Aibling off the military base. The Friedrichs' marriage was a rocky one from the start. Their first informal separation occurred in June 1990, but only lasted a weekend. The Friedrichs informally separated for a second time in March 1991. For the majority of this separation, Mr. Friedrich and his parents retained physical custody of Thomas. Mrs. Friedrich lived on the military base. In early May 1991, while still separated, the Friedrichs agreed that Thomas would accompany his mother on a ten-day visit to her parents' home in Ironton, Ohio. Upon Thomas's return to Germany, the Friedrichs reunited, and Thomas lived with both of them until late July 1991.

On the evening of July 27, 1991, the Friedrichs had a heated argument at their apartment. During the argument, Mr. Friedrich ordered Mrs. Friedrich to leave the apartment with Thomas and put most of their belongings in the hallway, including some of Thomas's toys. Mrs. Friedrich, however, did not leave the apartment until the next morning when she obtained assistance from friends in the United States Army. Together, they took Thomas and removed her possessions to on-base visiting quarters, where she lived with Thomas for the next four nights, until August 1, 1991. Mr. Friedrich did not interfere with the removal of Mrs. Friedrich's possessions or with the removal of his child. He explained that he was intimidated by the soldiers and wanted to avoid a scene in front of Thomas.

The on-base visiting quarters are not designed for permanent residence and the daily rate is expensive. Therefore, Mrs. Friedrich immediately sought alternative, less expensive accommodations. Under military regulations, Mrs. Friedrich could not live in the barracks on the base with her son. Mrs. Friedrich testified that she quickly concluded that she had nowhere to live with her son in Germany and that her only recourse was to return to the United States. In the late evening of August 1, 1991, without Mr. Friedrich's permission, consent or knowledge, Mrs. Friedrich left Bad Aibling en route to the United States with Thomas.

Between the time she left the family apartment on July 28, and the time she left Bad Aibling on August 1, 1991, Mrs. Friedrich met with Mr. Friedrich at least twice to discuss their separation and Thomas's welfare. On July 29, 1991, Mr. Friedrich visited with Thomas for four hours. On August 1, 1991, the Friedrichs planned specific times for Mr. Friedrich to visit with Thomas during the following week.

Mrs. Friedrich arrived in Ironton, Ohio on August 2, and initiated a divorce action in Lawrence County, Ohio on August 9, 1991. Although the court issued a Letter Rogatory to the appropriate German authorities, Mr. Friedrich claims that he never received the letter or any notice of the judicial proceedings in Lawrence County, Ohio. On August 11, 1991, Mrs. Friedrich returned to Germany without her son and immediately sought an emergency discharge from the United States Army. On August 28, 1991, the Lawrence County, Ohio, Court of Common Pleas issued a temporary order in favor of

Mrs. Friedrich and ordered that Thomas not be removed from Ohio until further order of the court. On September 15, 1991, Mrs. Friedrich was discharged from the United States Army, and she returned to her parents' home in Ironton, Ohio.

Mr. Friedrich discovered that Thomas had been removed to the United States on August 3, 1991, and filed a claim in Germany seeking to obtain parental custody soon afterward. On August 22, 1991, a Municipal Court-Family Court in Rosenheim, Germany granted Mr. Friedrich parental custody of Thomas. Mrs. Friedrich did not receive notice of that judicial proceeding.

Mr. Friedrich filed this action on September 23, 1991, alleging that Mrs. Friedrich had wrongfully removed Thomas from Germany in violation of the Hague Convention on Civil Aspects of International Child Abduction. On January 10, 1992, the district court denied Mr. Friedrich's claim.

II

The Convention on Civil Aspects of International Child Abduction was adopted by the signatory nations in order "to protect children internationally from the harmful effects of their wrongful removal or retention and to establish procedures to ensure their prompt return to the State of their habitual residence, as well as to secure protection for rights of access." Hague Convention, Preamble. The United States ratified the Convention on April 29, 1988. Germany is also a signatory nation to the Convention. Pursuant to Article 19 of the Convention and section 2(b)(4) of the Act, a United States district court has the authority to determine the merits of an abduction claim, but not the merits of the underlying custody claim. It is important to understand that "wrongful removal" is a legal term strictly defined in the Convention. It does not require an ad hoc determination or a balancing of the equities. Such action by a court would be contrary to a primary purpose of the Convention: to preserve the status quo and to deter parents from crossing international boundaries in search of a more sympathetic court.

* * *

[A]s a threshold matter, Mr. Friedrich must prove by a preponderance of the evidence that 1) Mrs. Friedrich removed Thomas from his "habitual residence," and 2) Mr. Friedrich was exercising his parental custody rights over Thomas at the time of removal, or that he would have exercised his rights but for the removal, under the law of the state of Thomas's habitual residence. If Mr. Friedrich meets this burden, Mrs. Friedrich may fall back on one of the four affirmative defenses. The district court held that Mr. Friedrich failed to prove both parts of the test. Instead, the court found that 1) Thomas's habitual residence was "altered" from Germany to the United States when Mr. Friedrich set some of Thomas's belongings out in the hallway on July 27, 1991, and 2) Mr. Friedrich "terminated" his custody rights when he "unilaterally expelled" Mrs. Friedrich and Thomas from the apartment. The district court did not reach the merits of any affirmative defenses.

III

A

The Convention does not define "habitual residence." Little case law exists on the Convention in general; no United States cases provides guidance on the construction of "habitual residence." The British courts have provided the most complete analysis. In Re Bates, No. CA 122.89, High Court of Justice, Family Div'n Ct. Royal Court of Justice,

United Kingdom (1989), the High Court of Justice concluded that there is no real distinction between ordinary residence and habitual residence. Id. at 10. The court also added a word of caution: "It is greatly to be hoped that the courts will resist the temptation to develop detailed and restrictive rules as to habitual residence, which might make it as technical a term of art as common law domicile. The facts and circumstances of each case should continue to be assessed without resort to presumptions or pre-suppositions." Id. (quoting Dicey & Morris, The Conflicts of Laws 166 (11th ed.)). We agree that habitual residence must not be confused with domicile. To determine the habitual residence, the court must focus on the child, not the parents, and examine past experience, not future intentions.

Thomas was born in Germany to a German father and an American mother and lived exclusively in Germany except for a few short vacations before Mrs. Friedrich removed him to the United States. Mrs. Friedrich argues that despite the fact that Thomas's ordinary residence was always in Germany, Thomas was actually a habitual resident of the United States because: 1) he had United States citizenship; 2) his permanent address for the purpose of the United States documentation was listed as Ironton, Ohio; and 3) Mrs. Friedrich intended to return to the United States with Thomas when she was discharged from the military. Although these ties may be strong enough to establish legal residence in the United States, they do not establish habitual residence.

A person can have only one habitual residence. On its face, habitual residence pertains to customary residence prior to the removal. The court must look back in time, not forward. All of the factors listed by Mrs. Friedrich pertain to the future. Moreover, they reflect the intentions of Mrs. Friedrich; it is the habitual residence of the child that must be determined. Mrs. Friedrich undoubtedly established ties between Thomas and the United States and may well have intended for Thomas to move to the United States at some time in the future. But before Mrs. Friedrich removed Thomas to the United States without the knowledge or consent of Mr. Friedrich, Thomas had resided exclusively in Germany. Any future plans that Mrs. Friedrich had for Thomas to reside in the United States are irrelevant to our inquiry.

The district court appears to agree that before the argument of July 27, 1991, Thomas was a habitual resident of Germany. The district court, however, found that Thomas's habitual residence was "altered" from Germany to the United States when Mr. Friedrich forced Mrs. Friedrich and Thomas to leave the family apartment.

Habitual residence cannot be so easily altered. Even if we accept the district court's finding that Mr. Friedrich forced Mrs. Friedrich to leave the family apartment, no evidence supports a finding that Mr. Friedrich forced Mrs. Friedrich to remove Thomas from Germany; Mr. Friedrich was not even aware of the removal until after the fact. Thomas's temporary three-day stay on a United States military base did not transfer his habitual residence to the United States, even if it was precipitated by Mr. Friedrich's angry actions in a marital dispute. As a threshold matter, a United States military base is not sovereign territory of the United States. The military base in Bad Aibling is on land which belongs to Germany and which the United States Armed Services occupy only at the pleasure of the German government.

More fundamentally, Thomas's habitual residence in Germany is not predicated on the care or protection provided by his German father nor does it shift to the United States when his American mother assumes the role of primary caretaker. Thomas's habitual residence can be "altered" only by a change in geography and the passage of time, not by changes in parental affection and responsibility. The change in geography must occur before the questionable removal; here, the removal precipitated the change in geography. If we were to determine that by removing Thomas from his habitual residence without Mr. Friedrich's knowledge or consent Mrs. Friedrich "altered" Thomas's habitual residence, we would render the Convention meaningless. It would be an open invitation for all parents who abduct their children to characterize their wrongful removals as alterations of habitual residence.

This is a simple case. Thomas was born in Germany and resided exclusively in Germany until his mother removed him to the United States on August 2, 1991; therefore, we hold that Thomas was a habitual resident of Germany at the time of his removal.

B

The district court also found that Mr. Friedrich "terminated his actual exercise of his parental custody rights" when he "unilaterally" expelled Mrs. Friedrich and Thomas from his residence. We are doubtful that the evidence supports a finding that Mr. Friedrich unilaterally expelled Mrs. Friedrich and Thomas from the family apartment. It is undisputed that during the heated argument on July 27, 1991, Mr. Friedrich removed some and maybe even all of Thomas's toys from the apartment. Yet, Mrs. Friedrich and Thomas remained in the apartment through the night. Mrs. Friedrich was the one who actually removed Thomas from the residence and did so with the help of the United States Army.

Even if we accept the district court's finding that Mrs. Friedrich removed Thomas from Mr. Friedrich's residence only because she was forced to do so by Mr. Friedrich, we doubt that Mr. Friedrich terminated his custody rights. Mr. Friedrich continued to have contact with both Mrs. Friedrich and his child. Mr. Friedrich assisted Mrs. Friedrich in establishing quarters on the base and helped her move Thomas's crib on to the base. On July 29, 1991, Mr. Friedrich visited his child for four hours. On August 1, 1991, Mr. Friedrich met with Mrs. Friedrich to discuss the future of their relationship and the custody of Thomas. Although they gave conflicting accounts of the meeting, both stated that plans were made for Mr. Friedrich to visit Thomas within the next week.

Under the Convention, whether a parent was exercising lawful custody rights over a child at the time of removal must be determined under the law of the child's habitual residence. Hague Convention, Article 3. We have determined that Thomas was a habitual resident of Germany when Mrs. Friedrich removed him to the United States. Neither the district court, nor either party on appeal, applied German custody law to the above facts. At oral argument, however, both parties agreed that German custody law is similar to American law. Under American law, custodial rights can only be terminated by judicial action, or by circumstances much more extraordinary than those presented here. We would be surprised if Mr. Friedrich's actions terminated his custody rights under German law, but we do not make that factual determination. Instead, we remand to the district court with instructions to make a specific inquiry as to whether, under German law, Mr. Friedrich was exercising his custody rights at the time of Thomas's removal.

* * *

For the foregoing reasons, we REVERSE the district court's denial of the petition and REMAND the case to the district court with instructions to determine whether, under

German law, Mr. Friedrich was exercising his custody rights over Thomas at the time of the removal and to consider any affirmative defenses Mrs. Friedrich might raise.

THOMAS D. LAMBROS, Chief District Judge, dissenting.

* * *

With regard to the treaty itself, Article 13 provides:

> ...the judicial or administrative authority of the requested State is not bound to order the return of the child if the person, institution or other body which opposes its return establishes that-a the person,...having the care of the person of the child was not actually exercising the custody rights at the time of removal or retention...

In defining the rights of custody, Article 5 of the Convention includes rights relating to the care of the person of the child and the right to determine the child's place of residence. By expelling the child from the apartment, petitioner gave up his right to determine the child's place of residence which means that there was no right of custody to assert in the district court. Since there was no right of custody because petitioner gave it up, there was no breach of the rights of custody. Thus, removal was not wrongful under the terms of The Convention.

For these reasons, I believe the district court's decision should be affirmed.

Notes

1. For comment on the principal case see Adair Dyer, The Internationalization of Family Law, 30 U.C. Davis. L. Rev. 625, 640 (1997): "[T]he concept of 'actual exercise' [of custody rights] probably does not exist in the domestic laws of most states. Therefore it is, almost by necessity, a concept that is subject to an autonomous international interpretation. Thus the express reference [in *Friedrich*] to German law was troubling."

2. Ponath v. Ponath, 829 F. Supp. 363 (D. Utah 1993). The court denied the father's motion pursuant to the Convention to return his child to Germany. The parents had met in Utah when the father visited there from Germany. They married and lived in Utah for 14 months, including 4 months after their child was born. The family then flew to Germany to visit the father's family. They traveled on round trip tickets. The mother had suggested a 6-month open ticket, but the father said they would return to Utah within 3 months. The child traveled on a United States passport. The father obtained employment in Germany and began construction of a house there. At the end of 3 months, the mother expressed a wish to return to the United States, but did not return with the child until a year after arriving in Germany. The court found that the mother and child "were detained in Germany against her desires by means of verbal, emotional and physical abuse." The court also found, however, that some months after the mother desired to return to the United States, the father told the mother "that, if she desired to live without him as her husband and as the minor child's father, she and the child could leave Germany." The court denied the father's motion on the ground that Utah, not Germany, was the child's habitual residence when the mother returned to the United states, and on the "alternative basis...that [the father] gave his consent for [the mother] to return to the United States with the minor child." With regard to "habitual residence," the court said:

> Although it is the habitual residence of the child that must be determined, the desires and actions of the parents cannot be ignored by the court in making

that determination when the child was at the time of removal or retention an infant. The concept of habitual residence must, in the court's opinion, entail some element of voluntariness and purposeful design. * * * In this case, what began as a voluntary visit to petitioner's family in Germany, albeit an extended visit, might be viewed by the court as a change of habitual residence of the minor child but for respondent's intent and desire to return to the United States with the minor child and petitioner's willful obstruction of that purpose. Petitioner's coercion of respondent by means of verbal, emotional and physical abuse removed any element of choice and settled purpose which earlier may have been present in the family's decision to visit Germany. The aim of the Hague Convention is to prevent one parent from obtaining an advantage over the other in any future custody dispute. Friedrich v. Friedrich, 983 F.2d 1396, 1402 (6th Cir. 1993). For the court to grant petitioner's motion, and thereby sanction his behavior in forcing continued residence in Germany upon respondent, and through her, the minor child, would be to thwart a princip[al] purpose of the Hague Convention. In the court's view, coerced residence is not habitual residence within the meaning of the Hague Convention.

3. In re J., A Minor, [1990] 2 A.C. 562, [1990] 3 W.L.R. 492, [1990]. 2 All E.R. 961 (H.L. 1990). The parents, United Kingdom citizens, emigrated to Australia where they met, cohabited, had a child, but did not wed. Over two years after the child, J, was born, the mother left Australia without notifying the father. She took the child with her to England where she intended to reside indefinitely and not return to Australia. Twenty-two days after the mother had left Australia, the father obtained an order from an Australian Family Court judge awarding the father sole custody of the child. The father's application in England for return of the child under the Convention was dismissed and this dismissal was affirmed by the Court of Appeal and by the House of Lords. The opinion in the House of Lords held that the removal of the child from Australia was not wrongful because under Australian law, until the father obtained the custody order, the sole right of custody of the illegitimate child was in the mother. The retention of the child in England after the Australian custody order was not wrongful because by that time Australia was no longer the child's "habitual residence." On this last point, the opinion stated:

> [T]here is a significant difference between a person ceasing to be habitually resident in country A, and his subsequently becoming habitually resident in country B. A person may cease to be habitually resident in country A in a single day if he or she leaves it with a settled intention not to return to it but to take up long-term residence in country B instead. Such a person cannot, however, become habitually resident in country B in a single day. An appreciable period of time and a settled intention will be necessary to enable him or her to become so. During that appreciable period of time the person will have ceased to be habitually resident in country A but not yet have become habitually resident in country B. * * * [W]here a child of J's age is in the sole lawful custody of the mother, his situation with regard to habitual residence will necessarily be the same as hers.

In re S, [1998] A.C. 750 (H.L. 1997), distinguished In re J and held that the Hague Convention was violated when the maternal grandmother, who had removed an illegitimate child from England to Ireland before the father obtained an order of an English court granting him custody, refused to return the child. The court held that the grandmother had no power to change the child's habitual residence. Therefore the child was still habitually resident in England when the father obtained the custody decree and the grandmother's failure to return the child as ordered by the English court was a wrongful "retention" of the child within the meaning of Article 3 of the Convention.

In re H, [2000] 2 W.L.R. 337 (H.L. 2000), held that an Irish court was "an institution or any other body" possessing custody rights within the meaning of Convention article 3(a). Therefore the mother had wrongfully removed her illegitimate child from Ireland after the father had filed a petition with the court for custody of the child.

In re A, [1996] 1 W.L.R. 25, [1996] 1 All E.R. 24 (Family Div.), held that the children had acquired a habitual residence in Iceland where the father, a United States serviceman from Michigan, was stationed and where the family lived for two years before the mother took the children to England. Because Iceland was not a Convention signatory, the court declined to make an order under Convention standards and denied the father's request for return of the children to Michigan, where he had begun divorce proceedings. The court found that return to Michigan was not in the best interests of the children. The children had lived in Michigan with the father's parents for three months between the time the father left his service post in England and they joined him in Iceland.

Feder v. Evans-Feder, 63 F.3d 217 (3rd Cir. 1995) stated:

> [W]e believe that a child's habitual residence is the place where he or she has been physically present for an amount of time sufficient for acclimatization, and which has a 'degree of settled purpose' from the child's perspective. We further believe that a determination...must focus on the child and consists of an analysis of the child's circumstances in that place and the parent's present, shared intentions regarding their child's presence there.

Id. at 224. The court found that the child had acquired a habitual residence in Australia where he had lived with his parents, United States citizens, for six months before he returned to the United States with his mother, purportedly for a family visit. The mother had no intention of returning to Australia and filed for divorce in Pennsylvania. The court vacated the trial court's denial of the father's petition for return of the child and remanded for consideration of the mother's contention that the court should invoke the article 13(b) "intolerable situation" exception.

For a German case refusing to order the return of an Illegitimate child, see Amtsgericht Hamburg-Altona, Beschluá vom September 11, 1991, AZ 351F 128/91 (the father was not exercising his custody rights in Spain because after the separation of the parents, the mother provided the child with care and education, and by taking the child to Germany the mother only made it harder for the father to exercise his visitation rights, but she did not deny these rights).

The United States and other countries have complained that Germany is not fulfilling its Convention obligations. There is criticism of decisions of German courts as not applying the Convention properly and taking at least a year to reach a decision. Even when a court orders return of a child, Germany has complied only 65 percent of the time with court orders to send a child back to a U.S. parent. In May 2000, at a meeting in Berlin, President Clinton raised these concerns with German Chancellor Schroeder.

In February 2000, The National Center for Missing and Exploited Children, based in Virginia, stated that Mexico has honored about 3 percent of U.S. requests under the Convention for return of a child. The Mexican Embassy declared this figure exaggerated and stated that Mexico had a 50 percent return rate.

4. Viragh v. Foldes, 612 N.E.2d 241 (Mass. 1993). Father and mother, Hungarians, lived in Hungary, a Convention signatory, with their two sons. They were divorced in Hungary. The mother was granted custody of the children and the father granted specified rights of visitation. The mother visited the United States where she married a dual citizen of the United States and Hungary and became pregnant with his child. She returned to Hungary and obtained a visa for entry into the United States as the wife of a United States citizen. Without informing the father of her plans, she returned to the United States with her two sons. At the time, she did not intend to live permanently in the United States, thinking that her second husband would return to Hungary, but she subsequently formed the intention to make the United States her home with the children of her first marriage. The father petitioned under the Convention for return of the children to his custody in Hungary or, in the alternative, that the mother be ordered to send the children to Hungary twice a year at her expense. The trial court instead ordered the mother to reimburse the father's expenses in coming to the United States to visit the children. The father claimed that he did not have the funds to purchase tickets for later reimbursement. The Supreme Judicial Court of Massachusetts remanded for submission of evidence "from which the Judge may craft an appropriate visitation order which recognizes the costs associated with visitation as well as the financial limitations of the parties." After the children had been removed to the United States, a Hungarian court had ruled that their best interests required that the mother retain custody. The court interpreted this as a declaration that, under Hungarian law, the mother's retention of the children in the United States was not wrongful. With regard to rights of access, the opinion states:

> The Convention distinguishes between "rights of custody" and "rights of access," and mandates return only when children have been removed or retained in breach of rights of custody * * * Art. 3; art. 12. * * * When a child has been removed or retained in breach of rights of custody, and no exceptions set forth in art. 13 have been established, the Convention mandates that the nation to which the child has been taken order the return of the child to its habitual residence "forthwith." Art. 12. In Contrast, the Convention does not mandate any specific remedy when a noncustodial parent has established interference with rights of access. Rather, nations are instructed in art. 21 to "promote the peaceful enjoyment of access rights and the fulfillment of any conditions to which the exercise of those rights may be subject," as well as to "take steps to remove, as far as possible, all obstacles to the exercise of such rights."

The Report of the Special Commission to study the operation of the Convention, cited in the notes following the Convention supra in this chapter, states that at the January 19, 1993 session, The First Secretary of the Permanent Bureau of the Hague Conference on Private International Law accepted the criticism that the Convention "does not offer sufficient protection to rights of access."

5. On remand in *Friedrich*, the trial court ordered the mother to return the child to the father in Germany, but stayed the order pending appeal. Finally on March 13, 1996, four and a half years after the father filed suit in the United States under the Convention, the Sixth Circuit affirmed and ordered return "forthwith." 78 F.3d 1060, 1070 (6th Cir. 1996). The court held that "if a person has valid custody rights to a child under the law of the country of the child's habitual residence, that person cannot fail to 'exercise' those custody rights...short of acts that constitute clear and unequivocal abandonment of the child." Id. at 1066. The court affirmed the trial court's

rejection of the mother's argument under Convention Article 13(b) that return would expose the child to psychological harm and held that such harm did not include the child's attachment to family and friends in Ohio during the pendency of the action.

Section 2: Exceptions to the Duty to Return

Tahan v. Duquette
613 A.2d 486 (N.J. App. 1992)

KESTIN, J.A.D.

In a prior appeal in this matter, Duquette v. Tahan, 252 N.J.Super. 554, 600 A.2d 472 (App.Div.1991), we held that the Convention on the Civil Aspects of International Child Abduction, adopted at The Hague on October 25, 1980 (the Convention), was effective in the United States as a treaty and applied to the parties. The case was remanded for a limited purpose: "to determine the applicability of the exceptions contained in Article 13b, particularly the second paragraph of that subarticle." Id. at 563, 600 A.2d 472.

The Convention requires the return of a child to the place in which the child habitually resided immediately before a wrongful removal or retention. We determined that the plaintiff, Fred Tahan, was obliged under the terms of the Convention and the statute implementing it, 42 U.S.C.A. § 11601 et seq., to return the child to the defendant, Michelle Duquette, in the Province of Quebec. Under the Convention, the merits of a custody dispute are to be decided in the place of habitual residence by a tribunal with subject matter jurisdiction.

Article 13 of the Convention, however, excuses the duty to return under specified circumstances. One of these, set out in subparagraph b, is "a grave risk that his or her return would expose the child to physical or psychological harm or otherwise place the child in an intolerable situation." In remanding, it was our expectation that this issue would be resolved promptly and that the situation of the parties would, juridically at least, be quickly stabilized. The record discloses, instead, that the single, limited issue on remand was not addressed until more than seven months had expired.

On June 24, 1992, the proceeding opened with the court's request for an offer of proof from the plaintiff. Counsel responded that plaintiff would rely upon the testimony of four witnesses. A court-appointed clinical psychologist who had prepared a psychological and bonding evaluation of the parties and the child would testify concerning the subject matter of his report. The plaintiff himself and his present wife would also testify, addressing the child's "dreams and his desires, his nightmares and fears", as well as his family relationships. The fourth person the plaintiff proposed to call was the child's teacher during the preceding school year "who has probably spent more time with [the child] in the last nine months than anyone other than his father, his step-mother and his baby sister." The purpose of all the foregoing testimony, according to counsel, was to give the court an opportunity "to consider how this child will be affected by the decision today... We have to look at the psychological harm that [the child] will suffer..." Counsel noted that the motivations of the parties would be explored, and concluded: "the clear and convincing evidence...will show that there is a grave risk of psychological harm to [the child] if this court disrupts his life now by compelling his return to Canada."

After hearing the response of defense counsel, the trial court ruled that the Article 13b inquiry, concerning physical or psychological harm or otherwise placing the child in an intolerable situation, was not intended to cover factual matter which was subject to being considered in a plenary custody hearing. To do so, the trial judge opined, would be to usurp jurisdictional prerogatives reserved by the Convention to the courts of Quebec. The court ruled, accordingly, that the proffered testimony would not be heard. The trial court went on to describe the Article 13b inquiry as being limited to the question whether there exists in the place of habitual residence such "internal strife" or unrest as to place the child at risk. The trial judge explained that, in his view, the focus of the Article 13b inquiry was exclusively upon the jurisdiction involved and not upon the individuals.

The court ordered the child to be turned over to the defendant for return to Canada two days later. The trial court denied a stay pending appeal. The next day, we stayed the order pending appeal and subsequently denied defendant's motion to vacate the stay. We now affirm the ruling of the trial court and vacate the stay. The trial court shall, within ten days, enter an appropriate order establishing the details concerning the early return of the child to the defendant.

We agree with the trial judge that the Article 13b inquiry was not intended to deal with issues or factual questions which are appropriate for consideration in a plenary custody proceeding. Psychological profiles, detailed evaluations of parental fitness, evidence concerning lifestyle and the nature and quality of relationships all bear upon the ultimate issue. The Convention reserves these considerations to the appropriate tribunal in the place of habitual residence, here Canada, specifically Quebec. No court on a petition for return should intrude upon a foreign tribunal's subject matter jurisdiction by addressing such issues.

Nevertheless, it is clear that Article 13b requires more than a cursory evaluation of the home jurisdiction's civil stability and the availability there of a tribunal to hear the custody complaint. If that were all that were required, the drafters of the Convention could have found a clear, more direct way of saying so.

Although we are not bound by the decisions of courts in other states or by the manner in which a treaty has been interpreted in other nations, a proper regard for promoting uniformity of approach in addressing a treaty of this kind requires that the views of other courts receive respectful attention. We are satisfied from our review of cases from various American and foreign jurisdictions cited by the parties that this precise issue has not been squarely addressed in an authoritative manner. We are satisfied further that the view we express on this question comports with conceptual principals embodied in the Convention which have informed the decisions of other courts in interpreting and applying the Convention.

To hold, as the trial court did, that the proper scope of inquiry precludes any focus on the people involved is, in our view, too narrow and mechanical. Without engaging in an exploration of psychological make-ups, ultimate determinations of parenting qualities, or the impact of life experiences, a court in the petitioned jurisdiction, in order to determine whether a realistic basis exists for apprehensions concerning the child's physical safety or mental well-being, must be empowered to evaluate the surroundings to which the child is to be sent and the basic personal qualities of those located there. The last paragraph of Article 13 says as much: "In considering the circumstances referred to in this Article, the judicial and administrative authorities shall take into account the information relating to the social background of the child provided by the Central Authority or other competent authority of the child's habitual residence."

Here, however, the plaintiff indicated no intention to address the surroundings and those located there in his proofs. Every element of his proffer went to issues which, under the Convention, may only be addressed in a plenary custody proceeding in Quebec.

The failure of the trial judge to interview the child was not plain error. To the contrary, an interview with the judge, under the circumstances before the court, could not have served a useful purpose. Article 13 of the Convention excuses the duty to return if a child of appropriate age and maturity objects. This standard simply does not apply to a nine-year old child.[1]

* * *

Affirmed. We remand to the trial court for entry of such orders as are necessary to effectuate this decision. We do not retain jurisdiction.

Notes

1. B. V. B., [1993] 2 All E.R. 144, [1992] 3 W.L.R. 865 (Ct. App. 1992). English spouses moved to Canada and became Canadian citizens. Four years later, their child was born. Ten years after the move to Canada, the father filed for divorce. The court granted the mother interim custody and gave the father access rights pending further custody proceedings. Without notice to the father, the mother removed the child to England. The Canadian court then made an ex parte order for the immediate return of the child. The father petitioned in England for the return of the child under the Hague Convention, which had been incorporated in English law by the Child Abduction and Custody Act of 1985. The trial judge denied the remedy on the ground that since the father only had access rights, the removal of the child was not unlawful and, under Article 13, there was a grave risk that the child would be placed in an intolerable situation because the mother was subsisting on charity and public welfare and in Canada and received no child support from the father. The Court of Appeal reversed and ordered that the child "be returned forthwith to the jurisdiction of the" Canadian court. With regard to the meaning of "rights of custody" in Article 3(a), the court said "the [Canadian] court itself had a right of custody at this time in the sense that it had the right to determine the child's place of residence..." With regard to the meaning of "intolerable situation" in Article 13(b), the court said:

> [A] very high degree of intolerability must be established in order to bring into operation art. 13(b)... [T]he facts of this case do not come anywhere near to the level of intolerability which is required when considering the provisions of art. 13. It must also be borne in mind that art. 13 does not oblige the court to decline to order the return of the child even if grave risk of an intolerable situ-

---

1. Plaintiff has moved to supplement the record with a certification of the court-appointed psychologist who evaluated the parties and the child. The certification endeavors to establish that this nine-year old child possesses the requisite maturity to lodge an effective objection to his return to Canada. The motion to supplement the record is granted. After carefully reviewing the certification submitted, we have determined that the material offered does not establish the proposition which it seeks to advance.

ation is established. It provides a discretion to the judge to consider whether the return is an appropriate order to make in all the circumstances.

Re F, [1995] 3 W.L.R. 339, [1995] 3 All E.R. 641 (C.A.), did invoke the "intolerable situation" exception in the light of the father's physical abuse of both mother and child.

Blondin v. Dubois, 189 F.3d 240 (2d Cir. 1999). The mother alleged that the father physically abused children that the mother removed from France. The district court refused to return the children on the ground that return would subject the children to grave risk of harm. The Second Circuit vacated the decision and remanded, stating: "the Hague convention requires a more complete analysis of the full panoply of arrangements [under French law] that might allow the children to be returned to the country from which they were (concededly) wrongfully abducted, in order to allow the courts of that nation an opportunity to adjudicate custody." Id. at 242.

Contrary to the approach in B. v. B., above, several German courts have refused to return children removed to German by their mother on the ground that the children have spent most of their time with their mother, that return would result in psychological harm, and that the Article 13(b) "intolerable situation" exception applies. Amtsgericht Bad Kreuznach, Beschluá vom March 6, 1992, AZ 9F 63/92; Amtsgericht Ludwigshafen, Beschluá vom December 13 1991, AZ 5dF 223/91; Amtsgericht Saarbrücken, Beschluá vom July 7, 1991, AZ 40F 177/91. A French decision taking this approach is District Attorney in the Strasbourg District Court v. Shamee, Colmar District Court, Second Civil Division, Judgment of March 12, 1993. The Report of the meeting of the Special Commission to study the operation of the Convention, referred to in the notes following the Convention in this chapter, states that during the afternoon session of January 20, 1993, "[o]ne expert suggested that [Art. 13(b)] might be used in cases where a very young child has spent a large part of his/her life with the abducting parent and would not remember the other parent. Others considered this to be an unacceptable use of the provision."

2. Re S, [1993] 2 All E.R. 683 (Ct. App. 1992). Husband and wife had lived in Borneo, France and Norway before returning to live in Paris. The father was a petroleum engineer whose work took him to many parts of the world. The mother was English. The child's mother tongue was English. She was 10 years old at the time of proceedings under the Convention. She had a high IQ but suffered from speech difficulties. Psychologists and a speech therapist advised that she should be educated in English rather than French. The mother and father separated and the mother, without notice to the father, took the child to England. The father's petition under the Convention for return of the child was denied by the trial judge and the refusal was affirmed on appeal. This denial was based on the child's statement that she did not want to go back to France because having to speak French aggravated her speech problems. The Court of Appeal said:

> [T]hat part of art. 13 which relates to the child's objections to being returned is completely separate from paragraph (b) [intolerable situation]. [I]f the court should come to the conclusion that the child's views have been influenced by some other person, e.g. the abducting parent, or that the objection to return is because of a wish to remain with the abducting parent, then it is probable that little or no weight will be given to those views. Any other approach would be to drive a coach and horses through the primary scheme of the Hague Convention. * * * On the other hand, where the court finds that the child or children have valid reasons for their objections to being returned, then it may refuse to order the return.

The court also stated that although the child was only 10 years old "[t]here was evidence which entitled [the trial judge] to find... that she had attained an age and degree of maturity at which it was appropriate to take account of her views." The Explanatory Report by Elisa Perez-Vera, cited in the notes Following the Convention, supra this chapter, states:

> [A]ll efforts to agree on a minimum age at which the views of the child could be taken into account failed, since all the ages suggested seemed artificial, even arbitrary. It seemed best to leave the application of this clause to the discretion of the competent authorities.

Report, ¶ 30 (English translation by the Permanent Bureau of the Hague Conference on Private International Law).

3. Re A, [1992] 1 All E.R. 929 (Ct. App. 1992). Mother and father lived in Australia where they had married after emigrating from England. Nine years later they divorced. They had experienced repeated marital difficulties and at one point had returned to England before moving back to Australia. The Australian divorce court did not make a decree concerning the custody of the couple's two children and declared itself satisfied with the arrangement that the mother and father had made-residence with the mother and access for visits by the father. Without informing the father of her plans, the mother returned to her parents' home in England with the two children. She sent a telegram to the father stating that she had come to England for a rest. Three days later the father wrote a letter stating that although what the mother had done was illegal, for the children's sake he was not going to contest the matter. He asked that his letters and presents be given to the children and that he be informed of their progress. He also wrote that the mother and boys were welcome to stay with him at any time: "[y]ou may want a holiday one day or you may even want to try Australia again." The mother responded informing the father that she intended to remain in England indefinitely. In the meantime, he began proceedings under the Convention for return of the children. The father contends that he did not tell the mother of his action under the Convention for fear that she would move and become impossible to locate. The mother opposed return on the grounds that return would place the children "in an intolerable situation" within the meaning of Article 13(b) and that the father has "acquiesced in the removal or retention" under 13(a). The trial judge rejected both of these contentions and ordered that the children be returned. The Court of Appeal reversed and remanded for the trial judge to exercise his discretion under 13(a), finding, two to one, that the father had acquiesced. On the issue of acquiescence, Lord Donaldson, Master of the Rolls, stated:

> [T]he father's letter * * * is incapable of any construction other than a clearly expressed acquiescence and * * * was so construed and believed by the mother. * * * The father cannot be heard to say that he had an intention not to acquiesce which he kept secret from the mother, any more than in other circumstances it would be open to the mother to say, and perhaps to prove, that the father had at one time had an intention to acquiesce which was kept secret from her.

* * *

> The question has been raised of whether an acquiescence can be withdrawn. I think that it cannot, in the sense that once there is acquiescence the condition set out in art. 13 is satisfied. On the other hand an apparent acquiescence fol-

lowed immediately by a withdrawal may lead the court to question whether the apparent acquiescence was real or whether it was the product of emotional turmoil which would not reasonably be interpreted as real acquiescence. That apart, the only relevance of the time which elapses between acquiescence and a purported withdrawal of the acquiescence is in the context of the exercise of a discretion whether to return the child to the jurisdiction of the courts of country A in order to enable those courts to make decisions as to its future. In this case this period lasted from 27 September [when the mother received the father's letter] until 6 December 1991 when the proceedings were served upon the mother.

Lord Donaldson also stated than in exercising discretion on remand, the Family Division judge should be mindful that:

It is only if the interests of the child render it appropriate that the courts of country B rather than country A shall determine [the child's] future that there can be any exception to an order for its return. This is something quite different from a consideration of whether the best interest of the child will be served by its living in country B rather than country A. That is not the issue unless paragraph (b) [intolerable situation] of art 13 applies. The issue is whether de-

Chapter 10

Letters of Credit

Introduction

A letter of credit issued by a bank is one of the most important tools in facilitating international commercial transactions. Much international litigation has concerned letters of credit.

Although a letter of credit need not be issued by a bank (Uniform Commercial Code 5-102(a)(9)), typically a letter of credit is a document signed by a bank officer and contains a promise that the bank will pay a sum of money to the addressee, or "beneficiary," under stated circumstances. The credit is issued by the bank at the request of its customer, or "applicant," as one form of extending the bank's credit to that customer. If the customer wishes to purchase goods or services, but is unable or unwilling to pay cash in advance, and the seller is unwilling to sell on the customer's credit, the letter of credit is a way that the seller can be assured of payment if the seller meets the conditions specified in the credit. [On the other end of the transaction, the buyer of goods or services may insist on a letter of credit guaranteeing the seller's performance. For simplicity, this note focuses on the buyer's obligations.]

A letter of credit differs from a simple guaranty of payment in that the bank is promising to pay the sum stated subject only to the conditions set out in the credit. If these conditions are met, the bank must pay, even though the buyer, its customer, would have a perfectly good defense to payment and probably a claim against the seller for breach of contract. The conditions stated in the credit are such that the bank can determine simply by inspecting certain documents submitted to it by the seller whether the conditions have been met. The documents do not guarantee that the seller has kept its contract with the buyer. If, the documents specified in the credit are submitted to the bank, but in fact the seller has not properly performed the contract, the bank must pay and leave the dispute for its customer, the buyer, to settle. Bank would pay seller on inspecting the documents that seller presented to it and satisfying itself that these documents complied with the credit; then the bank would be entitled to be reimbursed by its customer, the buyer; then buyer would have to recover from seller. One important effect of a letter of credit is to put the seller "in funds" while the dispute with buyer is being litigated or otherwise settled.

The letter of credit is the third of three contracts connected with the sales transaction. The first contract is between buyer and seller specifying the obligations of the parties and providing for the furnishing of a letter of credit by one or both parties. The second contract is the contract between the buyer and its bank, in which they agree on the terms of the credit and the buyer promises to reimburse the bank if, but only if, the bank pays the seller after the seller has presented the documents specified by the buyer and listed by the bank in the credit. The third contract, the letter of credit, is independent of the first contract between buyer and seller. The bank promises to pay the seller (the "beneficiary") under different, and far easier to determine conditions, than does the buyer: the bank will pay on presentation of the stated documents, period.

The most common form of letter of credit is the "documentary" credit. "Documentary" means that certain pieces of paper, in addition to the draft, or demand for payment, are specified in the credit as required for presentment in order for payment to be due.

There is a distinction between standby letters of credit and commercial letters of credit. Under the standby letter, the bank promises to pay if its customer does not perform. In other words, one of the documents required is a certification that the bank's customer has defaulted. Under the commercial credit, the bank, not its customer, has a direct obligation to pay on submission of the required documents. Commercial credits are commonly used for sales of goods. United States banks issue about six times more standby than commercial letters.

Unlike banks in many other major commercial powers, United States banks have historically been denied the power to issue guarantees on behalf of their customers for the accommodation of third parties. For example, the Glass-Steagall Act of 1933, also known as the Banking Act of 1933 (Act of June 16, 1933, ch. 89, 48 Stat. 162), sets out the powers of national banks. The power of guaranty is not among the powers granted. See 12 U.S.C. §24, subdivision 7. A commercial or standby letter of credit is not deemed a "guaranty" within the doctrine making bank guarantees ultra vires, in part because the obligation to pay on the credit is insulated from the performance of the underlying contract.

The Uniform Customs and Practice for Documentary Credits (UCP), is a detailed list of provisions to which most letters of credit are expressly made subject. Without this kind of incorporation by reference, every credit would have to be many pages in length. The provisions in the UCP are arrived at by consultation and agreement between commercial associations all over the world. After agreement, the UCP is published by the Commission on Banking Technique and Practice of the International Chamber of Commerce, which has its headquarters in Paris, but has offices in over 80 countries. The UCP is revised from time to time as new problems and technology require. The latest revision was in 1993. The 1993 revision was spearheaded by a Working Group composed of international bankers, law professors, and banking lawyers.

Another important source of letter of credit law is Article 5 of the Uniform Commercial Code (UCC). New York has a non-uniform provision (UCC 5-102(4)), which states that "unless otherwise agreed" Article 5 does not apply if the UCP does. Alabama and Missouri copied this New York provision. As of January 1, 1997, none of these three states had adopted the 1995 revision of Article 5. This exception is unfortunate and in these states the credit should provide for application of Article 5. Article 5 and UCP overlap to some extent, but primarily cover different issues.

The New York exception, that UCC Article 5 does not apply if the UCP does, was caused by the fear of a New York bankers' organization, the Clearing House Association, that Article 5 would interfere with international trade and that only the UCP, which the organization was instrumental in drafting, should govern. This fear has proven to be unfounded.

In 1995 the National Conference of Commissioners on Uniform States Laws and the American Law Institute approved a revision of Article 5, which is under consideration by state legislatures. Unless otherwise indicated, references in the Notes of this chapter are to the 1995 revision.

On December 11, 1995, the UN General Assembly passed a resolution adopting the Convention on Independent Guarantees and Stand-by Letters of Credit, G.A. Res. 50/48, U.N. GAOR, 50th Sess. Agenda Item 143, U.N. Doc. A/RES/50/48 (1996). The convention will enter into force on the first day of the month following the expiration of one year from the date the fifth instrument of ratification or accession is deposited with the UN Secretary-General. The Convention was prepared under the auspices of the United Nations Commission on International Trade Law (UNCITRAL). On June 21, 1999, the International Chamber of Commerce endorsed the Convention.

The coordination of the International Financial Services Association and the participation of major international financial institutions and law firms has produced the International Standby Practices (ISP98). The text was submitted to UNCITRAL for its endorsement at its Plenary Session in 2000. The reason for the ISP98 is that the UCP did not deal adequately with standby letters of credit. See James E. Byrne, The International Standby Practices (ISP98): New Rules for Standby Letters of Credit, 32 UCC L.J. 149 (1999).

For discussion of letters of credit and guarantees used in international trade, see Javier Camacho De Los Rios, The New ICC Regulations on Contract Bonds, 30 Int'l Law. 1 (1996); Alberto Giampieri & Giovanni Nardulli, Enforceability of International Documentary Letters of Credit: An Italian Perspective, 27 Int'l Law. 1013 (1993); Boris Kozolchyk, The Financial Standby: A Summary Description of Practice and Related Legal Problems, 28 UCC L.J. 327 (1996).

For discussion of arbitration to resolve letter of credit disputes, see William W. Park, Arbitration in Banking and Finance, 17 Ann. Rev. Banking L. 213 (1998).

Section 1: Compliance with Terms of the Letter

Banco Espanol de Credito v. State Street Bank and Trust Co.,
385 F.2d 230 (1st Cir. 1967), cert. denied, 390 U.S. 1013 (1968)

COFFIN, Circuit Judge.

This suit began as a claim by appellant, a Spanish bank (Banco Espanol), against appellee, a domestic bank (State Street), for the latter's allegedly wrongful refusal to accept and pay two drafts drawn upon it pursuant to two irrevocable commercial letters of credit. Each letter was issued by State Street at the behest of its customer, Robert Lawrence, Inc. (Lawrence), a Boston clothing concern. Banco Espanol was designated the advising bank and two Spanish suppliers (Alcides and Longuer) were named as beneficiaries. The cases were consolidated for trial in the district court sitting without a jury and, following judgment for State Street, appellant took these appeals.

The issue is whether State Street, whose letters of credit, as amended, called for the presentation of an inspection certificate by a named firm stipulating "that the goods are in conformity with the order", was justified in refusing to honor the drafts of Banco Espanol on the ground that the inspection certificate did not meet the terms of the letters of credit.

The transaction was initiated by Lawrence to finance the purchase of raincoats, beach jackets, knit shirts, and cardigans from Alcides and Longeur. Based upon preliminary arrangements apparently worked out by an intermediary, of which more later, Lawrence obtained two irrevocable letters of credit from State Street. One letter covered Lawrence orders Nos. 101, 102, and 103 for beach jackets, outer coats and cotton garments in the revised final amount of $105,630, and the other covered Lawrence order No. 100 for wool knit shirts and cardigans in the revised final amount of $13,320. Both letters constituted Banco Espanol the correspondent bank, and required signed invoices, customs invoices, inspection certificates, and full sets of clean on board ocean bills of lading dated not later than March 31, 1963.

* * *

Supervigilancia, on March 26, executed its two certificates of inspection. It divided each certificate into two parts. The first part tended to the matter at hand saying that (1) it had carried out its inspection

> "* * * basing ourselves on the details shown in the orders or Stocksheets Nos. [100], 101, 102 and 103 * * * and in the samples that were handed to us by the Requirer [Alcides and Longuer], that corresponded, according to his sayings ratified in presence of a Public Notary, to the samples seen and approved by the Delegate of Firm ROBERT LAWRENCE INC, during his stay in Barcelona, and with are mentioned in the notes appearing in orders Stock-sheets Nos. [100], 101, 102 and 103, where there is a note reading:

"COATS or JACKETS * * * TO BE AS SAMPLE INSPECTED IN SPAIN";

that (2) the letters of credit required it to certify "THAT THE GOODS ARE IN CONFORMITY WITH THE ORDER"; that (3) a ten per cent random sample had been taken; and that (4) the "whole * * * [was] found conforming to the conditions estipulated [sic] on the Order-Stock-sheets."

The second part of each certificate contained a chronological account of the cabled messages we have summarized, followed by this language: "Requirer * * * is formally requiring us for delivering this certificate what we are doing today under reserves, not as far as the goods are concerned, which correspond to the samples seen and produced referred to at the beginning of this certificate, but to the existing difference between both interested parties as per the quoted cables."

All documents were presented to Banco Espanol, which honored them and made payment or the equivalent on March 28 and 29. On April 3 State Street cabled its refusal to accept the drafts on it "because accompanying inspection certificates non conforming with terms of credits which require certificates certifying goods are in conformity with the orders". A later letter amplified its position by specifying that the certificates merely indicated conformity to samples alleged by the seller to "correspond" to other samples allegedly approved by the buyer and that the certificates were issued "under reserves".

The district court sustained this position, referring to the requirement that documents strictly conform to letter of credit provisions, and pointing out that each certificate failed in three respects: (1) that it merely certified that the goods conformed to "conditions"—which left it unclear if the conformity was to the whole of the order or only part; (2) that there was a doubt whether the "order-stock-sheet" was different from the order; and (3) that the certificate was confined to samples handed to the inspecting agency by a representative of the manufacturer. The court concluded that "* * * this was not the unqualified certificate required by the letter of credit and defendant bank was justified in its refusal to accept it."

We do not agree. Since, in our view, the third alleged defect noted by the court presents the most difficult problem, we shall deal with it first.

We note, at the outset, that an issuing bank's duty to honor a demand for payment is, to some extent, determined by statute. The Uniform Commercial Code, Mass.Gen.Laws ch. 106, §5-114(1) (1958), provides, in relevant part, that "An issuer must honor a draft or demand for payment which complies with the terms of the relevant credit regardless of whether the goods or documents conform to the underlying contract for sale or other contract between the customer and the beneficiary." This Code provision, however, simply codifies longstanding decisional law and does not assist us here in determining whether the inspection certificate submitted by Supervigilancia complied with the terms of the credit.

We take as a starting point the substantial body of case law which establishes and supports the general rule that documents submitted incident to a letter of credit are to be strictly construed. This is because international financial transactions rest upon the accuracy of documents rather than on the condition of the goods they represent. But we note some leaven in the loaf of strict construction. Not only does *haec verba* not control absolutely, but some courts now cast their eyes on a wider scene than a single document. We are mindful, also, of the admonition of several legal scholars that the integrity of international transactions (i.e., rigid adherence to material matters) must somehow strike a balance with the requirement of their fluidity (i.e., a reasonable flexibility as to ancillary matters) if the objective of increased dealings to the mutual satisfaction of all interested parties is to be enhanced.

* * *

What we face here is a matter of procedure which can, in the first instance, be structured by the purchasing party. How may a buyer in the international market place be assured before payment that his purchase as delivered is of the quality agreed upon by the parties? As buyers become more concerned about quality, this issue is likely to become more important. That there are so few cases or comments addressed to the issue of reasonable precautions to assure quality is indicative of the relatively novel status of the problem, at least so far as courts have dealt with it. We are mindful of the testimony in this case that an official of appellee, a busy bank, engaged in passing upon the issuance of 1,500 to 2,000 letters of credit a year for several decades, has encountered in this case his first experience with a letter of credit calling for a certificate of conformity to the order.

What are the realities of such a requirement on the part of the buyer? It is not enough that he receive the quantity of goods he ordered, nor that he receive goods capable of standard measure or grade. He must also, in such a case as this, receive them cut, tailored, sewn according to a style he has in mind. He must therefore rely on a sample he has seen and liked. Being in a distant part of the globe, the buyer must usually elect one of two alternatives. He may be present during the inspection process to verify the sample or he may select, with his seller's acquiescence, a person or firm in whom he has confidence to represent him. Unless he elects to be present, he is acting on faith- faith that the representative is capable and honest, and faith that the representative has the right samples or criteria to serve as a standard. Even if he mails an approved sample direct to the representative, he must rely on the integrity of the mails.

This act of faith-or its converse, the risk that merchandise will not turn out as hoped-is that of the buyer. As one contemporary student has written,

> "* * * there is one risk against which protection is required and which is less easy to guard against. That is the risk that the goods shipped may not comply with the terms of the sales contract as to quality. This is a risk which normally the buyer will have to bear * * * but * * * [he] can guard against the risk by requiring in his letter of request to the bankers that, in addition to the usual shipping documents, the vendor shall deliver a certificate of quality showing the goods to be as specified in the contract, signed by some responsible person at the place of shipment. The only risk then left to the buyer is that the person nominated to give the certificate may fail in his duty. But an entire absence of risk would mean an absence of business." A. G. Davis, The Law Relating to Commercial Letters of Credit, 3d ed., London, Sir Isaac Pitman & Sons Ltd., 1963, p. 19.

Or, in the words of other scholars,

> "The requirement of such other documents, and particularly certificates of analysis, quality, weight, and the like, is a reasonable precaution for a prudent buyer to take, since he may in this way obtain some measure of assurance that the merchandise is as ordered * * *. The bank is under no obligation and bears no responsibility for the accuracy of any such representations and certificates. Nevertheless, through selection of a reputable third party, the buyer does have a degree of assurance that the merchandise is as represented." Ward and Harfield, Bank Credits and Acceptances, 4th ed., Ronald Press, 1958, p. 45.

These observations go to the heart of this case. For the buyer here—Lawrence—was striving to assure the delivery of quality goods. To be sure, it deliberately postponed the problem when it caused the letters of credit to be issued without resolving the question of the inspecting agent. Then it naively sought to have the sellers accept one of its own representatives. It had long since sewn the seeds of dispute by sending to the sellers both "stock sheets" which were really orders and "orders" which were merely preliminary papers. When it finally reached agreement with the seller as to an inspecting agency, it neglected to specify precisely how it would conduct the inspection operation, leaving only the bland instruction that the goods must conform to orders. And, so far as the inspecting agency was concerned, the orders merely referred to samples that might very well have been inspected in Spain at some past time.

Consequently when faced on the eve of the shipping deadline both with a barrage of contradictory telegrams from the buyer and with samples which the sellers under oath stated "corresponded" with samples approved earlier by the buyer's representative in Barcelona, Supervigilancia had to act to the dissatisfaction of one of the parties to the basic contract. That it took the word, under oath, of the seller as to the appropriateness of the sample is no more than any inspector must ordinarily do. Unless the buyer is physically present (and Lawrence presumably could have arranged this during the frenetic two week period of cable traffic), the inspector must take someone's word that he is judging by the proper samples.

* * *

We see no significant difference in Supervigilancia being told by the manufacturers that the samples were those approved by the buyer and being told that they "corresponded" to such samples. * * * In effect, Lawrence in this case, by providing as a referent to the letter of credit requirement of conformity to orders merely the early cryptic description on the stock sheets ("Coats * * * to be as samples inspected in Spain"), procured no * * * reliable assurance of authenticity

* * *

To hold otherwise—that a buyer could frustrate an international transaction on the eve of fulfillment by a challenge to authenticity of sample—would make vulnerable many such arrangements where third parties are vested by buyers with inspection responsibilities but where, apart from their own competence and integrity, there is no iron-clad guarantee of the sample itself.

As for the argument that Supervigilancia's finding that the goods conform "to the conditions estipulated on the Order-Stock-sheets" is a meaningful variance from the terms of the letters of credit, we confess to semantic myopia. "The conditions" mean, as we read the certificates, all the conditions, hence the order itself. As for the dual use by the agency of the words "Order-Stock-sheets," we have already indicated both the nature and cause of the confusion and conclude that Supervigilancia acted solomonically in borrowing the substance of the stock sheets and the label of the "orders". We do not see how it could have done otherwise.

The remaining contention that "under reserves" has some mysterious meaning which infects the entire certificate is not borne out by the inapposite cases cited to us and is directly refuted by the limiting language immediately following- "not as far as the goods are concerned". Further reading of the document indicates clearly that the phrase was directed to the underlying dispute between buyer and seller, which could not be the concern of the advising bank.

We hold, therefore, that the inspection certificate in this case conformed in all significant respects to the requirements of the letter of credit.

* * * We reverse the judgment of the District Court and remand for such further proceedings, consistent with this opinion, as the court feels appropriate.

* * *

Notes

1. As the preceding case suggests, one important issue concerning payment under letters of credit is whether the documents presented to the issuer by the seller must strictly comply with the terms of the letter, or whether a looser standard, something like "substantial compliance," is sufficient. The preceding case holds that the documents "are to be strictly construed" but then states that "there is some leaven in the loaf of strict construction." UCP Art. 13(a) provides:

> Banks must examine all documents stipulated in the Credit with reasonable care, to ascertain whether or not they appear, on their face, to be in compliance with the terms and conditions of the Credit. Compliance of the stipulated documents on their face with the terms and conditions of the Credit, shall be determined by international standard banking practice as reflected in these Articles.

UCC 5-108(a) provides that "an issuer shall honor a presentation that, as determined by the standard practice referred to in subsection (e), appears on its face strictly to comply with the terms and conditions of the letter of credit." UCC 5-108(e) provides: "An issuer shall observe standard practice of financial institutions that regularly issue letters of credit. Determination of the issuer's observance of the standard practice is a matter of interpretation for the court. The court shall offer the parties a reasonable opportunity to present evidence of the standard practice."

Comment 1 to § 5-108 states: "The section adopts strict compliance rather than the standard that commentators have called 'substantial compliance,' the standard arguably applied in *Banco Espanol de Credito v. State Street Bank and Trust Co.*"—the preceding case.

In practice, much depends on the standards for determining whether documents that do not match exactly the stipulations in the credit nevertheless comply sufficiently and that payment is due. A recent survey of United States credit bankers reported "that 90% of the documents initially tendered contained discrepancies." Boris Kozolchyk, Strict Compliance and the Reasonable Document Checker, 56 Brooklyn L. Rev. 45, 48 (1990). UCP art. 14(c) provides that the issuing bank "may in its sole judgment approach the Applicant for a waiver of the discrepancy(ies)." Nevertheless, the Preface to the UCP states "[s]ome surveys indicate that approximately fifty per cent of the documents presented under the Documentary Credit are rejected because of discrepancies or apparent discrepancies. This diminishes the effectiveness of the Documentary Credit * * *. The marked increase in litigation involving Documentary Credits has also been of great concern."

The doctrine of strict compliance, permits the bank to determine quickly whether to pay, simply by inspecting the tendered documents and without becoming involved in any dispute concerning the sufficiency of the seller's performance of the contract of sale. UCP Art. 13(b) and UCC 5-108(b) allow the bank a reasonable time, not exceeding seven banking days.

2. The opinion in the preceding case states that "Banco Espanol was designated the advising bank." Since Banco Espanol paid when presented with the stipulated documents, it was apparently also a "confirming bank."

UCC 5-102(a)(1) defines "adviser" as "a person who, at the request of the issuer, a confirmer, or another adviser, notifies or requests another adviser to notify the beneficiary that a letter of credit has been issued, confirmed, or amended." UCC 5-107(c) sets out the obligations of an adviser: "An adviser that is not a confirmer is not obligated to honor or give value for a presentation. An adviser undertakes to the issuer and to the beneficiary accurately to advise the terms of the letter of credit, confirmation, amendment, or advice received by that person and undertakes to the beneficiary to check the apparent authenticity of the request to advise." UCP art. 7(a) provides that an advising bank "shall take reasonable care to check the apparent authenticity of the Credit which it advises. If the bank elects not to advise the credit, it must so inform the issuing Bank without delay."

A "confirming bank" is a bank other than the issuer that "undertakes, at the request or with the consent of the issuer, to honor a presentation under a letter of credit issued by another." UCC 5-102(a)(4). As the case indicates, a bank may be both an advising bank and a confirming bank. A form in common use contains a box to check if the bank elects to advise a credit and a different box to check if the bank in addition assumes the obligations of a confirming bank.

UCP art. 10(b) provides that "[p]resentation of documents must be made to the Issuing Bank or the Confirming Bank, if any, or any other Nominated Bank." A "nominated bank" is a bank authorized by the issuer or a confirming bank to effect payment on presentation of the proper documents. A nominated bank authorized by the issuer is sometimes referred to as a "drawee bank." See UCP art. 9(a)(iii)(b).

3. When, as in the preceding case, one of the documents is a certificate that the goods conform with the contract, the doctrine that the issuer's obligation to pay is independent of the performance of the underlying contract is somewhat compromised. The case explains the commercial justification for the use of inspection certificates.

4. Can the beneficiary of a letter of credit obtain jurisdiction over a distant issuer to sue the issuer for wrongful dishonor of the beneficiary's draw? Moog World Trade Corp. v. Bancomer, S.A., 90 F.3d 1382 (8th Cir. 1996), holds that "a bank issuing a commercial letter of credit at the request of its customer, payable at the bank's office, does not without more subject itself to personal jurisdiction in a distant forum, such as a court where the letter of credit beneficiary resides." Id. at 1387. The case collects authority in accord. Seaconsar Far East Ltd. v. Bank Markazi Jomhouri Islami Iran, [1994] 1 AC 438, [1993] 3 W.L.R. 756, [1993] 4 All E.R. 456 (H.L.), holds that jurisdiction exists in England over an Iranian bank that had promised to pay a Hong Kong company on presentation of documents to a London Bank.

Section 2: Enjoining Payment

Trans Meridian Trading Inc. v. Empresa Nacional de Comercializacion de Insumos
829 F.2d 949 (9th Cir. 1987)

Before WALLACE, HALL and LEAVY, Circuit Judges.

LEAVY, Circuit Judge.

This action involves a letter of credit issued by Banque Indosuez in favor of Banco Continental at the request of Trans Meridian Trading Inc. (TMTI). Banco Continental has demanded payment on the letter of credit. TMTI seeks to enjoin Banco Continental from demanding payment and Banque Indosuez from making payment. The district court denied TMTI's motion for a preliminary injunction. This court granted TMTI's request for a stay pending appeal. We now affirm the district court's decision and lift the stay.

FACTS

Defendant Multinacional Latinoamericana de Comercializacion de Fertilizantes (MULTIFERT) is a Panamanian company that acts as a bid solicitation agent for various Latin American countries. It solicited a bid from TMTI to supply fertilizer to Empresa Nacional de Comercializacion de Insumos (ENCI). TMTI is a California corporation. ENCI is a corporation wholly owned by the government of Peru.

On July 7, 1986, TMTI submitted its bid to MULTIFERT. As a condition of bid submission, TMTI was required to post a bond in favor of ENCI and MULTIFERT. At

TMTI's request, Banque Indosuez-Los Angeles issued the bid bond through Banque Indosuez-Panama. In consideration therefor, Banque Indosuez-Los Angeles issued letter of credit no. 1441-SB (LC 1441-SB) in favor of Banque Indosuez-Panama for $100,400.

In its bid, TMTI required that ENCI's payment be by an irrevocable and confirmed letter of credit issued by a prime United States bank. The bid also stated that if ENCI failed to post such a letter of credit, the fertilizer shipment would be delayed.

On July 14, MULTIFERT accepted, on behalf of ENCI, a portion of TMTI's bid involving large quantities of fertilizer. The acceptance restated ENCI's obligation to establish a letter of credit at a prime United States bank prior to shipment. TMTI sent MULTIFERT a draft format for the letter of credit that ENCI should post, stating a proposed value of $3,638,932.50 and noting shipping dates for the two shipments necessary to fill ENCI's order.

The contract also required TMTI to post a performance bond in favor of ENCI through a bank in Lima totaling six percent of the contract price, or $205,239. Banque Indosuez-Los Angeles arranged the issuance of a performance bond in favor of ENCI through Banco Continental. Banco Continental is located in Lima and describes itself as "indirectly owned by agencies of the government of Peru." In consideration for the performance bond, Banque Indosuez-Los Angeles issued letter of credit no. 1459-SB (LC 1459-SB) for $205,239 to Banco Continental on behalf of TMTI.

Under LC 1459-SB, Banque Indosuez was obligated to pay Banco Continental $205,239 upon Banco Continental's presentation of two documents: (1) Banco Continental's certification that it had been called upon to pay under the performance bond, and (2) an original statement "purportedly signed by the Gerente General of ENCI" that TMTI had been awarded the fertilizer contract but failed to deliver the fertilizer. LC 1459-SB also stated that "it is a condition of this letter of credit that our standby letter of credit no. 1441- SB...is now null and void." Finally, LC 1459-SB provided that "this credit is subject to the Uniform Customs and Practice for Documentary Credit (1983 Revision) International Chamber of Commerce (Publication no. 400)."

* * *

From July 28 through August 12 TMTI and ENCI or MULTIFERT exchanged telexes regarding vessel nomination, shipping dates, and ENCI's posting letters of credit. ENCI apparently believed it had a contractual shipping window of August 1-15 for the first shipment, whereas TMTI believed it had no obligation to confirm shipment dates until ENCI posted an acceptable letter of credit. ENCI opened two letters of credit in favor of TMTI, however, TMTI found them unacceptable because they were not opened at a prime United States bank. TMTI claims it arranged at least one vessel and shipping date, but was forced to cancel because it had not received an acceptable letter of credit from ENCI.

On August 15, TMTI advised ENCI of its vessel nominations for loading approximately August 25-September 5 and September 10-20. TMTI also requested that ENCI open new letters of credit and amend those already opened.

On August 16, the New York Times reported that the International Monetary Fund had declared Peru ineligible for new loans. TMTI expressed concern about this report.

On August 18, ENCI notified TMTI that it considered the contract cancelled because of TMTI's failure to ship within the contract period.

On August 22, ENCI requested payment from Banco Continental on the performance bond. That same day, Banco Continental requested payment of $205,239 from

Banque Indosuez-Los Angeles under LC 1459-SB. Banco Continental certified to Banque Indosuez that all terms and conditions of the letter of credit had been met and that the relevant documents were being forwarded.

On August 26, TMTI filed this action against ENCI, MULTIFERT, and Banque Indosuez claiming breach of contract and fraud. On August 27, the district court issued a temporary restraining order (TRO) enjoining Banque Indosuez from paying under either letter of credit and set a preliminary injunction hearing for September 5. Banque Indosuez and TMTI notified Banco Continental of the TRO on August 27 and 29.

On September 5, Banco Continental paid ENCI under the performance bond. On September 13, TMTI filed its first amended complaint, adding Banco Continental as a defendant.

TMTI claims that Banco Continental's request for payment under LC 1459-SB was fraudulent. TMTI alleges Banco Continental knew or should have known that the documents ENCI presented to it falsely stated that all the terms and conditions of LC 1459-SB had been met when, in fact, TMTI had not failed to perform under the contract. TMTI alleges that because ENCI and Banco Continental are controlled by the Peruvian government, and because of a financial crisis facing Peru, "a scheme was developed whereby ENCI and Banco Continental would defraud [TMTI] by having ENCI induce [TMTI] to delay the first shipment of [fertilizer] and then have Banco Continental make a fraudulent demand for payment upon Banque Indosuez under Letter of Credit No. 1459-SB."

TMTI contends it is entitled to a preliminary injunction because:

(1) LC 1459-SB provides that the law governing the transaction is the Uniform Customs and Practice for Documentary Credit (UCP), which TMTI argues allows the district court to enjoin payment on letters of credit;

(2) If California law applies, California law allows an injunction prohibiting either the issuer from paying on a letter of credit or the beneficiary from demanding payment on a letter of credit; and

(3) TMTI has demonstrated it meets the requirements for a preliminary injunction.

The district court held that California law governs the transaction, that it does not allow the court to enjoin letters of credit, and that TMTI is not entitled to a preliminary injunction.

On appeal, TMTI specifies the conditions of LC 1459-SB which it believes were not met: (1) LC 1441-SB had not been voided when Banco Continental demanded payment, and (2) no evidence was produced in district court that the original statement purportedly signed by the Gerente General of ENCI stating that TMTI had failed to perform was delivered to Banque Indosuez.

In response, Banco Continental claims: (1) it had no involvement whatsoever in LC 1441-SB, and (2) the Gerente General's statement was not produced as evidence in the district court because TMTI did not raise it as an issue until this appeal.

* * *

B: Injunction of Letters of Credit Under California Law

Letter of credit law is premised on the principle that the letter of credit is independent of the underlying contract. U.C.C. § 5-114, official code comment ¶ 1. "The commercial viability of letters of credit depends on their ability to provide an assurance of payment." *Agnew v. Federal Deposit Ins. Corp.*, 548 F.Supp. 1234, 1238 (N.D.Cal.1982).

California Commercial Code section 5114 governs this transaction and for the most part is consistent with the Uniform Commercial Code (U.C.C.). Under both, the issuer must inspect the documents accompanying the demand to see that they comply with the conditions stated in the letter of credit. If the beneficiary qualifies as a holder in due course or bona fide purchaser of the letter of credit, the issuer must honor the demand, without exception. If the beneficiary does not rise to the level of a holder in due course, the issuer has the discretion to honor or reject a payment demand if the customer notifies the issuer that there is fraud, forgery, or another defect not apparent on the face of the documents.

Here, however, the California and the U.C.C. diverge. The U.C.C. provides that in the latter instance, a court may enjoin payment upon demonstration of fraud, forgery, or other defect. Significantly, the California legislature intentionally prohibited the injunction of payment under a properly demanded letter of credit by omitting from § 5114 the language from the U.C.C. allowing injunctions. The legislative history explains why this provision was omitted:

> By giving the courts power to enjoin the honor of drafts drawn upon documents which appear to be regular on their face, the Commissioners on Uniform State Laws do violence to one of the basic concepts of the letter of credit, to wit, that the letter of credit agreement is independent of the underlying commercial transaction.

Agnew, 548 F.Supp. at 1238 (quoting official comment to Cal.Comm.Code § 5114 (West 1964)).

* * *

Thus, under California law, if Banco Continental presents Banque Indosuez with the two documents specified in LC 1459-SB (certification of payment demand by ENCI and statement from the ENCI Gerente General), Banque Indosuez may pay Banco Continental under the letter of credit. No evidence was presented to the district court that the documents were not presented as specified to Banque Indosuez. On appeal TMTI argues no evidence was presented to the district court showing that the Gerente General's statement was presented to Banque Indosuez, implying it was not. However, TMTI is the party alleging fraud and seeking the preliminary injunction. It was TMTI's burden to prove the specified conditions were not met.

* * *

TMTI next argues that Banco Continental's demand was fraudulent, because it knew or should have known that ENCI's demand on Banco Continental was fraudulent. TMTI claims Banco Continental should have known this because: (1) the underlying contract specified that the opening of an acceptable letter of credit by ENCI was a condition of shipment, (2) ENCI called on Banco Continental to pay at too early a date to determine whether TMTI had failed to perform because the first shipment could have been en route, and (3) the second shipment date had not arrived.

In the only case in this circuit discussing what showing of fraud would suffice to permit injunctive relief, the court concluded that "courts ... have refused to enjoin payment absent 'a clear showing of active intentional fraud' or 'evil intent,' as opposed to a dispute over performance of a contract." *Wyle* [*v. Bank Melli of Tehran, Iran*] 577 F.Supp. [1148] at 1162 [(N.D. Cal. 1983)](quoting *KMW Int'l v. Chase Manhattan Bank*, 606

F.2d 10, 16 (2d Cir.1979) and *American Bell Int'l v. Islamic Republic of Iran*, 474 F.Supp. 420, 425 (S.D.N.Y.1979).

As the district court found, TMTI did not show that Banco Continental knew of any intentional fraud by ENCI. Banco Continental had no duty to investigate the factual basis for ENCI's demand. The correspondence between TMTI and ENCI and MULTIFERT shows substantial disagreement about the shipping window dates. There is no evidence that Banco Continental knew or should have known any shipping dates.

TMTI also bases its argument that Banco Continental's demand was fraudulent on an alleged conspiracy between ENCI and Banco Continental to defraud TMTI in connection with Peru's financial crisis. TMTI relies on *Wyle* to demonstrate that California law allows injunctions in such an instance. However, *Wyle* is distinguishable. First, the *Wyle* court stated that while it declined to make a factual finding, substantial evidence existed "to support plaintiff's claims concerning an Iranian policy of demanding payment on letters of credit without regard to whether payment is justified on the facts underlying the guarantee arrangements." 577 F.Supp. at 1154. TMTI has not shown any such policy by the Peruvian government. As the district court noted, it would be unreasonable to infer a fraudulent pattern of calling on letters of credit orchestrated by the Peruvian government based on one such call, especially when a genuine contractual disagreement seems to exist.

Second, the *Wyle* court found that if it did not issue an injunction, the plaintiff would have no remedy available in the Iranian courts and no assets existed in the United States against which to enforce a judgment. Id. at 1165. As noted by the Fifth Circuit, the Iranian crisis presented a unique situation, prompting many courts to grant injunctions of payment on letters of credit demanded by Iranian entities because resort to Iranian courts would be futile. *Enterprise Int'l, Inc. v. Corporacion Estatal Petrolera Ecuatoriana*, 762 F.2d 464, 473 (5th Cir.1985). However, in other situations where foreign courts provide even a potential legal remedy, injunctions are rarely issued because "sophisticated investors knowingly undertake such risks as political upheaval or contractual breach in return for the benefits to be reaped from international trade." Id. at 474. TMTI has not shown that it cannot get relief in a Peruvian court.

Finally, the district court noted that given the special facts in *Wyle*, Bank Melli, the letter of credit beneficiary, knew or had reason to know of the fraud. *Wyle*, 577 F.Supp. at 1163. As discussed above, no showing has been made that Banco Continental knew or should have known of any fraud.

TMTI's final argument is that even if California law prohibits the court from enjoining Banque Indosuez from paying on the letter of credit, it does not prohibit the court from enjoining Banco Continental from demanding payment.

* * *

Given California's seemingly strong policy honoring letters of credit, it would be illogical to thwart it so easily by enjoining the beneficiary, not the issuer.

* * *

C: Merits of TMTI's Preliminary Injunction Motion

Because we agree with the district court's conclusion that California law prohibits it from issuing an injunction, it is unnecessary for this court to evaluate the merits of TMTI's motion.

CONCLUSION

The district court properly applied California law. California law does not permit the issuance of an injunction in this letter of credit transaction.

AFFIRMED.

Notes

1. UCC § 5-114(2), permitting enjoining payment on a letter of credit, as it read before the 1995 revision, provided:

> (2) Unless otherwise agreed when documents appear on their face to comply with the terms of a credit but a required document does not in fact conform to the warranties made on negotiation or transfer of a document of title (Section 7-507) or of a certificated security (Section 8-306) or is forged or fraudulent or there is fraud in the transaction:
>
> a) the issuer must honor the draft or demand for payment if honor is demanded by a negotiating bank or other holder of the draft or demand which has taken the draft or demand under the credit and under circumstances which would make it a holder in due course (Section 3-302) and in an appropriate case would make it a person to whom a document of title has been duly negotiated (Section 7-502) or a bona fide purchaser of a certificated security (Section 8-302), and
>
> b) in all other cases as against its customer, an issuer acting in good faith may honor the draft or demand for payment despite notification from the customer of fraud, forgery or other defect not apparent on the face of the documents but a court of appropriate jurisdiction may enjoin such honor.

As the preceding case indicates, California omitted the last clause in § 5-114(2)(b), beginning with "but."

The warranty referred to in UCC § 7-507 includes the warranty that a document of title is genuine and in § 8-306 includes the warranty that a security is genuine and not materially altered.

In the 1995 revision, injunction against honor is governed by §5-109(b). An injunction is permitted only if:

> (1) the relief is not prohibited under the law applicable to an accepted draft or deferred obligation incurred by the issuer;
>
> (2) a beneficiary, issuer, or nominated person who may be adversely affected is adequately protected against loss that it may suffer because the relief is granted;
>
> (3) all of the conditions to entitle a person to the relief under the law of this State have been met; and
>
> (4) on the basis of the information submitted to the court, the applicant is more likely than not to succeed under its claim of forgery or material fraud and the person demanding honor does not qualify for protection under subsection (a)(1). [Subsection (a)(1) protects a nominated person, confirmer, holder in due course of a draft drawn under the letter of credit, or assignee of the issuer's or nominated person's deferred obligation, who has given value, confirmed, taken the draft after acceptance, or taken for value, and in good faith].

Comment 4 states:

There are at least two ways to prohibit injunctions against honor under this section after acceptance of a draft by the issuer. First is to define honor [the performance of the issuer's undertaking] to occur upon acceptance and without regard to later payment of the acceptance. Second is explicitly to agree that the applicant has no right to an injunction after acceptance-whether or not the acceptance constitutes honor.

With regard to § 509(b)(1), § 5-116 (a) provides: "The liability of an issuer for action or omission is governed by the law of the jurisdiction chosen by an agreement in the form of a record signed or otherwise authenticated by the affected parties or by a provision in the person's letter of credit. The jurisdiction whose law is chosen need not bear any relation to the transaction."

Section 5-111(e) provides: "Reasonable attorney's fees and other expenses of litigation must be awarded to the prevailing party in an action in which a remedy is sought under this article.

The UCP does not mention enjoining payment on a letter of credit.

2. Southern Energy Homes, Inc. v. AmSouth Bank of Alabama, 709 So.2d 1180 (Ala. 1998), affirmed the trial court's dissolving of an order restraining payment of a letter of credit. The court found that the applicant had an adequate remedy at law in Germany against the German beneficiary and stated: " Clearly, a dispute exists between [the applicant] and [the beneficiary] based on the underlying contract. However, '[f]raud claims should not become surrogates for breach of contract claims.' [John] Dolan, [The Law of Letter of Credit: Commercial and Standby Credits] ¶ 7.04(4)(c) [rev. ed. 1996)]. To invoke the fraud exception in this case would require an inquiry into the underlying contract, further disrupting the important commercial functions of credit law."

State ex rel Barclays Bank PLC v. Hamilton County, Court of Common Pleas, 660 N.E.2d 458 (Ohio 1996), holds that because the plaintiff did not join the beneficiary as a party, the trial court does not have subject-matter jurisdiction of an action to enjoin an English bank from paying under a letter of credit.

Deutshe Ruckversicherung AG v. Walbrook Insurance Co., [1996] 1 W.L.R. 152, [1996] 1 All E.R. 791 (C.A.), discusses English standards for enjoining a bank from paying or a beneficiary from requesting payment on a letter of credit, but concludes that on the facts of the case the beneficiary should not be enjoined because there was insufficient proof of the beneficiary's fraud. "[T]he court will not grant an injunction restraining a bank from paying under a letter of credit unless the court is satisfied that there is a clear prima facie case that the beneficiary is acting fraudulently in drawing on the credit." [1994] 1 All E.R. at 196. In order to enjoin the beneficiary, the plaintiff "must prove that if the [beneficiary] draw[s] on the letters of credit, [it] will do so fraudulently in the knowledge that [it has] no right to payment under them." Id. at 197.

Foxboro Co. v. Arabian American Oil Co.
805 F.2d 34 (1st Cir. 1986)

Before BOWNES and TORRUELLA, Circuit Judges, and CARTER, District Judge.

TORRUELLA, Circuit Judge.

This appeal concerns the propriety of a preliminary injunction to prevent the honoring of an international letter of credit. Because plaintiff has failed to demonstrate irreparable harm, we reverse the district court and vacate the preliminary injunction.

I: The Contract and Letter of Credit

In March 1984 plaintiff, The Foxboro Company ("Foxboro"), a Massachusetts corporation, contracted with the Arabian American Oil Company ("Aramco"), a Delaware corporation, to provide a process control system for the Qasim Refinery in Saudi Arabia. Under the agreement Foxboro was to receive certain scheduled payments upon reaching specified contractual milestones. Foxboro had the option of allowing Aramco to retain a percentage of the payments as security, or of providing a bank guarantee to Aramco equal to the amount Aramco could retain. The contract provided that disputes be governed by Saudi Arabian law and be subject to arbitration.

Foxboro elected to provide the bank guarantee, which was issued by Saudi American Bank ("Samba") to Aramco. The Samba guarantee was itself secured by a letter of credit issued by Citibank on Foxboro's behalf. This "four-way" security is a typical commercial arrangement for American contractors doing business in the Middle East.

In March 1985 Aramco terminated the contract for "convenience," as it was authorized to do under the contract. In February 1986, after eleven months of negotiation over post-termination obligations, Aramco made a demand on the Samba bank guarantee, and Samba, in turn, made a demand on the Citibank letter of credit. Foxboro sought a temporary restraining order to prevent the execution of the letter of credit or bank guarantee. Foxboro alleged that the demand on the guarantee was fraudulent. The district court granted the restraining order, 634 F.Supp. 1226, and thereafter issued the preliminary injunction which is the subject of the appeal in this case.

* * *

Foxboro and Aramco are disputing their financial obligations under the contract. Honoring Aramco's demand on the bank guarantee, and Samba's demand on the letter of credit, will transfer money from Foxboro to Aramco, but will not change the merits of the underlying claim. The principal legally cognizable injury to Foxboro is that it will have to seek recovery of these sums through the contractually agreed upon forum. We do not find irreparable injury where only money is at stake and where the plaintiff has a satisfactory remedy at law to recover the money at issue. See *Itek Corp. v. First Nat'l Bank*, 730 F.2d 19, 22 (1st Cir.1984).

In *Itek* we affirmed the granting of a preliminary injunction to prevent the honoring of a letter of credit. But Itek involved a contract with the imperial government of Iran that was interrupted by the Iranian revolution and the seizing of the American hostages. Allowing the letter of credit to be honored in that case would have created irreparable harm; the plaintiff would have had no adequate remedy at law during the throes of the revolution. This case presents a far different situation.

The parties contracted to be bound by Saudi Arabian law and to use Saudi Arabian arbitration in resolving disputes between them. International arbitration provides Foxboro an adequate remedy, as do the Saudi Courts. Indeed, the underlying contract dispute is currently being arbitrated at Foxboro's behest.

Foxboro may also sue Aramco in federal court for any harm done to it by the allegedly fraudulent demand on the bank guarantee and letter of credit. Aramco is a Delaware corporation wholly owned by four United States corporations. Foxboro has not demonstrated that Aramco would be unwilling or unable to pay any judgment debt, or that Aramco lacks sufficient assets in the United States to cover any such debt. Foxboro thus has several avenues open to recover any money due from the allegedly fraudulent demand.

The district court found that Foxboro would suffer two forms of irreparable injury if the demand on the bank guarantee and letter of credit were honored. First, Aramco would achieve on "unfair advantage in the ongoing negotiations...between the parties". And second, Foxboro's business reputation would suffer. Neither of these harms, nor the two combined, are sufficient to constitute irreparable injury in this case.

The contract clearly contemplates that Aramco would have an advantage in negotiations. That advantage was the purpose of the retainage or bank guarantee provision. Whether that advantage is "unfair" in this case depends on whether the Aramco demand on the bank guarantee was "fraudulent." See *Itek*, 730 F.2d at 23-24. If the demand was fraudulent, Foxboro may recover the damages flowing from the fraud in federal court. Thus, an unfair negotiating advantage will not irreparably harm Foxboro.

The claimed harm to Foxboro's business reputation presents a more interesting issue. Foxboro claims that Aramco's fraudulent demand will make it more expensive for Foxboro to obtain letters of credit in the future. Whether the demand on the bank guarantee and letter of credit does so depends on how courts treat these credit instruments. If an injunction against an allegedly fraudulent demand can be easily obtained, then the party who is unable to secure such an injunction may be presumed to be subject to a proper demand and, thus, a credit risk in the future. But, if such injunctions are difficult to obtain, the failure to obtain one says nothing about the propriety of the demand on the letter of credit.

As we indicated in *Itek*, an injunction to impede the honoring of a letter of credit is an extraordinary remedy that should rarely be granted. This is so because their near inviolableness is an important element of trust underlying a large segment of international commerce. In contrast, however, the failure to obtain injunctive relief should have little or no consequence for Foxboro's reputation. In fact, it could very well be argued that seeking to prevent payment of an irrevocable letter of credit could have more drastic consequences on the movant's long range business reputation. The district court's contrary finding was speculative. Like the Fifth Circuit, "we are reluctant to accept the district court's inferences that payment on a letter of credit will embroider a permanent 'scarlet letter' on the bodice of the bank's customer." *Enterprise International, Inc. v. Corporacion Estatal Petrolera Ecuatoriana*, 762 F.2d 464, 474-75 (5th Cir.1985).

We fail to see how the demand on the letter of credit will prejudice Foxboro in future business deals. Letters of credit are independent of the underlying contract. Aramco's demand says no more about the merits of any dispute based on the underlying contract than would a complaint filed in court.

Accordingly, the order of the district court below is reversed and the preliminary injunction vacated.

Section 3: Political Risks

Note

In the preceding case, the court refers to the problems arising from letters of credit issued in favor of Iranian beneficiaries before the revolution. The rest of the materials in this chapter indicate how this extraordinary situation was dealt with. The United States eventually issued regulations forbidding payment to an Iranian entity and required the issuer to pay on the letter of credit into a blocked account (31 CFR 535.416 and 31 CFR 535.568(b)) pending settlement of the dispute by the Iran-United States Claims Tribunal. This Tribunal sat in the Hague and was established by agreement between the United States and Iran through the good offices of Algeria.

In this time of political upheaval in many parts of the world, it is likely that such problems will arise again.

Harris Corp. v. National Iranian Radio and Television
691 F.2d 1344 (11th Cir. 1982)

JAMES C. HILL, Circuit Judge:

National Iranian Radio and Television ("NIRT") and Bank Melli Iran appeal from a district court order granting plaintiff-appellee Harris Corporation preliminary injunctive relief. The court enjoined: (1) NIRT from making a demand on Bank Melli under a certain bank guaranty letter of credit; (2) Bank Melli from making payment to NIRT under that letter of credit; and (3) Bank Melli from receiving payment from Continental Illinois National Bank and Trust Company ("Continental Bank") under a standby letter of credit issued by Continental Bank in favor of Bank Melli.[1] The appellants challenge the jurisdiction of the district court, assert a lack of proper venue, and argue that the court abused its discretion by ordering preliminary relief. After careful consideration of the issues presented, we affirm.

I: The Facts

On February 22, 1978, the Broadcast Products Division of Harris Corporation entered into a contract with NIRT ("the contract") to manufacture and deliver 144 FM broadcast transmitters to Teheran, Iran, and to provide related training and technical services for a total price of $6,740,352. Harris received an advance payment of $1,331,470.40, which was to be amortized over the life of the contract by deducting a

---

1. The preliminary injunction also (a) directs Harris to maintain a blocked account in the amount of the letter of credit, $674,035.20, in accordance with the Iranian Assets Control Regulations, 31 C.F.R. § 535.568 (1980), (b) enjoins distribution or removal of any funds from the blocked account, (c) directs the attachment of the blocked account for Harris's benefit, and (d) continues a bond requirement of $674,035.20. Appellants do not challenge these provisions.

percentage of the payment due upon shipment of the equipment or receipt of the services and training from the balance of the advance.

Pursuant to the contract, Harris obtained a performance guarantee in favor of NIRT from Bank Melli, an agency of the State of Iran. The guarantee provides that Melli is to pay NIRT any amount up to $674,035.20 upon Melli's receipt of NIRT's written declaration that Harris has failed to comply with the terms and conditions of the contract. The contract between Harris and NIRT makes the guarantee an integral part of the contract and provides that NIRT must release the guarantee upon termination of the contract due to force majeure. Before Melli issued the guarantee it required that Harris obtain a letter of credit in Melli's favor. Continental Bank issued this standby, which provides that Continental is to reimburse Melli to the extent that Melli pays on the guarantee it issued. Harris, in turn, must indemnify Continental Bank to the extent that Continental pays Melli.

From August 1978 through February 1979, Harris shipped to Iran 138 of the 144 transmitters (together with related equipment for 144 transmitters) and also conducted a 24-week training program in the United States for NIRT personnel. In February 1979, the Islamic Republic of Iran overthrew the Imperial Government of Iran. After the overthrow, one shipment of goods which Harris sent could not be delivered safely in Iran. Harris notified NIRT, by telex dated February 27, that those goods were taken to Antwerp, Belgium, and Sharjah, United Arab Emirates.

* * *

Negotiations on contract modifications continued during the summer and fall of 1979. On August 18, 1979, Harris formally advised NIRT of the additional costs it had incurred with respect to the goods that had been reshipped from Antwerp, and Harris requested payment for the additional amount in accordance with the contract's force majeure clause and with a letter from NIRT authorizing Harris to reship the goods.

On November 4, 1979, Iranian militants took 52 hostages at the United States Embassy in Teheran. Harris received no further communications from NIRT after the seizure of the hostages.

Harris completed the remaining six transmitters in November 1979 and inventoried them for future delivery. Harris * * * has argued that disruptive conditions created by the Iranian revolution initially prevented shipment of the final six transmitters. Subsequently, Harris contends, it was unable to ship the materials as a result of the Iranian Assets Control Regulations [promulgated by the United States] effective November 14, 1979.

* * *

On June 3, 1980, Continental Bank received a telex from Melli reporting that NIRT had presented Melli with a written declaration that Harris had failed to comply with the terms of the contract and stating that NIRT had demanded that Melli extend or pay the guarantee. Melli demanded that it be authorized to extend the guarantee and that Continental Bank extend its corresponding letter of credit to Melli, or else Melli would pay the guarantee and demand immediate payment from Continental.

In response to the demand by Melli, Harris sought and obtained the preliminary injunction at issue in this case. On July 11, 1980, Harris filed a verified complaint against NIRT and Melli in the United States District Court for the Middle District of Florida, seeking to enjoin payment and receipt of payment on the guarantee and receipt of payment on the letter of credit. The complaint also sought a declaratory judgment that the contract underlying the guarantee and the letter of credit had been terminated by force majeure. The court granted a temporary restraining order on June 13, 1980, pending a hearing on Harris's motion for a preliminary injunction.[9]

On June 16, 1980, a copy of the TRO was mailed to Melli's counsel and on the following day was hand-delivered to Melli's branch office in Manhattan. On June 20, 1980, three days after receipt of the June 13th TRO at its Manhattan branch office, and despite the restraint against payment contained in the TRO, Melli telexed Continental Bank that it had paid the full amount of the guarantee "after receipt of a demand for payment from the National Iranian Radio and Television stating that there has been a default by Harris Corporation * * *." The telex also demanded that Continental pay Melli by crediting Melli's London office with the amount of the letter of credit. After a hearing on August 15, 1980, the district court issued the preliminary injunction at issue here.

* * *

IV: The Preliminary Injunction

A: The Framework for Review

The appellants contend that the district court erred in entering the preliminary injunction against payment or receipt of payment on the NIRT-Melli guarantee letter of credit and against receipt of payment on the Melli-Continental letter of credit. The four prerequisites for the injunction are: (1) a substantial likelihood that the plaintiff will prevail on the merits; (2) a substantial threat that the plaintiff will suffer irreparable injury if the injunction is not granted; (3) threatened injury to the plaintiff must outweigh the threatened harm that the injunction may cause to the defendant; and (4) granting the preliminary injunction must not disserve the public interest. In reviewing these factors, a court must keep in mind that the granting of the preliminary injunction rests in the sound discretion of the district court and will not be disturbed on appeal unless there is a clear abuse of discretion.

B: Substantial Likelihood of Success on the Merits

The merits of this case involve letter of credit law. Harris asserts that the existence of force majeure terminated its obligations under the contract with NIRT, making illegitimate NIRT's subsequent attempt to draw upon the performance guarantee issued by Melli. The appellants respond by relying upon a fundamental principle of letter of credit law: the letter of credit is independent of the underlying contract. Harris advanced two ways to overcome this barrier to enjoining a letter of credit transaction.

First, Harris asserts that the independence principle was modified by the parties here. It points to those paragraphs of its contract with NIRT which make "the bank guarantees" an "integral part" of the contract and which state that NIRT shall release all guarantees upon termination of the contract due to force majeure. Harris contends that it has demonstrated a substantial likelihood that force majeure occurred and terminated both the contract and the guarantee.

---

9. Following entry of the TRO, Harris advised Continental Bank that payment on the letter of credit would aid and abet violation of the restraint imposed on Melli. Continental Bank responded that Harris's creation of a blocked account "discharged" Continental's obligation under the letter of credit and that Continental had so advised Melli.

* * *

We choose not to rely upon Harris's first line of argument, for we hesitate to hold that the letters of credit were automatically terminated by the operation of the contractual provisions. Accepting Harris's first argument would create problems; a bank could honor a letter of credit only to find that it had terminated earlier. While parties may modify the independence principle by drafting letters of credit specifically to achieve that result, there is no assertion by Harris that the performance guarantee or the letter of credit contain provisions (conditions) which would modify the independence of the banks' obligations. Since the banks were not parties to the underlying contract, it would appear that the contractual provisions relied upon by Harris would have the same effect as a warranty by NIRT that it would not draw upon the letter of credit issued by Melli if the contract were to terminate due to force majeure.

The second avenue pursued by Harris is the doctrine of "fraud in the transaction."[19] Under this doctrine, a court may enjoin payment on a letter of credit, despite the independence principle, where there is shown to be fraud by the beneficiary of the letter of credit. Unfortunately, one unsettled point in the law is what constitutes fraud in the transaction, i.e., what degree of defective performance by the beneficiary justifies enjoining a letter of credit transaction in violation of the independence principle?

Contending that a narrow definition of fraud is appropriate, the appellants assert that an injunction should issue only upon a showing of facts indicating egregious misconduct. They argue that fraud in the transaction should be restricted to the type of chicanery present in the landmark case of *Sztejn v. Henry Schroeder Banking Corp.*, 117 Misc. 719, 31 N.Y.S.2d 631 (Sup.Ct.1941), where a seller sent fifty crates of "cowhair, other worthless material, and rubbish with intent to simulate genuine merchandise and defraud [the buyer]." 31 N.Y.S.2d at 633.

The appellants further contend that Harris does not and cannot allege conduct on the part of NIRT or Melli that would justify a finding of fraud under *Sztejn*. The egregious conduct, they assert, was by Harris. They state that it was Harris which failed to ship the remaining goods, unreasonably refused to extend the letter of credit obtained from Continental, and deliberately abandoned and destroyed the underlying contract. In contrast, they point out that they informed Continental that they would have been satisfied if the letter of credit had been extended long enough for Harris to complete

---

19. As did the parties, we use the "fraud in the transaction" terminology broadly to encompass any type of fraudulent conduct in the letter of credit transaction. (U.C.C. §5-114(2) uses the term to describe a sort of fraud external to the complying documents presented to an issuer as a part of a demand for payment on a letter of credit.) The U.C.P. is silent on the availability of remedies to a plaintiff alleging that fraud is involved in a beneficiary's demand on a letter of credit. Nonetheless, we are of the opinion that the "fraud in the transaction" doctrine as it has been developed in commercial law, and as it is now reflected in U.C.C. §5-114(2), is applicable in a case such as this, where the appellants have not alleged and shown that foreign law controls and makes resort to the doctrine impermissible. Cf. *KMW International v. Chase Manhattan Bank*, 606 F.2d 10, 15 n. 3 (2d Cir. 1979) (applicability of U.C.P. rather than U.C.C. "does not...take away from the point that apparent 'fraud in the transaction' or fraudulent documentation may be a defense under either the U.C.C. or the U.C.P."); *United Bank Ltd. v. Cambridge Sporting Goods Corp.*, 41 N.Y.2d 254, 360 N.E.2d 943, 947 n. 2, 392 N.Y.S.2d 265 (1976) ("The Uniform Customs and Practice, where applicable, does not bar the relief provided for in section 5-114 of the code."). Other courts in the United States have consistently reached this result. See Comment, Enjoining the International Standby Letter of Credit: The Iranian Letter of Credit Cases, 21 Harv. Int'l L.J. 189, 202-03 & n. 69 (1980) (criticizing the courts for failing to consider that foreign law might apply).

performance. According to the view of NIRT and Melli, all that Harris has-taking its assertions as true-is an impossibility defense to an action on the underlying contract.

Appellants' arguments are not persuasive in the context of this case. *Sztejn* does not offer much direct guidance because it involved fraud by the beneficiary seller in the letter of credit transaction in the form of false documentation covering up egregiously fraudulent performance of the underlying transaction. That does not mean that the fraud exception should be restricted to allegations involving fraud in the underlying transaction, nor does it mean that the exception should be restricted to protecting the buyer in the framework of the traditional letter of credit. The fraud exception is flexible, and it may be invoked on behalf of a customer seeking to prevent a beneficiary from fraudulently utilizing a standby (guarantee) letter of credit.

Thus, the independent contracts rule does not make a fraudulent demand completely irrelevant to a bank's obligation to honor a standby. The differences between the allegations in this case and those in *Sztejn* merely require us to focus on the conduct of the buyer rather than the seller as we evaluate the beneficiary's conduct in light of the terms of the particular documents involved in the demand.

In order to collect upon the guarantee letter of credit, NIRT was required to declare that Harris had failed to comply with the terms and conditions of the contract. Harris contends that NIRT intentionally misrepresented the quality of Harris's performance; Harris thus asserts fraud as it has been defined traditionally.

We find that the evidence adduced by Harris is sufficient to support a conclusion that it has a substantial likelihood of prevailing on the merits. The facts suggest that the contract in this case broke down through no fault of Harris's but rather as a result of problems stemming from the Iranian revolution. NIRT apparently admitted as much during its negotiations with Harris over how to carry out the remainder of the contract. Nonetheless, NIRT sought to call the performance guarantee. Its attempt to do so necessarily involved its representation that Harris had defaulted under the contract. Yet the contract explicitly provides that it can be terminated due to force majeure. Moreover, NIRT's demand was made in a situation that was subtly suggestive of fraud. Since NIRT and Bank Melli had both become government enterprises, the demand was in some sense by Iran upon itself and may have been an effort by Iran to harvest undeserved bounty from Continental Bank. Under these circumstances, it was within the district court's discretion to find that, at a full hearing, Harris might well be able to prove that NIRT's demand was a fraudulent attempt to obtain the benefit of payment on the letter of credit in addition to the benefit of Harris's substantial performance.

C: Irreparable Injury

The district court did not abuse its discretion in finding a substantial likelihood of irreparable injury to Harris absent an injunction. Harris has sufficiently demonstrated that its ability to pursue a legal remedy against NIRT and Melli (i.e., to recover the proceeds of the standby) has been precluded. It is clear that the Islamic regime now governing Iran has shown a deep hostility toward the United States and its citizens, thus making effective access to the Iranian courts unlikely. Similarly, the cooperative response of agencies of Iran to orders of a United States court would be unlikely where the court's order would impose a financial obligation on the agencies. Harris's possible resort to the Iran-United States Claims Tribunal does not, in our eyes, ameliorate the likelihood of irreparable injury for purposes of this requirement for preliminary relief.

D: The Balance of Harms

Neither appellant argues that the preliminary injunction has caused or will cause it any harm. Since there would otherwise be a likelihood that Harris would suffer irreparable injury, the balance of harms weighs heavily in Harris's favor.

E: The Public Interest

In a Statement of Interest filed with the district court on July 16, 1982, the United States indicated, that new amendments to the Iranian Assets Control Regulations governing letter of credit claims still permit American litigants to proceed in United States Courts and to obtain preliminary injunctive relief. The supplementary information explaining the changes provides a good indication that preliminary injunctions such as the one entered here are in the public interest:

> Iran filed more than 200 claims with the Iran-U.S. Claims Tribunal (the "Tribunal") based on standby letters of credit issued for the account of United States parties. United States nationals have filed with the Tribunal a large number of claims related to, or based on, many of the same standby letters of credit at issue in Iran's claims. Other United States nationals have litigation pending in United States courts concerning some of these same letters of credit.
>
> The purpose of the amendment is to preserve the status quo by continuing to allow U.S. account parties to obtain preliminary injunctions or other temporary relief to prevent payment on standby letters of credit, while prohibiting, for the time being, final judicial action permanently enjoining, nullifying or otherwise permanently disposing of such letters of credit.
>
> Preservation of the status quo will provide an opportunity for negotiations with Iran regarding the status and disposition of these various letter of credit claims. Preservation of the status quo for a period of time also permits possible resolution in the context of the Tribunal of the matters pending before it. The amendment will expire by its terms on December 31, 1982.

Supplementary Information, Iranian Assets Control Regulations, "Judicial Action involving standby letters of credit," to be codified at 31 C.F.R. §§ 535.222(g) and 535.504 (July 1, 1982).

Melli has charged, however, that the entry of a preliminary injunction here would threaten the function of letters of credit in commercial transactions. Admittedly, that has given us pause, for it would be improper to impose relief contrary to the intentions of parties that have contracted to carry out their business in a certain manner. Some might contend that the use of the fraud exception in a case such as this damages commercial law and that Harris could have chosen to shift the risks represented in this case. Under the circumstances, however, we disagree. First, the risk of a fraudulent demand of the type which Harris has demonstrated a likelihood of showing is not one which it should be expected to bear in light of the manner in December 9, 1993 which the documents in this transaction were structured. Second, to argue that Harris could have protected itself further by inserting special conditions in the letters of credit and should be confined to that protection is to ignore the realities of the drafting of commercial documents. Third, unlike the first line of argument presented by Harris, the issuance of a preliminary injunction based on a showing of fraud does not create unfortunate consequences for a bank that honors letters of credit in good faith; it is up to the customer to seek and obtain an injunction before a bank would be prohibited from paying on a letter of credit. Finally, foreign situations like the one before us are exceptional. For these reasons, the district court's holding is not contrary to the public interest in maintaining the market integrity and commercial utility of guarantee letters of credit.

V: Conclusion

The requisite jurisdictional elements either exist in this case or have been waived, and the requirements for preliminary injunctive relief have been met. Accordingly, the decision of the district court is

AFFIRMED.

Declaration of Algeria Concerning Settlement of Claims by the United States and Iran
20 ILM 230 (1981)

The Government of the Democratic and Popular Republic of Algeria, on the basis of formal notice of adherence received from the Government of the Islamic Republic of Iran and the Government of the United States of America, now declares that Iran and the United States have agreed as follows:

Article I

Iran and the United States will promote the settlement of the claims described in Article II by the parties directly concerned. Any such claims not settled within six months from the date of entry into force of this agreement shall be submitted to binding third-party arbitration in accordance with the terms of this agreement. The aforementioned six months' period may be extended once by three months at the request of either party.

Article II

1. An International Arbitral Tribunal (the Iran-United States Claims Tribunal) is hereby established for the purpose of deciding claims of nationals of the United States against Iran and claims of nationals of Iran against the United States, and any counterclaim which arises out of the same contract, transaction or occurrence that constitutes the subject matter of that national's claim, if such claims and counterclaims are outstanding on the date of this agreement, whether or not filed with any court, and arise out of debts, contracts (including transactions which are the subject of letters of credit or bank guarantees), expropriations or other measures affecting property rights * * * excluding claims arising under a binding contract between the parties specifically providing that any disputes thereunder shall be within the sole jurisdiction of the competent Iranian courts * * *.

Article III

1. The Tribunal shall consist of nine members or such larger multiple of three as Iran and the United States may agree are necessary to conduct its business expeditiously. Within ninety days after the entry into force of this agreement, each government shall appoint one-third of the members. Within thirty days after their appointment, the members so appointed shall by mutual agreement select the remaining third of the members and appoint one of the remaining third President of the Tribunal. Claims may be decided by the full Tribunal or by a panel of three members of the Tribunal as the President shall determine. Each such panel shall be composed by the President and shall consist of one member appointed by each of the three methods set forth above.

2. Members of the Tribunal shall be appointed and the Tribunal shall conduct its business in accordance with the arbitration rules of the United Nations Commission on International Trade Law (UNCITRAL) except to the extent modified by the parties or by the Tribunal to ensure that this agreement can be carried out. The UNCITRAL rules for appointing members of three-member Tribunals shall apply *mutatis mutandis* to the appointment of the Tribunal.

3. Claims of nationals of the United States and Iran that are within the scope of this agreement shall be presented to the Tribunal either by claimants themselves, or, in the case of claims of less than $250,000, by the Government of such national.

4. No claim may be filed with the Tribunal more than one year after the entry into force of this agreement or six months after the date the President is appointed, whichever is later.

* * *

Article IV

1. All decisions and awards of the Tribunal shall be final and binding.

2. The President of the Tribunal shall certify * * * when all arbitral awards under this agreement have been satisfied.

3. Any award which the Tribunal may render against either government shall be enforceable against such government in the courts of any nation in accordance with its laws.

Article V

The Tribunal shall decide all cases on the basis of respect for law, applying such choice of law rules and principles of commercial and international law as the Tribunal determines to be applicable, taking into account relevant usages of the trade, contract provisions and changed circumstances.

Article VI

1. The seat of the Tribunal shall be The Hague, The Netherlands, or any other place agreed by Iran and the United States.

2. Each government shall designate an agent at the seat of the Tribunal to represent it to the Tribunal and to receive notices or other communications directed to it or to its nationals, agencies, instrumentalities, or entities in connection with proceedings before the Tribunal.

3. The expenses of the Tribunal shall be borne equally by the two governments.

4. Any question concerning the interpretation or application of this agreement shall be decided by the Tribunal upon the request of either Iran or the United States.

* * *

Note

The UNCITRAL Model Law on International Commercial Arbitration is set out in chapter 11, infra page 528.

Chapter 11

Arbitration

Introduction

International arbitration has become a preferred method of resolving disputes that arise out of transnational commercial transactions. Arbitration has several features that make it attractive compared with litigation. The parties can select arbitrators who are knowledgeable concerning relevant trade usages and can be expected to give proper attention to documents and arguments and to render a decision in a reasonable time. Thus the parties can recreate something like the atmosphere Lord Mansfield created in England in the mid 18th Century by impaneling juries of merchants in commercial cases. The merchant juries not only decided the cases but also frequently rendered "special verdicts" on trade usages.

Furthermore, arbitration can be confidential and, arbitration awards are likely to be easier to enforce than judgments. The United States has no generally applicable judgment recognition treaty with any other country and except for regional treaties, such as the EEC Convention on Jurisdiction and Judgments set out in Chapter 1, section 1, there are no widely ratified multilateral judgment-recognition treaties. In contrast, as of January 1, 2000, the United Nations or "New York" Arbitration Convention, set out page 69 supra, had been ratified by 109 countries. The Inter-American or "Panama" Arbitration convention, set out following this note, had been ratified by 16 members of the Organization of American States.

As note previously (supra page 274 Note 8), the Foreign Sovereign Immunities Act and the Federal Arbitration Act, by eliminating sovereign immunity and the act of state doctrine, provide incentives to use arbitration agreements in dealings with foreign sovereigns. Also previously noted (id.), these arbitration agreements may be preferable to conciliation or arbitration under the Convention on Settlement of Investment Disputes (infra page 516) with its "Article 52 problem." This article (infra page 524) creates an appeals process within the International Centre for Settlement of Investment Disputes in which the parties do not pick the panel members.

International arbitration has attracted a specialized bar of superb lawyers who are at ease participating in arbitration anywhere in the world. They know and understand one another. International commercial arbitration is sometimes referred to as "Rolls Royce" justice. It should not be surprising that it can be very expensive. A report of interviews with close to 300 academics and practitioners concludes that "[i]n the past 20 years, 'international commercial arbitration' has shifted from an informal, compromise-oriented justice dominated by European academics to a U.S.-style, formalized, 'offshore litigation.'" Yves Dezalay & Bryant Garth, Fussing about the Forum: Categories and Definitions as Stakes in a Professional Competition, 21 L. & Soc. Inquiry 285, 295 (1996).

The materials in this chapter supplement the materials on arbitration in chapter 1, section 2: Scherk v. Alberto-Culver Co.; the United Nations Convention on Recognition and Enforcement of Foreign Arbitral Awards; Mitsubishi Motors Corp. v. Soler Chrysler-Plymouth, Inc.; Rhone Mediterranee Compagnia Francese v. Lauro, and the notes accompanying those materials.

Section 1: Conventions and Model Law

Inter-American Convention on International Commercial Arbitration

(Opened for signature January 30, 1975; entered into force for the United States, October 27, 1990; reprinted in 14 ILM 336 (1975) and in a note following 9 U.S.C.A. § 301.)

The Governments of the Member States of the Organization of American States, desirous of concluding a convention on International commercial arbitration, have agreed as follows:

Article 1. An agreement in which the parties undertake to submit to arbitral decisions any differences that may arise or have arisen between them with respect to a commercial transaction is valid. The agreement shall be set forth in an instrument signed by the parties, or in the form of an exchange of letters, telegrams, or telex communications.

Article 2. Arbitrators shall be appointed in the manner agreed upon by the parties. Their appointment may be delegated to a third party, whether a natural or juridical person.

Arbitrators may be nationals or foreigners.

Article 3. In the absence of an express agreement between the parties, the arbitration shall be conducted in accordance with the rules of procedure of the Inter-American Commercial Arbitration Commission.

Article 4. An arbitral decision or award that is not appealable under the applicable law or procedural rules shall have the force of a final judicial judgment. Its execution or recognition may be ordered in the same manner as that of decisions handed down by national or foreign ordinary courts, in accordance with the procedural laws of the country where it is to be executed and the provisions of international treaties.

Article 5. 1. The recognition and execution of the decision may be refused, at the request of the party against which it is made, only if such party is able to prove to the competent authority of the State in which recognition and execution are requested:

a. That the parties to the agreement were subject to some incapacity under the applicable law or that the agreement is not valid under the law to which the parties have submitted it, or, if such law is not specified, under the law of the Sate in which the decision was made, or

b. That the party against which the arbitral decision has been made was not duly notified of the appointment of the arbitrator or of the arbitration procedure to be followed, or was unable, for any other reason to present his defence; or

c. That the decision concerns a dispute not envisaged in the agreement between the parties to submit to arbitration; nevertheless if the provisions of the decision that refer to issues submitted to arbitration can be separated from those not submitted to arbitration, the former may be recognized and executed; or

d. That the constitution of the arbitral tribunal or the arbitration procedure has not been carried out in accordance with the terms of the agreement signed by the parties or, in the absence of such agreement, that the constitution of the arbitral tribunal or the arbitration procedure has not been carried out in accordance with the law of the State where the arbitration took place; or

e. That the decision is not yet binding on the parties or has been annulled or suspended by a competent authority of the State in which, or according to the law of which, the decision has been made.

2. The recognition and execution of an arbitral decision may also be refused if the competent authority of the State in which the recognition and execution is requested finds:

a. That the subject of the dispute cannot be settled by arbitration under the law of that State; or

b. That the recognition or execution of the decision would be contrary to the public policy ("ordre public") of that State.

Article 6. If the competent authority mentioned in article 5.1.e. has been requested to annul or suspend the arbitral decision, the authority before which such decision is invoked may, if it deems it appropriate, postpone a decision on the execution of the arbitral decision and, at the request of the party requesting execution, may also instruct the other party to provide appropriate guarantees.

Article 7. The Convention shall be open for signature by the Member States of the Organization of American States.

* * *

Article 13. The original instrument of this Convention, the English, French, Portuguese and Spanish texts of which are equally authentic, shall be deposited with the General Secretariat of the Organization of American States.

* * *

Notes

1. The Convention went into force in the United States when implemented by chapter 3 of the Federal Arbitration Act, 9 U.S.C. §§ 301-307. 9 U.S.C. § 304 imposes a reciprocity requirement that "an award made in the territory of a foreign State shall… be recognized and enforced under this chapter only if that State has ratified or acceded to the Inter-American Convention." § 305 provides that if both the Inter-American ("Panama") and United Nations ("New York") Arbitration Conventions are in force in the country in which the award was made, the Inter-American Convention applies "[i]f a majority of the parties to the arbitration agreement are citizens of a State or States that have ratified or acceded to the Inter-American Convention," otherwise the United Nations Convention applies. As of January 1, 2000, Argentina, Chile, Colombia, Costa Rica, Ecuador, Guatemala, Mexico, Panama, Peru, the United States, Uruguay, and Venezuela had ratified both the Inter-American and the United Nations Conventions.

2. The Inter-American Convention, unlike article III(3) of the United Nations Convention, does not state grounds on which a court may refuse to order arbitration, but does, in article 5, state the grounds for refusing recognition and execution of an award (see United Nations Convention article V). The Inter-American Convention does, in article 3, provide a procedure for conducting the arbitration if the parties do not specify a procedure. Article 1 limits the Inter-American Convention to commercial transactions- a limitation that the New York Convention permits as a reservation (article I(3)), and the United States has made this reservation.

3. The North American Free Trade Agreement between Canada, Mexico, and the United States, Dec. 17, 1992, 107 Stat. 2057, provides for panel arbitration as the basic mechanism for the settlement of disputes between the parties. See id. chapters 19 (Review and Dispute Settlement in Antidumping and Countervailing Duty Maters) and 20 (Institutional Arrangements and Dispute Settlement Procedures). Although these procedures are not for use by private parties, article 2022 provides:

> 1. Each Party shall, to the maximum extent possible, encourage and facilitate the use of arbitration and other means of alternative dispute resolution for the settlement of international commercial disputes between private parties in the free trade area.
>
> 2. To this end, each Party shall provide appropriate procedures to ensure observance of agreements to arbitrate and for the recognition and enforcement of arbitral awards in such disputes.
>
> 3. A Party shall be deemed to be in compliance with paragraph 2 if it is a party to and is in compliance with the 1958 United Nations Convention on the Recognition and Enforcement of Foreign Arbitral Awards or the 1975 Inter-American Convention on International Commercial Arbitration.

Convention on the Settlement of Investment Disputes Between States and Nationals of Other States
(Opened for signature Aug. 27, 1965, 17 UST 1270, TIAS 6090, 575 U.N.T.S. 159, reprinted in 4 ILM 532 (1965))

PREAMBLE

The Contracting States

Considering the need for international cooperation for economic development, and the role of private international investment therein;

Bearing in mind the possibility that from time to time disputes may arise in connection with such investment between Contracting States and nationals of other Contracting States;

Recognizing that while such disputes would usually be subject to national legal processes, international methods of settlement may be appropriate in certain cases;

Attaching particular importance to the availability of facilities for international conciliation or arbitration to which Contracting States and nationals of other Contracting States may submit such disputes if they so desire;

Desiring to establish such facilities under the auspices of the International Bank for Reconstruction and Development;

Recognizing that mutual consent by the parties to submit such disputes to conciliation or to arbitration through such facilities constitutes a binding agreement which requires in particular that due consideration be given to any recommendation of conciliators, and that any arbitral award be complied with; and

Declaring that no Contracting State shall by the mere fact of its ratification, acceptance or approval of this Convention and without its consent be deemed to be under any obligation to submit any particular dispute to conciliation or arbitration,

Have agreed as follows:

Chapter I: International Centre for Settlement of Investment Disputes

Section 1: Establishment and Organization

Article 1

1. There is hereby established the International Centre for Settlement of Investment Disputes (hereinafter called the Centre).

2. The purpose of the Centre shall be to provide facilities for conciliation and arbitration of investment disputes between Contracting States and nationals of other Contracting States in accordance with the provisions of this Convention.

Article 2

The seat of the Centre shall be at the principal office of the International Bank for Reconstruction and Development (hereinafter called the Bank). The seat may be moved to another place by decision of the Administrative Council adopted by a majority of two-thirds of its members.

Article 3

The Centre shall have an Administrative Council and a Secretariat and shall maintain a Panel of Conciliators and a Panel of Arbitrators.

Section 2 : The Administrative Council

Article 4

1. The Administrative Council shall be composed of one representative of each Contracting State.

* * *

Section 4: The Panels

Article 12

The Panel of Conciliators and the Panel of Arbitrators shall each consist of qualified persons, designated as hereinafter provided, who are willing to serve thereon.

Article 13

1. Each Contracting State may designate to each Panel four persons who may but need not be its nationals.

2. The Chairman [of the Administrative Council] may designate ten persons to each Panel. The persons so designated to a Panel shall each have a different nationality.

Article 14

1. Persons designated to serve on the Panels shall be persons of high moral character and recognized competence in the fields of law, commerce, industry or finance, who may be relied upon to exercise independent judgment. Competence in the field of law shall be of particular importance in the case of persons on the Panel of Arbitrators.

2. The Chairman, in designating persons to serve on the Panels, shall in addition pay due regard to the importance of assuring representation on the Panels of the principal legal systems of the world and of the main forms of economic activity.

* * *

Chapter II: Jurisdiction of the Centre

Article 25

1. The jurisdiction of the Centre shall extend to any legal dispute arising directly out of an investment, between a Contracting State (or any constituent subdivision or agency of a Contracting State designated to the Centre by that State) and a national of another Contracting State, which the parties to the dispute consent in writing to submit to the Centre. When the parties have given their consent, no party may withdraw its consent unilaterally.

2. "National of another Contracting State" means:

(a) any natural person who had the nationality of a Contracting State other than the State party to the dispute on the date on which the parties consented to submit such dispute to conciliation or arbitration as well as on the date on which the request was registered pursuant to paragraph 3 of Article 28 or paragraph 3 of Article 36, but does not include any person who on either date also had the nationality of the Contracting State party to the dispute; and

(b) any juridical person which had the nationality of a Contracting State other than the State party to the dispute on the date on which the parties consented to submit such dispute to conciliation or arbitration and any juridical person which had the nationality of the Contracting State party to the dispute on that date and which, because of foreign control, the parties have agreed should be treated as a national of another Contracting State for the purposes of this Convention.

3. Consent by a constituent subdivision or agency of a Contracting State shall require the approval of that State unless that State notifies the Centre that no such approval is required.

4. Any Contracting State may, at the time of ratification, acceptance or approval of this Convention or at any time thereafter, notify the Centre of the class or classes of disputes which it would or would not consider submitting to the jurisdiction of the Cen-

tre. The Secretary-General shall forthwith transmit such notification to all Contracting States. Such notification shall not constitute the consent required by paragraph 1.

Article 26

Consent of the parties to arbitration under this Convention shall, unless otherwise stated, be deemed consent to such arbitration to the exclusion of any other remedy. A Contracting State may require the exhaustion of local administrative or judicial remedies as a condition of its consent to arbitration under this Convention.

Article 27

1. No Contracting State shall give diplomatic protection, or bring an international claim, in respect of a dispute which one of its nationals and another Contracting State shall have consented to submit or shall have submitted to arbitration under this Convention, unless such other Contracting State shall have failed to abide by and comply with the award rendered in such dispute.

2. Diplomatic protection, for the purposes of paragraph 1, shall not include informal diplomatic exchanges for the sole purpose of facilitating a settlement of the dispute.

Chapter III: Conciliation

Section 1: Request for Conciliation

Article 28

1. Any Contracting State or any national of a Contracting State wishing to institute conciliation proceedings shall address a request to that effect in writing to the Secretary-General who shall send a copy of the request to the other party.

2. The request shall contain information concerning the issues in dispute, the identity of the parties and their consent to conciliation in accordance with the rules of procedure for the institution of conciliation and arbitration proceedings.

3. The Secretary-General [of the Secretariat] shall register the request unless he finds, on the basis of the information contained in the request, that the dispute is manifestly outside the jurisdiction of the Centre. He shall forthwith notify the parties of registration or refusal to register.

Section 2: Constitution of the Conciliation Commission

Article 29

1. The Conciliation Commission (hereinafter called the Commission) shall be constituted as soon as possible after registration of a request pursuant to Article 28.

2. (a) The Commission shall consist of a sole conciliator or any uneven number of conciliators appointed as the parties shall agree.

(b) Where the parties do not agree upon the number of conciliators and the method of their appointment, the Commission shall consist of three conciliators, one conciliator appointed by each party and the third, who shall be the president of the Commission, appointed by agreement of the parties.

Article 30

If the Commission shall not have been constituted within 90 days after notice of registration of the request has been dispatched by the Secretary-General in accordance with paragraph 3 of Article 28, or such other period as the parties may agree, the Chairman shall, at the request of either party and after consulting both parties as far as possible, appoint the conciliator or conciliators not yet appointed.

Article 31

1. Conciliators may be appointed from outside the Panel of Conciliators, except in the case of appointments by the Chairman pursuant to Article 30.

2. Conciliators appointed from outside the Panel of Conciliators shall possess the qualities stated in paragraph 1 of Article 14.

Section 3: Conciliation Proceedings

Article 32

1. The Commission shall be the judge of its own competence.

2. Any objection by a party to the dispute that that dispute is not within the jurisdiction of the Centre, or for other reasons is not within the competence of the Commission, shall be considered by the Commission which shall determine whether to deal with it as a preliminary question or to join it to the merits of the dispute.

Article 33

Any conciliation proceeding shall be conducted in accordance with the provisions of this Section and, except as the parties otherwise agree, in accordance with the Conciliation Rules in effect on the date on which the parties consented to conciliation. If any question of procedure arises which is not covered by this Section or the Conciliation Rules or any rules agreed by the parties, the Commission shall decide the question.

Article 34

1. It shall be the duty of the Commission to clarify the issues in dispute between the parties and to endeavour to bring about agreement between them upon mutually acceptable terms. To that end, the Commission may at any stage of the proceedings and from time to time recommend terms of settlement to the parties. The parties shall cooperate in good faith with the Commission in order to enable the Commission to carry out its functions, and shall give their most serious consideration to its recommendations.

2. If the parties reach agreement, the Commission shall draw up a report noting the issues in dispute and recording that the parties have reached agreement. If, at any stage of the proceedings, it appears to the Commission that there is no likelihood of agreement between the parties, it shall close the proceedings and shall draw up a report noting the submission of the dispute and recording the failure of the parties to reach agreement. If one party fails to appear or participate in the proceedings, the Commission shall close the proceedings and shall draw up a report noting that party's failure to appear or participate.

Article 35

Except as the parties to the dispute shall otherwise agree, neither party to a conciliation proceeding shall be entitled in any other proceeding, whether before arbitrators or in a court of law or otherwise, to invoke or rely on any views expressed or statements or admissions or offers of settlement made by the other party in the conciliation proceedings, or the report or any recommendations made by the Commission.

Chapter IV: Arbitration

Section 1: Request for Arbitration

Article 36

1. Any Contracting State or any national of a Contracting State wishing to institute arbitration proceedings shall address a request to that effect in writing to the Secretary-General who shall send a copy of the request to the other party.

2. The request shall contain information concerning the issues in dispute, the identity of the parties and their consent to arbitration in accordance with the rules of procedure for the institution of conciliation and arbitration proceedings.

3. The Secretary-General shall register the request unless he finds, on the basis of the information contained in the request, that the dispute is manifestly outside the jurisdiction of the Centre. He shall forthwith notify the parties of registration or refusal to register.

Section 2: Constitution of the Tribunal

Article 37

1. The Arbitral Tribunal (hereinafter called the Tribunal) shall be constituted as soon as possible after registration of a request pursuant to Article 36.

2. (a) The Tribunal shall consist of a sole arbitrator or any uneven number of arbitrators appointed as the parties shall agree.

(b) Where the parties do not agree upon the number of arbitrators and the method of their appointment, the Tribunal shall consist of three arbitrators, one arbitrator appointed by each party and the third, who shall be the president of the Tribunal, appointed by agreement of the parties.

Article 38

If the Tribunal shall not have been constituted within 90 days after notice of registration of the request has been dispatched by the Secretary-General in accordance with paragraph 3 of Article 36, or such other period as the parties may agree, the Chairman shall, at the request of either party and after consulting both parties as far as possible, appoint the arbitrator or arbitrators not yet appointed. Arbitrators appointed by the Chairman pursuant to this article shall not be nationals of the Contracting State party to the dispute or of the Contracting State whose national is a party to the dispute.

Article 39

The majority of the arbitrators shall be nationals of States other than the Contracting State party to the dispute and the Contracting State whose national is a party to the dispute; provided, however, that the foregoing provisions of this article shall not apply if the sole arbitrator or each individual member of the Tribunal has been appointed by agreement of the parties.

Article 40

1. Arbitrators may be appointed from outside the Panel of Arbitrators, except in the case of appointments by the Chairman pursuant to Article 38.

2. Arbitrators appointed from outside the Panel of Arbitrators shall possess the qualities stated in paragraph 1 of Article 14.

Section 3: Powers and Functions of the Tribunal

Article 41

1. The Tribunal shall be the judge of its own competence.

2. Any objection by a party to the dispute that that dispute is not within the jurisdiction of the Centre, or for other reasons is not within the competence of the Tribunal, shall be considered by the Tribunal which shall determine whether to deal with it as a preliminary question or to join it to the merits of the dispute.

Article 42

1. The Tribunal shall decide a dispute in accordance with such rules of law as may be agreed by the parties. In the absence of such agreement, the Tribunal shall apply the law of the Contracting State party to the dispute (including its rules on the conflict of laws) and such rules of international law as may be applicable.

2. The Tribunal may not bring in a finding of *non liquet* on the ground of silence or obscurity of the law.

3. The provisions of paragraphs 1 and 2 shall not prejudice the power of the Tribunal to decide a dispute *ex aequo et bono* if the parties so agree.

Article 43

Except as the parties otherwise agree, the Tribunal may, if it deems it necessary at any stage of the proceedings,

(a) call upon the parties to produce documents or other evidence, and

(b) visit the scene connected with the dispute, and conduct such inquiries there as it may deem appropriate.

Article 44

Any arbitration proceeding shall be conducted in accordance with the provisions of this Section and, except as the parties otherwise agree, in accordance with the Arbitration Rules in effect on the date on which the parties consented to arbitration. If any question of procedure arises which is not covered by this Section or the Arbitration Rules or any rules agreed by the parties, the Tribunal shall decide the question.

Article 45

1. Failure of a party to appear or to present his case shall not be deemed an admission of the other party's assertions.

2. If a party fails to appear or to present his case at any stage of the proceedings the other party may request the Tribunal to deal with the questions submitted to it and to render an award. Before rendering an award, the Tribunal shall notify, and grant a period of grace to, the party failing to appear or to present its case, unless it is satisfied that that party does not intend to do so.

Article 46

Except as the parties otherwise agree, the Tribunal shall, if requested by a party, determine any incidental or additional claims or counter-claims arising directly out of the subject-matter of the dispute provided that they are within the scope of the consent of the parties and are otherwise within the jurisdiction of the Centre.

Article 47

Except as the parties otherwise agree, the Tribunal may, if it considers that the circumstances so require, recommend any provisional measures which should be taken to preserve the respective rights of either party.

Section 4: The Award

Article 48

1. The Tribunal shall decide questions by a majority of the votes of all its members.

2. The award of the Tribunal shall be in writing and shall be signed by the members of the Tribunal who voted for it.

3. The award shall deal with every question submitted to the Tribunal, and shall state the reasons upon which it is based.

4. Any member of the Tribunal may attach his individual opinion to the award, whether he dissents from the majority or not, or a statement of his dissent.

5. The Centre shall not publish the award without the consent of the parties.

Article 49

1. The Secretary-General shall promptly dispatch certified copies of the award to the parties. The award shall be deemed to have been rendered on the date on which the certified copies were dispatched.

2. The Tribunal upon the request of a party made within 45 days after the date on which the award was rendered may after notice to the other party decide any question which it had omitted to decide in the award, and shall rectify any clerical, arithmetical or similar error in the award. Its decision shall become part of the award and shall be notified to the parties in the same manner as the award. The periods of time provided for under paragraph 2 of Article 51 and paragraph 2 of Article 52 shall run from the date on which the decision was rendered.

Section 5: Interpretation, Revision and Annulment of the Award

Article 50

1. If any dispute shall arise between the parties as to the meaning or scope of an award, either party may request interpretation of the award by an application in writing addressed to the Secretary-General.

2. The request shall, if possible, be submitted to the Tribunal which rendered the award. If this shall not be possible, a new Tribunal shall be constituted in accordance with Section 2 of this chapter. The Tribunal may, if it considers that the circumstances so require, stay enforcement of the award pending its decision.

Article 51

1. Either party may request revision of the award by an application in writing addressed to the Secretary-General on the ground of discovery of some fact of such a nature as decisively to affect the award, provided that when the award was rendered that fact was unknown to the Tribunal and to the applicant and that the applicant's ignorance of that fact was not due to negligence.

2. The application shall be made within 90 days after the discovery of such fact and in any event within three years after the date on which the award was rendered.

3. The request shall, if possible, be submitted to the Tribunal which rendered the award. If this shall not be possible, a new Tribunal shall be constituted in accordance with Section 2 of this chapter.

4. The Tribunal may, if it considers that the circumstances so require, stay enforcement of the award pending its decision. If the applicant requests a stay of enforcement of the award in his application, enforcement shall be stayed provisionally until the Tribunal rules on such request.

Article 52

1. Either party may request annulment of the award by an application in writing addressed to the Secretary-General on one or more of the following grounds:

(a) that the Tribunal was not properly constituted;

(b) that the Tribunal has manifestly exceeded it powers;

(c) that there was corruption on the part of a member of the Tribunal;

(d) that there has been a serious departure from a fundamental rule of procedure; or

(e) that the award has failed to state the reasons on which it is based.

2. The application shall be made within 120 days after the date on which the award was rendered except that when annulment is requested on the ground of corruption such application shall be made within 120 days after discovery of the corruption and in any event within three years after the date on which the award was rendered.

3. On receipt of the request the Chairman shall forthwith appoint from the Panel of Arbitrators an ad hoc Committee of three persons. None of the members of the Committee shall have been a member of the Tribunal which rendered the award, shall be of the same nationality as any such member, shall be a national of the State party to the dispute or of the State whose national is a party to the dispute, shall have been designated to the Panel of Arbitrators by either of those States, or shall have acted as a conciliator in the same dispute. The Committee shall have the authority to annul the award or any part thereof on any of the grounds set forth in paragraph 1.

4. The provisions of Articles 41 to 45, 48, 49, 53 and 54, and of Chapters VI and VII shall apply *mutatis mutandis* to proceedings before the Committee.

5. The Committee may, if it considers that the circumstances so require, stay enforcement of the award pending its decision. If the applicant requests a stay of enforce-

ment of the award in his application, enforcement shall be stayed provisionally until the Committee rules on such request.

6. If the award is annulled the dispute shall, at the request of either party, be submitted to a new Tribunal constituted in accordance with Section 2 of this chapter.

Section 6: Recognition and Enforcement of the Award

Article 53

1. The award shall be binding on the parties and shall not be subject to any appeal or to any other remedy except those provided for in this Convention. Each party shall abide by and comply with the terms of the award except to the extent that enforcement shall have been stayed pursuant to the relevant provisions of this Convention.

2. For the purposes of this Section, "award" shall include any decision interpreting, revising or annulling such award pursuant to Articles 50, 51 or 52.

Article 54

1. Each Contracting State shall recognize an award rendered pursuant to this Convention as binding and enforce the pecuniary obligations imposed by that award within its territories as if it were a final judgment of a court in that State. A Contracting State with a federal constitution may enforce such an award in or through its federal courts and may provide that such courts shall treat the award as if it were a final judgment of the courts of a constituent state.

2. A party seeking recognition or enforcement in the territories of a Contracting State shall furnish to a competent court or other authority which such State shall have designated for this purpose a copy of the award certified by the Secretary-General. Each Contracting State shall notify the Secretary-General of the designation of the competent court or other authority for this purpose and of any subsequent change in such designation.

3. Execution of the award shall be governed by the laws concerning the execution of judgments in force in the State in whose territories such execution is sought.

Article 55

Nothing in Article 54 shall be construed as derogating from the law in force in any Contracting State relating to immunity of that State or of any foreign State from execution.

Chapter V: Replacement and Disqualification of Conciliators and Arbitrators

Article 56

1. After a Commission or a Tribunal has been constituted and proceedings have begun, its composition shall remain unchanged; provided, however, that if a conciliator or an arbitrator should die, become incapacitated, or resign, the resulting vacancy shall be filled in accordance with the provisions of Section 2 of Chapter III or Section 2 of Chapter IV.

2. A member of a Commission or Tribunal shall continue to serve in that capacity notwithstanding that he shall have ceased to be a member of the Panel.

3. If a conciliator or arbitrator appointed by a party shall have resigned without the consent of the Commission or Tribunal of which he was a member, the Chairman shall appoint a person from the appropriate Panel to fill the resulting vacancy.

Article 57

A party may propose to a Commission or Tribunal the disqualification of any of its members on account of any fact indicating a manifest lack of the qualities required by paragraph 1 of Article 14. A party to arbitration proceedings may, in addition, propose the disqualification of an arbitrator on the ground that he was ineligible for appointment to the Tribunal under Section 2 of Chapter IV.

Article 58

The decision on any proposal to disqualify a conciliator or arbitrator shall be taken by the other members of the Commission or Tribunal as the case may be, provided that where those members are equally divided, or in the case of a proposal to disqualify a sole conciliator or arbitrator, or a majority of the conciliators or arbitrators, the Chairman shall take that decision. If it is decided that the proposal is well-founded the conciliator or arbitrator to whom the decision relates shall be replaced in accordance with the provisions of Section 2 of Chapter III or Section 2 of Chapter IV.

Chapter VI: Cost of Proceedings

Article 59

The charges payable by the parties for the use of the facilities of the Centre shall be determined by the Secretary-General in accordance with the regulations adopted by the Administrative Council.

Article 60

1. Each Commission and each Tribunal shall determine the fees and expenses of its members within limits established from time to time by the Administrative Council and after consultation with the Secretary-General.

2. Nothing in paragraph 1 of this article shall preclude the parties from agreeing in advance with the Commission or Tribunal concerned upon the fees and expenses of its members.

Article 61

1. In the case of conciliation proceedings the fees and expenses of members of the Commission as well as the charges for the use of the facilities of the Centre, shall be borne equally by the parties. Each party shall bear any other expenses it incurs in connection with the proceedings.

2. In the case of arbitration proceedings the Tribunal shall, except as the parties otherwise agree, assess the expenses incurred by the parties in connection with the proceedings, and shall decide how and by whom those expenses, the fees and expenses of

the members of the Tribunal and the charges for the use of the facilities of the Centre shall be paid. Such decision shall form part of the award.

Chapter VII: Place of Proceedings

Article 62

Conciliation and arbitration proceedings shall be held at the seat of the Centre except as hereinafter provided.

Article 63

Conciliation and arbitration proceedings may be held, if the parties so agree,

(a) at the seat of the Permanent Court of Arbitration or of any other appropriate institution, whether private or public, with which the Centre may make arrangements for that purpose; or

(b) at any other place approved by the Commission or Tribunal after consultation with the Secretary-General.

Chapter VIII: Disputes between Contracting States

Article 64

Any dispute arising between Contracting States concerning the interpretation or application of this Convention which is not settled by negotiation shall be referred to the International Court of Justice by the application of any party to such dispute, unless the States concerned agree to another method of settlement.

* * *

Notes

1. In order to encourage private investment abroad, the Executive Directors of the International Bank for Reconstruction and Development submitted this Convention to governments that were members of the Bank. The United States ratified the Convention in 1966 and the Convention entered into force the same year. As of January 1, 2000 it had been ratified in 131 countries. For a detailed account of its operation, see Ibrahim F.I. Shihata & Antonio R. Parra, The Experience of the International Centre for Settlement of Investment Disputes, 14 ICSID Rev. 299 (1999).

2. There is provision for mandatory recognition of an arbitration award rendered pursuant to the Convention (Article 54(1)) but this does not derogate from any law relating to immunity of the State from execution (Article 55).

Model Law on International Commercial Arbitration

(As adopted by the United Nations Commission on International Trade Law (UNCITRAL) on June 21, 1985; Report of UNCITRAL on the Work of its Eighteenth Session, 40 U.N. GAOR Supp. (No. 17), Annex 1, at 81-83, U.N. Doc. A/40/17 (1985), reprinted in 24 I.L.M. 1302 (1985); Legislative history, Report id. ch. II, pp. 5-65, reprinted in 24 I.L.M. 1314 (1985))

Chapter I: General Provisions

Article 1: Scope of Application

(1) This Law applies to international commercial arbitration, subject to any agreement in force between this State and any other State or States.

(2) The provisions of this Law, except Articles 8, 9, 35 and 36, apply only if the place of arbitration is in the territory of this State.

(3) An arbitration is international if:

(a) the parties to an arbitration agreement have, at the time of the conclusion of that agreement, their places of business in different States; or

(b) one of the following places is situated outside the State in which the parties have their places of business:

(i) the place of arbitration if determined in, or pursuant to, the arbitration agreement;

(ii) any place where a substantial part of the obligations of the commercial relationship is to be performed or the place with which the subject-matter of the dispute is most closely connected; or

(c) the parties have expressly agreed that the subject-matter of the arbitration agreement relates to more than one country.

(4) For the purposes of paragraph 3 of this article:

(a) if a party has more than one place of business, the place of business is that which has the closest relationship to the arbitration agreement;

(b) if a party does not have a place of business, reference is to be made to his habitual residence.

(5) This Law shall not affect any other law of this State by virtue of which certain disputes may not be submitted to arbitration or may be submitted to arbitration only according to provisions other than those of this Law.

Article 2: Definitions and Rules of Interpretation

For the purposes of this Law:

(a) "arbitration" means any arbitration whether or not administered by a permanent arbitral institution;

(b) "arbitral tribunal" means a sole arbitrator or a panel of arbitrators;

(c) "court" means a body or organ of the judicial system of a State;

(d) where a provision of this Law, except Article 28, leaves the parties free to determine a certain issue, such freedom includes the right of the parties to authorize a third party, including an institution, to make that determination;

(e) where a provision of this Law refers to the fact that the parties have agreed or that they may agree or in any other way refers to an agreement of the parties, such agreement includes any arbitration rules referred to in that agreement;

(f) where a provision of this Law, other than in Articles 25(a) and 32(a), refers to a claim, it also applies to a counter-claim, and where it refers to a defence, it also applies to a defence to such counter-claim.

* * *

Article 5: Extent of Court Intervention

In matters governed by this Law, no court shall intervene except where so provided in this Law.

Article 6: Court or Other Authority for Certain Functions of Arbitration Assistance and Supervision

The functions referred to in Articles 11(3), 11(4), 13(3), 14, 16(3) and 34(2) shall be performed by... [Each State enacting this model law specifies the court, courts or, where referred to therein, other authority competent to perform these functions.]

Chapter II: Arbitration Agreement

Article 7: Definition and Form of Arbitration Agreement

(1) "Arbitration agreement" is an agreement by the parties to submit to arbitration all or certain disputes which have arisen or which may arise between them in respect of a defined legal relationship, whether contractual or not. An arbitration agreement may be in the form of an arbitration clause in a contract or in the form of a separate agreement.

(2) The arbitration agreement shall be in writing. An agreement is in writing if it is contained in a document signed by the parties or in an exchange of letters, telex, telegrams or other means of telecommunication which provide a record of the agreement, or in an exchange of statements of claim and defence in which the existence of an agreement is alleged by one party and not denied by another. The reference in a contract to a document containing an arbitration clause constitutes an arbitration agreement provided that the contract is in writing and the reference is such as to make that clause part of the contract.

Article 8: Arbitration Agreement and Substantive Claim before Court

(1) A court before which an action is brought in a matter which is the subject of an arbitration agreement shall, if a party so requests not later than when submitting his first statement on the substance of the dispute, refer the parties to arbitration unless

it finds that the agreement is null and void, inoperative or incapable of being performed.

(2) Where an action referred to in paragraph 1 of this article has been brought, arbitral proceedings may nevertheless be commenced or continued, and an award may be made, while the issue is pending before the court.

Article 9: Arbitration Agreement and Interim Measures by Court

It is not incompatible with an arbitration agreement for a party to request, before or during arbitral proceedings, from a court an interim measure of protection and for a court to grant such measure.

Chapter III: Composition of Arbitral Tribunal

Article 10: Number of Arbitrators

(1) The parties are free to determine the number of arbitrators.

(2) Failing such determination, the number of arbitrators shall be three.

Article 11: Appointment of Arbitrators

(1) No person shall be precluded by reason of his nationality from acting as an arbitrator, unless otherwise agreed by the parties.

(2) The parties are free to agree on a procedure of appointing the arbitrator or arbitrators, subject to the provisions of paragraphs 4 and 5 of this article.

(3) Failing such agreement,

    (a) in an arbitration with three arbitrators, each party shall appoint one arbitrator, and the two arbitrators thus appointed shall appoint the third arbitrator; if a party fails to appoint the arbitrator within 30 days of receipt of a request to do so from the other party, or if the two arbitrators fail to agree on the third arbitrator within 30 days of their appointment, the appointment shall be made, upon request of a party, by the court or other authority specified in Article 6;

    (b) in an arbitration with a sole arbitrator, if the parties are unable to agree on the arbitrator, he shall be appointed, upon request of a party, by the court or other authority specified in Article 6

(4) Where, under an appointment procedure agreed upon by the parties,

    (a) a party fails to act as required under such procedure, or

    (b) the parties, or two arbitrators, are unable to reach an agreement expected of them under such procedure, or

    (c) a third party, including an institution, fails to perform any function entrusted to it under such procedure, any party may request the court or other authority specified in Article 6 to take the necessary measure, unless the agreement on the appointment procedure provides other means for securing the appointment.

(5) A decision on a matter entrusted by paragraph 3 or 4 of this article to the court or other authority specified in Article 6 shall be subject to no appeal. The court or other authority, in appointing an arbitrator, shall have due regard to any qualifications required of the arbitrator by the agreement of the parties and to such considerations as are likely to secure the appointment of an independent and impartial arbitrator and, in the case of a sole or third arbitrator, shall take into account as well the advisability of appointing an arbitrator of a nationality other than those of the parties.

Article 12: Grounds for Challenge

(1) When a person is approached in connection with his possible appointment as an arbitrator, he shall disclose any circumstances likely to give rise to justifiable doubts as to his impartiality or independence. An arbitrator, from the time of his appointment and throughout the arbitral proceedings, shall without delay disclose any such circumstances to the parties unless they have already been informed of them by him.

(2) An arbitrator may be challenged only if circumstances exist that give rise to justifiable doubts as to his impartiality or independence, or if he does not possess qualifications agreed to by the parties. A party may challenge an arbitrator appointed by him, or in whose appointment he has participated, only for reasons of which he becomes aware after the appointment has been made.

Article 13: Challenge Procedure

(1) The parties are free to agree on a procedure for challenging an arbitrator, subject to the provisions of paragraph 3 of this article.

(2) Failing such agreement, a party who intends to challenge an arbitrator shall, within 15 days after becoming aware of the constitution of the arbitral tribunal or after becoming aware of any circumstance referred to in Article 12(2), send a written statement of the reasons for the challenge to the arbitral tribunal. Unless the challenged arbitrator withdraws from his office or the other party agrees to the challenge, the arbitral tribunal shall decide on the challenge.

(3) If a challenge under any procedure agreed upon by the parties or under the procedure of paragraph 2 of this article is not successful, the challenging party may request, within 30 days after having received notice of the decision rejecting the challenge, the court or other authority specified in Article 6 to decide on the challenge, which decision shall be subject to no appeal; while such a request is pending, the arbitral tribunal, including the challenged arbitrator, may continue the arbitral proceedings and make an award.

Article 14: Failure or Impossibility to Act

(1) If an arbitrator becomes *de jure* or *de facto* unable to perform his functions or for other reasons fails to act without undue delay, his mandate terminates if he withdraws from his office or if the parties agree on the termination. Otherwise, if a controversy remains concerning any of these grounds, any party may request the court or other authority specified in Article 6 to decide on the termination of the mandate, which decision shall be subject to no appeal.

(2) If, under this article or Article 13(2), an arbitrator withdraws from his office or a party agrees to the termination of the mandate of an arbitrator, this does not imply acceptance of the validity of any ground referred to in this article or Article 12(2).

Article 15: Appointment of Substitute Arbitrator

Where the mandate of an arbitrator terminates under Article 13 or 14 or because of his withdrawal from office for any other reason or because of the revocation of his mandate by agreement of the parties or in any other case of termination of his mandate, a substitute arbitrator shall be appointed according to the rules that were applicable to the appointment of the arbitrator being replaced.

Chapter IV: Jurisdiction of Arbitral Tribunal

Article 16: Competence of Arbitral Tribunal to Rule on Its Jurisdiction

(1) The arbitral tribunal may rule on its own jurisdiction, including any objections with respect to the existence or validity of the arbitration agreement. For that purpose, an arbitration clause which forms part of a contract shall be treated as an agreement independent of the other terms of the contract. A decision by the arbitral tribunal that the contract is null and void shall not entail *ipso jure* the invalidity of the arbitration clause.

(2) A plea that the arbitral tribunal does not have jurisdiction shall be raised not later than the submission of the statement of defence. A party is not precluded from raising such a plea by the fact that he has appointed, or participated in the appointment of, an arbitrator. A plea that the arbitral tribunal is exceeding the scope of its authority shall be raised as soon as the matter alleged to be beyond the scope of its authority is raised during the arbitral proceedings. The arbitral tribunal may, in either case, admit a later plea if it considers the delay justified.

(3) The arbitral tribunal may rule on a plea referred to in paragraph 2 of this article either as a preliminary question or in an award on the merits. If the arbitral tribunal rules as a preliminary question that it has jurisdiction, any party may request, within 30 days after having received notice of that ruling, the court specified in Article 6 to decide the matter, which decision shall be subject to no appeal; while such a request is pending, the arbitral tribunal may continue the arbitral proceedings and make an award.

Article 17: Power of Arbitral Tribunal to Order Interim Measures

Unless otherwise agreed by the parties, the arbitral tribunal may, at the request of a party, order any party to take such interim measure of protection as the arbitral tribunal may consider necessary in respect of the subject-matter of the dispute. The arbitral tribunal may require any party to provide appropriate security in connection with such measure.

Chapter V: Conduct of Arbitral Proceedings

Article 18: Equal Treatment of Parties

The parties shall be treated with equality and each party shall be given a full opportunity of presenting his case.

Article 19: Determination of Rules of Procedure

(1) Subject to the provisions of this Law, the parties are free to agree on the procedure to be followed by the arbitral tribunal in conducting the proceedings.

(2) Failing such agreement, the arbitral tribunal may, subject to the provisions of this Law, conduct the arbitration in such manner as it considers appropriate. The power conferred upon the arbitral tribunal includes the power to determine the admissibility, relevance, materiality and weight of any evidence.

Article 20: Place of Arbitration

(1) The parties are free to agree on the place of arbitration. Failing such agreement, the place of arbitration shall be determined by the arbitral tribunal having regard to the circumstances of the case, including the convenience of the parties.

(2) Notwithstanding the provisions of paragraph 1 of this article, the arbitral tribunal may, unless otherwise agreed by the parties, meet at any place it considers appropriate for consultation among its members, for hearing witnesses, experts or the parties, or for inspection of goods, other property or documents.

Article 21: Commencement of Arbitral Proceedings

Unless otherwise agreed by the parties, the arbitral proceedings in respect of a particular dispute commence on the date on which a request for that dispute to be referred to arbitration is received by the respondent.

Article 22: Language

(1) The parties are free to agree on the language or languages to be used in the arbitral proceedings. Failing such agreement, the arbitral tribunal shall determine the language or languages to be used in the proceedings. This agreement or determination, unless otherwise specified therein, shall apply to any written statement by a party, any hearing and any award, decision or other communication by the arbitral tribunal.

(2) The arbitral tribunal may order that any documentary evidence shall be accompanied by a translation into the language or languages agreed upon by the parties or determined by the arbitral tribunal.

Article 23: Statements of Claim and Defence

(1) Within the period of time agreed by the parties or determined by the arbitral tribunal, the claimant shall state the facts supporting his claim, the points at issue and the relief or remedy sought, and the respondent shall state his defence in respect of these particulars, unless the parties have otherwise agreed as to the required elements of such statements. The parties may submit with their statements all documents they consider to be relevant or may add a reference to the documents or other evidence they will submit.

(2) Unless otherwise agreed by the parties, either party may amend or supplement his claim or defence during the course of the arbitral proceedings, unless the arbitral tribunal considers it inappropriate to allow such amendment having regard to the delay in making it.

Article 24: Hearings and Written Proceedings

(1) Subject to any contrary agreement by the parties, the arbitral tribunal shall decide whether to hold oral hearings for the presentation of evidence or for oral argument, or whether the proceedings shall be conducted on the basis of documents and other materials. However, unless the parties have agreed that no hearings shall be held, the arbitral tribunal shall hold such hearings at an appropriate stage of the proceedings, if so requested by a party.

(2) The parties shall be given sufficient advance notice of any hearing and of any meeting of the arbitral tribunal for the purposes of inspection of goods, other property or documents.

(3) All statements, documents or other information supplied to the arbitral tribunal by one party shall be communicated to the other party. Also any expert report or evidentiary document on which the arbitral tribunal may rely in making its decision shall be communicated to the parties.

Article 25: Default of a Party

Unless otherwise agreed by the parties, if, without showing sufficient cause,

(a) the claimant fails to communicate his statement of claim in accordance with Article 23(1), the arbitral tribunal shall terminate the proceedings;

(b) the respondent fails to communicate his statement of defence in accordance with Article 23(1), the arbitral tribunal shall continue the proceedings without treating such failure in itself as an admission of the claimant's allegations;

(c) any party fails to appear at a hearing or to produce documentary evidence, the arbitral tribunal may continue the proceedings and make the award on the evidence before it.

Article 26: Expert Appointed by Arbitral Tribunal

(1) Unless otherwise agreed by the parties, the arbitral tribunal

   (a) may appoint one or more experts to report to it on specific issues to be determined by the arbitral tribunal;

   (b) may require a party to give the expert any relevant information or to produce, or to provide access to any relevant documents, goods or other property for his inspection.

(2) Unless otherwise agreed by the parties, if a party so requests or if the arbitral tribunal considers it necessary, the expert shall, after delivery of his written or oral report, participate in a hearing where the parties have the opportunity to put questions to him and to present expert witnesses in order to testify on the points at issue.

Article 27: Court Assistance in Taking Evidence

The arbitral tribunal or a party with the approval of the arbitral tribunal may request from a competent court of this State assistance in taking evidence. The court may execute the request within its competence and according to its rules of taking evidence.

Chapter VI: Making of Award and Termination of Proceedings

Article 28: Rules Applicable to Substance of Dispute

(1) The arbitral tribunal shall decide the dispute in accordance with such rules of law as are chosen by the parties as applicable to the substance of the dispute. Any designation of the law or legal system of a given State shall be construed, unless otherwise expressed, as directly referring to the substantive law of that State and not to its conflict of laws rules.

(2) Failing any designation by the parties, the arbitral tribunal shall apply the law determined by the conflict of laws rules which it considers applicable.

(3) The arbitral tribunal shall decide ex aequo et bono or as amiable compositeur only if the parties have expressly authorized it to do so.

(4) In all cases, the arbitral tribunal shall decide in accordance with the terms of the contract and shall take into account the usages of the trade applicable to the transaction.

Article 29: Decision-making by Panel of Arbitrators

In arbitral proceedings with more than one arbitrator, any decision of the arbitral tribunal shall be made, unless otherwise agreed by the parties, by a majority of all its members. However, questions of procedure may be decided by a presiding arbitrator, if so authorized by the parties or all members of the arbitral tribunal.

Article 30: Settlement

(1) If, during arbitral proceedings, the parties settle the dispute, the arbitral tribunal shall terminate the proceeding and, if requested by the parties and not objected to by the arbitral tribunal, record the settlement in the form of an arbitral award on agreed terms.

(2) An award on agreed terms shall be made in accordance with the provisions of Article 31 and shall state that it is an award. Such an award has the same status and effect as any other award on the merits of the case.

Article 31: Form and Contents of Award

(1) The award shall be made in writing and shall be signed by the arbitrator or arbitrators. In arbitral proceedings with more than one arbitrator, the signatures of the majority of all members of the arbitral tribunal shall suffice, provided that the reason for any omitted signature is stated.

(2) The award shall state the reasons upon which it is based, unless the parties have agreed that no reasons are to be given or the award is an award on agreed terms under Article 30.

(3) The award shall state its date and the place of arbitration as determined in accordance with Article 20(1). The award shall be deemed to have been made at that place.

(4) After the award is made, a copy signed by the arbitrators in accordance with paragraph 1 of this article shall be delivered to each party.

Article 32: Termination of Proceedings

(1) The arbitral proceedings are terminated by the final award or by an order of the arbitral tribunal in accordance with paragraph 2 of this article.

(2) The arbitral tribunal shall issue an order for the termination of the arbitral proceedings when:

> (a) the claimant withdraws his claim, unless the respondent objects thereto and the arbitral tribunal recognizes a legitimate interest on his part in obtaining a final settlement of the dispute;
>
> (b) the parties agree on the termination of the proceedings;
> (c) the arbitral tribunal finds that the continuation of the proceedings has for any other reason become unnecessary or impossible.

(3) The mandate of the arbitral tribunal terminates with the termination of the arbitral proceedings, subject to the provisions of Articles 33 and 34(4).

Article 33: Correction and Interpretation of Award; Additional Award

(1) Within 30 days of receipt of the award, unless another period of time has been agreed upon by the parties:

> (a) a party, with notice to the other party, may request the arbitral tribunal to correct in the award any errors in computation, any clerical or typographical errors or any errors of similar nature;
>
> (b) if so agreed by the parties, a party, with notice to the other party, may request the arbitral tribunal to give an interpretation of a specific point or part of the award.

If the arbitral tribunal considers the request to be justified, it shall make the correction or give the interpretation within 30 days of receipt of the request. The interpretation shall form part of the award.

(2) The arbitral tribunal may correct any error of the type referred to in paragraph 1(a) of this article on its own initiative within thirty days of the date of the award.

(3) Unless otherwise agreed by the parties, a party, with notice to the other party, may request, within 30 days of receipt of the award, the arbitral tribunal to make an additional award as to claims presented in the arbitral proceedings but omitted from the award. If the arbitral tribunal considers the request to be justified, it shall make the additional award within 60 days.

(4) The arbitral tribunal may extend, if necessary, the period of time within which it shall make a correction, interpretation or an additional award under paragraph 1 or 3 of this article.

(5) The provisions of Article 31 shall apply to a correction or interpretation of the award or to an additional award.

Chapter VII: Recourse Against Award

Article 34: Application for Setting Aside as Exclusive Recourse Against Arbitral Award

(1) Recourse to a court against an arbitral award may be made only by an application for setting aside in accordance with paragraphs 2 and 3 of this article.

(2) An arbitral award may be set aside by the court specified in Article 6 only if:

(a) the party making the application furnishes proof that:

(i) a party to the arbitration agreement referred to in Article 7 was under some incapacity; or the said agreement is not valid under the law to which the parties have subjected it or, failing any indication thereon, under the law of this State; or

(ii) the party making the application was not given proper notice of the appointment of an arbitrator or of the arbitral proceedings or was otherwise unable to present his case; or

(iii) the award deals with a dispute not contemplated by or not falling within the terms of the submission to arbitration, or contains decisions on matters beyond the scope of the submission to arbitration, provided that, if the decisions on matters submitted to arbitration can be separated from those not so submitted, only that part of the award which contains decisions on matters not submitted to arbitration may be set aside; or

(iv) the composition of the arbitral tribunal or the arbitral procedure was not in accordance with the agreement of the parties, unless such agreement was in conflict with a provision of this Law from which the parties cannot derogate, or, failing such agreement, was not in accordance with this Law; or

(b) the court finds that:

(i) the subject-matter of the dispute is not capable of settlement by arbitration under the law of this State; or

(ii) the award is in conflict with the public policy of this State.

(3) An application for setting aside may not be made after three months have elapsed from the date on which the party making that application had received the award or, if a request had been made under Article 33, from the date on which that request had been disposed of by the arbitral tribunal.

(4) The court, when asked to set aside an award, may, where appropriate and so requested by a party, suspend the setting aside proceedings for a period of time determined by it in order to give the arbitral tribunal an opportunity to resume the arbitral proceedings or to take such other action as in the arbitral tribunal's opinion will eliminate the grounds for setting aside.

Chapter VIII: Recognition and Enforcement of Awards

Article 35: Recognition and Enforcement

(1) An arbitral award, irrespective of the country in which it was made, shall be recognized as binding and, upon application in writing to the competent court, shall be enforced subject to the provisions of this article and of Article 36.

(2) The party relying on an award or applying for its enforcement shall supply the duly authenticated original award or a duly certified copy thereof, and the original arbitration agreement referred to in Article 7 or a duly certified copy thereof. If the award or agreement is not made in an official language of this State, the party shall supply a duly certified translation thereof into such language.

Article 36: Grounds for Refusing Recognition or Enforcement

1) Recognition or enforcement of an arbitral award, irrespective of the country in which it was made, may be refused only:

    (a) at the request of the party against whom it is invoked, if that party furnishes to the competent court where recognition or enforcement is sought proof that:

        (i) a party to the arbitration agreement referred to in Article 7 was under some incapacity; or the said agreement is not valid under the law to which the parties have subjected it or failing any indication thereon, under the law of the country where the award was made; or

        (ii) the party against whom the award is invoked was not given proper notice of the appointment of an arbitrator or of the arbitral proceedings or was otherwise unable to present his case; or

        (iii) the award deals with a dispute not contemplated by or not falling within the terms of the submission to arbitration, or it contains decisions on matters beyond the scope of the submission to arbitration, provided that, if the decisions on matters submitted to arbitration can be separated from those not so submitted, that part of the award which contains decisions on matters submitted to arbitration may be recognized and enforced; or

        (iv) the composition of the arbitral tribunal or the arbitral procedure was not in accordance with the agreement of the parties, or, failing such agreement, was not in accordance with the law of the country where the arbitration took place; or

        (v) the award has not yet become binding on the parties or has been set aside or suspended by a court of the country in which, or under the law of which, that award was made; or

    (b) if the court finds that:

        (i) the subject-matter of the dispute is not capable of settlement by arbitration under the law of this State; or

(ii) the recognition or enforcement of the award would be contrary to the public policy of this State.

(2) If an application for setting aside or suspension of an award has been made to a court referred to in paragraph 1(a)(v) of this article, the court where recognition or enforcement is sought may, if it considers it proper, adjourn its decision and may also, on the application of the party claiming recognition or enforcement of the award, order the other party to provide appropriate security.

Notes

1. The Model Law is intended to assist states in shaping their arbitration law to facilitate proceedings pursuant to a multilateral arbitration convention such as the United Nations Convention set out in Chapter 1, section 2. Article 8(1), on grounds for refusal to refer the parties to arbitration, tracks Article II(3) of the UN Convention, but adds detail as to the timeliness of the request for referral, and Article 36, on grounds for refusing recognition or enforcement of an award, tracks Articles V and VI of the UN Convention. For the most part, however, the Model Law supplies necessary details as to the procedure for conducting the arbitration and provides valuable insights into the nature of international arbitration. As of August 30, 2000, the UNCITRAL Web site <http://www.uncitral.org/en_index.htm> indicates that legislation based on the Model Law has been enacted in twenty-eight countries and in two special administrative regions of China (Australia, Bahrain, Bermuda, Bulgaria, Canada, Cyprus, Egypt, Germany, Guatemala, Hong Kong (special administrative region of China), Hungary, India, Iran, Ireland, Kenya, Lithuania, Macau (special administrative region of China), Malta, Mexico, New Zealand, Nigeria, Oman, Peru, Russia, Singapore, Sri Lanka, Tunisia, Ukraine, United Kingdom (in Great Britain, Northern Ireland, and Scotland), and Zimbabwe; and that in the United States, four states have legislation based on the Model Law (California, Connecticut, Oregon, and Texas). Heather A. Purcell, State International Arbitration Statutes: Why They Matter, 32 Tex. Int'l L.J. 525, 529 n.19 (1997), adds Ohio and North Carolina as states with statutes based on the UNCITRAL Model law.

For comment on the German Act, which applies to any dispute "involving financial interests" and to all proceedings taking place in Germany whether or not of an international character, see Georges R. Delaume, Germany: Act on the Reform of the Law Relating to Arbitral Proceedings, 37 I.L.M. 790 (1998).

2. Article 28(3) provides that "[t]he arbitral tribunal shall decide *ex aequo et bono* or as *amiable compositeur* only if the parties have expressly authorized it to do so." These concepts derive from civil law tradition and enable an arbitrator to decide according to the arbitrator's concept of what is fair and reasonable under the circumstances, rather than according to legal rules linked to a particular national system. The doctrines are likely to have most influence in awarding damages and interest. A related doctrine is that of *lex mercatoria*, customs and usages of international trade common to all or most industrial states or, at least, to those states connected with the parties or the transaction. Some commentators have adversely criticized such doctrines on the ground that they introduce an undesirable element of uncertainty. See William W. Park, Neutrality, Predictability and Economic Co-operation, 12 J. Int'l Arbitration 99, 106 (December 1995) (stating that "[n]either the lender nor the borrower will want disputes resolved according to an adjudicator's intuitive sense of fairness"); Karen S. Weinberg, Equity in Inter-

national Arbitration: How Fair is "Fair"?, 12 B.U. Int'l L.J. 227, 253 (1994) (concluding that "the advocates of *lex mercatoria* and *amiable composition* have effectively carved predictability and uniformity out of existence, replacing them with subjective systems that serve only the interests of the arbitrator and are inconsistent both in application and effect").

Deutsche Schachtbau und Tiefbohrgesellschaft m.b.H. v. Ras Al Khaimah National Oil Co., [1987] 2 All E.R. 769, [1987] 3 W.L.R. 1023 (Ct. App. 1987), reversed on another issue, [1988] 2 Lloyd's Rep. 293; [1990] 1 A.C. 295; [1988] 3 W.L.R. 230; [1988] 2 All E.R. 833 (H.L. 1988). The court stated that it was not against public policy to enforce in England an award of arbitrators in Switzerland based on "the proper law to be decided by the arbitrators and...not...confined...to national systems of law." [1987] 2 All E.R. at 779. The court noted that the parties intended to give the arbitrators this freedom, intended "to create legally enforceable rights and obligations," and that the resulting agreement was "sufficiently certain to constitute a legally enforceable contract." Id. The court also noted that the issue was addressed only because counsel informed the court that "this was a matter of considerable importance to those engaged in international commerce," but that "in the instant case the decision of the arbitrators rested primarily, if not exclusively, on findings of fact..." Id.

Naviera Amazonica Peruana, S.A. v. Compania Internacional de Seguros del Peru, [1988] 1 Lloyd's Rep. 116 (Ct. App. 1987). The dispute between the parties concerned the reasonable amount of premiums for insurance of four vessels. The premiums were for a period after the policy had expired and the parties had agreed that coverage would be extended on a monthly basis. A printed term of the policy stated that the City of Lima had jurisdiction over all disputes, but a typed clause that had been added to the policy stated that disputes would be subject to arbitration under conditions and laws of London. Another printed clause stated that in the event of conflict between printed and typed clauses, a typed clause would prevail. The vessel's owners moved the court below to appoint arbitrators to conduct the arbitration in England. The court denied the motion, holding that the proper interpretation of the contract was that the parties intended that the forum would have to be in Lima, but that the arbitrators there would apply English law. The Court of Appeal reversed holding that the typed clause was intended to choose England for both the forum and the applicable law. The Court of Appeal explained its conclusion on the ground that:

> English law does not recognize the concept of a "de-localized" arbitration or of "arbitral procedures floating in the transnational firmament unconnected with any municipal system of law" *Bank Mellat v. Helliniki Techniki S.A.*, [1984] Q.B. 291 at 301 (Court of Appeal). Accordingly, every arbitration must have a "seat" or locus arbitri or forum which subjects its procedural rules to the municipal law which is there in force. * * * "Where the parties have failed to choose the law governing the arbitration proceedings, those proceedings must be considered, at any rate prima facie, as being governed by the law of the country in which the arbitration is held, on the ground that it is the country most closely connected with the proceedings." Dicey & Morris on the Conflict of Laws (11th ed.) vol. 1 at p. 539. * * * I cannot see any reason for doubting that the converse is equally true. Prima facie, i.e. in the absence of some express and clear provision to the contrary, it must follow that an agreement that the curial or procedural law of an arbitration is to be the law of X has the consequences that X is also to be the "seat" of the arbitration.

[1988] 1 Lloyd's Rep. at 119-20.

Section 2: Judicial Assistance and Interference

Introduction

A State must strike the proper balance between granting arbitration proceedings independence and autonomy and policing against gross abuses of the arbitration process or providing interim remedies in aid of that process. No one is likely to incur the costs in time and money of international arbitration in a State whose courts stand ready to adjudicate the award de novo.

Article V(1)(e) of the United Nations Arbitration Convention permits refusal to recognize and enforce an award if the award "has been set aside or suspended by a competent authority of the country in which, or under the law of which, that award was made." The Model Law on International Commercial Arbitration, in Article 34(2), sets out various grounds on which a court may set aside an arbitral award. The Convention on the Settlement of Investment Disputes, in Article 52(1)(e), adds "corruption on the part of a member of the Tribunal," although this may be taken account of in Article 34(2)(b)(ii) of the Model Law-conflict with public policy. The Model Law also permits judicial assistance including interim protection (Article 9), appointment of an arbitrator if the parties' process fails (Article 11(3)(a)), and adjudicating challenges to arbitrators' qualifications or actions (Articles 13(3) and 14(1)), or to the tribunal's jurisdiction (Article 16(3)).

England has struggled to find the proper balance between encouraging efficient and independent arbitration and policing against abuses. The Arbitration Act 1950 §21 permitted the High Court to direct an arbitrator to state questions of law or "an award or any part of an award, in the form of a special case for the decision of the High Court." This section was repealed by Arbitration Act 1979 §1(1). The 1979 Act permits an appeal from an arbitral award "with the consent of all parties; or * * * with leave of the court," which cannot be granted "unless [the court] considers that * * * the determination of the question of law concerned could substantially affect the rights of one or more of the parties * * *" (Section 1(3)). Further appeal from the decision of the High Court cannot be obtained unless "the High Court or the Court of Appeal gives leave; and it is certified by the High Court that the question of law to which its decision relates either is one of general public importance or is one which for some other special reason should be considered by the Court of Appeal." (Section 1(7)). More significantly with regard to international arbitration, §3 permits parties to arbitration that is not "domestic" (arbitration is not domestic if any party is an individual who is a national of or is habitually resident in any State other than the United Kingdom or is a corporation incorporated in or whose central management is in any State other than the United Kingdom) to use their arbitration agreement to exclude appeal from the arbitral award on questions of law. If the dispute involves Admiralty jurisdiction or arises out of a contract of insurance or a commodity contract, §4 permits such exclusion agreements only after the commencement of the arbitration. *The Nema* (the next principal case) and the notes following that case assist in determining how effective the 1979 Act had been in strengthening the autonomy of arbitral proceedings in England. (Section 8(4) provides that the Act "forms part of the law of England and Wales only.")

On January 31, 1997, Arbitration Act 1996 (c 23) took effect in England, Wales, and Northern Island. It makes available in a single source a restatement of English arbitration law.

Under the Act, the parties may agree to allow the arbitral tribunal to decide the dispute in accordance with considerations agreed to by the parties or determined by the tribunal rather than under the law of a specific jurisdiction. (§ 46(1)(b)).

The parties may agree not to permit an appeal on a point of law. (§ 69). If the parties do not agree to waive appeals on points of law, a party may so appeal only with the agreement of all other parties or with leave of the court. (§ 69(2)). The court may grant leave to appeal only if the court is satisfied that the question substantially affects the rights of a party and either that "the decision of the tribunal on the question is obviously wrong" or that "the question is one of general public importance and the decision of the tribunal is at least open to serious doubt." (§ 69(3)). The court shall not exercise its power to set aside the award on a point of law unless it is satisfied "that it would be inappropriate to remit the matters in question to the tribunal for reconsideration." (§ 69(7)).

A party may apply to a court for an order declaring an award made by the tribunal to be of no effect in whole or in part "because the tribunal did not have substantive jurisdiction." (§ 67)

A party may also challenge an award in court "on the ground of serious irregularity affecting the tribunal, the proceedings, or the award." (§ 68(1)). Such serious irregularities include the failure of the tribunal to "act fairly and impartially... giving each party a reasonable opportunity of putting his case." (§§ 33, 68(2)).

All grounds for appeal from an arbitral award are lost if the aggrieved party did not raise the objection with the arbitral tribunal as soon as that party had reason to know of the grounds for objection. (§§ 31 (objection to tribunal's jurisdiction) 73 (all grounds for objection)).

Section 9 authorizes a court in which proceedings have been brought to stay the proceedings so far as they concern a matter that the parties have agreed to submit to arbitration. The Act is silent as to whether a party may appeal a decision not to stay the proceedings. Inco Europe Ltd. v. First Choice Distribution, [2000] 1 W.L.R. 586 (H.L. 2000), held that there is a right of appeal.

For comment on the 1996 Arbitration Act, see William W. Park, The Interaction of Courts and Arbitrators in England: The 1996 Act as a Model for the United States?, 1998 Int'l Arbitration L. Rev. 54.

Pioneer Shipping Ltd. v. B.T.P. Tioxide Ltd. ("The Nema")
[1981] 2 All E.R. 1030, [1981] 3 W.L.R. 292 (House of Lords)

[The owners of a ship chartered it to the charterers for six or seven voyages. A labor strike in Canada prevented loading the ship for the second voyage. The charterers agreed to release the ship to the owners for a single voyage. At the end of this voyage, the strike continued in Canada and the owners refused the charterers' demand for return of the ship. The parties submitted their dispute to arbitration. The arbitrator decided that the contract had been frustrated and that the owners could retain possession of the ship. On appeal, the High Court held that the contract had not been wholly frustrated and allowed the appeal. On further appeal, the Court of Appeal restored the arbitrator's award and the charterers appealed to the House of Lords. The House of Lords dismissed the appeal.]

LORD DIPLOCK. My Lords, this is the first case to come before this House under the new procedure for judicial review of arbitrator's awards that was instituted by the Arbitration Act 1979. Leave to appeal was given by an Appeal Committee of the House itself. This was not because of any intrinsic general importance of the points of law involved in the arbitrator's award. If ever there were a case which under the new procedure ought never have been allowed to get any further than the arbitrator's award, this was one. The reason why leave was given to bring the matter before this House was because the proceedings in the instant case and in cases that have come before the Commercial Court since the judgment of the Court of Appeal [1980] Q.B. 547 was given, show that there exist significant differences of opinion between the individual judges themselves who sit in the Commercial Court, and between one of them at least and the guidelines laid down in the instant case, by Lord Denning M.R. (with whom Watkins L.J. agreed) as to the considerations which should influence the judge in deciding how to exercise his discretion under section 1 of the Arbitration Act 1979 to grant or to refuse leave to appeal to the High Court on a question of law arising out of an arbitrator's award.

The dispute submitted to the arbitration of a London maritime arbitrator of great experience arose between charterers and owners under a consecutive voyage charterparty.

* * *

My Lords, the particular circumstance[s] in which the parties wanted a quick decision as to where they stood as respects the future employment of the Nema are, no doubt, exceptional. In my view, they are in themselves sufficient to make a grant of leave to appeal from the arbitrator's award under section 1 of the Arbitration Act 1979 an unjudicial exercise of the discretion conferred upon the judge by that section. Such was the view of those who were then the two most senior judges of the Commercial Court and such (on second thoughts) was the view of Lord Denning M.R.; but the dispute had other characteristics that are likely to recur in other cases and have caused those divergences of views as to the weight that should be given to them in deciding how to exercise that discretion.

* * *

[T]he terms of the charterparty and its addenda that are relevant to the disputed issue of frustration are unique; it is almost inconceivable that they will be found again in any other charter. The same may be said of the events that preceded and led up to the dispute between the parties. If one were seeking to exemplify what is meant by the convenient neologism "a one-off case" it would be hard to find a better exemplar than the case that is now before your Lordships.

Of course the dispute involves some question of law. It is difficult to conceive of a dispute under a charterparty that does not do so. The dispute is likely to be about what the parties have agreed shall be their respective legal rights and obligations in events that have actually happened or, it may occasionally be, in events that it is anticipated may happen. The answer must depend upon the true construction of the agreement between the parties; and in English jurisprudence, as a legacy of the system of trial by juries who might not all be literate, the construction of a written agreement, even between private parties, became classified as a question of law. The object sought to be achieved in construing any commercial contract is to ascertain what were the mutual intentions of the parties as to the legal obligations each assumed by the contractual words in which they (or brokers acting on their behalf) chose to express them; or, perhaps more accurately, what each would have led the other reasonably to assume were the acts that he was promising to do or to refrain from doing by the words in which the promises on his part were expressed. In the case of a "one-off contract" where the exact combination of words and phrases that fall to be construed has not only never been used before and so did not possess an already established meaning of which each party was entitled to assume the other knew when he entered into the contract, but is also unlikely to be used in future by any other parties, it is not self-evident that an arbitrator or arbitral tribunal chosen by the parties for his or their experience and knowledge of the commercial background and usages of the trade in which the disputes arises, is less competent to ascertain the mutual intentions of the parties than a judge of the Commercial Court, a Court of Appeal of three Lords Justices or even an Appellate Committee of five Lords of Appeal in Ordinary. A lawyer nurtured in a jurisdiction that did not owe its origin to the common law of England would not regard it as a question of law at all. This, I believe, was all that Lord Denning M.R. meant to convey by his vivid, if somewhat less than tactful, phrase: "On such a clause, the arbitrator is just as likely to be right as the judge—probably more likely" ([1980] Q.B. 547, 564G).

* * *

My Lords, the great majority of international maritime and commercial contracts which contain a London arbitration clause, and typically those falling within the categories of disputes in respect of which it is, at least for the time being, forbidden by section 4 of the Arbitration Act 1979 to enter into an "exclusion agreement" covering disputes that have not already arisen, are made on standard printed forms on which the particulars appropriate to the contract between the actual parties are inserted, and any amendments needed for reasons special to the particular contract are either made to the printed clauses or dealt with in added clauses, which sometimes may themselves be classified as standard. Business on the Baltic, the insurance market and the commodity markets would be impracticable without the use of standard terms to deal with what are to be the legal rights and obligations of the parties upon the happening of a whole variety of events which experience has shown are liable to occur, even though it be only rarely, in the course of the performance of contracts of those kinds.

* * *

My Lords, when contracts are entered into which incorporate standard terms it is the interests alike of justice and of the conduct of commercial transactions that those standard terms should be construed and treated by arbitrators as giving rise to similar legal rights and obligations in all arbitrations in which the events have given rise to the dispute do not differ from one another in some relevant respect. It is only if parties to commercial contracts can rely upon a uniform construction being given to standard terms that they can prudently incorporate them in their contracts without the need for detailed negotiation or discussion. Such uniform construction of standard terms had been progressively established up to 1979, largely through decisions of the courts upon special cases stated by arbitrators. In the result English commercial law has achieved a degree of comprehensiveness and certainty that has made it acceptable for adoption as the appropriate proper law to be applied to commercial contracts wherever made by parties of whatever nationality. So, in relation to disputes involving standard terms in commercial contracts an authoritative ruling of the court as to their construction which is binding also upon all arbitrators under the sanction of an appeal from an award of an arbitrator that has resulted from his departing from that ruling performs a useful function that is lacking in that performed by the court in substituting for the opinion of an experienced commercial arbitrator its own opinion as to the application of a "one-off" clause to the particular facts of a particular case. It was this useful function that it was the plain intention of the Act of 1979 to preserve by section 4, for at least an experimental period during which it would be subject to scrutiny by the Commercial Court Users' Committee to see whether the new provisions of sections 1 and 2 relating to leave to appeal from arbitrators' awards and the determinations of preliminary points of law would operate in practice to prevent the continuance of abuses that has become notorious of recent years under the previous system of case stated.

My Lords, in the instant case there arose out of the arbitrator's award the two interdependent questions of law * * * One, which I shall call the question of divisibility was a question of construction of the charterparty and in particular the "one-off" clauses in addendum 2; the other was the question of frustration which, as was held unanimously by this House in *Tsakiroglou & Co. Ltd. v. Noblee Thorl G.m.b.H.* [1962] A.C. 93, is never a pure question of fact but does in the ultimate analysis involve a conclusion of law as to whether the frustrating event or series of events has made performance of the contract a thing radically different from that which was undertaken by the contract, however closely that conclusion of law may seem to follow from a commercial arbitrator's findings as to mercantile usage and the understanding of mercantile men about the significance of the commercial differences between what was promised and what in the changed circumstances would now fall to be performed.

* * *

My Lords, in weighing the rival merits of finality and meticulous legal accuracy there are, in my view, several indications in the Act itself of a parliamentary intention to give effect to the turn of the tide in favour of finality in arbitral awards (particularly in non-domestic arbitrations of which the instance case is one), at any rate where this does not involve exposing arbitrators to a temptation to depart from "settled principles of law." Thus section 1(1) removes a former threat to finality by abolishing judicial review (formerly certiorari) for error of law on the face of the award. Section 1(3) withdraws the previous power of an arbitrator to accede to a request to state his award in the form of a special case if such request was made by any party to the reference. It is notorious, particularly after the decision of the Court of Appeal in *Halfdan Grieg & Co. A/S v. Sterling Coal & Navigation Corporation (The Lysland)* [1973] Q.B. 843, that, if such request were made it was virtually impracticable for an arbitrator to refuse it.

* * *

Section 3 gives effect to a reversal of public policy in relation to arbitration as it had been expounded more than half a century before in *Czarnikow v. Roth Schmidt & Co.* [1922] 2 K.B. 478. Exclusion agreements, which oust the statutory jurisdiction of the High Court to supervise the way in which arbitrators apply the law in reaching their decisions in individual cases, are recognised as being no longer contrary to public policy. In principle they are enforceable, subject only to the special limitations imposed, for the time being, by section 4 in the case of awards made in respect of certain limited classes of contracts which, important as they are to the role of London as a forum for international arbitrations represent what is numerically only a small fraction of the total arbitrations, large and small, that take place in England.

* * *

Even in respect of contracts falling within these classes, however, exclusion agreement may be made and will be enforceable if entered into after the dispute arose. What is not enforceable is an exclusion agreement covering possible future disputes under the contract before they have arisen. Nevertheless, when a dispute under the contract has arisen and the award of an arbitrator made, an appeal to the High Court on a point of law arising out of it is not as right; it is still subject to the discretion of the judge under section 1(3)(b).

My Lords, it seems to me quite evident that the parliamentary intention evinced by section 4 in maintaining for the time being a prohibition on pre-dispute exclusion agreements only was to facilitate the continued performance by the courts of their useful function of preserving, in the light of changes in technology and commercial practices adopted in various trades, the comprehensiveness and certainty of English law as to the legal obligations assumed by the parties to commercial contracts of the classes listed, and particularly those expressed in standard terms; it was not Parliament's intention to encourage appeals from arbitrators' awards even under those classes of contracts where such appeal would not fulfil this purpose.

* * *

[A]s Lord Denning M.R. summarised it in dealing with the question of frustration in the instant case: to justify interference with the arbitrator's award it must be shown (i) that the arbitrator misdirected himself in law or (ii) that the decision was such that no reasonable arbitrator could reach.

Where, as in the instant case, a question of law involved is the construction of a "one-off" clause the application of which to the particular facts of the case is an issue in the arbitration, leave should not normally be given unless it is apparent to the judge, upon a mere perusal of the reasoned award itself without the benefit of adversarial argument, that the meaning ascribed to the clause by the arbitrator is obviously wrong; but if on such perusal it appears to the judge that it is possible that argument might persuade him, despite first impression to the contrary, that the arbitrator might be right, he should not grant leave; the parties should be left to accept, for better or for worse, the decision of the tribunal that they had chosen to decide the matter in the first instance. The instant case was clearly one in which there was more than one possible view as to the meaning of the "one-off" clause as it affected the issue of divisibility [of the contract as it affected voyages in different seasons when the port was not frozen.] It took two days' argument by counsel before the learned judge to satisfy him that the arbitrator was wrong on this and upon the interdependent question of frustration, four days' argument before the Court of Appeal to convince them that the judge was wrong and the arbitrator right and over three days' argument in trying to persuade this House to the contrary, even though it was not found necessary to call upon the respondent to address us on the merits.

* * *

For reasons already sufficiently discussed, rather less strict criteria are in my view appropriate where questions of construction of contracts in standard terms are concerned. That there should be as high a degree of legal certainty as it is practicable to obtain as to how such terms apply upon the occurrence of events of a kind that it is not unlikely may reproduce themselves in similar transactions between other parties engaged in the same trade, is a public interest that is recognised by the Act particularly in section 4. * * * But leave should not be given even in such a case, unless the judge considered that a strong prima facie case had been made out that the arbitrator had been wrong in his construction; and when the events to which the standard clause fell to be applied in the particular arbitration were themselves "one-off" events, stricter criteria should be applied on the same lines as those that I have suggested as appropriate to "one-off" clauses.

The other question of law arising out of the award in the instant case if the construction of the charterparty as respects the "divisibility" of the adventures for the 1979 season and the 1980 season respectively were to be decided in favour of the owners, as the arbitrator held it should, was whether in the events that had happened by September 26, 1979 (which were very much "one-off" events), the adventure for the 1979 season had by then become frustrated. Disputes on questions whether contractual obligations have been put an end to by frustration and the somewhat analogous questions as to whether one party to a commercial contract is entitled to refuse to continue to perform his own obligations under the contract in consequence of a fundamental breach or breach of condition by the other party, are frequent subjects of commercial arbitration.

* * *

In deciding how to exercise his discretion whether to give leave to appeal under section 1(2) what the judge should normally ask himself in this type of arbitration, particularly where the events relied upon are "one-off" events, is not whether he agrees with the decision reached by the arbitrator, but: does it appear upon perusal of the award either that the arbitrator misdirected himself in law or that his decision was such that no reasonable arbitrator could reach? While this should, in my view, be the normal practice, there may be cases where the events relied upon as amounting to frustration are not "one-off" events affecting only the transaction between the particular parties to the arbitration, but events of a general character that affect similar transactions between many other persons engaged in the same kind of commercial activity; the closing of the Suez Canal, the United States soya bean embargo, the war between Iraq and Iran, are instances within the last two decades that spring to mind. Where such is the case it is in the interests of legal certainty that there should be some uniformity in the decisions of arbitrators as to the effect, frustrating or otherwise, of such an event upon similar transactions, in order that other traders may be sufficiently certain where they stand as to be able to close their own transactions without recourse to arbitration. In such a case, unless there were prospects of an appeal being brought by consent of all the parties as a test case under section 1(3)(a), it might be a proper exercise of the judge's discretion to give leave to appeal in order to express a conclusion as to the frustrating effect of the event that would afford guidance binding upon the arbitrators in other arbitrations arising out of the same event, if the judge thought that in the particular case in which leave to appeal was sought the conclusion reached by the arbitrator, although not deserving to be stigmatised as one which no reasonable person could have reached was, in the judge's view, not right. But such was far from being the instant case.

For all these reasons this was the sort of case in which in my opinion leave to appeal from the arbitrator's award ought never to have been given.

* * *

Notes

1. Antaios Cia Naviera SA v. Salen Rederierna AB ("The Antaios"), [1985] A.C. 191, [1984] 3 W.L.R. 592, [1984] 3 All E.R. 229 (House of Lords):
[The owners of The Antaios wanted to avoid a charter agreement because charter fees had risen sharply. The owners claimed a right to rescind the charter agreement because

the charterers had allegedly issued inaccurate bills of lading. Pursuant to the charter agreement, the issue of whether the owners were privileged to withdraw the vessel was referred to arbitration in London. The arbitrator ruled for the charterers. The owners appealed to Judge Staughton, a High Court judge who denied the appeal, but granted an appeal to the Court of Appeal from his denial to determine whether he had applied proper standards on when to permit an appeal from arbitration. The Court of Appeal affirmed the High Court judge and the owners appealed to the House of Lords. The House of Lords affirmed.]

Lord Diplock.

* * *

My Lords, I think that your Lordships should take this opportunity of affirming that the guideline given in *The Nema* that, even in a case that turns on the construction of a standard term, "leave should not be given...unless the judge considered that a strong prima facie case had been made out that the arbitrator had been wrong in his construction" applies even though there may be dicta in other reported cases at first instance which suggest that on some question of the construction of that standard term there may among commercial judges be two schools of thought. I am confining myself to conflicting dicta, not decisions. If there are conflicting decisions, the judge should give leave to appeal to the High Court, and whatever judge hears the appeal should in accordance with the decision that he favors give leave to appeal from his decision to the Court of Appeal with the appropriate certificate under § 1(7) as to the general public importance of the question to which it relates; for only thus can be attained that desirable degree of certainty in English commercial law which § 1(4) of the 1979 Act was designed to preserve.

* * *

This brings me to "the § 1(6A) question" canvassed in Staughton J's second judgment of 19 November 1982: when should a judge give leave to appeal to the Court of Appeal from his own grant or refusal of leave to appeal to the High Court from an arbitral award? I agree with him that leave to appeal to the Court of Appeal should be granted by the judge under § 1(6A) only in cases where a decision whether to grant or to refuse leave to appeal to the High Court under § 1(3)(b) in the particular case in his view called for some amplification, elucidation or adaptation to changing practices of existing guidelines laid down by appellate courts, and that leave to appeal under § 1(6A) should not be granted in any other type of case. Judges should have the courage of their own convictions and decide for themselves whether, applying existing guideline, leave to appeal to the High Court under § 1(3)(b) ought to be granted or not.

In the sole type of case in which leave to appeal to the Court of Appeal under § 1(6A) may properly be given the judge ought to give reasons for his decision to grant such leave so that the Court of Appeal may be informed of the lacuna, uncertainty or unsuitability in the light of changing practices that the judge has perceived in the existing guidelines; moreover, * * * the judge should also give the reasons for the way in which he had exercised his discretion.

However, save in the exceptional case in which he does give leave to appeal to the Court of Appeal under § 1(6A) because it falls within this limited category, a judge ought not normally to give reasons for a grant or refusal under § 1(3)(b) of leave to appeal to the High Court from an arbitral award. He should follow the practice that has been adopted in your Lordships' House ever since a would-be appellant from a judgment of the Court of Appeal was required to petition this House for leave to appeal to it when leave to do so had not been granted by the Court of Appeal itself. It has been the practice of this House, at the close of the short oral argument on the petition, to say no more than that the petition is allowed or refused as the case may be.

Save in very exceptional circumstances, which I find myself unable at present to foresee, I can see no good reason why a commercial judge in disposing of an application under §1(3)(b) should do more than that, and several good reasons why he should not. In the first place, he is not himself deciding at this stage the question of law arising out of the award which usually involves a question of construction of a commercial contract. He is simply deciding whether the case is of a kind that is recognised, under the current guidelines laid down by appellate courts, as suitable to be admitted to appeal. In the second place, it adds to the already excessive volume of reported judicial semantic and syntactical analysis of particular words and phrases appearing in commercial contracts which judges are inveigled to indulge in by the detailed oral arguments which it appears to be current practice to allow on applications under § 1(3)(b), whereas all that the judge has to decide on the application is: first, is this dispute, on the one hand, about a one-off clause or event, or, on the other hand, about a standard term or an event which is a common occurrence in the trade or commercial activity concerned? If it is the former, he must then consider whether the arbitrator was in the judge's view so obviously wrong as to preclude the possibility that he might be right; if it is the latter, he must then consider whether a strong prima facie case has been made out that the arbitrator was wrong. Unless the answer he would give to the question appropriate to the type of case to which the application with which he is concerned is Yes, he should refuse leave to appeal.

* * *

2. Channel Tunnel Group Ltd. v. Balfour Beatty Construction Ltd., [1993] 1 All E.R. 664 (House of Lords):

[Under a contract for construction of the Channel tunnel, the concessionaires, who held the concession granted by England and France for the construction and operation of the tunnel, were entitled to issue orders for additional work not covered by the compensation terms of the contract. If the concessionaires and contractor could not agree on the price for the additional work, the dispute was to be referred to a panel of experts and, if the parties were not satisfied with the panel's decision, settled by arbitration in Brussels under the rules of the International Chamber of Commerce. In the meantime, the contractor was obliged to continue work. A major item of additional work, a cooling system, was ordered by the concessionaires. The parties could not agree on the price and the contractor threatened to suspend work on the cooling system unless the concessionaires agreed and paid the contractor's proposed price. The concessionaires did not agree and instead commenced an action in the High Court for an interim injunction restraining the contractor from suspending work on the cooling system. The contractor applied for a stay of this action on the ground that the action was in violation of the agreement to arbitrate. The judge refused to grant a stay and the contractor appealed. The Court of Appeal allowed the appeal and granted the stay. The concessionaires appealed to the House of Lords, which dismissed the appeal.]

Lord Mustill.

* * *

[T]he court does have power in the present case to grant the injunction for which the [concessionaires] contend, notwithstanding that their action has been stayed. Whether this is a power which the court ought to exercise in the circumstances of the present case is an entirely different matter.

* * *

[T]he injunction claimed from the English court is the same as the injunction claimed from the panel and the arbitrators, except that the form is described as interlocutory or interim. In reality its interim character is largely illusory, for as it seem to me an injunction granted in November 1991, and a fortiori an injunction granted today [January 21, 1993], would largely pre-empt the very decision of the panel and arbitrators whose support forms the raison d'être of the injunction. By the time that the award of the panel or arbitrators is ultimately made, with the [contractors] having continued to work meanwhile it will be of very modest practical value, except as the basis for a claim in damages by the [contractors] * * *.

* * *

There is always a tension when a court is asked to order, by way of interim relief in support of an arbitration, a remedy of the same kind as will ultimately be sought from the arbitrators; between, on the one hand, the need for the court to make a tentative assessment of the merits in order to decide whether the plaintiff's claim is strong enough to merit protection, and on the other the duty of the court to respect the choice of tribunal which both parties have made, and not to take out of the hands of the arbitrators (or other decision-makers) a power of decision which the parties have entrusted to them alone.

* * *

The parties chose an indeterminate "law" to govern their substantive rights [the contract stated that it was "governed by and interpreted in accordance with the principles common to both English law and French law, and in the absence of such common principles by such general principles of international trade law as have been applied by national and international tribunals"]; an elaborate process for ascertaining those rights; and a location for that process outside the territories of the participants. This conspicuously neutral "anational" and extra-judicial structure may well have been the right choice for the special needs of the Channel tunnel venture. But whether it was right or wrong, it is the choice which the parties have made. The [concessionaires] now regret that choice. To push their claim for mandatory relief through the mechanisms of [the contract] is too slow and cumbersome to suit their purpose, and they now wish to obtain far reaching relief through the judicial means which they have been so scrupulous to exclude. Notwithstanding that the court can and should in the right case provide reinforcement for the arbitral process by granting interim relief, I am quite satisfied that this is not such a case, and that to order an injunction here would be to act contrary both to the general tenor of the construction contract and to the spirit of international arbitration.

[The parties have since agreed that the arbitrators will apply the UNIDROIT Principles of International Commercial Contracts. The International Institute for the Unification of Private Law (UNIDROIT), with headquarters in Rome, published the Principles in 1994 as a codification of the lex mercatoria. (law of merchants). The lex mercatoria consists of the customs and practices of participants in international commercial transactions.]

3. Coppée-Lavalin SA/NV v. Ken-Ren Chemicals & Fertilizers Ltd., [1995] 1 A.C. 38, [1994] 2 W.L.R. 631, [1994] 2 All E.R. 449 (H.L.). The House of Lords held that an Eng-

lish court can support an ICC arbitration in England by ordering, as an interim measure, security for costs, but should do so only in exceptional circumstances. The court then split 3-2 as to whether this was an appropriate case in which to make the order. A bare majority held that the order should issue because not only was one party insolvent, but also that party's claim was being funded by the Kenyan government, which would gain if that party prevailed, but would bear no responsibility for costs if that party was not successful. At the conclusion of the arbitration, an order by the arbitrators for costs in favor of the solvent party would therefore, without security, be meaningless.

Hewlett-Packard Co. v. Berg, 61 F.3d 101 (1st Cir. 1995), held that despite absence of specific authority in article VI of the U.N. ("New York") Convention on the Recognition and Enforcement of Foreign Arbitral Awards, supra page 69, and the use of "shall" in 9 U.S.C. §207 dealing with confirmation, a court can stay confirmation of a foreign arbitration award pending arbitration of a claim for a set-off.

In Marc Rich & Co. v. Società Italiana Impianti P.A., Case C-190, July 25, 1991, [1991] E.C.R. I-3855, the Court of Justice of the European Communities held that the exclusion of "arbitration" from the Brussels Convention (art. 1(4), supra page 19), meant that an English court need not dismiss an action seeking appointment of an arbitrator although an Italian court was "first seised" (art. 21, supra page 24) of an action by the other party seeking a declaration that it was not liable.

Section 3: Awards of the Iran-United States Claims Tribunal

Ministry of Defense of the Islamic Republic of Iran v. Gould Inc.
887 F.2d 1357 (9th Cir. 1989), cert. den., 494 U.S. 1016 (1990)

O'SCANNLAIN, Circuit Judge:

We are asked to determine whether an award against an American corporation entered by the Iran-United States Claims Tribunal can be enforced in federal court. The district court ruled that subject matter jurisdiction to enforce such award vests under the New York Convention and the Federal Arbitration Act. We agree.

* * *

I

In the early 1970s, when somewhat more tranquil relations prevailed between the United States and Iran, the Ministry of War of the Imperial Government of Iran and Hoffman Electric Corporation entered into two contracts whereby Hoffman agreed to provide and install certain military equipment. The Iranian revolution disrupted progress payments and performance called for under the agreements. In early 1980, Hoffman filed an action against Iran for breach of contract in the United States District Court for the Central District of California, eventually obtaining a writ of attachment on Iranian assets held in the United States to satisfy its claim. See *Security Pacific Nat'l Bank v. Government & State of Iran*, 513 F.Supp. 864, 866 (C.D.Cal.1981). After President Reagan issued [an] Executive Order suspending all claims in U.S. courts, however, the district court vacated the attachment and dismissed without prejudice Hoffman's action "subject to the right of any party to move to reopen the action at any time prior to the entry and satisfaction of a judgment of the Arbitral Tribunal...on the grounds that the settlement has failed of its essential purpose." Id. at 884. [See Note 1 following this case.]

Hoffman in turn filed Claims 49 and 50 with the Tribunal at the Hague, seeking damages from Iran for breach of contract. In response, in a series of actions over the next year, Iran filed Statements of Defense to both of Hoffman's claims, and pursuant to Art. II, sec. 1 of the Claims Settlement Declaration, filed counterclaims for breach of contract in which it sought in excess of $80 million against Hoffman. By way of counterclaim, Iran also sought to obtain certain military radio equipment in Hoffman's possession. During the pendency of the proceedings before the Tribunal, Hoffman was merged into Gould Marketing, Inc. ("Gould"), a wholly-owned subsidiary of Gould International, Inc. ("GII").

The Tribunal eventually issued a consolidated final award in Claims 49 and 50 in which it ruled that Gould was to pay $3.6 million and return the military radio equipment to Iran. The monetary award in favor of Iran constituted a net accounting of the amounts the Tribunal found that Iran owed Gould under Claim No. 49 and that Gould owed Iran under the counterclaim to Claim No. 49.

Unlike the provision creating the Security Account at the escrow bank, the funds of which are to be used for the sole purpose of securing the payment of claims against Iran, the Accords provide no specific vehicle for the enforcement of awards in favor of Iran. Thus, following the Tribunal's judgment, Iran sought a ruling that the United States government was required to satisfy awards issued under the Accords in Iran's favor by filing a "Request for Interpretation" with the Full Tribunal, pursuant to Art. II(3) of the Claims Settlement Declaration. Request of the Islamic Republic of Iran for Interpretation, Iran-U.S. Claims Tribunal, Case A/21, July 1985, reprinted in Iranian Assets Lit.Rep. 10,897, 10,901-02 (1985).

The Full Tribunal determined that the United States had no such specific obligation under the Accords. *Islamic Republic of Iran v. United States*, Case No. A/21, 14 Iran-U.S.C.T.R. at 330. Nonetheless, the Tribunal went on to state that it considered the United States to have a more general obligation to provide some sort of enforcement mechanism for such awards "within its national jurisdiction."

* * *

II

The Tribunal's ruling led to the filing of the current action in the United States District Court for the Central District of California, in which Iran seeks confirmation and enforcement of its award against Gould. Gould responded to the petition by filing a motion to dismiss on the ground that the district court lacks subject matter jurisdiction to decide such a matter. Gould set forth three grounds in support of its motion. First, it argued that because Iran is not recognized formally by the United States government, neither it nor any of its instrumentalities may maintain any action in a United States Court. Second, it argued that because the Algiers Accords are not self-executing, no federal question exists over which the district court can assert jurisdiction. Third, it argued that because the Tribunal proceedings leading up to the award in favor of Iran did not comply with certain terms of the New York Convention, the district court improperly exercised jurisdiction under 9 U.S.C. §203.

The district court granted Gould's motion in part and denied it in part. The court held that it did not possess federal question jurisdiction over the matter, stating that it considered itself to be bound by language of this court concerning the nonself-executing nature of the Accords in *Islamic Republic of Iran v. Boeing Co.*, 771 F.2d 1279 (9th Cir.1985). Nonetheless, the court held that it did have jurisdiction over the petition under [9 U.S.C.] section 203, as a consequence of its ruling that the Tribunal's award satisfied the requirements of the New York Convention.

Both parties moved for certification of an immediate appeal to this court. Gould moved for interlocutory review of the issue of whether the district court properly could enforce the Tribunal award under the New York Convention; Iran moved for interlocutory review of the issue of whether the Algiers Accords are self-executing. The district court granted both motions, and issued an order certifying both questions for an immediate appeal.

We agreed to hear these interlocutory appeals pursuant to 28 U.S.C. § 1292(b).

III

In New York in 1958, the United Nations facilitated the creation of an international agreement providing for enforcement of foreign arbitral awards. Convention on the Recognition and Enforcement of Foreign Arbitral Awards, 21 U.S.T. 2517, T.I.A.S. No. 6997, 330 U.N.T.S. 38 ("the New York Convention" or "the Convention"). Party-States to the Convention agree to "recognize arbitral awards as binding and enforce them in accordance with [their own] rules of procedure." New York Convention, Art. III. The United States became a party to the Convention in 1970, and Congress soon after enacted legislation implementing the provisions of the Convention into domestic law, codified as Chapter II of the Federal Arbitration Act, 9 U.S.C. sections 201-208.

As part of this legislation, Congress vested federal district courts with original jurisdiction over any action or proceeding "falling under the Convention," as such an action is "deemed to arise under the laws and treaties of the United States." 9 U.S.C. § 203. The starting point for our interpretation is a supplementary statutory provision which provides that an "arbitral award arising out of a legal relationship, whether contractual or not, which is considered as commercial, including a transaction, contract, or agreement described in section 2 of this title, *falls under* the Convention." 9 U.S.C. § 202 (emphasis supplied). The provision goes on to except from the definition of "falls under" certain awards made pursuant to a domestic legal relationship which have no foreign nexus. Id.

Under the plain meaning of the statute then, three basic requirements exist for jurisdiction to be conferred upon the district court: the award (1) must arise out of a legal relationship (2) which is commercial in nature and (3) which is not entirely domestic in scope. These three conditions are clearly satisfied here.

Congress has provided that the New York Convention, with minor modifications, shall be enforced in United States Courts. 9 U.S.C. § 201. Article I discusses the scope of the Convention, stating that it "shall apply to the recognition and enforcement of arbitral awards made in the territory of a State other than the State where the recognition and enforcement of such awards are sought, and arising out of differences between persons, whether physical or legal...[and those awards] not considered as domestic awards in the State where their recognition and enforcement are sought." Article I, ¶1. The Convention defines "arbitral awards" to include those "made by permanent arbitral bodies." Article I, ¶2. The United States imposes an additional related condition on the award: it must be "made in the territory of another Contracting State." 21 U.S.T. 2566, reprinted at notes following 9 U.S.C.A. § 201. Because of the "shall apply" language of Article I, we read these requirements into the jurisdictional mandate of section 203.

The Tribunal's award satisfies these requirements as well. That is, the Tribunal sits at The Hague, which is in the Netherlands, which is a contracting State. In addition, the award is obviously not domestic in nature because Iran is one of the parties to the agreement.

IV

Gould sets forth two basic arguments to support its position that the district court lacks jurisdiction over the enforcement of the award under the Convention. First, relying on language in Articles II and IV, Gould argues that the Convention applies, and hence, jurisdiction to enforce exists, only as to those awards that derive from an arbitral agreement in writing to which the parties voluntarily submitted. It contends that the Accords documents themselves do not satisfy this requirement. Second, Gould argues that the arbitral award was not arrived at in compliance with the Convention's supposed requirement that the proceedings be subject to a "national" arbitration law.

A

The Convention does make several pronouncements concerning the form of the agreement leading up to the award. For example, it places upon each contracting State the obligation to recognize an arbitral agreement in writing between the parties. Convention, Article II, ¶ 1. In addition, the party seeking enforcement must file with the court "[t]he original agreement referred to in article II... or a duly certified copy thereof." Convention, Article IV, ¶ 1(b). These provisions do indeed seem to indicate that the award referred to in section 203 emanate from a written agreement.

We construe the Accords themselves as representing the written agreement so required, on the strength of the President's authority to settle claims on behalf of United States nationals through international agreements.

* * *

Moreover, even if the United States government lacked authority to enter into the agreement in writing required under the Convention, we find persuasive the argument that Gould, in filing its claim and arbitrating it before the Tribunal, "ratified" the actions of the United States.

B

The second basic argument Gould makes is premised on language contained in Article V, which lists the defenses available to the party against whom enforcement of a Tribunal Award is sought. Gould asserts that these defensive provisions contain an implicit requirement that the Convention applies only to arbitral awards made in accordance with the national arbitration law of a Party State. In particular, Gould seeks to buttress its position by looking to Article V, ¶ 1(e), which provides that the party against whom enforcement is sought may establish that enforcement should not be granted if it can show that "the award has not yet become binding on the parties, or has been set aside or suspended by a competent authority of the country in which, or *under the law of which*, that award was made." New York Convention, Article V, ¶ 1(e) (emphasis supplied). Gould argues that this subparagraph would be rendered devoid of practical meaning if the Convention calls for the recognition of awards other than those which are made under a foreign municipal law. Thus, it concludes that because the Tribunal's award in favor of Iran was a creature of international law, and not national law, it does not "fall under" the Convention pursuant to section 203.

Section 203 does not contain a separate jurisdictional requirement that the award be rendered subject to a "national law." Language pertaining to the "choice of law" issue is not mentioned, or even alluded to, in Article I, which lays out the Convention's scope of applicability. In addition, although it is a close question, the fairest reading of Convention itself appears to be that it applies to the enforcement of non-national awards. Indeed, a Dutch court has so held. See *Societe Europeenne d'Etudes et d'Enterprises v. Socialist Federal Republic of Yugoslavia*, HR (Hoge Raad der Nederlanden) NJ 74, 361 (1974) (hereinafter "*Societe*"). In *Societe*, the Hoge Raad, the highest court of the Netherlands, reversed the Court of The Hague, which had ruled that the Dutch trial court erred in recognizing an arbitral award that was not issued according to the law of Switzerland. The Hoge Raad held that the strictures of Article V do not come into effect unless and until "the party against whom the award is invoked furnishes proof of the existence of one of the impediments specified under (a) to (e) [in Article V]." Id. at 1006-07. "The relationship between the award and the law of a particular country need only be examined in the framework of an investigation to be carried out following a plea that the impediments mentioned in Article V(1) exist...in respect of which questions may arise which can be answered only with reference to the law of a particular country." Id.

In addition, allowing the parties to untether themselves from a pre-existing "national law" still leaves certain safe-guards in place to guard against enforcement of an otherwise unfair arbitration award. The Convention contains several due process protections requiring notice and the opportunity to be heard as well as a defense to guard against enforcement of awards contrary to public policy. Article V, ¶¶ 1(b), 2(b). Also, while the Tribunal at times may function as a forum for the resolution of interstate disputes, e.g., when it is called upon to render an opinion as between the United States and Iran under Article II, § 2 of the Claims Settlement Declaration, it primarily is concerned with the resolution of private law rights based on contractual arrangements relating to the provision of goods and services. Article II, ¶ 1. It certainly has served this latter function in this case.

Finally, as they are laid out, the defenses seem to apply to arbitral awards made pursuant to municipal domestic law or those made pursuant to law of the parties' choosing, as in this case. In particular, Article V ¶ 1(d) allows a party against whom enforcement is sought to defend against enforcement if "the arbitral procedure was not in accordance with the agreement of the parties, *or*, failing such agreement, was not in accordance with the law of the country where the arbitration took place" (emphasis supplied).

Although this language seems to be at loggerheads with that of Article V ¶ 1(e) concerning "the country...under the law of which, [the] award was made," it is possible to reconcile the two provisions in accordance with an interpretation that holds that the Convention applies to "non-national law" awards. That is, if the parties choose not to have their arbitration governed by a "national law," then the losing party simply cannot avail itself of certain of the defenses in subparagraphs (a) and (e).

Thus, we conclude that an award need not be made "under a national law" for a court to entertain jurisdiction over its enforcement pursuant to the Convention.

V

The district court properly denied that portion of Gould's motion to dismiss for lack of jurisdiction over this matter under 9 U.S.C. §203, because the award of the Iran-United States Claims Tribunal that Iran seeks to enforce "falls under" the New York Convention. Because we conclude that jurisdiction exists under section 203, we do not reach the question of whether there was jurisdiction under 28 U.S.C. §1331 [Federal Question]. Therefore, we do not consider Iran's cross-appeal on the question of whether the Algiers Accords are self-executing.

AFFIRMED.

Notes

1. The Declaration of Algeria Concerning Settlement of Claims by the United States and Iran, referred to in the opinion, is set out at the end of Chapter 10, supra page 510. The "New York" Convention referred to in the opinion is set out In Chapter 1, section 2. For background on the Declaration of Algeria, see the note following Foxboro Co. v. Arabian American Oil Co., supra page 504.

2. The opinion in the preceding case is an example of a tendency to enforce international arbitral awards in the spirit of Mitsubishi Motors Corp. v. Soler Chrysler-Plymouth, Inc., a principal case in Chapter 1, section 2. See note 1 following Mitsubishi Motors. Cf. Meisels v. Uhr, 593 N.E.2d 1359 (N.Y. 1991) (enforcing the decision of a Beth Din, a Jewish religious court, and holding that the agreement to submit to arbitration by a Beth Din "all the disputes between them as well as on [the] three buildings [in which the parties were partners]" was an enforceable broad arbitration agreement).

Iran Aircraft Industries v. Avco Corp., 980 F.2d 141 (2d Cir. 1992), refused to enforce an award by the Claims Tribunal on the ground that the Tribunal denied the United States party the opportunity to present its claim. The court held that Article IV(1) of the Declaration establishing the Tribunal, which states that "[a]ll decisions of the Tribunal shall be final and binding," (supra page 511) did not bar consideration of objections to enforcement provided for in the New York Convention. Article V(1)(b) of the New York Convention (supra page 70) provides that a court may refuse to recognize and enforce an arbitration award if "[t]he party against whom the award is invoked was...unable to present his case."

3. Commentators have differed on whether the awards of the Iran-United States Claims Tribunal are an important source of information on international arbitration, or whether the Tribunal is a unique institution whose awards contain no lessons for general application. See David D. Caron, The Nature of the Iran-United States Claims Tribunal and the Evolving Structure of International Dispute Resolution, 84 Am. J. Int'l L. 104 (1990). For a study of the Tribunal's work by a judge appointed by the United States, see George H. Aldrich, The Jurisprudence of the Iran-United States Claims Tribunal (1996).

Table of Cases

Principal cases in **bold** type.

A, Re, 479, 485
A. Ahlstrom Osakeyhtio v. Commission of the European Communities, 386
Abebe-Jira v. Negewo, 411
Adams v. Cape Industries PLC., 244
Adra v. Clift, 411
Air Crash Disaster, In Re, 185, 198, 210, 290, 292, 460
Air Crash Disaster at Boston, In re, 185
Air Crash Disaster Near New Orleans, In re, 198, 210, 460
Air Crash Disaster Near Roselawn, In Re, 290, 292
Air France v. Saks, 444, 450
Airbus Industrie G.I.E. v. Patel, 94
Aker Verdal A/S v. Neil F. Lampson, Inc., 164
Al-Zouhayli v. Al-Zouhayli, 471
Aldy v. Valmet Paper Machinery, 292
Alejandre v. The Republic of Cuba, 325
Alfred Dunhill of London, Inc. v. Republic of Cuba, 272, 308
Alghanim & Sons v. Toys , 76, 394
Allen v. Lloyd's of London, 396
Allendale Mutual Ins. Co. v. Bull Data Systems, Inc., 93
Allied Bank International v. Banco Credito Agricola de Cartago, 274
Aluminum Co. of America, United States v., 341, 346
Alvarez-Machain v. United States, 414
Ambatielos v. Foundation Co., 237
Amchem Products Inc. v. British Columbia (Workers' Compensation Board), 95
American Banana Co. v. United Fruit Co., 263, 341, 345, 346, 365, 400
Amtsgericht Bad Kreuznach, Beschluá vom March 6, 1992, 484

Amtsgericht Ludwigshafen, Beschluá vom December 13 1991, 484
Amtsgericht Saarbrücken, Beschluá vom July 7, 484
Anderson v. Metropolitan Life Ins. Co., 15
Antaios Cia Naviera SA v. Salen Rederierna AB, 547
Antoine v. Atlas Turner, Inc., 291
Anton Piller K.G. v. Manufacturing Processes Ltd., 139
Argentine Republic v. Amerada Hess Shipping Corp., 294, 307, 316, 409, 418, 425
Asahi Metal Industry Co., v. Superior Court, 7
Asbestos Insurance Coverage Cases, In re, 140, 157
Asplundh Tree Expert Co. v. Bates, 72
Asta Medica, S.A., In re Application of, 137
Atlantic Harvesters of Namibia (PTY) Ltd. v. Unterweser Reederei GMBH of Bremen, 54
Atlantic Star, 224
B. V. B., 483
Bachchan v. India Abroad Publications, Inc., 186, 253
Baker v. LeBoeuf, Lamb, Leiby & Macrae, 69
Baker Marine (Nigeria), Ltd. v. Chevron (Nigeria), Ltd., 77
Banco Espanol de Credito v. State Street Bank and Trust Co., 489, 494
Banco Nacional de Cuba v. Farr, 271
Banco Nacional de Cuba v. Sabbatino, 261, 315, 423
Bank Mellat v. Helliniki Techniki S.A., 540
Bank Melli Iran v. Pahlavi, 254

Bankston v. Toyota Motor Corp., 109
Banque Francaise du Commerce Exterieur v. Rio Grande Trading, Inc., 60
Barclays Bank PLC, State ex rel, v. Hamilton County, Court of Common Pleas, 501
Baris v. Sulpicio Lines, 219
Barkanic v. General Administration of Civil Aviation of People's Republic of China, 291
Barone v. Rich Bros. Interstate Display Fireworks Co., 15
Bayer, In re Application of, 138
Beanal v. Freeport-McMoran, Inc., 410
Benton Graphics v. Uddeholm Corp., 138
Bergesen v. Joseph Mueller Corp., 75
Bersch v. Drexel Firestone, Inc., 390, 395
Bhatnagar v. Surrendra Overseas Ltd., 183, 200
Bi v. Union Carbide Chem. & Plastics Co. Inc., 199
Blondin v. Dubois, 484
Boit v. Gar-Tec Products, Inc., 14
Bolchos v. Darrel, 411
Boosey & Hawkes Music Publishers, Ltd. v. Walt Disney Co., 187
Borden Inc. v. Meiji Milk Products Co., 199
Brane v. Roth, 164
Brannigan v. Davison, 157
Bremen, The v. Zapata Off-Shore Company, 47
British Airways v. Laker Airways Ltd., 94, 355
British Nylon Spinners, Ltd. v. Imperial Chemical Industries, 371
Brittingham v. Ayala, 44
Bruce Terminix Co., In re, 74
Bryks v. Canadian Broadcasting Corp., 292
Burnham v. Superior Court, 30, 45, 421, 424
Butte Mining PLC v. Smith, 400
Cajun Elec. Power Co-op v. Triton Coal Co., 94
Calbaceta v. Standard Fruit Co., 210
Callejo v. Bancomer, S.A., 273, 291, 308
Canada Trust Co. v. Stolzenberg, 156
Capital Currency Exchange, N.V. v. National Westminster Bank PLC, 347
Carbon Black Export v. The S. S. Monrosa, 55
Cardenas v. Solis, 238
Carnival Cruise Lines v. Shute, 54, 58
Castanho v. Jackson Marine, Inc., 224
Central Bank of Denver v. First Interstate Bank, 394

Chadade Steamship Co., Petition of, 56
Chambers v. Nasco, Inc., 210
Channel Tunnel Group Ltd. v. Balfour Beatty Construction Ltd., 549
Chick Kam Choo v. Exxon Corp., 212, 214
China Trade & Development Corp. v. M.V. Choong Yong, 93
Chromalloy Aeroservices, In re Arbitration between and Arab Republic of Egypt, 77
Chuidian v. Philippine National Bank, 294
Cicippio v. Islamic Republic of Iran, 325
Circuit City Stores, Inc. v. Adams, 72
Citibank N.A. v. Wells Fargo Asia Ltd., 279
Citro Florida, Inc. v. Citrovale, S.A., 55
Committee of United States Citizens Living in Nicaragua v. Reagan, 118
Compagno v. Commodore Cruise Line, Ltd., 54
Compania Mexicana de Aviacion, S.A. v. United States District Court, 291
Competex, S.A. v. Labow, 171
Concept Generation International v. Nippon Design Network, 248
Connelly v. T.T.Z. Corp, 187
Connor v. McGough, State ex rel, 7
Consolidated Gold Fields PLC v. Minorco, S.A., 395
Continental Bank NA v. Aeokos Cia Naviera SA, 94
Coppée-Lavalin SA/NV v. Ken-Ren Chemicals & Fertilizers, 550
Corporacion Mexicana de Servicios Maritimos v. M/T Respect, 292
Couzado v. United States, 400
Cox v. Hozelock, Ltd., 15
Craft v. Campbell Soup Co., 72
Credit Agricole Indosuez v. Rossiyskiy Kredit Bank, 44
Credit Suisse v. United States District Court, 278
Crosby v. National Foreign Trade Council, 382
CSR Ltd. v. Cigna Ins. Australia Ltd., 95
CSR, Ltd. v. Link, 15
Cunningham v. Quaker Oats Co., 183
Daliberti v. Republic of Iraq, 325
Denty v. Smithkline Beecham Corp., 401
Derby & Co. v. Weldon, 44
Detamore v. Sullivan, 257, 259
Deutsche Schachtbau und Tiefbohrgesellschaft m.b.H. v. Ras Al Khaimah National Oil Co., 540
Deutshe Ruckversicherung AG v. Walbrook Ins. Co., 501

Doe v. Unocal Corp., 278, 410
Doe I v. Karadzic, 424
Don Docksteader Motors, Ltd. v. Patal Enterprises, Ltd., 259
Doster v. Carl Schenk A.G., 138
Dow Chem. Co. v. Alfaro, 210
Dresser Industries v. Underwriters at Lloyd's of London, 212
Drexel Burhham Lambert Group v. Committee of Receivers, 333
Dumez Batiment SA v. Hessische Landesbank, 29
Eastern Airlines, Inc. v. Floyd, 450, 458
Eckert International Inc. v. Government of Fiji, 334
Effron v. Sun Line Cruises, Inc., 54
El Al Israel Airlines, Ltd. v. Tseng, 457
El Universal v. Phoenician Imports, Inc., 163
El-Fadl v. Central Bank of Jordan, 294
El-Hadad v. United Arab Emirates, 292
Equal Employment Opportunity Cmm'n v. Arabian Amer. Oil Co., 399
Erie R.R. v. Tompkins, 171, 177, 233, 266
Estate of Marcos Human Rights Litigation, In re, 409, 410
Estate of Marcos v. Hilao, 294, 410, 414
Eurim-Pharm GmbH v. Pfizer, Inc., 375, 377
Europa S.A. v. R. Esmerian, Inc, 138
Europcar Italia, S.p.A v. Maiellano Tours, Inc., 76
Evans Marshall & Co., Ltd. v. Bertola S.A., 61
Evolution Online Systems, Inc. v. Koninklijke PTT Nederland N.V., 56
Export Group v. Reef Industries, 292
F, Re, 484
F & H.R. Farman-Farmaian Consulting Engineers Firm v. Harza Engineering Co., 278
Fairchild, Arabatzis & Smith, Inc. v. Prometco Co., Ltd., 253
Farrell v. Long, 30
Feder v. Evans-Feder, 479
Federal Insurance Co. v. Richard I. Rubin & Co., 293
Federal Trade Commission v. Compagnie de Saint-Gobain-Pont-A-Mousson, 110
Fehn, U.S. S.E.C. v., 394
Ferens v. John Deere Co., 184
Filartiga v. Pena-Irala, 294, **403,** 416
Fireman's Fund Ins. Co. v. Cho Yang Shipping Co., 61
Firestone Tyre and Rubber Co., Ltd. v. Lewellin, 245
First National Bank of Chicago, United States v., 152
First National City Bank v. Banco Nacional de Cuba, 277
First Options of Chicago, Inc. v. Kaplan, 72
Fishman v. Delta Air Line, Inc., 450
Flatow v. Islamic Republic of Iran, 325
Fleming v. Yamaha Motor Corp., 109
Forti v. Suarez-Mason, 411
Founding Church of Scientology v. Verlag, 181, 198
Fox v. Board of Supervisors of L.S.U., 212
Foxboro Co. v. Arabian American Oil Co., 502, 556
Friedrich v. Friedrich, 472, 477, 478
Frolova v. Union of Soviet Socialist Republics, 292, 327
Fuentes v. Shevin, 37, 44
Galu v. Swissair, 272
Gannon v. Payne, 89
Gasperini v. Center for Humanities, 183
Gates Learjet Corp. v. Jensen, 198
Gates v. Victor Fine Foods, 293
Gau Shan Co., Ltd v. Bankers Trust Co., 93
Gaubert, United States v., 332
Gemini Capital Group, Inc. v. Yap Fishing corp., 188
General Atomic Co. v. Exxon Nuclear Co., Inc., 156
General Electric Capital Corp. v. Grossman, 290
Genesco, Inc. v. T. Kakiuchi & Co., Ltd., 85
Gerding v. Republic of France, 291
Gertz v. Robert Welch, Inc., 186
Gilbert v. Gulf Oil Corp., 43, 49, 174, 193, 209, 211, 214
Gilbertson, Her Majesty v., 251
Goldstar (Panama) S.A. v. United States, 409
Gonzalez v. Naviera Neptuno A.A., 199
Good Hope Chemical Corp., In re, 163, **165,** 271
Goodman Holdings v. Rafidain Bank, 304
Goto v. Malaysian Airline System Berhad, 15
Gould, Inc. v. Pechiney Ugine Kuhlmann, 290
Grand Jury Proceedings, In re, 155, 157
Graphics v. Uddeholm Corp., 138
Grupo Mexicano de Desarrollo, S.A. v. Alliance Bond Fund, Inc., 44

Grupo Portexa v. All American Marine Slip, 273
Gschwind v. Cessna Aircraft Co., 200
Guidi v. Inter-Continental Hotels Corp., 188
H, Re, 478, 479
Haaruis v. Kunnan Enterprises, Ltd., 93
Haldimann v. Delta Airlines, Inc., 461
Ham v. La Cienga Music Co., 14
Handelskwekerij G.J. Bier v. Mines de Potasse d'Alsace, 28
Hansen v. American National Bank, 237
Harris Corp. v. National Iranian Radio and Television, 504
Harris v. Balk, 36, 37, 45
Harrison v. Wyeth Laboratories Division of American Home Products Corp., 188
Harrods, (Buenos Aires) Ltd., In re, 225
Hartford Fire Insurance Co. v. California, 362, 370
Haynsworth v. The Corporation, 68
Hedrick v. Daiko Shoji Co., 10, 14
Heino v. Harper, 18
Helicopteros Nacionales de Colombia, S.A. v. Hall, 1
Her Majesty (see name of opposing party)
Hernandez v. Air France, 459
Hewitson v. Hewitson, 247
Hewlett-Packard Co. v. Berg, 551
Hilao v. Estate of Marcos, 294, 410, 414
Hill v. Showa Denko K.K., 15
Hilton v. Guyot, 91, 134, **227**, 234, **239**, **251**
Holden v. Canadian Consulate, 333
Holland v. Lampden-Wolfe, 304
Honduras Aircraft Registry, Ltd. v. Government of Honduras, 273
Hough v. P&O Containers Ltd., 56
Howe v. Goldcorp Investments, Ltd., 396
Hudson v. Hermann Pfauter GmbH & Co., 138
Hunt v. Coastal States Gas Producing Co., 272
Husserl v. Swiss Air Transport Co., 443
Hutson v. Fehr Bros., 10, 14
IIT v. Vencap, Ltd., 404, 411
Imperial Chem. Indus., United States v., 374
In re (see name of party)
In re Application of (see name of party)
Indistrie Tessili Italiana Como v. Dunlop AG, 224
Industrial Risk Insurers v. M.A.N. Gutehoffnunshutte GmbH, 76
Inkley, United States v., 248

Insurance Antitrust Litigation, In re, 377
Insurance Corp. of Ireland, Ltd. v. Compagnie des Bauxites de Guinee, 156
International Association of Machinists v. Organization of Petroleum Exporting Countries (OPEC), 312
Iragorri v. International Elevator, Inc., 188
Iran Aircraft Industries v. Avco Corp., 556
Ison v. E.I. Dupont de Nemours & Co., 185, 211
Itoba, Ltd. v. Lep Group, 396
Iwanowa v. Ford Motor Co., 411
J, In re, 478
J.J. Ryan & Sons, Inc. v. Rhone Poulenc Textile, 85
Jaffe v. Snow, 254
Jazini v. Nissan Motor Co., 34
Jet Holdings Inc. v. Patel, 239
John v. MGN Ltd., 186
John Doe I v. Unocal Corp., 278
Joseph v. Office of the Consulate General of Nigeria, 326
Jungquist v. Sheikh Sultan Bin Khalifa Al Nahyan, 294
K. S. Line Corp, In Re Complaint of, 56
Kadic v. Karadzic, 412, 415
Kauthar SDN BHD v. Sternberg, 394
Kawasaki Heavy Indus., Ltd. v. Superior Court of Guam, 109
Keaty v. Freeport Indonesia, Inc., 55
Keeton v. Hustler Magazine, 3, 10, 29
Kelly v. Syria Shell Petroleum Development B.V., 295
Kernan v. Kurz-Hastings, Inc., 15
Kinney System Inc. v. Continental Ins. Co., 200
Klaxon Co. v. Stentor Electric Mfg. Co., 211
Klinghoffer v. S.N.C. Achille Lauro, 409, 421
Knab v. Republic of Georgia, 333
Knickerbocker Ice Co. v. Stewart, 217, 219
Koehler v. Bank of Bermuda, Ltd., 7
Kollias v. D & G Marine Maintenance, 400
Kotam Electronics, Inc. v. JBL Consumer Products, Inc., 85
Kreimerman v. Casa Veerkamp, S.A. de C.V., 102
Krys v. Lufthansa German Airlines, 449
Kulko v. Superior Court, 4, 30
Kuwait Airways Corp. v. Iraqi Airways Co., 318
La Seguridad v. Transytur Line, 198
LaBella v. Burlington Northern R.R., 212
Lafontant v. Aristide, 293, 425

Laino v. Cuprum S.A. de C.V., 102
Laker Airways Ltd. v. Sabena, Belgian World Airlines, 347, 392
Lander Co. v. MMP Investments, Inc., 75
Lauro Lines S.R.L. v. Chasser, 61
Leasco Data Processing Equipment Corp. v. Maxwell, 64, 156, 395
Letelier v. Republic of Chile, 292, 319
Letter Rogatory, In re, 138
Linton v. Airbus Industrie, 293
Lipcon v. Underwriters at Lloyd's, 68
Littrell v. United States, 304, 318
Liu v. Republic of China, 291, 324
Lony v. E.I. DuPont De Nemours & Co., 185
Lotus, Re S.S., 338
Louring v. Kuwait Boulder Shipping Co., 45
Lubbe v. Cape PLC, 200
Lucchino v. Foreign Countries of Brazil, et al, 379
Mabud v. Pakistan International Airlines, 460
MacShannon v. Rockware Glass Ltd., 222, 224
Magnin v. Teledyne Continental Motors, 187
Malev Hungarian Airlines, In re Application of, 137
Mangattu v. M/V Ibn Hayyan, 292
Marc Rich & Co. v. Società Italiana Impianti, 551
Mareva Compania Naviera S.A. of Panama v. International Bulk Carriers, S.A., 44
Martin v. Republic of South Africa, 311
Mastrobuono v. Shearson Lehman Hutton, Inc., 73
Matsushita Elec. Indus. Co. v. Zenith Radio Corp., 379
Matusevitch v. Telnikoff, 186, 254
Maxwell Communication Corp., In re, 60
McCarthy v. Northwest Airlines, 460
McClenon v. Nissan Motor Corp. U.S.A., 109
McGee v. International Life Insurance Co., 45
McGlinchy v. Shell Chemical Co., 374
MCI Telecommunications Corp. v. Alhadhood, 318
McKnett v. St. Louis & S.F. Ry., 212
Meisels v. Uhr, 556
Melia v. Les Grands Chais de France, 109
Mercedes-Benz AG v. Leiduck, 44
Metro Industries v. Sammi Corp., 370

Mexico City Aircrash of October 31, 1979, In re, 460
Midland Bank v. Laker Airways, 94, 362
Millangos v. George Frank (Textiles), Ltd., 164
Miller v. American Dredging Co., 218
Miller v. Davis, 211
Miller v. Honda Motor Co., 30
Milliken v. Pratt, 345
Milosslavsky v. United Kingdom, 186
Ministry of Defense of the Islamic Republic of Iran v. Gould Ind., 278, 295, 551
Miskow v. Boeing Co., 211
Mitsubishi Motors Corp., v. Soler Chrysler-Plymouth, Inc., 55, 77, 514, 556
Mitsui & Co. (USA) v. Mira M/V, 61
Moats, United States v., 291
MOL, Inc. v. The Peoples Republic of Bangladesh, 316
Moog World Trade Corp. v. Bancomer, 495
Mukoda v. The Boeing Co., 16
Mullane v. Central Hanover Bank & Trust Co., 101, 110
Munzer v. Munzer-Jacoby, 231
Murray v. British Broadcasting Corp., 187
Murray v. The Schooner Charming Betsy, 118
Mushikiwabo v. Barayagwiza, 411
Myers v. The Boeing Co., 185
National Broadcasting Co. v. Bear Stearns & Co., 138
Naviera Amazonica Peruana, S.A. v. Compania Internacional de Seguros del Peru, 540
Neste Chemicals SA v. DK Line SA, 94
Neuchatel Swiss General Ins. Co. v. Lufthansa Airlines, 93
New York Times v. Sullivan, 186
Nicol v. Tanner, 251
Nieman v. Dryclean U.S.A. Franchise Co., 401
Nippon Paper Industries Co., United States v., 370
Nolan v. Boeing Co., 213
Noriega, United States v., 293
North South Finance Corp. v. Al-Turki, 400
Northon I v. Mansei Kogyo Co., 246
Northwest Airlines, Inc. v. American Airlines, Inc., 94
O'Gilvie v. United States, 247
Ocasek v. Flintkote Co., 290
Offshore Logistics, Inc. v. Tallentire, 215, 217, 219
Oil Spill by the Amoco Cadiz, In Re, 164

Olsen by Sheldon v. Government of Mexico, 292
Overseas Union Ins. Ltd. v. New Hampshire Ins. Co., 94
Owens Bank Ltd. v. Bracco, 94, 247
P, In re, 471
Pan Am Corp., In re, 213
Paul v. Avril, 411, 412
Pennzoil Products Co. v. Colelli & Associates, Inc., 15
Peralta v. Heights Medical Center, Inc., 101
Peré v. Nuovo Pigone, Inc., 290
Peregrine Myanmar Ltd. v. Segal, 187
Persinger v. Islamic Republic of Iran, 292
Pescatore v. Pan American World Airways, 457
Petrire v. Spantax, S.A., 461
Phillips v. Eyre, 345
Picketts v. International Playtex, Inc., 185
Pink, United States v., 263, 273
Pinsky v. Duncan, 45
Pioneer Container, The, 57
Pioneer Shipping Ltd. v. B.T.P. Tioxide Ltd. ("The Nema"), 542
Piper Aircraft Co. v. Reyno, 173, 193, 208, 209, 220, 222, 223
Plum Tree, Inc. v. Stockment, 55
Ponath v. Ponath, 477
Pravin Banker Associates, Ltd. v. Banco Popular Del Peru, 278
Prevot, In Re, 487
Princess Caroline of Monaco v. Publisher of the Magazines "B" and "G", 246
Princz v. Federal Republic of Germany, 305
Prudential Real Estate Affiliates, Inc v. PPR Realty, Inc., 219
Ramirez v. United States, 247
Randolph v. Budget Rent-A-Car, 332
Rantzen v. Mirror Group Newspapers, 186
Ravelo Monegro v. Rosa, 210
Re (see name of party)
Reading & Bates Construction Co. v. Baker Energy Resources Corp., 247
Regina v. Bow Street Metropolitan Stipendiary Magistrate, 293
Rein v. Socialist People's Libyan Arab Jamahiriya, 325
Rendall-Speranza v. Nassim, 334
Republic of Argentina v. Weltover, Inc., 300, 308
Republic of Kazakhstan v. Biedermann International, Application of, 138
Republic of Nicaragua v. Standard Fruit Co., 85
Republic of Philippines v. Westinghouse Electric Corp., 273
Request for International Judicial Assistance for the Federative Republic of Brazil, In re, 138
Rhone Mediterranee Compagnia Francese v. Lauro, 86, 514
Richards v. Lloyd's of London, 68
Richards v. United States, 291
Riggs National Corp. v. Commissioner of Internal Revenue Service, 278
Riley v. Kingsley Underwriting Agencies, Ltd., 68
Rivendell Forest Prod. v. Canadian Pacific, Ltd., 211
Roby v. Corporation of Lloyd's, 68
Rodriguez De Quijas v. Shearson/American Exp., Inc., 68
Rosenberg Bros. & Co. Inc. v. Curtis Brown Co., 7
Royal Bank Of Canada v. Trentham Corp., 254
Royal Bed & Spring Co., Inc., v. Famossul Industria e Comercio de Moveis, Ltda., 210
Russell v. CSX Transp., Inc., 212
S, Re, 484
S&R Co. of Kingston v. Latona Trucking, Inc., 74
Saadeh v. Farouki, 212
Salabaschew v. TRW, Inc., 187
Salomon v. A. Salomon & Co. Ltd., 246
Sanchez-Espinoza v. Reagan, 412
Sar Schotte GmbH v. Parmus Rothchild Sarl, 34
Sarrio S.A. v. Kuwait Investment Authority, 94
Saudi Arabia v. Nelson, 305, 425
Scherk v. Alberto-Culver Company Co., 61, 514
Schertenleib v. Traum, 181, 211
Schlobohm v. Schapiro, 6
Schoenbaum v. Firstbrook, 394
Scottish Air International v. British Caledonian Group, 188
Seaconsar Far East Ltd. v. Bank Markazi Jomhouri Islami Iran, 239, 495
Seifert v. U.S. Home Corp., 85
Shaffer v. Heitner, 34, 45, 46, 238
Shevill v. Presse Alliance S.A., 29, 186
Showa Denko K.K. v. Pangle, 15
Sibaja v. Dow Chemical Co., 207
Siderman de Blake v. Republic of Argentina, 324

Sidhu v. British Airways, 459
Siemer v. Learjet Acquisition Corp., 6
Silvious v. Pharaon, 103
Simon, In re, 60
Singh v. A.G. Daimler-Benz, 212
Slater v. Mexican Nat'l R.R., 345
Smith Kline & French Laboratories Ltd. v. Bloch, 219
Smith v. Socialist People's Libyan Arab Jamahiriya, 325
Smith v. United States, 400, 405
Smith/Enron Cogeneration Limited Partnership, Inc. v. Smith Cogeneration, Int'l, Inc., 75
SNI Aérospatiale v. Lee Kui Jak, 94, 225
Societe Internationale Pour Participations Industrielles Et Commerciales, S.A. v. Rogers, 140
Societe Internationale v. Kennedy, 146
Societe Nacionale Industrielle Aérospatiale v. United States District Court, 126
Society of Lloyd's v. Baker, 247
Soleimany v. Soleimany, 86
Somportex Ltd. v. Philadelphia Chewing Gum Corp., 232
South Carolina Ins. Co. v. Assurantie Maatschappij de Zeven Provincien NV, 138, 162
Southern Energy Homes, Inc. v. AmSouth Bank of Alabama, 501
Southern Pacific Co. v. Jensen, 217, 219
Southern Ry. v. Goodman, 212
Southway v. Central Bank of Nigeria, 292
Spatz v. Nascone, 55
Srl v. British Airways, 460
Stamm v. Barclays Bank of New York, 68
Stangvik v. Shiley Inc., 185
State ex rel (see name of party)
Stephens v. National Distillers & Chem. Corp., 305
Sterling Drug, Inc. v. Bayer AG, 400
Stevens v. Head, 183
Strasbourg District Court v. Shamee, 484
Straub v. A.P. Green, Inc., 291
Strawbridge v. Curtiss, 212
Subafilms Ltd. v. MGM-Pathe Communications Co., 401
Sulewski v. Federal Express Corp., 461
Sun v. Taiwan, 311
Swibon, The, 56
Swiss American Bank, Ltd., United States v., 17
Tabion v. Mufti, 333
Tahan v. Duquette, 481

Tahan v. Hodgson, 239
Taylor v. LSI Logic Corp., 187
Tel-Oren v. Libyan Arab Republic, 409
Temperature Systems, Inc. v. Bill Pepper, Inc., 6
Timberlane Lumber Co. v. Bank of America, 339, 364, 370
Tonga Air Service v. Fowler, 254
Torres v. Southern Peru Copper Corp., 210
Totalplan Corp. of America v. Colborne, 400
Tracer Research Corp. v. National Environmental Services Co., 85
Trans Meridian Trading Inc. v. Empresa Nacional de Comercializacion de Insumos, 495
Transaero Inc. v. La Fuerza Aerea Boliviana, 295
Treinies v. Sunshine Mining Co., 237
Trinh v. Citibank, N.A., 279
Turner Entertainment Co. v. Degeto Film GmbH, 93
Union Carbide Corporation Gas Plant Disaster at Bhopal, India, In re, 191, 192
Union Ins. Soc'y of Canton, Ltd. v. S.S. Elikon, 56
United Nuclear Corp. v. General Atomic Co., 156
United Rope Distributors, Inc. v. Kimberly Line, 6
United States (see name of opposing party)
United States Securities and Exchange Commission v. Carrillo, 17
United World Trade Inc. v. Mangyshlakneft Oil Production Assoc., 304
Uranium Antitrust Litigation, In re, 146, 156
Van Cauwenberghe v. Biard, 198
Van Dusen v. Barrack, 178, 179, 184
Vandelune v. 4B Elevator Components Unlimited, 15
Vasquez-Velasco, United States v., 400
Verlinden B.V. v. Central Bank of Nigeria, 295
Vermeulen v. Renault, U.S.A., 292
Villar v. Crowley Maritime Corp., 219
Vimar Seguros y Reaseguros, S.A. v. M/V. Sky Reefer, 57, 69
Viragh v. Foldes, 480
Volkswagen, A.G. v. Valdez, 156
Volkswagenwerk Aktiengesellschaft v. Schlunk, 103
Volt Information Sciences v. Board of Trustees of Stanford University, 73

W.S. Kirkpatrick & Co., Inc. v. Environmental Tectonics Corp., Int'l, 279, 346
Wallace v. Korean Air, 450
Weinstein v. Volkswagen of America, Inc., 110
Weiss v. Routh, 211
Wells Fargo Asia Ltd. v. Citibank N.A., 279
Westend Development Co. v. Westend Amusement Corp., 238
Westinghouse Corp., In re, 156, 356
Weston Compagnie de Finance de d'Investissement v. La Republica del Ecuador, 305
Wilco v. Swan, 68
Wiwa v. Royal Dutch Petroleum Co., 410
Wolf v. Federal Republic of Germany, 292, 318
Wolf v. Harry Cox B.V., 224
Wolgel v. Mexicana Airlines, 461
World Tanker Carriers Corp. v. M/V Ya Mawlaya, 17
X v. Y, 44, 238
Xuncax v. Gramajo, 411
Yunis, United States v., 338
Zelger v. Salinitri, 28
Zicherman v. Korean Air Lines Co., 454
Zoelsch v. Arthur Andersen & Co., 388
Zschernig v. Miller, 382

Index

References are to pages.

ACT OF STATE DOCTRINE
Antitrust defense, 312-318, 339-341, 381
Application and exceptions, 261-280
    Bernstein exception, 264, 269
    Commercial, 273
    No state action, 272
Comity, relation to doctrine, 275-276
Hickenlooper amendment, 271-272
Intangible property, 274-280
    Bank accounts, 279-280
    Situs, 276-280
Sovereign immunity, relation to doctrine, 312-318, 381
State or federal standard, 266

ADMIRALTY
Airplane crash, 454-457
Bareboat charter, 89
Carriage of Goods by Sea Act, 57, 61
Limitation fund, 56
Ship Mortgage Act, 284, 288
Time charter, 89
Vessel Owner's Liability Act, 56

AIRPLANE ACCIDENTS
See International Flights

ALIEN TORT STATUTE
Suit against foreign sovereign under, 316, 408-409
Suit against the United States under, 409

ANTI-SUIT INJUNCTION
Anti-Injunction Act, 214-219
Conflict of Jurisdiction Model Act, 92
Enjoining suit in another forum, 48-49, 62-64, 89-95, 163, 214-225, 347-350, 355-362
Parallel proceedings, 89-95

ANTITRUST LAW
See Extraterritorial Application of Law

ANTON PILLER ORDER
English practice, 139

ARBITRATION
Agreement to arbitrate, 57-89
Antitrust violation, 77-86
Arbitral institutions, 73
Beth Din, 556
Choice of law, 73, 535, 539-540
Compared with litigation, 513
Conciliation, 519-521, 525-526
Convention on the Settlement of Investment Disputes Between States and Nationals of Other States, 516-527
Drafting agreement, 72-75
English Arbitration Act, 74-75, 541-542
Decision as amiable compositeur, 535, 539-540
Decision ex aequo et bono, 535, 539-540
Federal Arbitration Act, 75-76, 515
Fraudulently induced agreement, 65
Inter-American Convention on International Commercial Arbitration ("Panama Convention"), 72, 514-515
Iran-United States Claims Tribunal, 504, 508, 510-511, 551-556
Judicial assistance and interference, 541-551
Lex mercatoria, 539
Local awards not considered "domestic", 75-76
Model Law on International Commercial Arbitration, 528-539
North American Free Trade Agreement, 516
Public law violation, 61-69, 77-86
Securities law violation, 61-69

Sovereign immunity from execution to enforce award, 274, 283, 525
United Nations Convention on the Recognition and Enforcement of Foreign Arbitral Awards ("New York" Convention), 69-89, 515, 541, 552-556

CALVO CLAUSE
Defined, 7

CARRIAGE OF GOODS BY SEA ACT
Effect on choice-of-forum clause, 57-61

CHILD ABDUCTION
European Convention on Recognition and Enforcement of Decisions Concerning Custody of Children, 472
Hague Convention on the Civil Aspects of International Child Abduction, 463-486
   Acquiescence in removal, 477, 485-486
   Burden of Proof, 469-470
   Consent to removal, 477, 485-486
   Child objects to return, 466, 484-485
   Choice of law, 477
   Explanatory report, 470
   Federal regulations, 470
   "Habitual resident" defined, 472-479
   Hague Conference Report, 470
   Intolerable situation as reason not to return child, 466, 481-486
   Legal analysis, 470
   Rights of access and custody distinguished, 480
   Rights of custody actually exercised, 476, 480
   Special Commission Report, 470, 480
Inter-American Convention on International Repatriation of Children, 472
International aspects, 463-486
International Child Abduction Remedies Act, 469-470
Uniform Child Custody Jurisdiction Act, 471
Uniform Child Custody Jurisdiction and Enforcement Act, 471

CHOICE OF LAW
Airplane crash, 456-457
Alien Tort Statute, 408, 412
Approach to currency conversion, 168-169
Arbitration, 73, 535, 539-540
As factor in forum non conveniens, 175-178, 181, 183-184, 190-191, 194-195, 210-211
Contractual, 73, 82-83
Damages, 182-184
Extraterritorial application of law, 345-346, 369
Foreign Sovereign Immunities Act, 291
Hague Convention on the Civil Aspects of International Child Abduction, 456
Modern theories, 17
State or federal rule, 207-219
Vested rights, 345

CONFLICT OF LAWS
See Choice of Law

CONVENTIONS AND AGREEMENTS
Australia-United States Agreement on Cooperation in Antitrust Matters, 386
Bermuda II (Agreement between U.S. and U.K. Concerning Air Services), 352-354, 357-359
   English courts do not construe, 357
European Community-United States Agreement on Antitrust Cooperation and Coordination, 385-386
European Convention on Recognition and Enforcement of Decisions Concerning Custody of Children 472
Friendship Commerce, and Navigation treaties, 187
General Agreement on Tariffs and Trade, 385
Hague Conference on Private International Law, 101
Hague Convention on the Civil Aspects of International Child Abduction, 463-486
Inter-American Convention on International Commercial Arbitration, ("Panama Convention"), 72, 490
Inter-American Convention on International Repatriation of Children, 472
Inter-American Convention on Letters Rogatory, 101-102
International Guaranty Letters and Standby Letters of Credit, 489
Japan-United States Agreement on Semiconductor Trade, 382-385
Jurisdiction and Enforcement of Judgments ("Brussels"), 19
Lugano, 28
Organization for Economic Cooperation and Development, 379
Service Abroad, 96-101
   Mail provision, 109
   Special Commission Report on, 109
Settlement of Investment Disputes Between States and Nationals of Other States, 516-527
Taking of Evidence Abroad, 119-163
   Effect on Federal Rules of Civil Procedure, 126-137
   Special Commission Report on, 136

Unification of Certain Rules Relating to International Transportation by Air ("Montreal Convention"), 436-443
Unification of Certain Rules Relating to International Transportation by Air ("Warsaw Convention"), 427-436, 443-461
United Nations Convention on the Recognition and Enforcement of Foreign Arbitral Awards ("New York Convention"), 69-89, 516, 527-528
Vienna Convention on Consular Relations, 331-333
Vienna Convention on Diplomatic Relations, 332-333

CURRENCY CONVERSION
"Choice of law" approach, 168-169
Conversion date when debt owed in foreign currency, 163-171
Satisfaction of judgment by paying judgment of another country, 171
Uniform Foreign-Money Claims Act, 164-165

DEROGATION
See Forum Selection

EUROPEAN COMMUNITY
See European Economic Community

EUROPEAN ECONOMIC COMMUNITY
Members, 28

EUROPEAN FREE TRADE ASSOCIATION
Members, 28

EUROPEAN UNION
See European Economic Community

EVIDENCE
Anton Piller order, 139
Blocking statutes, 116-117, 128, 133, 139-163, 357-362
Discovery on jurisdictional issue, 156
Hague Convention, 119-163
  Effect on Federal Rules of Civil Procedure, 126-137
  Special Commission Report on, 136
Obtaining from abroad, 110-163
  Pre-trial discovery, 126-163
Obtaining in U.S. for use abroad, 137-138

EXTRATERRITORIAL APPLICATION OF LAW
Antitrust law, 335-388
  Act of state, 339-341, 381
  Sovereign compulsion, 339, 378-379
  Sovereign immunity, 380-381
Bases, 335-401
  Effects, 335, 337-338, 386-387
  Nationality, 335-336, 349, 353
  Passive personality, 338
  Territorial, 335-336, 348-349, 353
  Universal jurisdiction, 338
Comity, 336, 342-345, 376, 378, 392-393
Conventions and agreements, 352-354, 357-359, 385-386
Choice-of-law analysis, 345-346, 369
Department of Justice Guidelines, 377-378
Effects abroad caused by United States defendants, 375, 377, 388-396
Export commerce, 374-378
Federal Tort Claims Act, 400
Foreign branches and subsidiaries, 397-398
Foreign Trade Antitrust Improvements Act, 375-378
International law, 338, 368
Organization for Economic Cooperation and Development recommendations, 379
Public law other than antitrust and securities, 397-401
Securities law, 337, 388-397
  Modification of registration requirements, 397
State law, 379-382
Sovereign compulsion, 339, 378-379
Treble damages, 386

FOREIGN SOVEREIGN IMMUNITY
See Sovereign Immunity

FOREIGN PLAINTIFFS
See also Forum Non Conveniens
Forum shopping, 173-225
  Within EEC, 184
Mid-Atlantic formula, 183
Reasons why United States is magnet forum, 178, 182-184, 219-220
  Defamation exception, 186
Suits by, 173-225
  Against foreign sovereigns, 295-303
  Alien Tort Statute, 403-413, 415-426

FORUM NON CONVENIENS
Alien Tort Statute, 404, 408, 423-424
Basis for closing forum, 43, 48-49, 173-207
Choice of law as factor, 175-178, 181, 183-184, 190-191, 194-195, 210-211
Conditions for dismissal, 191-198
Convention on Jurisdiction and Enforcement of Judgments ("Brussels Convention"), 225

English development, 200-207, 224-225
Foreign Sovereign Immunities Act, 299
Friendship, Commerce, and Navigation treaties, 187
Interlocutory appeal, 198-199
Japanese development, 207
Private factors, 175
Public factors, 175, 204-206
Standard for review of trial judge, 180, 185, 198-199
State or federal law applicable, 177, 207-214
Suits by foreign plaintiffs, 173-225
Torture Victim Protection Act, 423-424
Transfer under 28 U.S.C. § 1404(a), 55, 178-179, 184-185
Warsaw Convention, 460

FORUM SELECTION
Arbitration agreement, 57-89
Contractual, 47-89
Convention on Jurisdiction and Enforcement of Judgments ("Brussels"), 23
Derogation and prorogation distinguished, 55
Interlocutory appeal from refusal to enforce agreement, 61

GENERAL JURISDICTION
See In Personam Jurisdiction

GMBH
Defined, 138

INCONVENIENT FORUM
See Forum Non Conveniens

INJUNCTION
See Anti-Suit Injunction

IN PERSONAM JURISDICTION
Consent to jurisdiction, 55
Contesting, 232-236, 239, 244
Discovery on jurisdictional issue, 156
Exorbitant, 19-20, 30, 236-237
General jurisdiction, 1-7, 19
Over foreign defendants, 1-34
Over foreign sovereigns, 281, 296, 303-304
Piercing corporate veil, 32-34, 244-246
Service outside United Kingdom, 238-239
Specific jurisdiction, 3, 20
Transient presence, 30
Uniform Foreign Money-Judgments Recognition Act, 252-253
Warsaw Convention suit, 460

IN REM JURISDICTION
Convention on Jurisdiction and Enforcement of Judgments ("Brussels"), 19-20, 22, 27-28
Quasi in rem, how differs from in rem, 36
Over property of foreign defendants, 45-47
Over property of United States defendants, 34-45

INTERNATIONAL FLIGHTS
Bumping, 461
Choice of law, 456-457
Damages resulting from, 427-461
IATA Agreement, 436, 443
Montreal Convention, 436-443
   Removal of recovery limits, 436-443
Warsaw Convention, 427-436, 443-461
   "Accident" defined, 444-450
   Airline employees, 460-461
   Civil Aeronautics Board Order, 433-435
   "Destination" defined, 461
   "Disembarking" defined, 459-460
   "Embarking" defined, 460
   Forum non conveniens, 460
   Guatemala City Protocol, 435, 448
   Hague Protocol, 434-435
   In personam jurisdiction over airline required, 460
   Kuala Lampur Agreement, 436, 443
   Mental anguish, 450-454, 457-458
   Montreal Agreement, 433-435
   Montreal Protocols 3 & 4, 435, 448
   Notice of, 428, 434
   Parties not protected by, 443
   Personal injury, 450-454, 457-458
   Pre-emptive effect, 457-459
   Property damage, 430-432
   Punitive damages, 443
   "Ticket" defined, 428
   Venue for suit, 432, 460-461
   Willful misconduct, 432

INTERNATIONAL INSTITUTE FOR THE UNIFICATION OF PRIVATE LAW (UNIDROIT)
Principles of International Commercial Contracts, 73, 550

INTERNATIONAL LAW
Alien Tort Statute, 316
Effect on domestic legislation, 118-119
Jus Cogens, 118, 325
State responsibility for acts of individuals, 408-409
Sources, 405-406

INDEX

JUDGMENTS
Bases for non-recognition, 227-259
   Conditional appearance, 232-233, 236
   Federal or state standard, 234, 239
   Fraud, 239-244, 247, 252-253
      Intrinsic, extrinsic distinguished, 247, 253
   Lack of personal jurisdiction, 232-236, 239, 244
   Natural or substantial justice, 241-244
   Public law, 248-251
      Criminal law, 248-251
      Taxes, 250-251
   Public policy, 229, 246-247, 252-254
      Punitive damages, 246-247
   Reciprocity, 230-231, 234, 254-257
   Uniform Foreign Money-Judgments Recognition Act, 252
"Clawback" acts, 361-362
Comity, 228, 234
Currency conversion when debt owed in foreign currency, 163-171
Foreign judgments determining validity of forum judgments, 237-238
Foreign judgments affecting interests in forum property, 238
Recognition and enforcement, 25-27, 196-198, 227-259
Registration of U.S. judgments in Canada, 238
Satisfaction by paying judgment of another country, 171
Uniform Foreign Money-Judgments Recognition Act, 251-259
   Notice of proceeding, 257-259

JURA NOVIT CURIA
Defined, 236

JURISDICTION
See In Personam Jurisdiction, In Rem Jurisdiction, Jurisdiction to Enforce, Jurisdiction to Prescribe

JURISDICTION TO ADJUDICATE
See In Personam Jurisdiction, In Rem Jurisdiction

JURISDICTION TO ENFORCE
Defined, 335

JURISDICTION TO PRESCRIBE
Bases, 335-401
Limitations, 335-339

LETTERS OF CREDIT
"Advising bank" defined, 494
"Beneficiary" defined, 487
"Commercial letter" defined, 488
"Confirming bank" defined, 494
Convention on International Guaranty and Standby Letters of Credit, 489
Declaration of Algeria Concerning Settlement of Claims by the United States and Iran, 510-511
Documentary conditions, 488-495
   Compliance, 489-495
   Defined, 488
"Drawee bank" defined, 495
Enjoining payment, 495-504
Guaranty distinguished, 487
International Chamber of Commerce, 488
International Standby Practices, 489
International transactions, 487-511
Iran-United States Claims Tribunal, 504, 508, 510-511, 551-556
Iranian Assets Control Regulations, 504, 509
"Nominated bank" defined, 495
Political risks, 504-511
"Standby letter" defined, 488
Uniform Commercial Code, 487-501
Uniform Customs and Practice, 488, 493-495, 501
United Nations Commission on International Trade Law (UNCITRAL), 489, 511
United States banks' limited powers, 488
   Glass-Steagall Act, 488

LIMITATION FUND
In admiralty, 56

LITVINOV ASSIGNMENT
Transfer of funds under, 273

MAREVA INJUNCTION
English practice, 44

NOTIFICATION AU PARQUET
Discussed, 105-110

PERSONAL JURISDICTION
See In Personam Jurisdiction

PROROGATION
See Forum Selection

QUASI IN REM
See In Rem Jurisdiction

RES JUDICATA
See Judgments

RESTATEMENT OF FOREIGN RELATIONS LAW
Naming of editions, 156
Section 102, 119
Section 401, 335
Section 402, 335
Section 403, 336, 366, 368-370
Section 414, 397-398
Section 415, 336-337, 366
Section 416, 337, 394
Section 442, 139-140

SECURITIES LAW
See Extraterritorial Application of Law

SERVICE OF PROCESS
Federal Rules of Civil Procedure, 102-103
Foreign sovereigns, 286-287
Hague Convention on Service Abroad, 96-101
  Mail provision, 109
  Special Commission Report on, 109
Inter-American Convention on Letters Rogatory, 101-102
Mail service, 102, 109
Notice and opportunity to be heard, 110
Notification au parquet, 105, 110
Public law enforcement, 101
Validity of service, 96-119

SHIPMENT TERMS
F.A.S., 170, 271
Guide to Incoterms, 170

SOVEREIGN IMMUNITY
Act of state doctrine, relationship, 312-318, 381
Alien Tort Act, 293
Antitrust prosecution, 380-381
Burden of proof, 291
Foreign Sovereign Immunities Act, 281-334, 379, 381
  Choice of law, 291
  Constitutionality, 295-300
  Forum non conveniens, 299
  Differences in treatment of foreign state and agency of state, 291
History, 298-300
Immunity of foreign sovereigns from suit, 281-334
  By foreign plaintiffs, 295-303
  Exceptions, 282-286, 300-318
    Commercial, 300-333, 380-381
    Tort, 282-283, 319-332

  Discretionary function, 283, 330-332
  Scope of employment, 282, 329-330, 332
  Waiver, 282, 325, 327-328, 333-334
Immunity of sovereigns from attachment of property, 287-289, 319-324
  Exceptions, 287-289, 319-324
In personam jurisdiction over foreign sovereign, 281, 296, 303-304
Interlocutory appeal, 291
International Organizations Immunities Act, 334
Jury trial, 281, 290
Piercing corporate veil, 321-322
Punitive damages, 285, 290
Restrictive theory of, 297-298, 300
Service of process, 286-287
Tate letter, 297
Time for determining status, 290-291
Torture Victim Protection Act, 293, 423
Venue, 289-290
Vienna Convention on Consular Relations, 331-333
Vienna Convention on Diplomatic Relations, 332-333

SPECIAL DRAWING RIGHTS
Defined, 435
Measure of compensation under Montreal and Warsaw Conventions, 435-436, 438-439

SPECIFIC JURISDICTION
See In Personam Jurisdiction

UNIDROIT
Principles of International Commercial Contracts, 73, 550

UNITED NATIONS COMMISSION ON INTERNATIONAL TRADE LAW (UNCITRAL)
Letters of credit, 489, 511
Model Law on International Commercial Arbitration, 528-540